Best Prac

Asylum and Human Rights Appeals

The publication and distribution of this text has been made possible
by the financial support of the following:

The Nuffield Foundation

Electronic Immigration Network

INRIC (Immigration and Nationality Research and Information Charity)

Immigration Advisory Service

Refugee Legal Centre

Doughty Street Chambers

Garden Court Chambers

Immigration Law Practitioners' Association

The Medical Foundation for the Care of Victims of Torture

Renaissance Chambers

From the Immigration Services Commissioner

As Immigration Services Commissioner, it is my duty to promote good practice by those who provide immigration advice or immigration services. It is for that reason that I warmly welcome the practical emphasis in this Guide and particularly the key points that conclude each of its sections. It will be sure to give real assistance to practitioners in their continuing endeavours to provide quality advice and representation in the fast changing world of asylum and human rights law.

As a regulator, I believe we must focus on the competence of advisers and their ability to represent the interests of their clients. We aim to be able to define and assess quality within each advice-giving organisation. We are working strenuously towards this goal. As we do so, we will undoubtedly make use of this Best Practice Guide in developing our standards, refining the way we measure the quality of work undertaken by advisers, exploring different ways of promoting quality, and working with other regulators and funders involved in the field of immigration advice.

John Scampion CBE
Immigration Services Commissioner

Best Practice Guide to

Asylum and Human Rights Appeals

Mark Henderson

with a foreword by
Lord Justice Sedley

REFUGEE LEGAL GROUP

Published by the Immigration Law Practitioners' Association
in association with the Refugee Legal Group.

© Mark Henderson 2003

Best Practice Guide to Asylum Appeals (first edition) 1997
Best Practice Guide to Asylum and Human Rights Appeals 2003

Further copies of this text are available from ILPA
Lindsey House, 40–42 Charterhouse Street
London EC1M 6JN
Tel 020 7251 8383   Fax 020 7251 8384
Email info@ilpa.org.uk   www.ilpa.org.uk

ILPA is the UK's professional association of immigration lawyers,
advisers and academics practising or engaged in immigration,
asylum and nationality law.

The **Refugee Legal Group** is a forum for discussion and information
exchange among practitioners and others concerned for the
interests of asylum seekers within the UK's asylum process.

The electronic edition of this book is published by the
Electronic Immigration Network: www.ein.org.uk

ISBN 1 90183 308 9

A CIP record for this book is available from the British Library

Cover design by Carol Brickley
Typeset by Boldface, London
Printed by Unwin Brothers, Old Woking, GU22 9LH

Summary contents

Full contents

Foreword

by Lord Justice Sedley

The framers of the 1951 Geneva Convention almost certainly thought that the provision they were making was temporary and would become redundant as the world order became stable again. But what once appeared to be a reducing flow of displaced persons in a world which was slowly recovering its sanity had instead by the end of the century become a human flood. The collapse of civil order and the re-emergence of local and national tyrannies has caused people in their thousands – sometimes millions – to flee to safer places. A huge growth in air travel and the increasing permeability of land frontiers have contributed to these population movements.

In the closely-governed states of the developed world, the flow has been mingled with a stream – nobody knows how large – of economic migrants, serviced by a shadowy industry of agents and advisers, for whom asylum is simply a visa. It is the task of weeding them out, along with the smaller number of people whose claim, though bona fide, does not come within the Convention, which places today's huge burden on the adjudication process. Even so, it is worth keeping the burden in perspective. Countries like Kenya, which have not adopted the 1951 Convention, are host to millions of refugees who have crossed the frontiers to find relative safety in encampments where life is barely sustainable. Who would apply the adjective 'bogus' to them?

The work of representing those who have not been accepted as refugees on the Home Office's initial screening is as arduous as any branch of legal practice I know. Resources are scarce, instructions are often confused, corroboration is hard to come by and some, when it comes, is fake. The pressure of time is constant, and the law is almost as constantly changing, often in response to political pressures.

Practitioners live with the knowledge that the seamless story may well be a try-on, and that people who are incoherent or whose stories are incredible may well be telling the truth. Adjudicators have to remind themselves or be reminded that in real life the improbable is constantly happening. But there is no acid test of veracity. All our system can aspire to do is afford a scrupulously fair hearing to each claim.

It is here that the role of asylum practitioners is critical. We know that theirs is a field which has been dogged by malpractice and incompetence. It is now emerging from that blight, but it remains afflicted by another one – the lack of any accepted standard for interpreters. I repeat the call I made in introducing the first edition of this guide for the adoption of the Nuffield system of training and accreditation of interpreters, without which no system of adjudication can be sure that it is always according asylum-seekers their most basic entitlement, a fair hearing.

Good practice takes time and trouble, but it is never wasted. It shows in the standing and reputation of practitioners, in the respect in which opponents and tribunals hold them, and above all in the satisfaction of doing a job well. In the end, by avoiding disasters, it also saves money.

Because this guide is directed to people who advise and represent asylum-seekers within a system that sits uneasily between adversarial and inquisitorial modes of trial, its approach is inevitably one-sided. But that is all the more reason for it to be read and used both by those who handle and present cases for the Home Office and by members of the Immigration Appellate Authority. For the former, it is not a question of being forewarned and forearmed against the enemy's plans. For the Home Office, as for judicial decision-makers, it is a question of assisting and encouraging good practice by meeting it half-way; for the end which everyone working in this field surely shares is ensuring so far as is humanly possible that no genuine refugee is ever denied a safe haven.

It is this which remains the international obligation entered into by the United Kingdom at what seemed to be the end of one of the most terrible periods of human history. Fifty years and more on, in a world repeatedly scarred by cruelty, there is little ground for continuing to believe that it was an end. Even if all we are now able to do is pick up some of the pieces, there is every reason to do so conscientiously, remembering that the rule of law is for us as well as for others.

Stephen Sedley
The Rt Hon Lord Justice Sedley
Royal Courts of Justice
August 2003

Preface

> *It has been said time and again that asylum cases call for consideration with 'the most anxious scrutiny'... That is not a mantra to which only lip service should be paid. It recognises the fact that what is at stake in these cases is fundamental human rights, including the right to life itself.* (**Sivakumar**, per Dyson LJ)

The stakes in asylum and human rights appeals are higher than any other field of litigation. Since the *Best Practice Guide to Asylum Appeals* (the predecessor to this text) was published in 1997, the caselaw on what 'anxious scrutiny' means in practice has grown exponentially. So has the complexity of conducting appeals. Yet the exceptional stakes are matched by the exceptional political pressures both on appellants and the appeal process which hinder the effective preparation and determination of these cases.

Two themes run through this book. Firstly, the hearing is only the end of the process. Good advocacy at the hearing can win an appeal (and bad advocacy can lose it). But it is more likely that the appeal was won or lost on the preparation beforehand.

Secondly, the appeal system is just that, not a second round of primary decision making. It provides a means of testing whether Home Office decisions violate the UK's international obligations. It should not be employed to shore up inadequate Home Office decision-making by drawing adjudicators into trying to formulate a better case against the appellant than the Home Office could manage. Such a distortion of the appeal process only generates cost and delay and so provides ammunition to its detractors. The operation of this jurisdiction is also hampered by what appears to be a systemic inability on the part of the Home Office to engage in sensible negotiation to define and confine issues in advance; its propensity to present a different case at the hearing from any that was disclosed in advance; and a frequent failure to comply with judicial directions. The IAT has on one occasion been driven to remark that its conduct went 'beyond mere institutional incompetence, into the realm of an institutional culture of disregard for adjudicators' (para 9.18; see also paras 48.17, 48.27).

Neither appellants nor their lawyers can force the Home Office to make quality decisions or to litigate responsibly. But the best way to counter attacks on the appeal system, and to ensure that 'the highest standards of fairness' apply in practice, is to focus attention upon the Home Office's accountability for its decisions and its conduct in an adversarial system, and to discourage adjudicators from being drawn into acting as primary decision makers. In the words of the IAT, it should be made 'perfectly clear to... the Home Office that they cannot simply leave it to adjudicators to make bricks without straw on their behalf' (para 48.11).

This publication deals with the conduct of asylum and human rights appeals. (See *Making an Asylum Application: a best practice guide*, published by ILPA, for the initial application to the Home Office.) The text is structured in roughly chronological order, starting with the Home Office's decision, followed by procedure, evidence, and presentation of the appeal before the adjudicator, and then proceedings before the IAT and statutory review. It aims to provide the practical advice and information required to conduct each stage of the appeal according to best practice.

The book is about practice and procedure, not substantive law. It is no substitute for the sound knowledge of asylum and human rights law that any representative must acquire. Nevertheless, no effort is made to artificially exclude points of substantive law where these are intrinsic to the practical conduct of the appeal. The only criterion used is what will most assist in rendering the presentation of the appeal more effective.

The aim is to be of as much use to as many practitioners as possible. Not everything will be relevant to every practitioner. Some will be embarking upon practice in the field from scratch. Others will be more experienced practitioners who have encountered a specific problem for which they want ideas quickly. Some practitioners will work only on certain aspects of the litigation. However, that makes it even more important to appreciate the process as a whole, and why choices made at one stage will reverberate many stages (and sometimes many years) down the line.

Practitioners vary in their knowledge and experience of civil litigation. Different elements of the appeal process vary in their difficulty and complexity, and the nature of this text inevitably varies accordingly. But as few assumptions as possible are made about the practitioner's legal background. Two assumptions are made: first, that for those appellants who are without means, public funding will cover the proper conduct of the appeal (and so cannot constitute an excuse for bad practice); second, that the litigation is approached with a commitment which is commensurate to the issues at stake.

Social welfare and support issues for appellants are beyond the scope of this guide since they are beyond the power of adjudicators and the IAT. But dealing with such issues is not an optional extra. It is integral to best practice in the preparation of an appeal. It is facile, for example, to go to great lengths to provide a supportive environment for taking a torture survivor's statement, yet ignore her living conditions outside the interview room. The latter are likely to have the greater effect on her mental state and her ability to give instructions and to prosecute her appeal. If you are not able to provide social welfare advice, it is essential to make arrangements to ensure that your client has access to it.

Legal developments have resulted in some of the chapters of this book being revised (and in some cases rewritten) several times during its preparation. Reference has already been made to the explosion of caselaw in recent years affecting all aspects of procedure and evidence. Since 2000, there has also been the developing jurisprudence on the Human Rights Act. Fundamental questions relating to the interpretation of the Immigration and Asylum Act 1999 were resolved by the Court of Appeal only in 2002 – the same year as a new appeals regime was introduced by the Nationality, Immigration, and Asylum Act 2002. It will be a challenge for the courts to clarify the new law before it in turn is replaced. At time of writing, the Government has already announced plans to revamp the appeals system yet again, adding to the four major acts of parliament which the last decade has already witnessed. It indicates to the practitioner both the difficulty and the necessity of keeping abreast of developments.

The publishers and I would like to thank all the organisations who have funded and supported the publication and distribution of this book at a time when there are many competing demands on their resources.

I would also like to thank numerous people for discussing and researching points, commenting on or proofing the text, and for supporting the project through some difficult days. They include (with apologies to those omitted) Mark Symes, Nick Oakeshott, Alasdair Mackenzie, Rick Scannell, Julia Gasparro, Mark Phillips, Andrew Nicol, David Rhys Jones, Sonal Ghelani, Chris Randall, Jawaid Luqmani, Judith Farbey, Simon Cox, Tony Paterson, John Dean, Tony Good, Martin Rady, Vicky Wong, and Edwin and Jane Henderson. The

Immigration Team and the clerks and staff at Doughty Street have been as supportive and tolerant as ever. I am also grateful to the staff of the IAA who dealt with my requests with courtesy and professionalism and to HH Judge Hodge, the Chief Adjudicator for his time in meeting me and addressing my queries. It goes without saying that the IAA neither requested nor were offered any indication of the contents of the text.

The book was originally completed a year ago, but by the time arrangements were in place for publication in early summer 2003, intervening legal developments demanded what amounted to a new edition. Producing it during the heat of summer 2003 was an unenviable task and I must pay particular tribute to the contribution of Bojana Asanovic, who worked extraordinary hours editing, proofing and indexing the text and providing numerous ideas. A substantial debt of gratitude is also owed to our designers and typesetters at Boldface, and to Carol in particular. She remained an island of calm in a sea of chaos and fraught nerves, and implausibly understanding in the face of every provocation we could throw at her. Boldface's support for this project, including opening on several weekends to get it finished, went well beyond the call of duty.

Responsibility for remaining errors and omissions is, of course, my own.

Mark Henderson
Doughty Street Chambers
August 2003

Abbreviations and terminology

Abbreviations

asylum seeker This term is used to refer to any person who claims that her expulsion will violate the Refugee Convention or the ECHR.

HOPO The Home Office may be represented at an appeal either by its own official, known as a Home Office Presenting Officer (HOPO), or by counsel (or occasionally by both). For brevity, the acronym HOPO is used to refer to any person representing the Home Office in an appeal.

Other abbreviations used in the text:

APIs [Home Office] Asylum Policy Instructions

CA Court of Appeal (or, where it appears in the reference for a practice direction, 'Chief Adjudicator')

CLR Controlled Legal Representation

CPR Civil Procedure Rules

Col Column [of Hansard]

ECHR European Convention on Human Rights

EIN Electronic Immigration Network

ELR Exceptional Leave to Remain/ Enter

GCC [LSC] General Civil Contract

IAA Immigration Appellate Authority

IAS Immigration Advisory Service

IAT Immigration Appeal Tribunal

IDIs [Home Office] Immigration Directorates' Instructions

ILPA Immigration Law Practitioners' Association

LSC Legal Services Commission

OEM [Home Office] Operation Enforcement Manual

OGN [Home Office] Operational Guidance Note

OISC	Office of the Immigration Services Commissioner
OSS	Office for the Supervision of Solicitors
RLC	Refugee Legal Centre
RLG	Refugee Legal Group
SIAC	Special Immigration Appeals Commission
SSHD	Secretary of State for the Home Department
UNHCR	United Nations High Commissioner for Refugees

Gender

The publishing organisations have concluded that *she* should be used to refer to asylum seekers and refugees, in recognition that women make up the majority of the world's refugee population, while everyone else should be referred to as *he*. Each should be understood as including the other gender unless the context indicates otherwise.

Legal references

References to the 2002 Act are to the Nationality, Immigration and Asylum Act 2002.

References to the 1999 Act are to the Immigration and Asylum Act 1999.

References to rules are to the Immigration and Asylum Appeals (Procedure) Rules 2003 unless otherwise stated.

References to Symes & Jorro are to Asylum Law and Practice by Symes & Jorro (Butterworths, 2003).

Cases are referred to in the body of the text by a single name. Where necessary in order to differentiate cases, they are further identified by year and/or court. They are listed alphabetically in the Table of Cases by the name used in the body of the text (followed by the full name in brackets if it begins differently).

'Neutral citations' are stated where they exist. These start with the year in square brackets, followed by the court, identified by the following abbreviations:

UKIAT	Immigration Appeal Tribunal
EWHC Admin	Administrative Court
EWCA Civ	Court of Appeal (Civil)
UKHL	House of Lords

Note that IAT determinations issued during 2003 up to the date of implementation of IAT Practice Direction No 10 (see chapter 29) continue to display the neutral citation [2002].

The following abbreviations are used for law reports and periodicals:

AC	Appeal Cases
QB	Law Reports: Queen's Bench Division
WLR	Weekly Law Reports
All ER	All England Law Reports
INLR	Immigration and Nationality Law Reports
Imm AR	Immigration Appeal Reports
SOPIAT	Statements of Principle of the Immigration Appeal Tribunal
EHRR	European Human Rights Reports
Cr App R	Criminal Appeal Reports
Lloyd's Rep	Lloyd's Law Reports

Unreported decisions of higher courts pre-dating the neutral citation system are identified by the date of judgment followed by the court reference number. IAT decisions are identified by their reference number (known as the 'brackets number'). By convention, they are referred to by the name of the asylum seeker whether she was the appellant or respondent before the IAT.

Table of cases

Table of practice directions

Nationality, Immigration and Asylum Act 2002
Table of sections

Immigration and Asylum Appeals (Procedure) Rules 2003

Table of rules

Home Office policy
Table of APIs and IDIs

The present version of the APIs published on the Home Office's website identifies sections and sub-sections of the APIs only by name and has no numbered reference system. The following table lists the paragraphs of this text which refer to the APIs and, in the opposite column, identifies the relevant passage from the APIs by the name of the section, followed (if applicable) by the name of the sub-section, and then the paragraph number or annex. The IDIs retain chapter and section numbers which are used in the table. Otherwise, the IDIs are tabulated in the same format. The references have been verified on the Home Office website as of July 2003.

1 Analysing the refusal letter

1.1   The disturbing quality of many Home Office 'reasons for refusal' letters has been highlighted in a series of reports by Asylum Aid (*No Reason at All* and *Still No Reason At All*). The IAT has emphasised the importance to the effective operation of the appeal process of proper decision making at first instance. In *Horvath*, it emphasised that:

> the lack of skilled and professional care in reaching the initial decision necessarily places extra burdens on adjudicators. In this case,...(the adjudicator) was in effect having to reach a decision on the claim almost as if he were the original decision-maker. Some jurisdictions operate such a system, in Canada for example. But the UK has a different system, with the initial decision being taken by officials on behalf of the Secretary of State. It is incumbent upon these officials to give each and every case anxious scrutiny.

1.2   The purpose of the Home Office refusal letter is to set out its case for the appeal. The IAT states that:

> The refusal letter... should, if possible, identify the matters in issue and should make clear (a) what facts (if any) are found in the applicant's favour, and (b) what matters (if any) are rejected as untrue. If the Secretary of State is saying in an asylum appeal that he does not need to decide on the truthfulness of the appellant's account because, even if the account is true, any fear is not well-founded, that should be made clear. In order to avoid misunderstanding, the Secretary of State should make clear if he disbelieves an applicant when he says that he left his country because of fear. We strongly suggest that the use of the words 'credible' or 'credibility' should be avoided. If the Secretary of State believes that an applicant is not telling the truth either generally or about particular matters, he should say so. If he is prepared to assume the truth of the account given but rejects the claim because the alleged fear is not well-founded, he should say that that is his view. To describe such a claim as 'not credible' is to misuse the English language.
> *(Carcabuk & Bla)*

1.3   Unfortunately, many refusal letters fail to comply with these require-ments. The Home Office's guiding principle is more often to 'dispute everything' as 'not credible', often over several pages. A clear state-ment of issues that the Home Office does *not* feel able to dispute is rare. This practice substantially increases the cost and complexity of appeals.

1.4   A significant part of the refusal letter often consists of allegations of 'discrepancies' based on a minute analysis of the claimant's testimony in the Home Office interview and her statement. Many such allega-tions can be shown to be unfounded but all require rebuttal.

1.5   An even larger part may be devoted to assertions of 'implausibility'. The proposition that protection should be refused to those whose per-secutors behaved illogically, surprisingly or bizarrely might itself appear bizarre to us. In fact we might expect to be surprised by their behaviour. Neither might we wish to refuse protection to victims of persecution, simply because we think that we would have behaved dif-ferently. However, the Home Office commonly rejects claims on this basis. It will urge the adjudicator to conclude that the sensible persecu-tor or sensible victim would have done things differently. In ***Kasolo***, the IAT criticised this practice by reference to the following comments by Lord Bingham:

> *An English judge may have, or think he has, a shrewd idea of how a Lloyds Broker or a Bristol wholesaler, or a Norfolk farmer, might react in some situation which is canvassed in the course of a case but he may, and I think should, feel very much more uncertain about the reactions of a Nigerian merchant, or an Indian ships' engineer, or a Yugoslav banker. Or even, to take a more homely example, a Sikh shopkeeper trading in Bradford. No judge worth his salt could possibly assume that men of dif-ferent nationalities, educations, trades, experience, creeds and tempera-ments would act as he would have done or even – which may be quite different – in accordance with his concept of what a reasonable man would have done.*

1.6   But the Home Office claims to have a 'shrewd idea' about the reactions of the reasonable sadistic secret policeman, the reasonable corrupt prison guard, and the reasonable 'genuine refugee'. You will find that the behaviour of the 'genuine refugee' tends to vary from case to case so as to create a 'damned if you do, damned if you don't' effect.

1.7   That, of course, is before one even reaches the question of whether the claimant's fears are presently well-founded. This will also be the sub-ject of detailed claims about present human rights conditions in the country or origin. These will bear a varying relationship to reality.

Some will consist of standard assertions dropped, word for word, into every refusal letter issued in respect of your client's country of origin. Legal arguments will also be advanced, again of varying validity. You need to be able to differentiate between those allegations that could damage you in the absence of rebuttal, and those that are legal or factual nonsense.

1.8 This section deals with the initial analysis of the refusal letter – the start of the appeal preparation – and tactics for dealing with some of the commonest allegations. It can be no substitute, however, for a sound knowledge of asylum and human rights law.

Initial steps

1.9 Get your client in as soon as possible to obtain her instructions and comments on the refusal letter. The allegations and assertions it contains may appear even more bizarre to your client, and you will have to explain that she is not being singled out for this treatment.

1.10 The initial application to the Home Office is outside the scope of this guide (see *Making an asylum application: a best practice guide* (ILPA, 2002). Whoever represented your client should have checked the Home Office interview record with her for accuracy (essential now that the Home Office refuses to read its notes back at the end of the interview: see para 36.20). Any necessary representations on accuracy and omissions should then have been advanced to the Home Office. If this has not happened, you should go through the interview notes with her as soon as possible. If any issues arise about their accuracy, a dated statement should be taken. If there are serious concerns about the interview, it is valuable to raise these at an early stage (even though, in reality, the prospects of a satisfactory response from the Home Office are slim). Always check the summary of your client's claim in the refusal letter (which is sometimes inaccurate and/or misleading) against the statements and interview records which were before the Home Office.

Disputes about past facts
Alleged Discrepancies

1.11 The Home Office has adopted a variety of procedures for its initial decision on asylum claims in recent years. It continues to alter these regularly. At time of writing, the most common procedure is to issue a 'Statement of Evidence Form' (SEF) which poses detailed questions about the claim. This has to be returned to the Home Office in English within 14 days. A substantive interview will then be arranged (sometimes after a considerable delay).

1.12 The 14 day time limit for submission of completed SEFs means that representatives commonly do not have enough time to take full instructions on the claim. Unfortunately, some representatives complete the form based on hurried and unchecked instructions through fear of being refused on non-compliance grounds. Even if there are no actual mistakes in the information that is submitted, giving incomplete details is often worse than no details at all. The Home Office will argue that because some events have been detailed in the initial SEF, it follows that the *every* event would have been detailed had it occurred.

1.13 If the claimant's answers at the asylum interview produce information that did not appear in the SEF (or any subsequent statement), the Home Office is likely to allege that the new information is fabricated. This is apparently because *'A genuine refugee could be expected to give a consistent account of her persecution.'* No evidence or research is ever offered to support this assertion as to how the genuine refugee acts (the expert learning is in fact to the contrary – para 26.13), but it will be made as a matter of course especially (and most inappropriately) where the new information relates to torture.

1.14 It is not a view shared by the IAT which has noted that 'it is, of course, well-known that asylum applicants frequently do not tell the full story or indeed the true story on arrival after they have claimed asylum' (**Adong**). Indeed, the Home Office has conceded as much with respect to torture victims when it published the following on its website:

> The reluctance of a genuine victim of torture to talk in detail about their experiences should not be held against them in assessing the credibility of their claimed fear. However, where claims to have been tortured are advanced only at a very late stage in the process, this may have a bearing on the applicant's overall credibility.
>
> Caseworkers and interviewers must remain alert and receptive to the difficulties and barriers victims of torture may face in expressing highly traumatic experiences.
>
> Potential embarrassment and humiliation about recounting their experiences are difficulties which may need to be overcome. This is particularly difficult in the atmosphere of officialdom. Those who have suffered at the hands of their own authorities may distrust officials here, despite travelling to this country to seek refuge. In many ways, this is an intractable problem, but common sense, awareness and sensitivity can minimise its influence.

1.15 That contrasts with many refusal letters which allege that the fact that someone has sought asylum in the UK in itself demonstrates that she can have no distrust of any UK official.

1.16 In *Kasolo*, the Home Office admitted that the full asylum interview was an opportunity to expand upon information previously provided, not an opportunity to catch the asylum seeker out, and the IAT accordingly overturned an adjudicator who had relied on failure to provide information at an earlier stage.

1.17 If your client has been subjected to a full interview shortly after arrival without advice or representation, you may well wish to argue that it is unsafe to rely on the interview notes. In *Uhumwango-Asembu*, the IAT considered a case where the Home Office had attacked credibility on the basis of a failure to mention details in an interview which were subsequently disclosed upon appeal. The IAT concluded that:

> The asylum applicant and the interviewer each have a real part to play in the investigative process (see paras 198–200 of the UNHCR Handbook). In considering the effect of a decision which derives its personal facts from a single interview, the proximity of that interview to arrival and the then circumstances of the applicant must be taken into account... The interview was not structured but effectively commenced with a request that the appellant states 'what particular event caused you to leave your own country' and then proceeded by way of question and answer arising from the information so elicited. The interview is therefore effectively led by the interviewer but its parameters are set by the response to the initial question. In those circumstances, the question is to what extent a failure to provide the detailed information which might follow from a more structured approach can be regarded as undermining credibility.

1.18 It found the adjudicator's acceptance of the Home Office's credibility allegations to be unsatisfactory because

> There was no evaluation of the degree to which they were foreshadowed in what was said at interview nor any real consideration of the degree to which such an interview could in the circumstances in which it was carried out, be expected to produce such a full explanation of the basis of claim.

1.19 The *converse* of the allegation discussed above is also common: the refusal letter will complain that information provided in a SEF or accompanying statement was not *repeated* in the interview. It is difficult to attribute good motives to the Home Office when one considers that the claimant is given the following standard assurance by the immigration officer about the purpose of the interview:

> *I have read all the information in the SEF form you sent us. There is no need for you to repeat this information today. This interview gives me the opportunity to ask you for some further details on the information in the SEF.* (Standard introduction to Home Office interview record following SEF)

1.20 The IAT has emphasised that a decision maker should have regard to the context of any interview, and particularly what the claimant was told about its purpose, when determining whether the omission of information is significant (e.g. *Salim*).

1.21 Sometimes, the claimant may be criticised for failing to give details, even though the Home Office interviewer asked for none. For example, your client may have been asked if she were detained. She answers 'Yes, for a month.' The interviewer, rather than asking for details, moves on to his next question. It is then alleged in the refusal letter that if your client had really been detained for a month, she would have given more details about it.

1.22 Where actual inconsistent statements are alleged (as opposed to a failure to mention a point at any particular stage), the allegation may result from misunderstanding or misrepresentation of your client's statements. For example, what was expressed as a rough guess by your client may be transformed by the refusal letter into a concrete statement. Leading questions may be used to lead inconsistent answers.

1.23 Very often, the claimant will be given no opportunity to comment on a perceived inconsistency between answers during the interview. The answers will simply be stored up for presentation in the refusal letter as unexplained discrepancies. Such practices are pursued, despite assurances from the Home Office that it follows (and the IAT's direction that it *should* follow) the UNHCR handbook. The Handbook states that:

> *While an initial interview should normally suffice to bring an applicant's story to light, it may be necessary for the examiner to clarify any apparent inconsistencies and to resolve any contradictions in a further interview, and to find an explanation for any misrepresentation or concealment of material facts.* (paragraph 199)

1.24 It is, in any event, a basic principle of fairness that perceived discrepancies should be put to a claimant before being held against her. In *Uruthiran*, the IAT noted that:

> *[G]iven the shared burden of investigation, the failing by the Home Office themselves to have picked the point up when it emerged in the interview and sought elucidation tends to demonstrate a propensity towards a con-*

frontational type of interview which is both unacceptable and contrary to the guidelines included in the UNHCR Handbook. These guidelines are in our view sensible, practical, and ensure a proper and fair investigation of a claim which does not depend for its outcome upon the awareness of an individual claimant of what he should do or alternatively the availability to a claimant of an experienced representative present at an interview.

1.25 The Home Office's APIs contain sensible advice, seldom followed by the Home Office in practice:

The caseworker, when assessing an application, should consider whether there is any reason to doubt the credibility of the applicant. Where credibility is in doubt, the applicant should be given the opportunity to explain the reasons behind their actions or statements.

Where the applicant has been given no opportunity to explain inconsistencies, care should be taken about using the inconsistencies to question credibility.

As noted above, question marks over an applicant's credibility do not negate their claim to asylum if other objective evidence demonstrates a reasonable likelihood of persecution should they be returned.

Discrepancies, exaggerated accounts, and the addition of new claims of mistreatment may affect credibility. However, they may equally reflect a concern on the part of the applicant, or their advisers, to bolster a claim due to a very real fear of return. Applicants should be given the opportunity to explain any apparent discrepancies and the reasons for any changes in their accounts.

1.26 The unfairness in not putting discrepancies at the time is not cured by the point being put months or years later at the appeal when it is obviously far more difficult to explain (if it is even remembered), and the lapse of time may be relied upon by the Home Office as providing opportunity to fabricate an answer. In *Salim*, the IAT said that:

It seems to us that in the second interview if there are discrepancies with the first, the appellant should then be given the chance to explain why. That opportunity would be more telling whichever way the responses went when the matter came on appeal.

Allegations arising from other asylum claims

1.27 Refusal letters have been known to allege discrepancies between the information given by the claimant and confidential information from the files of other asylum seekers (particularly relatives). This again is directly contrary to Home Office policy which is that:

> *Caseworkers should not seek to discredit one applicant's claim by refer-ring in a Reasons for Refusal Letter or elsewhere, to information provided in confidence by another applicant, unless that information is already in the public domain. Such action represents a clear breach of our confiden-tiality statement as it may allow a third party to deduce the original source of the information. This applies even where we leave out those details which specifically allow the other person to be identified.*
>
> *This applies to applicants who are related, such as husbands and wives, and have separate applications. Even where one directly contradicts the other, details from the claim of one family member should not be used to discredit another family member in a Reasons for Refusal Letter unless the matter is already in the public domain.* (APIs)

1.28   The policy applies regardless of whether the present claimant was pre-viously a dependent on the other asylum seeker's claim.

1.29   Note, however, that the Home Office considers that its confidentiality undertaking lapses once an appeal has been dismissed. It then claims to be free not only to make use of the determination but also to dis-close any other information previously provided to it by the claimant during the course of her claim, regardless of whether the information was even mentioned in the determination. This freedom to disclose previously confidential information expressly embraces disclosure to other asylum seekers via their refusal letters. The only exception is where the adjudicator directed that the public be excluded from the hearing of the appeal (see chapter 32 where the policy is set out). You may need to warn your client about this disturbing policy.

1.30   Where confidential information *has* been included in a refusal letter in breach of the Home Office's confidentiality undertaking, Home Office policy is to remove it:

> *If we become aware of a case where a caseworker has disclosed informa-tion that should not have been disclosed, then we must not continue to rely on that information at any subsequent appeal hearing… The case should be looked at again to ascertain whether the decision will stand without the information in question and whether further consideration/ investigation is necessary.* (APIs)

Political sophistication

1.31   The refusal letter might claim that '*The Secretary of State was of the opin-ion that your understanding of the aims of the organisation was extremely basic and therefore did not believe that you had the involvement which you claimed.*'

1.32   The asylum interview on which that statement is based may have included a series of sometimes ludicrously simplistic questions about the ideology of the organisation. Your client answers the simplistic questions. The refusal letter then alleges that your client's understanding of the aims and objectives of the organisation is simplistic!

1.33   Alternatively, the Home Office will criticise a 'foot soldier' who attended demonstrations or provided food and shelter because she cannot give a blow by blow account of past splits in the organisation or the derivation of its ideology. An interviewing officer may demand that a young Kurdish villager explain whether the party for which she distributed leaflets adopts the Russian, Chinese, or Albanian model of socialism. Your client will not know what the interviewing officer is talking about (though neither, it has to be said, may the interviewing officer). The Home Office appears to have little conception of the way such activists are recruited or the manner in which the organisation presents itself to them. It would of course be more startling if such a claimant were able to pontificate on such topics.

Implausibility

1.34   On a vast array of topics, the refusal letter will say that the Secretary of State considers that someone would have acted differently in the scenario your client describes and, solely on that basis, conclude that your client's account is a lie. The Secretary of State may consider that the local police would not have released your client if they were still suspicious of her; that officials would not have accepted bribes to release her or allow her through immigration control; that she would not have been arrested just because her family were active; that guerillas would not have anything against her just because she refused to help them; or that drug barons would not pursue her to a particular town.

1.35   Since no evidence is provided to support such allegations of implausibility, it can only be assumed that they are based either on what the Secretary of State would do if he was a prison guard, a guerilla or a drugs baron, or on how he believes a reasonable prison guard, guerilla, or drugs baron would behave. How the Secretary of State works this out is never revealed. Equally, the refusal letter will claim that the Secretary of State knows how your client would and would not have acted in her country of origin, for example, how much torture she would take without confessing, or whether she would risk returning to her village to see her mother one last time if she was really so frightened of the authorities.

1.36 These allegations of implausibility may directly contradict each other. For example, one paragraph may allege that the appellant's 'low level' activity for her organisation was insufficient to provoke the adverse interest of the authorities. But another paragraph will claim that it was both legitimate and expected that the authorities would wish to apprehend someone who had supported an 'illegal organisation' in the manner claimed by your client.

1.37 Sometimes, the refusal letter will be contradicted by the Home Office's own reports. For example, claims by activists from Turkey have been regularly rejected on grounds that it is implausible that the claimant would have been tortured then released without charge, rather than charged under 'the Turkish Penal Code or the strict Anti-Terror Law'. Yet, the Home Office's own contemporaneous Operational Guidance Note on Turkey (January 2002) recognised both the prevalence of torture and the prevalence of arbitrary detention without charge and quoted the statistic that 95% of detainees are released without charge.

1.38 The Home Office commonly claims that an asylum seeker's ability to leave her country with her own passport is inconsistent with a fear of persecution. In *He*, Schiemann LJ noted that:

> Another pillar [of the case against the appellant] seems to be that he left on his own passport. That at best goes to show that he is not wanted for any outstanding offences. Given that it is to be assumed that the passport was obtained by bribery it does not even go that far. In any event, it tells us nothing of the likelihood of persecution on return. History contains examples of regimes which persecute a minority in their home country but are content for them to leave their home country. Their attitude is: we just do not want them here.

Lack of corroboration

1.39 Despite your client having submitted a detailed witness statement to the Home Office, the refusal letter will often state that '*The Secretary of State notes that you have provided no evidence of your claim.*' As pointed out by the IAT on several occasions (e.g. ***Kasolo***), this allegation is simply wrong. Her statement is evidence. What the Home Office appears to mean is that the asylum seeker has provided no additional evidence to corroborate her own testimony. However, it is well established that an asylum seeker's claim should not be dismissed simply because she fails to provide corroboration. The UNHCR Handbook states that:

> Often, however, an applicant may not be able to support his statements by documentary or other proof and cases in which an applicant can provide evidence of all his statements will be the exception rather than the

rule. In most cases a person fleeing from persecution will have arrived with the barest necessities and very frequently even without personal documents. Thus, while the burden of proof in principle rests on the applicant, the duty to ascertain and evaluate all the relevant facts is shared between the applicant and the examiner. Indeed, in some cases, it may be for the examiner to use all the means at his disposal to produce the necessary evidence in support of the application. Even such independent research may not, however, always be successful and there may also be statements that are not susceptible of proof. (paragraph 196)

1.40   On occasion, the Home Office has made completely unreasonable or impractical demands that asylum seekers obtain documentary proof from the country of origin. On the other hand, its own obligations to assist in this respect (although only with the consent of the claimant) appear to have escaped it.

1.41   If the claimant is lucky enough to be able to produce corroborating documentary evidence, that is seldom the end of her troubles. The evidence is liable to be dismissed simply as 'self-serving' (which the IAT has noted is a nonsensical characterisation: see para 16.14). The refusal letter may then assert in Kafkaesque terms that the corroborating evidence cannot be accepted without corroborating evidence.

Timing of flight

1.42   If the claimant remained in her country for any period after first being attacked or ill-treated then it will usually be alleged that the reasonable refugee could be expected to leave her country at the earliest opportunity. This may well sit in the same refusal letter as a paragraph claiming that the first incident was of insufficient gravity to justify claiming protection, or that her release from detention should have left her with nothing to worry about.

1.43   On the other hand, if your client left immediately after her problems developed, it will be said that there is no proof that she would have suffered any further problems had she stayed. For example, a claimant who fled following a two week detention in Sudan was told that her decision to flee was 'hasty and ill-conceived' (*Still no reason at all*, p.33). It is not uncommon to find the same refusal letter containing one allegation that the claimant left too early, and another that she left too late.

1.44   The allegation regularly derives from a misunderstanding of the cause of the claimant's flight. For example, the Home Office may complain that the claimant remained in her country for a year after being detained despite her never actually having suggested that this detention was the trigger for her flight. The Home Office may have little regard to factors such as a claimant's reluctance to abandon her home or family. Nor does it find it easy to recognise any middle ground between somebody who leaves at the first sign of trouble and someone who fights to the death.

Choice of country of asylum

1.45 If the claimant passed through any other country on her way to Britain, it will be alleged that '*a genuine refugee would be expected to apply for asylum in the first safe country she reached*'.

1.46 The Home Office does not offer any justification for this allegation. There would have been no need to claim asylum in a transit country unless she was detained in the transit country and faced with refoulement. Given that she successfully passed through the transit country undetected, it is difficult to see the logic behind the Home Office's argument. The Home Office has never produced any empirical evidence to support it.

1.47 Nor has it any basis in law. Professor Hathaway – recognised by the House of Lords as the leading academic authority on the Convention – states that there is no requirement upon a refugee to claim asylum in the first country which they reach. He points out that the Convention could have imposed such a requirement but did not. He concludes that 'The basic standard unequivocally refutes the legitimacy of a so-called 'direct flight' requirement' (*Law of Refugee Status*, pp. 46–50). That is also UNHCR's position. In *Adimi*, the English courts finally rejected the argument, Simon Brown LJ stating that he was persuaded by the *travaux préparatoires* to the Convention, UNHCR, and the writings of leading commentators that an element of choice was indeed open to refugees as to where they claimed asylum. Newman J said in the same case that:

> The Convention is a living instrument, changing and developing with the times so as to be relevant and to afford meaningful protection to refugees in the conditions in which they currently seek asylum. Apart from the current necessity to use false documents, another current reality and advance, occurring since 1951, is the development of a readily accessible and worldwide network of air travel. As a result there is a choice of refuge beyond the first safe territory by land or sea. There have been distinctive and differing state responses to requests for asylum. Thus there exists a rational basis for exercising choice where to seek asylum. I am unable to accept that to recognise it is to legitimise forum shopping.

1.48 Even if the Home Office argument did have some basis in law, it is unclear how it envisages that asylum seekers would judge the relative safety of various third countries – particularly when litigation over the years demonstrates how difficult the Home Office itself has found this task. It is often hard to believe that even the Home Office considers the third country is really safe. Sometimes, the supposedly safe third country turns out not even to be a signatory to the Refugee Convention. Finally, the previous Home Secretary himself disputed that asylum seekers are drawn to the UK by its favourable laws and policies (a finding supported by Home Office research). He concluded instead that:

> The reason particular individuals and groups choose a particular country in which to seek asylum are many and various, including historical links and similar cultural factors. (Letter from Home Secretary, *Daily Telegraph* 21.1.99)

When the claim was lodged

1.49 Claiming asylum after arrival, even days after arrival, is according to the Home Office '*contrary to the behaviour which could reasonably be expected of a genuine refugee*'. No evidence is offered. If someone successfully effects entry to the country – whether legally or illegally – and *then* presents themselves voluntarily to the Home Office to seek asylum, it is difficult to understand how that demonstrates that they do not need it. The IAT has recognised that:

> '*It seems to us entirely understandable that a potential refugee would think it far preferable to obtain admission before applying for asylum than applying at the airport.*' (**Latif Mohammed**)

1.50 A similar point has been made by the Court of Appeal (which also quoted the above passage):

> *Care should be taken before placing undue weight on an untruth told at the point of entry in order to get into this country. There may in certain cases be good reasons for telling that untruth. Cases will vary depending on their facts and the personality involved. Some people arriving in this country may be in fear or may have very little understanding of what is required of them.* (**Wakene**, per Swinton Thomas LJ)

1.51 In **Adimi**, Simon Brown LJ quoted with approval UNHCR guidance to the effect that:

> *given the special situation of asylum seekers, in particular the effects of trauma, language problems, lack of information, previous experiences which often result in a suspicion of those in authority, feelings of insecurity, and the fact that these and other circumstances may vary enormously from one asylum seeker to another, there is no time limit which*

can be mechanistically applied or associated with the expression [claiming asylum] 'without delay'.

1.52　If someone has been granted leave to enter or remain in another capacity for a substantial period, she may be understandably reluctant to subject herself to the distress and uncertainty of the asylum process for so long as she has this alternative protection from refoulement. That is particularly so since a refusal in the asylum process could lead to curtailment of her leave and hasten her expulsion. She may hope that she will be able to return to her country in time.

Activities in Britain

1.53　This is another 'damned if you do, damned if you don't' category. If your client has taken part in political activities in the UK, these are likely to be dismissed as 'self-serving'. If she has not, it may be said that this is inconsistent with her claimed political commitment in her home country.

1.54　The Court of Appeal held in **Danian** that a claim cannot be rejected on the basis that the risk flows from activities which were 'self-serving' (or 'unreasonable', or even carried out in bad faith). The sole question is whether these activities create a real risk of article 3 ill-treatment or persecution for a Convention reason.

Economic motivation

1.55　The refusal letter commonly asserts that the claimant is an economic migrant. Questions and answers in the asylum interview may be twisted in an effort to produce a basis for this allegation. Consider, for example, the following exchanges from a Home Office asylum interview, quoted in *Still no reason at all*:

> 1/ Interviewer:　*How did you intend to support yourself in the UK?*
>
> Claimant:　　　*When I came here I knew nothing. I believe that given the chance to work I would.*
>
> Interviewer:　　*Did you think you would be able to work in the UK when you left…?*
>
> Claimant:　　　*I hoped.*
>
> 2/ Interviewer:　*What will you do if (asylum) granted?*
>
> Claimant:　　　*I will be grateful. Try to work at anything?*

> Interviewer: *If refused?*
>
> Claimant: *I think it will be very difficult to return to [my country]. I cannot return because of the danger to my family. I have faith in the UK being a democratic country and upholding human rights.*

These were sufficient in each case for the Home Office to allege that the claim was based on a 'desire for economic betterment not a fear of persecution'.

1.56 Your client may well have had a perfectly reasonable quality of life in economic terms in her home country (particularly compared to her quality of life as an asylum seeker in the UK). Alternatively, her economic difficulties may flow from discrimination or the adverse interest of the authorities.

Claims about country conditions and risk

1.57 The Home Office produces standard paragraphs about conditions in particular countries of origin which it often inserts into refusal letters regardless of the facts of the individual's case. They are seldom sourced. They will range from claims that democratic elections are on the horizon to more picturesque assertions about farmers feeling safe enough to return to their fields. It will often be alleged that government ministers do not approve of human rights abuses by their security forces or that such abuses are not government policy. It will likely ignore clear evidence that abuses continue despite this condemnation, or claim that they may be disregarded because they are the result of 'indiscipline'. In *Jayakumaran*, Taylor J commented:

> '*I ask what solace it is to the victim to hear that he is being persecuted by soldiers out of control rather than the government if this be the case.*'

1.58 Often there will not be a clear divide between 'the government' and 'soldiers out of control'. Particular organs of state may be willing to condemn human rights abuses while other organs of state perpetrate them. One part of the security forces may torture while another does not. Different state organisations may be bitterly opposed to each other. In *Kinuthia*, the Court of Appeal confirmed that it is a misdirection in law to conclude that the availability of 'recourse' after the claimant has been maltreated by the security forces can constitute sufficient protection for the purposes of the Refugee Convention.

Minimising past harm and present risk

1.59 Past persecution and ill-treatment will commonly be dismissed by the Home Office on the ground that the claimant has not shown that she will suffer such treatment again. It is of course impossible for the claimant to prove that she will suffer the same treatment that she has already suffered. But that is not the test. In **Demirkaya**, the Court of Appeal cited with approval the following passage from Professor Hathaway's *The Law of Refugee Status*:

> *Where evidence of past maltreatment exists, however, it is unquestionably an excellent indicator of the fate that may await an applicant upon return to her home. Unless there has been a major change of circumstances within that country that makes prospective persecution unlikely, past experience under a particular regime should be considered probative of future risk...*
>
> *In sum, evidence of individualised past persecution is generally a sufficient, though not a mandatory, means of establishing prospective risk.*

1.60 The Court held (per Stuart-Smith LJ) that:

> *In my judgment, if it is the opinion of the Tribunal that there has been such a significant change that the appellant is no longer at risk, it is incumbent upon them to explain why it is so.*

1.61 Another common Home Office argument is that 'While you claim to have been arrested repeatedly and ill-treated, you were on your own account released each time without charge because the authorities had no evidence and the Secretary of State does not therefore believe you are of any adverse interest to the authorities.'

1.62 Claimants often indicate, when asked why they were not charged or convicted, that they do not think that the authorities had the necessary evidence. This may be correct. However the Home Office may portray this as acceptance that the authorities have no further interest in, suspicion of, or desire to obtain evidence against the claimant, which is not usually what she meant at all.

1.63 You can of course simply point to the fact that your client has been repeatedly detained as indicating risk of repetition. But the central weight that the Home Office repeatedly puts on the absence of any charge (regardless of torture) is particularly strange. The right not to be detained without charge is, according to international human rights law, there to protect the *detainee*. Arbitrary extra judicial detention may well be a feature of the tyranny from which your client flees. The security forces may use detention and torture in order to intimidate, punish, and obtain information, and disregard due process of law because they consider themselves above it. That, one would have thought, was part of the claimant's case rather than the Home Office's case.

1.64   Some Home Office assertions are more bizarre altogether. The following is taken from *No reason at all*:

> *The Secretary of State noted that you claimed that soldiers... came to your house... arrested your father and shot your brother who later died although you managed to escape through a window. The Secretary of State noted your claim that the soldiers were firing wildly within the house, and he considered that the shooting of your brother was therefore not necessarily a deliberate act. He further noted that they did not shoot your father who was the most politically active member of your family.*

Non-state risks

1.65   The law relating to risk from non-state actors has been the subject of substantial litigation. At time of writing, it is being reviewed once again by the Court of Appeal in **Bagdanavicius**. Yet the Home Office still manages to incorporate criteria into its refusals for which there is no support in any caselaw, and which can be discarded before you start collating evidence to deal with the remainder. This is a common standard paragraph from a refusal letter in a non-state case:

> *With regard to the attacks that you claim have been perpetrated on you by non-state groups, the Secretary of State would point out that, in general, he takes the view that such individuals cannot be regarded as 'agents of persecution' within the terms of the Refugee Convention. In order to bring yourself within the scope of the Convention, you would have to show that these incidents were not simply the random actions of individuals but were a sustained pattern or campaign of persecution directed at you which was knowingly tolerated by the authorities, or that the authorities were unable, or unwilling, to offer you effective protection. In the opinion of the Secretary of State, this has not been established in your case. The Secretary of State does not consider that the authorities' inability to apprehend the perpetrators can be construed as complicity in, or support for, such attacks. He considers that you should seek redress through the proper authorities before seeking international protection.*

1.66   There is no authority for the proposition that past harm from non-state actors must constitute 'a sustained pattern or campaign of persecution'. Ask the HOPO to identify his authority. Ask him also for the authority supporting a requirement that a refugee must 'seek redress through the proper authorities' before seeking asylum. It is similarly unnecessary to show 'complicity in, or support for, such [non-state] attacks'.

1.67   The Home Office will often allege that sufficient protection exists in countries where there is no proper rule of law, no independent judicial system, and brutal and arbitrary security forces. It will rely upon statements of government ministers and government 'initiatives' without any assessment of their effect on the ground.

1.68   Do not be surprised if half the refusal letter is aimed at showing that your client is not at any risk from the government, even if the risks claimed are purely non-state.

Refugee Convention reason/exclusion/legitimate interest

1.69   It is fairly unusual for the refusal letter to contain an explicit allegation that the claimant is excluded from the Refugee Convention by reason of article 1F (but see chapter xx). More usual is an allegation that the security forces' interest in the claimant was 'legitimate' because of the claimant's support for an illegal/terrorist organisation. What the Home Office apparently wants to say is that she is not being persecuted because the security forces are conducting a legitimate investigation into terrorism. However, torture can never amount to legitimate investigation (*Ravichandran*). One motive of the persecutor may be to combat 'terrorists'. But the infliction of torture may give rise to a factual inference that a Convention reason was also in play (*Sivakumar*, per Lord Hutton).

1.70   The 'legitimate interest' argument may be used not only against supporters of armed opposition groups but even against those involved in peaceful political opposition simply on the basis that the state authorities have declared such activities 'illegal'. The Home Office may allege that security forces were only doing their duty in arresting your client due to the illegal nature of her activities, and that this is 'prosecution not persecution', or even that arrest for illegal activities does not come within the Refugee Convention. Clearly, the fact that the state has outlawed her activities will be part of her case – yet the refusal letter may not only appear to legitimise such laws but view them as the answer to the claimant's case.

Internal protection alternative

1.71   The Home Office regularly relies on an internal protection alternative ('internal flight') for no apparent reason except that your client has not actually been persecuted in the area to which the Home Office suggests she goes. This is often as sensible as suggesting that someone who escaped from police in London will not be of interest to police in Newcastle. It will usually be perfectly reasonable for your client to assume that once she comes to the adverse attention of a state's security forces in her home area, she cannot look to those same authorities for protection in any other area. In UNHCR's guidance on the subject, it states that 'UNHCR has long held that the possibility of internal relocation cannot be a relevant consideration where the feared agent of persecution is a state agent, as these are presumed to be able to act throughout the country' though this presumption may be rebutted by evidence to show that the state has lost control of a particular area (see UNHCR Position Paper: *Relocating Internally as a Reasonable Alternative to Seeking Asylum – (The So-Called 'Internal Flight Alternative' or 'Relocation Principle')*). That position is reflected by Professor Hathaway's Michigan Guidelines to which the Court of Appeal referred with approval in *Canaj.*

1.72 There is in any event the additional question of how your client might reach the proposed area of internal protection. The Home Office may have to be reminded that your client is not actually in the country of origin – its proposed internal protection alternative often assumes the contrary. Its proposal might be viable were it planning to drop your client on a deserted beach in the dead of night so that she could reach the 'safe' area undetected. It might be less viable if (as is more likely) the Home Office is planning to fly her into the main airport into the arms of the security forces.

1.73 The question of whether it is unreasonable or unduly harsh to expect the claimant to go to the 'safe' area generally receives cursory, if any, attention. (See para 20.19 for how to apply this test.)

The Home Office's human rights analysis

1.74 The separate consideration of human rights provisions at the end of this chapter reflects the treatment it receives in the average refusal letter. The issue generally appears as an addendum, indeed often a single paragraph which asserts that the claimant does not qualify for protection under any of the articles of the ECHR.

1.75 Where individual articles of the ECHR are dealt with at all, it will often be simply by reference back to the reasons for refusing asylum, however inapplicable they are. For example, an article 3 claim may be dismissed by reference to a discussion which centred upon absence of Convention reason, or upon the proposition (particular to the Refugee Convention) that generalised risk from civil war should be excluded from consideration.

1.76 Where the refusal letter does engage in discussion of human rights provisions, it will often get them spectacularly wrong. This is worth taking up with the Home Office. For example, the Home Office rejected one claimant in the following terms:

> The Secretary of State has considered your claims under Article 3 in which you claim that your mental state would deteriorate. However, the Secretary of State considers that depression, post-traumatic stress disorder or mental illness cannot amount to inhuman and degrading treatment even when the condition deteriorates on return.

1.77 That proposition is contrary to the European Court's caselaw (**Bensaid**) as well as common sense. The Medical Foundation complained about this assertion, stating that:

> Those who suffer from post-traumatic stress disorder have their symptoms exacerbated whenever memories of the trauma are triggered… To return the person to the environment in which they were traumatised may expose them to constant reminders, thus causing a catastrophic deterioration in their psychological state. For the Secretary of State to send such a person to a situation where their memories will be repeatedly triggered is unacceptable and inhuman in the article 3 sense…

> In our opinion knowingly aggravating depression, post traumatic stress disorder and mental illness may constitute inhuman and degrading treatment. (Letter from Hopkins and Peel, dated 12 February 2002).

1.78 The Home Office responded to the effect that:

> …we share your view that circumstances may arise in which it may be possible to demonstrate that the United Kingdom would be in breach of its obligations under Article 3 to return a person suffering, for example, from post-traumatic stress disorder to their home country. In short, the views set out in the offending paragraph do not reflect the policy of the Secretary of State.

> (Home Office instructors) will emphasise to caseworkers that bald general statements of the type you identified are not appropriate in this very complex area of caselaw.

1.79 If family life is in issue, the Court of Appeal's decision in **Mahmood** will be invoked like a Mantra, regardless of its applicability to the facts of the case. See **Shala** (para 42.101) for the Court of Appeal's discussion of the flaws inherent in this practice. To the extent that article 8(2) is addressed at all, it is usually by standard paragraphs asserting that the decision is justified by the need to maintain immigration control. Without more, the Home Office's argument is circular. The 'maintenance of immigration control' can only require the removal of someone whom the Home Office has already decided needs to be removed.

Is that it?

1.80 The Home Office has in the past given the following written assurance to the Asylum Rights Campaign which had 'expressed concern about Presenting Officers raising fresh reasons for refusal':

> *Presenting Officers are instructed to confine themselves to the reasons for refusal and the factual information which supports them, for example records of interview.*

1.81 There is nothing to stop HOPOs dealing with new issues which arise at the hearing. However, HOPOs regularly seek to advance different (and even contradictory) reasons for refusal at the hearing from those disclosed in the refusal letter. Such conduct adds to the cost of preparing an appeal as a conscientious representative has not only to meet the case that has been made in the refusal letter, but whatever alternative case the HOPO might try to advance in the appeal. Fairness requires that an asylum seeker is given notice of the reasons for which her claim has been rejected, and she is entitled to the full reasons not just some of them. See chapter 9 for seeking to clarifying the case you have to meet.

1 Analysing the refusal letter
Key points

- Analysing the refusal letter is the first stage in your appeal preparation. The letter is supposed to set out the Home Office's case.

- Its contentions may cover

  - ☐ disputes over past facts, including alleged discrepancies or implausibility,
  - ☐ claims about human rights conditions in the country of origin and absence of risk,
  - ☐ legal arguments.

- Get your clients comments on the refusal letter at the outset. Check that representations were made about any defects in the Home Office asylum interview. If not, take a dated statement covering these.

- Check the Home Office's factual summary of your client's claim.

Disputes about past facts

- Is an alleged 'discrepancy' based simply on the fact that further information was presented during the course of the claim? Did the Home Office actually request the further information during the asylum interview?

- Did the Home Office provide an opportunity to comment on perceived discrepancies during the interview?

- Has it relied on confidential information from another asylum seeker's claim?

- Does it criticise lack of detail when none was requested at the asylum interview?

- Where actual inconsistent statements are alleged, has the Home Office misunderstood or misrepresented those statements?

- Are credibility challenges based on lack of political sophistication fair and realistic?

- What basis has been offered for allegations of implausibility? Are they contradicted by other claims made in the refusal letter?

- Has the claim been dismissed for want of corroboration? Is corroborative evidence dismissed as 'self-serving'?

- Do criticisms of the timing of the appellant's escape disclose a failure to grasp the reasons for her flight?

- Has any basis been shown for allegations that failure to claim in a third country or failure to claim immediately upon arrival is inconsistent with a genuine fear of persecution?

- Are allegations of economic motivation based on a fair reading of the asylum interview?

Claims about country conditions and risk

- Do the Home Office's claims about country conditions reflect the independent evidence?

- Has it paid proper regard to past persecution when assessing future risk?

- Are its assertions about sufficiency of protection from non-state actors realistic?

- Are claims of Art 1F exclusion or 'prosecution, not persecution' consistent with the caselaw?

- Is a claimed internal protection alternative realistic? Does it take account of the method by which the Home Office proposes to expel your client?

- Have human rights arguments been properly appreciated and addressed?

2 Non-compliance refusals

2.1   If the Home Office alleges that the claimant has failed to comply with its procedures, it may reach a decision on the initial claim without completing the normal determination process. These 'non-compliance refusals' have increased dramatically in recent years.

2.2   The increase has largely resulted from the 14 day deadline imposed for completion of a Standard Evidence Form (SEF). Not only was the time limit unreasonably short, but the Home Office was too inefficient to recognise when the form was returned. Many non-compliance refusals were therefore issued where the SEF had in fact been returned within the deadline.

2.3   In *Haddad*, the IAT held that the Home Office could never refuse a claim on grounds of non-compliance alone. It must always reach a decision on the merits on the basis of the information available to it. However, where the refusal results from alleged non-submission of a SEF, the information with which the Home Office needs to deal on the merits is likely to be minimal.

2.4   The IAT also held in *Haddad* that an adjudicator could not dismiss the appeal on the ground that the allegation of non-compliance was well-founded or simply on the evidence that was before the Home Office when the non-compliance refusal was issued. The adjudicator must determine the asylum/human rights appeal on the merits on the material which is placed before him.

Flawed non-compliance refusals

2.5   Where the allegation of non-compliance turns out to be mistaken, the Home Office has accepted that it must withdraw the non-compliance refusal and reconsider the claim (Home Office's statement of reasons, approved by the Court in *R v SSHD, ex parte Karaoglan*, 4 May 2001).

2.6   The APIs recognise that non-compliance refusals based on failure to attend an interview may also transpire to be incorrect:

> *If a non-compliance refusal has been made on the basis that the applicant failed to attend for interview and it subsequently turns out that either the interview invitation was never despatched or was despatched to the wrong address then the refusal should be withdrawn as above and another interview arranged.*

2.7 In **Nori**, the Home Office had withdrawn its flawed non-compliance refusal. The IAT concluded that there was consequently no lawful basis for the refusal of leave to enter against which the appeal had been brought (given that the asylum claim was now undetermined):

> *Once the decision on which the appeal was based had been withdrawn, no appeal could proceed. In those circumstances, the adjudicator's purported decision on that appeal is in our view a nullity... If the Secretary of State decides on the merits that he will refuse the application, and therefore will issue a fresh decision to refuse leave to enter, then Mr Nori will have his appeal rights based on that decision.*

Tactics

2.8 Regardless of whether you consider the non-compliance refusal to be justified, you should always lodge grounds of appeal in order to protect your client's position. If you can show that the non-compliance refusal was based on incorrect facts, you can then write to the Home Office requiring it to withdraw its decision and reconsider your client's claim on the merits.

2.9 Where the Home Office does not withdraw its non-compliance refusal of its own accord, it is not always in your interests to press it to do so. The main *disadvantages* of a non-compliance refusal are that you lose the initial consideration of your claim, the adjudicator becomes the first decision maker (sometimes without any advance notice of the Home Office's case), and there is no right of appeal on the facts against what has become the first decision (appeal to the IAT is on a point of law and requires permission).

2.10 However, the withdrawal of the non-compliance refusal will mean delay if the Home Office then refuses on the merits. Where the Home Office is issuing more or less pro forma refusal letters for a particular category of claimants with little regard to their individual facts, the benefits of an initial consideration by the Home Office may be illusory.

2.11 The adjudicator has no power to 'remit' the claim to the Home Office or direct that it reconsider the claim, whether or not the non-compliance refusal was justified (see *Haddad* above and *Mwanza*). But whether or not the non-compliance refusal was justified, you (and the adjudicator) are entitled to some disclosure of the Home Office's case. The adjudicator is entitled to direct that the Home Office state the grounds upon which it is opposing the appeal, as long as he does not require the Home Office to 'reconsider' the case (see the IAT's decision in *Razi* and the discussion at para 9.11).

2.12 Sometimes, the Home Office will claim that its allegation of non-compliance is relevant to the adjudicator's assessment of credibility. This will often be unfounded, particularly where the allegation is simply the late submission of a SEF (given the difficulties in finding a representative and completing the SEF within 14 days).

2 Non-compliance refusals
Key points

- The Home Office may not refuse a claim on non-compliance grounds alone without considering the merits on the basis of any material already before it.

- It has undertaken that where a non-compliance refusal is shown to be flawed, it will withdraw the decision and reconsider.

- If the Home Office withdraws the refusal of asylum, the underlying refusal of leave to enter will be rendered unlawful, and the appeal against that decision will be terminated.

- An adjudicator must always determine an appeal on the merits: he has no power to remit the matter to the Home Office for reconsideration. He can, however, require the Home Office to disclose any grounds for opposing the appeal.

- The merits of pressing the Home Office to withdraw a non-compliance refusal will depend on the circumstances of the case.

3 'Clearly unfounded' certificates

3.1 The most urgent point to check when you receive the refusal letter is whether the claim has been certified as 'clearly unfounded'.

3.2 The complex certification regime under the 1999 Act (sch 4, para 9) has been repealed. The repeal does not formally affect certificates issued prior to 1 April 2003, but Home Office policy is to withdraw all remaining certificates prior to or at the hearing (Home Office Instruction on 'Withdrawal of Certificates made under Sch. 4 Immigration and Asylum Act 1999'). You need not therefore devote effort to challenging any such certification in the refusal letter.

3.3 However, what has replaced it is much more dangerous. The effect of a 'clearly unfounded' certificate under s.94 of the 2002 Act is that your client is denied any in-country appeal before being expelled to her country of origin. She may bring an appeal from her home country but the Court of Appeal noted in *ZL* that this is 'scant consolation' when she has already been removed to the country where she fears persecution and human rights abuses. Such appeals are not covered by this text.

3.4 The only means of preventing the Home Office removing your client without an effective appeal on the merits is to judicially review its certificate. This chapter gives a summary of some of the procedures and issues involved up to the consideration of the permission application on the papers. But these cases are complex, the Home Office tends to fight them hard, and the extraordinarily tight time limits applied to claimants mean that a mistake can be disastrous. They should be undertaken only if you are experienced in bringing judicial review proceedings. Otherwise, refer the judicial review to someone else.

The test for certification

3.5   While the consequences of a s.94 certificate are dire, the test for certification is correspondingly exacting. In **Razgar**, the Court of Appeal emphasised the 'very high threshold' that has to be met before a claim can be characterised as 'clearly unfounded', explaining that:

> *The Secretary of State cannot lawfully issue such a certificate unless the claim is bound to fail before an adjudicator. It is not sufficient that he considers that the claim is likely to fail on appeal, or even that it is very likely to fail.*

3.6   If your client is from a designated country, the Home Office is required by s.93(3) to issue a certificate if the claim is clearly unfounded. For other countries, he has a discretion whether or not to certify a claim that is clearly unfounded.

3.7   Section 94(4) designates the following countries: Cyprus, Czech Republic, Estonia, Hungary, Latvia, Lithuania, Malta, Poland, Slovak Republic, and Slovenia. Section 94(5) provides that:

> *(5) The Secretary of State may by order add a State, or part of a State, to the list in subsection (4) if satisfied that –*
>
> *(a) there is in general in that State or part no serious risk of persecution of persons entitled to reside in that State or part, and*
>
> *(b) removal to that State or part of persons entitled to reside there will not in general contravene the United Kingdom's obligations under the Human Rights Convention.*

3.8   At time of writing, the following additional countries have been designated: Albania, Bulgaria, Serbia and Montenegro, Jamaica, Macedonia, Moldova, and Romania (Asylum (Designated States) Order 2003); Brazil, Ecuador, Bolivia, South Africa, Ukraine, Sri Lanka and Bangladesh (Asylum (Designated States) (No. 2) Order 2003). The designation of a country may be challenged by judicial review if the criteria in s.94(5) are not met.

3.9   In **ZL**, the Court of Appeal held that the threshold test for determining whether a claim is clearly unfounded should be applied in the same way whether or not the country is designated. The practical effect of designation is nevertheless very significant. Home Office policy up to 8 June 2003 was not to certify claims from non-designated countries. Since that date, it is engaged in what it describes as a 'managed roll out of case-by-case certification of claims from residents of non designated states' (letter from Home Office to IAS, 17 June 2003). At time of writing, it remains rare for a claim from a non-designated country to be certified. On the other hand, most claims from designated countries are certified, and you should be prepared for this.

3.10 In *ZL*, the Court of Appeal held that on judicial review of a clearly unfounded certificate, the Court will determine for itself whether an appeal would be bound to fail:

> *We have... concluded that a [decision on whether a claim is clearly unfounded] is one which the court is as well placed as the Home Secretary to take, and we go on to review the evidence in that light...*

> *the test is an objective one: it depends not on the Home Secretary's view but upon a criterion which a court can readily re-apply once it has the materials which the Home Secretary had. A claim is either clearly unfounded or it is not...*

> *... If... the claim cannot on any legitimate view succeed, then the claim is clearly unfounded; if not, not.*

3.11 This means that the Court should be prepared to have regard to relevant evidence in determining this objective test whether or not it has been considered by the Home Office.

3.12 Almost all certificates presently issued are in respect of claimants who have been processed through the Oakington fast track procedure. The initial determination of such claims is supposed to be completed in seven days (although in reality, the Home Office has taken much longer to issue some decisions where it intends to certify the claim). The Court of Appeal concluded in *ZL* that the fast track procedure was fair in the context of what the claimant must do to avoid certification:

> *We would emphasise once again that the object of the fast-track procedure is to give applicants the chance to demonstrate that they have, or may have, an arguable case. We consider that the procedure affords them a fair opportunity to do this.*

3.13 The Court noted that:

> *[I]n some cases medical evidence will be required to support a protection claim and... in such circumstances, it is likely to prove impossible to bring a suitably qualified medical expert onto the site in the time available. In such cases, and in analogous cases, we would expect it to be recognised that the fast-track procedure is not appropriate and the decision deferred.*

3.14 It also stated that:

> *[I]n a case where the authenticity of documents remains in doubt and the issue of their authenticity is critical, we do not see how a claim can properly be declared clearly unfounded.*

3.15 As to country expert evidence, the Court of Appeal accepted that it would not be possible for a claimant herself to obtain and adduce expert evidence in the time permitted by the fast track process. However, it was influenced by the fact that representation from the RLC and IAS is available onsite at Oakington and these organisations collate expert evidence as an 'ongoing process' and it is not simply driven by individual applications. Different considerations may apply to claims certified outside the Oakington procedure.

3.16 In view of the high threshold test, it should be unnecessary at this stage to obtain expert evidence going to the plausibility of your client's account. It will not ordinarily be possible for the Home Office to say that an adjudicator would be bound to reach one credibility finding or another after hearing oral evidence. The Court of Appeal in *ZL* pointed out, in response to concerns about the time required to obtain expert evidence on country conditions, that:

> *The individual's own experience may raise a question as to whether, at least in the part of the country from which he has come, persecution is occurring... In such a case the applicant's claim will not be clearly unfounded and the claim should not be certified.*

Tactics and procedure

3.17 If the claim has been certified, the immediate priority is to check whether removal directions have been issued: this will determine the degree of urgency.

3.18 You then have to analyse the refusal letter to determine whether the Home Office has demonstrated that an adjudicator would be bound to dismiss the appeal. If its reasoning does not establish this test, you can then apply for public funding to challenge the certificate by judicial review.

3.19 Refusal letters tend to be longer than the norm where a s.94 certificate is issued. They are also far more likely to quote country evidence and IAT caselaw (sometimes copiously). This is often in support of an argument that there is a 'sufficiency of protection' in the country of origin. The citation of IAT caselaw is liable to be selective, raising serious issues of propriety in the context of a fast track procedure with such catastrophic potential consequences. One of your initial tasks in these circumstances will be to perform a search of relevant IAT caselaw to determine whether it is as adverse and uniform as the Home Office claims.

3.20 The Home Office usually accepts that it cannot rely on its views on credibility in order to show that the appeal would be bound to fail. Work through your client's account carefully to check whether the Home Office has failed to appreciate relevant elements. As indicated by the Court of Appeal, your client's experiences of ill-treatment may contradict the Home Office's claims that persons such as your client are at no real risk. It may have missed or downplayed facts which exacerbate future risk, e.g. the extent to which your client was targeted individually.

3.21 There may well be aspects of the Home Office's reasoning that can be addressed through further representations and evidence. Expert analysis of the refusal letter can be invaluable in order to deal with the Home Office's contentions on matters such as sufficiency of protection. Your client may also be able to add relevant evidence, particularly if the Home Office has given no prior notice of adverse points on which it intends to rely in the refusal letter.

3.22 However, you should not delay challenging the refusal letter if you already have sufficient grounds to do so. The Home Office usually rejects any request to defer removal in order to allow for further evidence in response to the refusal letter: such evidence can be submitted after you have lodged judicial review proceedings (thereby protecting your client from expulsion in the meantime).

3.23 If the Home Office appears to have done enough to justify its certificate on the basis of the evidence already before it, you must consider whether there is further evidence (e.g. expert evidence) that could be obtained to show that the appeal is arguable. If so, you should contend strongly to the Home Office that fairness demands that you have a reasonable opportunity to submit evidence in response to the refusal letter. If the Home Office refuses a reasonable request to permit you to obtain specific relevant evidence, this refusal may itself give grounds for judicial review.

3.24 Home Office policy is that once you indicate that you are applying for public funding with a view to seeking judicial review, it will defer removal for three working days. Within that time, you must not only seek and obtain public funding, but prepare and lodge the judicial review papers and notify the Home Office of the Administrative Court reference number.

3.25 Plainly, this leaves little time. Devolved powers by which solicitors can themselves authorise emergency public funding are not available in these cases. The LSC undertakes to turn around applications for public funding within 24 hours and, if public funding is refused, to arrange for a Funding Review Committee to hear the appeal on the same day or the next day.

3.26 Counsel can be instructed through Legal Help to provide an advice on the merits. You should be proactive in your application to the LSC in order to address its concerns. If public funding is refused, it may be very difficult in the timescale to arrange representation before the Funding Review Committee, but attendance by someone familiar with the issues can have a very substantial impact on the prospects of success. If it is impossible to arrange representation, it is essential to make written submissions addressing the LSC's reasons for refusing public funding. If funding is refused, the Funding Review Committee may be the only tribunal to have considered the merits of your client's asylum/human rights case before she is expelled.

3.27 Once the judicial review is lodged and the reference number communicated to the Home Office, you must again be proactive in ensuring that removal directions are cancelled. Do not rest until you have specific confirmation of this. Home Office procedures are far from infallible and it has been known to remove claimants by mistake after a judicial review has been lodged. If this happens, you need to contact the Treasury Solicitor urgently before the flight lands in the country of origin. The Treasury Solicitor will normally arrange for your client to be brought straight back. If not, an emergency application to the duty judge will be required.

3.28 The only body that escapes stringent time limits in this procedure is the Home Office. It regularly takes the full three weeks ordinarily allowed for lodging the Acknowledgement of Service. Use this time to obtain and submit any further relevant evidence.

3.29 The Acknowledgement of Service may well be accompanied by a new refusal letter countering the points made in your Claim Form and in any further evidence or representations you have submitted. The procedure operated at present involves an Administrative Court judge deciding whether to grant or refuse permission on the papers on the same day as the Home Office Acknowledgement of Service is received. This means that the judge may be invited to refuse permission on the basis of a new decision by the Home Office which you have not had any opportunity to consider. You should make immediate representations to the Administrative Court seeking a reasonable opportunity to respond to the fresh decision letter before permission is considered. If the Administrative Court does not defer consideration on the papers, the judge may at least be more inclined to list for oral hearing rather than dismissing the application on the papers. This is important in securing representation for the client since the LSC regularly withdraws public funding once there is a refusal of permission on the papers.

3.30 If consideration on the papers does result in permission being refused, you will have to make a further application to the LSC to extend public funding for an oral renewal. The Home Office's Acknowledgement of Service and any further refusal letter together with the judge's reasons must be addressed in detail in the grounds accompanying the public funding application. If the judge has relied on new points taken by the Home Office to which you had no opportunity to respond, then this should be emphasised (together with how you intend to respond to them).

3 'Clearly unfounded' certificates
Key points

■ Upon receipt of the refusal letter, check whether a clearly unfounded certificate has been issued. If it has, your client will be expelled without any appeal unless that certificate can be challenged in the Administrative Court. Such a challenge must be handled by someone experienced in bringing judicial review proceedings.

■ The Home Office may only certify a claim as clearly unfounded if an appeal would be *bound* to fail. It will not ordinarily be possible to say that an adjudicator would be bound to make one credibility finding or another after hearing oral evidence.

■ If your client is from a designated country, her claim is very likely to be certified if it is dismissed. You should be prepared for this.

■ Analyse the refusal letter to determine whether the Home Office has shown that an appeal is bound to fail. Are its references to country evidence and IAT caselaw selective? Has it overlooked or downplayed aspects of your client's account which may exacerbate risk?

■ Further representations and evidence may be appropriate to address the Home Office's reasoning, but it is unlikely to defer removal voluntarily to allow for this. Do not delay taking steps to challenge the certificate if you have sufficient grounds to do so.

■ The Home Office will defer removal for three working days once you indicate an intention to seek judicial review. The LSC will determine a public funding application within 24 hours and if refused, place the matter before the Funding Review Committee on the same or the next day. Representation before the committee is vital.

■ After lodging the judicial review, insist on confirmation that removal directions have been cancelled: the Home Office has been known to remove people by mistake.

■ Obtain and submit any further evidence as soon as possible after lodging the judicial review.

- The Administrative Court generally determines the permission application on the same day that it receives the Acknowledgement of Service. If that is accompanied by a new decision letter, request an opportunity to respond before permission is determined.

- If permission is refused on the papers and you seek public funding for an oral renewal, you must include a detailed response to the Home Office Acknowledgement of Service and any fresh decision letter and to the reasons given by the judge on the papers.

4 Lodging the appeal

The notice of appeal

4.1 An appeal can be lodged against any 'immigration decision' listed in s.82 of the 2002 Act on any of the grounds listed in s.84 (which include asylum and human rights grounds). See chapter 52 for asylum upgrade appeals brought under s.83.

4.2 By r.6(2), the notice of appeal must be served on the respondent (not the IAA) unless the appellant is in detention, in which case the notice can be served on 'the person having custody of him' (r.6(3)).

4.3 Rule 8 deals with lodging an appeal against any immigration decision post-dating 1 April 2003:

> *Form and contents of notice of appeal*
>
> 8. *(1) The notice of appeal must be in the appropriate prescribed form and must –*
>   *(a) state the name and address of the appellant; and*
>   *(b) state whether the appellant has authorised a representative to act for him in the appeal and, if so, give the representative's name and address.*
>
> *(2) The notice of appeal must set out the grounds for the appeal and give reasons in support of those grounds.*
>
> *(3) The notice of appeal must be signed by the appellant or his representative, and dated.*
>
> *(4) If a notice of appeal is signed by the appellant's representative, the representative must certify in the notice of appeal that he has completed the notice of appeal in accordance with the appellant's instructions.*

4.4 It is important to ensure that the notice of appeal is properly completed to avoid the Home Office alleging that no valid appeal has been made. If a defect in the notice is subsequently detected, whether the defect is fatal will depend on a consideration of the leading case of

Jeyeanthan (see para 44.16). An adjudicator should strive to avoid dismissing an asylum/human rights appeal on technicalities.

Grounds of appeal

4.5   The practical benefits of serving detailed grounds of appeal are in many cases limited. The appeal papers may languish in the Home Office for many months or more before even being transferred to the IAA (para 6.2). Conditions may change by the full hearing. Prior to the hearing, you will be directed to produce a skeleton argument which should set out your case. An advocate may wish to pursue points that were not apparent when the appeal was lodged. It is better not to draft long but hasty grounds which advance arguments on which you later have second thoughts, or which are inconsistent with those subsequently advanced by your advocate at the hearing.

4.6   The Rules state that the notice should include 'grounds for the appeal' and 'reasons in support of those grounds' (r.8(2) above). The distinction between a 'ground' and a 'reason in support' will largely depend on your phraseology. There is no point whatsoever in including three pages of 'standard' arguments in support of a generic asylum/human rights case. They will not assist the adjudicator and are likely only to irritate him if he reads them at all. If you are lodging an asylum/human rights appeal, your grounds/reasons should include allegations to the effect that:

● The Secretary of State's decision is in breach of the United Kingdom's obligations under the Refugee Convention because I will be at real risk of persecution for a Convention reason if removed in consequence of the decision.
● The Secretary of State's decision is unlawful under s.6 of the Human Rights Act 1998 and/or my removal from the United Kingdom in consequence of the decision would be unlawful under s.6 because my human rights will be breached.

4.7   It may also be useful to include a ground of appeal to the effect that 'the decision is otherwise not in accordance with the law' (s.84(1)(e)). If you are contending that the immigration decision is unlawful on public law grounds because it is inconsistent with Home Office policy, you should identify the relevant policy in your grounds of appeal. (Section 88, headed 'Ineligibility', provides that a person may not appeal under s.82(1) against any of the immigration decisions listed in s.88(1) if the immigration decision against which she wishes to appeal was taken on the ground that the person had sought leave to enter/remain for a purpose other than one which is permitted by the Immigration Rules. However, where a person *has* a right of appeal under s.82(1), and that appeal is before the adjudicator, s.88 does not purport to restrict his jurisdiction (indeed, his duty) to consider any of the grounds of appeal listed in s.84.) Other grounds listed in s.84 of the 2002 Act may be appropriate in a particular appeal. But the above should ensure that your grounds do not limit the future development of your asylum or human rights case. Rule 11 allows an appellant to vary grounds with the permission of an adjudicator. But it should not be necessary to make an application under this rule so long as you have not limited yourself to a particular asylum or human rights argument in your original grounds. (The position is different in the IAT: see chapters 43 and 46.)

4.8   There will be circumstances, however, where it is important to raise specific matters in the grounds of appeal. This may apply where you are raising significant new factual matters or complaints about how your client was treated by the Home Office. If the point touches on credibility, the HOPO may argue at the appeal that an adverse inference should be drawn from the failure to raise the point in the grounds. The alternative, if you are not yet decided whether to disclose the material, is to prepare a dated statement or note which can be produced to establish the date upon which your client supplied the material.

4.9   Where there has been a failure to follow Home Office policy or impropriety at the interview, it will be valuable to raise these in the grounds even if the prospects of a constructive response from the Home Office are forlorn. You can point to the reference in the grounds (and the absence of any Home Office response) in order to highlight to the adjudicator how seriously you viewed the matter. If the flaw is particularly serious, consider also making a formal complaint to the Home Office.

4.10   Home Office policy is that it will not usually respond to grounds which comment on the reasons for refusal. It claims that it will respond to *new* issues, but that does not often reflect the practice (para 9.3). Where the Home Office *does* serve a supplementary refusal letter following receipt of the appeal, it seldom assists in narrowing the issues. The Home Office may propose that you submit *further* grounds of appeal in response to its supplementary refusal letter. Most often, there is neither procedural need nor much utility in doing so.

4.11   The response to a one-stop notice is discussed in chapter 5.

Time limits and late appeals

4.12   Rule 7 states that:

(1) A notice of appeal by a person who is in the United Kingdom must be

> *given –*
>
> *(a) if the person is in detention under the Immigration Acts when he is served with notice of the decision against which he is appealing, not later than 5 days after he is served with that notice; and*
>
> *(b) in any other case, not later than 10 days after he is served with notice of the decision.*

The notice must be received within the time limit, not merely sent (r.54(6)). Rule 56 provides that only 'business days' are counted: this excludes weekends, bank holidays, Christmas Day, 27–31 December, and Good Friday.

4.13 If the time limit appears to have expired, you should take steps to lodge a notice of appeal immediately. Rule 10(1) provides that:

> *Where a notice of appeal is given outside the applicable time limit in rule 7, the appellant must –*
>
> *(a) state in the notice of appeal his reasons for failing to give the notice within that period; and*
>
> *(b) attach to the notice of appeal any written evidence upon which he relies in support of those reasons.*

4.14 The requirement to include both reasons for lodging out of time and any written evidence upon which you rely may conflict with the aim of lodging the appeal as quickly as possible. Do not delay more than necessary lodging the notice of appeal in order to prepare representations and evidence addressing the out of time point. Such delay may prejudice your client if you have to ask an adjudicator to extend time. Instead, submit the notice of appeal, and indicate that representations and evidence in respect of the delay are in preparation and the date on which they will be forwarded.

4.15 The Home Office as well as the adjudicator has power to extend time. Rule 10(2) states that:

> *Where the respondent receives a notice of appeal outside the applicable time limit, he may treat the notice as if it had been given in time, if satisfied that by reason of special circumstances it would be unjust not to do so.*

4.16 If you think that the notice of appeal may appear to be out of time but you contend that it is being lodged within 10 days of receipt of the immigration decision, you should address this with your notice of appeal in order to pre-empt an out of time allegation.

Procedure for an out of time allegation

4.17 Rule 10(3–10) provides:

(3) Where the respondent receives a notice of appeal which he contends has been given outside the applicable time limit, and does not treat the notice as if it had been given in time, he must –

   (a) file with the appellate authority –

      (i) the notice of appeal;

      (ii) a copy of the notice of the decision against which the appellant is appealing and any document served on the appellant giving reasons for that decision; and

      (iii) a copy of the notice which he serves on the appellant under sub-paragraph (b); and

   (b) at the same time, serve on the appellant a notice stating that –

      (i) he is treating the notice of appeal as being given out of time; and

      (ii) he is sending the notice of appeal to the appellate authority for an adjudicator to decide whether to extend the time for appealing.

(4) If the appellant contends that the notice of appeal was given in time he may file with the appellate authority written evidence in support of that contention.

(5) Written evidence under paragraph (4) must be filed –

   (a) if the appellant is in the United Kingdom, not later than 3 days;

   ...

   after the appellant is served with a notice under paragraph (3)(b).

(6) If the appellant files evidence under paragraph (4), an adjudicator must decide whether the notice of appeal was given in time.

(7) Where the notice of appeal was given out of time, the adjudicator may extend the time for appealing if satisfied that by reason of special circumstances it would be unjust not to do so.

(8) The adjudicator must decide the issues in paragraphs (6) and (7) –

   (a) without a hearing; and

   (b) on the basis of the documents filed by the respondent and any written evidence filed by the appellant.

(9) The appellate authority must serve notice of the adjudicator's decision on the parties.

(10) If the adjudicator decides that the notice of appeal was given in time, or he extends the time for appealing, rule 9 shall apply.

4.18   Under the 2000 Procedure Rules, an adjudicator would determine an out of time allegation at a hearing. However, r.10(8)(a) purports to prohibit an adjudicator from holding a hearing in order to decide the matter. Moreover, written evidence must be submitted within three days of being given notice by the Home Office that it is contending that the appeal is out of time.

4.19   The potential for unfairness and inaccurate decision-making is acute. If you are aware that the appeal has been lodged out of time, you should have prepared your evidence when you lodged the appeal. However, if the allegation comes as a surprise, the three days permitted to submit evidence may well be woefully inadequate.

4.20   The absence of any entitlement to a hearing is especially serious on two grounds. Firstly, it leaves no procedure in the Rules by which the adjudicator can notify the appellant of his concerns and the appellant can address them. The adjudicator will essentially be acting as primary decision maker upon the appellant's evidence since the Rules do not envisage any response from the Home Office. It is a fundamental requirement of fairness that there should be 'a reasonable opportunity to deal with and to explain any matter which [is] to be relied on against' the appellant (Q). Secondly, if any issue arises about the appellant's credibility, the adjudicator will have no opportunity to assess this in person.

4.21   The adjudicator's acceptance of an out of time allegation will terminate the appellant's asylum/human rights appeal. If for good reason, you are unable to submit all the material evidence within three days or if the issues raised cry out for a hearing, you may wish to submit that the r.10 procedure is unfair and unsafe and therefore inconsistent with human rights and unlawful. If he accepts this submission, the adjudicator should be obliged to modify his procedure so that it meets human rights requirements.

Issues

4.22   Where you submit that the appeal is not out of time because the notice of decision was received late, you should invite the Home Office to produce evidence of how the claim was served. The Immigration (Notices) Regulations 2003 (reg 7(1)) state that a notice may be:

   a) *given by hand;*

   b) *sent by fax;*

   c) *sent by postal service in which delivery or receipt is recorded to:–*

      i) *an address provided for correspondence by the person or his representative;*

ii) where no address for correspondence has been provided by the person, the last-known or usual place of abode or place of business of the person or his representative.

4.23 Regulation 7(4) provides that a notice served by post will be deemed to have been received on the second working day after it was posted. However, if your client asserts that he did not receive it until later, then there ought to be an evidential burden on the Home Office to produce the delivery receipt: there would otherwise be little utility in the requirement imposed by reg 7(1)(c) to effect service by post by recorded delivery. If it does not respond to your enquiry, ask the IAA for a direction that it does so, failing which the out of time allegation should be dismissed.

4.24 The most common cause of appeals being lodged out of time is error by representatives. The IAT's caselaw indicates that adjudicators should extend time where the fault lay with the representative rather than the appellant: see e.g. *Abaci*, *Minta-Ampofo* and *Mapuranga*. In the latter case, the IAT held that:

We have accepted that the failure of a representative, if not attributable to the client, and if the client has behaved reasonably is capable of amounting to a special circumstance.

4.25 In the context of the anxious scrutiny that must apply to asylum/ human rights appeals, and the potentially disastrous consequences of removing someone whose appeal has not been considered on the merits, adjudicators will usually be inclined to extend time in the absence of deliberate abuse.

4.26 If the adjudicator refuses to extend time, this amounts to a final determination of your appeal, so you can seek permission to appeal from the IAT. (The Home Office has no right of appeal against a decision to extend time.) The appeal will be limited to a point of law, but see the discussion in chapter 43 for the IAT's power to consider fresh evidence in the interests of justice. This may be particularly important in light of the defects in the r.10 procedure discussed above.

Representation

4.27 Rule 46 deals with representation in appeals. Rule 46(1) provides that an appellant may be represented by anyone not prohibited from doing so by s.84 of the 1999 Act. If you are unsure whether this applies to you, check your position immediately. You could be committing a criminal offence. Rule 46(3) provides that no determination or other step by the IAA will be invalidated simply because a party was represented by someone who was not authorised under s.84.

4.28 Rule 46(4–8) provides that:

> *(4) Where a representative begins to act for a party, he must immediately notify the appellate authority of that fact.*

> *(5) Where a representative is acting for a party, he may on behalf of that party do anything that these Rules require or permit that party to do.*

> *(6) Where a representative is acting for a party appealing against a relevant decision, the party is under a duty –*

>> *(a) to maintain contact with his representative until the appeal is finally determined; and*

>> *(b) to notify the representative of any change of address.*

> *(7) Where a representative ceases to act for a party, the representative and the party must notify the appellate authority and every other party of that fact, and of the name and address of any new representative (if known).*

> *(8) Until the appellate authority is notified that a representative has ceased to act for a party, any document served on that representative shall be deemed to be properly served on the party he was representing.*

4.29 Rule 54(3) also states that unless a rule expressly requires otherwise, service on someone who has notified the IAA that he is acting as a representative will be deemed to constitute service on the appellant.

4.30 The potential dangers arising from these provisions are obvious. Impress upon your client the necessity of keeping in touch and providing up to date contact details. If you cease to act for any reason, you must notify the IAA and the Home Office immediately.

What happens next?

4.31 As discussed in chapter 6, it may be some time before the Home Office transfers the papers to the IAA. The period for which the papers sit in the Home Office may far exceed the period between receipt of the IAA's notice and the full hearing. If there is lengthy preparation required, e.g. a report from the Medical Foundation for which there is currently a long waiting list, you should therefore be pursuing these steps now rather than waiting for the notice of hearing.

4 Lodging the appeal
Key points

- The notice of appeal must be lodged with the respondent or a person having custody of the appellant.

- Your grounds/reasons should encompass a general allegation that expulsion will violate the Refugee Convention and the ECHR so as not to limit the future development of the appeal.

- Do not produce pages of standard submissions in the grounds of appeal.

- Circumstances in which you should raise a specific point in the grounds of appeal may include:

  - □ where the Home Office may otherwise allege that late disclosure affects credibility (alternatively, take a dated statement), and
  - □ where you are alleging a failure to follow Home Office policy or impropriety at the interview.

- The notice of appeal must be received within 10 business days (or 5 business days if the appellant is in detention) of service of the immigration decision.

- If the Home Office serves an immigration decision by post, it must use recorded delivery. The burden is on you to show that it was received more than two working days after postage but you can ask the Home Office to supply the delivery receipt.

- Either the Home Office or the Adjudicator has power to extend time by reason of special circumstances.

- If you are out of time, the reasons and any supporting evidence should be supplied with the notice of appeal.

- If the Home Office alleges that you are out of time, r.10 requires you to serve evidence within three days of receipt of its notice. The adjudicator should then determine the matter without a hearing. This procedure raises acute concerns about fairness and in certain circumstances, may be unlawful.

- Error by a representative should justify an extension of time.

- A refusal to extend time may be appealed to the IAT.

- You must impress upon your client the need to provide up to date contact details. If you cease to act, you must inform the IAA immediately.

■ It may be a long time before you receive a notice of hearing from the IAA. If lengthy evidential preparation is required, this time should be utilised.

5 One stop procedure

5.1 The stated intention of the 2002 Act is to enable all outstanding issues relating to a person's entitlement to enter or remain in the UK to be dealt with in one appeal.

5.2 The 'one stop procedure' has been simplified from that contained in the 1999 Act. Your client may be served with a one stop notice under s.120 of the 2002 Act where:

(a) he has made an application to enter or remain in the United Kingdom, or

(b) an immigration decision within the meaning of section 82 has been taken or may be taken in respect of him. (s.120(1))

5.3 The notice may:

require the person to state –

(a) his reasons for wishing to enter or remain in the United Kingdom,

(b) any grounds on which he should be permitted to enter or remain in the United Kingdom, and

(c) any grounds on which he should not be removed from or required to leave the United Kingdom. (s.120(2))

5.4 The Home Office's APIs state that:

Section 120 … provides for a one-stop warning notice to be served on any applicant at any time. It also allows us to serve a warning notice on a person who has not made an application, but in respect of whom an immigration decision may be made. This covers enforcement situations in which, before taking removal action, we want to oblige someone formally to tell us if they have any reasons for remaining in the UK. 'Immigration decision' here means any of the decisions listed in section 82(2) … It does not apply to a decision to grant humanitarian protection or discretionary leave following the refusal of asylum; there is no point in serving a one-stop notice on a person who will be remaining in the UK for the foreseeable future and whose circumstances may change in the meantime.

The warning must be given in writing. It will require the recipient to state any additional grounds for wanting to enter or remain in the United Kingdom that have not previously been mentioned in connection with an application. It will warn the applicant of the penalties that may result from non-compliance with this requirement. There is no time limit within which the applicant must return a statement of additional grounds, and no obligation for IND to wait for a statement before making a decision. However, in each case the caseworker should tell the applicant how long it will be before a decision is taken. The caseworker is free to set an appropriate deadline that is reasonable in the circumstances of the case, but care should be taken to treat applicants equitably and standard periods should be given. The statement must be considered if it arrives late, even if an appeal has been lodged, and a supplementary refusal letter issued if appropriate.

It is in the applicant's interest to participate in the process, partly because full information will allow us to make an informed decision and partly because the adjudicator is obliged (under section 85(2)) to consider anything raised in a one-stop statement. Non-compliance opens up the possibility that IND will issue a certificate under section 96. The effect of a certificate is to prevent the applicant from appealing against refusal on any of the grounds included.

There is no statutory requirement to serve the one-stop warning on people with any particular immigration status or at any particular point in the application process (as there was under the 1999 legislation). There is no obligation to serve the warning at all, although if we fail to do so we may not be able to certify a later claim. In asylum cases the warning should be served at an early stage, usually as part of the induction procedure, when the applicant's rights and responsibilities are explained. The notice should be issued together with a form on which the applicant can explain any additional grounds. A careful note should be made of the date and means of service, and a copy of the notice should be retained on file in case of litigation later. It will be safest to serve the one-stop warning notice with other papers where possible.

Unsuccessful applicants who have a right of appeal in the UK should usually be given a one-stop warning with the refusal notice and appeal form. The one-stop warning notice can be served as a paragraph within the notice of decision or the reasons for refusal letter. There is a box on the appeal form in which the appellant can enter any additional grounds.

5.5   There are no provisions in the 2002 Act (as there were in the 1999 Act) limiting your ability to advance submissions at the appeal that you did not raise in a one stop notice.

5.6   Section 85(2–3) provides that an adjudicator should consider any matter raised in a one stop statement which constitutes a ground of appeal listed in s.84(1). However, if you have followed the advice in the previous chapter to include in your grounds of appeal general allegations to the effect that expulsion will violate the Refugee Convention and the ECHR, that will be sufficient to enable you to advance any asylum or human rights submissions. Section 84(4) in any event states that:

> *an adjudicator may consider evidence about any matter which he thinks relevant to the substance of the decision, including evidence which concerns a matter arising after the date of the decision.*

5.7   Any pure immigration grounds (i.e those which raise neither asylum nor human rights issues) should be raised in response to a one stop notice. These are outside the scope of this text. The opportunities to obtain leave to enter/remain on non-human rights grounds are anyway likely to be limited for most asylum seekers.

5.8   For an asylum/human rights appellant, the main impact of the one stop procedure will be felt only if she seeks to bring a second appeal.

5.9   However, severe adverse consequences may apply to any family member who does not raise an asylum or human rights ground in response to a s.120 notice. If they subsequently make a claim in their own right, the Home Office may issue a certificate under s.96 to deny them any appeal on the merits. If you are instructed by anyone affected, you must take instructions on their individual circumstances if you have not already done so. If you are not instructed, you should advise your client of the risk and suggest that her family members take advice. See also para 54.24.

5 One stop procedure
Key points

■ The intention of the 2002 Act is to enable all outstanding matters to be dealt with in one appeal.

■ As long as you alleged in your grounds of appeal that removal will violate the Refugee Convention and the ECHR, you will not be precluded from raising any asylum or human rights argument at the appeal, regardless of whether it was included in a one stop statement.

■ Family members who do not respond to a one stop warning, and who later make an asylum/human rights claim in their own right, may be denied any appeal on the merits.

6 The start of the appeal procedure

Getting started

6.1 As indicated in chapter 4, the notice of appeal is lodged with the Home Office rather than directly with the IAA. This is for administrative reasons (and to ensure that the Home Office knows immediately that an appeal has been lodged so that it does not try to remove the appellant).

6.2 The Rules require the Home Office to forward the notice of appeal to the IAA (r.9–10). However, they do not state when the Home Office must do this. In practice, it may be many months (sometimes extending into years) before the Home Office sends the notice of appeal and other appeal papers to the IAA.

6.3 The appeal is triggered by you lodging your notice of appeal with the Home Office in accordance with the Rules. The failure of the Home Office to send the notice of appeal to the IAA does not deprive an adjudicator of jurisdiction to hear the appeal. Nor should the Home Office, as respondent, dictate when the appeal is heard. However, it is reasonably clear that the Home Office does not simply transfer notices of appeal in date order, but is instead seeking to take advantage of the procedure to dictate when particular appeals should be heard. In *Lokko*, the IAT held that:

> the fact that the notice of appeal is by the Procedure Rules served on the respondent cannot lead to the conclusion that the control of the proceedings are thereby vested in the respondent...

6.4 While most appellants will be anxious to have their appeals resolved, some will have more urgent reasons than others. The most urgent cases are often where the appellant needs to establish she is a refugee so as to be entitled to family reunion. Family members may be living in desperate and sometimes dangerous circumstances overseas.

6.5 If you write to the Home Office to request that it forward the appeal notice promptly, you will usually prompt neither action nor a response. You can bring a claim for judicial review of the Home Office's failure to transfer the notice of appeal. The lodging of such a claim is often sufficient to persuade the Home Office to act.

6.6   Alternatively, the IAT stated in **Pui Yu Wong** (following **Lokko**) that if the Home Office fails to transmit the notice of appeal to the IAA, it is open to an appellant to lodge the notice of appeal with the IAA directly. If your appeal is of no greater urgency than most other appeals, the IAA may decline to expedite it. The IAA does not presently have capacity to work its way through the entire backlog of appeals that have now accumulated at the Home Office.

6.7   However, the question of which appeals should be prioritised should be for the IAA, not the Home Office. If there are particular grounds for expedition, the IAA ought to be prepared to prioritise that appeal: it certainly should not permit the respondent to dictate the timing of the hearing. You can therefore lodge the notice of appeal with the IAA, provide submissions as to why the appeal ought to be expedited, and ask it to issue a notice of hearing. If it declines your application, that decision, along with the refusal of the Home Office to forward the appeal papers, may be susceptible to judicial review.

The first communication: notice of hearing and standard directions

6.8   The first communication that you receive from the IAA is normally a notice of hearing together with the standard directions. The notice of hearing will include notice of the 'first hearing' and the full hearing. You may find that the appeal has been listed at a hearing centre far from the appellant. This problem will be exacerbated if the IAA implements current proposals to hear more appeals from London appellants in other parts of the country. ILPA has strongly objected to these proposals, pointing to the difficulties that may arise, including:

- Appellants may have to travel long distances when they have scant resources or understanding of English or the transport system.
- They will arrive at the hearing centre after an arduous and tiring journey which may begin in the early hours of the morning: their appeal may not then start until the afternoon.
- These issues will be especially acute for families, unaccompanied minors, pregnant women and those in ill health.
- Witnesses (factual and expert) will often also be based in London, and may be unable to travel long distances.

6.9   The practice of listing appeals in other parts of the country adds substantially to the cost of appeals. If it will cause unfairness to your client, you may wish to apply for a transfer to a hearing centre nearer where she lives. (See, e.g. *Kaur*, in which the IAT criticised the refusal to transfer the appeal to London where there was an 'overwhelming case' based on the appellant's disability and the fact that appellant, witnesses and representative were all based in London.)

6.10   The Standard Directions are:

> *The appellant is required to complete the attached form, headed Reply and to return it to the Immigration Appellate Authority... 7 days before the date of the First Hearing.*
>
> *The following documents are to be filed by the party indicated... 7 days before the date of the Full Hearing.*

App	Resp.	
√		*Witness statements of the evidence to be called at the hearing, such statements to stand as evidence in chief at the hearing.*
√	√	*A paginated and indexed bundle of all the documents to be relied on at the hearing with a schedule identifying the essential passages.*
√		*A skeleton argument, identifying all relevant issues including Human Rights claims and citing all the authorities to be relied on.*
√		*A chronology of events.*

> *Copies of all documents are to be provided to every other party to the appeal. Copies of documents in a language other than English must be accompanied by a full certified translation.*
> (CA8 of 2001, 27 July 2001)

6.11   The documents mentioned in the standard directions are addressed separately (see in particular chapters 12 and 15 on Witness Statements, chapter 27 on Bundles, and chapter 28 on Skeleton Arguments and Chronologies).

6.12   The Notice also contains the following statement:

> *If the appellant or his representative does not attend the first hearing the Adjudicator may determine the appeal in the absence of the appellant unless there is a satisfactory explanation of his absence. The Adjudicator will accept the return of a Reply in which boxes A and D are fully completed as a satisfactory explanation for not attending the First Hearing.*

6.13   Box A of the Reply contains the following statement:

> *I request a hearing of the appeal and I certify I am **in all respects** ready to proceed.*

6.14   It also asks how many witnesses you intend to call, whether an interpreter ought to be provided, and if so, in what language and dialect. You are required to give a time estimate and details of any further documentary evidence that you intend to adduce.

6.15   Box D contains the following statement:

> *I have been authorised to represent the appellant at the hearing of this appeal and I am satisfied that all necessary financial and other arrangements have been made to enable me to do so.*

6.16   The alternatives are Box B (should you not require a hearing of the appeal) and Box C which requires you to state your reasons if you are 'currently **not ready** to proceed.'

6.17   The Practice Direction governing the standard directions states that:

> 1   ... [S]tandard directions are to be issued with the first notice of hearing sent to the parties in all appeals listed for hearing before adjudicators...
>
> 2   ... [T]he direction requiring the filing of witness statements provides that such statements shall stand as evidence in chief at the hearing.
>
> 3   The standard direction is not intended to interfere with an adjudicator's discretion to conduct the substantive appeal hearing in the most appropriate way depending upon the facts of the individual case. In normal circumstances a witness statement should stand as evidence in chief. There may be cases where it will be appropriate for appellants or witnesses to have the opportunity of adding to or supplementing their witness statement. Parties are referred to the judgment of the Court of Appeal in ... **Singh**.
>
> 4   At any first hearing the adjudicator will make such further directions as may be necessary. If a party is not able to comply with any of the standard directions he must attend the first hearing. (CA8 of 2001)

6.18   It also warns parties of the potential consequences under the Rules of failure to comply with directions.

6.19   The consequences of failing either to attend the first hearing or submit an acceptable reply are dire. In **Butt**, the High Court stated that:

> *The documentation makes it clear that the advisers had two options: either to attend on [the first hearing] or to certify that the case was now*

ready to proceed. The advisers took neither of those options. That there-
fore gave the adjudicator power to proceed to hear the appeal on [the first
hearing].

6.20   As discussed in chapter 8 on Adjournment, many representatives sign
        certificates of readiness to avoid attending the first hearing, even
        though they do not know whether the evidence will be ready by the
        full hearing. If you subsequently need to apply for an adjournment in
        order to complete these enquiries, the certificate of readiness may be
        held against you.

6.21   Where counsel is instructed to represent at the hearing, his first task
        will often be to advise on evidence. Ideally, this would be done before
        the reply was submitted to the IAA, but the time limit for lodging the
        reply means that such early instruction is the exception rather than
        the rule.

6.22   The safest route, where you have any doubt about whether you will be
        ready to proceed, is to attend the first hearing. Explain that you hope
        to be ready but that you are still seeking evidence which may or may
        not require an adjournment – even if you do not at that stage have any
        specific requests concerning listing or directions. This is obviously
        inefficient. Some representatives have adopted a practice in recent
        years of amending the certificate in the Reply form to state that while
        they are not ready to proceed immediately, they expect to be ready by
        the date listed for the substantive hearing (or else they give reasons
        why they do not expect to be ready and seek a later listing). They ask
        the IAA to inform them if it nevertheless wishes them to attend the
        first hearing. The IAA seldom requests attendance where it is provided
        with this information (although if it does so, it is imperative that you
        do attend). This practice is manifestly preferable to the practice of
        some representatives of certifying untruthfully that they are in all
        respects ready to proceed.

6.23   If the case is complex and it is already clear that you will require sub-
        stantially more time for preparation, or if you are seeking detailed
        and/or unusual directions, you ought to attend the first hearing. The
        judge in ***Butt*** described the purpose of the procedure as:

>   *to promote efficiency… by ensuring that either an acceptable Certificate*
>   *of Readiness is produced, so that all relevant matters have been*
>   *addressed, or to ensure that the matter comes before the adjudicator at an*
>   *early date so that the adjudicator can take all necessary steps to ensure*
>   *that the case is heard as soon as reasonably and fairly possible.*

6.24   Unfortunately, some representatives' experience of the first hearing
        has been at odds with the intention that it be an effective case man-

agement tool. The strongest criticism has been that the point of the first hearing was to handle cases which were not susceptible to the standard listing procedure. Despite this, adjudicators have been known to insist on arbitrary hearing dates, even where the appellant has proposed a detailed timetable and there has been no suggestion that this timetable is unreasonable. The Chief Adjudicator has indicated (at a meeting with the RLG) that this is not how first hearings ought to work.

6.25   If you attend with a fully prepared timetable and the adjudicator rejects it without satisfactory reason, you will have little option but to renew your adjournment request nearer the hearing (see further chapter 8). You will, by your attendance, have avoided prejudicing that application by inappropriately signing a certificate of readiness. You may also wish to write to the Chief Adjudicator setting out your concerns.

6.26   There are other instances where the first hearing ought to be valuable. In *Carcabuk & Bla*, the IAT held that:

> At any preliminary hearing before an adjudicator, doubts about what matters are in issue should be resolved. If the refusal letter or the explanatory statement is less than clear, that is the time to discover in what respect (if any) the Secretary of State is asserting that the appellant is not telling the truth.

6.27   It is also a good opportunity to apply for directions such as those suggested in chapters 9 and 10, including particulars, skeleton arguments, and a typed transcript of the interview.

6 The start of the appeal procedure
Key points

- The Home Office may take months (or even years) to transfer the notice of appeal to the IAA. It appears to be taking advantage of the procedure to seek to control when appeals are heard.

- If there are grounds for expediting your appeal, you can
  - ☐ judicially review the failure of the Home Office to forward the appeal papers, or
  - ☐ lodge a copy of the notice of appeal directly with the IAA and ask it to expedite the hearing.

- The appeal may be listed in a hearing centre far from the appellant, witnesses, and representative. If this will cause unfairness, apply for a transfer.

- Standard directions will be issued with the notice of hearing.

- The notice requires you either to certify that you are ready to proceed or attend the first hearing. Failure to do either may result in the appeal being determined at the first hearing.

- Signing the certificate of readiness where you have grounds to believe that you will not actually be ready to proceed may well prejudice a subsequent adjournment application.

- For cases that are not susceptible to standard listing, the first hearing ought to (but may not) provide an effective case management tool.

- Attend with full details of the steps you are taking to prepare the appeal and, preferably, a proposed timetable.

- The IAT has held that the first hearing should also provide an opportunity to clarify the issues in dispute. You may use it to apply for directions against the Home Office.

7 Exceptions to the right to a hearing

7.1 Rule 12 states that:

Every appeal must be considered at a hearing before an adjudicator, except where –

(a) the appeal –

 (i) lapses pursuant to section 99 of the 2002 Act;

 (ii) is treated as abandoned pursuant to section 104(4) of the 2002 Act;

 (iii) is treated as finally determined pursuant to section 104(5) of the 2002 Act; or

 (iv) is withdrawn by the appellant in accordance with rule 42; or

(b) a provision of these Rules or of any other enactment permits or requires an adjudicator to dispose of an appeal without a hearing.

7.2 This chapter addresses these exceptions.

Determination without a hearing

7.3 Rule 45 details the circumstances in which an adjudicator can dispense with a hearing:

(1) An adjudicator or the Tribunal may, subject to paragraphs (2) and (3) of this rule, determine an appeal without a hearing if –

(a) all the parties to the appeal consent;

(b) the party appealing against a relevant decision is outside the United Kingdom or it is impracticable to give him notice of a hearing and, in either case, he is unrepresented;

(c) a party has failed to comply with a provision of these rules or a direction of the appellate authority, and the adjudicator or Tribunal is satisfied that in all the circumstances, including the

extent of the failure and any reasons for it, it is appropriate to determine the appeal without a hearing; or

(d) the adjudicator or Tribunal is satisfied, having regard to the material before him or it and the nature of the issues raised, that the appeal can be justly determined without a hearing.

(2) Where paragraph (1)(c) applies and the appellant is the party in default, the adjudicator or Tribunal may dismiss the appeal without substantive consideration, if satisfied that it is appropriate to do so.

(3) Where paragraph (1)(d) applies, the adjudicator or Tribunal must not determine the appeal without a hearing without first giving the parties notice of his or its intention to do so, and an opportunity to make written representations as to whether there should be a hearing.

7.4   Note that r.45(1)(b) applies only when the adjudicator is satisfied that she is unrepresented.

7.5   With respect to r.45(1)(d), there ought to be no circumstances other than those falling within r.45(1)(c) where it would be just to dispense with a hearing without the appellant's consent (see *Gioshev* and *S (1998)* (para 7.13)).

Failure to comply with directions/rules

7.6   Rule 45(1)(c) and r.45(2) apply only where a party has failed to comply with a provision of the Rules or a direction. Rule 45(1)(c) empowers an adjudicator to determine the appeal without a hearing but only where he is 'satisfied that in all the circumstances, including the extent of the failure and any reasons for it, it is appropriate to determine the appeal without a hearing'. Rule 45(2) contains the more draconian power to dismiss the appeal without substantive consideration where it is the appellant that is in default. (This introduces a new bias into the procedure rules in favour of the Home Office. Previously, the rules were even-handed in this respect: they also permitted an adjudicator to allow an appeal without consideration of the merits where the Home Office was in default.)

7.7   The IAT has encouraged adjudicators to avoid determining appeals without consideration of the merits wherever possible. In *Gonzales*, the IAT stated that:

It cannot be used as a punitive measure with no regard for the overriding objective...

7.8   This is set out in r.4 which states that:

> *The overriding objective of these Rules is to secure the just, timely and effective disposal of appeals and applications in the interests of the parties to the proceedings and in the wider public interest.*

7.9   The IAT added that:

> *[An adjudicator] must then consider all the relevant circumstances and these will include the extent of the failure and reasons for the failure. Other relevant circumstances would, in our view, also include the nature of the direction which had not been complied with and the potential or real effect of non compliance on parties.*

7.10   It further pointed out that the powers to dispense with a hearing and dismiss without substantive consideration were discretionary, even where the preconditions set out in the rules were made out, and that the parties should have an opportunity to make representations on the appropriate disposal:

> *The discretion must be exercised reasonably, fairly and justly.*

7.11   In **Ishaq Saqi Muhammad**, the IAT also emphasised that where non-compliance has been established, the adjudicator should strive to determine the appeal on the merits having regard to the overriding objective and the anxious scrutiny which an asylum or human rights appeal merits. It stated that 'where there is material before an adjudicator which sets out the substance of the appellant's claim, it will normally be preferable to consider' determining the appeal on its merits. In the instant case, there was evidence before the adjudicator on which she could have made an assessment and she erred in giving no reason (nor could the IAT perceive any reason) for not determining the appeal on the basis of the evidence. (See also **Senigeur** in which the IAT urged adjudicators not to dispose of 'perfectly ordinary non-appearance cases without consideration of the merits, in view of the likely delay and expense in putting things right'.)

7.12   While determination on the merits without a hearing is preferable to determination without consideration of the merits at all, the IAT has also stated in **Meflah** that:

> *where both the appellant and the representative are present at the hearing an adjudicator should exercise extreme caution before deciding to determine an appeal without a hearing because of failure to comply with directions.*

> *In the present case the failure did not go to any essential part of the case and the course taken by the adjudicator is unsustainable. This is not a case in which there is a huge amount of documentary evidence and such documentary evidence as there was, was itself mainly paginated. Further*

the appellant and his representative being present the omission of a dec-laration as to whether the appellant was adopting the interview as his evidence and the lack of proof of evidence cannot possibly provide grounds for sending the appellant away without allowing him to present his case. In our view the adjudicator's action in this case was a misuse of the power conferred by the rules. Such misuse is likely to bring the power to give directions into contempt.

7.13 It follows that where you are guilty of non-compliance with directions or rules, you should argue strongly that the adjudicator should never-theless determine the appeal on its merits if there is (despite your non-compliance) sufficient material before him to do so. The question then arises whether the adjudicator should determine the appeal with or without a hearing. He should only decide to dispense with a hearing if he satisfies himself by reference to the material before him and the nature of the issues that the appeal can be justly determined on the papers. That 'draconian step' will seldom be justified where credibility is in issue and the appellant is present and prepared to give evidence. In *S (1998)*, Sullivan J held that:

Where the appellant's credibility is in issue and he is present and wishes to give evidence, it would only be in rare cases that a special adjudicator could properly be satisfied that the appeal could be disposed of justly without a hearing.

Hearing the appeal in the absence of a party

7.14 Rule 44 sets out circumstances in which an adjudicator can proceed with a hearing in the absence of a party:

(1) An adjudicator or the Tribunal must hear an appeal in the absence of a party or his representative, if satisfied that the party or his represen-tative –

(a) has been given notice of the date, time and place of the hearing; and
(b) has given no satisfactory explanation for his absence.

(2) Where paragraph (1) does not apply, an adjudicator or the Tribunal may hear an appeal in the absence of a party if satisfied that –

(a) a representative of the party is present at the hearing;
(b) the party is outside the United Kingdom;
(c) the party is suffering from a communicable disease or there is a risk of him behaving in a violent or disorderly manner;

> (d) the party is unable to attend the hearing because of illness, acci-
> dent or some other good reason;
>
> (e) the party is unrepresented and it is impracticable to give him
> notice of the hearing; or
>
> (f) the party has notified the appellate authority that he does not
> wish to attend the hearing.

7.15 Rule 44(2) grants a discretion to proceed with the hearing in the absence of a party if the party has been properly notified (see below). But r.44(1) obliges the adjudicator to proceed with a hearing in those circumstances if there is no satisfactory explanation for the absence of a party *or his representative*. So as long as the appellant's representative is in attendance, r.44(1) does not require the adjudicator to proceed simply because the appellant herself has not attended without explanation. If there is no evidence that the appellant has deliberately failed to attend, an adjudicator will usually agree to adjourn the appeal for a short period to enable any explanation to be submitted (para 8.31). It is therefore very important that the representative attend: even if an adjournment is refused in those circumstances, the representative will be entitled to make submissions.

7.16 In *Feghali*, the IAT considered the position where an adjudicator had concluded a hearing in the absence of the appellant but then agreed to consider documentation submitted by the appellant after the hearing. The IAT said that it would be open to an adjudicator hearing an appeal in the absence of a party to indicate that he would accept submission of material within a certain period after the hearing. But if he did not do so, and then entertained post-hearing submissions, he was effectively reopening the hearing. He therefore had to reconsider whether to hear from the appellant.

7.17 In light of the severe consequences for the appellant of proceeding in her absence, the IAT requires the rule to be complied with strictly. In *Khmelkevich*, it stated that:

> [The adjudicator] does not say whether or not he is satisfied that due notice of the time and place of the hearing has been given. We have little doubt that it was but, where an asylum seeker is to be deprived of his right to give oral evidence and to have an appeal determined in his absence, it seems to us that it is at least incumbent on the Special Adjudicator to make it clear that the formalities of the rules have been complied with. Secondly, the mandatory sub-rule … applies only if there is no satisfactory explanation for the absence of the party concerned. In this case there manifestly was such an explanation before the Special Adjudicator. There is no suggestion that what was contained in the medical certificate supplied was not accepted by him. Whilst it has in the

past been properly considered that a certificate that an appellant is not fit to attend work is not appropriate to explain absence from a hearing, the doctor specifically stated the Appellant was not fit to attend an interview. That is to put the ability to attend anywhere at a very low level and, simply as a matter of common-sense, must extend to a court appearance at which evidence subject to cross-examination is to be given. Whilst we accept that adjudicators must be vigilant in ensuring that explanations for absence are reasonable, this is to impose far too high a duty on the Appellant.'

7.18   Note that where r.44(1) does not apply, r.44(2) does not mandate – or even, without more, entitle – the adjudicator to proceed in the absence of the appellant. He must have regard to the overriding objective in r.4.

7.19   In particular, r.44(2)(d) does not entitle an adjudicator to proceed in the absence of the appellant whenever it is established that she is too ill to attend the hearing. On the contrary, that will normally be good grounds for an adjournment. However, there will come a stage where the prospects of her being well enough to attend within a reasonable period are sufficiently remote to justify proceeding under this provision. In **Tahir Iqbal**, Collins J said that:

[A] balance may, in certain circumstances, have to be drawn between the need for the appellant to be heard in order to be able to put forward his appeal in a proper manner and the need for an appeal to be disposed of in a reasonable time. One can imagine examples where, if he was unfit for a period of years, it would be unreasonable to expect the matter to be deferred. But, as I see it, in considering an adjournment, an Adjudicator must always have in mind fairness to both parties but, in particular in asylum cases such as this, the need for fairness to the applicant to enable him to put forward a meaningful appeal.

7.20   In light of the provisions on closure (r.13), it will be particularly important to present medical evidence showing when the appellant will be well enough to attend where the duration exceeds six weeks.

7.21   See also applying for an adjournment on the ground that the appellant is unable to attend (paras 8.27–8.33).

Withdrawal of appeals

7.22   Rule 42 provides that:

(1) An appellant may withdraw an appeal –

   (a) orally, at a hearing; or

(b) at any time, by filing written notice with the appellate authority.

(2) If an appellant withdraws an appeal, the appellate authority must serve on the parties a notice that the appeal has been recorded as having been withdrawn.

7.23 Where an appellant disputes that she previously withdrew her appeal, she must be given the opportunity to present her case to that effect, and there should then be a determination with reasons deciding whether or not the appeal was withdrawn (*El-Tuyeb*). The Home Office's policy on withdrawal of appeals is as follows:

1. *The appellant has appealed to the appellate authorities, not to the Home Office. Consequently, no withdrawal will be effective until the appellate authorities have accepted it. Even when the appeal is withdrawn in court, with a presenting officer present, any enforcement action must wait until the appellate authorities have issued a written acknowledgement of the withdrawal…*

   Sometimes we may invite an appellant to withdraw the appeal. This should only be done with great caution, since it can adversely affect the appellant's subsequent rights of appeal and leave us open to accusations of coercion…

2.1 *Appeals not yet passed to the appellate authorities*

   Rule 9 of the Procedure Rules requires us to pass specified documents (the appeal bundle) to the appellate authorities. There is no clause absolving us from doing so if the appeal is withdrawn before the IAA have been made aware of the case…

2.3 *Withdrawal of appeals by representatives*

   Correspondence from the appellant's representatives purporting to withdraw an appeal can only be accepted as a proper withdrawal if the representatives have the express authority of the appellant to act on the appellant's behalf. If the same representatives submitted the appeal, it will normally be appropriate to accept any subsequent correspondence from them stating that the appeal is to be withdrawn. Care should be taken when an appellant has sought to instruct a number of representatives during the course of the application. In cases of doubt, the appellant personally should be asked to confirm the withdrawal in writing. Again, the final decision to accept or reject a withdrawal from a representative rests with the appellate authorities…

5. *REOPENING WITHDRAWN APPEALS*

   Although a withdrawn appeal cannot be reinstated, it is possible for an appellant to argue that the appeal was not withdrawn properly, and therefore is still extant. Since the withdrawal will have been seen and accepted by the appellate authorities, it is up to them to consider re-opening the appeal. The appellant should therefore be advised to contact the Clerk to the Adjudicator, and any enforcement action should be suspended until the outcome is known. (APIs)

7.24   Since the withdrawal is not effective until accepted by the IAA, communication to the Home Office of an intention to withdraw the appeal does not commit the appellant until that withdrawal is communicated to and accepted by the IAA. The potential importance of this point is illustrated by *El-Tuyeb*:

> *[T]he withdrawal notice had not reached the appellate authority until the hearing itself. It could not therefore be said that the appeal was withdrawn until that moment. It was clear from the background of the case and the presence of counsel to argue the appeal that, whatever the effect of the 'withdrawal' letter to the Home Office, that had been overtaken by subsequent actions by those representing the appellant and it is necessarily to be implied from those actions that any withdrawal there had been had itself been withdrawn. There was therefore, in the Tribunal's view, no withdrawal of this appeal.*

> *We add only this, that where a withdrawal of an appeal is contested, the adjudicator must allow an opportunity to put the case against withdrawal. This reflects the fundamental principle that each party should be able to put the case before the adjudicator, and the need for this is particularly so where a notice of withdrawal is presented on the day of the hearing.*

7.25   So a notice withdrawing an appeal which is sent to the Home Office can be cancelled at any point until it is received by the Appellate Authority. But if a valid withdrawal has been received by the IAA, it is not possible to reinstate the appeal by demonstrating that your client now wishes to pursue it (*Adewole*).

7.26   The commonest scenario in which you will face a disputed withdrawal is where your client's previous representatives are alleged by the Home Office or the IAA to have withdrawn your client's appeal. You should write immediately to the IAA, copied to the Home Office, informing them that your instructions are that the appeal has not been withdrawn. If the purported withdrawal was sent to the Home Office and has not yet been communicated to or dealt with by the IAA, then that should be the end of the matter. The Home Office must be informed to ensure that it suspends any enforcement action (APIs, above).

7.27   If the purported withdrawal *has* been received by the IAA, the question will be whether it was a valid withdrawal. You cannot 'undo' a valid withdrawal. If the notice withdrawing the appeal came from her previous representatives and your client's instructions are that they acted improperly, you should obtain a statement from your client to that effect. Where the IAA has received a document signed by your client purporting to withdraw the appeal, you will have to

> establish, on the balance of probabilities, that he had instructed his representative either not to present the letter of withdrawal, which he had signed, or to have it, in some way, withdrawn, in order for him to satisfy us that his original letter of withdrawal had been improperly used by his representatives and that it ought to have been cancelled. (*Adewole*)

7.28 If you find that the purported withdrawal has already been considered by an adjudicator and a notice issued to the effect that the appeal has been withdrawn, the IAA is likely to say that the matter may not be reopened before an adjudicator. The only way to pursue the appeal will be to seek permission to appeal to the IAT against the decision that the appeal was withdrawn. The IAT is now restricted to considering points of law (although that may not exclude the admission of fresh evidence in the interests of justice: para 43.19).

7.29 The remaining option is to lodge a fresh appeal (assuming that there is a decision against which you can appeal). If the appeal was validly withdrawn, there is no other option. It is likely that the Home Office will certify the new appeal (see chapter 51). You will need to show the circumstances in which the appeal was withdrawn, and why that should not be held against the appellant.

Appeals deemed to be abandoned or finally determined

7.30 Rule 43 deals with abandonment of appeals. It provides that:

> *(1) The parties to a pending appeal must notify the appellate authority if an event specified in section 104(4) or (5) of the 2002 Act takes place.*
>
> *(2) Where the appellate authority treats an appeal as abandoned pursuant to section 104(4) of the 2002 Act, or finally determined pursuant to section 104(5) of the 2002 Act, it must –*
>
> > *(a) serve on the parties informing them that the appeal is being treated as abandoned or finally determined; and*
> > *(b) take no further action in relation to the appeal.*

7.31 Section 104(4) provides that:

(4) An appeal under section 82(1) shall be treated as abandoned if the appellant –

(a) is granted leave to enter or remain in the United Kingdom, or
(b) leaves the United Kingdom.

(5) An appeal under section 82(2)(a), (c), (d), (e) or (f) shall be treated as finally determined if a deportation order is made against the appellant.

7.32   The relevant decisions to which s.104(5) applies are:

- refusal of leave to enter the United Kingdom,
- refusal of a certificate of entitlement under section 10 of this Act,
- refusal to vary a person's leave to enter or remain in the United Kingdom if the result of the refusal is that the person has no leave to enter or remain,
- variation of a person's leave to enter or remain in the United Kingdom if when the variation takes effect the person has no leave to enter or remain,
- revocation under section 76 of this Act of indefinite leave to enter or remain in the United Kingdom.

7.33   The previous Rules conferred on an adjudicator a power to treat an appeal as abandoned where he was satisfied, including by reference to a failure to comply with directions, that the appellant is no longer pursuing the appeal. That power has been omitted from the present rules. The deliberate omission of a previous express power strongly suggests that no continuing power can be implied to treat an appeal as abandoned in any circumstances other than those listed in r.43.

7.34   A notice issued under r.43 to the effect that an appeal has been abandoned can be appealed to the IAT: **Gremesty**.

7.35   Rule 41 provides that:

(1) If the Secretary of State or an immigration officer issues a certificate under section 96, 97 or 98 of the 2002 Act which relates to a pending appeal, subject to paragraph (4) he must file notice of the certification with the appellate authority.

(2) Where a notice of certification under section 96(1) or (2), 97 or 98 of the 2002 Act is filed, the appellate authority must notify the parties that the appeal has lapsed in accordance with section 99.

7.36   See chapter 51 for certificates issued under s.96 and chapter 14 for certificates issued under s.97. An asylum/human rights appeal cannot be certified under s.98.

7 Exceptions to the right to a hearing
Key points

■ Unless one of the exceptions in r.12 applies, the appellant is entitled to a hearing of her appeal.

■ In deciding whether to dispense with a hearing on the merits by reason of failure to comply with directions, the adjudicator must be guided by the overriding objective in r.4.

   ☐ Where there has been a failure to comply with directions, he must give the parties an opportunity to make representations as to the appropriate means of disposal.

   ☐ He should not dismiss the appeal without consideration of the merits as a punitive measure: he should strive to determine the appeal on the merits if he has sufficient material on which to do so.

   ☐ Where appellant and representative are present and ready to proceed, and it is practical to hear the appeal on the merits despite the failure to comply with directions, the adjudicator should do so.

■ Rule 44(1) obliges an adjudicator to proceed with a hearing only if neither the appellant nor her representative have attended. In light of the severe consequences, the rule must be complied with strictly.

■ While short-term illness will normally be a good ground for an adjournment, there will come a point where the prospects of the appellant being well enough within a reasonable period are sufficiently remote to justify proceeding in her absence under r.44(2)(d).

■ An appeal can only be withdrawn by written notice to the IAA or orally at the hearing. A letter to the Home Office is not an effective withdrawal.

■ Where an appellant disputes that the appeal has been withdrawn, the adjudicator must determine the issue.

■ If the appeal has been validly withdrawn, it cannot be reopened, and a new claim is the only option.

■ The Rules no longer confer upon the adjudicator any power to treat an appeal as abandoned, except where it is deemed to be abandoned by s.104(4) of the 2002 Act.

8 Adjournment

8.1 The timing of the hearing may be critical to whether the appeal can be determined fairly and safely. In **Ghaly**, Sedley J said that:

> *Questions for adjournment by inferior tribunals receive in many cases a closer scrutiny from this court than a Wednesbury rationality test because the question frequently throws up fundamental questions of fairness. If the maxim that both sides are to be fairly heard is to have any effect, it means that each side has to have a fair opportunity of preparing to deal with what the other side has to say.*

8.2 Adjournment of adjudicator hearings is addressed by r.40 and r.13. R.40 states:

> *(1) Subject to any provision of these Rules or of any other enactment, an adjudicator or the Tribunal may adjourn the hearing of any appeal or application.*
>
> *(2) An adjudicator or the Tribunal must not adjourn a hearing on the application of a party, unless satisfied that the appeal or application cannot otherwise be justly determined.*
>
> *(3) Where a party applies for an adjournment of a hearing, he must –*
>
> > *(a) if practicable, notify all other parties of the application;*
> > *(b) show good reason why an adjournment is necessary; and*
> > *(c) produce evidence of any fact or matter relied upon in support of the application.*
>
> *(4) Where a hearing is adjourned, the appellate authority –*
>
> *(a) must fix a new date, time and place for the hearing; and*
> *(b) may give directions for the future conduct of the appeal or application.*

8.3 Rule 13 deals with the procedure for setting a 'closure date'. It does not alter the test for granting a first adjournment under r.40. It is intended however to discourage second adjournments and adjournments of more than six weeks. These are dealt with in the discussion of 'Closure' at para 8.21 below.

Making an application

8.4 The Chief Adjudicator's Practice Direction on Adjournments states that:

1 *Applications for the adjournment of appeals listed for hearing before an adjudicator must be made not later than 4.00pm one clear working day before the date of hearing. For the avoidance of doubt, for example, where a case is listed for hearing on a Friday, the application must be received by 4.00pm on Wednesday.*

2 *Full reasons including any supporting documentation must be filed with the application and, where practicable, served on the other party. The application must be made to the Regional Adjudicator or Centre Adjudicator for the region where the appeal is listed for hearing.*

3 *Any application made later than the time limit set out in paragraph 1 must be made to the adjudicator at the hearing so will require the attendance of the party or the representative of the party seeking the adjournment. It will only be in the most exceptional circumstances that late applications for adjournments will be considered without the attendance of a party or representative.*

4 *Parties and representatives must not assume that an application, even if made in accordance with paragraph 1, will be successful. They must always check with the appellate authority the outcome of any application. If an adjournment has not been granted and a party fails to attend the hearing, the adjudicator will proceed with the hearing if there is no satisfactory explanation of absence…* (CA7 of 2001)

8.5 It is important that you comply with the requirements of r.40(3) and the Practice Direction. Applications for adjournment are sometimes rejected simply because the representative failed to offer a new date for hearing. Try to give a date upon which you consider you will be ready to proceed. This should be realistic, because if you get the adjournment and are still not ready on the date you offered, you will need a cogent explanation for any further adjournment request.

8.6 If the need for the adjournment arises because the Home Office has failed to do something, you should normally accompany your adjournment application with a request for a direction requiring the Home Office to do it by a specified date. Otherwise, in the absence of an undertaking from the Home Office, the adjudicator can have no confidence that the adjournment will achieve the desired result.

8.7 Comply with the time limit for making the application (4pm one clear working day before the hearing) if you want to have any chance of avoiding attendance at the hearing.

8.8 The Practice Direction requires that the application be served on the Home Office where practical. This should be done by fax to the relevant HOPO Unit. You should also try to speak to the HOPO in order to explain your request and address any concerns that the HOPO has. This can be a frustrating and unrewarding experience, one of the many occasions on which the difficulty in persuading anyone at the Home Office to take responsibility for an appeal until the day before the hearing causes real problems. However, if a HOPO has been allocated, or if a duty HOPO is willing to find the file, his agreement to the adjournment application will increase the prospects of success considerably.

8.9 Most paper adjournment applications are refused. You must assume that the adjudicator will pick up your application expecting to refuse it. It is therefore not enough simply to state the reason you need more time (e.g. you are investigating further evidence) in the expectation that a sympathetic adjudicator will consider it self-evident that the matter should be adjourned. You need to formulate your application as if it were a written submission rather than a simple letter conveying the necessary information. You must impress upon the adjudicator why your application, unlike many others, needs to be granted. Anticipate the likely grounds of refusal. Explain, if appropriate, why you could not have completed the task in the time available: for example, you were unaware of the existence of the evidence, or you are dealing with a point only recently taken by the Home Office. Remember that r.40 requires you to 'produce evidence of any fact or matter relied upon in support of the application'.

8.10 Most representatives are not in a position to present the appeal when they sign the certificate of readiness in response to the standard directions (see paras 6.20–6.23). Many sign because they believe they will be ready in time for the full hearing. However, the certificate of readiness may be held against you if you subsequently find you have to apply for an adjournment because evidence is not ready. Unless it is obvious, you should anticipate this by explaining why the delay in preparing the evidence was not foreseeable when you signed the certificate of readiness.

8.11 If there is no good reason why you need an adjournment other than your own mistake, (e.g. overlooking an obvious line of enquiry), then the best thing is to say so openly and argue that your client should not be prejudiced by your mistake (see para 8.50 below). In this case, the second limb of any adjournment request becomes even more important.

8.12 As well as explaining what you would do with the additional time, you **must** explain why the appeal could not be justly determined on the date fixed. If you are presently seeking further evidence, you must justify to the adjudicator why it would be unsafe to proceed without that evidence. Explain how it will assist you to prove your case, or how it will refute an allegation made by the Home Office. You must convince the adjudicator that if the appeal was determined without this evidence, there would be a real risk of getting it wrong.

8.13 As indicated in the Practice Direction, if a paper application is refused, you *should* attend the hearing, and you should have decided what to do in the eventuality that you are unsuccessful in renewing your application orally. Study the refusal on the papers. Sometimes, the adjudicator will invite you to renew it at the hearing and indicate the points that he considers you must overcome.

8.14 Adjudicators vary as to the extent to which they are prepared to hear an adjournment application where the facts and grounds do not differ from the application which has already been refused on the papers. Some adjudicators will effectively hear the application afresh and may well grant it even though it had been refused on the papers. Others will not entertain the application unless you can point to some matter which was not before the adjudicator who refused the paper application.

8.15 Where you believe an adjournment to be necessary in the interests of justice, you should pursue the request forcefully and with determination. Beware of sounding antagonistic. Nevertheless, in certain circumstances, it may be appropriate to point out that any saving of time will be illusory if the determination of the appeal is consequently unsafe and so vulnerable to challenge. Adjudicators regularly put the same point to the HOPO.

8.16 The IAT has emphasised that anxious scrutiny of asylum claims requires that the appellant is able to present her case to the full (*Stolintchena*). It held that adjudicators should follow the guidance laid down by the Divisional Court in **Martin**. The issue in that case was whether a magistrates' court acted unfairly in refusing a request for an adjournment made at the hearing on behalf of one of the parties (a barrister). The grounds for the application were that work commitments prevented him being present and that he had been unable as yet to obtain potentially relevant evidence. The Divisional Court rejected the challenge. It identified the following seven factors as relevant:

- The importance of the proceedings and their likely adverse consequences to the party seeking the adjournment;
- The risk of the party being prejudiced in the conduct of proceedings if the application is refused;

- The risk of prejudice or other disadvantage to the other party if the adjournment is granted;
- The convenience of the court;
- The interests of justice generally in the efficient dispatch of court business;
- The desirability of not delaying future litigants by adjourning early and thus leaving the court empty;
- The extent to which the party applying for the adjournment had been responsible for creating the difficulty which had led to the application.

8.17   Simon Brown LJ stated that the proceedings were 'at the lower end of the scale of importance' and that the court was entitled to have regard to its own convenience (the court had no alternative business which it could take). Buckley J relied on the interests of the opposing party in bringing a 'relatively trivial piece of litigation' to a close, the fact that the applicant had in fact had months to prepare his case, and that he was a person 'well-versed in the ways of the law'. He said:

> The principles of natural justice that are prayed in aid in support of this application demand no more than that a party to litigation should be given every reasonable opportunity to prepare and present his case.

8.18   Because the Divisional Court accepted that the importance (or in that case, the lack of importance) of the litigation was a primary factor in determining whether fairness demanded an adjournment, it is clear that any significant risk that an appellant may be prejudiced in presenting her appeal – in view of the potentially horrendous consequences of such prejudice – may require that adjournment is granted in order to achieve the just determination of the appeal. Following *Martin*, also of relevance will be whether the court's time would be wasted or whether the adjudicator has other matters to hear. The IAA usually lists more appeals than there is time for an adjudicator to hear.

8.19   If an adjournment is granted and it is important that a particular advocate conduct the hearing, remember to check that the new date is suitable. The Deputy Chief Adjudicator has stated that:

> I accept entirely that it is good practice to liaise wherever possible with the representatives involved in any particular case when arranging a date. It is my own practice to note, when Counsel appear, Counsel's telephone number and the name of Counsel's clerk so that Listing at the IAA can liaise with Counsel's clerk to agree a mutually convenient date... [L]isting should strive to agree a mutually convenient date when a case should be listed. (Letter dated 15 January 2002 to Glazer Delmar, solicitors)

8.20   As well as the interests of justice, if you are publicly funded, you can point to the additional expense to the public purse which briefing a new advocate would involve.

Statutory closure

8.21   Rule 13 deals with the 'Closure date'. It applies to adjournments before an adjudicator but not the IAT. It provides that:

> *(1) Rule 40 applies to the adjournment of an appeal to an adjudicator, subject to the following provisions of this rule.*
>
> *(2) Subject to paragraph (3), where an adjudicator adjourns the hearing of an appeal, the adjudicator must give directions fixing a date (the 'closure date') by which an adjudicator must either –*
>
> *(a) hear the appeal; or*
> *(b) determine the appeal without a hearing.*
>
> *(3) Paragraph (2) does not apply where the appellate authority has fixed and notified the parties of a first hearing date and a subsequent hearing date, and the first hearing is adjourned.*
>
> *(4) The closure date –*
>
> *(a) must be fixed according to the individual circumstances of the case; but*
> *(b) subject to paragraphs (6) and (8), must be not more than 6 weeks after the date of the adjourned hearing.*
>
> *(5) The new date fixed for the hearing in accordance with rule 40(4) must be on or before the closure date.*
>
> *(6) An adjudicator may fix a closure date which is more than 6 weeks after the date of the adjourned hearing, or may vary a closure date –*
>
> *(a) if all the parties consent; or*
> *(b) in exceptional circumstances, if the adjudicator is satisfied by evidence filed or given by or on behalf of a party that –*
> *(i) the appeal cannot be justly determined within 6 weeks, or by the closure date where one has already been fixed; and*
> *(ii) there is an identifiable future date by which the appeal can be justly determined.*
>
> *(7) A senior adjudicator may (either before or after the closure date has passed) vary the closure date for an appeal if no adjudicator is or was available to hear or determine the appeal by that date.*
>
> *(8) The Chief Adjudicator may in exceptional circumstances –*

(a) *direct that, in such classes of case as he shall specify, the time within which pending appeals must be heard or determined in accordance with paragraph (2) shall be extended by such period as he shall specify; and*

(b) *accordingly modify the orders fixing a closure date which have been made in those appeals.*

8.22 An adjudicator is required to fix a 'closure date' when he adjourns an appeal. That closure date should not be more than six weeks away unless

- all parties consent, *or*
- 'in exceptional circumstances', he is satisfied that the appeal cannot be justly determined within six weeks. He must still be satisfied that there is an identifiable future date upon which the appeal can be justly determined.

The same test applies in respect of an application to vary a closure date previously set.

8.23 In practice, an adjudicator is unlikely to set the initial closure date significantly earlier than six weeks: the IAA struggles to relist hearings within six weeks in many centres. A 'senior adjudicator' (see r.2 for the definition) can extend the closure date if there is no adjudicator available to hear the appeal.

8.24 You will have to meet the additional tests in r.13 only if you need an adjournment of more than six weeks or, if a closure date has already been set, you need a further adjournment beyond that date. The basic hurdle is the same: you must show that the appeal could not otherwise be justly determined. The additional qualification is that this will apply only in 'exceptional circumstances'. The effect of this is that there is a presumption that the appeal can be justly determined within the closure date or within six weeks if none has already been set. You will have to rebut that presumption. The evidence and issues will be the same. But note that you must be able to show how the problem will resolve by an identifiable future date so as to enable the appeal to be heard.

8.25 The rule refers to an adjudicator hearing the appeal or determining the appeal on the papers within the closure date. However, he will only be able to determine the appeal on the papers rather than hold a hearing if the criteria in r.45 are made out (see para 7.3).

Circumstances in which adjournment may be necessitated

8.26 The following are among the most common circumstances in which an adjournment may be necessitated (although in no particular order). Some circumstances, such as being unrepresented or the representative having withdrawn at the hearing, are by definition not circumstances in which you will be making the resulting adjournment application. However, they are included here for ease of reference. If your client has instructed you after the adjudicator hearing, you will need to assess whether an adjournment ought to have been granted.

Absence of appellant

8.27 You must have regard to the provisions of r.44 (see para 7.14), in particular r.44(1) which mandates an adjudicator to proceed with the appeal if neither you nor the appellant attend without satisfactory explanation.

8.28 If your client is too unwell to attend court, you need to obtain a medical certificate confirming this. Often, a HOPO will oppose adjournment on the ground that the medical certificate is unsatisfactory, for example because it does not establish that your client's illness actually prevents her attending court. In *Chisthi*, the IAT adopted the following passage by Bingham LJ in *Merner*:

> *The Court is not obliged to accept any excuse, however unconvincing it may be. If the Court suspects the grounds to be spurious or believes them to be inadequate, the Court should ordinarily express doubts and thereby give the defendant the opportunity to resolve those doubts. It may call for better evidence or require further enquiries to be made or adopt any other expedient fair to both parties. The ultimate test must always be one of fairness and if a defendant claims to be ill and with apparently responsible medical reports in support of his claim, the Court should not reject that claim and proceed to hear the case in the defendant's absence without satisfying itself that the claim may properly be rejected and that no unfairness will thereby be done.*

8.29 Often, problems arise simply because the doctor has not realised that his medical certificate may be subjected to challenge by the HOPO in adversarial proceedings and has therefore failed to pre-empt potential criticisms. HOPOs sometimes appear to think that asylum seekers who do not even speak English should be expected to advise doctors upon what issues must be expressly covered in the certificate.

8.30   You should, however, check the certificate before submitting it. Check firstly that it expressly states that your client cannot attend the appeal hearing (as opposed to 'work' which is the box a doctor is often inclined to tick). Unless it is self-evident from the illness, the certificate ought also to explain what the effects of her illness are which prevent her attending. If the certificate does not do so, try to contact the doctor yourself to ask for these issues to be covered. If your application for an adjournment is refused on the papers, or if there is no time to make a paper application, then it is crucial that you attend the hearing even if your client cannot. If you do not, an adjudicator may feel obliged to proceed under r.44(1).

8.31   If the adjudicator who refused the application has made adverse comments about the medical certificate, it is vital that you try to address these prior to the hearing. If there is no time to have these addressed or if the adjudicator at the hearing remains unconvinced, you may ask the adjudicator to delay determining the appeal for a period to allow the submission of further medical evidence. In *Awadh*, the IAT approved this course. But it held that the adjudicator must either invite submissions on the merits at the first hearing or, if he did not do this, provide an opportunity for submissions should he be unsatisfied by the further medical evidence.

8.32   The same approach may be adopted when faced with the unexplained non-appearance of an appellant who had previously shown every sign of pursuing her appeal.

8.33   See also the discussion of the power under r.44 to proceed with the hearing in the absence of a party (para 7.19).

Absence of representative

8.34   An adjudicator should not normally refuse an adjournment when the appellant's advocate becomes unavailable for good reason at short notice. Illness of a representative should, in contrast to an appellant, be accepted at 'face value' (at least assuming that the representative is 'reputable'): *Muia*.

8.35   In *Okiji*, the adjudicator had refused an adjournment application based on counsel's illness, commenting that 'I found it extraordinary that an adjournment request was received because a counsel was indisposed. The normal practice of the bar is to send somebody else to take the brief, even at one moment's notice.' The IAT disagreed:

> As the Tribunal has said many times before, where a representative gives
> a good reason for failure to attend, an adjudicator should hesitate long

before accepting that an adjournment is not necessary. Further, where it is reported to an adjudicator that counsel had been taken suddenly ill, in many circumstances it would not be reasonable to expect another counsel to take over the case at a moment's notice. While the late handing over of the conduct of a case may be consistent with the traditions of the Bar, it is not always consistent with the interests of the appellant.

Withdrawal of representative

8.36 Where an advocate withdraws his representation during a hearing (other than because the appellant dispensed with his services), an adjournment should be granted. In **Kandeepan**, the adjudicator had refused to adjourn when counsel for the appellant withdrew during the course of the hearing. The IAT held that:

[T]he manner in which the Adjudicator then proceeded with the hearing demonstrated a striking lack of judgment as to what was the appropriate course to adopt in the interests of justice and fairness. There was no question of the Appellant having dispensed with the services of his Counsel during the course of the hearing which might have justified the continuation of it. In these circumstances, the only proper course was for the Adjudicator to adjourn the hearing before her.

See also **Dirisu**.

Appellant unrepresented

8.37 The IAT has held in several determinations that:

Whether or not an appellant is articulate the need for representation if [it] is wanted appears almost axiomatic given the obligation to give the most anxious scrutiny to cases of this kind. (Ajeh)

8.38 These decisions were criticised in a judicial review permission application, **Bogou**. The criticism was that the IAT had not expressly had regard to the relevant test in the Procedure Rules for adjournment. It is submitted that the criticism is not well-founded. The IAT concluded that representation was an 'almost axiomatic' precondition for anxious scrutiny of asylum appeals. That would appear to make clear that it considered that the appeal could not be justly determined without an adjournment to permit proper representation.

Further evidence required

8.39 You will have to show firstly that you have not unreasonably delayed in obtaining the evidence and secondly that the appeal cannot be justly determined without the evidence. If you have instructed local lawyers to try to obtain documents in the country of origin, explain when you instructed them and show how you acted with reasonable expedition to follow up this line of enquiry. If you have been trying to track down a witness abroad, explain what steps you have taken already. If these have so far been unsuccessful, explain what further steps you intend to take and why you still believe that you will ultimately be successful.

8.40 In **Macharia**, Peter Gibson LJ said that:

> There may be circumstances where, in the interest of justice, or for the effective disposal of the appeal, it would be proper to grant an adjournment, particularly in a case where it is the asylum seeker putting in the further evidence. Throughout, the Tribunal has to bear in mind that an asylum decision has potentially grave consequences for the asylum seeker whose very life may be put at risk by an adverse decision...

8.41 In *F*, Silber J said that the same principle applied in a human rights context, and that if to refuse an adjournment

> would have inevitably prevented the claimant from putting forward relevant and potentially cogent evidence in favour of her appeal, [t]hat to my mind, constitutes a powerful factor in favour of granting an adjournment or at least proceeding but offering to consider the report before producing his [determination].

He identified the cause of the lateness and degree of disadvantage to the respondent or the IAA as significant factors.

8.42 Where further documentary evidence will not affect the oral examination of witnesses, submission of that evidence after the hearing may address any perceived prejudice to the Home Office or inconvenience to the IAA which might otherwise arise from an adjourned hearing. In *F*, Silber J said that:

> [W]here a Special Adjudicator is being asked to adjourn a hearing because a report said to be relevant is about to become available and has not previously been available for understandable reasons, he ought to consider not merely whether to grant an adjournment but also if he does not whether he will agree to consider the report after the hearing and then if he believes it to be relevant to receive and consider submissions on it.

8.43 However, the Chief Adjudicator has discouraged adjudicators from taking this course except in exceptional circumstances because the IAA administration often fails to forward the material to the adjudicator in time. See para 39.20 for the procedure advised in Adjudicator Guidance Note No 4 to deal with this.

Witness unavailable

8.44 An adjournment should normally be granted when a material witness – whether expert or factual – is unavailable for good reason on the fixed date but will be able to attend within a reasonable period.

8.45 If the Home Office objects to an adjournment on this ground, you may invite the Home Office to accept the witness' written statement. If it does so, then oral evidence from the witness is unnecessary. If it wishes to dispute the witness' evidence, it will be more difficult for the Home Office to oppose an adjournment to permit oral evidence.

8.46 It is, however, important that you check the witness' availability as soon as you decide to call him, and that you make any application to the court promptly. Impress on the witness that if he subsequently becomes unavailable then he must tell you immediately. See further chapter 25 on expert witnesses. Issues that arise where the witness has an outstanding asylum claim are addressed in chapter 15.

Being taken by surprise by arguments/ evidence from the Home Office

8.47 In *Macharia*, Peter Gibson LJ emphasised the need for a

> *safeguard…requir[ing] a party other than the party producing new evidence to have a fair opportunity to deal with that evidence, and that must entail that he has time both to consider the material and also to see whether any further relevant material needs to be adduced to counter the new evidence.*

8.48 The IAT has also held that where the Home Office produces evidence late, you should be entitled to an adjournment to seek evidence to rebut it (see e.g. *Tambwe*).

8.49 Adjournment may also be necessitated where the HOPO is permitted at a late stage to put in issue a point which was not previously in dispute between the parties. Remember, however, that your primary submission in those circumstances should usually be that the Home Office should not be permitted to change its case at such a late stage. In *Carcabuk* the IAT concluded that:

> *A concession can be withdrawn but, if a HOPO seeks to do this, the adjudicator must be satisfied that the appellant will not be prejudiced if the hearing continues and should only allow an adjournment if persuaded that there was good reason to have made and to withdraw the concession.*
>
> *If a concession made before an adjudicator is to be withdrawn before the Tribunal, the Home Office must notify the appellant in good time.*

Adjournments will not be granted to allow for such withdrawals without good reason.

Mistake by representative (whether you or a previous representative)

8.50 If the need for adjournment arises through the failings of an appellant's representatives, then in the clear absence of an effective remedy against the representative and the potential adverse consequences to the appellant of her representative's conduct, it should seldom be just to refuse an adjournment in order to remedy the prejudice. Refer to the cases quoted at paras 42.78 and 42.79.

8.51 In the past, the Home Office have relied upon the House of Lords' decision in *Al-Mehdawi* for the (unattractive) proposition that appellants must suffer the consequences of their representative's mistakes. The Court of Appeal held in *Haile*, that the decision does not apply to asylum cases (see para 42.80).

8.52 You may again refer to *Martin* where the Divisional Court found that a significant factor in determining the fairness of the refusal to adjourn was that the party was himself an experienced barrister. The contrast with the vulnerability of the asylum seeker and her dependence on her representative could hardly be greater.

To await decisions in other cases

8.53 In the Court of Appeal and Administrative Court, it is often considered sensible to adjourn cases behind a lead case where they raise common issues, whether the lead case is in the same court or a higher court. However, you will often hear adjudicators say that they have a policy of not adjourning appeals to await decisions in other cases. It appears odd that adjudicators should not be prepared to adjourn in circumstances in which the Court of Appeal and Administrative Court consider it sensible, and the policy is not universally applied. Indeed, cases are regularly adjourned in the IAT to await other decisions of the IAT, particularly starred decisions.

8.54 The appropriateness of adjournment depends upon the relevance of the lead case and the imminence of judgment. The more detail that you can give on both counts, the better your chances. Adjournment will be most appropriate where the point in issue in the pending decision will affect the evidence that needs to be given in the present appeal, or the test that the fact-finder must apply.

8.55 You must reassure the adjudicator that he is not being asked to adjourn the appeal when you have no idea when the other case will be heard, and only a sketchy idea of its relevance. The strongest scenario will be where the case has already been heard and only judgment is awaited.

Challenging a remittal by the IAT

8.56 If you originally won your appeal, the Home Office may have appealed and succeeded in having the determination set aside and the matter remitted for rehearing. There is no right of appeal to the Court of Appeal against this decision, the remedy being judicial review (para 49.24). Because commencing judicial review proceedings does not automatically stay the appeal, you may have to apply for the remitted appeal before the adjudicator to be adjourned pending the outcome of the judicial review (see further para 49.26). Practice has been to adjourn the hearing provided judicial review proceedings have already been lodged.

Conditions recently changed in the country of origin

8.57 The Home Office sometimes applies for an adjournment when conditions have recently deteriorated in a country of origin. Its motivation would appear to be the hope that conditions will improve again by the time the appeal is relisted. That is an impermissible approach. The adjudicator is required to determine the appeal on the basis of country conditions as of the date of hearing.

8.58 However, you will occasionally have to apply for an adjournment as a result of recently changed circumstances in the country of origin. This is not because you hope that circumstances will change again before the appeal is heard, but because you have had insufficient time to obtain evidence, most often expert evidence, as to the implications of the changed conditions for your client.

Adjournment applications by the Home Office

8.59 You ought to be offered an opportunity to make representations on any Home Office application for an adjournment. It will often make such an application where it has been directed to do something within a particular period and has failed to do it. You may wish to argue alternatively that the Home Office should be prevented from advancing the allegation to which the direction was relevant.

8.60 If it appears that the IAA has granted the Home Office an adjournment without giving you the opportunity to comment, you may complain and ask for the matter to be reconsidered.

8.61 The HOPO may try to obtain an adjournment on the basis that he is prejudiced by having insufficient time to consider your evidence because of its late submission. The reality is that the file was probably not allocated to the HOPO until the day before the hearing. Countering such applications is discussed at para 27.13.

8.62 The IAA has been known to accede to applications to adjourn appeals from a particular country en masse, most recently Iraqi cases following the start of Gulf War II. If you have sufficient evidence of present country conditions, you may wish to challenge such adjournments.

Adjournments by the IAA

8.63 An adjudicator may adjourn a hearing despite neither party having made such an application and even if both parties object to the adjournment. The adjudicator must still show that the test in r.40(2) has been met, and his decision will be challengeable (as in *No. 19* where both appellants and the Home Office brought judicial review proceedings against the IAT's decision to adjourn).

8.64 It will however be rare for an adjudicator to adjourn of his own motion. In the past, some adjudicators have done so when the Home Office has not instructed a HOPO to attend because the adjudicator feels a HOPO would assist. However, the IAT has now established that an adjudicator should not normally adjourn on this ground (see chapter 40). Indeed, the adjudicator cannot lawfully adjourn the appeal where the Home Office is unrepresented and has given no satisfactory explanation for not attending (*Demeter;* r.44(1)). Where an adjudicator decided to issue a witness summons of his own motion (a power which should also be exercised sparingly, see para 9.45), he would also probably have to adjourn the hearing. The IAT has on occasion adjourned the hearing so as to direct that the parties seek further country information which it deemed necessary in order to properly determined the appeal (e.g. *limi*).

8.65 Sometimes, a hearing will be adjourned simply due to lack of court time, lack of adjudicators, or the court files having been mislaid. This may be unforeseeable and unavoidable. However, if the appeal is adjourned in circumstances *which should have been foreseeable and avoidable*, then you may wish to ask the IAA to pay your client's costs thrown away. The IAA's policy is to pay compensation for costs thrown away when a hearing is adjourned through its own fault. It produces a newsletter which includes reports of applications for compensation and the decisions it has reached. In an appropriate case, a refusal to pay compensation could be challengeable by means of judicial review, though you would have to weigh carefully whether the cost of the application was justified by the amount at stake. One example where this course might be considered is where the appellant is paying privately for representation at the appeal, and the costs thrown away by adjournment may render her unable to pay for further representation.

Dealing with the refusal of an application

8.66 If your adjournment application is refused, you must decide whether to challenge the refusal to adjourn immediately or whether to proceed with the appeal and then, if appropriate, raise the refusal to adjourn as part of your application for permission to appeal. There is no direct appeal to the IAT against the refusal of an adjournment, so the only means of challenge prior to the appeal being determined is judicial review of the refusal to adjourn.

8.67 As indicated by the quotation in para 8.1 above, adjournment may raise acute issues of fairness. The High Court has on occasion been willing to entertain applications for judicial review of a refusal to adjourn, and indeed to entertain urgent applications for an interim injunction prohibiting the adjudicator from proceeding with the hearing. For example, an interim injunction was granted by the Administrative Court in *Hwez*, prohibiting the hearing of an Iraqi Kurd's asylum appeal during 2001 pending the judicial review challenge to the refusal to adjourn.

8.68 Bringing immediate judicial review proceedings will only be appropriate where your adjournment application raises a point of principle and/or where waiting to appeal the final determination is clearly not a sensible remedy. The latter may apply where the refusal has placed the appellant in a particularly invidious position in terms of the conduct of the hearing, and risks causing prejudice which the IAT could not remedy effectively on appeal. The grant of an adjournment to the Home Office may also cause prejudice that cannot be remedied on appeal, e.g. where its real ground for adjournment appears to be the hope that conditions may subsequently improve in the country of origin.

8.69 Home Office barristers sometimes advance the misconceived argument that a claimant must show that it was perverse to refuse to adjourn. In *Ghaly*, Sedley J confirmed that the issue is procedural fairness, not rationality (para 8.1).

8.70   If you are refused an adjournment and the circumstances are not such as to merit an immediate challenge (or an injunction is refused), or if your adjournment application is refused at the hearing so that you have no time to apply for an injunction, you will be faced with the question of how (if at all) to conduct the appeal. Your options are either to present the hearing as best you can, withdraw your representation, or offer no evidence. It will seldom be helpful or appropriate to withdraw your representation or to offer no evidence if you have any instructions upon which you can present the appeal. Consider in advance what you will do if the adjournment is refused.

8.71   You will invariably decide to proceed with the hearing where the adjournment application related to a discrete piece of evidence which did not affect your ability to lead the rest of your evidence. (Note, however, that it is important to continue your efforts to obtain the evidence despite the refusal of the adjournment. If you get it before the determination is promulgated, you should submit it to the IAA anyway. If not, you will want to present it to the IAT on any permission application: chapter 43.)

8.72   If your client has attended, but has instructed you that he is too ill to give evidence, you may decide not to call your client (making it clear that you are doing so because he is too ill) and simply make submissions. Obviously, if your client is not there, you will take the same course.

8.73   The most difficult situations often arise where an advocate is instructed to meet his client on the day and no interpreter attends with the result that the advocate is unable to take instructions. If the appeal is publicly funded, there is no excuse for not arranging a conference prior to the date of the hearing. Similarly, there is no excuse for not arranging to have an interpreter at the hearing if the appeal is publicly funded. If you do find yourself in the unfortunate position of being briefed to meet your client for the first time on the day of the hearing and you have been unable for whatever reason to take instructions, you have a difficult decision to make if your adjournment request is refused. If you have a full witness statement and written instructions, and your client has indicated a desire to give oral evidence, you may decide to take the risk of calling your client to allow cross-examination. But you cannot lead evidence if you do not have adequate instructions.

8.74   You may in those circumstances indicate that you are unable to call your client due to inadequate instructions and your inability to communicate with her. You should therefore make any submissions you can on the refusal letter and any documentary evidence. It will not normally be appropriate to say that you offer no evidence if there is some evidence before the adjudicator. You must not of course withdraw the appeal. (You will anyway be unable to get instructions to that effect.) You may in extreme cases inform the adjudicator that you do not feel that you have sufficient instructions to represent the appellant and are therefore withdrawing. However, the effect of that decision may be that the appellant is cross-examined by the HOPO without any representative, so the better course will normally be to invite the adjudicator to determine the matter on the papers and then appeal the determination if appropriate.

8.75 Continuing the hearing should not prejudice you in challenging on appeal the adjudicator's refusal to adjourn. You will have asked the adjudicator to note that you are continuing under protest and will have renewed your request for an adjournment at every appropriate point in the hearing. You will have drafted a note immediately after the hearing, detailing how your client was prejudiced, and recording what was said at the hearing.

8 Adjournment
Key points

- In order for an adjournment application to comply with r.40 and the relevant Practice Direction, it should:
  - ☐ be made within the time limit,
  - ☐ be served on the Home Office,
  - ☐ include both full reasons and any further evidence required to establish any fact upon which you rely.

- Most paper adjournment applications are refused: your application must include cogent submissions showing
  - ☐ why further time is needed, *and*
  - ☐ why the appeal cannot otherwise be justly determined.

- Principles of natural justice demand that a party should have every reasonable opportunity to prepare and present his case. Relevant factors in determining an adjournment application include the importance of the litigation and the degree of inconvenience or prejudice to the Court and the opposing party.

- If the adjournment is necessitated by the Home Office's failure to do something, accompany your adjournment application with a request for a direction that it remedy its failure by a specified date.

- If an adjournment has not been granted on the papers, you *must* attend the hearing.

- 'Statutory closure' does not affect the test for a first adjournment of up to six weeks.

- An application for an adjournment exceeding six weeks, or any application that involves varying a closure date that has already been fixed, may be granted only if:
  - ☐ all parties consent, or
  - ☐ the adjudicator is satisfied 'in exceptional circumstances' that the appeal cannot be justly determined within six weeks (or by the closure date already fixed) *and* there is an identifiable future date when the appeal can be justly determined.

Circumstances in which an adjournment may be necessitated

■ The appellant or her representative are absent from the hearing.

■ The representative withdraws during the hearing.

■ The appellant has not been able to obtain representation.

■ Material evidence is not yet available.

■ A material witness cannot attend.

■ The Home Office has advanced a new case or new evidence without notice.

■ Errors have been made by the present, or a previous representative.

■ There is a pending decision in a higher court that will affect the evidence that needs to be led or the test that the fact-finder should apply in evaluating that evidence.

■ The hearing results from a remittal by the IAT, and that remittal is being challenged by judicial review.

■ There has been a change of circumstances in the country of origin about which further evidence is required.

Home Office applications for adjournment

■ You are entitled to make representations opposing the adjournment. Ask for the decision to be reconsidered if you have been denied that opportunity.

■ The Home Office should not be granted an adjournment in the hope that conditions in the country of origin will improve.

■ The HOPO may claim that he is prejudiced by receiving your evidence late: the reality is that he is unlikely to have received the file until the day before the hearing.

■ The adjudicator may not adjourn an appeal where the Home Office has failed to attend and has given no satisfactory explanation for its absence.

Adjournment on the adjudicator's own motion

■ An adjudicator can adjourn an appeal of his own motion, but only if the test in r.40(2) is met.

■ He may not adjourn on the ground that the Home Office has no present intention to remove the appellant.

■ The IAA's policy is to pay compensation for costs thrown away where its own error necessitates adjournment.

Challenging an adjournment decision

■ The refusal (or grant) of an adjournment can be challenged immediately only by judicial review.

■ This will normally be appropriate only where an important point of principle arises or the prejudice may not be capable of being remedied by appealing the adjudicator's final determination.

■ Only in exceptional circumstances may it be justified to withdraw from the hearing or offer no evidence when adjournment is refused. You should otherwise present the appeal as best you can (if necessary, simply on submissions) while reserving your right to challenge the refusal to adjourn before the IAT.

9 Narrowing the issues and seeking disclosure

9.1   This jurisdiction is adversarial. The IAA has encouraged the parties to define and narrow the issues in dispute. The Procedure Rules are designed to facilitate that. Fairness in any event entitles you to know the opposing party's case. However, appellants (and the IAA) can face endemic, indeed systemic obstacles in persuading the Home Office to disclose its case on the relevant issues with sufficient clarity sufficiently in advance.

Home Office skeleton arguments

9.2   The Home Office commonly argues that it need not produce a skeleton argument setting out its case because the refusal letter fulfils that role. Practice Direction CA1 of 2002 requires that a skeleton argument should 'define and confine the areas in issue'. The IAT has directed that the refusal letter should state exactly what is and is not in dispute. But the Home Office seldom complies (para 1.3). One paragraph of the refusal letter may even rely upon facts which another paragraph appears to dispute.

9.3   While the refusal letter is problematic enough as a guide to the Home Office's position at the date of the decision, it is no guide at all to its position on subsequent developments. The Home Office often fails to serve any response to post-decision submissions and evidence. The APIs claim that the Home Office will serve a supplementary letter where any 'relevant new issues have been raised (either new evidence, including medical reports, or a new basis of claim)'. Practice often falls far short of stated policy. It also states that additional (one stop) grounds raising new issues will prompt a supplementary letter but that it will not usually respond to 'grounds of appeal which comment on our reasons for refusing the application'.

9.4   Attempts to engage in sensible discussion with a HOPO in order to narrow or even define issues much in advance may well be futile. You will be lucky to find anyone at the Home Office prepared even to talk about the case more than a day or so before the hearing – no matter how much the appeal has developed since the refusal letter.

9.5   One way of teasing out the details of the Home Office case is to seek a direction that the Home Office serve a proper skeleton argument, in particular if they intend to advance any contention not set out in the refusal letter. Rule 38(5)(e)(iii) permits an adjudicator to direct 'a skeleton argument which summarises succinctly the submissions which will be made at the hearing and cites all the authorities which will be relied on, identifying any particular passages to be relied on'. Indeed, all appellants are now required to lodge 'a skeleton argument, identifying all relevant issues including Human Rights claims and citing all the authorities to be relied on'.

9.6   The Home Office's APIs state that:

> *Directions may require a skeleton argument. Unless the request relates to specific points, we should simply refer to reasons for refusal letter and any supplementary letter(s). It is not necessary for caseworkers to provide or refer to precedent cases. What is being sought is the paperwork on which our decision is based: the evidence backing up our assertions.*

9.7   It is unclear what basis the Home Office could have for claiming that it is unnecessary to refer to the caselaw upon which it relies. The Procedure Rules expressly state that a skeleton should incorporate the caselaw relied upon and it is required of all appellants. The APIs include a sample skeleton argument for a fictional case as an example of good practice. It is instructive. Its structure is as follows:

- The Home Office concedes in the light of 'further evidence' that the appellant was a member of his organisation and was active as claimed.
- It concedes that 'higher level' activists of that organisation 'may well' be at risk of persecution.
- It contends, however, that less prominent members are not at risk and supports this contention by reference to reports from Amnesty International.
- It therefore opposes the appeal on the sole ground that the appellant is not sufficiently prominent to be at risk.

9.8   This example demonstrates how a skeleton argument from the Home Office may assist. It identifies what is and is not in dispute and the evidence upon which the Home Office will rely to resolve the dispute. It saves everyone time and effort. Contrast it with the structure of the average refusal letter. You might refer an adjudicator to the Home

Office' sample skeleton to illustrate the utility of a skeleton argument in contrast to the refusal letter.

Seeking further details of the Home Office's case

9.9   Of course you cannot be sure that any skeleton argument which is produced will correspond to the standards of clarity set out in the APIs. You may therefore seek more specific directions in order to narrow the issues and identify what is in dispute by seeking 'further details' of the Home Office case pursuant to r.38(5)(d)(iii). (In older versions of the Rules and much of the caselaw, 'further details' were described as 'particulars'.)

9.10   The Home Office has on occasion adopted the bizarre position that it is justifiable for it to oppose an appeal while declining to disclose its case for opposing it. It has relied upon a decision of the Court of Appeal in **Mwanza**. The Court held that a direction to the Home Office to issue a 'fresh refusal letter' was *ultra vires* because it required the Home Office to take a substantive step (i.e. embark on a reconsideration). The Rules only permitted directions in respect of procedural issues.

9.11   That decision was deprecated on its facts by the IAT in **N'Da**. But its limited application was also emphasised by the IAT in **Razi**. In that case, the Home Office had refused the claim on non-compliance grounds and the adjudicator directed that it serve

> *a note of any reasons for refusing the substantive asylum application. Failing compliance, consideration may be given to disposing of the appeal in accordance with Rule 33 [of the 2000 Procedure Rules].*

9.12   The Home Office did not comply. The Adjudicator therefore treated its decision as withdrawn. The Home Office appealed. The IAT dismissed the appeal. It held that '[The adjudicator] was not requiring the Home Office to take a changed view of the case'. He was simply requiring it to 'give whatever reasons they might have for maintaining their decision' so that the appeal could be determined on the merits:

> *That was the proper procedural purpose for which [the adjudicator] gave his direction. It clearly came to the same thing as an order for particulars, familiar to civil practitioners, which essentially requires a party to give details of his own case.*

9.13   In **Emlik**, the Administrative Court approved **Razi**, holding that the IAT 'were clearly right in that case in distinguishing **Mwanza**' (per Silber J). See also **Zaier**, in which Auld LJ pointed to **Razi** as illustrating how a direction expressed as a requirement that the Home Office particularise its case might achieve the same result in practice as an (impermissible) direction requiring the Home Office to take a fresh decision. In the same case, Clarke LJ emphasised the adjudicator's 'extensive' and 'ample powers' to make appropriate directions, including that the Home Office particularise its case, notwithstanding that he could not order a reconsideration or fresh decision by the Home Office. The disagreement with *Razi* expressed by another division of the IAT in *C (Yugoslavia)* was limited to the consequences of non-compliance with directions under the previous 2000 Rules rather than the nature of the power to make directions.

9.14 The proposed direction should however be carefully phrased, both to improve the prospects of it being ordered and to decrease the prospects of the Home Office successfully challenging it. What an adjudicator may not do is direct that the Home Office take a substantive step such as to reconsider the case and make a new decision or to reinterview the appellant no matter how sensible or necessary that step may appear. What he can do is direct the Home Office to disclose details of its case: its reasons for maintaining that the appeal should be dismissed. If the case plainly requires a change of view, then the Home Office will either have to change its view, or expose its position as untenable.

9.15 Suppose the Home Office's original decision was based on the assertion that your client could live in rebel-held Narnia. Narnia has now fallen to the government. You may not ask the adjudicator to direct the Home Office to reconsider its decision to refuse asylum. That would be to imply (according to *Mwanza*) that the Home Office must take a different view. But the adjudicator *can* direct the Home Office to disclose its reasons for opposing the appeal in light of the fall of Narnia. The Home Office is entitled to respond to the direction by stating that its case remains unchanged. But if so, the disclosure of that fact may enable the adjudicator to resolve the appeal expeditiously against the Home Office. If on the other hand, the Home Office has changed its reasons then, as the IAT recognised, you are entitled to notice of its new case. The same reasoning applies if you have put forward further evidence particular to your client which demands a response.

9.16 The Home Office actually recognises that this is the correct position. The APIs state that:

> *Where representations are made, any new issues not previously taken into account should be given full consideration in the light of all earlier information and a response given so that the Immigration Appellate Authority (IAA) will have an opportunity to consider them at the appeal*

hearing. Early consideration of new evidence may avoid having an appeal hearing adjourned by the appellate authority for further consideration by IND.

...

If the refusal of the application is maintained, the Home Office will have to be able to demonstrate to the IAA that it has decided to maintain its decision only after considering the further representations, including all the relevant evidence submitted to it by the applicant both before and after the initial decision.

9.17 An example of how such a direction might be phrased is:

The Home Office is required to lodge with the Appellate Authority further details of whether, and if so on what grounds it continues to oppose the appeal. Those grounds should in particular state whether (and if so on what grounds) it challenges the following evidence relied upon by the appellant...

(For a further example, see the direction issued by the IAT in *Zaire*.)

9.18 Do not assume that the Home Office will necessarily comply. In *Razi* (which had been adjourned on several occasions without compliance by the Home Office), the IAT commented that taking the 'charitable view' that the Home Office's conduct 'was no more than institutional incompetence, it is hard to imagine any other department of state in this country where such incompetence would be tolerated'. It added, however, that:

This begins to go beyond mere institutional incompetence, into the realm of an institutional culture of disregard for adjudicators, who are the primary judicial authority in this country for making sure that immigration powers are efficiently, as well as fairly exercised. That does not serve the public interest, which the Home Office are there (we think) to represent.

9.19 It concluded that the adjudicator was justified in treating the decision as withdrawn. That course is no longer available under the present Procedure Rules. However, there are alternative measures available to the adjudicator in the face of non-compliance by the Home Office.

9.20 Rule 38(5)(f)(iv) empowers the adjudicator to limit 'the issues which will be addressed at the hearing'. You will often wish to seek a further direction that should the Home Office fail to comply with the order to provide further details of its case, it should be precluded from putting forward a new case at the hearing. Such an approach hugely facilitates the efficient and cost-effective disposal of appeals, avoiding appellants having to amass evidence at public expense or arrange experts to attend hearings only for it to transpire that the Home Office does not, or cannot take issue with the point. In **Nori**, the IAT noted that:

> *It may be that if the Secretary of State fails to carry out any investigation himself or to reach any conclusion himself, the adjudicator will have to make his decision on the basis of uncontroverted evidence from the appellant or without permitting the Secretary of State, if he has failed to comply with directions, to put in any material himself.*

9.21   The first hearing may provide an opportunity to define the issues or, if the Home Office cannot offer a sensible response, to seek an appropriate direction (see **Carcabuk & Bla**).

9.22   As with other litigation, the Home Office's first attempt to detail its case may be unclear or incomplete and you are entitled to ask for further details in these circumstances. This is distinct from asking for disclosure of its evidence (which is dealt with below). You are seeking to identify what claims the Home Office does and does not make. You will often want to know not only what is in dispute, but why. That will help you gauge how seriously you need to take the assertion, and how much effort and expense you need to devote to countering it.

9.23   You might, for example, want further details of the Home Office's case in order to enable your expert to engage with the Home Office's reasoning. If it alleges that your client wrongly identified the leader of a rebel organisation, it may assist in establishing its error if the Home Office is directed to identify who it claims the leader is. Sometimes, it will be helpful to explore the implications of the Home Office's case. By compelling the Home Office to follow through its argument to its logical conclusion, you may persuade it – or at least the adjudicator – of its absurdity, or may expose the unattractiveness of the underlying assumptions. You can also force the Home Office to engage with inconvenient aspects of the case.

9.24   You can of course present the evidence and make the submission without seeking further details. But by forcing the Home Office to commit itself to the full extent of its argument, the rebuttal of that case is more persuasive. Even if the request is refused, you have focussed minds upon the validity of the Home Office's case whereas the Home Office will often wish to focus minds anywhere but. You may even persuade the Home Office to abandon such allegations altogether (or occasionally to concede the case). The following appeared in a refusal letter quoted in *No Reason at All*:

> *'The Secretary of State... considered your account of crossing the Zaire River by canoe at night to be totally implausible. The Secretary of State is aware of the size, strength and considerable dangers posed by the river such as shifting sandbanks and crocodiles.'*

9.25 Confronted with a request for further details of the alleged crocodile population, the Home Office was unable to comply. It withdrew the allegation, but then – illustrating the potential drawback in seeking such a direction – produced a wholly new set of allegations to support its refusal. Such a response is a real risk in some cases. It illustrates the major proviso to the above discussion: just because the Home Office has not presented its case properly does not necessarily make it your job to force it to do so.

9.26 The appellant will have an understandable sense of injustice if he successfully discredits the reasons for refusal only to find that the Home Office puts forward new allegations upon which it chose not to rely in the original decision. She may well think that the Home Office is concerned simply to conjure up any reason which might allow it to maintain its original refusal. You will not want to encourage this unattractive practice on the part of the Home Office. For this reason, you should consider the likely response to such directions. You have no obligation to help the Home Office evade the defects in its case. You have to make a decision on the facts of each case whether your client is best served by seeking a direction in advance or simply attacking these defects in your skeleton and submissions.

Disclosure of evidence

9.27 The one standard direction which does apply to the Home Office is the requirement that it serve a bundle of the evidence upon which it will rely seven days in advance of the hearing. It often serves only its Country Assessment or other Home Office document (and seldom in time). The issues arising from such reports (including issues of disclosure) are discussed in chapter 17.

9.28 Under the CPR r.31.6, a party to civil litigation is required to provide disclosure of documents

> which adversely affect his own case; adversely affect another party's case; or support another party's case…

9.29 There is no express requirement in the Procedure Rules upon the Home Office to disclose relevant evidence in its possession (other than that which it must include in the Respondent's bundle – see chapter 10). As a public authority, it would be manifestly unfair, and itself inconsistent with the appellant's human rights, were the Home Office to withhold material which assisted the appellant's case. The Administrative Court has confirmed that, at its lowest, the Home Office has a duty 'not knowingly to mislead in the material he places before the

Adjudicator or the IAT' and that "knowingly' embraces that which he ought to have known' (*Cindo*). Those principles were taken from third country cases, and in *Konan*, Simon Brown LJ said that the Home Office's 'obligation in a full asylum appeal... may well be higher'.

9.30 One would hope it would be rare that there was a conscious decision by the Home Office to withhold material adverse to its case. However, the Home Office is not known for reaching consistently reasonable conclusions on the probative value of evidence. It may convince itself that a document in its possession does not assist the appellant whereas a reasonable observer may draw a very different inference.

9.31 This issue was considered by the panel of adjudicators which heard the Afghan hijacking case. The panel declined to issue a specific direction to the effect that the Home Office should disclose any document favourable to the appellant in the absence of grounds to suspect that the Home Office held such documents. However, it considered that the Home Office was in any event under a continuing duty throughout the process to disclose any evidence which came into its possession which an adjudicator might reasonably consider indicated that the appellants were at risk.

9.32 As well as seeking information about the Home Office's position on material matters, you can, through a request for further details, seek information about what evidence the Home Office has available to it. An adjudicator 'may give directions to the parties relating to the conduct of any appeal' (r.38(1)) which may 'in particular, relate to any matter concerning the preparation for a hearing' (r.38(5)(a)). The IAT has held that it 'must be right' that its power is 'wide enough to enable the Tribunal to make directions relating to the evidence it wishes to have placed before it' (*A, B, C, and D*). It therefore made a direction in that case that the Home Office permit inspection of a particular piece of documentary evidence.

9.33 Such requests can be used effectively to obtain disclosure by seeking further details of what material documents the Home Office has in its possession, and the contents of such documents. For example in the *Al-Mass'ari* case concerning the proposed expulsion of a Saudi dissident to a small Caribbean island in order to appease Saudi Arabia, the Chief Adjudicator ordered that further details be provided of the substance of communications between the governments of the United Kingdom and Dominica. The Home Office's complaint that this was an impermissible direction to disclose evidence was rejected.

9.34 You should write to the Home Office requesting the further details and stating a reasonable period for it to respond, failing which you will apply for a direction. The request should be as focussed as possible to avoid the risk of it being dismissed as a 'fishing expedition'. Where you suspect that the Home Office intends to rely upon evidence at the hearing, and you wish to have that evidence more than a week in advance of the hearing in order to prepare a response, you can also seek a direction that it particularise any evidence upon which it intends to rely to support a particular allegation.

9.35 If the further details relate to an allegation which is central to the reasons for refusal, and the Home Office refuses to comply with the direction, then it would be quite appropriate to urge the adjudicator to use his power to prevent the Home Office pursuing the allegation at the hearing.

Witness summonses to obtain disclosure of documents

9.36 A witness summons may also be used to compel a Home Office official to attend before the adjudicator with a particular document. The Home Office actually disputes this in its IDIs. They state that:

> An order for a witness to attend with documents which is intended purely to obtain the documents (for example where the summons is issued for a person to attend who has had no dealings with the case) should be resisted by relying on the case of **Care**, in which it was held that the appellate authorities have no power to issue a witness summons solely to discover documents. Where the summons is addressed to the Secretary of State, enquiries should be made to find out what evidence is in dispute to allow the appropriate person to attend.

9.37 The IDIs are simply, and inexplicably wrong. Contrary to the Home Office's claims, the case of **Care** referred to in the IDIs *approves* the use of witness summonses for this purpose. Further approval comes from the House of Lords in **Abdi and Gawe.** Lord Lloyd found that there was no general duty of disclosure upon the Home Office (at least in a third country case) because an adjudicator 'can always exercise his powers to ask for particulars of the Secretary of State's case, or to require a witness to attend and produce documents.'

9.38 In any event, r.47(1) itself states that:

> An adjudicator or the Tribunal may, by issuing a summons ('a witness summons'), require any person in the United Kingdom –
>
> (a) to attend as a witness at the hearing of an appeal; and
> (b) subject to rule 48(2), at the hearing to answer any questions or produce any documents in his custody or under his control which relate

> *to any matter in issue in the appeal.*

9.39 Rule 48(2) provides simply that:

> *An adjudicator or the Tribunal may not compel a party or witness to give any evidence or produce any document which he could not be compelled to give or produce at the trial of a civil claim in the part of the United Kingdom in which the hearing is taking place.*

9.40 The IDIs also suggest that:

> *The witness should not... agree to disclose any documents which IND would not normally disclose.*

9.41 This could amount to an incitement to Home Office officials to commit the criminal offence of failing to comply with a witness summons (s.106(4-5) of the 2002 Act). The only limitation on the adjudicator's power to direct the production of documents are those relating to the law of privilege.

Witness summonses for oral examination

9.42 The other purpose for which you might summons a Home Office official is to question him. Witness summonses have in the past been sought against Home Office interpreters and occasionally interviewing officers where the appellant alleges either that the interpreting was inadequate or that the interview has not been properly recorded. The Home Office's IDIs state that:

> *A witness summons may be requested where the appellant's representatives wish to dispute the contents of an interview report, a PCU call-note or the accuracy of a translation. The presenting officer will resist this request in the first instance by relying on the fact that the Home Office has prepared an explanatory statement or reasons for refusal letter and a bundle of documents, which together provide a record of the facts relating to the decision and the reasons for it. It should be argued that since the standard of proof is not that of a criminal court, the report of an immigration officer or a caseworker should be admissible without the presence of the author. The presenting officer should therefore ask the adjudicator or Tribunal whether they would be prepared to accept a signed statement from the IO or caseworker indicating that the report is a true account of the interview/visit to PCU/etc.*

9.43 A 'signed statement' simply asserting that the interview notes are accurate should, of course, carry little weight. But before requesting a witness summons, think carefully about what you will achieve by questioning the person. If you summons a witness, then he will normally be treated as your witness. That means your examination will be treated as examination in chief and you will not be permitted to ask leading questions on contentious issues. It also means that the HOPO's examination will be treated as cross-examination. He will therefore be permitted to put leading questions, notwithstanding that the witness' sympathies lie with the Home Office rather than the appellant.

9.44 The rule in civil litigation is that you can only cross-examine such a witness if he is declared hostile. That requires not only that the witness is giving unfavourable answers, but that he has no desire to tell the truth. It may be difficult to persuade an adjudicator to make such a declaration in respect of a Home Office employee. Adjudicators are not bound by any rules of evidence, and there is no reason why this rule should be applied inflexibly to asylum and human rights appeals. However, there is no IAA caselaw on the subject.

9.45 In *Kesse*, the Court of Appeal concluded that the IAT or an adjudicator had power to summons a witness where neither party had applied for a summons. However, it stated that a tribunal should hesitate long before exercising the power when the summons was not supported by either party. You cannot ask the adjudicator to issue the summons himself so as to avoid the rule that you cannot cross-examine a witness that you have summonsed (see *Prendi*, para 30.15).

9.46 It follows therefore that you have to decide whether you will be able to elicit the necessary evidence from the witness without leading questions. You will need to have considerable confidence that the witness will have no option but to admit the necessary facts.

9.47 There might be occasions when you wish to summons the author of the refusal letter. There is authority indicating that refusal letters can be treated as evidence. Where the allegations in the refusal letter appear to be misleading or raise potential improprieties, you ought to be within your rights to seek a summons against the author in order to investigate the basis for his assertions. However, you would again need to think carefully about how you would formulate your examination effectively in the face of an unhelpful witness and given the restrictions which may be imposed on your examination. In many cases, you will be better off simply pointing out that the refusal letter is a wholly unsatisfactory piece of evidence which should be given little weight.

9.48 As indicated above, to disobey a witness summons without reasonable excuse is a criminal offence. In circumstances where an employee of the respondent is defying an order of the court, it will also be appropriate for the adjudicator to draw the strongest adverse inference against that party.

9.49 Note that you are liable for the travelling expenses of a witness in respect of whom you have obtained a summons. Rule 47(2-3) provides that:

> *(2) A person is not required to attend a hearing in obedience to a witness summons unless –*
>
> *(a) the summons is served on him; and*
> *(b) the necessary expenses of his attendance are paid or tendered to him.*
>
> *(3) If a witness summons is issued at the request of a party, that party must pay or tender the expenses referred to in paragraph (2)(b).*

9.50 The IDIs give the following further guidance to Home Office officials who are summonsed:

> *WHERE A WITNESS SUMMONS IS ISSUED*
>
> *The person named on the summons should attend. Failure to do so is an offence. An IND official called by the appellant should not speak to the appellant's representative before giving evidence. The witness should not be cross-examined by that representative... Any attempt at cross-examination should be strongly resisted by the presenting officer.*

9 Narrowing the issues and seeking disclosure
Key points

■ Efforts to define and narrow the issues between the parties are to be encouraged. They reduce both the cost of appeals and the risk of unfairness.

■ Representatives face systemic obstacles in persuading the Home Office to clarify its case or otherwise engage in useful discussion prior to the hearing.

■ The Home Office argues that its refusal letter serves the same role as a skeleton argument. The IAT has held that the refusal letter should define the issues in dispute. In reality, it seldom does.

■ Seeking a direction that the Home Office produce a skeleton argument may assist to define the issues.

■ An adjudicator may not direct the Home Office to reconsider its decision. But fairness requires it to disclose its case for opposing the appeal. An adjudicator is entitled to direct that the Home Office give 'further details' of its case.

■ Directions may also require the Home Office to detail the basis for its allegations and the evidence that supports them.

■ If the Home Office fails to comply with a direction, the adjudicator is empowered to preclude the Home Office from relying on the argument or relevant evidence at the appeal.

■ The Home Office is (at least) under a duty not to mislead in the material it places before the adjudicator, whether knowingly or in light of what it ought to have known.

■ A direction for 'further details' may require the Home Office to detail relevant evidence in its possession. The IAT has held that the power to give directions encompasses directions as to the evidence that should be before the court.

■ The Home Office can be required to produce evidence in its possession through the issue of a witness summons.

■ A witness summons may also be used to require the attendance of a person for oral examination. However, if the summons is issued on your application, you will not normally be permitted to cross-examine the witness.

10 The respondent's appeal papers

10.1 Rule 9 states:

> *(1) Subject to rule 10 [see below], the respondent must file with the appellate authority any notice of appeal which is served on him, together with a copy of –*
>
> > *(a) the notice of the decision against which the appellant is appealing, and any other document which was served on the appellant giving reasons for that decision;*
> > *(b) any –*
> > > *(i) record of an interview with the appellant; or*
> > > *(ii) other unpublished document,*
> > > *which is referred to in a document mentioned in sub-paragraph (a); and*
> > *(c) the notice of any other immigration decision made in relation to the applicant in respect of which he has a right of appeal under section 82 of the 2002 Act.*
>
> *(2) The respondent must serve on the appellant, as soon as practicable after filing documents under paragraph (1) –*
>
> > *(a) a copy of all the documents filed with the appellate authority; and*
> > *(b) notice of the date on which they were filed.*

10.2 Rule 10 provides that where the Home Office contends that an appeal is out of time, its duties under r.9 are triggered only if and when an adjudicator decides that the appeal was in time or extends time.

10.3 Check the appeal papers when you receive them to ensure that they include everything required by r.9.

10.4 The reference in r.10(1)(d) to providing 'any notes of an asylum interview' is not further explained, but should encompass all interviews conducted by the Home Office in connection with its determination of the asylum claim. It presumably includes interviews conducted on human rights issues. (Note that the Practice Direction on Trial Bundles (para 27.2) requires the Home Office to include in its bundle notes of any other interview with the appellant.) On its face, this might be interpreted to include screening interviews. However, the Home Office has given an assurance that the screening interview will not be used in the determination of the asylum claim and it is on the basis of this assurance that the LSC does not normally fund representation at the screening interview.

10.5   The Home Office's policy is that:

> Details of relatives provided at our request and for our records, such as on the SEF... and during the interview should not be disclosed as this could conceivably place the applicant's family in jeopardy if it got into the wrong hands. These details should be omitted from copying and collation of the appeals papers... However any information volunteered about an applicant's family as part of their account may be disclosed. (APIs)

10.6   Nevertheless, if these details reveal anything prejudicial to the appellant's case, then the HOPO has been known to supply copies at the hearing and try to cross-examine on them. You may well object to this practice as contrary to the Home Office's published assurances. But it is as well to check the details from your own records or else request copies from the Home Office for your records.

10.7   Also check that pages of interview notes have not been omitted accidentally. This sometimes happens when an interviewer has continued a note on the reverse side of the page, but only one side has been copied.

10.8   If the Home Office notes are illegible, you should seek a direction from the IAA that the Home Office provide a typed transcript. Adjudicators are no more keen than you to have important documents presented in illegible scrawl rather than typescript.

10.9   The Home Office's policy is to include *all* documentation that has been submitted to it in support of the claim. This was confirmed to ILPA at a meeting with the Home Office Appeals Group on 15 May 2003 in response to concerns that documents were being regularly omitted from the appeal papers. The Home Office stated that:

> If representations are lodged before a decision is made, they should be included within the Home Office bundle and should be covered by the refusal letter. If representations and documents [are] lodged after the Home Office refusal, copies should also be included in the bundle provided they reach the Home Office before the bundle is prepared. If further pertinent representations have been made, the Home Office should review the case and these documents should also be included in the bundle. (minutes, para 7)

10.10 It is particularly important to check that documents submitted to the Immigration Service port have been included in the bundle: these are amongst the documents most often omitted (due to lack of communication between the port and the Home Office).

10.11 Rule 10(1)(a) also requires the Home Office to produce any unpublished document referred to in the immigration decision appealed against or in a document giving reasons for that decision (i.e. in this context, the reasons for refusal letter). The Home Office's APIs state that 'all documents, excluding statutory material, referred to' in the refusal letter must be included in the appeal papers.

10.12 In *Macit*, the IAT indicated that the obligation was not limited to documents referred to by name. Where the refusal letter gave particulars about the Secretary of State's 'understanding' that something was the case, the rule required him to provide any document which formed the basis of that 'understanding'.

10 The respondent's appeal papers
Key points

- Check the Respondent's appeal papers when they arrive.

- All records of interview are to be included. However, the Home Office has given assurances that screening interviews will not form part of the asylum determination process.

- Home Office policy is to omit details of relatives from the appeal papers. Beware that some HOPOs will nevertheless seek to adduce these at the hearing.

- Its policy is to include all documentation submitted to it in support of the claim but such documents are in practice regularly missed.

- The appeal papers must include any unpublished document referred to in the refusal letter: Home Office policy is to include any document other than statutory material.

- The IAT has stated that it is unnecessary for these purposes that the document is referred to by name in the refusal letter.

11 Taking instructions

11.1 Unless your client is going to give evidence in English, it is vital that you use an experienced professional interpreter when taking instructions for the purposes of preparing the witness statement for the court.

11.2 You should establish at an early stage in what language your client is most fluent. This will not necessarily be the language which your client used for Home Office interviews or which has appeared adequate for taking instructions. Check that both language and dialect are right. Ask her. The fact that the language spoken in different areas has the same label is not necessarily any indication that speakers from those areas will be able to understand each other. In relation to some dialects, it may be effectively impossible for someone to properly understand and convey meaning unless they have lived in the area and amongst the people who speak it. Try to ensure that the interpreter is familiar with cultural differences, as well as the language (see further chapter 34).

11.3 It is not satisfactory to use someone your client has brought along from her community. That person may well be more knowledgeable about the country of origin, and able to explain apparently surprising aspects of your client's story more convincingly than can your client. His expert knowledge may be invaluable to the preparation of your client's claim. But that is part of the problem in a representative using him to interpret. At worst, encouraged by the fact that the interpreter has all the answers, the representative will be tempted to direct questions to the interpreter, e.g. 'How was she able to escape?' and the interpreter will start providing an answer without even translating the question. The representative will merely accept the answer – presumably because he assumes that his client will give the same answer. You should always address questions directly to your client, and insist that these are translated directly to your client, and the answer translated directly back.

11.4 But simply giving this instruction is not enough to prevent exchanges such as the following:

> Rep: 'The Home Office is saying that the authorities would not have arrested you repeatedly just because you attend one demonstration. Were you surprised that they kept on arresting you just because you had attended one demonstration?'
>
> Interpreter: [Translates into client's language]
>
> Client: It did happen. I was arrested three times and tortured on every occasion.
>
> Interpreter: [in English] You see... [and continues to provide an explanation of why this might have happened]

11.5 Your client has not answered the question. The interpreter has realised this, and is giving you the answer you are looking for. However, you assume that he is merely translating the client's answer. An even more dangerous position is where your client understands the question but gives an answer that the interpreter thinks is misconceived or will not please you, so the interpreter alters or elaborates upon the answer when he translates it to you. The interpreter's answer will go in the statement. You may not realise that your client does not properly understand – or even perhaps agree with – what her statement says until she departs from her statement in oral evidence. Whereupon the HOPO is able to claim she is lying.

11.6 The interpreter may be able to add to your understanding of conditions in her country of origin. That information may well help you in presenting the case. However, the interpreter must be reminded to clearly differentiate between comment or additional information on the one hand and on the other, the direct translation that is his primary task. Your client is going to be cross-examined on her statement. The interpreter will not be able to answer these questions for your client.

11.7 Always try to ensure that your client is comfortable with a particular interpreter. Ask her whether she has any other concerns about which interpreter is used (though bear in mind that she may not feel comfortable explaining her concerns if she has to do so through the interpreter who is the subject of these concerns). Use common sense and your knowledge of the country of origin to identify in advance whether using a person of a particular ethnic origin, gender etc. may cause problems.

11.8 Be sensitive to the intrinsic difficulties in interpreting discussed in chapter 34. Where an interpreting problem or misunderstanding arises, you should encourage the interpreter to alert you to it. If these problems are discussed, it should increase the accuracy of the witness statement. Equally importantly, having been alerted to the difficulty, you will be better able to identify it if it reoccurs during oral evidence.

11.9 It is also important that the interpreter's English reflects the manner in which your client speaks as accurately as possible. For example, if the way your client speaks is simplistic, the interpreter should not interpret into sophisticated English. You want the statement to be as faithful as possible to the way your client speaks. You also need to be able to judge as far as possible from her language whether she is worried or uncertain about particular topics, and to be alert to any psychological difficulties your client may have (see chapter 26).

11.10 Provided the interpreter is competent, it is important if at all possible to use the same interpreter for taking the statement, pre-hearing conferences, and monitoring the hearing (see chapter 34).

11.11 Particularly where your client has suffered traumatic events, the environment in which she is interviewed is also important. The most *inappropriate* environment is a noisy office with repeated interruptions, and a caseworker and/or interpreter who is clearly pressed for time.

11.12 She should not normally be interviewed in the presence of family members and friends. She may feel inhibited from giving full details of her treatment or activities. Nor should she be asked in front of others whether she wants to be interviewed alone. She may feel inhibited from requesting this. It should be done, at least initially, as a matter of course.

11.13 The appeal may be won or lost on the strength of your client's statement. No amount of good advocacy at the hearing may remedy a careless mistake on the part of the caseworker while taking the statement. Appeals have trundled up through the courts for years while advocates argue at ever greater expense over the weight and construction to be placed upon alleged inconsistencies which arose solely because the caseworker taking the initial statement was cutting corners. It is therefore cost effective, as well as less dangerous for the appellant, to get it right first time.

11.14 *It is imperative that interviews are not rushed.* What is adequate will depend entirely upon the circumstances of the case. Asking 'How long does it take to complete an asylum seeker's statement?' is like 'How long is a piece of string?' Factors affecting the time required will include:

- the extent and nature of the allegations in the Home Office refusal letter;
- the extent to which your client's case turns upon the acceptance of her history;

- the extent and level of her activities;
- the extent of past ill-treatment;
- whether she is traumatised or ill or otherwise has difficulty in recollection or in understanding or focussing upon the material issues;
- how difficult is the interpreting;
- her level of education and understanding;
- the extent of past inconsistencies which need to be addressed and whether previously undisclosed information now has to be presented.

11.15 If the events are very straightforward, or the case is based largely upon factors other than the appellant's history, the statement may be finalised in one session. But if success rests on the acceptance of her history, that history is complex, and there are serious credibility issues, the statement may take many hours over different sessions and go through several drafts. There is nothing wrong with that. Cutting corners is a false economy. The important thing is not to keep to some arbitrary guideline, but to ensure that the time spent is appropriate to the nature of the case.

11.16 It is very easy when taking a statement through an interpreter to get the wrong end of the stick even in the simplest of cases, particularly if there is pressure on the caseworker to complete the statement. It can be very difficult to put aside preconceptions, whether from other cases or ordinary life which may distort the caseworker's understanding of what the client is trying to convey – particularly if such preconceptions seem to offer an easy way of conveying a sensible account to paper.

11.17 The open-focussed-closed method of questioning (sometimes known as the 'funnel technique') is usually the safest means of eliciting information. Begin with a completely open question ('What happened?'), then follow up with more focussed questions ('Can you explain why you did that?') which guide your client towards areas you need to explore but still require a substantial response. End with closed questions ('Could you see anyone else?') to check the facts you need to put in the statement and clarify the chronology. Then return to an open question to ensure that nothing has been missed, e.g. 'Did anything else happen?' Move on to the next point with another open question, 'What happened next?'

11.18 The circumstances in which this approach will not work are where your client is too unconfident or inarticulate to respond effectively to an open question. You will then have no option but to probe and prompt by offering her choices. If she relaxes during the interview, you may be able to return to a more open questioning technique.

11.19 Always ask one question at a time. You are unlikely to get a proper answer to a composite question, even if it survives the interpretation.

11.20 Never take the first answer you get without testing it. Approach the point from different angles. As a simple example, after eliciting the date of the last detention, ask how long she remained in the country after her release, and check that the two answers correspond. Ask what she was doing between the last detention and her escape, and be alert to any indication from the answer that the dates she had given are inaccurate. If you have been given dates for other events occurring around the same time, check the order in which they occurred rather than assuming this from the dates you are initially given. If you have a clear date for a particular event (e.g. marriage or the birth of a child), you can perform a similar check even though the event used for reference purposes is immaterial to the appeal.

11.21 Clients from different cultures (particularly if they use a different calendar) will often have much more difficulty in determining western dates than in putting material events in order and placing them in the chronology by reference to other events. If your interpreter is converting dates from a different calendar, mistakes are particularly likely. You should also record the date in your client's calendar so that she is not accused of inconsistency as a result of someone else's mistake.

11 Taking instructions
Key points

■ The quality of interpreting is critical.

■ Use an experienced professional interpreter, never someone provided by your client.

■ Check what language and dialect are best. Do not assume that those used in the past are adequate.

■ Check for any sensitivities on the part of your client as to which interpreter is used.

■ The interpreter can and should alert you to potential linguistic or cultural misunderstandings but must clearly differentiate between his own interventions and his primary responsibility of providing direct translation.

■ He should reflect as accurately as possible the way in which your client speaks.

■ Ensure that the environment in which the interview is conducted is conducive, particularly where the client is vulnerable. Do not interview the client in the presence of family and friends.

■ Never rush the interview. The amount of time required depends entirely on the characteristics of the client and nature of the case.

■ Beware of your own preconceptions distorting the interview. An open-focussed-closed method of questioning is the safest means of eliciting full and accurate information.

■ Always check the information by approaching the point from a different angle.

■ Be particularly careful to check the chronology where the client uses a different calendar.

12 Drafting the statement

Introduction

12.1 The Standard Directions require an appellant to lodge:

Witness statements of the evidence to be called at the hearing, such statements to stand as evidence in chief at the hearing.

12.2 Because her evidence in chief is to be given primarily in writing rather than orally, preparing the appellant's witness statement is one of the most important steps in the appeal. It is her presentation of her case to the adjudicator. A good statement can win an appeal and a careless one risks losing it. The statement will usually be far more important than the evidence you lead at the hearing.

12.3 There are a number of advantages to your client's statement standing as evidence in chief:

- She can tell her story in a relaxed setting, in her own time. That is particularly important if your client is inarticulate or unusually nervous and may not be capable of doing herself justice in oral evidence.
- Mistakes or misunderstandings between client and interpreter can be resolved before finalising the statement, rather than played out in front of the adjudicator where they may take on a wholly disproportionate significance.
- There is less risk of disputes arising later over the content of the witness' evidence if a statement is adopted as evidence in chief than if a recording of oral evidence at the hearing is relied upon instead.
- The HOPO's cross-examination will sometimes resemble a full examination in chief whether you have examined in chief or not – his rationale seemingly being that an inconsistency is bound to slip in somewhere. By using written witness statements, you avoid your client having to give the same oral evidence twice, and such

extensive cross-examination should leave sufficient scope for developing the evidence in re-examination if appropriate (see chapter 37).

12.4   There are also, of course, disadvantages. These are discussed in chapter 35 on examination in chief.

The purpose of the statement and dealing with past statements

12.5   The purpose of the statement will depend upon your assessment of the material submitted to the Home Office in support of the initial application.

12.6   If a statement has already been submitted to the Home Office, you need to determine whether that statement is a satisfactory account of your client's history up to that date. You do not want to find out that your client considers the initial statement inaccurate *after* you have adopted it as her appeal statement.

12.7   Whether or not you represented the client in the initial application, you need to check any statement previously submitted. The statement may have been rushed. A variety of procedures have been used in recent years by the Home Office for the initial application and some of these have required information to be presented within a very restricted period. SEFs have to be submitted within 14 days. If your client was detained in Oakington for processing, there will often have been no more than a day for the representative to take instructions, and no time to produce a proper statement. As indicated in the previous chapter, it is all too easy for a rushed representative to let his own preconceptions as to the likely nature of the case colour the statement. If the initial instructions were taken very shortly after a traumatic escape from the country of origin, the scope for inaccuracy is increased.

12.8   The statement may be accurate as far as it goes. But it may overlook important aspects of your client's case simply because these were not thoroughly investigated when the statement was taken. It is not sufficient to read through the statement paragraph by paragraph with your client asking her to confirm that it contains no inaccuracies (although you will have to do that at some stage). There is no substitute for reinterviewing the client, and checking the information through questions from different angles as described in the last chapter.

12.9   Should you determine that the statement does satisfactorily and accurately set out the case, the next step is to check it against the Home Office's asylum interview notes. This ought to have been done immediately following the interview and representations made to address any apparent inconsistency. However, this will often not have been done properly (or at all).

12.10 If you are satisfied that the existing statement accurately and appropriately covers all aspects of the case and that there is no inconsistency with the Home Office interview notes, the appeal statement can simply confirm the initial statement. But you will also have to provide any updating information and deal with those allegations in the refusal letter to which a response from your client is required (see below).

12.11 See chapter 13 for dealing with defects in statements which have already been disclosed, and inconsistent Home Office interview notes.

12.12 Unless a satisfactory statement has already been submitted, you should normally produce a full witness statement for the appeal. The adjudicator should have a stand-alone document setting out the appellant's history. He will not be able to engage properly with your client's evidence if he is forced to cross-refer between an initial unsatisfactory statement and a witness statement offering corrections, comments and additions.

Structure, style, and detail

12.13 The point of the witness statement is to tell your client's story, in so far as it is relevant to the appeal, in a credible and persuasive manner.

Structure

12.14 Often the best structure will be chronological. In a political case, the statement might be ordered as follows: her upbringing and background; the development of her beliefs and activities; any acts of persecution; the circumstances of her decision to flee; her escape from the country; any relevant post-arrival news from her country of origin; relevant post-arrival activities. Even if the appellant's fears arise on multiple grounds, for example race, political opinion and social group, these fears will often relate to a single story which is best told as a single story.

12.15 One drawback of a chronological statement can be to invite unwarranted emphasis on early events that now have little relevance to case. The HOPO, and sometimes the adjudicator, start worrying about an unrelated detention 20 years ago simply because it is the first thing they read in the statement.

12.16 That and other problems are addressed if the statement starts with an introductory paragraph summarising the claim, and explaining how the statement is structured and the relevance of each section. For example:

> *I escaped from my country after I was forced by the secret police to agree to inform upon my political colleagues. In this statement, I first explain my background and how I became politicised as a result of the human rights abuses that my family have long suffered at the hands of the state. Then I recount how I began my activities and why I stuck with these activities despite being detained on numerous occasions. I then describe how I was forced to agree to work for the state and why I came to accept, with the encouragement of my family, that the risks had so increased that I would be a fool to stay. After recounting my escape from my country, I describe how I have helped my organisation from the UK and the news that I continue to receive from my country. I conclude by setting out what I fear would face me were I to be expelled.*

12.17 An introductory paragraph, signposting how the statement is structured, is even more important if the statement is very lengthy and complex and the client's fears are based on an accumulation of inter-related or quite separate events and circumstances.

12.18 If your client faces various risks, and each relates to a distinct set of facts, the statement may be easier to follow if you deal with each ground in turn. For example, the appellant may fear racial attack, but also fear detention as a result of a relative's political activities. Or she may fear detention and ill-treatment upon arrival and if she survives that, absence of treatment for her illness. If they are effectively two separate stories, then it may be better to tell two separate stories, rather than switching between the two in chronological sequence. If your client wants to describe how the general situation deteriorated over a particular period, as well as telling her own personal story of that period, it is sometimes easier to deal with the two in turn.

12.19 The important thing is that whatever structure you choose is simple to follow both for your client and for the adjudicator.

Style

12.20 The statement must establish all facts within the knowledge of your client which are relevant to her present risk. But it is no good conveying the relevant facts if it is done in a way that provokes the reader to doubt them. Though he ought not to reject the statement without something rather more concrete, it is much better if the story 'rings true' to the adjudicator when he reads it.

12.21 It should ring true as her story. It should be her experiences from her perspective based on her perceptions. It should say what she did; what she experienced; what she thought; why she thought it. The aim should be a natural first person account with which the reader can even empathise in some small way, or at least feel that he has gained some insight or understanding. That will not happen if the reader is left constantly asking 'But how would she know?'; 'But why would she do that?'

12.22 By explaining from her own point of view her knowledge, beliefs, and feelings as the statement progresses, you ought to pre-empt any reasonable allegation of inconsistency and implausibility. It is much better to do it this way, rather than having a separate section aimed expressly at rebutting actual and potential allegations from the suspicious reader.

12.23 It should explain her own actions but – equally importantly – should not purport to explain the actions of others when she is in no position to do so. If she says what others were doing and (especially) why they were doing it, then unless it is obvious, she must explain what led her to that belief.

12.24 An immigration officer will often have posed questions to the client in the asylum interview that appear to require an explanation for the actions of third parties. A particularly silly example is referred to in chapter 36 on cross-examination. The appellant, shot while fleeing gunmen, was asked 'Why did they shoot you in the leg rather than the head?' A very common example in the asylum interview is 'Why were you released from detention?' Do not underestimate the perceived power relationship between claimant and questioner. When she believes her life and future depends upon the questioner's view of her, and the questioner requires information without any recognition that she may be unable to provide it, she is liable to try to do what she is told. Directed to explain the motivation of her guards, she will guess if she does not know. The guess might be 'They had no evidence.' The immigration officer never asks how she knows this. Rather, the answer is seized upon as evidence that she was in the clear.

12.25 The relationship between representative and client is not free from this danger. Do not adopt the same approach. Ask first whether she was told by anyone why she was being released. Then ask whether she has found out some other way. If the answer to both is negative, it is likely that she does not know. The statement can simply record that she was not informed why she was released. However, if the Home Office interview notes record her saying 'They had no evidence', the HOPO is likely to claim he has found a discrepancy. Since that is predictable, it saves everyone time if you anticipate it. Ask her about her answer to the immigration officer. If it transpires that she thought she was required to offer a guess, the statement can explain that.

12.26 The position would, however, be different if she had guessed at the time at the reason for her release and had acted upon it. The converse problem is where her unfolding perceptions and fears about the actions of others are necessary to explain her own actions, but these contemporaneous beliefs are not explained in the statement. The following is (obviously) not intended as a script, but to illustrate the difference between a good and bad statement.

12.27 A statement will sometimes say '*I had to be careful because they put me under surveillance.*' That simply invites the question 'how did she know?' That conclusion should be the culmination of what led up to it, e.g.: '*Outsiders seldom enter our neighbourhood but I and my neighbours started seeing strange men and strange cars loitering around my house. I then started looking out for such people following me, and saw on several occasions people and cars that I thought I had recognised before. I started to believe I was under surveillance.*'

12.28 Remember that having been told that she believed herself to be under surveillance, the subsequent narrative should address what happened to that belief. If the statement jumps to her attendance at secret meetings two months later, the reader will ask 'But why, when she believes she is under surveillance?' Nor should it simply record '*After two months, the surveillance stopped so I started my activities again.*' Rather than explaining, that again creates doubt: '*How would she know the surveillance stopped?*' She must explain what she thought and why she thought it, e.g. '*After a month, I stopped seeing these people, and my neighbours said the same. I refrained from any political activity for a further month, while remaining vigilant. I then decided that the surveillance had probably ended. While I could not be sure, the choice was to abandon my activities indefinitely or take the risk and I felt sufficiently confident to take the risk.*' It takes longer to explore her feelings in this way, but it makes the difference between an account that sounds natural and one that sounds contrived.

12.29 Similarly unsatisfactory is the statement '*Someone gave my name under torture so I had to flee.*' She must have known it in order to act upon it, yet she does not explain how she knew, and it is not obvious. Nor is it enough to say '*Friends informed me that someone gave my name under torture...*' because the reader may still be wondering 'How would they know?' If she knows, she should explain, e.g. *'My friends said they had heard through another detainee that someone had given my name under torture.'* But it is perfectly plausible that she may not know how her friends obtained this information. In that case, she should say so. That way, the reader is not expecting an answer at the hearing. But she should also say why she acted on the information nevertheless, e.g. *'My friends refused to tell me how they knew, but I have worked with them a long time, and I trusted them, so I believed them.'* Such simple explanations can make the difference between a statement that the reader understands and therefore believes and one that he does not understand and therefore suspects.

12.30 Of course, your client's experiences and beliefs may be so remote from that of the adjudicator that it appears both fruitless and misconceived to aim for this sort of understanding. This discussion is not intended to detract from the dangers (of which the IAT has warned adjudicators) of judging the experiences of refugees from the standpoint of the adjudicator's life experiences. However, so long as adjudicators continue to reject accounts on the basis that they cannot understand why the appellant would act as she did, then that, as well as putting the facts in evidence, must be the statement's aim.

12.31 The fact that it should be your client's own account from her perspective means that the style of the statement will vary according to the personality, education, culture, and experiences of the appellant. You should ensure that the statement reflects as far as possible the way your client speaks and the language in which she will give oral evidence.

12.32 Do not present the statement in emotional or passionate language when your client's language is actually matter-of-fact or under-stated. Do not use expansive, sophisticated or complicated language when your client is actually of little education. (Plainly, you are reliant on a skilled interpreter who can reflect your client's language.)

12.33 You should never embellish a witness' statement with standard passages which you think sound convincing and powerful – regardless of whether your client is happy to adopt the wording. Firstly, the adjudicator will have heard them before and may well recognise them. They will influence his opinion of the whole statement even though the remainder may be entirely the appellant's words. Secondly, if your client is able to explain your standard paragraphs at all in cross-examination, the explanation will likely sound equally artificial. A paragraph thanking the British Home Office for its kindness is unlikely to sound natural or credible.

12.34 It is not only the Home Office which has stereotyped ideas about genuine refugees. Perfectly credible clients with perfectly straightforward accounts have had their statements ruined by representatives dressing them up in what they believe to be the language and phraseology of a genuine refugee.

Detail

12.35 A refusal letter will often claim that an account is 'vague and lacking in detail'. There is a common belief that the credibility of an account increases with the amount of detail that is provided. Some Home Office caseworkers appear to believe that the genuine refugee will give a blow by blow account of her persecution, as if from the pages of a thriller, e.g.:

> 'I was grabbed from behind and pushed onto the ground. They were shouting something but I could not make it out. There were at least three of them standing around me. One put his boot on my head, and my nose felt it was going to break as it was pressed into the ground...'

12.36 The amount of detail that is appropriate depends, once again, upon the characteristics of your client. Some appellants are capable of providing this sort of detail (even where the task causes them great distress). Some adjudicators are swayed by such detail (and if the evidence is given orally, by the resulting distress). If the appellant is capable of relaying a detailed and consistent account of her torture, you should normally take it despite the pain it causes your client (though see para 12.40 as to mentally ill and disordered appellants).

12.37 However for fairly obvious reasons (to all except the Home Office), many victims of persecution are largely incapable of offering this kind of blow by blow account of their suffering. You must differentiate between clients who, though reluctant, are capable of giving detail but have not appreciated the importance, and those clients who are simply incapable of providing it.

12.38 There is a wealth of evidence (to which you can refer) about the effect that trauma may have on recollection (para 26.13). It is neither tactically sensible nor morally appropriate to attempt to force details out of clients who are actually unable to give a consistent or coherent account. But spend time talking around different subjects and understanding your client's capabilities. There is nothing wrong with going into details where she is able, and explaining that she cannot offer similar recall on other events (though she should explain, so far as possible, why). Detail is, in any event, a two-edged sword. A detailed and articulate account has on occasion been attacked as well-rehearsed and contrived, just as a hesitant, reluctant or vague account may be alleged to be fabricated.

12.39 Detail on matters such as political beliefs and activities will also vary according to the appellant. If your client is a sophisticated leading light in her movement who has played a significant role in its ideological splits, it will be effective to provide considerable detail about her political beliefs and the ideology and structure of her organisation. Indeed, it would be odd (and potentially dangerous) not to. If the appellant is an uneducated villager who assisted her organisation because it promised her food and protection from police harassment, then it would be odd if the statement did start to explore its ideological splits. She should explain, clearly and simply, why she supported the organisation and what it meant to her. That may not prevent the HOPO subjecting her to misconceived cross-examination about the organisation's ideology, but by setting out clearly the basis of her support and so the extent of her knowledge, you can challenge rather than encourage the HOPO's misconceptions.

Mentally ill or disordered appellants

12.40 Victims of torture and other traumas are liable to suffer from depression and/or PTSD. A traumatised client may be capable of relaying her account in a safe and supportive environment to someone who has won her trust, but incapable of repeating it under cross-examination conditions in a court room. The fact that she may be unable to repeat her account under cross-examination should not dissuade you from attempting to take a full statement. You can submit the statement without calling her to be cross-examined on it (see para 30.13).

12.41 You may well wish to have her examined first to find out whether it is medically advisable for you to attempt to take a statement. If your client is plainly traumatised, you ought to be facilitating treatment for her.

12.42 If your client is already under treatment, she may have given quite a full account of her experiences to her doctor or psychologist. If recounting it to you would risk exacerbating her symptoms, you may produce a report from the doctor setting out her history, together with a statement from her confirming its veracity.

Dealing with actual or potential allegations
Allegations in the refusal letter

12.43 Whether or not you decide to deal directly with allegations contained in the refusal letter, you should have these in mind while preparing the statement.

12.44 Your client may be able and anxious to respond to the refusal letter in her own words. She may have compelling things to say, even where it does not involve establishing further facts. If she wishes to do so, and is effective in doing so, then she ought to have the opportunity to answer the case against her in her own words. There is no guarantee that the HOPO will otherwise put the relevant questions to her in cross-examination.

12.45 But you do not necessarily need to incorporate her comments into the statement. As indicated in chapter 35, you will often want to lead some oral evidence in chief without being accused of regurgitating the statement. It is highly inadvisable to omit material facts from the statement in order that they be led in oral evidence. The omission may (however unfairly) be held against your client on credibility, even if it does not disturb the flow of the statement. While the adjudicator ought to allow reasonable examination in chief, some seek to limit it drastically. At worst, you may be prevented from putting the facts in evidence at all. Her response to the refusal letter can therefore be useful material for examination in chief. Your client can make her case to the adjudicator, rather than simply recounting fact, and it is not a disaster if the evidence is not permitted.

12.46 There is however no imperative that your client respond to every argument in the refusal letter. Some may require knowledge about legal or country issues which she does not have. She may not be confident in formulating the arguments even if she does have the necessary information. She may not be able to recognise and deal dismissively with allegations that deserve that treatment. If the allegations are wholly misconceived, you may simply mislead and unnerve your client by putting the Home Office allegations to her as if they were of substance. If told she has contradicted herself when she has not, she may feel compelled to offer some artificial explanation for a non-existent discrepancy which subsequently falls apart.

12.47 There may also be little that she can say about allegations of implausibility. She should not be pressurised into giving explanations for the actions of, say, the police because the refusal letter alleges (without evidence) that they would have acted differently. If all she can say is that it happened, then that is all she should say.

12.48 Now that a skeleton argument is required by the standard directions, it will usually be the best place to present arguments that are in reality in your words rather than your client's. There is no point in drafting a paragraph for your client in which she refers to expert and other evidence that you have gathered to demonstrate that the event is not implausible. It simply encourages cross-examination to which it is unfair to expect her to respond. That is especially so where such comments are standard rebuttals to standard paragraphs from the refusal letter. Inserting these into your client's witness statement, purportedly from her mouth, can only detract from the aim of a good statement: her story from her point of view.

12.49 Remember, however, that she must deal with her own state of mind if that is material to the allegation. The refusal letter might claim that she could not have passed through her country's immigration control if she was wanted by the police. You may want to submit expert evidence to confirm that this could have happened. But your client should also explain whether she thought that there was a risk at the time, and if so, why she decided to run it.

12.50 Where you want to add factual information to address a discrepancy in the refusal letter then, if possible, do so naturally in the narrative of the statement. If the refusal letter alleges she remained in the country too long after her decision to leave, she should explain what she was doing in the narrative rather than as an express response to the refusal letter. If the Home Office's point has any substance, then the answer ought to fit within the natural story. It is more effective if you point to the narrative to demonstrate how the allegation is unfounded, rather than to a paragraph expressly formulated to meet the allegation.

12.51 If it cannot fit within the narrative, then the statement should say something to the effect that *'I have been asked by my representative to comment on the suggestion that...'* This will firstly define what she is doing, so as not to suggest that she has taken it upon herself to respond to the refusal letter as a whole. It will secondly avoid any impression that she considers her actions to be odd, as might be the case if she simply said *'This was really not unreasonable because...'*

12.52 Sometimes, your client will have to refer to information provided by yourself or other sources in order to explain her present state of mind (for example, her fear of expulsion to a particular location or her ability to live in a particular part of the country). There is no objection to that. But she should say *'I am advised that...'*, so as to avoid misunderstandings and misconceived cross-examination.

Dealing with *potential* allegations or inconsistencies

12.53 Where you can envisage a point being taken against your client (whether by the HOPO or adjudicator) which has not been taken in the refusal letter, you should again deal with it in the narrative if you can do so without obstructing the natural flow of the statement. That flows from the rule that a good statement should not leave the reader thinking 'But why would she do that?' or 'That is different from what she said before!'

12.54 There are commonly recurring issues that you will want to ensure are covered by the statement if they may arise on the facts, whether or not any issue has been raised in the refusal letter. They commonly form lines of cross-examination. They include:

- why your client was released after any periods of detention (if she does not know, simply state that she does not know);
- (if appropriate) why she still felt in continuing danger despite being released;
- when she decided to leave the country, what made her decide to leave at that point, and (if not obvious) why she did not decide to leave sooner;
- why she did not try moving elsewhere in her country of origin;
- the circumstances of any delay between deciding to leave and actually leaving;
- what she did to avoid being captured during any period in which she believed she was in danger and (again if it is not obvious) why she is not confident that such tactics would work again;
- if she had any contact with the authorities while she was in danger, then what risks she considered were involved and (if any) why she took them;
- if she was at risk from non-state actors, whether she approached the authorities for protection, and if not, why not;
- if her fear is based on race or social group, whether she perceives other members of that group are suffering similar harm, and if not, why she believes herself to be at risk;
- if she failed to perform military service on political grounds or through fear of ill-treatment, whether siblings performed such service and if so, why and what happened to them;
- how her escape route was chosen and what risks she thought were involved;
- why she chose to come to the UK, or else how she ended up in the UK;
- whether she has had any contact with anyone in her country of origin since she left her country;

- if she has left her immediate family in the country of origin, whether she thinks they are at any risk and:
  - o if they are at risk, why she has left them (if they are her dependents) or why they have not fled themselves (if she knows);
  - o if they are not at risk, why that does not reassure her about her own position (if that might otherwise occur to the reader);
- What she now fears and, if applicable, why the passage of time since she left her country has not eased these fears;
- whether there is any part of the country in which she could live and be safe, and whether she could reach that place safely (including what would happen to her at the port to which the Home Office would expel her).

12.55 Where it is *not* possible to provide the answer without explaining the potential problem, you will have to decide whether it is worth signposting the problem in order to address it. This most commonly arises where a reader might perceive a discrepancy in past statements or interview notes but the point has not been taken in the refusal letter.

12.56 Do not assume without talking it over with your client that such a point cannot be satisfactorily addressed in the narrative. An apparent inconsistency may be down to the story being expressed in different ways. It is often possible, without distorting the statement, to include further information or rephrase the information so that the reader will realise that there is no real inconsistency.

12.57 Where that is impossible, you should introduce the point with words to the effect of *'I am asked by my representative...'* so as to avoid the impression that the client believed she had been inconsistent.

12.58 The advantages in dealing with such issues upfront are that you may promote an impression of openness and candour by voluntarily disclosing and addressing weaknesses. You ensure that the witness can explain these potential weaknesses in response to fair, straightforward questions in a more relaxed and sympathetic environment. Any cross-examination may be less effective if the point has already been recognised and dealt with.

12.59 The disadvantages are that you may signpost to the HOPO and the adjudicator an apparent concern about potential weaknesses that they had not actually perceived as damaging or had failed to notice altogether. By appearing to go out of your way to limit the damage, you may convey the impression that the discrepancy carries an importance that it does not deserve. If you do not consider the point could reasonably be taken, then addressing it may be perceived by the adjudicator as inconsistent with that stance. If you are confident that your client will be able to deal with any cross-examination, you may choose to leave it. The answer might appear more effective by being more spontaneous and catch the HOPO off guard.

12.60 However, be aware when making such a choice that even if the HOPO does not put a potential inconsistency in cross-examination, the adjudicator may be minded to rely upon it and upon the failure to offer an explanation. He may even do so without indicating his concern at the hearing. Whether that is unfair will depend upon the circumstances of the case (see *Maheswaran*, though note that the discussion was obiter as the Court found that the adjudicator had not in fact relied upon the discrepancy which had not been put).

12.61 The more clear the discrepancy appears on the papers, the greater the danger that the adjudicator will be entitled to rely upon it without notice. If you do not deal with a point in evidence in chief, and neither the HOPO nor the adjudicator raise it, you will not be able to address it in re-examination.

12.62 It is your duty to put the positive case which entitles your client to the protection of the Convention. This should include explaining points which, absent an explanation, would concern the reasonable reader. Whether to cover points which you consider unreasonable but which the HOPO (or adjudicator) might take anyway can be one of the most difficult questions faced in presenting an appeal. The above suggests the factors to be considered in reaching a decision. But there is no formula to the balancing act. It is a question of judgment in the circumstances of the individual case and the individual client.

12.63 Whatever you decide, avoid giving the impression that you are allowing the Home Office to dictate the ground upon which the case is fought by adopting its discrepancy culture and focussing upon a negative and nit-picking dissection of past statements and potential allegations rather than upon the central themes of the appellant's claim.

Final steps

12.64 The HOPO may well subject the written statement to a minute comparison against other documentation for potential discrepancies or inconsistencies. Despite the fact that you will have had such documentation in mind when preparing the statement, the final statement should be checked for consistency against:

- all Home Office interview notes;
- all statements and written representations previously submitted, whether by you or a previous representative;
- all documentary evidence specific to the client, for example dates of arrest warrants and letters from family members;
- any medical reports, other expert reports or character references which have been or may be submitted.

12.65 The final paragraph should be the CPR statement of truth: 'I believe that the facts stated in this witness statement are true.'

12.66 The statement should be signed and dated. In **Njehia**, the IAT gave the following guidance in respect of statements taken via an interpreter:

> *The proper procedure when taking a statement in a language other than English is for a competent interpreter, in the correct language and dialect, to read back the statement and for the maker of the statement then to sign it, confirming that the document has been read back in his or her own language. The interpreter should then append to the statement his own short statement that he has read back the contents of the document to the maker of the statement in his or her own language. That should then be signed and dated by the interpreter, whose name should be given.*

12.67 If you are instructing an advocate to present the hearing, *do not, if at all possible*, submit the statement without obtaining his input (which should be after he has seen the client in conference). That is especially so if you do not routinely attend appeals. The statement should always be reviewed by someone familiar with cross-examination in asylum and human rights appeals. Comments which appear unremarkable to a reasonable reader regularly excite a stream of cross-examination from a HOPO.

12.68 It is important that your client is provided with a copy of the statement, translated if he will not be giving evidence in English, in good time before the hearing.

12 Drafting the statement
Key points

- Any statement already submitted to the Home Office must be checked carefully by you and tested during an interview with your client. The time constraints applicable to the initial decision mean that an initial statement may have been rushed and so inaccurate, or at least incomplete.

- If it *is* accurate and complete, and it is consistent with the Home Office interview record, the appeal statement can adopt the initial statement and go on to provide updating information and respond to relevant allegations in the refusal letter.

- Otherwise, a stand-alone witness statement should normally be produced. An adjudicator should not have to cross-refer between an unsatisfactory initial statement and a witness statement containing comments and corrections.

- The best structure is usually chronological unless there are discrete bases for the claim that make more sense when dealt with separately. An introductory paragraph assists understanding and avoids unwarranted focus on the oldest events in a chronological statement.

- The statement must establish all relevant facts within the knowledge of the appellant. It should be *her* story from *her* perspective based on *her* experiences. By explaining the unfolding account from her own viewpoint, she ought to pre-empt any reasonable allegation of inconsistency or implausibility.

- She need not and should not speculate about the actions and motives of others if she is in no position to know. Conversely, she must describe what she thought at the time if that is necessary to explain her own actions.

- The style of the statement should reflect your client's personality, education, culture and experience and the way she speaks.

- Never embellish the witness statement with standard paragraphs.

- Where your client can provide detail about past ill-treatment, she should do so, even where it causes her distress. Do not force her to provide detail if she is incapable of doing so effectively and consistently.

- Detail about political activities and beliefs will vary according to the nature of the case: considerable detail should be expected from a sophisticated appellant; otherwise, a simple account of what her organisation meant to her.

- If the client is mentally ill or traumatised, you may be able to take a statement in a safe and supportive environment, even if she is not fit to give evidence in court. If in doubt, have her examined first. If she has given a full history during treatment, that can be set out in a medical report and the statement can simply confirm its veracity.

- Always have the Home Office case in mind when preparing the statement - irrespective of whether you decide to address allegations directly in the witness statement.

- Ensure that any material facts needed to answer the refusal letter are included in the statement, if possible in the narrative rather than a separate section.

- Where she can comment effectively on Home Office allegations in her own words, she can do so in the witness statement or in oral examination in chief.

- Do not insert arguments responding to the Home Office's case into the witness statement if they are in reality your arguments rather than your client's: they belong in the skeleton argument.

- There are many commonly recurring lines of cross-examination which can and should be pre-empted in the narrative of the witness statement.

- If a potential problem cannot be dealt with in the narrative, you must balance the disadvantages of highlighting it by addressing it expressly against the risk that an adjudicator might rely on it without notice: whether fairness *requires* him to give notice will depend on how obvious the potential problem is perceived to be.

- Check the witness statement for consistency against all other appeal documentation before submitting it.

- If you are instructing counsel to present the appeal, seek his input on the statement after he has seen the client in conference. The statement should always be reviewed by someone familiar with techniques of cross-examination prior to submission.

- The final version should be read back to the client in her own language, and signed by her. The interpreter should sign a statement confirming he has conducted the read-back.

- Provide the client with a written translation in good time before the hearing.

13 Presenting previously undisclosed information

13.1 As discussed at para 12.7, you may find that important aspects of the case were not properly presented in the initial application to the Home Office, either in the asylum interview or in any statement.

13.2 The Home Office regularly claims that the late disclosure of such matters raises credibility issues, particularly if it involves a complete departure from the case previously put. The first thing you have to do is to explain fully why the information was not put forward previously.

13.3 Non-disclosure will often be the result of inadequate or inappropriate representation. A woman may have felt unable to disclose sexual torture to a man. Insufficient time may have been allowed to elicit evidence of traumatic experiences. The appellant's mental health may have inhibited disclosure.

13.4 Your client may also have been reluctant to offer information because of concerns about where the information may end up. She may fear the Home Office making enquiries that could alert the authorities in her country of origin. Or she may be more concerned about disclosure to her own community. Examples are where your client has acted against the interests of opposition groups which are influential in her refugee community or where her claim is based on matters which might lead to discrimination on cultural/social/religious grounds from her community, e.g. sexual orientation, or where she has suffered sexual torture for which she fears she may be stigmatised. The IAA *Gender Guidelines* state that:

> *Torture, sexual violence and other persecutory treatment produce feelings of profound shame. This 'shame response' is a major obstacle to disclosure. Many victims will never speak about sexual violence or will remain silent about it for many years.*

13.5 You should explain the avenues available to protect the confidentiality of information provided in the appeal (although you may also have to warn her about the limitations of the Home Office's confidentiality undertaking: para 32.2). It may be useful to seek an appropriate direction at a first hearing so that your client can make her witness statement in the knowledge that the arrangements to keep her evidence confidential are already in place.

Non-disclosure at Home Office interview

13.6   Home Office interviews are often flawed. The closer an interview is conducted to a claimant's arrival in the UK, the greater the risk of mistakes and injustice. The risk is most acute if an interview is conducted at the port following arrival. The claimant is likely to have endured a dangerous journey, quite possibly putting her life at risk. Very often, such interviews are conducted without allowing the asylum seeker legal advice or representation. (Indeed, the Immigration Service has in the past insisted on conducting the interview before a legal representative arrives, even having been informed that he is on his way.) There are frequent accounts by asylum seekers of impropriety by the Immigration Service both before and during such interviews, the risk of which can only be exacerbated in cases where the Immigration Service insists on conducting the interview without legal representation. The interpreter (and interviewer) may be unsuitable on gender and other grounds.

13.7   The IAA *Gender Guidelines* state that delay in revealing full details of an asylum claim (and delay in claiming asylum) may be 'validly occasioned by other factors including many procedural and evidential factors' (para 5.43). They add that:

> There are many reasons, some of which are referred to above, why women in particular are not forthcoming with full information about their experiences which will be exacerbated if gender-sensitive interviewing procedures are not followed. Special care must be taken in relation to evidence pertaining to sexual violence; care must be taken before drawing any adverse inferences where an appellant, or other witness, has earlier described a rape as an attempted rape or as touching, beating or other ill-treatment or even as pain or illness.

13.8   Talk through with your client why she did not raise the matter at the interview. Be careful that she does not feel pressurised into giving a misleading explanation for why she did not disclose the information. For example, a client who did not reveal details of sexual torture because everyone in the room was male might not realise that this is an acceptable explanation, and so may simply say that she was never asked or she was not feeling well.

13.9   It may well be that no appropriate question was asked, and that will often be a perfectly good explanation. It is common, for example, for dates of detentions to be taken but no follow up questions asked about treatment during detention. It is equally common for apparent inconsistencies not to be put to the claimant, even if they are subsequently relied upon in the refusal letter. But you need to give detailed consideration to the interview notes. If your client says that she misunderstood a question, check whether that is borne out by the answer which is recorded. If it *does* appear that an appropriate question was asked, or the answer suggests that your client understood the point she was being asked to address, you will have to discuss with her whether the explanation can be maintained.

13.10 If your client says that the interviewer's or interpreter's tone was hectoring or inappropriate or the interpreter was difficult to understand, you may be able to find support for this assertion in the interview notes themselves. The immigration officer sometimes records his own inappropriate questions or comments. Answers may be recorded that are so obviously wrong as to indicate fundamental interpreting problems. The concerns are magnified if there is no evidence that such warning signs were acted upon by the interviewer.

13.11 There may also be a question over the accuracy of the interview notes. As discussed in chapter 36, the Home Office has now abandoned the readback procedure which it had previously accepted as an essential part of the interview. This greatly weakens the Home Office's position where accuracy is in dispute. It also removes any suggestion that your client should have been expected to clarify any answer during readback. The IAA's Gender Guidelines state that 'Where a woman has not been able to check the contents of her Home Office interview this may affect the reliability of that record.'

13.12 You should always check the Home Office notes against the notes taken by your client's representative if present. If you did not represent her in her initial application and previous representatives attended the interview, ask for the clerk's notes of the interview if these have not already been provided to you. (It is a requirement of the LSC that such a note is taken where the representation is publicly funded.)

13.13 Representation at interviews is crucial to the fairness of the process. Representatives often pick up misunderstandings by the interviewer that would otherwise distort the Home Office's decision. Representation also saves the time that would otherwise be spent in appeal determining factual disputes about what occurred at the hearing. The HOPO will often rely upon the representative's presence as evidence of the fairness of the interview. However, you will occasionally find that representation at the interview was incompetent. That is worse than useless for the client since the presence of a representative and his interpreter may confer an apparent legitimacy upon the interview whereas in reality, they did nothing to protect the claimant from improprieties. The quality of the clerk's note of the interview may give some guidance as to the quality of the representation. Check what protest was made at the interview about any impropriety and what instructions were taken from the client after the interview, and why no complaint was made after the interview. If the notes do not supply sufficient information, try to obtain the comments of the clerk who attended. If it appears that both clerk and interpreter were competent and they spotted no error, you will have to discuss with your client whether it is credible to maintain her complaint at this stage.

Non-disclosure in previous statement

13.14 You may find that a previous statement is inadequate and/or inaccurate. In those circumstances, you will have to take a full statement for the appeal *and* explain why the statement previously submitted cannot be relied upon. That may be because:

- the interpreter was incompetent;
- the interpreter altered the client's evidence during translation;
- the client was pressurised to say things which were untrue;
- the client was pressurised to avoid criticising particular organisations;
- the statement was taken by a representative who
  - ○ was not properly qualified for the job;
  - ○ allowed an inadequate time to take the statement;
  - ○ failed to ensure that the interpreter performed his role properly;
  - ○ failed to investigate relevant aspects of the case;
  - ○ filled in gaps or uncertainties by reference to his own preconceptions;
  - ○ Took the first answer he obtained without checking it through further questioning;
  - ○ failed to read the statement through with the client before submitting it. (As to the significance of the last step, refer to the IAT's guidance in *Njehia*, para 12.66.)

13.15 It is one of the ironies of this jurisdiction that the Home Office never tires of professing its concern about alleged incompetence and lack of scruples on the part of some representatives. Yet the moment the HOPO spots an omission or inconsistency which he thinks he can use to discredit the appellant, the representative who took that statement metamorphoses into a model of competence and commitment, quite incapable of fabrication or pressurising a witness to distort her story.

He may no longer even be an over-worked, under-paid, unqualified caseworker whose main aim (along with his similarly inept interpreter) is to get five pages of 'statement' typed out in the shortest time possible. According to the HOPO, it will be beyond doubt that this particular representative is a paragon of propriety and therefore similarly beyond doubt that any defect in the statement he took can only evidence the appellant's dishonesty.

13.16 You should therefore explain in as much detail as possible why the statement cannot be relied upon. If you simply assert that the previous representatives acted improperly or incompetently without giving any particulars, the adjudicator may accept the HOPO's claim that your allegations are made simply to dispose of an inconvenient statement.

13.17 The new witness statement should clearly set out what went wrong. Name the people involved. That is commensurate with the seriousness of the complaint. Explain in so far as relevant

- the circumstances in which the statement was taken;
- how long was allowed;
- the behaviour of the interpreter;
- what questions were asked and to what extent she was invited to offer additional information;
- whether the statement was translated back to her before she signed it and whether she had an opportunity to amend it.

13.18 If you have not received any file from the previous solicitors, or the file does not contain entries relevant to the statement, consider requesting these from the previous solicitors. The file is obviously unlikely to contain a confession that a representative or interpreter acted improperly. But the nature or absence of paperwork may indicate that proper procedures were not carried out. If the file lends support to your client's complaints, you may consider doing a witness statement yourself. (Since it is you who reviewed the file, this is preferable to including the information in your client's statement.)

13.19 You should consider reporting the previous representatives to the OISC and/or the OSS. This will not only assist future claimants. It will also emphasise to the adjudicator the gravity of your complaint through focussing upon the real issue of how your client has been endangered by the failings of her representative, rather than the advantage that the Home Office is seeking to extract from these failings.

13.20 If you are disclosing significant information late, especially if it is inconsistent with previous material, you should strive to include as much detail as possible in the witness statement.

13.21 There will be occasions when the new information being given by your client is not central to the case and does not affect the accuracy of the information already disclosed. Late disclosure may then be an unnecessary distraction. To include it may simply waste court time by encouraging prolonged cross-examination by the HOPO seeking to identify 'discrepancies' in peripheral detail. It is perfectly proper to suggest to your client that the information is not material to her case and is best left out of the appeal statement.

13.22 Genuine refugees may also seek to exaggerate their claims. A desperate fear of expulsion is not inconsistent with a willingness to embellish in order to escape refoulement – particularly if the Home Office has refused the claim with what appears to the refugee to be a ridiculous belittling of her fears and experiences. If you suspect this may be the case, you can take a dated statement (so that further delay should not be held against your client), but explain to her the allegations that will be made against her and give her time to reconsider before the material is disclosed. If the Home Office has not challenged credibility in the refusal letter, it will be particularly important to avoid giving the Home Office grounds to change its position (see para 30.4).

13.23 Equally however, you should not be overly frightened of unfair allegations of inconsistency from the Home Office. If your client has *relevant* evidence to give which has not yet been submitted then it will often be wrong to advise that it should not be submitted purely to avoid Home Office allegations of inconsistency. The IAT has been critical in cases such as *Kasolo* of such allegations based purely on an asylum seeker expanding on the reasons for which she seeks asylum. But you must be properly prepared to deal with the allegations which may arise.

13 Presenting previously undisclosed information
Key points

- Presenting previously undisclosed information will often prompt a new credibility challenge from the Home Office.

- It is essential to provide a full explanation of why the information was not advanced earlier. Common reasons are:

  ☐ inadequate representation,
  ☐ use of an inappropriate interpreter,
  ☐ the client's mental health and the effects of past trauma,
  ☐ a sense of shame about sexual torture,
  ☐ concern that the authorities in her country of origin may be alerted through Home Office enquiries,
  ☐ fear of stigma in her own community if the information gets out.

- Explain both what avenues are available to protect her confidentiality and the limits of the Home Office's confidentiality undertaking.

- Non-disclosure at Home Office interviews may be due to flaws or improprieties in the interviewing procedure or from the proximity of the interview to her arrival.

- If a previous witness statement which has already been submitted to the Home Office is unreliable or incomplete, you need to explain why.

- If the fault lies with previous representatives, the adjudicator is likely to take the submission more seriously if you identify and report these representatives.

- There is no obligation to disclose new information which is not central to the case unless it affects the accuracy of what has already been disclosed: to do so may provoke irrelevant cross-examination and detract from the real issues.

14 Armed opposition groups

14.1 Members, activists and supporters of armed opposition groups may have considerable fears about the consequences of disclosing their activities in evidence in their appeals.

14.2 The circumstances in which refugee status can be denied under article 1F of the Refugee Convention are deliberately narrow. The IAT has recognised that art 1F must be interpreted restrictively, and that adjudicators should not equate it with a simple anti-terrorist provision or adopt an 'exclusion culture' (*Gurung*). However, the same case encouraged the Home Office to allege art 1F exclusion more widely than the handful of cases in which it is presently raised.

14.3 It also indicated that adjudicators could raise the matter of their own motion where there was evidence indicating potential art 1F exclusion and, in an obvious case, should consider exclusion *before* assessing risk. While the parties must be warned that the adjudicator is raising the point and an adjournment may be appropriate in those circumstances, the adjudicator is entitled to have regard to the extent that membership of an armed organisation was raised in the refusal letter (even where art 1F exclusion was not alleged). The guidance in *Gurung* and the leading House of Lords case of *T* must be considered in detail in any case where art 1F may be raised. Even if the appellant's activities *are* sufficiently grave to engage art 1F, that will lead only to non-recognition as a refugee. Article 3 will still prohibit her expulsion if she faces a real risk of torture or ill-treatment.

14.4 An appeal under the 2002 Act cannot be 'brought or continued' if the Home Secretary issues a certificate under s.97 of the 2002 Act to the effect that the person's removal from the UK is in the interests of 'national security' or 'the relationship between the United Kingdom and another country' or the decision was taken

> *wholly or partly in reliance on information which in his opinion should not be made public –*

(a) in the interests of national security,

(b) in the interests of the relationship between the United Kingdom and another country, or

(c) otherwise in the public interest.

If a certificate is issued under this section, the asylum/human rights appeal must be heard by SIAC. Appeals to SIAC (which are uncommon) are governed by the Special Immigration Appeals Commission Act 1997 and are outside the scope of this text.

14.5 Recent UK anti-terror legislation has created additional fear and confusion. The Anti-Terrorism, Crime, and Security Act 2001 introduced detention without trial for 'suspected international terrorists' who are not British citizens and whom the Home Secretary believes are a threat to national security.

14.6 The Terrorism Act 2000 poses a serious and indeterminate risk to appellants. It bans a large number of organisations, including armed opposition groups with widespread support in major refugee producing countries and among UK refugee communities. The legislation is on its face of wide scope, criminalising *any* active support of a proscribed organisation in the UK. One of the most invidious aspects of the legislation is that those who are entitled to asylum as a result of their activities may be frightened into concealing them and thereby exposed to refoulement.

14.7 The list of proscribed organisations at date of publication (other than Irish organisations) is as follows:

- Kurdistan Workers' Party (Partiya Karkeren Kurdistan) (PKK)
- Revolutionary Peoples' Liberation Party – Front (Devrimci Halk Kurtulus Partisi-Cephesi) (DHKP-C)
- Liberation Tigers of Tamil Eelam (LTTE)
- International Sikh Youth Federation
- Harakat Mujahideen
- Egyptian Islamic Jihad
- Al-Gama'at al-Islamiya
- Armed Islamic Group (Groupe Islamique Armée) (GIA)
- Salafist Group for Call and Combat (Groupe Salafiste pour la Prédication et le Combat) (GSPC)
- Babbar Khalsa
- Al-Qa'ida
- Jaish e Mohammed
- Lashkar e Tayyaba
- Hizballah External Security Organisation

- Hamas-Izz al-Din al-Qassem Brigades
- Palestinian Islamic Jihad – Shaqaqi
- Abu Nidal Organisation
- Islamic Army of Aden
- Mujaheddin e Khalq [People's Mojahedin Organisation of Iran (PMOI)]
- Basque Homeland and Liberty (Euskadi ta Askatasuna) (ETA)
- 17 November Revolutionary Organisation (N17)
- Abu Sayyaf Group
- Asbat Al-Ansar
- Islamic Movement of Uzbekistan
- Jemaah Islamiyah.

(The Terrorism Act 2000 (Proscribed Organisations) (Amendment) Order 2001; The Terrorism Act 2000 (Proscribed Organisations) (Amendment) Order 2002)

14.8 Several organisations have been involved in legal challenges to their proscription. Who is, and as importantly, who is not on the list appears to owe as much to the Government's political priorities as a genuine assessment of the world's most violent and least legitimate organisations. Why, for example, is the People's Mojahedin Organisation of Iran banned for its armed opposition to the Iranian regime when the US State Department has declared the Iranian regime the world's number one terrorist sponsor? Such contradictions only increase confusion in refugee communities.

14.9 Even more alarming is the range of activities which are criminalised. These include:

- membership or professing membership – penalty up to 10 years imprisonment (s.11)
- inviting support for a proscribed organisation – up to 10 years (s.12)
- arranging or managing (or assisting in arranging or managing) a meeting of more than three people (public or private) which he knows is either to support a proscribed organisation, to further its activities, or is to be addressed by someone who is or professes to be a member – up to 10 years (s.12)
- addressing a meeting, where the purpose of the address is to encourage support for the proscribed organisation or its activities – up to 10 years (s.12)
- wearing in a public place any item of clothing or carrying or displaying any item which arouses reasonable suspicion that he is a member or supporter of a proscribed organisation – up to 6 months (s.13)

14.10 The above offences can only be committed in the UK. (Your client cannot be prosecuted for membership of a proscribed organisation outside the UK, although that might be used as evidence suggesting continued membership *in* the UK). However, other acts are criminalised even if committed only outside the UK (e.g. the country of origin). These include inviting funds, receiving funds, and using, possessing or providing money or property, where the person intends or has reasonable cause to suspect that the funds will be used to support a proscribed organisation (penalty up to 14 years imprisonment: s.15–16, 22) and incitement to carry out an act of terrorism which involves various offences of violence listed in s.59.

14.11 The offences of fund-raising (and also money laundering under s.18) apply not only to *any* assistance to a proscribed organisation, but also to fund-raising for any other organisation if the person intends or has reasonable cause to suspect that the funds are to be used for 'purposes of terrorism'. These are very widely defined in the Act (s.1). They include action which

a. involves serious violence against a person or serious damage to property or endangers another person's life or creates a serious risk to the health or safety of the public or a section of the public or is designed to interfere with or seriously disrupt an electronic system, if

b. the use or threat of the use of such action is made for the purpose of advancing a political, religious or ideological cause, and either it
   i. is designed to influence the government or to intimidate the public or a section of the public, or
   ii. involves the use of firearms or explosives.

14.12 That definition will include the activities of almost any armed opposition group and may include activities carried out by many organisations who would not reasonably merit the description 'terrorist'. Any involvement in fund-raising or providing funds for any organisation engaged in such activities is criminalised.

14.13 Conviction of an offence in the UK now carries an added risk by virtue of s.72 of the 2002 Act. In certain circumstances, this enables the Home Secretary to issue a certificate to the effect that there is a presumption that the appellant has been convicted of a 'particularly serious crime and constitute(s) a danger to the community of the United Kingdom' and so is excluded from the Refugee Convention under art. 33(2). It is for the appellant to rebut the presumption. The adjudicator must begin the appeal by considering the certificate and, if the appellant cannot rebut the presumption, must dismiss the asylum appeal.

14.14 It is also an offence for any person who receives information in the course of a trade, profession, business or employment not to disclose to the police any belief or suspicion he forms on the basis of that information that a person has been involved in fund-raising for a proscribed organisation or other terrorist purposes (as defined above). Privileged information obtained by a professional legal adviser is excluded from the offence. However, that defence may not extend to others who receive information which would normally be privileged, such as medical and other experts and interpreters. There is also no obvious reason why it should not apply to HOPOs or even adjudicators.

Advising your client

14.15 If your client's organisation has been engaged in armed activities (and particularly if it is proscribed under UK anti-terror legislation), you may find that she has been prevailed upon by previous representatives, interpreters, or community leaders to downplay or lie about the extent of her involvement. She may have been told that she risked being refouled if she reveals her true activities, or that she risks prosecution or indefinite detention without charge under anti-terror legislation.

14.16 You must advise her as to the risks and merits of disclosure. Many clients, once the law has been explained to them, will prefer to minimise the risk of refoulement by disclosing all the matters putting them in danger, despite any risks posed by art 1F and the legislation described above. (You will of course have to explain that while it is ultimately a matter for your client what she chooses to disclose, you cannot continue to represent her if she gives evidence to the court which she has instructed you is false.)

14.17 It is very difficult to advise clients properly on the risks posed by the Terrorism Act. It is not possible or proper to ignore the Act when you are proposing to disclose information which will incriminate your client in respect of a criminal offence carrying a heavy penalty. On the other hand, there have as yet been no known prosecutions based on information provided in asylum/human rights appeals. You *must* obtain specialised advice for your client if you are not in a position to provide it yourself.

Presenting new information about activities with armed groups

14.18 Where your client does decide to disclose her involvement, you will have to anticipate the likely credibility challenge from the Home Office based on late disclosure.

14.19 If the original advice not to disclose her activities came from someone associated with the armed organisation, your client may well be reluctant to follow the usual advice to give as much detail as possible about the guidance she was given (see para 13.17). In that case, you may wish to make early applications as discussed in chapter 32 so as to seek to reassure her as to the confidentiality of the information.

14.20 Where initial non-disclosure resulted from your client's fears of the consequences of admitting involvement with an armed organisation, it will often be useful to remind the adjudicator of the reasonableness of your client's fears. That is especially so where an armed organisation has recently become more acceptable to western governments. It is surprising how easy (and convenient) it is to forget the condemnation which the organisation previously attracted. For example, if representing someone in 1999 who had only recently revealed his involvement in armed resistance to the Serb authorities in Kosovo, you would probably have to remind the adjudicator that while NATO had fought alongside the KLA to oust the Serbs, the KLA had not long previously been stigmatised by western governments as a terrorist organisation.

14.21 (Remember also that the pendulum may have swung the other way. If the Home Office is attacking your client on the basis of her involvement in a terrorist organisation, it may be possible to point to past governmental support. For example, the Iranian PMOI is now proscribed as terrorist, yet in recent years has been invited to the Labour Party's annual conference.)

14.22 Although corroboration will always be useful where credibility is under attack (see chapter 16 on documents and chapter 15 on witnesses), armed organisations do not generally provide documentation, and it may be difficult to persuade witnesses to come forward. In those circumstances, a very detailed statement from the client is the best (and quite possibly the only) means of overcoming the credibility problems created by late disclosure.

14.23 A statement which simply notes that *'Contrary to my earlier account, I have actually been very involved at a very high level in guerrilla operations'*, provides far less protection against an adverse credibility finding than an account that goes into great, even verging on tedious, detail about her activities. Rather than the above bland sentence, you really do benefit from a blow by blow account: How did she get involved? How did she rise up through the ranks? How did she win sufficient trust to be given such high-level activities? Why was she chosen? How did she have (or gain) the necessary skills? Why did she take the risks? How did she get her instructions? Where did she go? How did she manage to travel? What exactly was her role? Who did she deal with?

14.24 Your client may obviously be unwilling to divulge details of names and places, particularly if her organisation is still involved in armed operations and/or is viewed antagonistically by western governments. However, while your client's initial reaction may be that she cannot reveal anything about her activities, if you talk it through with her, she may decide that she can give a fairly compelling account without divulging any information that would incriminate others. For example, she might be able to explain how a particular operation was carried out, but not the names or locations involved. In fact, a discussion of the former may establish her credibility far more effectively than the provision of names that the adjudicator will have no means of checking. If you do not make an effort to provide this sort of persuasive detail, you may have little else to bring to bear on credibility.

14.25 You will also want the statement to pre-empt so far as possible any points that may be taken against you on art 1F. Note the IAT's view in **Gurung**:

> [I]n deciding whether a person's membership of an organisation amounts to complicity in any crimes or acts proscribed by Art 1F, it is of crucial importance to examine the particular circumstances, taking account not only of factors concerning the individual and his specific role in the organisation but also that organisation's place and role in the society in which it operates. The more an organisation makes terrorist acts its modus operandi, the more difficult it will be for a claimant to show his voluntary membership of it does not amount to complicity.

14.26 In light of this, it may also be important to seek expert evidence on the 'organisation's place and role in the society in which it operates'.

14 Armed opposition groups
Key points

- Members, activists and supporters of armed opposition groups may not have disclosed the full extent of their case through fear of the consequences.

- Potential risks include an allegation of exclusion under article 1F of the Refugee Convention.

  ☐ The grounds for exclusion are restrictive and adjudicators should not adopt an 'exclusion culture'.

  ☐ However, the IAT has encouraged the Home Office to allege exclusion more often, and adjudicators may raise it of their own motion.

  ☐ Someone excluded under article 1F will still be able to challenge expulsion under article 3.

- The Home Office may issue a certificate on national security and other grounds to the effect that an asylum/human rights appeal may only be brought before SIAC.

- UK anti-terror legislation can create additional fear and confusion.

  ☐ The Anti-Terrorism, Crime, and Security Act 2001 permits detention without trial.

  ☐ The Terrorism Act 2000 imposes substantial sentences for membership and support for 'terrorist organisations': these include armed opposition groups with widespread support among minority communities in refugee producing countries.

- If your client has received a prison sentence of at least two years from a UK court, the Home Office may be able to issue a certificate creating a presumption that she is excluded from the Refugee Convention by article 33(2). The adjudicator must start by determining whether the appellant can rebut the presumption.

- Advise your client on the risks and merits of disclosure.

  ☐ Be alert to the possibility that she was given wrong-headed advice in the past.

  ☐ The risk of refoulement because potential dangers have not been appreciated will often outweigh those of an article 1F allegation.

  ☐ The client must receive specialist advice on any potential risks under UK anti-terror legislation.

□ It is for her to decide what to disclose, but you cannot present a case to the court which, on your instructions, is false.

■ If you are disclosing new information about activities with armed opposition groups at the appeal stage, you can expect credibility to be challenged.

□ A detailed statement is important since corroboration is unlikely to be straightforward.

□ Compelling detail can be advanced without disclosing names and places.

□ Explain the fears that prevented prior disclosure.

■ Pre-empt so far as possible potential article 1F allegations. Expert evidence may be required on the 'organisation's place and role in the society in which it operates'.

15 Other witnesses of fact and combined hearings

15.1 The Rules give an adjudicator the power to limit oral evidence, but he should not exclude the evidence of any witness whose evidence is admissible and relevant (*Hussain*).

15.2 Additional witnesses of fact can provide crucial collaboration where the appellant's credibility is in issue. Even if the evidence they can give is limited, it may be sufficient to preclude a blanket adverse credibility finding in respect of the appellant. If the adjudicator accepts that one aspect of the appellant's account is corroborated, that may favourably influence his view of other aspects of her evidence.

15.3 Do not automatically call family members and friends of the appellant just because they are there. You need to assess what their evidence will add to the appeal. Additional witnesses are not always helpful and may even be dangerous. The fact that an act of persecution was witnessed by your client's partner does not necessarily mean that she must give evidence of that fact. The HOPO will inevitably argue that her evidence should be given little weight because of her relationship to the appellant (see below), although he will equally criticise the opposite approach of *not* calling oral evidence from a family member who witnessed any relevant event. The HOPO may use cross-examination of the witness to embark on a fishing expedition to see if he can elicit any inconsistency in the witness' description of the event compared with that of the appellant. If both witnesses are discussing traumatic events from some time ago through interpreters, there is a real possibility that he will succeed.

15.4 On the other hand, if the proposed witness is not a very close relative, his evidence may provide particularly valuable corroboration. An adjudicator must make an assessment of each witness before him (see para 42.38) and consistency should be given weight in the same way as inconsistency. There will also be good reason to call the appellant's partner (or another close relative) where you decide they will give better evidence than the appellant. If the appellant is unable to give oral evidence because of her mental state, you may need to call someone else who can speak to her experiences. The same could apply if the appellant is a minor.

15.5 It will usually be appropriate to call a witness where he can give first hand evidence of a material event of which the appellant cannot give first hand evidence: for example, if the witness was interrogated about the appellant.

15.6 If there is a recognised refugee who can give material evidence, this will often represent particularly valuable corroboration. Having granted her asylum, the Home Office will find it much more difficult to attack the credibility of her evidence in relation to the present appeal. Even if she left the country of origin prior to the events which are in issue in the present appeal, she may be able to give evidence about how she heard of the events contemporaneously from your client or family members. That evidence (if accepted) may preclude a finding by the adjudicator that your client made up her account at some later date.

15.7 If such a witness was successful on appeal, consider submitting the determination. Even if a relative will not be giving evidence, it is often worth submitting her determination if she has won refugee status on appeal. That is particularly so where the adjudicator made findings of fact which are relevant to the determination of your own appeal (e.g. that the family as a whole are at risk). Check first whether there is anything in the factual summary which might be perceived as inconsistent with your client's evidence.

15.8 If the witness has been granted the now extinct status of ELR by the Home Office, the HOPO may argue that the basis upon which she was granted ELR is not known so no weight should be given to that grant. A similar problem has arisen in upgrade appeals where the Home Office refuses to confirm the basis upon which ELR was granted (chapter 52). It may be useful to provide the witness' asylum statement as well as his appeal statement (assuming there are no inconsistencies) and invite the Home Office to indicate whether there was any unconnected reason for granting ELR.

15.9 You should ensure that any friends or relatives who have been granted asylum, Humanitarian Protection, or ELR are interviewed to determine whether they can give helpful evidence.

Witnesses who have pending asylum claims/appeals

15.10 There are considerable complications involved in calling a witness who herself has an outstanding asylum claim or appeal. You should not do so without having full access to her papers, and satisfying your-self that she will give consistent evidence. But you will also have to explain to her, or invite her lawyers to advise her on the consequences for her own case of giving evidence.

15.11 You may have to consider applying for an adjournment in those cir-cumstances. In *Kimbesa*, Mr Kimbesa's two brothers had arrived in the UK and claimed asylum shortly before Mr Kimbesa's appeal hearing. Their cases were interlinked with his and an adjournment was sought so that they did not have to give evidence in Kimbesa's case before their own claims had been considered. That was refused. On judicial review, Jowitt J stated that:

> [T]he consequence of the Adjudicator declining to adjourn the matter would be that one of the two brothers, who very recently arrived within the jurisdiction (some three weeks before) would have his claim for asy-lum (his factual evidence) tested in a strenuous, adversarial situation at a time which all the relevant guidance would indicate was inappropriate. It is well recognised that normal practice dictates that before an account of an asylum seeker is tested in an adversarial situation, bearing in mind the stresses inevitably imposed upon persons of that character in a strange and different environment, he or she should be afforded every rea-soned opportunity to make representations and to give a full account of himself or herself in a less testing environment. That is, as I understand it, what [the appellant] was seeking to say to the Adjudicator on this occasion. 'He will be unfairly subjected to a test of his credibility. Unfairly because it is too early in his stay and he has not yet been afforded a sufficient opportunity to give a full account of himself and lodge any supporting material in a less testing environment.'

15.12 In *Rajan*, the IAT considered the circumstances in which it would be appropriate to adjourn appeals where concurrent asylum applications from family members were under consideration. It pointed to *Kimbesa* as an example of where it was unjust to refuse an adjournment. However, the IAT held that there was no general rule that appeals must be adjourned wherever there are concurrent asylum applications from family members under consideration by the Home Office. The IAT stated that:

> The reality is that an adjudicator must look at the words of Rule 31(1) [now r.40(2)] and will refuse an adjournment unless satisfied that refus-ing it would prevent the just disposal of the appeal. Of course, the exis-tence of concurrent applications by members of the family is a relevant consideration and it may, in an appropriate case, point to an adjourn-ment.

15.13 An adjournment application will therefore be appropriate where the family member's claim is interlinked with your client's, and her appeal has not yet been determined, or where the family member can give relevant evidence in your appeal, but her claim has still not been determined by the Home Office.

15.14 If, however, a family member's claim/appeal does not involve the same facts, or the potential witness' evidence is unlikely to be relevant to your own appeal, you are unlikely to be granted an adjournment, regardless of the closeness of the family relationship. In applying for an adjournment, you will have to fully explain how the cases are interlinked or what material evidence the potential witness can give.

15.15 Just because you might be entitled to an adjournment on this ground does not mean that you should apply for it. You will wish to weigh the factors discussed above as to the suitability of the potential witness.

Combined hearings

15.16 Rule 51 governs the power to hold combined hearings:

Hearing two or more appeals together

(1) Where two or more appeals to an adjudicator or to the Tribunal are pending at the same time, an adjudicator or the Tribunal may direct them to be heard together if it appears that –

(a) some common question of law or fact arises in each of them;

(b) they relate to decisions or action taken in respect of persons who are members of the same family; or

(c) for some other reason it is desirable for the appeals to be heard together.

(2) An adjudicator or the Tribunal must give all the parties an opportunity to make representations before determining appeals together under this rule.

15.17 The IAT has stated that combined hearings should be generally be used:

only… where the factual basis of each claim is so intertwined that it is only by considering them together that there can be a fair and proper evaluation of the evidence. In practice this is likely to be confined to family cases where each member relies on the same Convention reason or reasons arising out of a contemporaneous factual background.

15.18 Where this applies to two claims, one of which is before the adjudicator and the other has yet to be decided by the Home Office, the IAT stated that the adjudicator should give consideration to adjourning the hearing so that, if the second claim is refused, a combined hearing can be arranged. A similar view was expressed by Forbes J in **Kallova** who stated:

> It seems to me to be very unsatisfactory to deal with and dismiss one appeal of a family member, where that appeal is entirely identified in all relevant respects with a still current and outstanding appeal of another member of the same family. It is obvious that, if the father's outstanding appeal is successful (and there is no obvious reason for saying that it definitely will not be successful) then that outcome will produce an inconsistent result with the determination of this applicant's earlier, unsuccessful appeal. The adjournment of this applicant's appeal so that it could be heard at the same time as her father's later appeal was an obvious and sensible way to avoid any such risk of inconsistency. In my judgment, to reject the application to adjourn in circumstances such as these, which raise a real risk of such an inconsistency is arguably irrational.

15.19 Even in those circumstances, however, combined hearings may give rise to the substantial practical difficulties identified by the IAT in **Tabores**:

> Each appellant is then primarily concerned with giving evidence in relation to and in support of his own claim. The existence of unresolved discrepancies does not necessarily mean that all the deponents are not telling the truth; it may be that one is telling the truth and the other or others are not. Each principal appellant is entitled, even in a combined hearing, to have his case determined on its own merits. A principal appellant's appeal should not fail solely because he and another principal appellant cannot both be telling the truth.

> We do not say that in such circumstances combined hearings would never be appropriate. We think, however, that before proceeding with a combined hearing (even with the consent of the parties) an adjudicator would need to be very confident being able to perform the mental gymnastics involved in treating case A on its merits in the context of apparently contradictory evidence given in support of case B, and vice versa.

15.20 It also pointed to the additional concern that would arise if it were suggested that one of the appellants be excluded from the combined hearing while other appellants gave their evidence:

> We very much doubt whether this is... appropriate or proper in the case of principal appellants, even though they may be represented in the hearing room during their absence.

15.21 There will, of course, be circumstances in which it will be particularly unwise to apply for appeals of family members to be combined – an obvious example being where they have given inconsistent information to the Home Office.

15.22 Occasionally, the Home Office will also make an application for appeals to be joined under this rule (and the adjudicator can make a direction of his own motion). Rule 51(2) requires the adjudicator to give you an opportunity to make representations. You will obviously object to combined hearings where your client wishes to keep aspects of her history confidential, or where her evidence is sensitive. If there has been no proposal to combine the hearings, that also, of course, gives a family two chances to put their case to an adjudicator. If one appeal is successful, the rest of the immediate family should be granted status in line.

Presenting evidence from witnesses in other countries

15.23 If your client has relatives or acquaintances who have been granted refugee status in other countries, their evidence will be of similar value to someone granted asylum in the UK. The value of other potential witnesses will depend on the issues discussed above.

15.24 You should start by interviewing the potential witness by telephone to determine whether she can give material evidence. If she can, and particularly if she is a refugee, enquire whether it is practicable for her to come to the UK to give evidence. If it is and she is available for the date of the hearing, write to the IAA (copied to the Home Office) asking that it ensure that the appeal is heard on the date listed because a witness is attending from abroad. If she cannot make the date and her evidence is sufficiently important, ask for the date to be changed.

15.25 Appellants often submit letters from friends, relatives, and colleagues in the country of origin which contain information material to the appeal. The HOPO will often allege that they are 'self-serving' – by which he appears to mean that they are put forward to advance the appellant's appeal. In *Moyo*, the IAT stated that:

> *The only reason given by the Adjudicator for deciding to place no reliance on the letters submitted by the Appellant was that they were 'self serving'. This is not a good reason. If every document submitted by every party was to be rejected because it was 'self serving' it is likely that no documentary evidence would ever be admitted. Most documentary evidence is self serving in the sense that it assists the case of the party who submits it. The Adjudicator may have had better reasons for deciding not to place any reliance on the documents, but he has not said what these are and they are not obvious. (See also para 16.14.)*

15.26 The only circumstances in which this issue may validly arise is if the document purports to have been produced for some other purpose unconnected to the appeal. If you are presented with a letter which purports to be an ordinary communication between your client and friend or family, you need to get it translated and consider what the adjudicator will make of it. Is it worded in a way which appears unnatural or inappropriate in the context of the relationship between your client and the writer? Is it informing your client of matters which she might be expected to know already, or giving advice that appears obvious or unnecessary? Or does it include the sort of material one might expect in an ordinary letter? It is of course perfectly possible that what may appear contrived to the adjudicator is simply a result of translation and cultural differences. However, it is unwise to rely upon the adjudicator making such allowance, at least in the absence of expert evidence explaining the point.

15.27 If you have concerns, question your client about them. She may be able to explain them. On the other hand, she may readily accept that the letter was written with the court case in mind. She may simply have assumed that a letter to herself was the appropriate means of presenting information from her relative, and not appreciated that the adjudicator might suspect that its presentation in the form of an ordinary letter was an attempt to mislead him.

15.28 There is nothing wrong with people from the country of origin giving evidence in the appeal. Indeed, if it is relevant, and particularly if no-one in the UK can give first hand evidence, then they should do so. But there is no reason not to present that evidence in proper form – i.e. a witness statement – unless that is not practically possible. The exception is where it is necessary to establish in evidence the receipt of a particular letter in order to explain your client's contemporaneous state of mind.

15.29 You can take the statement over the telephone (unless, of course, you are able to travel to the country of origin to take the statement or instruct a local agent to do so). If practical, the statement should be translated and provided to the witness by post or fax who should then return a signed copy. If that is not possible, then you should have the completed statement translated to the witness over the telephone, including a statement of truth (see para 12.65) and a paragraph explaining that he is not in a position to sign it, but has had it translated, and approves its use in your client's appeal. You should also make a short witness statement explaining the circumstances in which you were able to contact the witness, and how the statement was taken and approved.

15.30 It will usually be apparent why the witness is unable to attend the hearing. (Indeed, if he is prepared to travel to the UK to attend the hearing, you should take care to address any suspicion that the ability to do so is inconsistent with your case). The fact that the evidence is presented in the form of a witness statement taken by a lawyer in itself adds weight. It demonstrates that you have interviewed the witness, and therefore decreases the risk that the witness' evidence (sometimes even his existence) may be questioned by the adjudicator if he forms an adverse view of the appellant's evidence.

15.31 The HOPO may of course argue that the evidence of a family member should be discounted. But it is an error to discount such evidence as a matter of course. In **Quijano**, the adjudicator had said that:

> No assistance is derived from the testimony of the Appellant's brother, whose interest in the success of the appeal is so manifest as greatly to diminish the value of his evidence and whose credibility I am therefore not prepared to accept.

15.32 The IAT held that:

> An adjudicator cannot dismiss evidence simply because the witness has an interest in the particular appeal. Were that so, no evidence of any appellant would ever be believed. The evidence must be assessed just as must an appellant's evidence and, while an interest in the proceedings may be a factor it certainly cannot ever be an exclusive ground for dismissing the accuracy of the evidence.

15.33 The point at para 15.28 also applies to evidence from lawyers and others who are not personally connected to your client but who have material evidence to give. If the evidence is coming from a lawyer, or someone holding a formal position, e.g. in an NGO, it is useful to submit a letter from the witness addressed to you on his letterhead (which can simply confirm his witness statement). But a witness statement from him in proper form should again increase the weight of his evidence (and will underscore the point that his evidence cannot be rejected unless the adjudicator has grounds to make an adverse credibility finding against him). Once again, your involvement in obtaining the evidence can only decrease the risk of it being blighted by the view the adjudicator forms of the appellant's own evidence.

Drafting the statement

15.34 Refer to chapter 12 on preparing the appellant's witness statement for general advice. It is particularly important to keep to the forefront of your mind what the witness is adding to your case, and to ensure that the witness' statement is directed towards those points. He should be clear about what he knows and does not know. If it is relevant for him to indicate his fears concerning your client's expulsion, he should be clear upon what he bases these fears.

15.35 This is particularly so if you will be calling the witness. If the statement wanders into less relevant matters, you will be in a less strong position to object if the HOPO embarks on a more general fishing expedition for discrepancies. To avoid this, the statement should clearly delineate the areas in which the witness can assist (for example, by pointing out that he has no detailed knowledge of the appellant's past detentions). Witnesses of fact should generally not purport to be country experts.

Whether to call oral evidence

15.36 Sometimes, a witness will come to light unexpectedly when there is no time to prepare a witness statement. You should never consider calling a witness to give oral evidence without seeing her and forming an opinion of her ability to give evidence. You should check what the response will be to foreseeable lines of cross-examination.

15.37 Very occasionally, you might decide to call an additional witness after the appellant has given evidence. This might happen when an appellant who you thought could give satisfactory evidence has actually given incoherent and inconsistent evidence or has failed to establish a vital fact. If there is someone available who you think could give better first hand evidence in the areas where the appellant has failed, you might now consider calling him. However, such a course is fraught with obvious danger, and should only really be considered when, after the appellant's evidence, you think you have little to lose. By far the better situation would be if you realised beforehand that your client would not give useful evidence and acted accordingly.

15.38 If you get yourself into the situation where you have not prepared a witness but decide due to unforeseen events during the hearing that you may have to call her, you should request an adjournment, rather than simply calling her and hoping for the best.

15.39 Witnesses of fact will normally be expected to remain outside the hearing room until their turn comes to give evidence.

15 Other witnesses of fact and combined hearings
Key points

■ Additional witnesses of fact may provide crucial corroboration where the appellant's credibility is in issue.

■ Where a witness can give first hand evidence of a material event at which the appellant was not present, the witness should normally be called.

■ The reliability of corroborative evidence from an immediate family member may be challenged on the ground of her closeness to the appellant. The HOPO is liable to embark on a fishing expedition for inconsistencies. However such evidence is important where:

  ☐ the witness can give better evidence that the appellant, or
  ☐ the appellant will not be called because of her mental condition or age.

■ Recognised refugees can make particularly valuable witnesses.

■ Where a material witness has an outstanding asylum claim, it may be necessary to seek an adjournment until that claim is determined.

■ Where the facts of two appeals are intertwined, a combined hearing could be appropriate. However, the IAT has identified serious difficulties in conducting such a hearing.

■ A combined hearing should be opposed where your client is concerned about confidentiality or her evidence is sensitive. It may not be in the interests of your client if the other appellant has given an inconsistent account in the past.

■ If a material witness is outside the jurisdiction, you should normally take a witness statement over the telephone. If the witness can travel to the UK for the hearing, make appropriate representations to the IAA concerning the listing.

■ If the client produces letters from friends or relatives from the country of origin, consider how these will be assessed by the adjudicator. A witness statement will usually be preferable unless it is necessary to establish receipt of the letter in order to explain your client's state of mind at the time.

■ Letters and evidence from family members cannot be dismissed by the adjudicator simply on the ground that they are related to the appellant. He must make a proper assessment of the credibility of the evidence.

■ Ensure that the witness statement remains focussed on what the witness knows and what he can add to the appeal.

■ Very occasionally and with great caution, you may seek to call an additional witness after the appellant has given oral evidence as a result of unexpected issues that have arisen during that evidence.

16 Documentary corroboration

Types of documentary evidence

16.1   Chapter 18 deals with general country reports. This chapter deals with documents which corroborate specific elements of your client's account, often documents which mention your client by name.

16.2   The obstacles that appellants face in obtaining such specific corroboration from the country of origin are formidable. Detention may well have been extra-judicial and the Home Office recognises that such detention will not be susceptible to documentary corroboration (Home Office OGN on Turkey: para 1.37). Your client may well have had no access to a lawyer. Doctors (if your client was able to obtain treatment) may be unwilling through fear to provide reports. Outlawed political or rebel organisations seldom issue membership cards or minutes.

16.3   It is because of such obstacles that the law prohibits the rejection of an asylum seeker's account simply because there is no corroboration. However, if an adjudicator might otherwise be justified in making an adverse credibility finding against your client, specific corroboration may make the difference between winning and losing.

16.4   The following are amongst the documents which may provide specific corroboration:

- documents issued by the authorities of the country of origin indicating adverse interest in the appellant such as
  - arrest warrants,
  - court documents,
  - documents corroborating past detention such as release orders,
  - call up papers;
- when dealing with non-state risks, evidence that attacks were reported to the authorities, such as police reports;
- confirmation from lawyers or NGOs (local or international) of past interventions in the case, e.g. attending a police station for the appellant or representing her in court;

- newspaper, other media or NGO reports naming the appellant or confirming an incident in which she was involved;
- evidence from hospitals or doctors confirming past injuries and treatment;
- evidence of membership of, or activities with opposition groups;
- confirmation of past employment, where that is relevant;
- evidence about lifestyle, e.g. salary or property ownership where it is alleged that the appellant is an economic migrant;
- letters from relatives, friends or colleagues in the country of origin.

Obtaining documentary evidence

16.5 Despite the difficulties, you should always make every effort to pursue whatever corroboration may be available unless the material facts are not in dispute. If an event does appear to be susceptible to corroboration yet none is produced, the adjudicator may – absent a satisfactory explanation – hold it against your client. The same may apply if your client claims to have been mentioned in documents which could have been but have not been obtained. (See, e.g. *Shanjarfi* where the IAT said that an adjudicator would be entitled to assume that a newspaper article could normally be obtained from its archive if the paper is still being published.)

16.6 Start by working through your client's history with her, exploring what documents might exist which could corroborate each material event that is in dispute, and what avenues might be explored to obtain such documents.

16.7 If your client was lucky enough to have a lawyer at some stage, then he will be a prime source. If practical, it is preferable that you approach the lawyer directly rather than asking your client to do it. This will help to dispel any suspicion, however unjustified, that an improper approach was made (see below). The same applies to approaching other sources, whether NGOs or individuals, including relatives. Wherever possible you, rather than your client, should make the arrangements. (See also para 15.30 re obtaining witness statements from the country of origin or other countries).

16.8 If your client has been the subject of formal court proceedings, e.g. charged or released on bail, it may be possible to make enquiries through official records. The same may apply if your client has instigated a complaint to the authorities. You may instruct a local lawyer to do this. You should obtain the specific consent of your client beforehand, and take care to ensure that the lawyer is genuinely independent. Where your client fears the authorities in the country of origin and those authorities have a record of suppressing opposition, it may be difficult to identify a lawyer who is both competent and genuinely independent. At worst, he may report the enquiry to the authorities.

16.9 Where there are respected local human rights organisations, as exist, say, in Turkey or Sri Lanka, they can advise on reputable lawyers. The human rights committees of the Bar Council and the International Bar Association may also be able to advise on lawyers. You should not approach the local bar association without first checking whether there is any suspicion that it is under the influence of the authorities.

16.10 If you have instructed an expert in the case, he may also be able to advise on sources of documentation, and give an indication of what sort of documentation might be available. Even if an expert is not formally instructed, he may be willing to help on such a point. See chapter 21 for identifying experts. Sometimes relatives can obtain such documents, but you must be sure of how they were able to obtain them, and that the ability to do so is not inconsistent with other parts of the case (see below para 16.57).

16.11 Newspaper reports mentioning the client may be available from the paper's archive (as indicated above). If there is a web-based archive for a foreign language news organisation, you can use an interpreter to search it.

16.12 As to letters from friends and relatives, if the purpose of the letter is simply to convey the writer's information to the Court, then where possible, this is best done by way of witness statement (see chapter 15). On the other hand, it may be important to demonstrate that your client received particular information at a particular time, for example, to explain the timing of the asylum claim, or to refute an allegation that an aspect of the case has recently been fabricated. Amongst the first advice you give your client should be to retain envelopes if there is any chance that the contents may be relevant.

Disputes over authenticity

16.13 The Home Office will often dispute the reliability of a document which, if accepted, establishes an important part of your client's account. Sometimes, the HOPO even argues that no weight can be placed upon corroborating evidence unless the adjudicator has *first* concluded that the appellant's account is credible. In ordinary litigation, it is of course precisely when a witness' credibility is in issue that corroboration is sought. Nor is the HOPO's line consistent with that often taken by the Home Office in its refusal letters. These often assert the following:

> *The Secretary of State notes that you have produced no documentary evidence to support your assertions. While an asylum seeker is not required as a matter of law to provide corroboration, the Secretary of State is not obliged to accept unsupported statements where he has doubts about your credibility.*

16.14 The obvious response is to urge the asylum seeker to obtain corroborative evidence from her country so as to satisfy the Home Office's concerns. Yet if the asylum seeker is successful, the HOPO's response is too often that he will not entertain the corroborating evidence because of his doubts about the person's credibility! The Kafkaesque approach is epitomised in the HOPO's allegation that corroborative documents are 'self-serving', attracting this comment from the IAT in *Rodriguez*:

> *If, by 'self-serving' the adjudicator means that they assist the appellant, then most documents produced by appellants would, by definition, be condemned in this way. In the absence of any more specific criticism 'self-serving' is not sufficient reason for not accepting that a document is reasonably likely to be genuine.*

16.15 Sometimes, the HOPO completes the vicious circle by claiming not only that documents cannot corroborate an account which is not independently credible, but that the submission of documents to corroborate such an account is further evidence that it is not credible! In *Gomez-Salinas*, Sullivan J stated that:

> *There certainly have been instances where adjudicators have said in respect of a document produced by the claimant 'I do not accept that the document is genuine, therefore, that casts doubt on the credibility of the claimant'. In such cases, where the special adjudicator has effectively cast a burden on the claimant to demonstrate that a document is genuine and then reached adverse credibility findings because the appellant has failed to discharge that burden, the courts have been prepared to quash adjudicators' decisions on applications for judicial review.'*

16.16 In *Davila-Puga*, Laws LJ accepted that an adjudicator may not apply the 'illegitimate compartmentalised approach' of reaching a view on the appellant's credibility as a 'distinct and prior exercise' to the assessment of the documentary corroboration (an approach described in *B* as putting 'the cart before the horse': see para 26.53). Laws LJ said:

> *I certainly accept that the genuineness of an asylum claim has to be judged by reference to the evidence as a whole, including... such documents as are relied on, unless of course they could, on the particular facts, be peremptorily dismissed as inauthentic.*

16.17 In *Tanveer Ahmed*, the IAT explained that the burden would fall upon the Home Office to prove that a document was a forgery only where the document was 'apparently reliable'. It considered that it would usually be unnecessary for the Home Office to contend that a document was forged in order to dispute its reliability. It summarised its guidance as follows:

> 1 *In asylum and human rights cases it is for an individual claimant to show that a document on which he seeks to rely can be relied on.*
>
> 2 *The decision maker should consider whether a document is one on which reliance should properly be placed after looking at all the evidence in the round.*
>
> 3 *Only very rarely will there be the need to make an allegation of forgery, or evidence strong enough to support it. The allegation should not be made without such evidence. Failure to establish the allegation on the balance of probabilities to the higher civil standard does not show that a document is reliable. The decision maker still needs to apply principles 1 and 2.*

16.18 The IAT emphasised that a document which is not a forgery may exhibit false information:

> *At its simplest we need to differentiate between form and content; that is whether a document is properly issued by the purported author, and whether the contents are true.*

So even where the Home Office does not contend that a document is forged, it may still contend that it is false in the sense that it purports to establish something which is false.

16.19 It is important to bear in mind this possibility. It may arise either through mistake or deliberate misrepresentation by the creator of the document. For example, a death certificate may be a genuine document but the subject is incorrectly named through an innocent mistake. Alternatively, the authorities might wish to publish false information about the death of a person who in reality remains in their custody or who had been killed by them. Or they may have been persuaded to do so in the interests of some other party, e.g. through bribery.

16.20 In practice however, it is not uncommon for the Home Office to contend forgery where it disputes the probative value of a document. Suppose that there is before the adjudicator a piece of evidence which on its face is a police document confirming that the appellant has been charged with membership of an illegal organisation. But it is the Home Office's case that the appellant has never been charged. The Home Office may contend that the information contained in the document is false even where it does not contend that the document is a forgery.

However, if it *is* the Home Office's case that the appellant was never charged, but the Home Office does *not* contend that the document was forged, then its submission (if it is logically coherent) *must* involve either of the following:

- that although the document emanated from the proper source, the information contained in the document is the result of an innocent mistake by the proper source, *or*
- that the proper source has deliberately published false information.

16.21 Unless the Home Office is able to point to specific evidence of mistake, an adjudicator is unlikely to be convinced by the first alternative. The prospects of the second contention being accepted should depend upon the facts and evidence in the particular case. One can well imagine that the police might wish to publish false documents incriminating someone in respect of a particular offence in order to facilitate his conviction. They might publish documents indicating that someone was wanted for a legitimate common law offence when he was actually wanted for illegitimate political reasons. But it is far less plausible that it would be in the interests of the police to issue a document falsely claiming that the appellant had been charged with membership of an illegal organisation.

16.22 The remaining alternative is that the police were persuaded by the appellant or those acting on his behalf to issue the document. The plausibility of such an allegation will again depend on the circumstances of the case. In some cases, it may be plausible. The IAT suggested in *Tanveer Ahmed*, that 'birth, death, and marriage certificates from certain countries... can be obtained from the proper source for a 'fee' but contain information which is wholly or partially untrue'. Whether that applied in your case would depend on the evidence, i.e. whether there was evidence that the proper source of the document you had produced would readily publish false information or provide false documents for a fee.

16.23 It may well be rather less common for the police in a particular country to charge a person (or purport to charge a person) for a 'fee'. Whether such a service was available in the particular country would again be a question of evidence. So would the equally important question of whether the particular appellant would have been in a position to purchase the service. An allegation that a poor villager from an oppressed minority race had purchased such a service might have little credibility, even where evidence suggested that such a service *was* available to those with establishment connections or large amounts of money.

16.24 Obtaining evidence on these matters will obviously not be straightforward and the above discussion highlights the need to know the Home Office's position so that you can prepare properly. If the Home Office alleges that a document is a forgery or that the proper source has published false information, you ought to be permitted advance notice of the basis of that claim. The Home Office may advance both arguments in the alternative. But if the HOPO declines to advance *either* position, he cannot rationally dispute the reliability of the document.

16.25 HOPOs have occasionally – and bizarrely – refused to disclose the Home Office's position on a document. That is irresponsible as well as unfair. The Home Office is not only the opposing party to the appeal: it is the public authority responsible for granting asylum to refugees, and is obliged to assess fresh evidence for that purpose. It cannot simply decline to form a view upon the reliability of a document which purports to establish a significant element of the claim.

16.26 It is worth reminding the HOPO of the fundamental principles of fairness in an adversarial hearing, and of fact finding in this jurisdiction. It is obviously for the appellant to advance his appeal. But that does not mean that there is no burden upon the Home Office to explain its opposition to the appeal, to dispute evidence only where it has proper grounds to do so, and to explain what these grounds are. That would be the position even were the Home Office an ordinary litigant, quite apart from the special duties that attach to it as a public authority charged with discharging the UK's human rights obligations. The adjudicator's job is to reach a view on the evidence as a whole. But he must do so according to basic *Karanakaran* principles. He may not discard evidence when assessing risk unless he has no real doubt that it does not represent the truth. These principles apply to evidential disputes over documents as to any other evidential dispute.

16.27 There may be cases where other evidence before the adjudicator establishes beyond real doubt that the information contained in the document cannot represent the truth. It is not necessary in those circumstances for the adjudicator to make a specific finding on whether the document is forged or whether the proper source has given false information. However, he will normally have to assess the likelihood that one or other is the case in order to reach a safe conclusion as to whether the document can be relied upon.

16.28 In *Mungu*, the Court of Appeal considered *Tanveer Ahmed* and Latham LJ (with whom the other members of the Court agreed) stated:

> *I accept that where an apparently genuine document is said to be a forgery, there will inevitably and in practice be an evidential burden on the*

Secretary of State to undermine the authenticity of the document. That accords with the general approach any court or tribunal will adopt to the resolution of such a factual issue.

16.29 The appellant in **Tanveer Ahmed** did not submit any expert evidence to support the apparent reliability of the document. Similarly, in **Davila-Puga**, Laws LJ pointed out that:

This is not a case, as sometimes happens, where the documents are essentially self-proving or are positively demonstrated to be authentic by reference to material, including expert evidence, that is independent of the appellant himself.

16.30 One can understand that an adjudicator faced with assessing the authenticity of a foreign document will feel more comfortable if he has some expert assistance. The benefits to the appellant are illustrated by the IAT's decision in **Benaissa**:

The assessment of the validity and effect of foreign documents is, as we are aware from our own experience, a matter of the very gravest difficulty. We have confidence that the Adjudicator was doing his very best to reach a conclusion, fair to both parties, derived from the evidence before him and his own not inconsiderable experience. In our judgment, however, the Adjudicator's conclusions on the Appellant's age cannot be sustained on the basis of the evidence before him. We agree with Mr Cox's submissions that that evidence pointed wholly in one direction, which was that the documents adduced in support of the Appellant's case were genuine. It is true that the Adjudicator found the Appellant's oral evidence entirely unsatisfactory, but that factor does not of itself, we think, render the documents any more likely to be unreliable. The Adjudicator was presented with documents, accompanied by a report from an expert who, whilst admittedly not a document examiner, was a person who claimed to have, and, indeed, if we may say so, appears to have displayed, considerable knowledge of Algerian administrative and bureaucratic, as well as linguistic, practice. The Adjudicator, faced with documents which in our view were not obviously forged, and which were supported in such terms, should have been very slow to reject both the documents and the expert opinion.

Defending the document

16.31 Your aim should be to produce evidence independent of your client's testimony which supports the reliability of the document. If you can obtain such evidence then you should at least succeed in placing an evidential burden upon the Home Office to show why the document should nevertheless be dismissed (see *Mungu* above). You will also be in a stronger position to seek a direction that the Home Office either accepts evidence or particularises why it remains in dispute. Unless the Home Office has accepted that a document is genuine, it will be open to the adjudicator to reject the document for reasons of his own. However, unless the defect which he identifies is obvious, he will normally act unfairly if he does reject the document without raising his concerns. If a potential defect is obvious, you should deal with it in advance.

16.32 The document's reliability may be supported in three ways:

- by the means by which you obtained the document;
- by enquiries in the country of origin to verify the document;
- by expert evidence as to whether the document is authentic.

16.33 These are dealt with in turn below.

The means by which it was obtained

16.34 You should involve yourself as much as possible in obtaining documentary corroboration rather than leaving it to your client. The manner in which you have obtained a document may be the best evidence of its reliability. It may well rebut an allegation that the document was forged by your client or obtained by your client through bribery. The case will be further strengthened when the document was obtained through a local lawyer instructed by yourself. That should obviate the need which might otherwise arise to instruct a local lawyer to try to verify the document or provide an expert report on its authenticity. You must provide a full explanation of how the document was obtained, and ask any agent used by you to do the same.

Enquiries in the country of origin to verify the document

16.35 If the document was not obtained through a prima facie reliable source, you may wish to try to instruct a local lawyer or NGO to make enquiries to try to verify it, e.g. through local court records. But see para 16.8 as to the difficulties in instructing a local lawyer.

Expert evidence as to whether the document is authentic

16.36 If it is not practical or safe to seek to verify the document through local enquiries, you should make every effort to obtain expert evidence on its authenticity. The best source may still be a lawyer based in the country of origin, or else familiar with the type of documentation that your client has produced. Country experts, or human rights organisations active in the country of origin may be able to do a report. You may be able to find a suitable expert through the *ILPA Directory of Experts, the Law Society Directory of Experts*, and other such directories.

Lawyers in other fields may also know of experts in general document verification. Interpreters from the country of origin can sometimes assist with verification.

16.37 Where documentary evidence goes primarily to your client's contemporaneous state of mind, it may be relevant simply to show that the document would have appeared authentic to a person in your client's position so that it is understandable that she would have acted on it.

16.38 You should obviously seek evidence to support the document's reliability before disclosing it to either the Home Office or IAA.

16.39 The Home Office approach to assessing documents is inconsistent. Sometimes, a HOPO will apply for an adjournment, arguing that it would not be safe to rely on a document until the Home Office had had an opportunity to 'authenticate' it. On other occasions, HOPOs will claim that the Home Office is incapable of investigating the authenticity of a document. Where the Home Office does make investigations, these may include comparing the document with similar documents in the possession of the Home Office and making enquiries in the country of origin. Sometimes, it will claim to have insufficient resources to investigate the document. Indeed, it has in the past issued Operational Guidance to its caseworkers in respect of at least one country to the effect that documents should not be verified because the Foreign Office charges for this service.

16.40 Where you have evidence which at least supports the apparent reliability of a document, you have stronger grounds to press the Home Office to indicate its reasons for alleging that the document is unreliable. If the Home Office declines to do so, you may seek a direction for further details (para 9.9). If it is suggested that the Home Office is under no obligation to disclose its views on a document, refer to the discussion at paras 16.24 above.

16.41 Disclosure of the Home Office's case in advance obviously assists you in countering it. For example in one case, the Home Office disclosed that the reason why it had concluded that a warrant was a forgery was that it was completed by hand. An expert was able to state that it was unlikely that the magistrate who completed the warrant would have typed it. After six adjournments, all instigated by the Home Office, the appellant was successful (*Still no reason at all*).

16.42 You also need to know whether it is contended that the proper source has provided false information (whether deliberately or mistakenly). You should seek expert evidence on the plausibility of any suggestion that your client could have persuaded the proper source to falsify the information (if there is no apparent reason why the source would present false information of its own accord).

16.43 Often, the Home Office's case will amount to little more than 'you can't trust foreign documents' (despite the fact that at other times, it criticises claimants for failing to produce such documents). This line of reasoning has even been accepted by adjudicators. In *Singh (IAT)*, the adjudicator had stated that he placed no reliance upon the documentary corroboration because 'He had formed the opinion from his own experience of hearing appeals of this nature from the sub-continent over several years... that documentary evidence emanating from there was of little value'. The IAT unsurprisingly condemned this stance:

> *We regard that approach as quite wrong. The adjudicator should have considered the evidence and indicated, if he placed little reliance thereon, that he did so for some good reason and in the light of the evidence in this particular case.*

16.44 Sometimes, the Home Office case descends to levels of acute absurdity. In one refusal letter, the Home Office claimed that no weight could be given to the newspaper articles submitted by the claimant because he was aware that a number of fake newspaper articles had been submitted in other cases (though he offered no evidence of this fact). The newspaper articles in question were from *The Times*' website. Since the Home Office could readily check these articles on the website, the allegation was presumably that the proper source had been persuaded to impart false information. Unsurprisingly, the Home Office were unable to explain how the appellant would have bribed or otherwise influenced *The Times* and its case was rejected. Often, the greatest benefit in forcing the Home Office to disclose its case is to demonstrate its absurdity.

Originals and copies

16.45 The importance of trying to obtain the original document (in the sense of the physical piece of paper originally issued by the proper source) rather than a copy made by someone else will depend upon any challenge to the document's reliability. If it is alleged that the document is a forgery, then it will depend on the grounds. If, as in the above example, the challenge is that it is handwritten rather than typed, it will be immaterial whether the document is an original or a copy. On the other hand, if the allegation relates to the type of paper used, then it will obviously be material to examine the physical document which was originally issued. If it is not contended that the document is a forgery, and the allegation is instead that the proper source published false information, questions of originals and copies will be of no relevance.

16.46 In the following discussion, the term 'original' is used to refer to the physical document that you or your client received (which may be the physical document issued by the proper source, an official copy, or a copy made by someone else, e.g. a local lawyer).

16.47 If the original was submitted to the Home Office in support of the initial asylum application, the Home Office probably still has it. If the authenticity of the document has not been accepted in the refusal letter, you may well want the original back if you are going to have it examined by an expert. Your requests to the Home Office may well go unanswered.

16.48 In *Abadi*, the Home Office had retained the original of an arrest warrant which the IAT noted was 'an important part, if not the centrepiece of the appellant's case'. The appellant requested a legible copy in order to verify it. The Home Office provided only a partially legible copy and partial translation. It actually refused to return the original of the document. The IAT noted that:

> It is clear that, at latest at the time of hearing before the Special Adjudicator, the appellant had a right to inspect the document of which the respondent had produced a copy in his bundle, and had a right also to make copies of the original document.

16.49 It stated that the failure to comply with the appellant's request for a fully legible copy and translation, together with the failure to make the original available to the Adjudicator represented a 'clear procedural irregularity, which... casts a shadow on the proceedings before the adjudicator'. It directed that:

> the respondent supply to the appellant forthwith a legible copy of the document... together with a full translation of that document and that the original document be available at any further proceedings in respect of this appeal.

16.50 In that case, the appellant had only required a legible copy in order to obtain evidence as to authenticity. If your expert wants to see the original, the Home Office ought to return it. If it fails to do so, you should request a direction from the IAA that it either confirm that it accepts the authenticity of the document or else returns the original to you.

Procedure

16.51 If you have obtained a document well before the hearing and are going to rely on it, it is worth sending a copy to the Home Office as soon as possible, together with a letter indicating that the original can be provided if necessary. The likelihood is that nobody at the Home Office will look at the document until the HOPO prepares the appeal (assuming it even gets to the HOPO). However, by submitting it as soon as possible, you pre-empt any argument from the HOPO that the time following service of your trial bundle was insufficient for the Home Office to assess the document and take a view.

16.52 The original should be available to the adjudicator who hears the appeal. Some representatives put the original into the bundle that goes to the Home Office (if it has not already been submitted). It is better not to send the original to the Home Office unless it specifically requests it. The Home Office may lose it. Or it may not be represented at the hearing. In either case, it will be unavailable to the adjudicator. The better course is to send a covering letter to the HOPO indicating that the original can be provided if he needs it in order to pursue his investigations. Consequently, the adjudicator's bundle should also contain a copy, rather than the original, with a covering letter indicating that the original will be made available at the hearing if the HOPO has not requested it in advance. Ensure there is a certified translation.

16.53 Always submit evidence as to how the document was obtained. If your client obtained it, she should explain how she did so in her witness statement. If you obtained it, you should prepare a witness statement explaining how it was done.

16.54 Make every effort to submit such documents at least in compliance with the standard directions. If you serve it within a week of the hearing, the HOPO may argue that it should either be excluded or that the Home Office should have an adjournment in order to assess the document. Contact the Home Office as soon as you have served the document to check that it has been received by the HOPO who will consider it. If you are informed that no HOPO has been allocated or the HOPO tells you that he has not yet started preparing the case, the HOPO will be in difficulty if he contends at the hearing that his lack of time to assess the document is your fault.

16.55 While you will resist any refusal to admit material documents, particularly if late submission was not your client's fault, it may be more difficult to resist an adjournment. If the Home Office does obtain an adjournment in order to assess a document, seek a direction that it notify you in advance of the next hearing if it disputes the reliability of the document, and if so on what grounds. If it raises alleged defects in the document only at the next hearing, that may necessitate a further adjournment. You would normally object where you have submitted the document in good time, and only at the hearing does the Home Office raise a challenge to the document which it could have raised earlier. At the very least, you should then be entitled to an adjournment in order to rebut the challenge. If you have asked the Home Office to provide objections in advance (and still more so if you have obtained a direction), you will be in a better position to argue that the adjudicator should not permit the late allegation.

16.56 Where the Home Office fails to disclose the evidence upon which it relies to dispute the document, it is of course open to you to apply for a witness summons in respect of the person who has made an allegation of forgery. This could require that he produce all evidence upon which he has relied. But see the s.108 procedure at para 16.61 below. Also, as indicated in chapter 9, if the Home Office has not presented its case properly, you should not necessarily try to force them to do so. It will often be sufficient and preferable to point out that the Home Office has provided no evidence whatsoever to support its allegations.

16.57 The HOPO may cross-examine your client about how a document was obtained and invite the adjudicator to draw adverse inferences from the answer. If the way in which the document was obtained could potentially be thought inconsistent with other parts of your case, you should address this in the witness statement. If the document was obtained by bribery, the HOPO will suggest that you cannot trust it because it was not obtained through normal channels. On the other hand, if it was obtained through normal channels, the HOPO will claim that normal channels would not have been available if the appellant was really wanted by the authorities. You can point out that this is one of the Home Office's 'damned if you do, damned if you don't' tactics.

16.58 If the HOPO pursues your client about how you or some other third party obtained a document, you should object that these are not questions that your client can address, and point the HOPO to the information which should be in your bundle.

Demonstrating that a document is false

16.59 It is another irony that on the one hand, documents relied upon by the appellant are regularly met with a bald allegation from the Home Office that you cannot trust documents from that country. However, if the foreign document is convenient to the Home Office, it will disparage any suggestion that it could either be forged or contain incorrect information.

16.60 The most common example is where your client used false travel documents of another country in order to reach the UK. If that country is one to which the Home Office thinks it can expel your client more easily, it will often refuse to accept that the document is unreliable as evidence of your client's nationality. In those circumstances, you may need to obtain an expert report to indicate that the document is unreliable. It should be sufficient to show a real doubt that the disputed travel document establishes the appellant's nationality.

Exclusion of the appellant where forgery is alleged

16.61 Section 108 of the 2002 Act states:

> Forged document: proceedings in private
>
> (1) This section applies where it is alleged –
>
> (a) that a document relied on by a party to an appeal under section 82, 83 or 101 is a forgery, and
> (b) that disclosure to that party of a matter relating to the detection of the forgery would be contrary to the public interest.
>
> (2) The adjudicator or the Immigration Appeal Tribunal –
>
> (a) must investigate the allegation in private, and
> (b) may proceed in private so far as necessary to prevent disclosure of the matter referred to in subsection (1)(b).

16.62 The predecessor to this section (para 6 of sch 4 of the 1999 Act) applied this procedure only to travel documents, visas, certificates of entitlement, and work permits.

16.63 The new provision is not so limited and could be applied to documents such as arrest warrants. The Explanatory Notes to the 2002 Act confirm that:

> the class of document which may be relevant has been extended since many types of document may be submitted in evidence and these may rely on sophisticated technologies. The security features, ways of forging or defeating them and forgery detection methods should not normally be divulged to the public. (para 268)

16.64 But s.108 *should not* automatically preclude disclosure of 'a matter relating to the detection of the forgery' simply because the Home Office claims that disclosure would not be in the public interest. The adjudicator should decide for himself whether the allegation that disclosure would be contrary to the public interest is made out. S.108(2)(b) per-

mits proceeding in private only 'so far as necessary' to prevent disclosure of a matter that would be contrary to the public interest.

16.65 The public interest itself must involve a balancing act between any
detriment that the Home Office is able to establish would flow from
disclosure, as compared with the obvious public interest in appeals
being conducted according to the highest standards of fairness.
Furthermore, s.108(2)(b) gives the adjudicator a discretion to proceed
in private, whereas the predecessor provision in the 1999 Act was
mandatory. A discretion must be exercised with regard to all relevant
factors, and the risk of unfairness through adopting this procedure
ought to be one of those factors.

16.66 The adjudicator must consider the Home Office's submissions on that
point in the absence of the appellant. But that does not mean that he
should not consider the appellant's submissions. The adjudicator
ought to entertain submissions from the appellant as to the importance of the document to the appellant's case and the prejudice resulting from exclusion.

16.67 If the adjudicator decides that disclosure would be contrary to the public interest then he must allow the Home Office to present its evidence
on forgery in the absence of the appellant. But once again, that does
not mean that he cannot entertain evidence from the appellant on forgery, or that he decide the issue as soon as he has heard the Home
Office's evidence.

16.68 In practice of course, the ability of the appellant to make submissions
both on the public interest and the authenticity of the document is
greatly impaired where he is not permitted to know the nature of the
case against him.

16.69 The provision applies only where the Home Office claims forgery. It
cannot rely on it where it is submitting evidence to the effect that a
travel document is genuine (see para 16.59 above).

16 Documentary corroboration
Key points

■ An adjudicator is not entitled to dismiss an appeal simply through lack of corroboration, but if credibility is in issue, obtaining corroboration may be crucial to its success.

■ If apparently available corroboration is not produced, then absent a good explanation, the adjudicator may draw an adverse inference.

■ Sources of documentary corroboration may include

☐ any local lawyer who represented your client,
☐ a local lawyer instructed by you (but take care to find one who is genuinely independent of the state),
☐ a country expert,
☐ the archives of news organisations,
☐ friends and relatives (but only if you cannot obtain the document through other means).

■ Where the reliability of a document is disputed, it should be assessed according to ordinary *Karanakaran* principles. Credibility should not be determined as a distinct and prior exercise to the evaluation of the documentary corroboration.

■ A document may be unreliable on two grounds: firstly, that it is forged and secondly, that it is issued by the proper source but contains information that is untrue.

■ Evidence supporting the reliability of a document may come from

☐ the means by which it was obtained (which should always be by yourself rather than your client where possible),
☐ enquiries in the country of origin to verify the document,
☐ expert evidence.

■ If you can establish the apparent reliability of a document, there will inevitably be an evidential burden on the Home Office to undermine its authenticity.

■ Argue strongly that you are entitled to disclosure of the Home Office's grounds for challenging the document's reliability.

■ The significance of whether you can obtain the physical document produced by its source will depend upon the grounds on which its reliability is disputed.

 ☐ The physical document that you received should be available for examination by the adjudicator.

 ☐ Do not send it to the Home Office unless specifically requested to do so: but provide it with a copy as soon as possible.

 ☐ If the original is already with the Home Office, you may need a direction that it produces it.

■ Always ensure that there is evidence of how the document was obtained and that this does not appear inconsistent with any element of your client's case.

■ It may be necessary to demonstrate that a document is *unreliable* if the Home Office relies on a false travel document to dispute nationality.

■ There is statutory provision for the adjudicator to proceed with the hearing in private where the Home office alleges a document is forged and that disclosure of its evidence would be contrary to the public interest. Urge the adjudicator to take account of the unfairness of this procedure when deciding whether to accede to the request.

17 Home Office evidence on the country of origin

Reports authored by the Home Office

17.1 The refusal letter will make many claims about country conditions, nearly always unsourced and unsupported. The IAT held in *Lakew* that:

> [I]f the Secretary of State makes assertions as to the circumstances of a particular country little if any weight can be given without evidence to support those assertions.

17.2 In most appeals, the Home Office now submits its 'Country Assessment'. These are documents prepared by the Home Office on the major refugee producing countries. They set out its views of that country, dealing in particular with common issues relating to asylum and human rights claims. It also produces shorter notes, known as Operational Guidance Notes (OGNs) or Bulletins.

17.3 These Home Office documents will offer a useful summary of its view, particularly given the difficulties involved in seeking any advance clarification from the Home Office about the issues in dispute. HOPOs have been known to make fairly far-fetched submissions about conditions in the country of origin. To serve evidence to anticipate every point which might be taken by a HOPO would require the sort of voluminous bundle that adjudicators are keen to avoid.

17.4 The Home Office reports vary in quality, some being less partial than others. But as they are subjected to a degree of public scrutiny, they are liable to be more even-handed than the HOPO's submissions. They can be used to identify points about the country of origin (like the prevalence of torture) which are accepted by the Home Office. It may therefore be possible to undermine the HOPO's submission simply by pointing out that it is not supported by his own evidence. You may even be able to contradict the claims in the refusal letter on the basis of the Home Office's reports.

17.5 The problems arise when the HOPO attempts to use the Home Office's own material to prove his case. As indicated above, little weight should be given to an unsubstantiated allegation by the Home Office. The HOPO may assert that the Country Assessment is 'sourced'. By this, he means that it includes references to various reports which it claims support the assertions in the Country Assessment. He will say that the assertion should be accepted because it is supported by the listed independent evidence. Yet he will not produce the independent documents as evidence but will simply invite everyone to accept the Home Office's paraphrasing of what they say.

17.6 If the appellant made various claims about the contents of independent reports – and then suggested that there was now no need to put these reports in evidence – she could expect vociferous objection from the HOPO. Unsurprisingly, he will not accept that what's sauce for the goose is sauce for the gander.

17.7 An appellant's prospects would be even worse if she produced a submission which did not even identify which report was said to support which assertion. Yet that is often the case with the Country Assessment. Each paragraph will conclude with a list of sources which are claimed to support the various assertions therein – but with no indication of which source supports which assertion. Some assertions may be uncontroversial, some highly controversial. The list of sources may include obviously reputable organisations, along with far more dubious sources. Not infrequently, you will find that the most controversial assertions are supported by the least reputable sources.

17.8 Or at least you would if the HOPO were prepared to tell the Court which organisation is alleged to support the particular assertion on which he relies. Often, the HOPO will not do so. Sometimes, your query will elicit the disturbing response that the HOPO does not know which of the listed sources supports the assertion. Plainly, little weight should then be attached to his submission.

17.9 The sources listed in the Country Assessments vary widely in reliability, independence, and accessibility. No-one would object on these counts to Amnesty International reports. Many might object to particular newspapers from the country of origin, especially in countries where the regime interferes with press freedom. Not infrequently, the source will simply be a letter to the Home Office from the Foreign Office.

17.10 These letters are often the basis for the most curious of Home Office claims. In 2000 and even into 2001, the Home Office were relying on a 'Bulletin' on Zimbabwe which asserted that:

> The F&CO comments that while there have been instances of ruling ZANU(PF) supporters harassing members of other political parties there

is no evidence of State-sponsored persecution of members or supporters of opposition parties.

17.11 The Home Office was not discouraged in maintaining this stance by the fact that Amnesty International had by 2000 found 'state sponsored terror' against the opposition or even by what it could read in the newspaper (e.g. 'Mugabe's terror squads "driven round by army"', *Daily Telegraph*, 31 May 2000; 'A campaign of terror… is being mounted with the specific approval of Robert Mugabe, Zimbabwe's president, against opponents of his regime', *Sunday Times*, 21 May 2000). The source for the Home Office's claims about the FCO's stance was actually a letter written by it in 1999.

17.12 Even if the letter from the Foreign Office turns out to be recent, it will often be unilluminating in terms of the sources and methodology by which it reached its view. The Court of Appeal has illustrated the dangers in a tribunal accepting claims from the Foreign Office which are not properly sourced. In **Drrias**, the IAT had described the British Embassy in Sudan as 'a wholly independent body' which would not make a claim 'unless it had very good reason'. On examination, the Court of Appeal found that the IAT had erred in being so impressed by the Embassy's methods, and concluded that the Embassy's information was actually 'of very little weight or worth'. In **Murugiath**, the IAT commented that:

> *The telex from the British High Commission in Colombo is… , we note, an avowedly partisan document, written from the point of view of the British Government, not that of an outside observer.*

17.13 The IAT has on occasion challenged the partiality of particular reports because they were produced by campaigning organisations or by lawyers who represent asylum seekers. The Home Office reports do not even come from its lawyers but from the respondent himself. They are produced by his own caseworkers, not by independent country experts. The caseworkers do not have the specialist expertise to investigate and report on countries of origin which is required of the staff of the Canadian independent documentation centre (DIRB) or any reputable human rights monitoring organisation. Most have graduated from deciding individual asylum claims and have never visited the country in question (though see para 17.22 below). If there is a conflict between an independent expert and the author of a Home Office report, it may well be appropriate to remind the adjudicator not simply that only one is independent (and carrying corresponding duties to the Court), but that only one is an expert.

17.14 If the Home Office claims that there is independent evidence that contradicts the independent evidence advanced by the appellant, then it should produce it, rather than purporting to paraphrase it. In fact, even the Home Office accepts that its Country Assessments are no substitute for consideration of the independent evidence. The introduction to each Country Assessment states that:

> It is intended to be used by caseworkers as a signpost to the source material, which has been made available to them.

17.15 According to the Home Office, this meets concerns raised by NGOs that caseworkers would otherwise use the Country Assessment as a substitute for consideration of the independent evidence. Its APIs similarly state that:

> Caseworkers have access to the source material cited in the text of the country assessments and should refer to this material for more detail about events or human rights abuses. CIPU retains copies of all the original source material referred to in the assessments.

Pre-hearing preparation

17.16 Home Office reports, including Country Assessments, OGNs, and Bulletins are available on the its website. The standard directions require the Home Office (like the appellant) to serve material seven days in advance. However, it often seeks to serve its reports at the hearing. As discussed above, you may anyway wish to make use of Home Office material in order to narrow the issues in dispute. You should therefore consider them in advance.

17.17 The problems in identifying the sources for particular assertions are described above. It could be that the most damaging allegation in the paragraph of a Country Assessment is supported by UNHCR – in which case you must treat it seriously – or an unknown publication in the country of origin – which will carry much less weight. You may consider seeking a direction for particulars so as to require the Home Office to identify the source of a damaging assertion, particularly if you think it unlikely that the statement came from any reputable source listed in the Assessment.

17.18 If you are able to review the source material, you may find that it is not consistent with the representation of it by the Home Office. One would hope that arises through inadvertence rather than design (although it highlights the importance of independent scrutiny of the evidence by adjudicators, rather than taking the Home Office's word for it). The more authoritative documents, such as Amnesty International reports, are usually available from the Internet. The less reliable material such as obscure publications or letters from the FCO is not. Its APIs state that the Country Assessments are 'entirely based on disclosable source material' and NGOs were promised (via the Home Office's Consultative Group on an Independent Documentation Centre) that this material would be made available.

17.19 If the source document is not accessible, you may therefore ask the Home Office for a copy of it. If the Home Office declines (or does not respond), it is open to you to seek a direction or a witness summons against the author of the Country Assessment (para 9.36). You might do so if you have reason to believe that the document will assist your case or that the Home Office may have misrepresented it.

17.20 However, there is no need for you to seek a direction or a witness summons simply because the source for an assertion is not readily identifiable, accessible or of obvious reliability. As discussed at chapter 9, it is not your job to prepare the Home Office's appeal, and this includes obtaining the evidence that it ought to have produced. The better course will often be to point out that the Home Office has not submitted the evidence, and argue that no weight can be placed on the Home Office's assertion in the absence of that evidence.

17.21 As indicated above, the OGNs usually make no attempt to source their assertions. The introduction to these notes states that they should be read in conjunction with the Country Assessment and the source material. Given the Home Office's assurances that the Country Assessments *themselves* are used as signposts to the source material, it is unclear what purpose the OGNs serve (once you exclude the suspicion that they are for caseworkers who cannot grasp the full Country Assessments). They are primarily for internal consumption and HOPOs do not usually produce them at appeal. However, it is worth checking whether there is an OGN on your country as occasionally, it paints a less rosy picture than the Country Assessment.

17.22 While it remains the case that most authors of the Country Assessments have never been to the country on which they are commenting, the Home Office has recently initiated country visits to major refugee producing countries. The first two countries to benefit from these visits were Turkey and Sri Lanka. The resulting reports appeared to lack any coherent methodology. They rely heavily on governmental sources, and non-governmental sources are not identified. But on some issues, again, the information is not entirely consistent with the line taken by the relevant Home Office Country Assessment.

Other documentary evidence

17.23 Where there is no Country Assessment on the country of origin, it is more common for the HOPO to produce a bundle of country evidence. These bundles seldom include Amnesty or Human Rights Watch reports. They are more likely to contain reports from national governments, including the relevant US State Department report (if the report contains any indication that the human rights situation is improving). Increasing co-operation amongst EU immigration authorities means that you are more likely to see their reports cited by the Home Office.

17.24 Many of the latter reports appear to carry no more weight, or tally no better with the independent evidence, than similar assertions made directly by the Home Office. Indeed, these Home Office assertions are apparently being quoted as 'objective evidence' by other EU immigration authorities. It will sometimes be necessary to point out that an unsupported assertion from one state's immigration authorities does not acquire an independent status simply because it is swapped around between other national immigration authorities. In *Chinder Singh*, the IAT expressed concern about the partiality of employees of the Canadian authorities, including its immigration service, who had commented on the country of origin. It said it would be 'circumspect' about accepting their evidence.

17.25 The US State Department reports are often more even-handed than those issued by EU authorities. But they are far from immune to the general objection to reports emanating from national governments that unlike independent human rights monitoring organisations, comment may be skewed by national (or government) interests. According to the US Lawyers Committee for Human Rights, these reports had been growing in accuracy and objectivity until 11 September 2001. But it reported to Congress on 30 April 2003 that the 'war on terror' had led to 'serious omissions and distortions', and 'many of these can be directly tied to a calculus of political expedience'. Indeed it was reported that the 2001 series of reports were delayed into March 2002, because the US Secretary of State had intervened personally 'amid some evidence of censorship – or at least soft-soaping – involving countries whose support is needed in the fight against terrorism' (*Guardian*, 5 March 2002). Similar concern has been expressed by US courts:

> [T]here is perennial concern that the (State) Department softpedals human rights violations by countries that the United States wants to have good relations with. (*Gramatikov*)

17.26 Unsurprisingly, the IAT has stated that if feels 'more comfortable' with the 'well-documented and sourced reports of NGOs (Amnesty and Human Rights Watch)' than the US State Department reports (*Mario*).

Home Office compliance with directions

17.27 The standard directions issued with the notice of hearing require the Home Office, like the appellant, to submit any documentation seven days in advance of the full hearing. Despite this, the HOPO often attempts to serve his material on the day of the hearing rather than in accordance with directions. There is a perception that some adjudicators appear more lenient towards this practice than to the non-compliance by the appellant.

17.28 Whether you object will depend upon how familiar you are with the Home Office's material and the extent to which it appears relevant and therefore needs to be addressed. If you have not seen it before, you will, at the very least, want an opportunity to read it before the appeal starts. In *Macharia*, the Court of Appeal was unimpressed by the argument that the fact that the material was in the public domain meant that it could be produced at the hearing without the appellant having an adequate opportunity to consider it.

17.29 If you are prejudiced by the late submission of documents with which you are not familiar and the HOPO can offer no satisfactory excuse, you may ask for the documents to be excluded. If that is refused, you should normally be entitled to an adjournment to consider the documents and whether you need to respond to them (see *Macharia*). If you have submitted your documentary evidence in good time rather than on the day of the hearing, your position will be strengthened.

17.30 The requirement in the standard directions to produce a schedule of essential passages from the bundle applies to the Home Office as well as appellants. The Home Office often fails to comply: where it does, the list is likely to be selective. Indeed, you can sometimes use other parts of its own bundle to rebut these passages. For example, the Home Office might refer to a report having stated that the Government has set up a commission of enquiry into torture or to government ministers having condemned human rights abuses as unacceptable. However, the same report might state that torture of detainees remains common.

17 Home Office evidence on the country of origin
Key points

- Unsupported claims by the Home Office about conditions in a particular country should be given little if any weight.

- The Home Office produces 'Country Assessments' and other documents on major refugee producing countries. These are useful in two respects:

  - ☐ Such documents provide a useful guide to the Home Office position, particularly when it cannot otherwise be persuaded to clarify its case in advance.
  - ☐ Where points are accepted in the Home Office Assessment, it can be used to undermine inconsistent submissions by the HOPO or even in the refusal letter.

- On the other hand, the Country Assessments are an inappropriate means of establishing disputed points.

  - ☐ The claimed sources vary considerably in terms of their independence and reliability. The most controversial claims often come from the most problematic sources.
  - ☐ The citations are such that it is often unclear which source is said to support which assertion (and the HOPO may be unable to offer clarification).

- The HOPO often asks the adjudicator to accept Home Office claims about what an independent source has reported without putting that report in evidence. That would be entirely unacceptable from an appellant, and will normally merit a strong objection.

- If the source material can be reviewed, you may find that it has not been accurately paraphrased in the Country Assessment.

- You may request, or alternatively seek a direction that the Home Office disclose source material which is not readily available.

- Other country evidence submitted by the Home Office is more likely to consist of material from national governments and immigration authorities, rather than independent human rights organisations.

- The Home Office seldom complies with the Standard Directions when submitting country material. If you are unfamiliar with the material and there is potential for prejudice, request either that the material be excluded or the hearing be adjourned.

18 Country information

Relevance

18.1 'Country information' is used here to refer to evidence about country conditions excluding expert evidence (section 4) and documentary corroboration (see chapter 16).

18.2 The importance of country information to the evaluation of present risk is obvious. But it is also critical to determining disputes over credibility. In *Ahmed*, David Pannick QC held that an adjudicator 'erred in principle' when she reached a conclusion on credibility in isolation from any conclusions as to relevant country conditions.

18.3 That also reflects the consistent caselaw of the IAT. In *Jeyakumar*, it noted that:

> In *Horvath*, the Tribunal reminded Special Adjudicators that the probative value of an asylum seeker's evidence must be evaluated in the light of what is known about the conditions in the country of origin. If a Special Adjudicator fails to relate an appellant's story to the background evidence on the appellant's country, he has necessarily applied the wrong approach in the case.

18.4 That applies regardless of (indeed, especially where) the adjudicator claims not to have believed a word the appellant said. In *Kavuma*, the IAT considered a finding by an adjudicator that 'The appellant's claim is so lacking in credibility that it is not incumbent upon me to consider the objective situation...' The following important passage from *Kavuma* is worth quoting at length:

> 22 ... The Special Adjudicator might have intended to say, but did not say, that after a detailed and anxious scrutiny of **all** the evidence in the appeal she had been drawn to the clear conclusion that she did not believe anything the appellant said that was material to the question of whether he has a well-founded fear of persecution for a Convention reason. He had not made out his case because she did not believe him. We emphasise 'all' the evidence, which should have included the objective country evidence.

23. There may be a very limited number of special circumstances in which the objective country evidence is of no relevance. For example, this might arise if the appellant was found not to be a citizen of and had not lived in the country where he claimed to fear persecution. However, in the vast majority of cases, the objective country evidence will not be totally irrelevant. This is such a case...

24. Passages in the judgments of Lord Justice Brooke and Lord Justice Sedley (in **Karanakaran**)... support this view;...

26. Lord Justice Sedley said, at page 30, 'The issues for a decision-maker under the Convention (whether the decision-maker is a Home Office official, a special adjudicator or the Immigration Appeal Tribunal) are questions not of hard fact but of evaluation: does the applicant have a well-founded fear of persecution for a Convention reason? Is that why he is here? If so, is he nevertheless able to find safety elsewhere in his home country? Into all of these, of course, a mass of factual questions enters: what has happened to the applicant? **What happens to others like him or her? Is the situation the same as when he or she fled?** Are there safer parts of the country? Is it feasible for the applicant to live there? Inseparable from these are questions of evaluation: did what happened to the applicant amount to persecution? If so, what was the reason for it? **Does what has been happening to others shed light on the applicant's fear? Is the home situation now better or worse?** How safe are the safer places? Is it unduly harsh to expect this applicant to survive in a new and strange place?' The emphasis is ours.

27. There are valid and important reasons which could have led to the conclusion that the Special Adjudicator did not believe anything the appellant said that was material to the question of whether he has a well-founded fear of persecution for a Convention reason. However, the Special Adjudicator should have looked at and made an assessment of the objective country information. Had she done so she might have concluded that what the appellant claimed had happened to him was not reasonably likely to happen in Uganda. She might have concluded that such events were reasonably likely to happen in Uganda but that, nevertheless, the appellant's credibility was so damaged that she did not believe anything he was saying which was relevant to his claim for asylum. It was not open to her to disregard the objective country information. The failure to do so makes the determination fatally flawed.

18.5 Researching and presenting the right country information is therefore one of the most important elements in the preparation of most appeals.

18.6   Adjudicators are often critical of the volume of country information which they receive in support of an appeal. But it is not volume in itself which is objectionable. In **Turgut**, the Court of Appeal remarked upon the heavy burden of considering over 1500 pages of material placed before it on the risk to expelled Turkish Kurdish asylum seekers. It heard two days of oral argument largely addressed to that documentary evidence. But it did not dispute the necessity of shouldering this heavy burden.

18.7   What *is* objectionable is irrelevant country information. You should not create a 'generic' country bundle containing every human rights report you can find on a particular country and simply add to it whenever a new country report appears. An adjudicator will be justifiably annoyed to be presented with a 'generic bundle' of several hundred pages, the relevance of which the advocate is unable to explain except as 'general background'. It may well be useful for an adjudicator (like a representative) to read a report in order to get an overview of a country with which he is unfamiliar. But he is unlikely to need (or be prepared) to read several hundred pages for that purpose.

18.8   That does not mean that a small country bundle will be appropriate in every case. Omitting relevant material is worse than including irrelevant material. In some cases, there is a large amount of relevant material on disputed issues which needs to be before the court. But the larger the bundle, the more likely an adjudicator will be to query it, so the more rigorous you need to be in satisfying yourself as to its relevance. Do not add anything to a country bundle without asking yourself what it adds to your case. In what circumstances will you need to rely on it? What is its purpose in this bundle?

18.9   An obvious first step would be to contact the Home Office to agree in advance what points about the country are in dispute, so that the country information can be limited to these issues (and perhaps its contents agreed). But the disinclination of the Home Office to engage in discussion more than a day before the hearing generally renders this impractical.

18.10   Some guidance as to the Home Office's position can be obtained from the country information which it produces, e.g. the Country Assessments and Operational Guidance Notes (chapter 17). If a Home Office report accepts that torture in detention is routine, there is no need to produce reports *solely* to establish this point. It may still, however, be necessary to produce the same report in order to identify who is at risk of detention.

18.11   If an issue is in dispute, you need not restrict yourself to one report supporting your argument. It will often be helpful to show that a number of reliable reports support your contention, in order to contrast that with the scant support for the Home Office position.

18.12 You may be advancing a number of alternative arguments to allow for whatever credibility finding the adjudicator makes. For example, you may not need much material to establish present risk on the basis of your client's past persecution (if that is accepted), but a great deal more material to show that she would also be at risk simply because of her ethnicity. If credibility is in issue, it all has to be before the adjudicator. But use your skeleton argument to explain why it is there.

18.13 You will often be relying on country information to show that your client's account of past ill-treatment is consistent with contemporaneous country conditions and so should be accepted. That may involve submitting older material from the period in which the events your client recounts occurred, even if the position has changed since.

Researching country information

18.14 The GCC, para 12.2, states:

Immigration Asylum: Country of origin material

You are required to maintain and utilise a generic pack of current material in relation to the country of origin of any client or clients on behalf of whom you are providing Controlled Work relating to their asylum application.

1. *Many offices deal with asylum applications on behalf of a number of applicants from the same country of origin. Being aware of the background in the country in question will be an important part of advising the client, presenting their case to the Home Office and advising on the prospects of success of any appeal. However much of this work will be generic for the group and will not need to be duplicated in relation to any individual applicants. The packs should contain information on matters such as the current political situation, government practices and any relevant Immigration Appeal Tribunal determinations in relation to the country of origin of the client.*

2. *The packs should contain information on matters such as the current political situation, government practices and any relevant IAT determinations in relation to the country of origin of the client.*

3. *For the avoidance of doubt, nothing in this rule is intended to prevent you from carrying out necessary or urgent work on behalf of a client from a country in relation to which you do not yet have a pack,*

although you would be expected to create a pack in due course as part of presenting the client's case to the Home Office. To some degree, the more clients you have from a particular country of origin, the more information would be expected to be contained in the pack. Thus, if you have only one or two clients from a particular country, the information contained in the pack could be confined to that relevant to their particular applications, with more information being added as more clients were acquired.

4. *We are currently looking into arrangements to provide the materials for generic packs to practitioners. However, until such arrangements are in place, one way to comply with the Rule would be for you to join the Refugee Legal Centre subscription service. Otherwise you should compile the pack using relevant information from such sources as the Electronic Immigration Network, US State Department, Amnesty, the Home Office, Human Rights Watch and UNHCR's ref world database.*

5. *Time spent compiling the pack cannot be claimed as Contract Work. However, any time reasonably spent considering its relevance to the particular case and/or updating it for the purposes of that case can be claimed.*

18.15 This pack may be the starting point for your research. But it should not be the endpoint. For the reasons set out above, you should resist the urge to simply photocopy this 'pack' for each appeal.

18.16 There are now a number of electronic resources which make it far easier to conduct effective research and to tailor the information you present to the issues that arise in the individual appeal.

CD-ROM based subscription services

18.17 The RLC's subscription service (to which the GCC refers) produces a CD-ROM containing the contents of the RLC's country information and legal intranet. You will find not only internet based reports but also scanned press, academic and expert reports. It also produces paper packs on countries of origin.

18.18 The Immigration Consortium Country Information Database (ICCID) produces a CD-ROM containing country reports in word format (facilitating the incorporation of quotations into your skeleton arguments). It also contains a powerful search facility and 'bundle maker' software to compile a bundle electronically for a particular appeal. Details are available via the EIN (see below).

18.19 UNHCR's Refworld 2003 is a four CD-ROM collection ranging from background country reports to legal position papers and guidelines (although the country information is also available on its website).

Web based resources

18.20 The EIN has a comprehensive collection of links to country information sites from around the world (www.ein.org.uk). It also has a large database of country reports on its own site (in association with ICCID) and members can download its bundlemaker software.

18.21 The European Country of Origin Information Network (ecoi.net) also brings together a wealth of reports, as does asylumlaw.org.

18.22 The country information section from UNHCR's Refworld database is available on its website at www.unhcr.ch/research/cio.

18.23 Check routinely for the latest material from major international human rights NGOs such as Amnesty International (www.amnesty.org) and Human Rights Watch (www.hrw.org). Some, including Amnesty, have an email service to which you can subscribe to receive press releases. The International Crisis Group (www.crisisweb.org) and Freedom House (www.freedom.org) often have useful information. Some NGOs specialise on specific countries, ethnic groups or issues, e.g. the Kurdish Human Rights Project (www.khrp.org) or the International Lesbian and Gay Human Rights Commission (www.ilghrc.org).

18.24 The Canadian independent documentation centre is well respected by adjudicators (DIRB: the Documentation, Information and Research Branch of the Immigration and Refugee Board, www.irb.gc.ca). Of reports produced by governments, the best known are the annual reports of the US State Department (www.state.gov/g/drl/hr/). You should also check the Home Office's own reports, though for a different purpose (see chapter 17). The reports of any national government should be treated with caution in light of the risk of distortion where accurate assessment is inconsistent with its national interests (para 17.25).

18.25 There is no substitute for searching the Internet yourself for the most recent information, particularly where country conditions are unstable.

18.26 Recent reports from reliable news media are often a good and graphic way of providing information on present dangers. They sometimes have more impact than the standard human rights reports which adjudicators are more used to seeing. They demonstrate the concern felt in the wider community about events. The information is direct and easily digestible.

18.27 News reports are, of course, essential where the situation is changing rapidly. Parties are under a particular duty in such circumstances to provide up to date information 'if necessary by reference to developments taking place the day prior to the hearing' (**Yasotharan**). They can be vital to rebut Home Office claims that conditions have improved recently – particularly where they post-date the material relied upon by the Home Office.

18.28 Always check for any very recent news reports on the country of origin. You can also do more focused searches, for example by an ethnic group or the name of an organisation, or individual. Where matters like the existence or nature of an organisation are in issue and it is not mentioned in the main country reports, finding such news reports can be invaluable.

18.29 The best and most authoritative site is that of the BBC (news.bbc.co. uk). This has an effective search engine. Other useful media sites include CNN's (www.cnn.com). Several UK broadsheet newspapers have comprehensive sites including the *Guardian* (www.guardian.co.uk), *The Times* (www.thetimes.co.uk), and the *Daily Telegraph* (www.telegraph. co.uk). Foreign newspapers sites like the *New York Times* (www. nytimes.com) are similarly valuable. Do not overlook web only resources such as Institute for War and Peace Reporting (www.iwpr. net). Some news websites also have an email alert service which can be tailored to provide news on a specific topic.

18.30 News organisations in the country of origin or nearby countries can offer information not picked up by western news sites (though plainly, their value depends upon affiliation and press censorship). Paperboy (www.thepaperboy.com) offers a superb portal for newspapers around the world. If the relevant newspapers are not available in English, you should arrange for someone (e.g. an expert or one of your interpreters) to monitor them or search for specific information.

18.31 Previously, nearly all major news resources on the internet were free to use. There is now a general move towards charging for content, particularly archive content (for example, *The Times* and Paperboy now charge for some services.) Depending on the requirements of the case, the charges may be justifiable as disbursements for the purposes of public funding.

18.32 You can also try one of the web's general search engines, of which the best is Google (www.google.com). This is most effective if you can search by name, e.g. for information on a particular organisation or individual or a particular event. You will often find the website of the organisation with which your client is involved, as well as more obscure reports and articles about it. This may well assist in establishing its nature and activities. If the site is in a foreign language, you will have to engage someone to translate it. (Facilities on search engines which purport to translate pages seldom produce anything comprehensible.)

18 Country information
Key points

- Country information is important not only to the assessment of present risk, but also to resolving disputes about past facts.

- An adjudicator's determination will be fatally flawed where he reaches credibility findings in isolation from his conclusions as to contemporaneous country conditions (or where he fails to evaluate the country conditions at all).

- The volume of country information required depends entirely on the issues that arise in the appeal. But the larger the volume of information, the more rigorous you should be in ensuring its relevance.

- Do not submit a 'generic bundle' for every appeal from a particular country of origin. Modern electronic research methods enable the country bundle to be tailored to each case.

- A large number of CD-ROM and web-based resources are now available to assist with country research.

- There is no substitute for searching the Internet yourself for the most recent news reports and other material, and for specific information to support your client's account.

19 Introduction

19.1   As discussed in chapter 1, much of the Home Office refusal letter may consist of claims that security forces, rebels, or refugees would not have acted in the manner reported by your client. This approach continues during the appeal. The HOPO, as if competing in a strange parlour game, will eschew evidence in favour of clever reasons suggesting what each would do next. However bizarre it may appear, you ignore such allegations at your (and your client's) peril. You should prepare to refute allegations of implausibility by the Home Office, and any similar point which you think may be taken by an adjudicator.

19.2   Your client is the obvious person to rebut allegations of implausibility. She was there after all and can give first-hand evidence. The Home Secretary was not there and usually offers no evidence whatsoever. But the Home Office may seek to denigrate your client's evidence as self-serving and partial. The HOPO will invite the adjudicator to make an adverse credibility finding purely on the basis that the account seems surprising – from which it can therefore be inferred that she is lying. If the adjudicator accepts this argument, then relying upon your client's credibility to rebut allegations of implausibility becomes a vicious circle.

19.3   Any suggestion that your client requires corroboration to succeed is a misdirection of law. But if the adjudicator is minded to disbelieve your client's evidence (a serious danger when evidence is given in a cross-cultural situation of experiences which do not appear from a UK perspective to make logical sense), then you may lose your appeal if you cannot corroborate your client's account. In the absence of documentary corroboration or corroborating witnesses of fact, expert evidence may be critical to the success or failure of the appeal.

19.4   Normally, courts admit expert evidence where the issue upon which it is given is outside the knowledge or experience of the fact finding tribunal and where the expert, through experience, training or qualifications, has acquired that knowledge and expertise. Often – one might say almost by definition – the issues which arise in an asylum or human rights appeal will be outside the ordinary experience of the fact-finding tribunal.

19.5 So much has been recognised by the Court of Appeal. Criticising the proposition that an adverse credibility finding rendered an expert report irrelevant, the Court commented in *Es-Eldin* (per Brooke LJ) that:

> *It must be extremely difficult for special adjudicators to form their view of credibility in relation to somebody who comes from a culture different from theirs and from a political background different from theirs. In those circumstances a special adjudicator always needs all the help that can be given by those who know more about such matters than he or she necessarily does.*

19.6 In *S (2002)*, the Court of Appeal said that:

> *In this field opinion evidence will often or usually be very important, since assessment of the risk of persecutory treatment in the milieu of a perhaps unstable political situation may be a complex and difficult task in which the fact-finding tribunal is bound to place heavy reliance on the views of experts and specialists.*

19.7 In *Gupreet Singh*, the expert in that case was described as 'plainly a respected and well informed academic expert on Indian affairs... and the sources of her relevant information are in the context substantial. This court should regard the uncontradicted material deriving from her in that light as sufficient in an asylum case to establish the facts which she states.' On other occasions, that Court has expressed concern about expert evidence, particularly uncontradicted expert evidence, being dismissed on inadequate grounds. (See e.g. *Kuranakaran*: '[It] was completely wrong for the tribunal in the present case to dismiss considerations put forward by experts of the quality who wrote opinions on this case as "pure speculation".')

19.8 On the other hand, the IAT has regularly complained about being faced with expert evidence which does not meet the standard normally expected by a court or from 'experts' who – at least on the face of the report submitted – do not appear to merit the title.

19.9 These views represent two sides of the same coin. Expert evidence is sometimes treated with irrational suspicion, if not hostility by the Home Office, and even in the appellate authority. Stories abound of points being taken against experts which would be seen as absurd in other jurisdictions – for example that expert evidence was unreliable because the expert was 'on a retainer' (in reality charged a fee) to the solicitors. (The Home Office Country Assessments seldom receive the same treatment, despite their authors being paid employees of the respondent.)

19.10 But some representatives must also shoulder blame for submitting inadequate evidence in inappropriate form. Sometimes, the wrong expert has been chosen, but more often there is nothing wrong with the expert (who nevertheless attracts the blame from the adjudicator): what is wrong is the complete absence of appropriate instructions and guidance from the representative. The unique gravity of the issues at stake in this jurisdiction render it more, not less important that wherever possible, expert evidence meets the normal standards expected by the courts.

19.11 A substantial section of this text is therefore devoted to expert evidence. The next chapter deals with the issues where country expert evidence can help; the chapter after that with identifying the right expert.

19.12 Chapter 22 sets out the guidance an expert needs to understand his role in the litigation and avoid eminently avoidable criticism from the court. Experts in other jurisdictions commonly attend courses to familiarise themselves with these points: these pointers will at least start to fill the gap. Chapter 23 deals with instructing the expert. If an expert's answers are deficient, it will often mean he was asked the wrong questions, or given the wrong information. It also discusses the preparation of his report for disclosure, an exercise which can lead to misunderstanding on both sides. Chapter 24 deals with the dangers of so-called 'recycling' of reports. Chapter 25 is about calling the expert to give oral evidence. The IAT has emphasised the benefits of an expert giving oral evidence, and it may make the difference between acceptance and rejection of his evidence. Chapter 26 deals with specific problems relating to medical evidence.

19 Introduction
Key points

■ Relying on your client's evidence to rebut allegations of implausibility can become a vicious circle.

■ The Court of Appeal has emphasised the importance of expert evidence in this jurisdiction.

■ Good expert evidence can win the appeal. However, the IAT is concerned about the quality of some expert evidence.

■ The gravity of the issues renders it more, not less important that expert evidence meets the standards required by the courts.

20 When to use expert country evidence

20.1 Issues where expert evidence will be needed fall into two main categories:

- the consequences of the proposed expulsion;
- disputes as to past events.

Some issues fall into both categories. The Home Office might assert that 'low-level' activists are at no risk in the country of origin. It then reasons from this not only that your client is not at risk if expelled, but that her evidence of past detentions as a 'low-level' activist must be false! The same expert evidence will refute both these allegations.

20.2 As always, distinguish between those Home Office arguments which may be taken seriously by an adjudicator and those which result from legal misconceptions or are so outlandish that you can safely deal with them yourself. But remember the question is not simply whether you think they are outlandish, but whether you can be confident that an adjudicator will think the same. The most surprising Home Office allegations are sometimes accepted by adjudicators – even absent any apparent expertise on the part of the maker of the allegation.

20.3 If in doubt, err on the side of caution. The qualifications or experience of an expert should enable him to arrive at a better appreciation of the material than either you or the Home Office. If your argument is rejected, you will be on stronger grounds to complain if the adjudicator rejected expert analysis rather than simply your own analysis.

The consequences of expulsion

20.4 You will often find evidence about the conditions your client will face in the main country reports from the likes of Amnesty, Human Rights Watch, and the US State Department. However, the Home Office will often argue that these documents do not address the particular circumstances of your client or you have not shown how your client will be affected by these abuses. You may well be able to counter this by making submissions upon the general material. However, evidence from an expert who has focussed specifically upon your client's circumstances will put you in a stronger position.

20.5 If there is a dearth of general material about an unfamiliar country, you may need expert evidence to provide the basic information that would normally be available from country reports.

Persecution and human rights abuses by the state

20.6 Examples of the many issues on which expert evidence might be sought are:

- what risks your client will face as a result of her perceived political position;
- whether a particular action will be perceived as political and/or a threat;
- whether her sexuality or ethnicity will place her at risk;
- whether the criminal offence for which she is wanted may put her at risk of ill-treatment during interrogation, detention conditions that will be inhuman or degrading, or an unfair trial;
- the consequences of exercising freedom of expression or association to which she is committed, or practising her religion;
- whether she will be at risk of ill-treatment as an expelled asylum seeker;
- whether dissident activities abroad are monitored, and whether your client's activities in the UK may place her at risk.

20.7 If you are assessing risk to members of a party, tribe, ethnic group, or religious order, of which there is little mention in the general country of origin material, expert evidence will again be especially important.

20.8 To meet the Home Office case, you might want to know

- whether the Government's statements on human rights are contradicted by its deeds;
- how effective are its investigations into human rights abuses by its security forces;
- whether it persecutes ordinary activists as well as prominent officials or whether persecution is common even against peaceful opponents;
- the risk of torture during detention and interrogation.

20.9 As indicated at para 1.59, a victim of past persecution should not normally be required to produce *additional* evidence of risk unless there has been a substantial change of circumstances for the better in the country of origin. However, not only HOPOs but adjudicators some-times suggest that simple passage of time will quell the home state's antipathy. In some cases, it will be better to err on the safe side by obtaining expert opinion on this proposition. You will be looking for an expert who can comment on the methods of the security forces, and can say whether they close files or lose interest after a period.

20.10 Of course, if there has – or the Home Office claims there has – been a fundamental change of circumstances in the country of origin then expert evidence may well be vital to establish that someone in your client's position will still be at risk.

20.11 Also common are assertions by the Home Office that the appellant is safe because she was detained without charge, or because she was released following detention (with or without torture): see para 1.61. Again, these are sometimes accepted by adjudicators so expert evidence is a sensible safeguard. The expert might indicate whether it is common practice for the security forces to repeatedly arrest and ill-treat people without charging them – whether for information gathering, informal punishment, or simply general intimidation – and whether those who have been detained in the past are at risk of being targeted in the future.

Non-state risks

20.12 The complexity of the legal issues which non-state risks raise are noted in paras 1.65–1.68. You will often want expert evidence on the factual issues. The expert can examine the degree of likelihood that your client will suffer serious harm notwithstanding any protection that will be on offer. He may conclude, for example, that despite the large number of arrests the police are making and the resources it has put into preventing the attacks upon a particular ethnic or religious group, these attacks continue and show no sign of abating.

20.13 However, the Home Office has argued that such evidence is insuffi-cient. It claims you need to go further than showing a real risk to your client by showing that there is no 'sufficiency of protection according to international standards'. This concept has proved elusive. But a suit-ably qualified expert may be able to address the effectiveness of sys-tems of protection both generally and in the context of your client's particular circumstances. He should say not only whether there is a developed criminal justice system with appropriate penalties for par-ticular offences, but whether the authorities possess both readiness and ability to operate it.

20.14 Relevant issues may include the extent to which the security forces themselves comply with international standards including human rights standards, the extent of corruption, the effectiveness of crime detection and prevention, and the extent to which direct protection is available to those most at risk (e.g. protection schemes for those who have been specifically targeted). Levels of protection might meet international requirements generally but not, for example, for women at risk from male relatives, transsexuals, or people from a particular ethnic group against whom the security forces are themselves prejudiced. As discussed in chapter 22, he should not in terms express an opinion upon whether there is, overall or for the individual client, a 'sufficiency of protection'.

20.15 On occasion, you will be faced with arguments that non-state entities constitute quasi-state authorities that are capable of providing sufficient protection from an international perspective (as has been argued in respect of Somalia and Iraqi Kurdistan). Such questions have been the subject of academic study by contemporary historians who may well be able to provide useful expert evidence.

Internal protection

20.16 The law relating to internal protection/internal flight in refugee cases is also not straightforward. The first question should be whether the proposed internal protection alternative is safe and accessible. UNHCR states that in determining whether internal protection is available,

> Factors which will be relevant to consider include, among others: the actual existence of a risk free area, which must be established by evidence: the stability of the area and the likelihood that safety will be a durable feature (at the time of the decision and the time of return); the accessibility of the area (both internally and from outside the country)...
> (UNHCR's Position Paper *Relocating Internally as a Reasonable Alternative to Seeking Asylum* (the so-called 'Internal Flight Alternative' or 'Relocation Principle'), para 14)

20.17 You would think that once you had shown you were of adverse interest to the state authorities, it would be obvious that you could not seek protection from these authorities in any part of the country they controlled. UNHCR agrees (para 1.71). But as pointed out there, the Home Office often makes the contention regardless. You might therefore ask an expert whether the police have access to nationwide records, whether they make enquiries with the police in a person's home area, what requirements there may be to register when one moves to a new area, or whether a person's ethnicity or other characteristics might attract attention if they tried to relocate in a different area.

20.18 It is, of course, a precondition of internal protection that your client can get to the proposed area safely. The expert may therefore comment upon what treatment she can expect at the location to which she is to be expelled; what checks will be carried out (including whether enquiries may be made with the authorities in her home area); and the risks and practicalities of onward travel. If she cannot access internal protection, it is not an alternative.

20.19 You will also want to examine whether the proposed internal protection alternative is unreasonable or unduly harsh. In *AE and FE*, the Court of Appeal revised this limb of the test. It held that human rights arguments based on a comparison of the appellant's circumstances in the UK and in the proposed area of internal protection are irrelevant to the test (although they may provide 'good grounds under the Human Rights Act'). Instead, the evidence must focus on a comparison of the appellant's circumstances in the area where she has a well-founded fear of persecution and the location of the internal protection alternative. This exercise may well benefit from expert evidence.

Destitution

20.20 If your client will face starvation and destitution upon expulsion then expulsion may well violate the ECHR. (Refer to the discussion on the threshold in this regard in *Q* and in *S, D & T*.) The case will be even stronger if your client is vulnerable, for example if she is pregnant or has a child or care of a child, or is elderly, ill, or disabled.

20.21 Your expert should be asked to deal with the possibilities of obtaining work, benefits, charitable aid, and support from friends, relatives and neighbours. Again, it is important for him to be aware of and consider your client's personal circumstances. Her particular circumstances, for example as a divorced woman with children, may render destitution more likely, but equally, if her statement reveals family or other possible support networks in the country of origin, the adjudicator will expect to be addressed on whether these could provide for her.

Civil war and lawlessness

20.22 You may well want an opinion on whether there is a real risk of serious harm arising from civil war, or the extent to which law and order has broken down and the resulting risks to the appellant. Your client may be at particular risk of, say, rape as a result of her particular circumstances.

Medical cases

20.23 The risks to a person's health if she is expelled may raise issues under articles 3 and 8 and may also be relevant (though less commonly) in asylum appeals. Medical expert evidence will obviously be required but related evidence from a country expert may be just as important. This is discussed further at para 26.23.

Other issues relating to cultural conditions

20.24 Relevant issues could include whether someone will be stigmatised by their local community, or whether absence of family will prevent her marrying and the consequences of that. If your client is a child or has care of children, you may wish to obtain expert evidence about what educational facilities may be available for them, particularly if they are well settled in the UK's education system.

20.25 Conditions which would not normally be sufficient in themselves to engage the ECHR may be relevant in meeting a Home Office argument as to the proportionality of interference with family or private life.

20.26 Where your client enjoys family life in the UK, you might obtain expert evidence as to the conditions her UK-based family would face in your client's country of origin, in order to argue that it would be unreasonable to expect her UK-based family to relocate there with her. This would include whether there would be sufficient health and educational facilities for any UK-based children and language and cultural problems. This will often go hand in hand with evidence from child psychologists and independent social workers which is discussed at chapter 26.

Disputes as to past events

Assertions about the behaviour of opposition groups and activists

20.27 As previously discussed, Home Office allegations of implausibility will often be based upon allegations about how the state authorities, opposition groups, your client or indeed anyone else would have acted in a particular situation. Sources will seldom be offered. Many are pure speculation by the caseworker. Some may be misunderstanding of books or articles intended for appreciation by experts. (Chapter 9 deals with requests for further details.)

20.28 Allegations as to how the security forces or opposition groups would have reacted in a particular situation may merit an expert response. The allegation might be that the claimant would not have operated for so long as a sympathiser without obtaining military training. The Home Office may also make claims as to how your client's opposition group would behave when your client fell out with it, e.g. *'The Secretary of State did not find plausible your assertion that this organisation would have pursued you simply because you left it without permission.'*

20.29 Expert evidence may ultimately be impossible to obtain on some of the more esoteric claims (experts tending to have a more realistic appreciation of their expertise than Home Office officials). In some cases, it will be useful simply for him to confirm that there is nothing in the relevant learning to support the Home Office's claim. You should still point out that the Home Office has produced no evidence to support its assertion in the face of your client's first-hand evidence to the contrary.

20.30 It will often be alleged that your client's political understanding is too basic when compared to her claimed involvement in her organisation. As indicated in chapter 1, the allegation may be based on the most basic or even facile questions by an immigration officer. You may consider seeking expert opinion on the depth of your client's political knowledge (and possibly on the adequacy of the immigration officer's questioning). In particular, you may wish your expert to comment upon the degree to which your client's political knowledge is consistent with her claimed involvement. You may well wonder whether it is really necessary to get an expert to point out that the appellant probably became involved because she was told, say, that the party would fight for her own people rather than because it adopted her favourite socialist model but experience shows that it is often better to be safe than sorry.

Escape

20.31 Allegations about the implausibility an appellant's escape route are common. For example, the Home Office's case may be that it is not possible for a wanted person to escape the country using false documents, or that the security forces guarding prisons will not accept bribes to release people.

20.32 Your client can obviously give evidence that this is exactly what happened. However, the HOPO may nevertheless urge the adjudicator to guess that the escape route would not have been feasible, or the guards would not risk taking a bribe, and dismiss the appeal accordingly. You could consider requesting further details of the material upon which the Home Office bases its claim (which are unlikely to be forthcoming). But adjudicators regularly accept Home Office claims about escape routes without evidence and it may therefore be important to have expert evidence on such assertions.

20.33 Experts will often be able to comment upon the prevalence of corruption on the part of state officials. It is a subject of academic study. An expert who can describe the mechanics by which bribery operates, for example in facilitating release from custody, will be particularly impressive. NGOs such as Amnesty may also have information on the feasibility of escape routes and methods from different countries. Refugees and interpreters, particularly if they have lived in the county of origin in recent years, can also be a useful source of information on this topic.

The appellant's actions

20.34 A range of other claims may be made by the Home Office about the plausibility of your client's actions – for example:

> The Secretary of State notes that you did not seek or receive any medical treatment for your alleged injuries, which he considered damaged the credibility of your claims to have been tortured.

20.35 You may want to obtain evidence to the effect either that there were no medical facilities available in the area; or that medical facilities in the area were under the control or influence of the security forces.

20.36 The Home Office might even dispute her torture on the basis that anyone so tortured would have confessed. Strange though such allegations may seem, they are often made and are on occasion accepted by adjudicators. Consider asking your expert how common it is for detainees such as your client to experience torture without making confessions.

20.37 A very common allegation is that the appellant would have left the country sooner if she had suffered the persecution she claimed. The expert might comment on how difficult, costly and time consuming organising an illegal exit from the country can be. She may also have been dedicated to her cause or prevented by family obligations from leaving. The expert might explain the particular strength of family obligations in her culture (see further below on cultural considerations).

Cultural misconceptions

20.38 Allegations from the Home Office about credibility are often based upon misconceived cultural assumptions. In those circumstances expert evidence, say, from an anthropologist who specialises in the particular country may be especially valuable.

20.39 Where your client is unable to say how her parents arranged her escape from detention or to recount her parents' political activities, this may be claimed to be so implausible as to render your client not credible. An expert might explain that cultural factors actually make it unlikely that your client would make such an enquiry of her parents or that her parents would disclose the information. The Home Office might also take a credibility point against your client on the basis that she waited until her husband's asylum claim had been refused before claiming asylum herself. An expert might again explain that this was culturally consistent.

Language

20.40 Expert evidence may be useful where it appears that an alleged discrepancy is in reality a product of error or inherent difficulty in interpretation. The intrinsic difficulties in interpreting, particularly between languages which have developed in very different cultures, are discussed in chapter 34.

20.41 Many HOPOs and some adjudicators do not appreciate these difficulties and the extent to which interpretation requires an exercise of judgment by the interpreter as opposed to a mechanical conversion.

20.42 That is quite apart from the possibility of errors resulting from the use of an under-qualified interpreter, or one who is inappropriate because he speaks a different dialect or because his cultural or ethnic background or gender inhibit communication. Note that these issues do not apply only to interpreters used in Home Office interviews and by the IAA. Your own role in choosing an interpreter is dealt with in chapter 11. But if issues have arisen as to the accuracy of a statement taken by a previous representative, you may also wish to investigate whether the interpreting was appropriate.

20.43 An experienced and reliable interpreter will be an obvious source of expert evidence on many of these questions. However, be careful that the interpreter is not making the same instinctive assumptions as had contributed to the original problem (e.g. equating police charging procedures that are not in fact equivalent). An anthropologist who is proficient in the language of the country or ethnic group he studies may be both more alert to these issues and better able to explain to the court the cultural context in which the problems arise.

20 When to use expert country evidence Key points

■ Expert evidence falls into two main categories: firstly, the consequences of expulsion and secondly, disputes about past facts.

■ Expert evidence on the consequences of expulsion may cover:

☐ risk from state authorities as a result of the appellant's own activities or her membership of a particular group,

☐ non-state risks and the degree of protection available,

☐ whether an internal protection alternative exists and whether it would be unduly harsh,

☐ the risk and consequences of destitution,

☐ the effects of civil war,

☐ absence of medical treatment,

☐ stigmatisation in the local community,

☐ cultural and other obstacles to a family resettling in the country of origin.

■ Expert evidence dealing with disputes about past facts may cover:

☐ allegations of implausibility in terms of the conduct of the appellant and anyone she encountered,

☐ whether the political sophistication of the appellant is consistent with her claimed involvement,

☐ the feasibility of escape routes,

☐ whether the appellant's actions were consistent with known practices and conditions in the country of origin,

☐ cultural misconceptions,

☐ interpreting errors and linguistic misunderstandings.

21 Choosing an expert

Who is an expert?

21.1 The range of experts in asylum and human rights appeals is limited only by the range of experiences to which appellants have been subjected, and the range of allegations and assumptions which may be made by the Home Office and the courts.

21.2 Neither are there set criteria by which you can judge whether a person is qualified to be an expert witness. What matters is that by qualifications, study or experience, that person has acquired expertise beyond that to be expected of the adjudicator.

21.3 You should be able to contrast your expert's expertise with, say, the author of the refusal letter or the Home Office Country Assessment who (unlike, for example, the researchers of the Canadian documentation centre) commonly lack any recognised qualifications or expertise.

21.4 Academics will often have relevant expertise. Anthropologists, sociologists and geographers may be able to assist with issues relevant to the establishment of a social group in an asylum case. They may comment upon risks from an appellant's own community for cultural or religious reasons, e.g. how a single mother will be treated by her community. Anthropologists may also be particularly helpful in exposing cultural misconceptions which underlie Home Office allegations of implausibility. An interpreter may be able to provide expert evidence as to the reliability of an apparent discrepancy.

21.5 A political scientist or modern historian might comment on the risks faced by a political party. Experts may be found amongst those who have worked with international organisations; human rights monitoring NGOs such as Amnesty and Human Rights Watch; or research organisations and 'think tanks' such as the Royal Institute of International Affairs (Chatham House). Journalists who have specialised in a particular country or region may also have built up substantial expertise, as may workers in the aid or development fields. The latter can be particularly useful in commenting on social and economic conditions (such as risk of destitution) or upon the availability of medical treatment. So may health professionals who have worked in the country of origin.

21.6 Some questions are of a similar nature to those which regularly arise in other jurisdictions such as the criminal courts. If an identity document is alleged to be forged, it may require forensic examination. If your client's claim to be the person in a particular photograph is rejected by the Home Office, you may want to consider facial mapping. Criminal lawyers can be a good source of experts in these areas.

21.7 Local lawyers may be useful not only for document verification but also for opinion as to the risks your client will run, or the conduct of particular state authorities (but see the discussion at para 16.8 as to the difficulty in finding an appropriate local lawyer).

21.8 It will be seen that you may need more than one expert. For example, you might need a political scientist to comment upon the risks that your client would be arrested for her political activities, and an anthropologist to advise upon whether life would be viable as a lone woman in her home village or to expose cultural misconceptions which have led the Home Office to doubt credibility. In the case (quoted at para 9.24) where the Home Office relied upon the crocodiles said to inhabit the River Zaire, you might have to instruct a zoologist.

21.9 That is not overkill. It is simply recognition of the huge variety of issues that human rights and asylum appeals (and the Home Office) may throw up. The court will only be assisted by an expert who possesses the right expertise. Rather than applying arbitrary limits, the aim should be to ensure that each expert is individually justified by the relationship between the issue in question and his expertise, having regard to the anxious scrutiny required of any asylum or human rights appeal.

21.10 But beware overkill. Satisfy yourself that the additional expert is really appropriate. That is not only on grounds of expense. Use of multiple experts on the same issue may backfire if their reports are seen as inconsistent. This will obviously be so if they give contradictory evidence, but inconsistency has been alleged simply because the experts do not all identify the same factors in reaching the same conclusion. If they are dealing with different issues from different expert perspectives, be clear about that.

21.11 You may want to call more than one expert from the same field to demonstrate a preponderance of expert opinion on a proposition that the Home Office disputes (just as you might wish to produce several human rights reports supporting the same line). That is often done in high profile cases or those intended to set a factual precedent on a particular issue. But proceed with caution. While you must not seek to disguise real divergence in view, you must guard against creating an appearance of inconsistency where there is none.

Locating an expert

21.12 The first source of experts is the ILPA *Directory of Experts on Conditions in Countries of Origin and Transit*. It lists experts on asylum related issues alphabetically and by country of expertise. The last paper edition is the second edition, published in 1997 but a new electronic edition is presently being produced by ILPA and the EIN. Check the EIN website for details and help make it comprehensive by submitting recommendations of experts to ilpaexperts@ein.org.uk.

21.13 General expert directories such as *The Law Society Directory of Experts* and the *UK Register of Expert Witnesses* list vast numbers of experts, but relatively few experts on refugee producing countries. They may be a useful source, however, on the type of issues which arise across jurisdictions, such as document verification. The Law Society, the Academy of Experts and other organisations run help lines, though these tend to be expensive.

21.14 Posting queries to other lawyers can be an effective means of finding an appropriate expert. The Refugee Legal Group has a large and popular electronic mailing list. EIN members can also use its Queries Bulletin Board (from which adjudicators are excluded). The RLC External Information Service holds copies of numerous expert reports which have been prepared for past cases. Only in certain conditions is it permissible or appropriate to reuse these (see chapter 24) but they can help to identify potential experts and offer an indication of the quality of the expert's written work. Personal contacts may also be useful, particularly if you know a representative with substantial experience of a particular country or a particular issue (e.g. gender or sexuality based human rights abuses).

21.15 It is sometimes difficult finding an expert in the UK on an unfamiliar country or a particularly specialised issue. There is, of course, no need for your expert to be UK-based (though a foreign-based expert may make oral evidence impractical). Email has made dealing with foreign experts far easier. Asylumlaw.org now has an international database of expert witnesses on its website.

21.16 Organisations such as Amnesty and Human Rights Watch may be able to point you to relevant experts. So may voluntary agencies and campaigning groups, both particular to the country of origin and to the category of persecution. Journalists might be identified by searching the websites of newspapers which often include the email address for the author of the article (see chapter 18 for further details). Look for published works (through library catalogues, including the online British Library catalogue, or even booksellers such as amazon.co.uk).

21.17 Recognised refugees can make valuable witnesses, particularly if, say, the refugee used the same escape method which is now being disputed by the Home Office. Ask your client about possible sources from within her community. But bear in mind that an adjudicator needs to have confidence in an expert's ability to provide an opinion which is not rendered unreliable by reason of the expert's personal beliefs and affiliations (see paras 23.33, 23.39).

Assessing the expert

21.18 Talk the case over with the potential expert on a no-names basis before instructing him. Try to get a feel for his knowledge, understanding, and common sense. Watch for any tendency to be dogmatic. Ask him how he justifies his expertise on the particular question. If he is defensive, uncomfortable or awkward when asked to do this – or if he cannot give you a sensible explanation – then he is probably not the right expert (especially if you wish your expert to give oral evidence).

21.19 The response of most social scientists to being asked if they are objective will be that objectivity does not exist. (See similarly the IAT in *Chinder Singh*: 'No document is absolutely unbiased.')

21.20 But you will wish to ensure that the expert is not partisan in a way which will detract from the reliability of his expert evidence, for example because his evidence is likely to be tainted by his sympathy for, or antipathy towards the present regime. Inclusion in, for example, the *ILPA Directory of Experts*, is not a guarantee that the expert will not be biased against your client's case or even asylum seekers in general.

21.21 Sometimes, the expert may be concerned about the implications for his work, or even his safety, if he gives expert evidence. The expert may fear that to give evidence will put him in danger, particularly if he is based in the country of origin. But he may also have less extreme concerns about his ability to enter and work in the country of origin, or about his, or his organisation's relationship with the local authorities, particularly if he is involved with aid or development. In those circumstances, you will wish to help him assess the risks, and if they are real, consider making an application to the court that the public be excluded from the hearing or that he not be identified in the determination (see further para 25.17).

21.22 Ask for a CV. The following will be of interest:

- Publications, especially recent and relevant ones.
- Journalism, particularly for media with a reputation for impartiality.
- Advising national or international bodies, and reputable NGOs. Obviously if an expert has at any stage advised the Foreign Office, or if the Home Office has relied upon their work, that will be of particular interest. The Canadian independent documentation centre, DIRB, is among foreign organisations perceived by the IAA as reliable.
- Academic discipline, postings and research, and work with research organisations and think tanks.
- Relevant work with reputable NGOs, particularly human rights monitoring but also in the aid and development fields.
- Time spent in the country (but see the next paragraph).

21.23 There is considerable misconception on the part of the Home Office and some adjudicators about the relevance of recent country visits. HOPOs will often submit that an expert is unreliable simply because he has not visited the country recently – apparently unaware that many authors of the Home Office Country Assessments have never visited the country at all!

21.24 Dr Anthony Good's study of expert evidence in this jurisdiction (*Undoubtedly an Expert?* published by the Journal of the Royal Anthropological Institute) notes that:

> *HOPOs also sometimes seek to discredit absent experts on the naively empiricist grounds that they have not been in the country concerned recently… There are of course circumstances where having recently conducted one's own field research would make a crucial difference, but having merely visited a country recently is of very limited significance. In general, if an expert has been accepted as such on the basis of a CV demonstrating prolonged study of and broad knowledge about a particular country or region, it hardly matters where they happened to be when reading or assessing a particular document or news report.*

21.25 If an expert has been able to go to oppressed areas and interview people in circumstances similar to the appellant, that will of course be intensely valuable. But recent Home Office 'fact-finding missions' consisting solely of visits to government and NGO offices in the capital city illustrate the limited value of many country visits. An expert may be able to monitor, investigate, and interpret relevant developments as or more effectively from London than he can from an international hotel in the country's capital. He applies expertise he may have built up over decades to interpret that information and place it in its proper context. An expert may also, of course, have been refused entry to oppressive countries because of his work, he may fear that the regime would seek to exploit any visit, or it may simply be too dangerous to visit.

21.26 Also of relevance will be any experience on the part of the expert in giving expert evidence by way of written reports and/or oral evidence. Past experience means that you can expect some understanding of the role he is expected to play and how to frame a report for litigation. However, the inadequacies of some instructing representatives mean that this cannot be assumed. If he is otherwise the right person, then you should not be put off by absence of previous experience as an expert. (Indeed, one sometimes finds an unjustified suspicion of experts on the part of the Home Office, and even the adjudicator, simply on the basis of a long track record of giving expert evidence in this jurisdiction.) What lack of such experience will alert you to is the need to give the fullest guidance to enable him to perform his role properly (see the following chapter).

21.27 A past record of giving expert evidence can also provide an opportunity to assess his abilities. Ask him which representatives he has worked for in the past, and whether he is aware of any previous judicial comment on his work.

21.28 Where you trust a representative who has previously instructed him to give you an accurate assessment, seek one. You may also be able to obtain from these representatives copies of the determinations in the cases where he has given evidence (adjudicator determinations, though public documents, do not appear on any database).

21.29 You can perform a search on the expert's name on the EIN's caselaw database and SOPIAT to check whether the IAT has commented upon previous reports. The EIN also contains some higher court decisions, but a search on Casetrack will be comprehensive. When considering adverse comment, bear in mind the comment elsewhere in this section that badly presented expert evidence may be the fault of the instructing representative rather than the expert. The IAT has been known more than once to change its mind about an expert when he has appeared before it in person. Rejection of expert evidence may also have been successfully appealed. (And see the IAT's warning in *Cherbal* (para 42.61) as to the caution adjudicators must exercise before dismissing an expert's report because similar evidence from him was not accepted in an earlier case).

21.30 Finally, check practicalities:

- fees (note that it is inappropriate for an expert, given his overriding duty to the court, to accept a fee which is contingent on the nature of the evidence or the outcome of the appeal);
- how long he will require to produce the report;
- if applicable, whether he will be prepared to give oral evidence and if so, his availability and fees for doing so.

21.31 You should consult your client where she is going to be interviewed by the expert (most commonly by medical experts but also where the expert is determining nationality/ethnicity – see para 23.22). Illegitimate discrimination on grounds of race, gender, sexual orientation, religion, or disability when choosing an expert is prohibited by the Law Society's Anti-Discrimination Code and the Bar Council's Code of Conduct. This means that you will have to judge whether complying with a request by a client to take account of such grounds in choosing an expert is illegitimate discrimination or legitimate concession to her particular vulnerability.

21 Choosing an expert
Key points

■ There are no set criteria by which to determine whether someone qualifies as an expert. What matters is that whether by formal study or experience, he has acquired an expertise which can assist the adjudicator to resolve a material issue.

■ Experts will come from a range of backgrounds, including academics, journalists, aid and developments workers, and local lawyers. In each case, ask if he has the right expert knowledge to answer your particular question.

■ The nature of the issues involved may require more than one expert, but beware of overkill.

■ Locate experts through

☐ the ILPA Directory of Experts on the EIN,
☐ general expert directories,
☐ posting queries on the EIN bulletin boards or the RLG mailing list,
☐ asylumlaw.org's international database of experts,
☐ relevant NGOs and campaigning organisations ,
☐ journalists covering the country,
☐ recognised refugees from that country.

■ Assess the expert:

☐ talk the case over on a no-names basis to get a feel for his expertise and his ability to give a balanced opinion,
☐ obtain a CV,
☐ check recent country visits, but remember these are only one factor in assessing his expertise,
☐ search on the EIN or Casetrack for past judicial comment on the expert,
☐ check availability and fees (a fee cannot be contingent on the success of the appeal).

■ Consult your client about choice of expert if she is to be interviewed by him, but distinguish between legitimate concession to her vulnerability and illegitimate discrimination.

22 The expert's role

Introduction

22.1 As noted in chapter 19, a constant theme of the IAT in recent years has been that expert evidence in asylum and human rights appeals should meet the same standards as apply in the civil courts. The rules about expert evidence in the civil courts are designed to increase the confidence which a court can place in an expert's opinion. In order to reduce the risk of your expert's opinion being wrongly rejected, it is therefore imperative that you ensure where possible that these standards are met.

22.2 However, asylum and human rights appeals do differ from civil litigation. One of the differences is the esoteric nature of the questions upon which expert evidence may be required. The only person able to give an authoritative opinion upon whether your client could have escaped detention in a particular manner may be a local human rights monitor who deals in life and death issues in a remote part of the country of origin, and who may even place himself at risk by assisting you. If you manage to obtain from him an informal fax that answers your point, that may be more persuasive than a perfectly presented expert report from someone in the UK who has less expertise. One would expect an adjudicator to understand in such circumstances that the reliability of the opinion was consistent with the informality of its presentation.

22.3 On the other hand – and contrary to what is sometimes supposed – the fact that it is an asylum and human rights appeal rather than a civil case does not excuse the presentation of a similarly informal fax when the expert is an established UK academic. Most commonly, expert evidence contravenes the civil rules not through necessity, but because of lack of awareness on the part of the expert as to what is required flowing from lack of awareness on the part of the representative.

22.4 Unless the expert's circumstances render it inappropriate or impractical to follow the ordinary rules applicable to expert evidence, the gravity of the issues in asylum and human rights appeals renders it more rather than less important that these rules are complied with. The effect of compliance ought to be to increase a court's confidence in your expert evidence, and therefore to reduce the risk of a wrong decision.

22.5   Unless you are instructing an expert who is trained or experienced in providing expert evidence for litigation, he will need guidance as to what the court requires from an expert. He cannot be expected to guess this, yet ignorance of the rules governing expert evidence can result in wholly avoidable criticism of your expert by the adjudicator. During the three month hearing of the asylum appeals of the victims of the Afghan aircraft hijacking in 2000, Home Office counsel cross-examined the appellants' expert on whether he was aware of the rules governing expert evidence laid down in the *Ikarian Reefer* (para 22.9 below). The IAT has similarly indicated that it expects an expert to be aware of these duties (e.g. *Zarour; Thambiah*).

22.6   Much of this guidance is of general application and can be recycled whenever you instruct a new expert. (If you cannot produce your own guidance covering the following points, you could even provide the expert with a photocopy of this chapter.)

The role of an expert and his duty to the court

22.7   Unless your expert is familiar with the asylum appellate process, you should start by explaining to him what is going on. An expert may not even realise that his evidence will be considered at an adversarial hearing. This is not only a courtesy to the expert, but should mean you get a better report due to his better understanding of his role and what is expected of him.

22.8   He must understand the rules which govern his evidence (and should state in his report that he understands them). His overriding duty as an expert witness is to the court rather than the party who instructs him (see CPR, r.35.3 and *Thambiah*). In *Slimani*, the IAT said:

> *While the principles which apply to expert witnesses called in High Court actions are not directly applicable, they give guidance when the weight to be attached to such evidence is considered. The most important are the need for independent assistance to the adjudicator or tribunal, the prohibition against assuming the role of an advocate and the need to specify the facts upon which an opinion is based: see **The Ikarian Reefer**, p.81–82 per Cresswell J.*

22.9 The IAT has elsewhere set out in full the duties and responsibilities of an expert witness derived from the *Ikarian Reefer*, and similarly indicated that it would apply these criteria when approaching expert evidence (*Saidi*). They are:

- Expert evidence presented to the court should be and should be seen to be the independent product of an expert uninfluenced as to the formal content by the exigencies of litigation.
- An expert witness should provide independent assistance to the court by way of objective unbiased opinion in relation to matters within his expertise.
- An expert witness in the High Court should never assume the role of advocate.
- An expert witness should state the facts or assumptions on which his opinion is based. He should not omit to consider material facts which detract from the concluded opinion.
- An expert witness should make it clear when a particular question or issue falls outside his expertise.
- If an expert's opinion is not properly researched because it considers that insufficient data is available then this must be stated with an indication that the opinion is no more than a provisional one.
- If after exchange of reports, an expert witness changes his view on a material matter, such change of view should be communicated to the other side without delay and when appropriate to the court.
- Where expert evidence refers to photographs, plans, calculations, survey reports or other similar documents, they must be provided to the opposite party at the same time as the exchange of reports.

22.10 The Civil Procedure Rules (Pt 35) provide further guidance on expert evidence in civil litigation which in light of *Slimani* should be followed (and is reflected in the guidance given below).

22.11 The expert must address his report to the Court. It must look like a report and should carry a heading such as 'Expert Report for presentation to the Adjudicator in the appeal of... '). It should not be in the form of a letter addressed to you (or to anyone else). Apart from the IAT wanting this level of formality, it again helps focus the expert's mind on the tone that is appropriate.

22.12 His report ought to contain an appropriate declaration as to his duty (see CPR, r. 35.10(2), *Thambiah*). The following is an example of the type of declaration which is appropriate (from the reports of Dr Good, the author of *Undoubtedly an Expert?*):

> *I am aware that in providing this report my overriding duty is to the court. I believe that the facts stated in this report are true, and that the opinions I have expressed are correct. I believe that I have dealt fully with those issues which have been drawn to my attention or which seem relevant to my understanding of this case. I have not omitted any facts of which I am aware which would have had a material effect on my conclusions as stated above. The absence of an expressed opinion on any particular point should not be construed as meaning that I have no opinion on that point. I would be happy to assist the court by clarifying any matter raised herein. My fee is not dependent on the outcome of this appeal.*

22.13 It is not, of course, necessary that the expert uses this wording but his declaration ought to cover these points.

The boundaries of expert opinion

22.14 This matter consistently troubles the IAT and adjudicators. It is central to the practical presentation of expert evidence, but it is impossible to deal with it effectively (both advising the expert and rebutting objections to his evidence) without some consideration of the relevant legal issues.

22.15 You may often hear it claimed that an expert's opinion infringes the 'ultimate issue rule'. This 'rule' was developed by the courts from the 18th Century. It was said to prohibit an expert from expressing an opinion on an issue which the court would ultimately be called upon to decide – the rationale was that an expert must not usurp the role of the Court as ultimate decision maker. It has been described as 'a mere bit of empty rhetoric' (Evidence (Chadbourn rev) para 1920) since a court is always free to disagree with the expert (provided its decision is open to it on the evidence as a whole). Its application has been described by the Court of Appeal (*Stockwell*) as 'vexed'. It is not hard to see why. Plainly, the court will have to reach a conclusion on all issues which are pertinent to the case. And an expert might be forgiven for thinking that his usefulness in the case rests upon the degree to which he can proffer expert opinion upon the most pertinent issues.

22.16 You will still on occasion find the 'rule' being invoked by HOPOs to dispute the admissibility of a particular expert opinion. It is useful, therefore, to point out that it was actually abolished in civil proceedings by the Civil Evidence Act 1972 (*M and R*). Although that Act did not apply to criminal proceedings, the Criminal Division of the Court of Appeal has effectively abandoned it. In *Stockwell*, Lord Taylor LCJ said that:

> *The rationale behind the supposed prohibition is that the expert should not usurp the functions of the jury. But since counsel can bring the witness so close to opining on the ultimate issue that the inference as to his view is obvious, the rule can only be… a matter of form rather than substance. In our view, an expert is called to give his opinion and he should be allowed to do so. It is, however, important that the Judge should make clear to the jury that they are not bound by the expert's opinion, and that the issue is for them to decide.*

22.17 This does not, however, mean that the expert is entitled to relay any opinion that he has formed on the case or your client. The additional scope it gives the expert to comment renders it all the more important that he understands and respects the limits of his expertise. But it does enable the expert to focus, unencumbered by technicalities, on the real test: does he possesses expertise on the issue beyond what may be expected from the court?

22.18 This test does not (any more than the ultimate issue rule would have done) entitle him to offer an opinion on whether someone is a refugee. His expertise may extend across a range of factual issues by which it is determined who the appellant is, what happened to him in the past, and what may happen to him in the future. But after all these factual issues are resolved, there remains the task of applying the legal standard to those findings of fact. As the IAT has pointed out, it remains the adjudicator's 'duty to test and evaluate the evidence in accordance with the legal criteria contained in the 1951 Refugee Convention. An expert is not a judicial decision-maker' (***Gomez***).

22.19 That principle applies equally to constituent elements of the legal definition. The expert should not offer a conclusion on whether the treatment your client faces amounts to 'persecution' (or in an article 3 case, whether it amounts to 'inhuman or degrading treatment'). Determining what factual events will or might occur is only the first stage in answering this question. The second stage is applying to that factual assessment legal standards which are dependent upon an understanding of refugee and human rights caselaw. The expert may well possess expertise beyond that of the court in conducting the first stage, the factual assessment. However, he should strive to convey all the opinions that his expertise permits without trespassing upon the second stage of applying the legal standard.

22.20 The distinction is not always straightforward to apply. Whether a claimant has a 'well-founded fear' of a particular event occurring depends on whether there is in fact a 'real risk' that it will happen. (The same 'real risk' threshold applies to article 3 claims.) So this issue is a constituent part of the test both for refugee status and article 3 protection. However, the probability that a particular event will occur in the country of origin in a given scenario is a matter which may well call for expert evidence. What needs to be determined is whether there is a real risk that it shall occur – an ordinary English phrase. Asking the expert to use a different formula in expressing his opinion simply through fear of treading on the court's toes is liable only to obfuscate his evidence on the question.

22.21 What distinguishes the issue 'is there a real risk that x will happen' from the issue 'does x constitute persecution' is that upon the former it is not possible – or useful – to draw a clear division between the assessment for which the expert may draw upon special expertise and the conclusion upon the legal test which the court must apply.

22.22 Another example is whether prison conditions meet international standards. To some extent, this involves applying legal standards found in international human rights law, but it involves other factors as well and is a test, for example, which the US State Department routinely applies in its country reports. Where your expert is a human rights monitor, it will not therefore be inappropriate to express an opinion on the question.

22.23 Similar scenarios arise in other jurisdictions. Even prior to the abandonment of the 'ultimate issue rule', experts in the criminal courts were regularly permitted to pronounce upon whether or not the defendant was suffering from 'diminished responsibility' – even though that was the final question for the court (*A and B Chewing Gum*). The modern view, as appears from **Stockwell**, is that so long as the court remembers that the final decision is for it, 'the expert is called to give his opinion and should be allowed to do so.'

22.24 The expert ought then to go as far as necessary – but no further – in order to provide the court with such assistance as his expertise qualifies him to give. The expert should ask at each stage 'In expressing this opinion, am I drawing upon expertise that the court cannot be expected to possess?'

22.25 That analysis also assists in addressing the particularly problematic issue of the extent to which an expert is entitled to offer an opinion relating to the appellant's credibility.

22.26 Traditionally, courts have held that whether or not a witness is telling the truth is a question upon which expert evidence will not be entertained. The justification was both that it would usurp the function of the court (in other words, the ultimate issue rule) and that the task was within ordinary experience so that no expert evidence was required. The courts were particularly concerned to ensure that a jury was left to determine credibility for itself.

22.27 Yet even in the criminal courts, barriers are now breaking down and psychiatric evidence relating to credibility (e.g. reliability of confessions) is increasingly admitted which would not have been admitted in the past. That is especially so where credibility is affected by issues such as age and mental condition which are outside the ordinary experience of a jury made up of ordinary adults. The same test applies: whether the opinion is based on expertise outside the ordinary experience of the court.

22.28 Both the Court of Appeal (para 19.5) and the IAT (para 1.5) have recognised that this will very often be the case in this jurisdiction where evidence comes from persons of very different cultures. The ordinary experiences of the refugee are also happily remote from those of an adjudicator who is unlikely to have endured the effects upon the mind of persecution and flight.

22.29 That said, the expert should normally be able to convey his expert opinion without expressing a direct opinion on the appellant's honesty. Expert evidence may be eminently appropriate to rebut allegations about the plausibility of the appellant's account and to expose associated cultural misconceptions. The expert may conclude that something is plausible in light of conditions in the country of origin, and consistent with or explicable by cultural or mental factors. But the court considers it important to distinguish between such expert opinions and the further step of reaching a conclusion that the witness is credible.

22.30 If an allegation of implausibility is the only basis upon which the account is questioned, then the inference to be drawn from rebuttal of that allegation will be clear. But it is still important that the expert leaves that inference for the court – that he goes no further than he must in order to convey his expertise. Such has been the concern in the Appellate Authority about experts overstepping the mark in this regard – and the connotations that the term 'credibility' has in this jurisdiction – that your expert will be wise to avoid the word altogether when commenting on such issues. (Without this advice, the expert may think he is acting perfectly within his expertise in concluding in the light of his own knowledge and expertise that an account is 'credible'.)

22.31 There will be cases where it is idle to pretend that the expert is not offering a direct opinion on whether the appellant is telling the truth. A prime example is where nationality or ethnicity is in dispute. An adjudicator is highly unlikely to have the expertise to resolve this based on questioning or observation. Typically therefore, an expert will interview the appellant and form a view based upon some combination of his answers, his language and dialect and his appearance as to whether his claimed nationality or ethnicity is genuine. That is not objectionable, even where (as was the case in the past for Kosovan Albanian claimants) the conclusion is effectively determinative of the appeal. Indeed, the expert's input is particularly vital where mistakes on such issues can lead to refoulement.

22.32 What matters is whether the expert is drawing upon special expertise or drawing purely upon common sense and common experience. If the latter, he should not express an opinion in evidence (regardless of the extent to which it may appear that common sense has escaped the author of the allegation). That does not, of course, prevent the expert making the point to the representative (whose job it is to make common sense submissions).

22 The expert's role
Key points

- The IAT requires experts and their evidence to meet the same standards that apply in the civil courts.

- Strive to meet these standards unless the expert's circumstances render that impractical.

- You are responsible for ensuring that the expert understands his duties as an expert witness, in particular:

  - ☐ his overriding duty is to the Court and his report must be addressed to the Court,
  - ☐ he should never assume the role of advocate,
  - ☐ he should offer his own independent opinion, uninfluenced by the exigencies of litigation,
  - ☐ the facts and assumptions on which his opinion is based should be stated, and he should not omit any material facts which detract from the concluded opinion,
  - ☐ he must state where an issue falls outside his expertise,
  - ☐ if he has insufficient data to offer more than a provisional opinion, he must say so,
  - ☐ if his view changes following submission of the report, then this should be communicated without delay.

- The expert should offer an opinion on any matter legitimately within his particular expertise but should not stray beyond that.

- Issues relating to credibility may well call for expert opinion, but the expert should be especially careful to demonstrate how his opinion derives from his expertise, rather than simply from common experience.

- He should seek to avoid expressing a direct opinion on overall 'credibility'.

23 The expert report

The expert's instructions

23.1 Instruct your expert as soon as possible. Do not leave it until days before the hearing. Even if delay does not place you in breach of directions, the more time you give an expert, the more impressive his report is liable to be – and vice versa. If you decide that your expert should give oral evidence (see chapter 25), it is also important to instruct him in time for you to make any necessary application to the court to have the case listed for his availability. If you are briefing counsel to present the hearing, do so in time to allow counsel to feed into the preparation of the expert evidence and advise on the report before it is disclosed.

23.2 The expert must be clear as to what he is being asked to do and (as importantly) what he is not being asked to do. The representative and the expert both have a role to play in ensuring that the expert evidence meets the requirements of the court and is therefore well received by it. An expert is not a lawyer, and is not to be expected to do your job. Some representatives have adopted a practice of simply sending all the papers on the file to an expert with a request that he does a report, but without any further guidance whatever as to what is expected. In those circumstances, it is unsurprising that an expert does not do himself justice in the eyes of the adjudicator.

23.3 It is similarly unsurprising when simply asked to comment upon the appeal papers that the expert will suppose that he is being asked to reach a conclusion on whether your client is telling the truth or even whether she is a refugee. He is not entitled to offer a conclusion on either question (see paras 22.14–22.32). By doing so, the expert only invites suspicion on the part of the adjudicator (however undeservedly) of those other opinions that he is entitled to offer.

23.4 It is up to you to frame your questions so that the expert is clear upon what issue his opinion is required. But it is neither necessary nor desirable to provide a mass of questions of such oppressive detail that the expert feels unable to fully develop his opinions on those matters which appear most relevant to him. It is, after all, part of the point of an expert that his training or experience enable him to recognise aspects of the case that you may have missed.

23.5   You need to consider what areas of the case would benefit from expert evidence (see chapter 20). You should explain the purpose of the report to the expert and set out clearly what questions you want him to answer.

23.6   Copies of correspondence between yourself and the expert, including instructions and draft reports, are normally privileged and an expert report need not include a verbatim account of either the expert's instructions or subsequent discussions. However, the report ought to set out 'the substance of all material instructions, whether written or oral, on the basis of which the report was written' (CPR, r.35.10(3)). The Court may not order disclosure of any document relating to his instructions or permit any questioning of the expert (other than by the party who instructed him) 'unless it is satisfied that there are reasonable grounds to consider the statement of instructions given [by the expert]... to be inaccurate or incomplete' (CPR, r.35.10(4)). The intention here was to find a balance between transparency as to the basis of instruction and permitting lawyer and expert to communicate reasonably freely. It has been almost unheard of for a civil court to order disclosure or permit cross-examination under this rule.

23.7   You should obviously ensure, regardless of the risk of disclosure, that your questions to the expert are fair and cannot be characterised as slanted or misleading: pose the question in a manner that you would not be embarrassed to have disclosed to the adjudicator.

23.8   The question may or may not be specific to your client. A general question might be whether those arrested at illegal demonstrations are likely to be recorded and of continuing interest to the authorities. A specific question might be whether the client's knowledge of the aims or structure of an organisation is consistent with her claimed involvement or what the chances are that such involvement will lead to her detention in the future. If the expert has been asked to comment on particular allegations in the refusal letter, then these allegations should be set out in the report along with the expert's comments.

23.9   You may wish the expert to consider alternative factual scenarios (in particular to cover the risk of the adjudicator making a blanket or partial adverse credibility finding in respect of your client's evidence). You could, for example, ask your expert to comment upon the degree of risk to your client:

- on the basis that her entire account is true;
- on the basis of just those facts for which there is corroborating evidence;
- and simply on the basis of her expulsion as a failed asylum seeker together with any facts which are undisputed such as her ethnicity.

23.10 Questions may be directed towards satisfying different tests in respect of different scenarios. You may consider, say, that if her account is accepted, your client is entitled to refugee status, but even if it is rejected, there will be issues under article 3.

23.11 Where your expert considers that your client will be at some risk even if part or all of her account is rejected, then it is important that he is instructed to set out that opinion so as to provide for this eventuality. You want to avoid having to ask the IAT to admit a supplementary expert report upon an application for permission to appeal or worse being reliant upon further representations to the Home Office.

23.12 What is important is that the expert clearly states in his report upon what factual scenarios he has based each opinion (including where he has been asked to proceed on the basis that the entire account is true). Being clear about the scenario upon which he is commenting will protect him from the common allegation that he has unquestioningly accepted the appellant's evidence as true thereby exhibiting partiality. (Also check, however, that the report is not inadvertently phrased in a manner which suggests that you or your expert expect an adverse credibility finding to be made).

23.13 Explain the legal context of the question to the expert, not to encourage him to tailor his opinion to the caselaw but because some understanding of context will assist him in understanding what is relevant. For example, if his report is to assist in determining whether a proposed internal protection alternative will be unduly harsh, some basic explanation of the unduly harsh test will enable him to avoid wasting time formulating opinions on matters which will be immaterial to whether the test is met.

23.14 An expert can advise you on your preparation and conduct of the case as well as providing a report for disclosure. You might, for example, seek his comments on a document which your client has obtained from the country of origin and which you are unsure whether to submit (see further chapter 16). Traditionally, communications with an expert are privileged to the extent that he is acting in an advisory capacity rather than an expert witness. The CPR require an expert to state only the 'substance of all material instructions... *on the basis of which the report was written*' [emphasis added]. If the expert who produces a report could not also advise privately on other issues, that would encourage the practice of solicitors instructing a second 'shadow expert' to avoid the risk of his advice being disclosed. However, the matter is not free from doubt. Any issue on which you ask your expert to act in an advisory capacity should be clearly differentiated from those issues that he will address as an expert witness.

23.15 The expert should, of course, be at liberty to conduct his own research and enquiries. His expertise may well enable him to do this more effectively and to pursue avenues which would not be available or apparent to a lawyer. Clearly, some lines of enquiry may risk jeopardising your client's confidentiality, most obviously where the expert proposes approaching contacts in the country of origin.

23.16 Emphasise to the expert that any case specific information that he is given is confidential unless you say otherwise. Give clear guidance as to what he is permitted to disclose when conducting his own enquiries, and in what circumstances he must revert to you for authorisation before releasing information. Alternatively, he may be able to advise you on further avenues for you to explore. Remember that you could be required to disclose any document to which the expert refers in his report.

Documentation accompanying the instructions

23.17 Ensure that you have given the expert all the documentation he requires to form his opinion. If it appears to the adjudicator that the expert was unaware of relevant material, he may give the expert's opinion less weight. The HOPO may submit that a report which comments upon plausibility (and is therefore relevant to credibility) cannot be relied upon unless the expert has considered all the statements and interview notes in the case.

23.18 The expert should have all the documentation that will be before the adjudicator unless it is plainly irrelevant to the issues raised in his instructions. Err on the side of caution. Where the documentation is voluminous, you can point in your instructions to what you consider most relevant. By providing it all, you ensure that he has had the opportunity – and more importantly is seen to have had the opportunity – to form his own view. An additional benefit of providing him with all your documentation is that he may through his expertise recognise aspects of a document (good or bad) or potential implications that you had missed.

23.19 Where the expert is not familiar with asylum appeals, give him some explanation of the standard documents and their purpose. Asylum interview notes may appear to you to be self-explanatory, but the expert may nevertheless appreciate an explanation of the purpose of the interview, at what stage it comes in the determination process, who conducts the interview, who attends etc. Whenever the provenance and relevance of supporting documentary evidence is not obvious on its face, this should be explained.

23.20 If you have not made up your mind whether to rely on a particular document, ask him to revert to you before referring to it in his report (any document to which he refers is potentially disclosable). Where witness statements are still in draft form, point this out to the expert. If he needs to refer to a statement in his report, it should be delayed until the final version of the statement is available.

Whether the expert should meet your client

23.21 HOPOs will sometimes suggest that a report from a country expert is less reliable because the expert has not met the appellant. With certain exceptions, this allegation is likely to be misconceived.

23.22 The main exception is where an expert has been instructed to give an opinion on your client's ethnicity/nationality. He will often need to interview her in order to form a view. You might also consider a meeting where the Home Office has alleged that your client's political knowledge is inconsistent with the extent of her claimed involvement. The most effective way for an expert to assess political knowledge may be to interview her, particularly where the asylum interview has been woefully inadequate. Many social scientists are now trained and experienced interviewers.

23.23 But in many other cases, a meeting with the client does not assist an expert in reaching an opinion on any question which is open to him, and it may increase the temptation to express an impermissible conclusion on whether your client is telling the truth. Since his role is to provide independent assistance to the court, a separate meeting with the appellant might even detract from that important appearance of impartiality even though nothing improper will have occurred. If he attends the hearing, your expert will of course have the same opportunity as the adjudicator to see your client give oral evidence (see para 25.30).

23.24 The expert may well ask questions about your client's history upon which you have to revert to your client, and you should seek full answers to such questions. (He may well see relevance in matters which you did not think were important.) And there is nothing to prevent them talking prior to the hearing where your expert attends court. But a formal meeting for the purpose of informing the report is often of dubious value. Generally, unless the expert needs to see your client in order to form his opinion, he should not do so. His report should always say whether or not he has met the client.

The report itself

23.25 To comply with the standards expected by the courts, all expert reports should contain the following:

- An account of the expert's qualifications, training and experience, such as are relevant to his ability to assist the court reliably on the issues raised by his instructions.
- A statement setting out the substance of his material instructions (whether written or oral). The statement should summarise those facts and instructions provided to the expert which are material to the opinions expressed in the report or upon which those opinions are based (see by analogy CPR rule 35.10(3) and para 23.6 above).
- What documentation he has considered.
- His conclusions upon each question posed in his instructions, separating facts, inferences drawn from facts, and opinion.
- An explanation of how the expert arrived at each answer, including particular aspects of his qualifications, training, experience or research which led him to the answer, and the sources upon which he has relied (see below).
- The declaration that the expert has complied with his duty to the Court and a 'statement of truth' (see the example at para 22.12).

23.26 The *Law Society Directory of Experts* gives the following guidance on the representative's duties upon receipt of the draft report:

C11.6 Preparing the report for disclosure

A report produced by even the best-briefed, best-informed expert may need some refinement before it is ready for disclosure to the other side.

This must not mean asking the expert to modify or distort his opinions. This section is solely about changes it is wholly legitimate to ask him to make for the sake of accuracy, completeness, clarity or consistency.

Once you have received the initial report, you will need to go through it, and refer it back to the expert for clarification if necessary.

Some reports may go through more than one draft. Make sure that your expert differentiates each version by dating it.

Do not accept any report at face value. Consider whether your expert's views are supported by the facts. Are there factors not covered? Are you convinced by his argument? If not, ask him to expand on it.

If it is favourable, assess it critically. Is he painting too rosy a picture of your case? What has he left out? Has he addressed all the issues? Where is the evidence to support what he says? Has he blurred the lines between fact and opinion? Do his comments stray outside his field, as determined by his qualifications and experience?

If there are inherent weaknesses in your case, consider whether the expert addresses these in his report. It is better for potential difficulties to be acknowledged and dealt with by reasoned arguments, rather than omitted. In any event, never be tempted to allow your expert to mislead the court.

You also need to check the report for clarity. Is it understandable to someone with no expertise in this particular field and no prior knowledge of the case? Is everything explained clearly and simply? You and he should be thinking of how you can help the judge by making things clearer...

Check it for consistency, even details, such as dates and times. Inconsistencies may be used to undermine the expert. You should also check spelling, punctuation and grammar.

Although you can and should ask your expert to make necessary changes to his report, you must be careful not to overstep the mark into writing it for him. Expert reports must not be 'settled' by the lawyers.

*In **Whitehouse v Jordan**, Lord Denning complained that a medical report had been settled by counsel. When the case went to the House of Lords, Lord Wilberforce stated:*

> *'While some degree of consultation between experts and legal advisers is entirely proper, it is necessary that expert evidence presented to the court should be, and should be seen to be, the independent product of the expert, uninfluenced as to form or content by the exigencies of litigation.'*

23.27 Unfamiliarity with expert evidence in this jurisdiction can lead to misunderstanding and unease about this process on the part of both experts and representatives. That sometimes results in experts being asked to make inappropriate changes, but more frequently has the opposite result whereby experts decline to engage in any discussion of the report and representatives feel awkward about making quite legitimate suggestions.

23.28 It is your job to ensure that the report properly addresses the issues in a manner which will be of assistance to the adjudicator. There is nothing wrong with raising a concern or putting a point to him. You may ask him if he agrees or disagrees with a particular proposition, as long as you do not ask him to misrepresent his own opinion.

23.29 If the expert will not be giving oral evidence (see paras 25.1–25.5), then he will be unable to defend the report in cross-examination. It is especially important in that case to put yourself in the position of the HOPO and consider whether any aspect of the report is inadequately explained or there is any ambiguity which might be exploited, and to ensure that the expert addresses those concerns in the final version of the report.

23.30 You will occasionally have to decide whether to submit a report which has both favourable and unfavourable aspects. You should not disclose the report if it does more harm than good. If the report is so damning that you feel you can no longer present your client's case, then the appropriate course will be to advise your client so that she can either withdraw her appeal or seek alternative representation.

23.31 Ask the following:

- Has he clearly answered each question you asked?
- Has he cited sources where appropriate or else explained why he cannot cite sources or otherwise how he has come to his conclusion?
- Is his conclusion justified by his reasoning?
- Does his report raise further questions in your mind?
- Has he expressed an opinion that he is not entitled to express?
- Is there irrelevant material or emotive comment?
- Does he clearly state the factual premises upon which he is commenting?
- Is information that he has reproduced from the material supplied to him, including the client's statement, accurate? (The HOPO may suggest that a mistake shows carelessness or, unjustifiably, a discrepancy on the part of the appellant going to credibility.)

Qualifications

23.32 It should be apparent from the report why the author's opinion should be preferred to that of someone (including the HOPO or the author of the Home Office Country Assessment) who lacks his expertise.

23.33 Particularly where the expert has a history of campaigning or is connected to a campaigning organisation, it is important that he avoids any suspicion of bias. The report's account of his qualifications and experience should highlight factors which support his ability to give an independent opinion, such as advising bodies which are manifestly independent, or bodies which take different approaches.

Sources

23.34 The source(s) for any statement should be cited wherever possible. The IAT has recognised that experts in this jurisdiction may not be able to identify all their sources. Problems do not only arise where identification may place the source at risk. Much knowledge in international affairs is exchanged through seminars and conferences held under the Chatham House Rule (whereby the information can be disclosed, but the identity and affiliation of the source is confidential). To ignore the knowledge that an expert acquires in this way will be unreasonable (as well as potentially dangerous).

23.35 The basis of an opinion may be accumulated experience over years or decades of study of the country. It is perfectly legitimate to prefer the opinion of a highly qualified person who has long studied the country to someone without these attributes.

23.36 What is important is that the expert explain how the information is derived, its reliability, and, if applicable, why he is not able to give specific sources. In so doing, he should not assume even the most basic knowledge on the part of the Home Office. In **Es-Eldin**, the Court of Appeal was plainly disturbed that an official representing the Home Office in an asylum appeal (and unhappily also the appellant's representative) had not heard of the Royal Institute for International Affairs (Chatham House). As a result, the adjudicator (who also did not know what it was) rejected the expert evidence.

23.37 The IAT gave the following guidance in **Zarour**:

> When it comes to quoting sources, a measure of judgment has to be exercised, both by country experts in what they do, and by adjudicators in what they expect...
>
> What we suggest on this point is that country experts should
>
> a) only use confidential sources where no open ones are available; b) give the best indication they can of the general nature of the source; and c) make it clear why it must remain confidential, and why no open source can be used.
>
> The rest must remain a matter of judgment for them and adjudicators.

23.38 The expert may regard the confidential source as adding weight to (or more authoritative than) the publicly available sources. Indeed, his value as an expert may rest in part upon his access to sources that are not available to the public. In those circumstances, it is suggested that he quote the publicly available sources and explain so far as possible the additional corroboration he has obtained from confidential sources.

Language

23.39 The report should not contain emotive or partisan language – regardless of whether the expert is within his area of expertise. It exposes him to the allegation that he is straying into the role of an advocate rather providing independent assistance to the court. The need to appear detached may not come naturally in this jurisdiction. One would hope that no-one, whatever his expertise, would be impartial about whether a refugee should be refouled to face death or torture. It is unsurprising that experts form strong views, given the juxtaposition they see between the cavalier absurdity of some Home Office arguments and the unique gravity of the matters in hand. The expert is not expected to divorce himself from humanity. Nevertheless, he must attempt to keep such feelings out of his report. Where emotive comments have crept in, suggest that they are removed. You must not, however, write passages of the report.

23.40 Any factual premise on which the comment is based should be expressed. If he has inadvertently included phraseology which suggests that he has assumed the truth of the appellant's account rather than proceeded on a given premise, point this out to him.

Consistency/accuracy

23.41 Any mistake in the expert's summary of your client's evidence may take on an unjustified significance. A mistake as to the date of some event in your client's history will usually be a slip on the expert's part, but a HOPO will be all too eager to present it as a significant discrepancy even where the expert has never met your client or been provided with any material which is not before the court. Though the adjudicator should recognise such mistakes as carelessness, it can only detract from the overall impression he forms of the expert evidence.

23.42 It is often unnecessary for the expert to reproduce your client's history, rather than simply to confirm that he has read her statement. It can encourage criticism that the expert has inappropriately identified with your client (particularly if emotive language has crept in) or approached the case with an unquestioning acceptance of her account as true.

23.43 Similarly, check that there is no unexplained inconsistency between the expert report and other country evidence which you propose submitting including, in particular, any other expert evidence. Submitting more than one expert report on the same topic can backfire if the experts highlight different factors when responding to the same question: this has in the past been sufficient to result in each report being rejected on the ground that they are inconsistent with each other! Where the experts have in fact been instructed to address different questions, you should check that this is apparent from their reports. If the questions overlap, then you may have to raise with each of them the points taken by the others. If the disagreement is apparent rather than real, then this should avoid giving a misleading impression of inconsistency. If the disagreement is real, then you should normally go with the expert you consider the more reliable rather than submitting inconsistent expert evidence. You cannot ask an expert to alter his opinion.

Presentation

23.44 Unless the expert's circumstances make it impossible, the court should receive a legible well presented copy of the report. Check punctuation, grammar, and spelling. Paragraphs should be numbered so they are easy to identify. Remember that if you are not calling your expert to give oral evidence, the report will be all the adjudicator has upon which to form an impression.

23.45 Consider seeking a direction that the Home Office indicate in advance whether the expert report is disputed and, if so, on what grounds it is disputed. In the absence of a direction, the Home Office may challenge the expert evidence only after the hearing is underway. If your expert has not attended the hearing, the adjudicator will be unable to hear his response to such a challenge. This may necessitate an adjournment application to obtain the expert's response. If the hearing is not adjourned and it transpires that the expert can show that the Home Office's challenge was misconceived, the matter may have to be pursued on appeal. It is far better for all involved if the Home Office is compelled to disclose any challenge in advance of the adjudicator hearing.

23 The expert report
Key points

- Instruct your expert as soon as possible.

- Do not simply provide the expert with the case papers and ask him to comment. Give clear (but not oppressively detailed) instructions which should include an explanation of the context in which your questions arise.

- Ensure that your instructions set out the issues fairly and are not slanted or misleading.

- If you ask him to comment on different factual scenarios, these should be set out in your instructions and the report.

- An expert can provide valuable assistance in an advisory role but this must be clearly differentiated from his role as an expert witness.

- Emphasise issues of confidentiality.

- Provide him with all relevant documentation (which will usually be all the papers in the appeal).

- Only arrange for the expert to meet your client if that will assist in forming an expert opinion (for example, in assessing ethnicity or nationality).

- Check the draft report to ensure that

  - ☐ it complies with the guidance from the courts as to what it should include,
  - ☐ the expert addresses your questions and explains how he reached his answers,
  - ☐ if he does not identify sources, he explains why,
  - ☐ his language is clear and not partisan,
  - ☐ any factual premise is expressed,
  - ☐ there are no mistakes in any summary of your client's account,
  - ☐ it is properly presented.

- You can and should discuss the draft report with the expert and suggest legitimate changes, but you must never ask him to distort his opinion.

- Consider seeking a direction that the Home Office disclose its position on the expert evidence in advance.

24 Re-using expert reports

24.1 Questions that require expert evidence range from those specific to the appellant's circumstances to those which arise in similar form in many appeals. Expert reports may be client based, issue based, or a mixture of the two. In the past, representatives have regularly submitted reports that were prepared for previous cases because the issue has arisen again in the present case. The practice has been of increasing concern to the IAT, and to some experts.

24.2 The IAT's concern is not only about confidentiality (it goes without saying that an expert report should not be reused without removing any text which would identify the original client). In *Slimani*, it said that:

> [T]oo often reports prepared for a specific case are relied on in other cases in which appellants from the same country are represented by the same advisers. This should not happen unless the report is stated to be general and the author is asked to confirm that he is content for it to be relied on. Apart from anything else, conditions change and views which may have been valid when the report was written might not be 12 months later.

24.3 In *Bouglouf*, it said that:

> The tribunal has in other cases deprecated the practice of using reports prepared for a particular case in others, unless the author is prepared to say that he or she agrees. It is said that it is too expensive to get a fresh report in every case. That is no excuse, particularly as it could hardly be expensive to obtain the agreement of the author that it can be used because it is of general application. This practice must cease and adjudicators and the tribunal will be entitled to attach very little if any weight to such reports.

24.4 Expert reports are sometimes recycled for perfectly understandable reasons. One can sympathise with the dilemma faced by counsel who is briefed the night before a hearing and has a recent expert report from another case which appears to answer a similar allegation being made in the present case. It may be impossible even to contact the expert in the time available, yet it is obviously of great concern if this information cannot be conveyed so that the allegation goes unanswered.

24.5 Unless you are in such an unhappy position, you should try to obtain a report from the particular expert which addresses the present case. This always carries more weight. If the expert is unable to provide another report, you may ask him to confirm that the previous report is of general application and if possible reproduce it as a general comment. You must at least request his permission to submit an anonymised version of the previous report. His consent cannot be assumed. Many experts now incorporate a standard stipulation into their reports to the effect that they cannot be reused without permission, and are reluctant to give such permission in light of previous adverse comments by the IAT.

24.6 If you are in the unhappy position of being instructed the night before, you should still attempt to contact the expert in order to explain the problem and ask whether the expert will consent to his report being disclosed, at least in order to support an adjournment application to obtain a case specific report. He may consent on the understanding that it is made clear that he has not seen the papers in the present case. However, the expert may not be contactable and your adjournment application may be refused. If the report stipulates that it is not to be reused, that must be respected. Otherwise, you have no choice but to offer an anonymised version of the original report if the adjudicator is prepared to consider it.

24.7 Where an expert can give valuable evidence upon a recurring issue but is not able to comment upon each individual appeal, you may consider obtaining an issue-based report from him which can be referred to in each case without specific authorisation. Paying for such a report may be more problematic than a report which is clearly attributable to an individual case.

24 Re-using expert reports
Key points

■ The IAT has expressed consistent concern about 'recycling' of expert reports and prefers to receive a report specifically directed to the appellant.

■ It will not consider a 'recycled' report at all unless the expert has given permission for it to be reused.

■ Always obtain an individual report where possible.

■ If that is impractical, strive to obtain the expert's consent to the use of a previous (relevant) report and ensure that it is anonymised.

■ Consider obtaining a report that is expressly issue-based rather than client-based to deal with issues that arise repeatedly in the same form.

25 The expert at court

Whether to call oral expert evidence

25.1   The IAT has indicated that it particularly values oral evidence from experts. It considers that the discipline imposed by oral examination, particularly cross-examination, is an important check upon the reliability of their evidence.

25.2   There are particular features of asylum and human rights appeals that often render oral expert evidence impractical. There may be a very small number of suitably qualified experts on a country which is presently generating a large number of appeals. It may not be practical even to obtain a written report on every appeal, still less have the expert give oral evidence at each hearing. Expert evidence may have to be sought from abroad, in which case attendance at the hearing may be ruled out by impracticality or cost.

25.3   This has been recognised by the Court of Appeal. In **Tarlochan Singh**, the Court considered a decision of the IAT in which it had rejected an expert report because the expert had not been available for cross-examination. Buxton LJ said that the author had been

> put forward as an expert, just as the authors of all the other [human rights] documents before the tribunal were put forward as experts. In the way in which this sort of inquiry is necessarily conducted in front of a tribunal, it is only rarely going to be the case that evidence is given by persons actually appearing in front of a tribunal rather than by reference to the reports of persons of greater or lesser weight – Amnesty International, the United Nations Commission on Refugees and the Canadian body used in this case. It was, therefore, not sufficient simply to reject [the expert's evidence] because he had not been cross-examined.

25.4   If the HOPO seeks to criticise the fact that an expert is not available for oral examination, you may also wish to point out that the Home Office urges reliance upon its 'Country Assessments' despite never offering the authors for cross-examination.

25.5   Nevertheless, the proposition that expert evidence should not be rejected on the ground that it was not given orally should not detract from the good reasons that exist for calling your expert.

25.6   Obviously, the ideal is that you seek to reach agreement on the expert evidence with the Home Office in advance. Unfortunately, you may well come up against the brick wall faced by anyone attempting to engage the Home Office in useful discussion prior to the hearing. The result is wasted time and expense. Consider therefore seeking a direction that the Home Office indicates whether, and on what grounds, the expert report is disputed (para 23.45).

25.7   Where you are lucky enough to be able to agree expert evidence in advance, it is unlikely that the expert's attendance at the hearing will be necessary. The Adjudicator should not go behind such an agreement (*Carcabuk & Bla*). If unforeseen issues subsequently arise at the hearing upon which the expert's comment is needed, it will normally be unfair to refuse an adjournment for that purpose.

25.8   If expert evidence is not agreed, then the benefits of calling your expert are several. As indicated above, the IAT often prefers to hear from experts. Where an adjudicator might otherwise be minded to reject an expert's opinion, the expert's ability to respond to cross-examination and the adjudicator's questions may persuade him otherwise. The IAT has on occasion changed its view of an expert after hearing oral evidence even where previous written reports had been rejected in strong terms.

25.9   The expert's presence will invariably focus the adjudicator's mind on his evidence. (Sometimes, an adjudicator fails to deal with an expert report at all in his determination, usually necessitating appeal.) Unless your expert presents badly, the adjudicator is less likely to be dismissive of an expert who appears before him. Equally, the HOPO is likely to feel more inhibited from making unjustified allegations against the expert, particularly if the expert has dealt with the HOPO's cross-examination satisfactorily. Indeed, some suspect that the very sight of the expert attending for cross-examination has influenced an unexpected settlement offer from the HOPO at the door of the court!

25.10 If your expert's evidence is nonetheless rejected, the fact that he dealt with whatever points were put to him in examination may well strengthen any appeal. It will be even less justifiable for an adjudicator to reject expert evidence on a point which has not been raised at the hearing if the adjudicator and HOPO had ample opportunity to put the point to the expert. (And see conversely the IAT's comment in

Kapela that the risk of not calling the expert is that the adjudicator is left with unanswered questions.)

25.11 Last but not least, if an unexpected issue arises during examination of the appellant or other witnesses, your expert will be there to comment on it. Similarly, where oral evidence departs from or adds to that contained in the witness statements, your expert will have seen that evidence and can say whether or not his opinion has altered. The HOPO cannot then seek to undermine the expert's opinion on the basis that it was reached in ignorance of the oral evidence.

25.12 Prior to making a final decision about whether or not to call oral expert evidence, there obviously has to be an assessment of how good a witness the expert will be. Indeed, where there is a choice of suitably qualified experts, this assessment may influence who to instruct. An expert may write thorough and reliable reports but be poor at performing in court.

25.13 You need to know how the expert will handle cross-examination. The best way to establish this is to ask some probing questions yourself. You should therefore see the expert, or at least have a substantial telephone conference, prior to deciding that he should give oral evidence.

25.14 If your expert is not going to give oral evidence, it is all the more important that you invite, and if necessary seek a direction that the Home Office either agrees the expert report or indicates what parts are disputed and on what grounds. You should also invite the Home Office to provide any written questions for your expert's consideration (a procedure which is formalised in the CPR). All these steps will render it less likely that the expert's opinion can be dismissed on grounds that he has not had an opportunity to rebut. But these steps can only happen if your expert is instructed, and his report prepared and served, in good time.

25.15 A further reason for deciding at the earliest possible stage whether your expert will give oral evidence is in order to check his availability and make any application to the Court concerning listing. The IAT has said that where an expert's evidence is prima facie relevant and an adequate reason is given for his unavailability on the date listed, there will be 'every ground' for granting an adjournment (*Kondo*). It is important that you inform the Court as soon as you are aware that there may be a problem with the expert's attendance.

25.16 The standard directions issued with the notice of first hearing require either that you indicate that the appeal is ready to proceed (and indicate how many witnesses you intend to call) or that you attend the first hearing. If you are still in the process of identifying an expert and you hope to call oral evidence, you should not certify that the case is ready to proceed. Instead, explain to the court why expert evidence is important, what steps have already been taken to obtain it, what further steps you plan to take, and an estimate of how long this will take. (You must be able to offer a date on which you should be ready to proceed.)

25.17 The possibility that your expert might be prepared to give evidence only on condition of anonymity was raised at para 21.21. If so, consider an application either that the public be excluded from the hearing, that the expert not be required to give oral evidence that may identify himself, and/or that he not be identified in the determination.

25.18 It would of course be possible to seek a witness summons in respect of your expert were he otherwise unwilling or unable to attend (though only if he is within the UK). But you should hesitate long before summonsing an expert (or any witness) against his will. It might be appropriate to obtain a summons where the expert himself was happy to appear but was being prevented from doing so, say, by his employer.

25.19 The IAT in *Zarour* said that it would have been prepared to issue a witness summons of its own motion against an expert whose report was in evidence before them. That possibility should be borne in mind. However, the Court of Appeal has indicated that the power of the IAT to summons a witness should be exercised sparingly. The IAT has also held in *Prendi* that an adjudicator should not issue a witness summons of his own motion simply to enable the HOPO to cross-examine a witness (which the HOPO could not do if he applied for the witness summons himself) – see para 30.15.

Preparation for the hearing

25.20 It is most important that you have a full conference with your expert prior to his appearance in court. The conference should not, unless unavoidable, take place on the day of the hearing. You should allow sufficient time for the expert to make any further enquiries or conduct any further research arising out of the conference. He may at least want some further period to reconsider the documentation in light of the potential challenges which are discussed. If he is unused to giving evidence, he will also appreciate being briefed on what to expect well before he reaches the doors of the court. The conference should, if at all possible, be conducted by the advocate who will present the hearing.

25.21 Experts in other jurisdictions commonly receive training in presenting expert evidence to a court, including cross-examination, and have sub-

stantial experience of it in practice. It is far less common in this jurisdiction (largely on grounds of cost). Before discussing case-specific
issues you should explain in some detail how an appeal hearing is conducted. When you are so familiar with the process, it is easy to forget
how ill at ease your expert may feel at the prospect of entering and performing in an environment of which he knows next to nothing.
Putting him at ease, even on simple things like how to address the
adjudicator, leaves him free to concentrate on the contents of his evidence.

25.22 You should also give general advice about presentation of oral evidence: listen to the question but direct the answer to the adjudicator;
speak clearly and pause sufficiently to allow the adjudicator to take a
note; consider carefully (and with an open mind) any proposition that
is put to him by the HOPO and (particularly) the adjudicator; avoid
emotive language or appearing partisan.

25.23 He should give his evidence in a calm and straightforward manner
(especially under aggressive cross-examination) and should avoid
appearing on the one hand nervous or uncertain, and on the other
hand arrogant or over-confident. Where a proposition is repeatedly
put with which he does not agree, he should express his disagreement
calmly and firmly but having explained his response, avoid being
drawn into an argument. If he realises that one of his earlier statements requires revision, then he should say so and explain why. He
should say if he does not know the answer to the question or if he considers that he is being asked to comment on a question outside his
remit.

25.24 In accordance with the practice as to witness statements, your expert's
written report will stand as his evidence in chief. This means that oral
examination in chief will be at best limited. Cross-examination will be
the primary, perhaps only environment in which the adjudicator is
able to assess the expert's oral evidence. It is imperative that any witness listens to the question and shows how he is answering it. But if
your expert is confident and capable of doing so properly, he also can
be advised to use the questions as a hook to advance relevant and
important points to the adjudicator, rather than following the common advice on cross-examination of saying as little as possible consistent with answering the question.

25.25 It is your job to foresee lines of cross-examination. You ought to know
what his views will be on any topic about which he is likely to be cross-
examined. Apart from forewarning you of any problems which can be
pre-empted in evidence in chief, it is a prerequisite to conducting an
effective re-examination.

25.26 Aims of cross-examination might be to persuade the expert to accept points favourable to the Home Office; to probe his knowledge by asking him about matters contained in the country reports; to portray his opinion as unbalanced when compared to the country reports; to suggest that he has insufficient evidence to justify his opinions; and to allege inconsistency between the expert's opinion and the actions or opinions of the appellant so as to support credibility challenges. An example of the latter would be where your expert is encouraged to agree that the appellant would have been in great danger during a particular period, from which the HOPO alleges that it is not credible that she did not try to escape earlier.

25.27 The passages at paras 23.26–23.44 on preparing a written report for disclosure apply equally to discussing the expert's oral evidence. You can and should tell the expert if the answers he gives are unclear, or seek further information if his answers appear unconvincing, and you may put points to him that he may have overlooked. But this process must not place him under any pressure to alter his opinion or trespass into 'coaching'.

25.28 His oral evidence is not a memory test. He should familiarise himself with his written report before the hearing. He should bring with him to the hearing all the documentation that he has been given (*and* his report). If he has not already been provided with the paginated bundle that is being used by the adjudicator, then he should be given the full bundle in the form that it was provided to the adjudicator, in time to familiarise himself with it (NOT when he arrives at the hearing). He should also get any further documentation such as chronologies and skeleton arguments, and any material served by the Home Office. If he was not referred to the Home Office's Country Assessment when preparing his report, he should be asked to consider it now as the HOPO may refer to it at the hearing despite not having served it in advance (see para 17.27).

25.29 The above discussion assumes that the expert report was prepared according to the best practice set out in the previous chapters. If an expert report was disclosed before you were instructed, that may not be the case and the report itself may be problematic. If so, a conference is all the more important, and an important part of the conference will be exploring what can be done to address the deficiencies in the original report through oral evidence or a supplementary report. Sometimes – through lack of guidance as much as any fault on his part – the report may be so flawed that it will be better to instruct another expert rather than attempt to retrieve the position through further evidence from the report's author.

The hearing
Examination in chief

25.30 The expert should normally give evidence after all witnesses of fact, and should be present to hear their evidence. Unlike a witness of fact, an expert's primary purpose is to give his opinion upon the factual evidence. This has to be explained to some HOPOs who, unused to expert witnesses, may wrongly suggest that the expert be excluded from the hearing until he gives evidence.

25.31 You should check with the adjudicator before you start examination in chief whether he has read the expert report and if not, invite him to do so before the expert is called. Your oral examination in chief should start by asking the expert whether he has modified any of the opinions in his report and if not, to confirm that he adopts the views contained therein. You may also wish to confirm whether he has met the appellant (other than at court).

25.32 If there is nothing further upon which you want him to comment or elaborate, that is sufficient examination in chief. As with witnesses of fact, it can be effective simply to offer him for cross-examination immediately (this sometimes discomforts the HOPO).

25.33 The potential drawbacks of this approach are twofold. Firstly, like other witnesses, if this is the first time the expert has given oral evidence, he should ideally have an opportunity to get into his stride by dealing with a couple of questions of which he has had advanced warning.

25.34 Secondly, the cross-examination may not be sufficiently relevant or extensive to allow the expert a full opportunity to impress his expertise upon the adjudicator through his oral presentation. The problem is exacerbated if the adjudicator does not have a clear recollection of the expert's written report when he hears the evidence. You may therefore decide to prepare a couple of questions which will give the expert an opportunity to demonstrate his expertise by expanding on the opinions in his report. But avoid inviting the objection that he is simply being asked to repeat information in his report (an objection that should not arise so long as your evidence in chief remains short and focussed).

25.35 There are circumstances in which you would be justified in conducting a longer examination in chief. These are:

- if developments have taken place in the country of origin which post-date the expert's report;

- if new issues have arisen during the hearing upon which he can give expert comment, such as a new allegation about implausibility or risk during the HOPO's cross-examination of the appellant. Where this is the case, you should if necessary request a short adjournment in order to discuss the point with your expert before he gives evidence.
- if there are problems with the written report which need to be remedied, or it does not deal with all the matters upon which the expert can give relevant evidence.

25.36 A similar dilemma may arise as with witnesses of fact: whether to deal with a potential problem in examination in chief or whether this simply draws unnecessary attention to it. Where there is a real risk that the problem will emerge later, whether in cross-examination or on the adjudicator's initiative, it is usually best to get it over with in examination in chief. If the expert's opinion has altered from that contained in the written report, you have, of course, no option but to raise it.

25.37 That approach is also consistent with the expert's over-riding duty to the court. It may actually assist the expert's credibility by impressing the adjudicator that he is taking this duty seriously and is anxious to be entirely straightforward. It may be much more damaging if such problems emerge only in cross-examination. However as with witnesses of fact, there is no need to dwell on issues which only a HOPO might suggest were problematic so that your examination in chief starts to resemble the HOPO's cross-examination.

25.38 The better a witness the expert is, the more general the questions can be, allowing the expert to develop his evidence himself. If your expert is more uncertain, the questions should be more specific so as to guide the expert away from repetition or irrelevance, (though the normal rule prohibiting leading questions applies).

25.39 In any event, you ought to give your expert prior notice of the areas you will cover. The only exception might be if you are (probably unfairly) refused a short adjournment to discuss with him a new issue which has arisen during the hearing and (after very careful consideration) you feel sufficiently confident to raise it with him 'raw' in examination in chief.

Cross-examination

25.40 See paras 25.22–25.26 for preparation for cross-examination. If your expert is a good and confident witness then he can (and therefore should) be left to deal with most inappropriate or misleading questions himself (for example, where the question proceeds on a false premise). You will have already probed with him foreseeable lines of cross-examination so it should only be the oddest of questions that takes him completely by surprise.

25.41 Where a HOPO persists with a question that the expert has explained is inappropriate, you may wish to intervene. He should not, for example, be pressed to reveal anonymous sources. While the CPR require that an expert's report state the substance of his instructions, they also prohibit cross-examination as to an expert's instructions unless the court rules that there are reasonable grounds to consider that his account of his instructions is incomplete or inaccurate (r.35.10(4) and see further para 23.6).

25.42 The expert should not be expected to have as detailed a recollection of your appellant's facts as you should. Intervene where the HOPO makes inaccurate references to the factual evidence, for example dates of detention or details of family members. You are also freer to check the HOPO's references against the documents, whereas the expert will be concentrating on composing his answer.

25.43 A HOPO sometimes objects to an expert referring to the views of others in his field, (for example, describing the consensus view on an issue) on the ground that the expert is giving hearsay evidence. There is of course no rule prohibiting hearsay evidence in any event but even in other jurisdictions, it is well established that an expert may refer to the learning of others in his field to support his opinion without infringing the hearsay rule. A HOPO may even object that the expert is stating his opinion rather than giving factual evidence! The only circumstance in which the HOPO may have a valid objection is where your expert strays beyond his expertise. Remind your expert beforehand of the points discussed in chapter 22 concerning what is and what is not appropriate.

Re-examination

25.44 Once again, the ordinary rules apply: the most impressive course is often not to re-examine at all. Even if your expert has been damaged in cross-examination, it will seldom be sensible to try to repair the damage unless you know what answer you will get. If the expert's answers have appeared ambiguous, then depending how thoroughly you have worked through the issues in conference, you may be able to formulate questions in a way that allows the expert to clarify matters.

25.45 Where an adjudicator has restricted your evidence in chief to the written report, re-examination may also enable you to offer your expert a better opportunity to impress the adjudicator through oral evidence on questions which arise from the HOPO's cross-examination and to ensure that the critical issues are at the forefront of the adjudicator's mind.

25 The expert at court
Key points

■ If you cannot agree expert evidence in advance, then calling the expert to give oral evidence has substantial advantages:

☐ the IAT has emphasised that it is preferable for an expert to be available for cross-examination,

☐ it has in the past reversed its assessment of an expert after hearing his oral evidence,

☐ the expert's ability to respond to cross-examination and questions from the adjudicator can determine whether his evidence is accepted or rejected,

☐ the expert will hear the rest of the evidence and so can comment on the full factual picture and on unexpected issues that arise during cross-examination of the appellant and other factual witnesses.

■ A pre-hearing expert conference is important so that you can

☐ assess how the expert will come across in court,

☐ explain how the hearing will be conducted,

☐ give general advice on how to present his evidence orally,

☐ check whether there are any issues in the report that need to be addressed in oral examination,

☐ explore what his response will be to foreseeable lines of cross-examination.

■ The expert, unlike factual witnesses, should be present during the factual oral evidence.

■ Check before the expert gives evidence that the adjudicator has read his report.

■ Start examination in chief by asking whether the expert has altered any opinion set out in the report. He may then be invited to expand upon these opinions in a short and focussed examination in chief.

■ A longer examination in chief may be appropriate to deal with

☐ developments in the country of origin that post-date his report,

☐ new issues that have arisen during the factual evidence,

☐ any problems with the written report.

- Intervene during cross-examination if the HOPO has his facts wrong.

- Your ability to re-examine effectively will depend on how thoroughly you explored the issues during the pre-hearing conference.

26 Medical reports

26.1 Much of the guidance on the role of an expert and the presentation of his evidence is equally applicable to the reports discussed in this chapter. But this chapter deals with issues specific to expert medical evidence. The term 'medical report' is used as a label for all expert evidence on physical or mental condition, whether or not the expert is a medical doctor (or, say, a psychologist). For convenience, two other types of expert evidence are discussed in this chapter. The first is expert evidence on medical facilities in the country of origin as this is usually submitted in conjunction with medical reports. The second is evidence from independent social workers as to the effects upon families of expulsion as this is often submitted in conjunction with psychological reports.

26.2 Medical evidence is commonly obtained to

- corroborate past ill-treatment;
- establish scarring, injuries or other conditions which will exacerbate risk from the authorities or non-state actors;
- explain an appellant's difficulties in giving evidence or recounting events;
- demonstrate the effect of expulsion upon a person's physical or mental condition or that of a member of her family.

26.3 In *Ibrahim*, the IAT emphasised to adjudicators that they must follow the IAT's guidance on medical evidence to the effect that:

Any medical report or psychiatric report deserves careful and specific consideration, bearing in mind, particularly, that there may be psychological consequences from ill-treatment which may affect the evidence which is given by the applicant. In the Tribunal's view, it is incumbent upon the adjudicator to indicate in the determination that careful attention has been given to each and every aspect of medical reports, particularly [as] these are matters of expert evidence which cannot be dismissed out of hand.

Corroborating past ill-treatment

26.4 A physical examination will normally be appropriate if your client reports significant past ill-treatment and credibility is in issue. The only basis for not obtaining a physical examination would be where there is no realistic possibility that the treatment reported by your client would have left any evidence.

26.5 Do not assume that because your client has no visible marks, there is no point in a physical report. A medical expert may detect after-effects of torture which are not apparent to a lay person. (Equally, do not make assumptions about the marks you can see. Ask your client about them. It may turn out that they have an innocent explanation.)

26.6 Some have unrealistic view of what medical evidence can do. It is virtually never the case that medical evidence can prove conclusively whether or not someone was tortured. Sometimes, adjudicators and HOPOs will suggest that the absence of medical evidence indicates that the appellant's account of torture is false. In *Junaid*, the IAT commented as follows:

> There is a further concern in that [the adjudicator] relied upon the absence of any medical report in relation to physical evidence of torture. The appellant's account was that the wounds had healed and there was effectively nothing substantial to show for what had happened to him. In our judgement, the way the Adjudicator approached that was again wrong. She should have considered first whether the evidence established that there would have been some sort of scarring and then and only then would it have been proper for her to have drawn the conclusion that the absence of scarring in some way militated against the account given by the appellant.

26.7 The Istanbul Protocol (see para 26.65) states that:

> To the extent that physical evidence of torture exists, it provides important confirmatory evidence that a person was tortured. However, the absence of such physical evidence must not be construed to suggest that torture did not occur, since such acts of violence against persons frequently leave no marks or permanent scars.

26.8 Despite this, the absence of medical evidence may raise suspicion in the adjudicator's mind that the reason there is no report before him is that the report which was obtained was negative. That risk is not obviated if the adjudicator does not refer to his suspicion in the determination. Where an expert indicates that the absence of positive medical evidence is not an indicator that the claimant's case is false, it may be worth serving the report.

26.9 Expert evidence on mental conditions, e.g. PTSD, may also corroborate past ill-treatment. In many countries, state agents are becoming increasingly sophisticated in inflicting torture by means that do not leave lasting physical evidence. This makes psychiatric corroboration of past ill-treatment increasingly important. For example, in Amnesty International's report 'Turkey: Torture and Impunity' (October 2001), it stated that:

> *Psychiatric reports have gained importance in the documentation of torture, since the security forces increasingly use psychological and other forms of torture which do not leave visible wounds, making torture allegations more difficult to verify.*

Characteristics going to present risk

26.10 Corroborating credibility may not be the only relevance of visible marks and scarring. Country evidence may indicate that visible scarring which is consistent with past torture or past combat may provoke the adverse interest of local security forces. Such scarring will be relevant regardless of whether it in fact had an innocent explanation. A medical report demonstrating scarring suggestive of past torture or combat may therefore be material, even where the scarring was actually caused in some other way. A report from a country expert may also be required in such cases as the real question is not simply what the scarring indicates to a medical practitioner but whether there is a real risk that the scarring may provoke the suspicions of the security forces. The IAT has also indicated that it is useful to make photographs of the scarring available to the adjudicator where this issue arises. (Medical photography is available from the Photography & Illustration Department, University College London, tel: 020 7380 9079.

26.11 Psychiatric and psychological reports may also be material to present risk. A person who is mentally ill or disordered may be less capable of withstanding intense interrogation without inadvertently incriminating herself. It may be claimed by the HOPO that your client can avoid ill-treatment by lying or concealing information when interrogated upon arrival. Such a proposition is obviously unattractive even in respect of a healthy appellant, but expert evidence may indicate that the appellant is in any event unlikely to be able to carry off such a deception (e.g. *Demirca*).

Reports on mental condition

26.12 The Istanbul Protocol states that:

> *A psychological evaluation and appraisal of the alleged torture victim is always necessary and may be part of the physical examination, or where there are no physical signs, may be performed by itself.* (para 103)

Even where your client does not report significant physical ill-treatment, be sensitive to the possibility that your client may be traumatised, disturbed or have other psychiatric or psychological difficulties, whether flowing from ill-treatment that she has not disclosed or some other reason. Listen to your client when you take instructions. Ask her how she is feeling, but do not unquestioningly accept her answer. Sometimes a client will have blanked out particular incidents. She may give what seem to be completely different accounts of an incident each time you speak to her. She may appear disturbed, unable to concentrate, unusually slow, unwilling to answer the questions you ask or incoherent. Such an assessment obviously requires an experienced and competent interpreter so that you get the best possible idea of how your client is expressing herself. As discussed in chapter 11, some interpreters consider their role not only to interpret but to render the language coherent and logical. If you do not recognise and prevent this, it means that you will probably miss problem signs.

26.13 The Home Office regularly alleges dishonesty on the ground that any genuine refugee should be able to give a consistent account of her ill-treatment over time. There is now a large body of expert learning to the contrary, see e.g.:

- *Discrepancies in histories presented by asylum seekers*, Stuart Turner (expert opinion, 16 August 1996, available from RLC's EIS database)
- *Discrepancies in autobiographical memories – implications for the assessment of asylum seekers: repeated interviews study*, Jane Herlihy, Peter Scragg, Stuart Turner (*British Medical Journal*, Vol 324)
- *The Psychological Sequelae of Torture – Use of Evidence in the Asylum Procedure*, Dietrich Kock and Deirdre Winter (Presentation to ELENA Conference, Berlin, December 2000 – available from RLC's EIS database)
- *Errors of Recall and Credibility: Can Omissions and Discrepancies in Successive Statements Reasonably be Said to Undermine Credibility of Testimony* (*Medico-Legal Journal*, Dr Juliet Cohen (2001) Vol. 69 Part 1, 25–34

26.14 An examination by a psychiatrist or psychologist may demonstrate that it is particularly inappropriate to expect consistency in view of your client's condition. It may go to explain past discrepancies relied upon by the Home Office and/or to explain your decision not to call oral evidence from your client.

26.15 Even when the examination is conducted by an expert, encouraging a trauma victim to recall and relive their experiences is dangerous. The Istanbul Protocol states that:

> *Despite all precautions, physical and psychological examinations by their very nature may re-traumatize the patient by provoking or exacerbating symptoms of post-traumatic stress by eliciting painful effects and memories… A subjective assessment has to be made by the evaluator about the extent to which pressing for details is necessary for the effectiveness of the report in court, especially if the claimant demonstrates obvious signs of distress in the interview.* (para 148)

26.16 Given the risks involved even in taking a history in a supportive environment, the expert may well advise that cross-examination in the context of an adversarial court hearing will pose an unacceptable risk. In those circumstances, it will usually be inappropriate to call your client to give oral evidence at the hearing (see further chapter 30).

26.17 A fear of stigma may make your client anxious to conceal past ill-treatment from relatives and her community, particularly sexual ill-treatment. You must always take instructions in the absence of friends and relatives (see chapter 11). Your client may be worried that referral for psychiatric examination will provoke unwelcome questions from relatives. It can help to tell close relatives who are also involved in the case that your client's examination is a routine measure. If confidentiality as regards relatives is an issue, be sure that any report is not sent to your client by post without express authorisation.

Treatment

26.18 Unfortunately, many representatives consider that their job is done once they have obtained the necessary forensic evidence and give little consideration to the therapeutic requirements disclosed by the report. Left to her own devices, the prospects of your client accessing therapeutic care are little better than the prospects that she would have obtained forensic evidence on her own. A large proportion of UK citizens who suffer mental illness or disorder fail to access appropriate treatment. The obstacles are magnified for an asylum seeker.

26.19 The expert report should contain an indication of any appropriate treatment. However, the overriding duty of a medical expert, like any other expert, is to provide independent assistance to the Court. Although the Medical Foundation is a special case, an expert witness will not normally view arranging treatment for your client as consistent with his role in the litigation. You should ensure that any recommendations are taken forward in conjunction with your client's GP. Referral to the Medical Foundation (if it did not produce the original report) may be considered, although its waiting lists for treatment are even longer than the waiting lists for forensic reports.

26.20 Facilitating treatment is obviously in the interests of your client. It will also avoid the HOPO attempting to discredit the forensic evidence on the ground that one would have expected her to be receiving treatment. Although he will not stand in the same shoes as an independent expert, a doctor who is responsible for your client's treatment may also be able to add valuable evidence for the appeal.

26.21 The extent of treatment in the UK will also be important in establishing the degree of private life enjoyed in the UK.

Challenging expulsion on medical grounds

26.22 The effects of expulsion upon the appellant's health may well raise issues under articles 3 and/or 8. Possible scenarios include the following:

- The appellant or her dependants are unable to access the treatment they need in the country of origin (either because it is not available generally or will not be available to them).
- The need to access treatment precludes moving to a part of the country which would otherwise be safe.
- The appellant's health prevents her working and so deprives her and any dependants of the means of survival.
- Some conditions (e.g. HIV/AIDS) provoke discrimination and stigmatisation.
- The act of forcible expulsion will trigger a relapse of a serious mental illness/disorder.
- Returning the appellant to the site of previous trauma will exacerbate her condition.
- Treatment which would not cross the requisite severity threshold for a healthy person will cross that threshold where the person is suffering from serious physical or mental conditions.

26.23 Medical evidence will commonly be advanced in tandem with supporting country evidence to establish the factual premise upon which the medical prognosis is based.

26.24 The Home Office sometimes seeks to discredit a medical expert's prognosis on the basis that it assumes matters about the country of origin that he is not qualified to know. It is important, therefore, that your medical expert sets out in his report the factual premise upon which he is commenting and indicates from where it is derived. If your medical expert does in fact have knowledge of country conditions (most usually, the availability of health care), then he should explain that knowledge in the same way as a country expert. If not, he should explain what information he has been given. This may be country evidence, including expert evidence, or simply your instructions. But if the latter, you will obviously have to support the statements made in the instructions by evidence.

26.25 It will be apparent from the scenarios listed above that a wide range of country evidence may be required in a medical case. Particularly where health care provision in the country of origin is in issue, it is often useful for your medical expert to liaise with your country expert. The process might start with a preliminary note from the medical expert as to what treatment is required. The country expert will then produce a report upon the extent to which such treatment will be available. On the basis of that report, the medical expert will produce a prognosis.

26.26 The Home Office commonly argues that what is material is the *theoretical* availability of treatment. In other words, the success or failure of the appeal of a destitute mother should turn on whether a rich person could obtain the treatment that she needs at vast cost. It claims support for this proposition from the case of *K*. *K* was actually a decision by the Court of Appeal on a permission application (so is neither binding nor should it normally be cited: *Senkoy*). To determine the appeal on such hypothetical questions appears contrary to the European Court's fundamental principle that the ECHR rights must be 'practical and effective rather than theoretical and illusory' (*Artico*). It also does not reflect the European Court's approach in the leading case of *Bensaid* which centered upon whether appropriate treatment would be available to Bensaid, not to someone in entirely different circumstances. However, *K* has been cited and followed by the IAT. It is therefore presently necessary for the expert to consider not only practical availability to the appellant but also whether the necessary treatment is available to *anyone* in the country of origin.

26.27 If the extent of health care in the country of origin is in dispute (for example, if the refusal letter claimed that some health care will be available), you may wish your expert to provide an alternative prognosis on the basis of the facts claimed by the Home Office. If the prognosis is sufficiently serious to raise human rights issues even on the Home Office's case, then alternative arguments should be advanced to allow for the possibility that the adjudicator prefers the Home Office's claims about the availability of treatment.

26.28 The medical report should set out

- your client's present condition;
- what, if any, treatment she is receiving;
- the prognosis with that treatment;
- the effects (if any) of the act of expulsion;
- the prognosis in the country of origin.

26.29 It is particularly useful in such situations to have information from the person with responsibility for your client's treatment in the UK.

26.30 In article 8 cases involving families with children, and particularly where proportionality is in issue, it will often be necessary to obtain expert evidence from a child psychologist as to the consequences for the children of their own expulsion or that of a parent. In *Mindoukna*, the IAT gave guidance on the type of issues that such a report could usefully cover:

> The trouble is that we do not have any reliably verified information about what the state of affairs in the family actually is, nor any expert help in predicting its future. As we hope everyone will come to realize, decisions in these cases are at least as important for the welfare of the child involved (even if that cannot be regarded as paramount), as any others. Where, as in this case, they may depend on significant recent developments, or other complications, in our view a short welfare report is required, from the local authority in whose area the child is living. Adjudicators should be asked by solicitors in such cases to make a request for one (assuming it has to come from them) in good time before the hearing. What the report should contain in this case, and how it should be dealt with, we shall discuss below.

> We should not want to be accused of telling experienced court welfare officers how to do their business; but, as welfare reports have not so far been usual in this field, we shall try to give some idea of what we should expect one to contain. Naturally there would be a personal interview with both the appellant and Cathy, together with a home visit so that Leon could be seen in his normal surroundings. Some confirmation that there is regular contact between Cathy's other children and their father would be desirable; but other than that there does not seem to be any special need to go into their situation. What would be particularly appreciated is some assessment of the probable long-term stability of the appellant's relationship with Cathy, and of the contribution he is making to caring for Leon.

26.31 Court welfare officers have now been replaced by 'children's guardians'. It is not possible to obtain a report from them in their official capacity unless there are ongoing proceedings in the family courts. However, a report from an independent social worker (many of whom also act as children's guardians) will perform the same role.

Instructing a medical expert

26.32 The Medical Foundation is the best known source of medical reports in asylum and human rights appeals. The Home Office states that:

> Its work has received recognition and support from a wide range of organisations, including the United Nations, the European Union, the British Medical Association and the British Council of Churches. The Home Office recognises the Medical Foundation as a bona fide organisation. (APIs)

26.33 Its policy is that only in 'exceptional circumstances' will it decline to postpone decisions in order to allow a Medical Foundation report to be obtained (APIs).

26.34 The IAT has also described the Medical Foundation as a 'most prestigious and reliable' body which has 'over the years accumulated a large body of expertise' (**Guney**). There are presently long waiting lists for reports from the Foundation.

26.35 There are a wide range of medical experts available, including many who are experienced in preparing medical reports for the purposes of litigation. The important thing to consider is exactly what you want and why you want it. Your expert should have the appropriate forensic expertise to analyse your client's injuries or condition and the ability to present his findings clearly and explain their relevance. The range of issues on which psychological evidence is accepted in the criminal courts is constantly expanding.

26.36 It can also pay to talk to personal injury solicitors. They are dealing on a regular basis with medical experts and will know not only where the expertise lies, but which experts are better able to produce that knowledge in a form which is useful and persuasive to a court. *The Law Society Directory of Experts* and other expert directories list vast numbers of medical experts. The Law Society also runs an experts helpline. APIL (the Association of Personal Injury Lawyers) has a directory based on recommendations by members. As you build up relationships with the medical experts you use, use them as sources of information on other experts. Talk to other lawyers in the field. Check whether your expert's reports have been the subject of comment by the IAT (see para 21.29).

26.37 As with other expert reports, you should be alert to the risk, particularly when using experts new to the field, that they will be politically unsympathetic to your client. Because the production of the medical report will almost invariably involve examination and interview, it is important to ensure that your client will be as comfortable as possible with the expert. The expert's gender may be particularly significant in relation to sexual torture. Take similar care with the interpreter.

26.38 The Home Office should address in the refusal letter any medical evidence already submitted. Obviously, if a medical report was submitted to corroborate a physical injury, but the refusal letter makes allegations about discrepancies which may be explained by your client's mental condition, it will be necessary to seek a further medical report prior to the appeal. You may also need a supplementary report on the same subject where, for example, the original medical report confirmed scarring consistent with torture but the refusal letter alleges that it could have been caused by some accident. Equally, your medical report might have detailed psychological problems yet the refusal letter nevertheless relies on discrepancies which are explicable by your client's condition. If so, you should get the expert to address directly the relevance of the alleged discrepancies.

Medical experts instructed by the Home Office

26.39 The Home Office does not normally advance expert medical evidence. It has been recorded that an experiment in seeking expert evidence to rebut Medical Foundation reports was abandoned when the Home Office found that its expert tended to corroborate the Foundation's findings (see Good, para 21.24).

26.40 During the summer of 2002, the Home Office began routinely submitting a 'generic' expert report headed *Notes for Assessing Psychiatric Injury in Asylum Seekers* by a Dr Neal. It made various claims about the diagnosis and treatment of PTSD in asylum seekers – including that refugees with PTSD were best treated by returning them to the site of their trauma. None of the claims was based on research into refugees, or even experience of examining asylum seekers on the part of the expert. Adjudicators were nevertheless invited to prefer this generic report to the report of an expert who had examined the appellant. Unsurprisingly, the IAT was unimpressed. In **Harunaj**, it said that:

> *Dr Neal had not seen the appellant and nor had he prepared a report specific to the appellant and if the basis of [the HOPO's] submissions to us*

[challenging the appellant's medical report] was to be based on the general notes for reassessing psychiatric injury in asylum seekers we could see no reason why these should be preferred by the Tribunal to a specific report relative to this appellant; we felt that we lacked the qualification to make any judgment relative to psychiatric matters, and certainly could not make a judgment based on general notes as opposed to a judgment between two medical practitioners, both of whom had had the benefit of a consultation with the appellant.

26.41 So offbeat did HOPOs' submissions become on the strength of their 'generic' report that they could be rebutted simply by reference to the Home Office's own statements. The Home Office has recognised in correspondence with the Medical Foundation that far from being the best thing for them, expelling a refugee suffering from PTSD may amount to inhuman or degrading treatment for the purposes of article 3 (see para 1.78). In fact, the psychiatrist subsequently wrote an open letter stating that he had given no authority for his paper to be relied upon by the Home Office in appeals.

26.42 Unfortunately, the HOPO's submission is often no less outlandish when (as is more often the case) he does not even have 'generic' expert evidence upon which to base a challenge to the appellant's medical expert. The HOPO may attack the conclusions of the most renowned psychiatrist on the basis of what appears to be no more than the HOPO's own 'medical' analysis. He commonly claims that the psychiatrist's diagnosis is defective because it is simply based upon whatever the appellant told him. The High Court has in the past been provoked to point out that:

*It is not appropriate for a civil servant without medical expertise to reach a conclusion contrary to that reached by a psychiatrist simply by drawing on his own native wit. (**Khaira**)*

26.43 This absurdly nihilistic approach to medical expertise is particular to the Home Office in this jurisdiction. It does not occur in those appeals where the Home Office actually submits its own psychiatric evidence. Indeed, during the adjudicator hearing of *Ahmadi*, leading counsel for the Home Office led expert evidence from two psychiatrists aimed at supporting an adverse credibility finding – an approach that somewhat undermines the common claim by HOPOs that psychiatrists can only accept whatever the appellant tells them.

The role of the medical expert

26.44 A medical expert is just that. He is not an expert on asylum and human rights law. It is your job to ensure that the report addresses the correct issues. Doctors accustomed to litigation in other fields may be accustomed to reaching conclusions according to the balance of probabilities, and to disregarding claims which cannot be established on the balance of probabilities. If you want to know whether there is a serious possibility that an injury was caused in a particular way, then you should ask the expert to address this (though you will, of course, welcome greater certainty where available).

26.45 Refer to the general discussion in chapter 22 about the boundaries of acceptable expert comment, particularly on credibility issues. The sensitivity of the IAA to inappropriate comment on credibility is no less strong in relation to medical experts than country experts. But it is unrealistic to pretend that medical experts are not concerned with credibility. Doctors assess credibility in the ordinary course of their work. The Medical Foundation's *Guidelines for the examination of survivors of torture* state that:

> *Consistency and credibility are continuously assessed as the interview and examination proceed. In coming to a conclusion, the doctor must make a series of judgments, assessing the subject's demeanour as well as the history and physical signs.* (p.41)
>
> *... All participants in the asylum process inevitably need to make some estimate of the applicant's credibility. The examining doctor is not excluded from this process of assessment and should have credibility in mind throughout the history-taking and examination and have made some personal assessment of it by the end.* (p.48)

26.46 This has been recognised by the IAT. In **Ademaj**, it noted that:

> *It is clearly the case that an adjudicator is in no sense bound by a medical report. He/she must make his/her own assessment of the credibility of witnesses. Equally however it is the case that [the medical expert] is bound in the context of... his examination of a patient in a case such as this to reach a conclusion as to the extent to which he accepts that what the patient says is credible in the context of his medical assessment of her. However, as we have said, though an adjudicator is not bound to accept the conclusions of a doctor, nevertheless he must pay serious attention to those conclusions in assessing the witness before him.*

26.47 Similarly, in **B (2002)**, Forbes J (who also referred to **Ademaj**) said that:

> *[I]t goes without saying that clinicians of the experience of [the psychia-*

trists whose reports were before the court] must be taken to be well used to assessing the truth or otherwise of assertions made by patients, particularly when assisted by appropriate objective forms of questionnaire and tests used for those purposes... [T]heir reports constitute a significant body of medical evidence which provides strong corroboration of the truth of the claims made by the claimant and his wife as to what had happened to them.

26.48 Medical experts have on occasion been criticised by HOPOs for offering an opinion upon the degree of likelihood that an injury was caused in a particular way. That is misconceived. It is the expert's job. What he must make clear however is that his assessment of the likelihood that the injury was caused in a particular way is based upon the application of his expertise, and *not* on any view he has formed as to the general credibility of the appellant's claim. The Medical Foundation Guidelines state that:

It is no part of the doctor's function to give an opinion as to overall credibility of the case, though it is quite in order to express an opinion as to whether the medical evidence supports the allegation of torture. (p.50)

26.49 The basic rule is that any conclusion that the expert reaches must be transparently justified by the expert's expertise. The report should never state '*I conclude that the appellant has been persecuted in the manner described*' or '*I conclude that the history given by the appellant is correct*' But if the expert is able so to conclude, the report may state that it is unlikely that an injury was inflicted by means other than those described by the appellant. That will often be highly material. For example, in *Yasotharan* the IAT said that:

*It seems to the Tribunal that where there is credible, reliable expert medical evidence that someone has been injured by a burning cigarette being applied to the skin (which to the **Sivakumaran** standard is the effect of the medical evidence before us), other possible causes than torture, in all but the exceptional case, can safely be excluded.*

26.50 While the HOPO may criticise an expert for having made some assessment of credibility, he is even more likely to advance the converse criticism, namely that the expert has simply adopted whatever the appellant told him.

26.51 Unfortunately, adjudicators are not immune from adopting a similar approach. An adjudicator sometimes appears to form an assessment of credibility independently of the medical evidence and then consider the value of the medical evidence in light of the fact that the appellant lied to the expert! Both the IAT and the Administrative Court have emphasised that to 'put the cart before the horse' in this way is the wrong approach. In *Faustino*, the IAT noted that:

> *[The Adjudicator] rejects the evidence from the Medical Foundation on the basis that having found the appellant is not credible his version of the events to the doctor cannot be true. This with respect seems to us to ignore totally the inherent value of a medical report which is in this case that there were injuries and they were consistent with the appellant's story.*

26.52 In the case of *B* (para 26.47), the Administrative Court was called upon to consider the following finding by an adjudicator: 'The medical reports of [the psychiatrists] refer to the clinical depression and post traumatic stress disorder of both applicants resulting from the rape incident. However, these reports were based upon the evidence which the appellant and his wife gave the doctors. I therefore attach little weight to the reports bearing in mind that I have found both the appellant and his wife to be without credibility.' Forbes J commented that:

> *It goes without saying that the Adjudicator was not bound to accept the medical evidence without question. However, if the medical evidence was to be rejected by her, it had to be rejected on a reasoned and proper basis. Moreover, in my view, it is clear from the authorities that the evidence in question should have formed part of the overall material to be taken into account by the Adjudicator when considering the credibility of the claimant and his wife, before any final conclusion was reached by the Adjudicator as to the truth of their claims.*

26.53 He accepted that the adjudicator had erred in dismissing the psychiatric evidence on 'a peremptory and unreasoned basis', and concluded that:

> *It is clear to me that the Adjudicator used her adverse findings of credibility with regard to the claimant and his wife as the means whereby to reject the important and significant evidence of [the psychiatrists]. That was putting the cart before the horse. [Their] evidence... was strongly corroborative of the truth of the account given by the claimant and his wife about the serious rape that was suffered by the wife. It was therefore necessary for the Adjudicator to take that evidence into account as part of her consideration of all the evidence, before coming to any conclusion as to the credibility of the claimant and his wife.*

Format and presentation of the report

26.54 This section should be read in conjunction with chapter 23. Also refer to the Medical Foundation's *Guidelines for the examination of survivors of torture*. Supply it to your expert if he is not already familiar with it. You should evaluate the report in light of the guidance in chapter 3 of that publication.

26.55 The medical expert should be willing to discuss his draft with you and respond to reasonable comments, so long as it does not lead to his opinion being distorted or misrepresented (see para 23.26 for general guidance). If you have concerns in relation to a Medical Foundation report which, for whatever reason, cannot be dealt with by the writer, then it is worth discussing them with one of the Foundation's full time staff.

26.56 The report should always start with a detailed explanation of the writer's qualifications. Do not assume that the HOPO or adjudicator will know what the string of initials after the expert's name mean. Nor can it be assumed that everyone will be familiar with which disciplines are appropriate to different issues: a HOPO may allege at the hearing that your expert does not hold the appropriate qualifications. Do not assume that your audience will be fully conversant with the distinction between psychiatrists and psychologists and when one or other is appropriate.

26.57 As with country experts, it is vital that a medical expert demonstrates what differentiates his analysis from that of a lay person. As indicated above, the HOPO is particularly likely to attack a medical report where the appellant's mental condition is used to corroborate past ill-treatment. It is therefore important that such experts are made aware of this, and that the report pre-empts any legitimate concern. This process is particularly important if the expert will not be giving oral evidence, and so will not have that opportunity to answer criticisms. The report must also demonstrate how the examination conducted formed a sufficient basis for the opinions expressed. The IAT has in the past questioned the value of a report based on a single short interview.

26.58 A medical report on a physical injury need not and should not regurgitate your client's entire account of her experiences in her country of origin. It need deal only with the matters upon which the expert is being asked to form a view. One would expect a physical report on evidence of torture to include a history of that torture. You would not expect it to include a history of the appellant's political activities. If the report does reproduce irrelevant detail of your client's case, you may ask the expert to omit it from the final report.

26.59 A report on the appellant's mental condition may involve taking a much fuller history from the patient and reproducing that history in the report. However, it should not consist merely of a long statement taken from the client followed by a short comment at the end. The history which is reproduced should still be limited to that which is relevant to the diagnosis, and should be closely tied to the diagnosis.

26.60 Always check any factual history in the report against your client's statement and interview. It may be that the inconsistency is symptomatic of the condition that the expert has diagnosed. But you nevertheless need to be aware of it. The HOPO may try to cross-examine on it and there is also the risk that the adjudicator may rely upon it, even if it has not been raised during the hearing.

26.61 As with other expert reports, presentation is important. Check spelling, punctuation and grammar.

26.62 Refer to para 23.45 concerning the presentation of expert evidence during the appeal process, and the desirability that it is served in time to seek a direction that the Home Office either indicate that it is not disputed or particularise the grounds upon which it is disputed. The Home Office states in its APIs on the Medical Foundation that:

> Where a Medical Foundation report is submitted after an application has been refused, the case should be reviewed before any appeal. If the report is persuasive it may be appropriate to grant asylum or Humanitarian Protection... If refusal is to be maintained a further letter to the applicant will be required explaining how the report has been considered and why the Secretary of State is not persuaded to reverse the decision...

26.63 If you need an adjournment to present medical evidence, you should ensure that the reasons are properly explained, for example the waiting lists of the Medical Foundation or experts of similar standing. The Home Office sometimes implies that such reports are available upon demand (see above para 26.33 for its own policy of agreeing postponements of decisions to await reports from the Medical Foundation except in 'exceptional circumstances'). You might also refer to the UNHCR Handbook's provision in relation to mentally disturbed asylum seekers that 'The examiner should, in such cases, whenever possible, obtain a medical report' (paragraph 208). At the appeal stage, the examiner is the adjudicator.

26.64 As with other experts, it will often be beneficial for the medical expert to be called to give oral evidence where his conclusions are disputed (see chapter 25).

Further reading

26.65 The following provide valuable guidance:

Guidelines for the examination of survivors of torture (2nd ed)
Medical Foundation for the Care of Victims of Torture

Examining Asylum Seekers: A Health Professional's Guide to Medical and Psychological Evaluations of Torture
Physicians for Human Rights (www.phrusa.org)
(An abridged version appears on the website)

Medical evidence: Guidance for Doctors and Lawyers
Produced jointly by the Law Society and the British Medical Association.

The Istanbul Protocol: Manual on the Effective Investigation and Documentation of Torture and other Cruel, Inhuman or Degrading Treatment or Punishment (UNHCR)

26 Introduction
Key points

- Medical evidence may

  - ☐ corroborate past ill-treatment,
  - ☐ establish attributes which will exacerbate risk,
  - ☐ explain difficulties in giving evidence or recounting events,
  - ☐ demonstrate the consequences of expulsion for the appellant's physical or mental condition or that of a family member.

- Do not assume that there will be no physical evidence of torture simply because there are no physical marks. Equally, do not make assumptions about scarring that you can see without checking whether it has an innocent explanation.

- Be alert when taking instructions for signs of mental illness or disorder.

- Physical scarring may attract adverse interest upon return. The appellant's mental condition may render him less able to withstand interrogation.

- Be sensitive to your client's concerns about confidentiality with respect to her relatives and her community.

- Ensure that she obtains appropriate treatment as well as arranging forensic examination.

- Establishing the consequences of expulsion for her health may involve country evidence as well as medical evidence.

- The Medical Foundation is widely recognised as a respected source of medical evidence but does not have the capacity to meet demand. A range of other medical experts are available.

- Where expulsion affects families with children, a report from an independent social worker as well as a child psychologist may be valuable.

- Issues relating to credibility often call for medical evidence. But you must be vigilant in ensuring that the limits of legitimate expert opinion are not exceeded.

- The report should demonstrate how the expert's opinion derives from his expertise and should pre-empt potential criticisms.

- Seek disclosure of any grounds upon which the Home Office challenges the medical evidence.

27 The trial bundle

27.1 The Standard Directions require that not less than seven days before the hearing, you should lodge with the IAA and serve on the Home Office:

> *a paginated and indexed bundle of all the documents to be relied on at the hearing with a schedule identifying the essential passages.*

27.2 Practice Direction CA1 of 2003 deals with Trial Bundles. It is set out in full below:

> *1. Parties shall have regard to the guidance, best practice and commentary below in the preparation of trial bundles for hearings before adjudicators.*

> *GUIDANCE*

> *2. Each party shall prepare the bundle on which it relies.*

> *3. The respondent's bundle shall consist of:*

>> *(a) The documents submitted to the appellate authority in accordance with the Procedure Rules from time to time in force.*
>> *(b) Notes of any relevant interview had with the appellant not included in (a) above.*
>> *(c) Such further documents as may be considered relevant.*
>> *(d) Any relevant country report which may be submitted at the hearing.*

> *4. The appellant's bundle shall consist of:*

>> *(a) A chronology to include the dates of incidents on which the appellant relies.*
>> *(b) All witness statements to be relied on as evidence.*
>> *(c) Any relevant documents on which the appellant relies as evidence, including country reports, expert and medical reports.*
>> *(d) Translations of any of the above documents.*
>> *(e) A skeleton argument.*

BEST PRACTICE

5. *The best practice for the preparation of bundles follows:*

    (a) *All documents must be relevant, be presented in logical order and be legible.*

    (b) *Where the document is not in the English language, a typed translation of the document must be inserted in the bundle next to the copy of the original document together with details of the identity and qualifications of the translator.*

    (c) *If it is necessary to include a lengthy document, that part of the document on which reliance is placed should, unless the passages are outlined in any skeleton argument, be highlighted or clearly identified by reference to page and/or paragraph number.*

    (d) *Bundles submitted must be paginated and have an index showing the page numbers of each document in the bundle.*

    (e) *The skeleton argument or written submissions should define and confine the areas at issue in a numbered list of brief points. Each point should refer to any documentation in the bundle on which the appellant proposes to rely and its page number.*

    (f) *Where reliance is placed on a particular case or text, photocopies of the case or text must be provided in full for the adjudicator and the other party.*

    (g) *Large bundles should be contained in a ring binder or lever arch file, capable of lying flat when opened.*

COMMENTARY

6. *Adjudicators recognise the constraints on those representing the parties in appeals at adjudicator level in relation to the preparation of trial bundles. The Direction does not therefore make it mandatory in every case that bundles in exactly the form prescribed must be prepared. If parties to appeals fail in individual cases to present documentation in a way which complies with the Practice Direction, it will be for the individual adjudicator to deal with any such issue.*

7. *Much evidence in asylum and immigration appeals is in documentary form. Representatives preparing bundles need to be aware of the position of the adjudicator who is coming to the case for the first time. The better a bundle has been prepared, the greater it will assist the adjudicator to reach a decision which is fair and in accordance with the law. Bundles should contain all the documents that the adjudicator will require to enable him or her to reach a decision without the need to refer to any other file or document.*

8. *It is not practical in appeals at adjudicator level to require there to be an agreed trial bundle. It remains vital that both parties inform the other at an early stage of all and any documentation on which they intend to rely.*

9. *The parties cannot rely on the adjudicator having judicial notice of any country information or background reports in relation to the case in question. If either party wish to rely on such country or background information, copies of the relevant documentation must be produced.*

10. *The Guidance Note for good practice on the preparation of trial bundles dated February 2000 is withdrawn.*

27.3 The adjudicator will appreciate some sort of order in the compilation of the bundle. It should at least differentiate between documents which are specific to the appellant and more general country information. The Practice Direction states that the skeleton argument should be included in the bundle. However, this may be impractical if the skeleton is being drafted by counsel and he needs to receive the bundle before he can do so. Adjudicators do not usually object to the skeleton being provided separately.

27.4 The bigger the bundle, the more important that it is properly presented. If you want the adjudicator to accept that a large bundle is carefully chosen rather than thrown together, help yourself by exhibiting care in its presentation. Always ensure that the pages and the pagination are legible. It creates an even better impression if you put it in a good condition ring binder with tabs dividing discrete sections accompanied by a detailed index. This will also comply with the Practice Direction. A large pile of papers held together by one treasury tag is cheaper to produce but far less easy for the adjudicator to use.

Schedule of essential passages

27.5 The standard directions require a 'schedule identifying the essential passages'. Again, the bigger the bundle, the more important that you do this. The adjudicator is unlikely to read hundreds of pages in full. Indeed, you are unlikely to be inviting him to read the whole thing if you are relying only on particular passages from particular reports. It will do your prospects no harm to have your key quotations available in convenient form when he turns to write his determination. This can be either in your skeleton argument (para 28.19) or a separate schedule. You may wish to check whether the adjudicator would like to receive the schedule in electronic form to facilitate quotation.

27.6 A schedule helps demonstrate the care you have taken over the material. It is also a useful check on the relevance of your bundle. You may need to include a report which does not appear in your schedule of key passages. But its absence should lead you to double-check what purpose it is actually serving.

27.7 ICCIID's and EIN's bundlemaker software (chapter 18) contains an automated function for highlighting and indexing key passages from country reports.

Lodging the bundle

27.8 The standard directions require the bundle to be served one week before the hearing. Rule 46(5) states that:

> An adjudicator or the Tribunal must not consider any evidence which is not filed or served in accordance with time limits set out in these Rules or directions given under rule 38, unless satisfied that there are good reasons to do so.

27.9 This represents a change of form rather than substance from the previous rules which gave adjudicators a discretion to prohibit reliance on evidence not filed in accordance with directions. (An adjudicator would anyway act unlawfully if he exercised a discretion without good reason.) There is no restriction on what may constitute a good reason. It should encompass not only the explanation for why the evidence was not served earlier but also the interests of justice in ensuring that all relevant evidence is considered in an asylum/human rights case, and absence of prejudice to the opposing party.

27.10 Other than in very high profile appeals, there is no real likelihood of either adjudicator or HOPO considering your bundle more than a day in advance. (Indeed, the papers are not dispatched to some hearing centres until the day before the hearing.) Adjudicators ought not to adopt a technical approach. The Chief Adjudicator stated on 15 May 2003 that:

> It is only on rare occasions that adjudicators in my experience decline to consider late filed evidence or documents. (letter to IAS)

27.11 You should make every effort to comply so far as possible with directions, and especially to avoid having to submit material on the day of the hearing. But it is never wise to submit an unfinished statement or report purely to comply with the standard directions. This may seriously jeopardise the prospects of the appeal succeeding. If, say, your country evidence is ready a week in advance but other evidence is not ready, you can serve the bundle of country evidence with a letter explaining that the remainder of the evidence will follow as soon as possible. The submission of some material will show that you are anxious to comply with directions so far as possible. You may also ask the IAA for an extension to be on the safe side.

27.12 Be aware that if you then submit further evidence that needs to be inserted into the bundle, nobody is likely to have done this for the adjudicator by the time the hearing starts. Time may therefore be wasted at the start of the hearing while the further material is inserted into the bundle. If there is a significant amount to be inserted at different points, it is often better to provide a second complete copy of the bundle.

27.13 Sometimes, the HOPO will object that he is prejudiced by your having lodged material within a week of the hearing because he has been left with insufficient time to consider it. He may argue either that it should be excluded or that he should have an adjournment. Further investigation very often reveals this argument to be disingenuous. The Home Office does not normally allocate appeal files to HOPOs until the day before the hearing. This will be well known to any representative who has ever tried to get the Home Office to consider material in advance. Indeed ILPA were informed at a meeting with the Home Office Appeals Group on 15 May 2003 that:

> *Unfortunately, there is no mechanism for Presenting Officers to consider cases earlier as they usually pick up the papers the day before. (Minutes, para 4)*

27.14 A good way of checking this is to telephone the HOPO Unit the day after you served the material on them and ask to discuss the case with the responsible HOPO. If you are told that a HOPO is yet to be allocated, or if the allocated HOPO tells you that it will be days before he picks up the file, you will be in a position to refute any subsequent claim that his lack of preparedness is the result of your late submission of evidence rather than Home Office inefficiency.

27.15 The HOPO will often make this submission even as he himself seeks to submit evidence on the day (most commonly a Country Assessment). You can point out that the HOPO is in no position to object if he is doing the same thing.

27 The trial bundle
Key points

- The standard directions require a paginated, indexed bundle with a schedule identifying essential passages to be submitted a week before the hearing.

- The Practice Direction on Trial Bundles gives detailed guidance as to what is required.

- The bigger the bundle, the more important it is to ensure that it is properly presented and referenced. Identifying the key passages will also increase the prospects of success.

- Every effort should be made to comply so far as possible with the time limit, but it is never wise to submit unfinished evidence.

- If parts of the evidence are not ready by the time limit, submit a partial bundle with an explanation that further evidence will follow as soon as possible.

- Claims by the HOPO that he has had insufficient time to consider your evidence may be revealed as disingenuous if it transpires (as it usually does) that he did not pick up the file until the day before the hearing.

28 Skeleton arguments and chronologies

28.1 Rule 38(5)(e)(iii) permits an adjudicator to direct that one or both parties provide

> *a skeleton argument which summarises succinctly the submissions which will be made at the hearing and cites all the authorities which will be relied on, identifying any particular passages to be relied on.*

28.2 The standard directions issued in adjudicator appeals require only the appellant to lodge

> *a skeleton argument, identifying all relevant issues including Human Rights claims and citing all the authorities to be relied on.*

28.3 Practice Direction CA1 of 2003 states that:

> *The skeleton argument or written submissions should define and confine the areas at issue in a numbered list of brief points. Each point should refer to any documentation in the bundle on which the appellant proposes to rely and its page number.*

28.4 If the parties are in other respects ready to proceed, it would seldom be reasonable for an adjudicator to refuse to hear the appeal on its merits simply because the appellant had not produced a skeleton argument. However, it is always valuable to start your appeal with a fair wind, and the value of a skeleton argument can be much more than simply demonstrating that you are anxious not to default on directions.

28.5 Assuming an adjudicator has done some pre-reading (i.e. read some papers before the hearing starts), he will have read the Home Office refusal letter if nothing else. While one hopes that he would discount the more outlandish points, there may be enough of substance (together with a misleading factual summary) to leave the adjudicator with a negative impression of your case. You are not usually invited to make an opening speech. If the adjudicator has nothing to set against the refusal letter when pre-reading, it will be closing submissions before you have the opportunity to rebut the refusal letter head-on.

28.6 If the adjudicator has started with a negative impression of your case, that may affect his interventions during oral evidence. If his interventions leave your client and other witnesses feeling uncomfortable or believing that the adjudicator is leaning against them, it may affect their confidence and the quality of their evidence. That in turn may influence the adjudicator's assessment of their evidence and reinforce any negative impression. It should not, of course, happen this way. But by providing a skeleton argument, you ensure that the adjudicator has an accurate factual summary, is alerted to the real issues, and that misleading allegations in the refusal letter are answered before they have an opportunity to infect the adjudicator's view of your client.

28.7 To have this effect, your skeleton must stand out as a document worth the adjudicator's attention during what may be very limited pre-reading time. In *Zarour*, the IAT said that:

> One good thing can be said about [counsel's] skeleton argument... , which is that it was short enough to make it reasonably clear how he put his case... This is usually not so with the skeleton arguments of counsel in this field, which are all too often so intolerably prolix that they may be better described as well-fleshed corpses, doing more to conceal than reveal what the case is about.

28.8 Some appeals, of course, are so complex that they require lengthy skeleton arguments. But the lengthier the skeleton, the more important it is to demonstrate to the adjudicator how the document is directed to answering the questions that he will have to answer – and is therefore worth prioritising. If you present a 30 page skeleton consisting largely of a 'cut and paste job' of generic legal and country submissions, the likelihood is that it will not get read (and will do your client little good if it is read).

28.9 Your skeleton will normally cover the following:

- factual summary, highlighting matters which are relevant to the consequences of expulsion;
- summary of claims of breach of either Convention;
- response to the arguments set out in the Home Office refusal letter;
- further relevant legal argument;
- guidance on the expert and country evidence.

Factual summary

28.10 Given that the standard directions also require provision of written witness statements, it is unnecessary for the skeleton to reproduce a detailed account of your client's history. Rather, it should start with a summary of the most material and compelling facts in your case. These should always include the main events which caused your client to flee and which give rise to her present fears. You may also highlight any unusual factors which may grab the adjudicator's attention, such as your client's particularly prominent position, or particularly disturbing treatment at the hands of the authorities. In a straightforward case, there is no need for this factual summary to extend beyond a few paragraphs.

Summary of the claim

28.11 Set out concisely why your client's expulsion will violate the Refugee and/or Human Rights Convention. The primary question is: what are the risks/consequences of expelling this person? Explain that in ordinary language. Then explain briefly how it will violate the UK's obligations. For example, *'The denial of medical treatment will constitute inhuman or degrading treatment (art 3) and/or a disproportionate interference with her private life in the sense of her moral and physical integrity (art 8).'*

Rebutting the refusal letter

28.12 Go through the refusal letter identifying every discrete point then either accept it, dispute it, or dismiss it as irrelevant. You should not pass over points simply because they appear to be absurd. If the Home Office has dismissed the claim on unreasonable grounds, you want to emphasise that fact rather than treat it with a sort of benevolent acceptance. It does no harm to impress upon the adjudicator that it is not acceptable for a meritorious case to be rejected on irrational grounds.

28.13 Some representatives deal with the refusal letter in a witness statement from the appellant. Often, there will be specific points that the appellant can make in evidence, and she should do so. Otherwise, it is your job to respond to the refusal letter. That is preferable to a witness statement purporting to be from the appellant but presenting arguments which obviously did not come from her. It also avoids the perception, often encouraged by the HOPO, that your client must personally have an answer for every allegation in the refusal letter (see also para 12.46).

28.14 Before giving your rebuttal, set out briefly the point to which you are responding. This enables the adjudicator to make sense of your skeleton without having to cross-refer to the refusal letter.

Legal argument

28.15 Do not drop standard paragraphs into every skeleton argument setting out the leading authorities on the Refugee Convention. Nothing is more likely to put the adjudicator off reading it. If there is a specific point to make about the application of an authority to the facts of your case, then explain what it is. For example, there is little point in including lengthy quotes from **Karanakaran** in every skeleton. However, you might need to explain how the **Karanakaran** approach (which is not always fully understood) should affect the evaluation of a particular piece of evidence (para 42.13).

28.16 If you are advancing an unusual or difficult legal argument, then you should set it out fully on paper. If an authority is genuinely relevant, then the relevant passages should be quoted rather than simply providing the references. The citation of authorities is discussed in the following chapter.

28.17 Grounds of appeal should have been sufficiently expansive so as not to limit the future development of the appeal (para 4.5). But by the time you draft your skeleton argument, you should be in a position to focus your submissions. Take a realistic view. If the accepted evidence is that pre-trial detention is accompanied by torture, it may be unnecessary to devote substantial effort to establishing that the trial will be unfair; if you get as far as establishing pre-trial detention, you should succeed on article 3. Conversely, if the evidence concerning torture in detention is sketchy, then you may well have to establish unfair trial.

28.18 Although the IAT's Practice Direction on the citing of Strasbourg authorities (para 46.89) does not apply to adjudicator appeals, the 'few simple points of guidance' set out by the IAT in **Dominguez** are equally applicable:

   1) *[Representatives] should take steps to acquaint themselves with any relevant human rights decisions of the Tribunal or the courts.*

   2) *They should not embark on arguments as to the position taken by Strasbourg jurisprudence without at least some rudimentary grasp of the relevant case law. Furthermore,... argument needs to be formulated and advanced in a plausible way.*

Country of origin evidence

28.19 The skeleton should offer a guide to the relevance of the documentary evidence that you have submitted. Set out the most relevant quotations in the skeleton (along with page references). This avoids the adjudicator having to note these when you make your oral submissions. A report should normally be submitted in its entirety, even if you only intend to quote a small part of it. This is one reason why bundles will often far exceed the number of pages upon which you intend to rely. Particularly if your bundle is large, it is unlikely that the adjudicator will have an opportunity to digest it whole. A document that sets out the key quotations for your case (for example, as to the prevalence of torture) can therefore substantially add to the persuasiveness of your bundle.

28.20 If you conduct a lot of appeals from a particular country which raise common issues, you may be able to reuse much of this material. But ensure that it is focussed on the issues that actually arise. It should not look to the adjudicator like a 'generic' submission.

Chronology

28.21 The chronology will normally consist of a summary of key dates (though a very detailed chronology may assist in a complex case). The dates will normally be taken from the witness statements. It should not include any dates that will have to be established by oral evidence. (All material facts should in any event be in the witness statement.) Some representatives add a proviso to the chronology to the effect that it is their own work and not evidence (in case the HOPO tries to put a mistake in the chronology to the appellant as an inconsistent statement).

28.22 An adjudicator may turn to the chronology for a summary of the claim even before looking at any skeleton argument. If it is not too long, you can incorporate the chronology into the skeleton.

28.23 Either way, the chronology is part of your case. It should tell your client's story in a sensible, straightforward and persuasive manner. The chronology of events should make sense to the adjudicator. It should not provoke unnecessary doubts at the outset. If the chronology states *'15/11/99: escaped from last detention; 28/2/00: fled the country'*, the adjudicator's first thought may be that there is an unexplained delay in departure. It is better to let the adjudicator know, however shortly, that this is not the case by inserting an entry such as *'16-11-99–27/2/00: remained in hiding with relative while family raised money to pay agent'*.

28 Skeleton arguments and chronologies
Key points

■ The standard directions require a skeleton argument in every appeal.

■ The adjudicator should be able to refer to your response to the refusal letter during his pre-reading.

■ The skeleton argument should be directed to the questions that the adjudicator will have to answer: a 'cut and paste' job setting out the standard authorities is unlikely to assist or even be read.

■ The skeleton argument should contain succinct summaries of

☐ the facts of the case, highlighting the events that caused the appellant to flee and those contributing to her present fears,
☐ the grounds on which expulsion will violate the UK's obligations.

■ Each argument in the refusal letter should be addressed: do not ignore the more absurd points.

■ While the original grounds of appeal may have been expansive, the skeleton provides the opportunity to focus your arguments.

■ Quote authorities only if they are directly relevant to the arguments in the present case. Unusual or difficult legal arguments should be set out in full.

■ The adjudicator may turn to your chronology for a summary of the facts. It should not leave unanswered questions.

29 Citing authorities and legal research

IAT determinations

29.1 IAT determinations of direct relevance to your appeal can provide considerable assistance. Some IAT determinations are now 'starred'. The status of starred decisions was the subject of comment by Laws LJ in *Sepet & Bulbul*:

> *I should make plain my clear view that (a) adjudicators should regard themselves as bound by starred decisions of the IAT, and (b) the IAT should itself follow an earlier starred decision unless it is satisfied that the decision is clearly wrong.*

29.2 Starred determinations may state that they are to be regarded as *binding* even by other divisions of the IAT. But in light of the above statement, you should not be precluded from attempting to persuade the IAT that a previous starred determination is clearly wrong.

29.3 Adjudicators will treat starred determinations as binding on a point of law. The recent PD No. 10 (below) states that non-starred determinations are not binding. However, the IAT has held that all determinations of the IAT are binding on points of law. In *Ekinci*, it stated that:

> *It is our clear and quite unequivocal view that adjudicators are bound by decisions of the Tribunal where they are clear and relate to a point of law.*

29.4 If there are conflicting decisions of the IAT, then unless one is starred, an adjudicator is free to elect which to follow: *Sivakarathas*.

29.5 Decisions by the IAT on factual issues (most commonly country of origin conditions) are not binding upon adjudicators but are of persuasive value. It may be an error of law for an adjudicator to decline to follow the IAT's factual assessment without giving reasons for doing so, especially if the IAT considered the same evidence. In *Manzeke*, the Court of Appeal held that adjudicators ought to give 'careful consideration' to such decisions in these circumstances, given:

the important function of the Immigration Appeal Tribunal in guiding special adjudicators into adopting a consistent approach to frequently occurring factual issues of this kind... (per Brooke LJ)

29.6 In *S (2002)*, the Court of Appeal considered a new move by the IAT to create a binding factual precedent. The IAT had held that its factual findings on the risk of persecution to ethnic Serbs in Croatia should henceforth be treated as binding in the absence of a change of circumstances in the country of origin. The Court of Appeal concluded that the notion of factual precedent, though 'exotic', was in the context of the IAT 'benign and practical'. However, it held that the duty to give reasons would be applied 'with particular rigour' to any factual precedent that it established.

29.7 Note that both the above judgments of the Court of Appeal were in the context of the IAT's historic wider jurisdiction encompassing factual as well as legal appeals. It is not clear what scope remains for factual precedents or guidance given the limitation of the IAT's jurisdiction to one of law.

29.8 A substantial change to previous practice in respect of the citation of IAT determinations was announced by IAT PD No. 10. The Practice Direction and accompanying notes are set out in full below:

CITATION OF DETERMINATIONS

1 *From 19th May 2003 the Immigration Appeal Tribunal will cease the practice of reporting and publishing all its determinations. From that time, determinations will be either 'reported' or 'unreported'. The decision whether to report a case is that of the Tribunal and is not perceived to be an issue in which the parties to the appeal have an interest.*

2 *Reported determinations will receive a neutral citation number of the form [2003] UKIAT 00001 and will be widely available. They will be made anonymous and will be cited by the neutral citation number. Determinations without a number in this form are unreported.*

3 *Unreported determinations will receive no neutral citation number. They will be sent to the parties but will not be published. Anonymous versions will be deposited in the Supreme Court Library. (Negotiations for an electronic depository are in progress.)*

4 *From the date of this Practice Direction, no unreported determination of the Tribunal, and no determination of an Adjudicator, may be cited in proceedings before any Adjudicator or the Tribunal unless either:*

(i) the Claimant in the present proceedings, or a member of his family, was a party to the proceedings in which the previous determination was issued, or

(ii) the Adjudicator or the Tribunal (as the case may be), gives permission.

5 Permission will be given only in exceptional cases, and even more rarely in relation to Adjudicator determinations. An application for permission to cite an unreported determination:

(i) must include a full transcript of the determination,

(ii) must identify the proposition for which the determination is to be cited,

(iii) must certify that that proposition is not found in any reported determination of the Tribunal, and has not been superseded by a decision of higher authority,

(iv) must be accompanied by a summary analysis of all other decisions of the Tribunal, and all available decisions of higher authority, relating to the same issue, promulgated in the period beginning six months before the date of the decision proposed to be cited and ending two weeks before the date of the hearing. This analysis is intended to show the trend of IAT decisions on this issue.

6 Determinations of the Tribunal published in 2002 and previous years will continue to be citable. From 1st May 2004, however, a party citing a determination bearing a neutral citation number prior to [2003] (including all series of 'bracket numbers') must be in a position to certify that the matter or proposition for which the determination is cited has not been the subject of a more recent, reported, Tribunal determination.

7. 'Starred' determinations of the Tribunal continue to have a special status. They are to be treated as binding by all Adjudicators and the Tribunal unless inconsistent with authority binding on the Appellate Authorities. Other determinations are not binding. The Tribunal will nevertheless attempt to secure consistency in its decision-making and to provide appropriate guidance to Adjudicators.

NOTES (These notes do not form part of the Practice Direction)

1 The number of determinations of the Immigration Appeal Tribunal is currently of the order of 6,000 per year and rising. With the exception of 'starred' decisions they are not binding on subsequent appeals.

2 *The large number of decisions, coupled with the increased numbers of judiciary at both levels of the Immigration Appellate Authority, has exacerbated problems of 'selective citation'. Adjudicators and panels of the Tribunal are shown Tribunal determinations in an attempt to persuade them that the instant case should be decided in a similar way. Whether intentionally or not, this process is often misleading, as there is no proper effort to survey the whole of the Tribunal output on a particular topic, or to discover whether there is any good reason for following one decision which is cited rather than others, not cited, which may be to the opposite effect.*

3 *By restricting the number of determinations capable of being cited at either level, the Tribunal intends both to promote consistency of decision-making and to give a reliable indicator of the current judicial thinking on frequently (and less-frequently) occurring issues. Determinations will not, however, be reported if in the Tribunal's view they contain no new principle of law or matter of real and generally-applicable guidance to parties, Adjudicators or the Tribunal, and no assessment of facts of such generality that others ought to have regard to it.*

4 *It should be emphasised that both Adjudicators and the Tribunal remain open to arguments that the reported decision or decisions should not be applied or followed. The effect of the Practice Direction is that such arguments will need to be supported by sound reasons, rather than by some previous decision.*

5 *The arrangements envisaged in the Practice Direction will be kept under review by the President and the Chief Adjudicator.*

29.9 In its response to the consultation on this Practice Direction, ILPA expressed concern on a number of grounds. The Practice Direction appears to subject determinations of equal authority to different levels of accessibility and rules as to citation. (It does not alter the special status of starred determinations.) No details are provided of the mechanism by which it will be determined whether a decision is 'reported' or 'unreported': it appears that the tribunal which heard and determined the appeal will not itself be empowered to hold that its determination should be 'reported'. More importantly, no criteria are stated by which this assessment will be made, nor any definition of the 'exceptional' circumstances in which an adjudicator should consider an unreported authority. ILPA indicated its concern that the procedure might add to the complexity of litigation and lead to further challenges where a tribunal declined to consider a relevant determination pursuant to the Practice Direction.

29.10 As of July 2003, only around 30 determinations of the IAT have been 'reported' out of several hundred. The EIN (which received all unreported determinations up to July 2003 but is not presently publishing them) has claimed that there is as yet no 'clear logic as to the basis for the demarcation between "reported" and "unreported"' (EIN Newsletter, Summer 2003). Given the tiny proportion of reported determinations, it seems unlikely that the unreported determinations all fall within the examples given at para 3 of determinations that are of no assistance other than to the parties.

29.11 ILPA noted in its comments on the draft Practice Direction that:

> The restriction of the IAT's jurisdiction to hearing appeals on the law renders it all the more important that the public access to its determinations is not restricted. [W]e consider that any such move would constitute a serious interference with public access to justice. It would have a particularly unfair effect in the present jurisdiction: while appellants representatives' access to determinations would in practice be greatly restricted, the Secretary of State, being a party to all appeals, would continue to enjoy the same ability to consider every determination issued by the IAT when deciding upon which he will seek to rely. That inequality is in itself a sufficient objection to any interference with the public availability of determinations.

29.12 The 'negotiations for an electronic depository' for unreported determinations which the final version of the Practice Direction announced have not borne fruit at time of writing. The requirement that the citation of an unreported authority should be accompanied by a summary analysis of all recent IAT determinations on the issue is impractical until the electronic depository is in operation. At the moment, the majority of current IAT determinations are available only from the Supreme Court Library. If you receive an unreported IAT determination which is of wider interest, you may submit it to ILPA, the RLG or the EIN.

29.13 The unnecessary citation of IAT determinations has certainly been a problem in the past, particularly determinations of appeals on the facts rather than on points of law. Indeed the Home Office had developed a practice of submitting 'generic' bundles for a particular country of up to 20 IAT determinations. The only relevance of these determinations appeared to be that they were about the same country and the Home Office won. That particular mischief ought to be addressed for the future by the restriction of the IAT's jurisdiction to one of law.

29.14 Determinations involving the appellant or family members may be cited without permission. (There is no definition of 'family member' so you can argue that it encompasses any relative's appeal.)

29.15 If you seek permission to cite an unreported IAT authority, the first step will be to comply so far as possible with the requirements in para 5 of the Practice Direction. You must provide a full transcript and identify the proposition that the authority supports. You should be able to certify that the proposition has not been superseded by any judgment of a higher court and is not to be found in any reported IAT determination (of which there are not yet very many).

29.16 For the reasons set out above, complying fully with para 5(iv) may be more difficult. Higher court authorities and reported IAT determinations are available on various websites (see below). However, an adjudicator should appreciate that it is unrealistic to expect a full survey of the IAT's unreported caselaw until the IAT concludes its negotiations to make these electronically available.

29.17 The adjudicator might well seek guidance as to how he should interpret the exceptionality criterion for considering an unreported determination, given that the Practice Direction offers no further definition. It is difficult to envisage circumstances in which an adjudicator would refuse to consider an IAT authority which contained a material proposition of law which did not appear in a reported determination. If a determination offers relevant guidance on the facts, you can refer to the 'careful consideration' that the Court of Appeal has held should be afforded to such guidance (*Manzeke*, above). You can refer the adjudicator to para 3 of the accompanying notes which suggests that the intention is simply to prevent citation of authorities that were particular to their own facts.

29.18 The instruction to cite a reported authority in preference to an unreported authority where they support the *same* proposition of law is good practice. However, ILPA indicated particular concern that the Practice Direction might be interpreted as preventing a tribunal being told about conflicting authorities where one or more were unreported. The consequences of such an interpretation would include that the IAT could not be made aware of a conflict of authority that the Court of Appeal would subsequently have to resolve.

29.19 If an adjudicator refuses permission to cite a relevant unreported authority which supports your submissions, and your submissions are subsequently rejected, this may constitute a ground of appeal.

Law reports and caselaw updates

29.20 There are two sets of specialist law reports: the *Immigration and Nationality Law Reports* (INLR) and the *Immigration Appeal Reports* (Imm

AR). The INLR also include foreign and Strasbourg caselaw and are now available on the web by subscription (including cases which have not yet appeared in the paper reports).

29.21 The RLC's monthly *Legal Bulletin* features summaries and commentaries on recent decisions of the IAT and higher courts. It is an effective means of keeping abreast of important asylum and human rights decisions before they work their way into law reports. The IAS publishes a similarly useful bulletin which also includes general immigration cases.

29.22 *Statements of Principle of the Immigration Appeal Tribunal* by Symes (RLC) is a CD-ROM based publication, updated quarterly, which contains every statement of principle issued by the IAT since 1993, comprehensively indexed. It has substantially aided the accessibility of the IAT's caselaw. You will often find an authority exactly on point and it should be consulted on any significant issue that arises in your appeal. Be careful, however, that a particular ruling has not been overturned on appeal, or overtaken by higher court caselaw or statutory changes. (These developments are not noted in the publication.)

Unreported higher court caselaw

29.23 For higher court authorities, the best free database is the British and Irish Legal Information Institute (BAILII). This contains all decisions of the Court of Appeal Civil Division and Crown Office List (the precursor to the Administrative Court) from 1996 to 1999. It also includes all 'handed down' decisions since 1999 (i.e. all decisions which were originally issued in paper form rather than given orally).

29.24 The best online subscription services for higher court caselaw are Casetrack (www.casetrack.com) and Lawtel (www.lawtel.co.uk). Lawtel provides daily email updates but is not comprehensive. Casetrack includes all transcripts of the Court of Appeal and Administrative Court along with a good search facility.

29.25 The EIN is the main source of IAT determinations, together with the most important higher court decisions. It aims to publish all IAT determinations other than those of no interest beyond the parties (although it is not, at time of writing, publishing 'unreported' determinations pending negotiations with the IAT). Paper versions of IAT determinations can be obtained via the RLC's subscription service.

Citation

29.26 The Court of Appeal has held that judgments on permission applications are not binding and should not normally be cited (see e.g. **Senkoy**). Notwithstanding this, many judgments on permission applications have been reported in the immigration law reports and they are regularly cited. However, if the HOPO argues that an adjudicator (or the IAT) is bound by such a judgment, you should point out his error.

Foreign caselaw

29.27 Professor Hathaway's website (www.refugeecaselaw.org) provides a selection of international decisions. It is particularly useful in conjunction with his textbook, *The Law of Refugee Status* (below), as cases are sorted according to the paragraph numbering of the book.

29.28 Asylumlaw.org has comprehensive links to European refugee caselaw, though for most, access will be limited by language. It also contains a database of skeleton arguments and written submissions used in other cases, searchable by country and issue. Canada, Australia, and New Zealand all have excellent free databases of caselaw. Links are on the EIN's Resources pages.

Human rights decisions

29.29 Judgments from Strasbourg are reported in the European Human Rights Reports (EHRR). Human rights judgments from the UK and other jurisdictions as well as Strasbourg can be found in an increasing number of other series.

29.30 For searching the Strasbourg caselaw, the European Court of Human Rights' own database, HUDOC, is often the best option. It contains every Strasbourg decision and is easy to use for case name and free text searches (although not as easy for more complex searches). Printouts from HUDOC are admissible in both the IAT and the higher courts. Publishers such as Butterworths and Lawtel now provide specialised online subscription databases covering Strasbourg caselaw.

Search techniques

29.31 As with searching for country information, the aim when searching caselaw databases is to find the word or phrase which is most likely to appear in decisions which interest you, and least likely to appear in those that do not interest you. If there is a leading authority on the point, searching by the name of that authority will often be most effective.

Textbooks

29.32 The authoritative UK immigration textbooks are *Macdonald's Immigration Law and Practice* by Macdonald and Webber (Butterworths, 5th ed, 2001) and *Immigration Law & Practice* by Jackson and Warr (Sweet & Maxwell, looseleaf). Both cover refugee and human rights law. The *JCWI Immigration, Nationality & Refugee Law Handbook* (2002 Edition) is an invaluable source of quick and effective advice, though not a substitute for the text books.

29.33 *Immigration, Asylum, and Human Rights* by Blake and Hussain (Blackstone's, 2003) provides detailed guidance on human rights issues in this jurisdiction. There is a plethora of general textbooks on human rights law, including *Human Rights Law and Practice* (Lester & Pannick). One of the most accessible and comprehensive is *European Human Rights Law* (Starmer).

29.34 At time of writing, there is no UK-centred textbook on refugee law, but this will change with the publication later this year of *Asylum Law and Practice* by Symes and Jorro (Butterworths, 2003). This should be an indispensable resource. *Refugees and Gender: Law and Process* by Crawley (Jordans, 2001) is a comprehensive guide to women's refugee claims. See also the IAA Gender Guidelines, available from the IAA's webiste or the EIN. *Caselaw on the Refugee Convention* by Symes (RLC, 2001) is a valuable casebook collecting extracts from major refugee law decisions from various countries, ordered by issue.

29.35 The main texts on international refugee law are *The Law of Refugee Status* by Hathaway (Butterworths, 1991) and *The Refugee in International Law*, by Goodwin-Gill (Oxford University Press, 2nd ed, 1996). Both texts have been extensively cited by higher courts in the UK. Hathaway has been described in the House of Lords as 'one of the leading figures in the academic field' (**Adan**, per Lord Lloyd). Any support you can find in either text for your arguments will be important.

29.36 The three volume Butterworths *Immigration Law Service* is a looseleaf publication which gathers statutory material, caselaw, and policy, together with commentary. *Blackstone's Immigration Handbook* by Phelan (new edition due 2003) collects the main statutory and treaty material, and you will often find it on the desks of the IAT and adjudicators.

Policy

29.37 Keep abreast of Home Office statements of policy and practice. This is not because these are particularly liberal, but because they are often more liberal than the stance taken by individual officials and HOPOs (who may well deny knowledge of particular Home Office statements). The APIs are quoted several times in this text and are available on the Home Office's website.

29.38 Other policy material is trickier to get hold of. The best way is through ILPA which provides a monthly mailshot to members including many useful Home Office letters and statements. The RLG's email list is also useful, as is the EIN.

29 Citing authorities and researching legal materials
Key points

■ Starred determinations will be binding on adjudicators and should be followed by the IAT unless clearly wrong. The IAT has in the past held that non-starred determinations bind adjudicators on points of law in the absence of conflicting authority.

■ Decisions by the IAT on similar facts should be afforded careful consideration, especially if the IAT considered the same evidence.

■ PD No. 10 on Citation of Determinations introduces a new distinction between 'reported' and 'unreported' determinations.

■ Unreported determinations may only be cited with permission (unless the appellant or a family member was a party to them). Permission will be granted in 'exceptional' cases.

■ An application for permission to cite an unreported determination

  ☐ must include a full transcript,
  ☐ must identify the proposition for which it is cited,
  ☐ must certify that the proposition is not to be found in any reported determination and has not been superseded by a decision of a higher court,
  ☐ must be accompanied by an analysis of all decisions of the IAT and higher courts on the same issue in the previous six months (excluding the two weeks prior to the hearing).

■ Neither the criteria for determining whether a determination is reported or unreported, nor the criteria for granting permission to cite an unreported determination appear in the Practice Direction.

■ An adjudicator ought not to refuse to consider a decision of the IAT that contains a material proposition of law not found in a reported authority. Neither should you be prevented from making the tribunal aware of a conflict of authority.

■ Presenting an analysis of the IAT's unreported caselaw over the last six months is impractical until these are made electronically available.

■ There are numerous sources of higher court, Strasbourg, and international caselaw, many of which are searchable electronically.

■ Note that judgments on permission applications by the Administrative Court or Court of Appeal are not binding.

■ Keep abreast of Home Office statements of policy and practice as they may be more liberal than the stance taken by an individual HOPO.

30 Whether to call the appellant

30.1   It is your client's case, and assuming she is capable of giving instructions, she may instruct you to call her, whatever you think of the idea. But part of your job is to offer advice on this question based on your experience.

30.2   Your client may have given a full account in her asylum interview and a statement submitted to the Home Office. The refusal letter may not have challenged her credibility, but instead alleged that on the basis of her account, her expulsion will not engage the UK's obligations. If her credibility has not been put in issue, and she has nothing material to add to the interview notes and written statements which were before the Home office, then there may be little point in calling her.

30.3   It may also lead to unnecessary problems. Some HOPOs appear to regard it as their job to cross-examine if given the opportunity, regardless of its relevance to the matters in issue. To call your client when credibility has not been challenged may simply prompt an aimless fishing expedition by the HOPO in which he will require your client to regurgitate evidence she gave long ago in the apparent hope that with the passing of time, the evidence will not come out exactly the same. It could also result in an adverse credibility finding by the adjudicator, based on an assessment of demeanour or mannerisms which are in fact explained by cultural differences or simply personality. If credibility is not challenged, then there is nowhere to go on credibility except downhill.

30.4   If you serve a witness statement for the appeal which contains new information (or even repeats old information in different form), the HOPO may use the new witness statement to suggest that matters have moved on from the decision letter, credibility is now in issue, and he wishes to cross-examine on the fresh statement. If a satisfactory statement was submitted to the Home Office in support of the initial claim and there is no need to provide further information to update it or address the refusal letter, you can simply adopt the initial statement rather than serving a redrafted witness statement.

30.5 Obviously, if further evidence is needed from the appellant about her history in order to counter the Home Office's arguments on risk, a new statement will be required. But if the Home Office did not challenge an initial statement, it can often do more harm than good to serve a new witness statement simply repeating the original information in more polished form.

30.6 If you are not calling your client to give oral evidence because credibility has not been put in issue, you should explain this at the outset of the hearing. This will give the adjudicator the opportunity to indicate if he has developed his own concerns about credibility on the material before him, so that you have a proper opportunity to deal with these. Depending on the nature of any concerns, you may need to reconsider whether to call the appellant.

30.7 Note that where the HOPO concedes that credibility is not in issue (as opposed to the refusal letter not having challenged it), the adjudicator is not entitled to go behind that concession regardless of what concerns he may express (*Carcabuk & Bla*). The refusal letter seldom expressly accepts credibility. Whether it is worth trying to elicit that confirmation from the HOPO will depend on the strength of the case and on the HOPO. Sometimes, the question appears to so discomfort the HOPO that he starts attempting to formulate grounds for putting credibility in issue, despite the fact that no point was taken by the Home Office.

30.8 If the HOPO does attempt to put credibility in issue at the start of the hearing, you should question his justification for doing so. You should also seek an indication of which parts of the evidence the Home Office is now said to dispute and why, so that you can consider your position. Occasionally, the HOPO refuses even to indicate on what ground he now claims that credibility is in issue. You then have to decide whether to tender your client for cross-examination merely so that the HOPO can embark on a fishing expedition of indeterminate length in the hope of finding something he can offer as a reason for disputing credibility.

30.9 Despite the inappropriateness of such practices, you should be wary of not calling your client in such a situation. The danger is that the adjudicator may reach an adverse credibility finding upon matters which were not aired in evidence at the hearing. The best course might be to indicate your willingness to tender your client for cross-examination but also indicate your concerns about doing so when the HOPO purports to dispute credibility without notice, and without offering any grounds for doing so. In light of the overriding objective "to secure the just, timely and effective disposal of appeals" (r.4), the adjudicator may agree that lengthy but irrelevant cross-examination is an abuse of court time (see para 36.31).

Not calling the appellant when credibility is disputed

30.10 If credibility is put in issue in the refusal letter, most representatives will choose at least to tender their client for cross-examination, however flimsy the basis upon which credibility has been disputed. If, however, your client is disturbed, incoherent, or repeatedly inconsistent, she may have psychological problems which would render it inappropriate for you to tender her. In such a situation, you should obviously arrange for a medical report and, if appropriate, treatment (see chapter 26).

30.11 If the medical examination indicates that your client has psychological problems such that she cannot be expected to give accurate and consistent evidence, or that to have her cross-examined would pose significant risks to her mental well-being, then you will be justified in not calling your client. A medical report should be submitted explaining the position.

30.12 If a medical examination does not disclose any recognised condition but you nevertheless think that there is little prospect that your client will do herself justice in cross-examination, then the decision whether or not to call her is far more difficult. You have to ask yourself how you think you are advancing your client's case by calling her in circumstances where your best assessment is that oral evidence is more likely to harm than assist your case. An adjudicator is not entitled to base an adverse credibility finding on the fact that the appellant was not tendered for cross-examination (see e.g. *Kaleem Ahmed*). But the absence of oral evidence does not preclude an adverse credibility finding, and there is a risk that the adjudicator may take points which might have been explained had oral evidence been given. It may also make the adjudicator suspicious of your client, even though he is not entitled to rely on that suspicion.

30.13 If you decide not to tender the appellant for cross-examination, you are still entitled (and obliged by the standard directions) to submit a written witness statement. The adjudicator is obliged to reach a proper assessment of the credibility of that evidence. It is all the more important in those circumstances that the statement should pre-empt foreseeable challenges (para 12.53). You should also invite the adjudicator to raise any points of concern so that you can deal with these in submissions.

30.14 It is open to the HOPO to apply for a witness summons to compel your client to give evidence. In *Prendi*, the IAT stated that:

> *Proceedings before the Appellate Authority are civil proceedings and (save where special provision is made) must be regarded as governed by the ordinary principles and practice relating to civil proceedings... [P]arties to civil litigation are competent and compellable... There is... no doubt in our view that the Home Office Presenting Officer was entitled to call the claimant as a witness if she chose to do so.*

30.15 However, the same rule will apply to the HOPO as would apply to you if you sought a witness summons. The appellant will be the HOPO's witness, so he may not cross-examine (see para 9.43). Though the Adjudicator has power to summons a witness of his own motion, he should not do so simply to avoid that rule. The IAT stated in *Prendi* that:

> *What [the HOPO] could not do, of course, was call [the appellant] in order only to cross-examine him; because a party cannot generally speaking cross-examine his own witness. We do not think it would be right for the Adjudicator (or the Tribunal) to call a party as a witness with the sole aim of enabling cross-examination to take place and so assisting that other party to win.*

30.16 It is highly unlikely that the HOPO will apply for a witness summons against the appellant. But though he is entitled to apply for one, the dicta in *Prendi* should not be understood as indicating that the adjudicator is obliged to grant it. Clearly, if medical evidence indicates that it would be inappropriate for your client to give evidence, you would oppose the HOPO's application, and it is unlikely that an adjudicator could reasonably grant it.

30.17 If your client is a child, particular considerations apply to deciding whether or not to call her. These are discussed in chapter 54.

30.18 The same sort of considerations as are discussed in this chapter can apply when deciding to call oral evidence from witnesses other than the appellant. This is discussed further in chapter 15.

30 Whether to call the appellant
Key points

Credibility not challenged in the refusal letter

■ If all material facts were established in the initial claim and credibility has not been challenged, there is often no need to call the appellant: doing so may simply prompt a lengthy but aimless fishing expedition from the HOPO in cross-examination.

■ Tell the adjudicator that you are not calling the appellant because credibility has not been challenged: this gives him the opportunity to raise any concerns which might lead you to reconsider.

■ If the HOPO concedes credibility, the adjudicator cannot go behind that concession regardless of any concerns of his own.

■ If the HOPO challenges credibility for the first time at the hearing without offering coherent grounds to do so, you will probably tender your client but express your concern about whether this is a constructive use of court time.

Credibility challenged

■ The normal course will be to call the appellant where the refusal letter has challenged credibility.

■ If your client's mental state renders cross-examination inappropriate, you should not call her, but should submit medical evidence.

■ If a medical examination discloses no recognised condition but you conclude that she could not do herself justice in cross-examination, your decision – although much more difficult – may be the same.

■ An adjudicator may not make an adverse credibility finding on the basis that the appellant did not give oral evidence. But the absence of oral evidence may limit the opportunity to explain adverse points.

■ If you are not calling your client, you remain obliged to submit a witness statement and it is especially important that the witness statement pre-empts foreseeable challenges.

■ It is open to the HOPO to seek a witness summons against the appellant but he will not be permitted to cross-examine. The adjudicator may not issue a summons of his own motion in order to avoid this rule.

31 Pre-hearing conference

31.1 A pre-hearing conference is an essential part of the appeal preparation. This should not take place on the day of the hearing itself. Given the gravity and complexity of the issues, it is unacceptable to brief an advocate to conduct the hearing without arranging such a conference. The only exception may be where it has already been decided that there is no prospect of oral evidence being led. The pre-hearing conference should take place before the witness statement is finalised in case it needs to be amended in light of the issues that arise at the conference. It should be attended by a representative of the instructing solicitors (preferably the person with conduct of the case). This will enable difficult issues to be worked through more effectively and efficiently at the conference. It is also important that the instructing solicitors have an independent record of their client's instructions on what are likely to be the most sensitive and problematic areas of the case (quite possibly areas in which the client has given conflicting instructions in the past). It is not appropriate to ask the interpreter to try to combine his own role with that of the solicitor's representative at the conference. Interpreting is a distinct and demanding job. It is not practical to expect the interpreter even to take a note of the conference.

31.2 Your client should have been provided with a translation of any statement already submitted and of the Home Office interview record if the latter raises any credibility issues. She should be reminded to bring these to the conference.

31.3 The conference should begin with a detailed explanation of what will happen at the hearing. That should include what the hearing room will look like, who will be there, what their roles are, and in what order things will happen. An appellant may worry about the most seemingly innocuous details, like whether she stands or sits and how she addresses the adjudicator. It is particularly important to explain the role of the court interpreter (see chapter 34).

Examination in chief

31.4 Explain that the adjudicator will have been provided with her witness statement, and that your first questions after establishing her name and address will be whether she is familiar with its contents and whether it is true. (She may otherwise become worried or confused by these first questions, particularly when in a heightened state of nervousness at the very start of her evidence.)

31.5 If you are going to ask supplementary questions, you should normally tell her what areas they will cover. Do not give her an exact list of questions that will constitute your examination in chief: this could be interpreted as rehearsing the witness. There is undoubtedly a risk that a nervous client with little else to think about will fixate upon these questions and how she is going to respond so that the answers ultimately sound both rehearsed and contrived.

31.6 You must, however, make sure during the pre-hearing conference that she is capable of answering the question confidently: ask your questions from different angles so as to satisfy yourself of the answers you will get to your examination in chief.

Cross-examination and re-examination

31.7 The majority of the appellant's oral evidence is likely to be spent dealing with cross-examination. She needs to be aware of this. She needs to understand that cross-examination represents her main opportunity to put her case personally to the adjudicator. She must listen to the questions and make sure that she answers them (or else explains why she cannot answer). But impress on her that answering the point is not the same as agreeing with the point: this is her opportunity to explain to the adjudicator why the Home Office is wrong. Do not assume that she will understand this. Contradicting a state official in a formal setting may not come naturally to your client and may have very different consequences in her home country.

31.8 You are not permitted to rehearse, practise, or coach a witness. Your role is to probe potential weaknesses in her evidence and assess how real these are. Your ability to re-examine effectively is entirely dependent on how thoroughly you have done this. You should find out what the answer will be to any follow up question you may ask in response to foreseeable lines of cross-examination. Apparent weaknesses may turn out on investigation to have arisen from omissions, misunderstandings or ambiguities in the draft witness statement. If so, it should be amended. Other responses may also be incorporated naturally into the narrative of the witness statement, thereby avoiding unnecessary cross-examination and court time. If they do not fit naturally within the narrative, they may be best left for re-examination if needs be.

31.9 You may well have to question your client robustly. The first time your client is asked a difficult question should not be by the HOPO in front of the adjudicator. The pre-hearing conference serves a different purpose from the interviews at which the statement was taken. Your purpose when taking the statement was to elicit all information relevant to her case and to ensure that you understood it before including it in the statement. You would allow her to speak about what she thought was important, regardless of its direct relevance to the question, and then come back to the question if necessary later.

31.10 However, you must now accustomise your client to the strictures which will govern her oral evidence. She will not be permitted to give evidence in that style at the hearing, particularly in cross-examination. She will have to learn to focus on and deal with the questions which are put. You need to tell her if she is not answering the question, and explain why she is not answering the question. She needs to understand the distinction between disagreeing with a point and failing to address it. It does her no service to give her free rein in the conference only for her to face constant interruptions from the adjudicator when she behaves in the same way in the hearing.

31.11 You should also explain common techniques of cross-examination such as leading questions. She should not allow the HOPO to force her into a 'yes' or 'no' answer where it is not as simple as that. (Conversely, she should not elaborate where the question can be dealt with by a single word.) She should not be put off by an aggressive or disbelieving tone on the part of the HOPO: he is not making the decision. Warn your client that those questions which are asked most aggressively may be those with the least justification. If she does not understand a question she should always say so rather than guess the answer. Explain that you may object if you consider a question to be unclear or unfair and a discussion may follow: the important thing for her is to concentrate on the question that is ultimately put.

31.12 Explain that you will be offered an opportunity to ask further questions in re-examination, but you may not need to do so (see chapter 37).

General advice on giving evidence

31.13 Your client will be concerned about giving her evidence in a manner which convinces the adjudicator. The IAT and the High Court have emphasised the dangers of making adverse credibility findings based on an assessment of oral evidence of a witness who speaks in a foreign language and is of a wholly different culture and background from the adjudicator. Given the difficulties in envisaging any safe method by which an adjudicator could dismiss oral evidence on the basis of demeanour, mannerisms, pattern of speech, or tone of voice, it is not possible – nor is it permissible – to give detailed guidelines on how to give evidence in a manner that will convince the adjudicator.

31.14 Rather than attempt to second guess the basis upon which an adjudicator may dismiss oral evidence, it is better to concentrate on assisting your client to give her evidence as confidently as possible. She should remember that she is talking *to* the adjudicator and putting *her* case. She should not pretend he is not there. If he puts a question to her, she should pay particular attention. He will be asking because he needs to know the answer, not as a means of supporting the case against her.

31.15 If your client is giving evidence in English, warn her that she may be interrupted if she starts speaking too quickly as everyone has to make a proper note. If she is using another language, explain the role of the court interpreter. She should always say if she has difficulty understanding him, either at the outset or at any point during her evidence. The court interpreter may interrupt if her answer is too long to interpret in one go.

31.16 Most adjudicators do not ask witnesses to give evidence on oath. However, if the witness wishes to do so, this should be permitted (***Nakhuda***). Ask her beforehand if she wants to give evidence on oath, and if so ensure that the IAA will have any necessary book available in the hearing room.

31.17 You should check whether she wishes to have the public excluded from the hearing, or steps taken to protect her identity (see chapter 32). Also check whether any of the other steps suggested in the IAA Gender Guidelines (para 5.6) may be appropriate, such as rearranging the hearing room to make it less formal, giving evidence via video link, provision of a female interpreter, or an all-female court. The latter involves not only a female adjudicator but the Home Office being directed to provide a female HOPO. Note, however, that anecdotal but consistent reports indicate that some of the worst examples of offensive cross-examination by HOPOs of victims of rape have occurred in the context of an all-female court.

31 Pre-hearing conference
Key points

- The pre-hearing conference is an essential part of the appeal preparation. It should take place before the witness statement is finalised.

- It is unacceptable to brief an advocate to conduct the hearing without arranging a prior conference. The only exception is if there is no prospect of oral evidence being led.

- A detailed explanation of what will happen at the hearing should be offered.

- Satisfy yourself that any planned examination in chief will be effective.

- Probe potential weaknesses in your client's evidence, both to enable you to re-examine effectively and to test the draft witness statement.

- Give general advice on cross-examination techniques and how your client should conduct herself.

- Rehearsing, practising, or coaching a witness is impermissible.

- Check whether your client wishes to give evidence on oath or to have the public excluded from the hearing or her identity protected.

32 Private hearings and anonymity

32.1 An adjudicator has the power to make provision to secure the anonymity of the appellant or a witness and, in certain circumstances, to conduct hearings in private. Explore with your client in advance of the hearing whether any such application is appropriate.

32.2 A decision to conduct the hearing in private has important consequences in terms of the Home Office's confidentiality policy. The APIs state:

> **When Does an Asylum Claim Enter the Public Domain?**
>
> *Once a failed asylum seeker has had their case heard openly before the appellate authorities, the claim can be said to be in the public domain and details of their claim may be included in other Reasons for Refusal Letters. Determinations may also be referred to, or annexed to another case. The information that may be used is not restricted to that which is specifically mentioned at the appeal hearing, or in the determination, but all the information given to us by the applicant/appellant in connection with the asylum application.*
>
> *If an appeal is outstanding, but has not yet had a hearing, it is not in the public domain and no reference to that claim should be made in the Reasons for Refusal Letter relating to another claim.*
>
> *If an appeal hearing is heard 'in camera' (i.e. hearing evidence in secret) then the matter has not passed into the public domain and details of that claim should not be mentioned in relation to another case.*

32.3 You will have to warn your client of the risk that the Home Office may disclose information that she had assumed was confidential. You may also have to explain the policy to the adjudicator. He may have no idea that the Home Office claims to be able to make public use not just of the determination, but also of whatever information and material the Home Office was given in support of the claim, regardless of whether it is mentioned in the determination.

32.4 Rule 50 states:

Admission of public to hearings

(1) Subject to the following provisions of this rule, every hearing before an adjudicator or the Tribunal must be held in public.

(2) Where an adjudicator or the Tribunal is considering an allegation referred to in section 108 of the 2002 Act, all members of the public must be excluded from the hearing.

(3) An adjudicator or the Tribunal may exclude any or all members of the public from any hearing or part of a hearing if it is necessary –

(a) in the interests of public order or national security; or

(b) to protect the private life of a party or the interests of a minor.

(4) An adjudicator or the Tribunal may also, in exceptional circumstances, exclude any or all members of the public from any hearing or part of a hearing to ensure that publicity does not prejudice the interests of justice, but only if and to the extent that it is strictly necessary to do so.

(5) A member of the Council on Tribunals or of its Scottish Committee acting in that capacity is entitled to attend any hearing and may not be excluded pursuant to paragraph (2), (3) or (4) of this rule.

32.5 By r.38(5)(i), an adjudicator can also make a direction to

make provision to secure the anonymity of a party or witness.

32.6 You may request that your client and/or a witness be identified in the determination by initials only. The IAT now refers to the claimant by initials in all determinations (see IAT PD No 10, para 29.8). Prior to that practice direction being adopted, the then President had stated that:

If we are asked to do so in an individual case, we will always ensure that the person concerned is referred to by a letter only.
(letter from Collins J to ILPA, 31 May 2002)

32.7 The Administrative Court and Court of Appeal also agree quite readily to refer to parties by initials if requested to do so. The Home Office does not normally raise any objection (although it sometimes emphasises that its consent should not be taken as any acceptance of the merits of the underlying asylum claim). There is no reason for an adjudicator to take a more restrictive approach to such applications.

32.8 The power under r.38(5)(i) 'to secure the anonymity of a party or witness' should also enable the adjudicator to direct that nothing be said in court which could identify the person to the public. This may be sufficient to assuage the concerns of a witness about giving evidence in public.

32.9 This new power (absent from previous versions of the Rules) to make directions to secure anonymity raises the question of whether adjudicators and the IAT can also impose reporting restrictions under s.11 of the Contempt of Court Act 1981. This provides that:

> *In any case where a court (having power to do so) allows a name or other matter to be withheld from the public in proceedings before the court, the court may give such directions prohibiting the publication of that name or matter in connection with the proceedings as appear to be necessary for the purpose for which it was so withheld.*

32.10 Section 19 of the same Act states that:

> *'court' includes any tribunal or body exercising the judicial power of the State...*

32.11 On its face, this would appear to include adjudicators and the IAT. However, the only relevant authority is a decision of the House of Lords (pre-dating the 1981 Act) of **AG v BBC**. It found that a local valuation court was not a 'court' for the purposes of the then common law of contempt of court because its function was essentially administrative rather than judicial. Each of the Law Lords gave separate speeches with their own emphases. Eliciting guidance on the present question is also not helped by the fact that the legal concepts involved have developed considerably in the intervening years. However, the general tenor of the judgments was towards a restrictive definition of 'court'. Further discussion is beyond the scope of this text. If reporting restrictions might be justified in the circumstances of your case, seek specialist advice. Do so quickly as reporting restrictions will generally be judged inappropriate where the information has already entered the public domain.

32.12 An order excluding the public under r.50 may at least prevent public knowledge of the contents of the evidence. In **D**, Dyson J held that the test for conducting proceedings 'in camera' (i.e. excluding the public) and the test for imposing reporting restrictions were the same:

> *whether the proposed derogation from open justice is necessary in order to prevent a real risk that the administration of justice will be rendered impractical.*

Rule 50(4) is presumably intended to reflect this test.

32.13 Dyson J also quoted the comments of Lord Donaldson MR in **H**:

> *In order that the citizens be not deterred from seeking access to justice through courts it is occasionally necessary to protect them from the conse-*

> *quences of public scrutiny of evidence, and in particular medical evidence, of a nature that such scrutiny would prove not only embarrassing but positively damaging to them.*

32.14 In *D* itself, the application was for an anonymity order under s.11 preventing publication or disclosure of any information that might reveal D's identity. D had advanced HIV disease, had overstayed, and had sought judicial review of his local authority's refusal to assist him under the National Assistance Act. Medical evidence indicated that public knowledge of his situation would endanger him psychologically. Dyson J held that:

> *In my judgment, for the purposes of the present case, D has to show that there is a real risk that, without the protection of anonymity, he will suffer real significant physical or mental harm.*

32.15 He considered that the medical evidence before him met that test. This highlights the need to ask your experts to address the question if you intend to rely on medical grounds as justifying a private hearing.

32.16 Any external physical risk to the appellant, a witness, or other persons, whether in this country or the country of origin, may also satisfy the test so long as the risk is a real one. You may present expert evidence about any monitoring by the authorities in the country of origin of the activities of dissidents abroad.

32.17 Rule 50(3)(b) specifically provides for the exclusion of the public in order to 'protect the private life of a party' or 'the interests of a minor'. The above caselaw will nevertheless remain relevant because the protection of private life will have to be balanced under article 8(2) with the public interest in open justice, and the party's rights under article 8 balanced with the rights of the media to freedom of speech under article 10. As Sedley LJ stated in *Douglas*, 'neither is a trump card'. Even in respect of the 'interests of a minor', a similar balancing exercise will be required. The child's welfare is not a 'paramount consideration' (*Re S*) although the specific reference in r.50(3)(b) reflects that a court may be more easily persuaded that the criteria for protection from publicity are satisfied in the case of a child.

32.18 There should be few cases in which the exclusion of the pubic will be necessary in the interests of public order or national security (r.50(3)(a)). Any risk to national security perceived by the Home Office as a result of public disclosure of the evidence in the appeal may result in it issuing a certificate requiring the appeal to be heard by SIAC (which has its own procedural rules).

32.19 If the IAA agrees to an application to exclude members of the public under r.50, you should ensure that measures have been taken to prevent the public entering before the hearing proper starts. The court clerk usually places a notice on the door. If you have a r.50 application that has not yet been considered, this should obviously be the first item you raise at the hearing. Similarly, if the IAA has agreed that the appellant may be known by initials, check that the paper lists displayed in the hearing centre reflect this.

32 Private hearings and anonymity
Key points

■ An adjudicator has power to make provision to secure the anonymity of the appellant or a witness (r.38(5)(i)). He may exclude the public from a hearing under r.50 if necessary:

  ☐ in the interests of public order or security,
  ☐ to protect the private life of a party or the interests of a minor,
  ☐ to ensure, exceptionally, that publicity does not prejudice the interests of justice.

■ Explore with your client in advance of the hearing whether any such application is appropriate.

■ A request that your client and/or a witness be identified in the determination only by initials should be readily granted by the adjudicator. The IAT refers to the claimant by initials in all its determinations.

■ The power to secure the anonymity of a party or a witness should encompass a power to prevent their identity being disclosed in open court. There may be scope to argue that this power gives rise to a further power to impose reporting restrictions under s.11 of the Contempt of Court Act 1981.

■ The public should be excluded from a hearing only where it is necessary in order to prevent a real risk that the administration of justice will otherwise be rendered impractical.

■ A real risk of real significant physical or mental harm through publicity will satisfy this test. If the risk is to your client's health, then medical evidence will be required. Any external physical risk to the appellant, a witness, or other persons, whether in this country or the country of origin, may also satisfy the test so long as the risk is a real one.

■ The protection of the private life of a party must be balanced against principles of open justice and the media's article 10 rights. The interests of a minor are not paramount but a court may be more easily persuaded that the criteria for protection from publicity are satisfied in the case of a child.

33 Opening the hearing

33.1   If you are lucky, you may be able to contact the HOPO by telephone in advance of the hearing date. Unfortunately, beyond confirming whether or not he has your material, the HOPO is very likely to indicate that he does not intend to familiarise himself with the file until the eve of the hearing. (As indicated in chapter 27, it may be helpful to note this if he subsequently tries to take a point on late submission of evidence.)

33.2   When you arrive at the hearing centre, you will be handed a form to complete confirming that you are not prohibited from providing representation under s.84 of the 1999 Act.

33.3   See the HOPO beforehand and check that you have everything he has submitted or plans to submit, and that he has everything you have submitted. You should also explore with the HOPO whether there is any scope to narrow or agree any issues. HOPOs vary greatly in the degree to which they will co-operate in defining the issues. It is not unknown for the HOPO to refuse even to discuss the case with you until the adjudicator enters the room on the ground that this would be 'unprofessional'!

33.4   The first thing you are likely to be asked by the adjudicator is to confirm whether you are ready to proceed with the hearing. At this point, you should indicate whether you have any adjournment request or an application to be put back in the list (for example, because a witness is late, or because the Home Office wants to submit further evidence upon which you need to consider your position). The HOPO will also make any adjournment application at this stage. Deal with any issues concerning exclusion of the public or anonymity (chapter 32).

33.5   The adjudicator will want to check that he and the parties have the same documents. Neither the HOPO nor the adjudicator can necessarily be relied upon to have everything that you have served on the Home Office and the IAA. You should therefore ensure that you are in

310 • Best practice guide to asylum and human rights appeals

a position to provide details of when and how your evidence was served.

33.6 If any attempt to engage the Home Office in useful negotiations has so far proved futile, the opening discussion provides a further opportunity to seek to define the issues. The HOPO will usually be asked whether he has anything he wishes to add to the refusal letter. Normally he will not, in which case you may confirm with him, in front of the adjudicator, that he is not raising any new issue at the hearing. You will normally object to any new basis for refusal being advanced at this stage if it could have been raised in advance.

33.7 If you have submitted evidence such as medical reports or documentary corroboration in compliance with directions and the Home Office has given no indication that it disputes them, you should object if the HOPO raises any specific objection to them at the hearing (for example, that an arrest warrant is forged, or that a medical expert's methodology is deficient).

33.8 The HOPO may openly justify the lack of prior notice on the ground that he was only briefed the day before the hearing. Your client will be nervous enough about facing cross-examination without you starting by needlessly antagonising the HOPO: he may privately be equally critical of the Home Office's conduct of the appeal, but powerless to do anything about it.

33.9 Your argument is with the Home Office, and the HOPO's admission assists you. If its failure to provide proper notice of its case is simply down to briefing the HOPO very late (rather than some unavoidable circumstance), that is a powerful argument in favour of not permitting the Home Office to advance new allegations for the first time at the hearing. The undesirability of any adjournment that fairness would otherwise require to enable you to respond to the new allegation is a further factor militating against the allegation being permitted.

33.10 If the refusal letter has made specific but unsourced allegations against your client, then you should query these at the start of the hearing (if you have not already done so). The same applies if an allegation appears to be based on a mistake or misunderstanding of the evidence. You can assume that the HOPO intends to cross-examine on the arguments set out in the refusal letter. There is no reason why your client should have to respond to misconceived and mistaken allegations, and it saves everyone time to sort these out at the start of the hearing.

33.11 If you have submitted evidence which refutes an assertion in the refusal letter, ask the HOPO if he will now withdraw it, and if not, what evidence he intends to call. HOPOs again vary in their approach to this process. But a reasonable HOPO will often withdraw the offending paragraphs from the refusal letter if you convince him that they are mistaken or insupportable. This process also reminds everyone that this is an appeal against the Home Office's decision rather than an unfettered investigation into your client's credibility and character.

33.12 See also para 30.6 for opening where you do not intend to call the appellant.

33 Opening the hearing
Key points

- Check that everyone has the correct documentation.

- Seek to clarify and define the issues. Object if the HOPO raises fresh issues without notice, especially if they would necessitate adjournment.

- If allegations in the refusal letter are clearly misconceived or mistaken, or if you have submitted evidence that refutes such allegations, ask the HOPO to reconsider his position.

34 Interpretation at the hearing

34.1 The Royal Commission on Criminal Justice noted in 1993 that 'Clearly, in the court setting, the highest standards of interpretation are called for.' The Royal Commission recommended that only trained and qualified interpreters be used in court, and the recommendation was accepted by the Government. In response, a National Register of Public Service Interpreters was established in 1994, administered by the Institute of Linguists with the support of the Home Office and the Lord Chancellor's Department (now the Department of Constitutional Affairs).

34.2 It is often assumed, not unnaturally, by appellants and representatives – and perhaps by some adjudicators – that only such interpreters are used for court work by the IAA. This is not the case. The IAA administration has made efforts to improve the quality of interpreters in recent years, but it remains the position that IAA interpreters do not need to have relevant qualifications or be members of the NRPSI. The only requirements are to be interviewed, to pass two 10 minute oral assessments, and attend a two day training course. Even this may be waived for uncommon languages.

34.3 The standard of interpretation is fundamental to the fairness of the appeal and the safety of the decision. While many court interpreters are committed people of a high standard who carry out their role with considerable sensitivity, there have also been numerous concerns expressed about the quality of some of the interpreters used by the IAA. The concerns have included insufficient knowledge of the witness' language, inadequate standard of English, inability to interpret properly (which is not the same as speaking both languages), and bias.

Obstacles to accurate interpreting

34.4 Interpretation is often assumed by HOPOs (and sometimes adjudicators) to be a mechanical process which, if properly conducted, involves no choice of expression on the part of the interpreter. That is not so. There is often no word or phrase in each language which is exactly equivalent. Where there is a phrase with an equivalent meaning, it might be quite different to the literal translation of the words used. These difficulties are naturally exacerbated where the languages reflect very different cultures. A central issue for the competent interpreter is when to depart from literal interpretation in order better to convey the intended meaning of the words used. Getting the balance wrong on either side can pose serious dangers to the integrity of the process.

34.5 To interpret well requires familiarity both with the topic under discussion and an understanding of the different cultures in question. Only then can the interpreter identify whether he is effectively conveying the true meaning. The court interpreter ought in particular to have a basic understanding of the legal and policing systems both of the country of origin and of the UK. Problems often occur when questions are put in the context of UK procedures and terminology with the expectation that there will be a simple equivalent in the country of origin.

34.6 There may be different interpretations of the word 'detained' in the appellant's language depending upon whether one is referring to arrest for questioning and release on the same day, detention overnight in a police station, or detention for a longer period in a prison. Arrest by a militarised police force may be translated into English by one interpreter as arrest by the police and by another interpreter as arrest by the army. The HOPO will then allege a discrepancy. HOPOs commonly ask whether the appellant has been charged with an offence. If there is no equivalent to the British procedure by which the police charge a suspect, the interpreter may, instead of indicating that there is no means of accurately interpreting the question, simply substitute what he considers the most similar procedure – commonly, whether the witness was ever brought before a court. The witness will answer no, and this answer will be interpreted and recorded as 'No, I was never charged with any offence.' Being charged and being brought before a court may have quite different connotations and implications. However, if you are not aware of the problem, and the court interpreter does not indicate that he has altered the question and answer, the court will be misled. The problem is exacerbated where more than one interpreter has been involved. There is then the risk that they substitute different procedures when interpreting the question, resulting again in an apparent but false discrepancy.

34.7 Different calendars also give rise to a host of problems. The interpreter may have grown into the habit over many years of performing a rough conversion when a date is mentioned, seeing it as part of the interpretation process. However, the foreign calender is unlikely to provide exact equivalents and what one interpreter identifies as August might be identified by another as September. Another fraught area is kinship terminology, there often being no equivalent description of particular relationships.

34.8 On the other hand, interpretation that is too literal can also pose dangers. For example, an activist may refer to fellow activists as 'friends'. She may say 'I was detained with my friends'. She is then asked how long she knew them, and when she responds that she had seen them for the first time when they were arrested, this is marked down as a discrepancy. The common thread is the failure to take account of the inherent difficulties in interpretation.

The court interpreter

34.9 It is important to set out all your requirements in respect of the court interpreter in the reply to directions (or as soon as possible in writing if you become aware of further requirements after the reply has been submitted). These may include language, dialect, gender, and nationality. Gender may be particularly important if the appellant will have to give evidence of sexual torture. Nationality may be important not only where it determines accent and dialect, but because it may be impossible to interpret accurately unless the interpreter is fully familiar with national systems and customs. The IAA's *Handbook for Interpreters* (below) states that interpreter should be aware of 'the general culture, social and political situations' in the country of origin.

34.10 In *Kaygun*, the IAT emphasised that an appellant should not be required to use an interpreter who speaks other than her first language, regardless of whether she is able to conduct a conversation in the interpreter's language. It said that:

> This is by no means the first time in which difficulties of interpretation have arisen where an appellant is giving evidence in other than his first language. Although, plainly, the appellant speaks good conversational Turkish, one of the problems, revealed time and again in these asylum appeals, is that someone who has a good conversational command of a language other than his own or first language, in the unfamiliar surroundings of the Courtroom, with the added stress of giving evidence in a matter of no small importance to an individual appellant, can run into difficulties.

34.11 There may be some circumstances in which your client's evidence may be more effective in English than in her first language. It is an inevitable consequence of giving evidence through an interpreter that an adjudicator will not engage with the evidence to the same extent as he can if the witness addresses him in his own language. It may also be useful to give evidence in English in a human rights appeal where the appellant's integration into British society is an important issue.

34.12 You should not suggest that the appellant gives evidence in English without satisfying yourself that she can do so effectively. In particular, she should not be distracted from the content of her answer by trying to formulate it in English. You may ask the court interpreter to remain in case the witness experiences problems with her English at any stage. The IAA *Guide to Adjudicators* on interpreters (below) states that 'the adjudicator should be wary of releasing the interpreter' where the witness starts giving evidence in English.

34.13 Some adjudicators will query whether they are permitted to adopt this approach or whether all evidence must be given in one language or the other. In *Humadi*, the IAT said that 'what is essential in order to prevent unfairness or detriment is that the appellant's evidence is given without distortion or inaccuracy' and that:

> *The mere fact that an adjudicator decides to receive evidence partly in English and partly in a witness' native language does not constitute an error of procedure.*

34.14 Provided that you state clearly what you require in terms of the court interpreter, these requirements should be respected. In *Cavasoglu*, the IAT said that:

> *In the view of the Tribunal, the decision as to whether or not an interpreter should be employed in a case, is a decision which can only be taken by the Appellant and his advisors, and it is not the function of an adjudicator to disagree with a decision that an interpreter should be employed at a hearing nor, indeed, is it the function of an adjudicator to express any view with regard to a request that an interpreter be employed. The Tribunal considers that the function of the adjudicator within this context of the conduct of the hearing is to comply with the wishes of the Appellant and his advisors so far as the provision of an interpreter is concerned. The decision as to whether an Appellant should give his evidence in the language of his country or any other nation is a matter for him and his advisors alone.*

34.15 The IAA assesses interpreters on its panel according to their qualifications, training and experience. Training and qualifications are graded on a skills points basis as follows:

- 10 points: Full member of the National Register of Public Service Interpreters (NRPSI);
- 7.5 points: Diploma of Public Service Interpreting (DPSI) [based on a nine month course], Interim Member of NRPSI, 'A' mark at IAA assessment, full member of Institute of Linguists and/or ITI, or recognised language degree;
- 5 points: DPSI in other options, 'B' mark at IAA assessment, member of IOL and/or ITI, recognised English degree, or reference with language assessment from the Metropolitan Police or a Local Authority;
- 2.5 points: C mark at IAA assessment, or non-assessed member of NRPSI

34.16 Experience is also graded out of 10, ranging from 10 points for an interpreter with over four years and 1500 hours of experience of interpreting for the IAA down to one point for someone with little or no interpreting experience.

34.17 As will be apparent, the court interpreter may have scored anything from 20 out of 20 down to three-and-a-half out of 20 in his combined grade, yet still be considered qualified to act as court interpreter. As part of its work to improve the standard of interpreting, the IAA introduced a policy in 2001 of booking the best interpreter available, according to this grading system (*Allocation of Interpreter Bookings: Providing the most appropriate interpreter for all hearings*, IAA, 2001).

34.18 However, the IAA has now reversed that policy, and will book the cheapest interpreter (in terms of travel expenses) in preference to a better qualified interpreter who is available for the hearing. It will also use an interpreter who is already booked at the hearing centre to interpret additional languages – irrespective of his skills grading in these languages – rather than book a second interpreter.

34.19 The reversal of its previous policy raises obvious concerns in the context of the 'highest standards of fairness' that are required in such appeals. You may have to explain this change of policy to the adjudicator if there are concerns about the court interpreter. The IAA *Guide for Adjudicators* on interpreters is presently being updated: the May 2002 version mentioned in para 5 of Adjudicator Guidance Note 3 (below) reflects the old policy to the effect that the IAA 'allocates bookings to the most skilled and experienced person'.

34.20 The IAA states that if the court interpreter is challenged, 'the ability and skill level of the interpreter present should be quickly verified [by the adjudicator] by speaking to the Interpreter Team Leader' (*Guide to Adjudicators*, May 2002). He may also question the interpreter. You are entitled to the same information. In **Kutukcu**, the IAT stated that:

Consideration of the ability or otherwise of an interpreter is of central importance to the adjudicator's assessment of the evidence. As with any other subject in that category, the parties need not only to know what the adjudicator is told, but see the relevant material for themselves. In this case that meant the interpreter's own words and demeanour when giving her qualifications and experience, apparently at some length. We cannot for the moment think of any case that might call for private communication between the interpreter and the adjudicator: with the best will in world, this one did not. The fact that a point has been raised which may be thought embarrassing is no reason to depart from the general rule of doing justice in the presence of both sides.

34.21 Ongoing assessment of interpreters relies upon adjudicators completing an assessment form at the hearing giving the court interpreter marks out of five on various questions. The latest version marks 'overall Standard of English (i.e. could you understand what was said); overall standard of interpretation (including fluidity, comprehension, and appropriate body language and tone of voice); adherence to IAA protocol (clarity and explanation of cultural references); professionalism; punctuality.' The previous form annexed to the IAA *Handbook for Interpreters* included a question about the interpreter's proficiency in the foreign language. This has been removed: the adjudicator is in as unsatisfactory a position to assess this as you would be if you attended without your own interpreter (see below).

34.22 To test whether the interpreting is satisfactory, the adjudicator will ask the interpreter to exchange some remarks with the witness before she gives evidence. The correct procedure is set out in Adjudicator Guidance Note No 3 which, for convenience, is set out in full below:

INTRODUCTION OF INTERPRETERS

1   *This guide provides a suggested form of words for the introduction of interpreters and appellants at the beginning of hearings.*

2   *Interpreters are booked by the IAA and they do not usually meet the appellant until they attend in court at the beginning of the hearing day. It is vital that the Adjudicator ensures that the appellant and the interpreter understand each other. This must be done in open court by the Adjudicator.*

3   *In the absence of any guidance several practices have developed. The most common is for an Adjudicator to say to an interpreter something like 'Do you understand each other'. The interpreter turns to the witness and says presumably, 'Do you understand me'. The appellant says something in reply and the interpreter confirms there is an understanding. Something rather more formal is likely to be more effective.*

It is bad practice to have no form of introduction of the appellant and the interpreter as has happened on occasions.

4 *The following format is suggested as a guide to Adjudicators. The purpose is for the Adjudicator to take an early and immediate control of the proceedings so that the Adjudicator establishes with the help of the interpreter that the appellant and the interpreter understand each other rather than leaving that to the interpreter.*

Adjudicators Pre Hearing Introduction

I am now going to hear your appeal. It will take the form of you being asked questions, first by your representative and then by Mr/Mrs.................. for the Home Office.

The important thing for you is to listen to the question carefully and just answer the question asked. If you have to give a long answer, please do so in small parts so that it can be interpreted properly. Please do not interrupt the interpreter when your answer is being interpreted.

Although the interpreter is sitting next to you, speak loudly and clearly to them. I would also like you to speak loudly enough for me to hear what you are saying. The interpreter will speak loudly and clearly to you.

If you do not understand anything please say so.

You will not be asked to give a full account of what happened to you in your country. This is detailed on the papers before me. I have to decide what is likely to happen to you if you went back. Don't feel too upset that you have not been asked to give a full account.

After the evidence has been given, the Presenting Officer and your representative will make their final submissions to me. The interpreter will do his best to interpret those as well.

Do you understand the interpreter?

Now to ensure that the interpreter understands you, I would like you to tell the interpreter how you arrived at court this morning. Tell the interpreter what time you left and some details of your journey here.

(To the Interpreter): Do you understand the witness?

This process should not take more than a couple of minutes.

5 *The IAA are shortly producing a guide for Adjudicators on interpreter*

services which will contain the above suggested form of words as an annex. The guide will be circulated.

6 *It is not good practice to ask an interpreter to explain the procedure in the court to the appellant. Nor should interpreters be used as experts or be asked to give advice.*

7 *There is no objection to appellant's representatives bringing in their own interpreter. Interpreting is a difficult job particularly when being done under pressure. An appellant's interpreter however must only communicate through the appellant's representative. If there is any disagreement with the court interpreter the appellant's interpreter can bring that to the representative's attention promptly. It may be appropriate to have the appellant's interpreter sit relatively close to the appellant's representative.*

8 *There are occasions when representatives ask for the assistance of the court interpreter to help communication with the client outside the court. So long as this does not involve anything contentious and does not entail the interpreter interpreting detailed instructions then this should not be regarded as objectionable.*

9 *Interpreters are the only people during hearings who speak all the time. They do need regular breaks and it is not best practice to leave it to the interpreter to ask for a break.*

34.23 The conversation about how the appellant got to court that morning (while an improvement on previous practice) is likely to be at a level of sophistication that could be handled in French by the average British school pupil. Having established this level of understanding, the interpreter is then expected to be capable of translating the witness' explanation of Marxist ideology. Not surprisingly, it does not always follow. What does often follow is absurdly literalist translation. Upon being challenged on the interpretation into nonsensical English, the interpreter may reply that they have been told to translate exactly what the witness has said. What he is actually doing, as the British school pupil learning French would do, is interpreting words without any regard to context.

34.24 The IAA's *Handbook for Interpreters* gives guidance on the court interpreter's conduct:

You should try to replicate the type of language that is being used, whether it be simple, formal, colloquial etc. If abusive or obscene language is used in the source language, you should use the English equivalent...

To aid in this, it is necessary that you maintain information on the gen-

eral culture, social and political situations in the countries from which the languages being interpreted originate...

You may intervene at the hearing for the following reasons:

- to seek clarification if you have not fully understood what [you have] been asked to interpret;

- to alert the Adjudicator that although the interpretation was correct, the question or statement may not have been understood;

- to alert the court to a possible missed cultural inference – such as when an item of information has not been stated but knowledge of which has been assumed;

- if someone is speaking indistinctly, too quickly or for too long without pausing to allow adequate consecutive interpreting...

An interpreter's duty is to interpret accurately and precisely. An interpreter must remain strictly impartial both before and throughout the proceedings...

Do:

- use the witness's exact words. If you cannot make a direct or exact interpretation, interpret it as accurately as possible in the witness's own words and then inform the Adjudicator what the phrase means. Your duty is to make sure the court understands what the witness is meaning.

- stop the witness or questioner at the end of each sentence as necessary and interpret sentence by sentence...

Don't:

- speak to a witness [or] appellant before or during the hearing except in the course of your official duties, unless the Adjudicator has given you permission. In particular, do not have untranslated discussions with a witness during the court session.

- use an English expression or phrase which is not an exact translation of the witness's own words.

- ask the witness what they mean by a particular answer. If you cannot understand what is meant by an answer, you must ask the Adjudicator if you can ask the witness to repeat or clarify their answer.

- try to anticipate what the witness is trying to say or give an answer other than what is being said.

- *let your own experience or views get in the way of how you interpret the evidence.*

34.25 Always address the witness directly. If clarification is required, you will normally ask the witness. If you need to ask the interpreter directly for clarification of something the interpreter said, address him as Mr/Madam Interpreter. If the question is anything more significant than whether you heard him correctly, you will normally indicate to the adjudicator first that you wish to seek clarification from the interpreter. This may be because your own interpreter has alerted you to the fact that there is a difficulty in the interpretation of a particular phrase or concept, or simply because the interpretation appears unclear or ambiguous.

34.26 The IAA *Guide to Adjudicators* points out that:

> *Cross examinations can be used to ask unexpected questions and the Adjudicator must take care that the interpreter is not used to interpret for example double negative questions that are difficult to interpret properly.*

34.27 The court interpreter should provide whispered simultaneous interpretation during exchanges between representatives and the adjudicator and during closing submissions. (He sometimes needs to be reminded to do this.)

34.28 The Adjudicator Guidance Note emphasises the need to give the court interpreter regular breaks. Interpreting court proceedings demands intensive concentration. If it appears that an interpreter who is otherwise satisfactory may be starting to make mistakes through tiredness, you should suggest to the adjudicator that he takes a break.

34.29 Always keep a note of the court interpreter's name. If a case is adjourned (for reasons other than defects in the interpreting), it should normally resume with the same interpreter. As indicated above, different interpreters may interpret the same word or phrase differently, and a change of interpreter mid-way through evidence may lead to changes in the interpreting which will suggest a false inconsistency on the part of the witness.

Your interpreter at the hearing

34.30 **You should always have your own interpreter present where the appellant (or any material witness) will not be giving evidence in English.** In terms of client care alone, it is less than satisfactory if your client cannot communicate with her advocate both before and after the hearing. In terms of your professional responsibility to present the appeal properly, it is unacceptable for an advocate to be unable to communicate with his client at court. Your duties include addressing last minute concerns from your client which may otherwise affect her confidence. You may also have to take instructions on new issues raised by the HOPO or adjudicator.

34.31 Unless you are fluent in the language in which your client will give evidence, it is even more important that you are able to monitor the court interpreting through your own interpreter. You are otherwise powerless to intervene if mistakes (which may be critical) are made. As the IAT noted in *Kaygun*:

> *It is not easy for an adjudicator who has no command of the language to pick up problems of this sort, nor indeed is there any reason why an appellant who has no command of English, or only a limited command, should himself be able to pick up problems of interpretation. A witness who requires the services of an interpreter ipso facto will be unlikely to appreciate the way in which his answers are being translated, and as a consequence will not be in a position to draw the problem to the adjudicator's attention. Similarly, unless the representative is fluent in [the appellant's language], then the representative will often not be aware that there is difficulty.*

34.32 The LSC gives the following guidance in the GCC:

> *Is it reasonable to allow an interpreter to attend with you at [the asylum interview], before the adjudicator, or before the IAT?*
>
> *Although interpreters are provided for hearings before the adjudicator and Immigration Appeal Tribunal, their function is to provide an interpreting service for the adjudicator/tribunal. It may therefore be appropriate to authorise an extension to enable you to communicate with the client and take instructions where there is no other suitable person (for example, family member or friend) to assist the client and you do not speak the relevant language to a sufficient standard.*
>
> *It is normally reasonable to authorise an interpreter to attend with you at the [asylum] interviews. Whilst the immigration services have their own interpreters attending at every interview, where necessary, it is still normally considered reasonable for the applicant to have an independent*

interpreter present as the interpreter provided by the Immigration Service may have an opposite opinion or opposing political affiliation to the applicant and may therefore be biased against the applicant. Interpreters cannot be instructed to attend in your absence. (para IM 3.5)

34.33 The latter considerations apply equally to appeal hearings, where the consequences of the evidence being tainted by inappropriate interpretation are even graver than at the asylum interview. The LSC recognises the need for a professional interpreter at the full hearing where the appeal is funded by CLR.

34.34 If at all possible, the interpreter who monitors the hearing should be familiar with the case. This is most easily done by booking the same interpreter for the pre-hearing conference and the hearing. Even if he is no better qualified than the court interpreter, his familiarity with the case and with any problems that have arisen previously means that he is more likely to be alert to the potential problems.

34.35 Your interpreter should sit beside you at the representative's desk in the hearing room so that you can communicate easily with each other without disrupting the proceedings. (The adjudicator will sometimes seek confirmation that he is a professional interpreter rather than a friend of the appellant, and ideally, he should be smartly dressed for the hearing.) Occasionally, an adjudicator may object to your interpreter sitting beside you. It will be appropriate to refer him to para 7 of the Adjudicator Guidance Note which points out that interpreting is a difficult job when done under pressure, there is no objection to the appellant's representative bringing his own interpreter, and that it may be appropriate to have that interpreter sit relatively close to the representative (para 34.22).

34.36 Your interpreter should immediately indicate to you either by a note or a whisper whenever something is going wrong. You should emphasise to your interpreter that he should not address the witness, court interpreter or adjudicator directly unless permitted to do so by the adjudicator. If he indicates to you that there is a problem that you need to discuss, ask the adjudicator for a moment to consult. Your interpreter should take a detailed note of any problems that are arising. He may be an important witness in future proceedings arising out of mistakes by the court interpreter.

34.37 If you do not have a professional interpreter, then an English speaking friend of the appellant is better than nothing. However, interpreting is a demanding and difficult profession, and the friend is likely to be of limited value. If such a friend warns you about a problem during the hearing, the adjudicator is likely to be unhappy that the concern comes from your client's friend rather than a professional interpreter.

34.38 You should not be in the position where you are presenting a hearing without your interpreter present. If you are put in that position, there is a grave danger that you will miss even very serious mistakes by the court interpreter. If the answers which are translated vary from those given in conference, you will have no way of knowing whether the problem is with the interpreter or your witness.

34.39 Warning signs include where the interpreter uses inarticulate or bad English whereas the witness was coherent and articulate in conference; where the answers translated differ markedly whereas the client has been entirely consistent up to the hearing; and where the answers do not reflect the knowledge and sophistication that you are aware that the witness possesses. You will face an extremely unsatisfactory dilemma in deciding whether to raise your suspicions about the interpreter. You risk the interpreter simply denying that there is a problem and you then have no way of gainsaying him: the only result may be to highlight the fact that the evidence has taken you by surprise.

Challenging the interpreting

34.40 If there appears to be a problem with the interpreting then you should normally raise it with the adjudicator immediately. Even if the mistake is tolerable in itself, if it later becomes necessary to replace the interpreter because of accumulating difficulties then it will be important that the adjudicator was made aware of the developing situation from the outset. If an isolated and minor error occurs in cross-examination which is not going to affect the development of the cross-examination, you may leave it to be cleared up in re-examination.

34.41 The IAT has indicated that the court interpreter is unlikely to be the best judge of the degree of comprehension between himself and the appellant, and that where there is a dispute, it is advisable for an adjudicator to adjourn either to replace the interpreter or to seek expert evidence as to the degree of comprehension (*Diarrassouba*).

34.42 Major refugee producing countries are, for obvious reasons, more likely than average to be deeply divided on grounds of ethnicity, tribe, religion, class or politics. The LSC points out that interpreters 'may have an opposite opinion or opposing political affiliation to the applicant and may therefore be biassed against the applicant' (see below). It is alarmingly common for court interpreters, when challenged about their interpreting, to seek to persuade the adjudicator that the witness is at fault. It is not unknown for interpreters to have alleged to adjudicators, in court, that the witness is lying and pretending not to understand the interpreter. There have also been cases where the appellant repeatedly complained that she was unwell but the interpreter ignored this and translated only the substantive answers to the representatives' questions.

34.43 Any claim by the interpreter in court that a witness is blameworthy should normally lead to the immediate halting of the hearing, to begin afresh with a new interpreter. It is fundamental to the court interpreter's role that he maintains strict impartiality throughout. You should always make a formal complaint, and, in an especially serious case, you may indicate that you will object to the interpreter's use in any future appeal in which you are involved.

34.44 If an adjudicator refuses all applications to at least adjourn in such circumstances, your client is left in the desperately unfair position of having to communicate with the court through an interpreter who is making allegations to the court about her evidence, or even her credibility. Even so, you should be wary of offering no further evidence in such circumstances. Assuming you have your own interpreter monitoring proceedings, then the better course will usually be to continue the evidence, objecting on each occasion on which the interpreting is inappropriate, and asking the adjudicator to note each objection. (You should politely continue to object where necessary, regardless of whether the adjudicator has indicated that he does not wish to hear any further objections relating to the standard of interpreting.) If you do not have your own interpreter at the hearing, then you and your client are obviously in a far worse position. However, even so, offering no further oral evidence should be a last resort. If there is a major problem with the court interpreter and the adjudicator refuses to adjourn, you may wish to state your concerns in writing to the Chief Adjudicator immediately after the hearing.

34.45 If the hearing has to be adjourned through defects in the interpreting, evidence should not normally resume part-heard. In *Ki-Lutete*, the IAT said that:

> *Where interpretation is found not to be satisfactory in almost all cases the evidence should then be started again.*

34 Interpretation at the hearing
Key points

■ The skills and professionalism of the court interpreter are fundamental to the fairness of the hearing. Interpreting is not a mechanical process.

■ Be sure to list all your requirements in respect of the court interpreter in the reply to directions, or as soon as possible thereafter. These may include language, dialect, gender, and nationality. These requirements should not normally be second-guessed by the IAA.

■ Your client is entitled to have an interpreter in her first language, not a second language in which she has conversational skills. In certain circumstances, you or your client may wish evidence to be given in English, but the court interpreter should not be released in case the appellant runs into difficulties in complex answers.

■ Court interpreters vary widely in their training and capabilities. Many are unqualified.

■ The IAA grades the court interpreter using skills points which are marked out of 20: a court interpreter may score anything from 20 out of 20 down to three-and-a-half out of 20.

■ The IAA has reversed its previous policy of allocating bookings to the most skilled and experienced person and now books the cheapest interpreter available (in terms of travel expenses). You may have to point out this change of policy to the adjudicator if concerns arise about the court interpreter.

■ If the court interpreter is challenged, his ability and skill level should be verified by the adjudicator. You are entitled to the same information and should be present if the adjudicator questions the interpreter about his qualifications.

■ The procedure for introducing interpreters is now governed by Adjudicator Guidance Note No 3. This states that the interpreter should ask the appellant about her journey to court in order to test comprehension. Problems may still arise later when more complex questions are put.

■ The IAA's *Handbook for Interpreters* gives guidance on the court interpreter's conduct.

- Always address the witness directly. If you need to clarify with the court interpreter anything more than whether you heard him correctly, indicate this to the adjudicator first.

- You should always have your own interpreter present where the appellant (or any material witness) will not be giving evidence in English. You may have to take instructions on points raised by the adjudicator or HOPO at the hearing. Without your interpreter, you will be powerless to intervene if the court interpreter is making critical mistakes.

- Your interpreter should sit beside you and alert you to any problem through a note or whisper. He should not address the adjudicator, court interpreter, or witness unless invited to do so by the adjudicator. He should make a full note of any error: he may have to give evidence in future proceedings.

- You should normally raise any interpreting issue with the adjudicator immediately, but an isolated and minor error during cross-examination may be cleared up in re-examination.

- It is fundamental to the court interpreter's role that he remains strictly impartial. Should he make any adverse comment about your client or another witness, ask for the hearing to be halted immediately and the interpreter replaced.

- If the adjudicator directs that the hearing continue with a court interpreter who has made allegations against your client, you should object strongly but offer no further evidence only as a last resort.

- If a hearing is adjourned because of interpreting errors, evidence should almost always start afresh at the adjourned hearing.

35 Examination in chief

35.1 The standard directions require that witness statements stand as evidence in chief at the hearing. The scope for examination in chief is therefore limited.

35.2 The advantages of written witness statements are listed in chapter 12. The main *disadvantage* in having a statement stand as evidence in chief is the weight that some adjudicators place upon an assessment of the appellant's performance in oral evidence. The HOPO is often permitted a free rein to conduct a lengthy cross-examination, repeating questions which have been dealt with in the witness statement, whereas your oral examination is restricted by the adjudicator on the ground that it is wasting time to repeat matters contained in the statement. Most of the oral evidence is therefore conducted on the HOPO's rather than the appellant's terms, dwelling on the issues that the Home Office rather than the appellant considers important. If the appellant is denied the opportunity to put her case directly to the adjudicator in chief, she may not be able to do herself justice answering narrow, negative questions in cross-examination. She will also have less opportunity to get into her stride before cross-examination starts.

35.3 You obviously need to lead oral evidence if material evidence is missing from the statement. Also, if the HOPO indicates that he will pursue different issues at the hearing from those raised in the refusal letter (and your objections are over-ruled), you may need to lead evidence on the new issues. Be wary, though, of turning your examination in chief into a mini cross-examination. This can be a particular risk if you feel it necessary to address potential discrepancies which were not dealt with in the witness statement. You should always ensure that any defensive questions on discrepancies are balanced by positive questions enabling the witness to argue her own case to the adjudicator and gain some confidence. Even when putting discrepancies, your tone and the way in which you phrase the question should be appropriate to the fact that you are addressing your own witness and, if applicable, to the fact that the alleged discrepancy you are putting is of little weight. Discrepancies may well be apparent rather than real. If you did not have an opportunity to do so in the witness statement (para 12.56), you may now be able to lead further details in examination in chief which establish, without highlighting your concern, that there is no real discrepancy.

35.4 Examination in chief is not simply an opportunity to remedy any shortcomings in the witness statement. One purpose of examination in chief is to accustom the witness to the court room and to addressing the adjudicator before she is subjected to cross-examination. Another purpose may well be to put questions to the appellant that give her the opportunity 'to bring to life the witness statement' (see below).

35.5 You should not be prevented from conducting an oral examination in chief simply because you have complied with a direction to submit a witness statement. Practice Direction CA8 of 2001 states that:

> *There may be cases where it will be appropriate for appellants or witnesses to have the opportunity of adding to or supplementing their witness statement. Parties are referred to the judgment of the Court of Appeal in* **Singh**.

35.6 **Singh** was a renewed application for permission to apply for judicial review. The applicant claimed that he ought to be allowed to give *all* his evidence orally, despite a direction that witness statements stand as evidence in chief. The Court of Appeal rejected the submission. However, Sir Patrick Russell stated:

> *That does not mean that at the hearing the applicant or his representative should not have the opportunity of adding to the witness statement anything that is necessarily supplementary to it. It may well be – indeed the papers in this case demonstrate it to be the case – that in the future conduct of this particular inquiry the adjudicator will permit some supplementary answers to be given in order to bring to life the witness statement which as a whole should stand as the evidence-in-chief.*

35.7 Peter Gibson LJ said that:

> *I too would emphasise that there is a discretion in the adjudicator conducting the hearing whether to allow some oral evidence, notwithstanding a direction in the form in which it has been given in this case. Such discretion may in an appropriate case be one which he ought to exercise in the interests of justice.*

35.8 You should not be prevented from supplementing the witness statement through oral examination, even where the HOPO indicates that he does not intend to cross-examine (**Petre**). The IAT held that it was 'fundamentally flawed' for the adjudicator to effectively hand the HOPO a 'veto' over whether or not the appellant could lead oral evidence, 'particularly' when he then went on to make an adverse credibility finding.

35.9 The ideal examination in chief allows the facts to unfold through a natural flow of question and answer. This is never easy to do in a court room under rules of evidence and gets much more difficult when using an interpreter. Particular vocabulary or phrases which you might use to put an English speaker at ease and to encourage spontaneity or a particular tone or mood may not survive translation, even with a properly qualified interpreter (see chapter 34).

35.10 Those questions which allow your client to put her case effectively to the adjudicator are also likely to be those questions which give her confidence. But you might want to start by dealing with uncontentious background details. Even going through her name and address can help.

35.11 Your client may be better talking about some things than others. It may be that your client is nervous and uncertain about dates but confident in describing details of particular detentions. If so, you may wish to take her to a particular detention in a way which will clearly identify it to her (not by date) and then let her recount events in some detail. Having been given an opportunity to tell the adjudicator about something she remembers well, she may be more relaxed about admitting confusion about something she does not remember. If the written witness statement does not deal with the reasons for refusal, you may well wish to address aspects in examination in chief (see para 12.45). The aim should be to take advantage of the opportunity to address the adjudicator personally and, in the words of *Singh*, 'to bring to life the witness statement'.

35.12 There are no formal rules of evidence. The adjudicator is responsible for his own procedure so long as he acts fairly but he will usually prevent you from leading your own witness on contentious issues. Though you will be permitted to lead on non-contentious issues, you may choose not to lead in order to allow your witness an initial opportunity to offer more than a one word response to a question that is not too demanding.

35.13 Leading questions are those which lead the witness towards a particular answer or which assume facts that are in dispute (or which the witness has not yet established in evidence). They can often be answered yes or no. Non-leading questions are those which do not suggest a particular answer and cannot usually be answered yes or no. Non-leading questions will usually start 'Who...', 'What...', 'Where...', 'Why...' or 'When...' If the question begins with 'Did...', then it may well be a leading question.

35.14 Leading is a relative term. The degree to which a question leads depends upon the extent to which it suggests an answer and the extent to which any facts which it assumes are disputed. *'Did you escape by bribing the security guard?'* obviously suggests how the witness escaped. *'How were you able to escape?'* does not suggest the method. But you are still leading (suggesting) the fact that she escaped unless the witness has already stated this. Even *'How did your detention end?'* leads the fact that the witness' detention ended. However, this fact is pretty obvious, as the witness is now sitting in front of you. Whether a question is 'too leading' is a matter of common sense and fairness. Ideally, the more contentious a fact is (or the more uncertain it appears that the witness will give that fact), the more important it is that the question does not assume or suggest that fact. Adjudicators vary in how much leading they accept, but it is not only to prevent the HOPO or the adjudicator interrupting that you avoid leading. Open questions will also give the witness the best opportunity to put her case to the adjudicator. The more the question leads a contentious answer, the less impressive the answer may appear. But be flexible. If your witness is nervous and inarticulate, some leading (so long as the adjudicator allows it) may ease her into her evidence and help her to focus to the ultimate benefit of the court.

35.15 You do not lead when you repeat a fact which the witness has already stated (or 'piggy-back' on her answers). This can help keep control of the evidence where you are pursuing a particular narrative but the witness is not sticking to the question. You repeat back the part of the witness' answer which you want to develop as a prelude to your next question, for example:

Q: *What did the soldiers do when they got to your house?*
A: *They broke the door down because you see we have no rights and have had none since 1963 and will have none until they are deposed.*
Q: *After they broke down the door to your house, what did they do next?*

This brings the witness back to the particular point you are developing, without criticising the witness for straying from the question, or provoking the adjudicator into criticising the witness.

35.16 Fixed choice questions, where you ask which of the offered alternatives are correct, are not leading as long as they do not suggest which alternative the witness should choose, e.g. *'Did you obey or disobey the order?'* These can also be useful where you want to control the witness and avoid expansive answers.

35.17 You are normally allowed to lead against your case. You lead against your case by asking a leading question which suggests an answer which is prejudicial to you, for example 'Did you make these detentions up?' Some advocates do this because they believe that putting the allegation in chief will deprive the HOPO's cross-examination of its impact. Sometimes a witness is at her best dealing with a direct allegation, and as discussed in the following chapter, HOPOs are notorious for not putting their case properly in cross-examination. It can certainly produce an engaging exchange with your witness.

35.18 However, there are important provisos. Firstly, you must ensure beforehand that your witness is aware of and comfortable with the tactic. Secondly, be careful that you do not unnecessarily emphasise a potential weakness by putting the allegation to your client. Thirdly, remember it is not your job to do the HOPO's job properly for him. Fairness may require that an allegation is put to the witness if the HOPO is going to rely on it in closing, particularly if it is not made in the refusal letter. It will often be ill-advised for you to help the HOPO by putting the point to your witness for him.

35.19 Never allow yourself to appear impatient because you are not getting the answer you are looking for. This will only damage your client's confidence, and will give the adjudicator a bad impression of you and potentially (and more importantly) your client.

35.20 If you are not getting the answers you are looking for, think about how your phrasing of the question might have led your witness to misunderstand the information she was being asked to give. Explain the topic you are dealing with as far as you can without too much leading. If you have asked a non-leading open question, consider a fixed choice question or a question which leads against your case. If you are not getting the answer you were expecting and cannot think of a way of rephrasing it which will explain the misunderstanding, then it is unlikely that simply repeating the question will solve rather than exacerbate the problem. If the answer is not essential then leave it. If the answer is essential then it may be that you can come back to the point once you have elicited further evidence which can then be used to explain the answer you are seeking without leading. As a last resort, you can try again in re-examination if the subject has been tackled in cross-examination.

35.21 The difficulties in controlling the witness are increased through the necessity to use interpreters. A question which may be adequately clear in English may not be adequately clear by the time it has been translated. Be particularly careful to avoid long questions, compound questions, and those involving double negatives. For example, instead of *'Why did you not flee until Easter even though you were arrested at Christmas?'* try, *'You were arrested at Christmas, but you fled at Easter. Why did you wait until Easter?'* Let the interpreter translate the statement before asking the question. As well as making the question clearer, this will give the witness more time to consider the issue before having to answer.

35.22 If you are asking more than a couple of questions, both control of the witness and comprehension by the adjudicator will be aided if you indicate the structure of your examination in chief and signpost each group of questions as you come to them. This will help your client and the adjudicator (and yourself) to understand where you are going and what you are trying to do. You can use the written witness statement as a framework and refer to it in guiding the witness to the issues with which you wish to deal.

35.23 You ought to be able to assume facts established in the written statement for the purposes of your oral examination, even if they are disputed by the Home Office, just as disputed facts can be assumed in your questioning once the witness has established them in her oral evidence: for example, *'You describe in your statement how you were arrested at the demonstration. How many people were arrested with you?'*

35.24 Some HOPOs and adjudicators may wrongly object to you referring to facts contained in the witness statement in this way. However (and as you should point out in the face of such an objection), an adjudicator might more validly object if you ask questions to elicit facts already established in the witness statement.

35.25 When you are supplementing a statement in this way, there is a danger that it may appear disjointed and difficult to follow – both to the adjudicator and your witness – if you jump about between different parts of the case. This may also make it less memorable. It is not usual for a statement to be read out in asylum/human rights appeals, but you should paraphrase or read enough of the statement to put your questions into context, and give some indication of what you are intending to add to the statement by each group of supplemental questions.

Examination in chief of other factual witnesses

35.26 Much of the above discussion will apply both to the appellant's examination in chief and to other factual witnesses. In getting the evidence in chief underway and in controlling it thereafter, you should make clear by signposting and by the way in which you phrase your questions how the evidence is adding to or corroborating that of the appellant. If you are careful to focus the witness upon the matters that she is establishing rather than straying into more general issues, you will be on stronger ground objecting if the HOPO pursues irrelevant matters in cross-examination.

35.27 If no statement from the witness was submitted in support of the initial claim to the Home Office, and the HOPO has served no skeleton argument, you may have no prior notice of the Home Office's response to the witness statement. It will usually be unfair for the HOPO to raise a challenge in closing submissions that he had not (at least) put to the witness in cross-examination. You need not relieve him of that responsibility by putting every potential allegation to the witness in examination in chief.

Examination in chief where there is no usable witness statement

35.28 If you are proposing to conduct a full examination in chief (i.e. taking the appellant or another witness through her entire account), it will be because something has gone wrong. It should only happen when you are instructed at the last minute (including being briefed as advocate at the last minute) and you find that there is either no witness statement or, upon taking instructions, that the witness statement is unusable. The application in those circumstances will always be for an adjournment on the basis that your client should not be prejudiced by the behaviour of her past (or current) representatives.

35.29 If that adjournment is refused, and you feel you have sufficient instructions to lead evidence, the adjudicator may urge you to allow the Home Office record of the asylum interview to stand as evidence in chief. The HOPO may put allegedly inconsistent statements in the interview notes to your client during cross-examination, whether or not they have been adopted in evidence in chief. However, if you have mistakenly agreed to the adoption of inaccurate interview notes, you will have unfairly prejudiced your client.

35.30 The Home Office has abandoned its previous practice of reading its interview notes back to the claimant to check their accuracy (para 36.20). You should not agree to the interview notes standing as evidence in chief unless you have both taken sufficient instructions from your client on her claim, and gone through the interview notes with her line by line. The adjudicator cannot force you to adopt the interview record.

35.31 If you have sufficient instructions, you can offer to conduct a full oral examination in chief. If you do not have sufficient instructions, and you are not in a position to adopt the Home Office interview notes (or a previous statement), and especially if the appellant is personally at fault, you will have no choice but to seek an adjournment. The adjudicator will otherwise lack the necessary factual evidence upon which to determine the appeal.

35.32 It is far more difficult to conduct a full examination in chief of your client than it is to examine witnesses in other jurisdictions. It is particularly difficult to get the examination in chief underway without leading. If you are examining the defendant in a criminal trial, all the relevant facts may have occurred on the one day, and you can start by asking the witness if she remembers any particular incident on that day. The material facts in an asylum/human rights appeal may be spread over many years or even the appellant's lifetime. They may involve not just her own experiences over those years but those of her family, community, and comrades.

35.33 Carefully work out the structure of your examination in chief, referring to the discussion on the structure of witness statements in chapter 12. Controlling the structure will be assisted by identifying the broad issues to which the questions will be directed. It will also help relax the witness, by making sure she always knows what is coming up: for example, *'I want to start with your upbringing and background... Now I'm going to ask some questions about your political activities... I'd like to ask some questions about the experiences of your family... Can I move on to ask you some questions about how you came to leave your country... Now I want to deal with events since you arrived in Britain...'* Signposting in this fashion should not be criticised as leading. It is obvious that she was born and brought up; it is presumably accepted that she had a family; it must be accepted that she left the country and that she is now in Britain. It might not be accepted that she had any political involvement, but if her claim is based on political involvement, then it is so obvious that she will give evidence of political involvement that you are unlikely to be criticised for leading into your questions. It would be different if you were to introduce your questions with *'I am now going to deal with your various responsibilities as the organiser for three branches of the IPK.'*

35.34 Open questions may enable the witness to develop her own story without further interruption, but to what extent this is practical and desirable depends on the witness. Will she keep to the point or digress? Will she give the right amount of detail or too little or too much? Will she go at a reasonable speed for the adjudicator? Does she have the presence to keep the adjudicator's attention during a long monologue without the interjection of a question? Is she articulate and confident?

35.35 If she is nervous, inarticulate, has a poor memory, or the evidence is complicated, then it is probably a good idea to limit open questions and keep tight control of the evidence. Short questions and answers can also be easier to follow and more engaging than a monologue.

35 Examination in chief
Key points

■ The standard directions require that a witness statement stand as evidence in chief. You should nevertheless be permitted to lead supplementary oral evidence, whether or not the HOPO wishes to cross-examine.

■ Your aims in examination in chief may be to

☐ allow the witness an opportunity to get into her stride before she is challenged in cross-examination,

☐ supplement the statement and 'bring it to life' through positive questions,

☐ address allegations in the refusal letter or new issues raised on the day by the HOPO.

■ You may not ask leading questions on contentious issues. Doing so will anyway render the answer less impressive. You may:

☐ ask fixed choice questions,

☐ lead against your case,

☐ lead on non-contentious issues,

☐ refer to facts which have already been established in oral evidence or in the witness statement.

■ If the witness has misunderstood your question, consider how it can be rephrased but do not simply repeat it. Do not display impatience if you are not getting the answers you expect.

■ Conducting examination in chief through an interpreter creates formidable difficulties in controlling the evidence for which you must allow and plan.

■ Examination in chief of other factual witnesses should not stray beyond the matters on which they can legitimately give evidence.

■ You should not be considering conducting a full examination in chief unless something has gone wrong and you are faced with conducting a hearing with no usable witness statement. A full examination in chief in an asylum/ human rights appeal is complex. If you do not have sufficient instructions to embark on it, you have no choice but to seek an adjournment.

36 Cross-examination

36.1 If you call your client, the HOPO is entitled to cross-examine her. (See chapter 30 for whether you should call her).

36.2 Now that witness statements are required as evidence in chief, most of your client's oral evidence will normally be spent dealing with cross-examination. That is therefore the main opportunity that your client has to communicate directly with the adjudicator and the main opportunity for the adjudicator to assess her as a witness. One of your most important roles as advocate is to try to ensure that cross-examination is as fair as possible and gives her a reasonable opportunity to answer the allegations against her.

36.3 Law students are taught that the first rule of cross-examination is to put your case to the witness. HOPOs, apparently, are not. It is common to sit through a long and rambling cross-examination of questionable relevance, only to find that the most contentious allegation made in the HOPO's closing submission is the one that he did not find the time to put to the witness. It may be (indeed one might like to think) that the HOPO on occasion feels embarrassed about putting the more offensive parts of his case to the appellant, for example that she fabricated rape. However, that only renders it more offensive when he raises the allegation in closing without giving her the opportunity to respond to it in evidence.

36.4 In *Vellupillai*, the IAT held that:

> It is fundamental... in our adversarial system of justice that adverse matters or potentially adverse matters are put to a witness. We do not say that each and every aspect of an Appellant's evidence ought to be cross-examined but the purpose of cross-examination is to clarify, expand or undermine a witnesses' evidence. A cross-examiner is entitled to accept evidence as true and not cross-examine on it but the cross-examiner should always take care to ensure that key aspects of the evidence in chief which are not accepted are challenged. That is the whole purpose of cross-examination.

36.5   In *Ezzi*, it said that:

> *If the cross-examiner does not accept the evidence given in chief, or considers that it is not truthful, any contrary proposition which the cross-examiner intends to make in submissions should be put to the witness in order to elicit his response thereto. If that is not done, the evidence in chief of the witness has not been challenged nor tested. The Tribunal is thereby denied the opportunity to have matters fully explored and the Tribunal may be left in some doubt as to where the truth may lie. Furthermore, while submissions made in respect of key matters which have not been raised or challenged in cross-examination may not be incompetent, they cannot have the forcefulness of submissions in respect of matters which have been addressed during the hearing of evidence. The proceedings must be conducted in a manner which is fair to both sides.*

36.6   Much cross-examination tends to traverse the same ground that has already been covered in the asylum interview, statement, or evidence in chief – apparently in the hope that an inconsistency can be elicited. The HOPO may seek confirmation of matters which have never been in dispute but which the HOPO believes assist his case, e.g. that she was never convicted of an offence. You should warn the witness that those sorts of questions will arise. Explanations may also be sought for the actions of the appellant (e.g. *'Why did you not leave the country earlier?'*), or third parties (e.g. *'Why did the police not arrest you?'*). Less frequently, the witness will be asked to comment on an allegation from the HOPO, usually that some part of the account is implausible.

Objecting to inappropriate cross-examination

36.7   This is one of your key roles at the hearing. It is imperative to concentrate on each question as it is asked so that you can object promptly where justified.

36.8   You should normally object to cross-examination if you consider the question is improper, unfair, irrelevant, confusing, misleading, based on a misunderstanding of the facts, or the HOPO is adopting a hectoring approach. Some representatives consider that a confident, articulate, sophisticated client can be left to deal with improper or confusing questions, effectively making her own objections. Others consider that regardless of the client's ability to deal with improper questions, part of the representative's duty is to do his best to ensure that proceedings are conducted fairly.

36.9   While you should not come across as overprotective of your client, do not decide to let an improper question pass unless you are very sure of your reasons. The fact that an adjudicator has over-ruled previous objections does not mean you should stop putting legitimate objections on record. It will be more difficult to challenge the fairness of cross-examination on appeal if you did not object at the time. Even if the objection is over-ruled, the HOPO will sometimes rephrase the question in a less objectionable way, and may at least think more carefully about how he puts future questions.

36.10 The risk of inappropriate cross-examination causing unfairness is much greater when vulnerable witnesses unused to formal proceedings are giving evidence through interpreters. Where an English speaking witness gives evidence in ordinary proceedings, he will be shown material documents during cross-examination and permitted to read alleged inconsistent statements and see the context in which they were made. Reviewing the relevant document is obviously useless to a non-English speaking witness. It is therefore critical that the cross-examiner is scrupulously fair in ensuring that any relevant document forming the basis of cross-examination is properly described and quoted before the witness is challenged on it.

Examples of potentially objectionable cross-examination

36.11 Some of the examples below apply particularly to cross-examination of the appellant, but the same principles apply to cross-examination of other witnesses.

Mistakes

36.12 Questions based on mistakes as to dates and the sequence of events are common. You should point out the HOPO's mistake before the witness has the opportunity to respond to the question.

36.13 If he refers to evidence in the papers which you do not recognise, ask for him to give the reference before the question is translated. The HOPO may introduce a question by making an assertion about the 'objective evidence' before the court, only for it to transpire that he is referring simply to a Home Office document. The witness should not be misled about the nature of the evidence to which she is being asked to respond.

36.14 Also check that the HOPO is reading from the interview notes correctly. The Home Office seldom provides a typed transcript of interview records unless directed to do so and expects the court to rely on a handwritten note. Mistakes in deciphering the handwriting may change the meaning of the note the HOPO is reading.

Not putting alleged inconsistent statements or putting them out of context

36.15 If the HOPO is going to ask a witness about something she is claimed to have said in a previous statement or interview, then the relevant passage should be read together with any further material necessary to put the passage in context. Particularly if the statement is being put as an alleged inconsistency, the HOPO should not be permitted to paraphrase it. If you feel that the extract read out by the HOPO is insufficient to enable the witness to understand the context, explain why the witness ought to be referred to additional passages before she answers the question.

36.16 Object if the HOPO appears to misrepresent your client's statements. For example the Home Office interview record may contain the following exchange:

Q: *What was the date of the detention you have just told me about?*
A: *I cannot remember, it was during the summer of 1988.*
Q: *Please can you be more specific? I want to know the date.*
A: *I think it may have been June 1988.*

36.17 The cross-examination may then be conducted as follows:

Q: *During which month were you detained in 1988?*
A: *I think it might have been July.*
Q: *July?*
A: *Yes*
Q: *At your asylum interview you said your detention was in June but now you say July. How do you explain this discrepancy?*

Objection: Point out that your client's answer at interview has been misrepresented, and ask the HOPO to read the full exchange before putting it to the appellant.

36.18 The HOPO may also fail to explain to the circumstances in which the appellant is alleged to have made the inconsistent statement. There may be notes of one or more Home Office interviews before the court, plus additional written statements, but the HOPO may simply ask the witness

> *So why did you say to the Home Office that you had no problems until 1990?*

Objection: The appellant cannot simply be shown the document as can an English speaking witness. The witness is entitled to know when and where she is alleged to have made the statement. The HOPO should therefore provide the date and nature of the interview, or the date of the statement and by whom it was submitted (e.g. by present or previous representatives).

Putting the Home Office interview notes as if they have been accepted by the appellant

36.19 Given the delays that commonly occur, the HOPO may be putting statements to the appellant that she is alleged to have made months or years previously. Before asking '*Why did you say that?*', it will usually be appropriate to ascertain whether the witness recalls saying it and/or accepts that she said it.

36.20 Home Office interviewers now refuse to read back their notes to the claimant at the end of the asylum interview in order to check their accuracy. The Home Office previously claimed that 'The read back is an essential part of the interview' (*Still No Reason at All*). The HOPO's tactic in cross-examination used to be to confirm that a read back was conducted and the record agreed by the appellant. Since the Home Office refuses to conduct this procedure which it previously accepted was 'essential' to establish the accuracy of the interview record, the HOPO should not put the interviewing officer's record to the appellant as if she has already approved it.

36.21 Sometimes, the HOPO will refer to a part of the interview note which the appellant's statement already explains is inaccurate. It is open to the HOPO to dispute what was said at interview. But he should not suggest that evidence is undisputed when that is not the case.

The discrepancy which is not a discrepancy

36.22 HOPOs will often ask a witness to explain a 'discrepancy' when there is no discrepancy to explain:

> *Today you said that your father had written to you saying that your brother had been arrested, but you said in your interview that you have had no contact with your family since leaving your country. How do you explain this discrepancy?*

Objection: the interview was long before the hearing. It may be that the appellant had not heard from her family at the date of the interview but has heard from them since. The HOPO has assumed a discrepancy which has not been established. He should at least be required to give the date on which the appellant had said that she had not heard from her family.

36.23 Another example is:

> *You say in your statement that you have been an activist since 1998, but in your asylum interview you said you sympathised with the organisation in 1996. Why are you telling a different story now from that which you told in your interview?*

Objection: The two are not inconsistent. She need not be an activist in order to be a sympathiser. This is a point that might be left to the witness if evidence were being given in English. But you cannot rely on the nuances surviving interpretation. Indeed, having been told by the HOPO that there is a discrepancy because she gave conflicting dates for the same activity, the court interpreter may assume that it is appropriate to use the same word from the appellant's language to describe the activity when translating each statement.

Criticising a 'failure' to provide information which had not previously been requested

36.24 The HOPO might say:

> *You've told us today that you were ill when you passed through Russia on your way to claim asylum in the United Kingdom, but you did not mention this during your asylum interview. Why have you just remembered now that you were ill in Russia?*

Objection: She was never asked during her asylum interview whether she was ill in Russia. The asylum interview record is the record of an interview, not a complete record of the appellant's life.

36.25 Another example is:

> *You have said today that you were tortured while you were detained, but you did not say you were tortured when asked about your detention during the asylum interview.*

Objection: The appellant was asked when she was detained at the interview and she answered. She was not asked how she was treated during her detention, and the interviewer may have moved straight onto a new topic (see further para 1.23). If the witness had a complete recollection in her head of an interview conducted some time ago, she could point this out herself. But it is unfair to expect this degree of recollection. If she has no clear recollection then she may assume that the

HOPO could not be criticising her in this manner unless she *had* been asked about her treatment during detention. At the very least, the HOPO should be asked to read the questions and answers which addressed this particular detention.

36.26 The HOPO may also allege that failure to repeat during the asylum interview information which was given in a previous SEF or statement represents a discrepancy:

> *In your SEF, you said you had been subjected to torture yet there is no mention of this in your subsequent interview.*

36.27 As indicated at para 1.19, this is a particularly dubious tactic when one considers the guidance commonly given by the Home Office at the interview to the effect that she need not repeat information already provided in the SEF, and that the purpose of the interview is rather to elicit 'some further details'. If such an allegation was included in the refusal letter, you should have objected in your skeleton argument. If the HOPO has not taken issue with the submission contained in your skeleton, point that out when you object during cross-examination.

36.28 If the HOPO is permitted to put the point at all, the least fairness should require is that he also read out the guidance that the appellant was given at the start of her interview. Again, it is unfair to assume that she will recall what guidance she was given at the time. If the question is allowed to be put as an omission for which an explanation is required then, unsurprisingly, your client may become confused as to why she would have omitted the incident if asked about it, and offer that perhaps she forgot. That answer is then held against her.

36.29 If you object to the witness being told there is a discrepancy in her statement when she simply did not answer a question that she was not asked, the HOPO will sometimes claim that a question at the end of the interview enquiring whether there is anything to add is sufficient for these purposes. The asylum interview may consist of a long list of questions over many hours. The asylum seeker will normally have been advised by her representative to restrict herself to answering the questions she is asked. The very detail of the interview may imply that the opportunity to add anything at the end refers to the questions which have been asked in the interview. It might be different if, at the end of the interview, the interviewer was to say: '*I have finished my questions but you are now required to make a statement before you leave describing all details of your claim that I have not asked you about: a failure to do so will be held against you when such details are provided later.*' But that, of course, is not what the asylum seeker is told.

36.30 A similar issue may arise over written witness statements. These are

usually drafted by a representative on the basis of one or more interviews with the appellant. As discussed in chapter 13 the methodology
and quality varies drastically. The HOPO may question the appellant
on the premise that she drafted the witness statement herself. As far as
the appellant is concerned, it would simply have constituted another
interview where she answered the questions that were put. The statement may not even have been properly checked prior to submission.
The reason why a point is not contained in her statement is most probably that her representative did not ask her about it. However, the
HOPO may put to the appellant that *'You had the opportunity to say
whatever you chose in your statement.'* To make such a claim, the HOPO
would first have to establish how the statement was taken. As indicated at para 13.15, the HOPO sometimes approaches this point with a
unique unwillingness to contemplate a representative following anything other than best practice.

Irrelevant questioning

36.31 Your client may have started her statement with her early life and early
problems, but made clear that it is not the basis of her present claim.
The HOPO may fail to understand this and start asking detailed questions about events which occurred decades ago. Apart from irrelevant
questions being inappropriate in principle, it will save valuable court
time if you point out to the HOPO that these matters do not form the
basis of the present claim. 'It is no part of (the advocate's) duty to
embark on lengthy cross-examination on matters which are not really
in issue' (*Simmonds*). In *Maynard*, the Court of Appeal noted that even
though counsel may be allowed more latitude in a criminal case, the
judge nevertheless had a 'duty to curb irrelevancy' and reiterated its
earlier dictum in *Kalia* to the effect that:

> The trial judge can and should do his utmost to restrain unnecessary, pro-
> longed cross-examination, and this Court will unhesitatingly support
> him when he does...

Raising new issues without notice

36.32 Sometimes, the explanation for a line of cross-examination which is
irrelevant to the Home Office's decision will be that the HOPO is planning on raising new reasons for refusal which did not form part of the
original decision. If this is the response to your query about the question's relevance, you will normally object. While it is unsatisfactory to
raise a new issue at the start of the hearing, it is even more so to raise it
for the first time during cross-examination when the absence of prior

notice has precluded you from taking instructions. You will be in a particularly strong position if you have sought details of the Home Office's case (chapter 9).

36.33 If the Home Office is not prevented from taking a new point at the hearing which it declined to take in the decision, it may well be unfair for that to be done without offering you an adjournment in order to take instructions and if necessary submit further evidence to deal with it. But given the general undesirability of adjournment, that should militate against the Home Office being permitted to take the new point at all – particularly if the HOPO can give no good reason why it was not raised in the decision or at least prior to the commencement of the hearing.

Questions to which the witness cannot be expected to know the answer

36.34 HOPOs repeatedly ask witnesses to explain the actions of third parties, e.g. 'Why did the police not search for you?' Your client is not the police. If the HOPO wants to 'know' why they did not search for her (assuming they did not), then it would be appropriate to ask the police. The appellant should not be asked questions which demand an explanation for the actions of others without establishing whether she is in a position to know. He should first establish if the appellant actually knows that the police did not search for her before enquiring 'Do you know why not?' If the question does not allow for the possibility that she does not know, an inexperienced witness may assume that she is required to provide the information and offer what is effectively a guess. If that guess is along the lines that the police did not have enough evidence or information, the HOPO may seize on this as confirmation that the appellant is at no risk. The dangers involved in this style of questioning are discussed further at para 12.24.

36.35 The HOPO may make more ambitious assumptions about the appellant's insight. In one case, described in *Still No Reason at All*, the appellant had been shot in the leg whilst fleeing Islamic gunmen. The HOPO's cross-examination was:

> *If they had really wanted to get you, why did they shoot you in the leg, and not the head?*

The adjudicator over-ruled the question.

HOPO giving evidence under the guise of cross-examination

36.36 The HOPO may use cross-examination to assert facts which are not even referred to in the refusal letter, never mind supported by evidence. If the HOPO wishes to lead evidence of those facts, then he may do so, whether documentary or oral, and, if oral, you will have the right to cross-examine whoever he calls. On at least one occasion when the HOPO was prevented from giving evidence during cross-examination, the HOPO responded by calling himself as a witness! The adjudicator accepted the HOPO as a credible witness and dismissed the appeal. The IAT allowed the appeal on the basis that the adjudicator erred in permitting a representative to give evidence (*Aitsaid*).

36.37 Examples of potential 'questions' include:

> *You say you were stopped by the Special Branch but that's not true because the Special Branch only operate in the capital.*

> *I suggest that there is no way that you would have been able to bribe your way through that airport given the security in place.*

Objection: Ask the HOPO if he is going to lead evidence about the areas in which Special Branch operates or on what security is in place at the particular airport. If he is not going to lead evidence to establish it, then he should not be asserting the 'fact'. Cross-examination is the wrong place for such assertions in any event. 'An advocate must not in the course of cross-examination state matters of fact or opinion... ' (*Archbold*, 2003, para 8–116).

Commenting on evidence instead of asking questions

36.38 The HOPO may make derogatory comments in response to the witness' answer such as 'I find that completely implausible.' If the HOPO has any comment to make on the evidence, then he should make it in his closing submissions. '[C]ross-examination must not be used for making comments, which should be confined to speeches' (*Archbold*, ibid).

36.39 By commenting, he may also be straying into giving evidence. If he alleges that something is likely, what is his basis for doing so: his knowledge or experience of the country of origin? If he wants to put to the witness that something is implausible then he should do so. A confident English speaking witness might understand that he is entitled to respond to such a comment. An asylum seeker may not do so and, worse, may regard it as some sort of conclusion on her evidence which may adversely affect her future evidence.

Hectoring approach

36.40 The HOPO may criticise the witness for not answering the question when she has plainly done so to the best of her ability. This is another unfair method of discomforting her. He may similarly demand that she answer yes or no to a question when the appellant is trying to explain that it is not that simple. You should also object if the HOPO interrupts an answer, particularly before it has been fully translated.

Breaching another asylum seeker's confidentiality

36.41 HOPOs have in the past made assertions in cross-examination that the witness' evidence regarding a particular event is inconsistent with that given in the claim of another asylum seeker (whether relative, friend, or acquaintance) who is not party to the appeal or represented at the hearing. That may well be contrary to the Home Office's own undertaking of confidentiality (see para 1.27). You should object immediately if it appears that the HOPO is breaching that undertaking.

Privilege

36.42 Communication between you (or any other representative) and your client concerning the preparation of your appeal is privileged. You may object to any question which would require the appellant to reveal such information. Communication between either you or your client and any expert may also be privileged (though see para 23.6 concerning the duty to disclose an expert's instructions).

36.43 It will not always be in your client's interests to object to the disclosure of privileged information. It may in fact be necessary, for example, to explain why a witness statement is unsatisfactory.

Unclear questions

36.44 The simplest, yet one of the most important objections you must make is to unclear, convoluted and ambiguous questions. If you are unsure what the HOPO is getting at, then there is little prospect that the witness will be able to guess correctly. Even if the question is tolerably clear in English, it may be incomprehensible by the time it has been translated. Adjudicators are also advised to intervene if a question in cross-examination is difficult to interpret, e.g. because it involves a double-negative (para 34.26).

Cross-examination of other factual witnesses

36.45 The HOPO will have had advance notice of the evidence of other factual witnesses through the service of their witness statements. The purpose of providing these statements in advance is to give the Home Office the opportunity to consider its position. If the HOPO neither indicates in advance that the evidence is disputed nor challenges the witness in cross-examination, fairness should not permit him to challenge it in closing submissions.

36.46 As indicated in chapter 15, the HOPO is quite likely to ask the witness questions about the *appellant's* evidence in the hope of eliciting an inconsistency. The witness should be warned not to guess at answers and that it is perfectly alright to explain that he does not know. If the HOPO persists, you should object.

36.47 Cross-examination of expert witnesses is dealt with in chapter 25.

36 Cross-examination
Key points

- If you call your client, the HOPO is entitled to cross-examine her: that cross-examination is likely to constitute the majority of her oral evidence.

- A fundamental purpose of cross-examination is to put the case against the witness and give her an opportunity to respond. Despite conducting lengthy cross-examination, many HOPOs fail to put their most damning allegations to the appellant, which they then attempt to raise for the first time in closing submissions.

- One of your most important roles as an advocate is to ensure that cross-examination is as fair as possible by objecting to inappropriate questions and comments. Examples may include the following:
  - [ ] questions based on a mistaken reading of the evidence (most commonly as to dates and the sequence of events),
  - [ ] failing to put alleged inconsistent statements or quoting them out of context,
  - [ ] putting Home Office interview notes as if they have been accepted by the appellant,
  - [ ] asserting that there is a discrepancy in the evidence that is not there,
  - [ ] criticising the appellant for 'failing' to provide information at the asylum interview when she had not actually been requested to provide it,
  - [ ] irrelevant questioning,
  - [ ] raising new issues without notice,
  - [ ] requiring the appellant to explain the actions of third parties,
  - [ ] asserting 'facts' or commenting on the evidence,
  - [ ] adopting a hectoring or unreasonable approach,
  - [ ] breaching another asylum seeker's confidentiality,
  - [ ] requiring the appellant to divulge privileged information,
  - [ ] unclear, convoluted or ambiguous questions.

- If the Home Office has not taken issue with the witness statement of a factual witness, and the HOPO does not challenge his evidence in cross-examination, it will be unfair to raise a credibility challenge against that witness for the first time in closing submissions.

37 Re-examination

37.1 When cross-examination is concluded, you will be asked whether you want to re-examine. It is an invitation not an order, and one to be regarded with some suspicion.

Risks of re-examination

37.2 Representatives sometimes re-examine far too much for their clients' good – especially where they have not prepared the ground properly in the pre-hearing conference. You do not demonstrate the strength of your case by the number of questions you ask in re-examination – sometimes, the reverse is true. Declining the invitation may indicate how little damage the HOPO's cross-examination has inflicted.

37.3 You can only ask questions in re-examination which arise out of the evidence given in cross-examination. It is not an opportunity to ask questions you forgot to ask in chief and which cannot be related to cross-examination (though if you do find yourself in this position, you will have to own up to your mistake and ask the adjudicator's permission to put the question).

37.4 If the witness for whatever reason has contradicted herself in cross-examination, further questioning may increase rather than limit the damage. Ask yourself whether you are digging yourself a deeper hole. Similarly, if the cross-examination has inflicted minimal damage, then the risks may well outweigh the possible gains of re-examining, as well as over-emphasising any damage.

37.5 The adjudicator's response to your objections to cross-examination may have been that you can clear it up in re-examination. Consider carefully whether or not you should do so. It may be better to point out in closing why the question was misleading and why it would be unsafe to rely on the response. The witness may have been confused by the misleading question and anxious about the answer she gave.

She may now be even more anxious about contradicting the earlier answer, and therefore feel forced to confirm her earlier answer rather than give the answer you expect. If she does so, you will have undermined the submission that you could otherwise have made about the unfairness of the original question.

37.6 If your witness has given new information in cross-examination upon which you have no instructions, and you fear that it appears prejudicial, then you may be tempted to ask questions which give the witness the opportunity to explain her previous answers in a better light. It is seldom wise to use re-examination to take fresh instructions from your client in front of the adjudicator. If you have thought of an obvious explanation for an apparently unsatisfactory answer, then you can and should offer that explanation in your closing speech to counter any adverse inference which the HOPO has sought to draw. You are prohibited from leading in re-examination as you are in examination in chief. You should avoid embarking on a tortuous series of non-leading questions which you hope will lead the witness to offer your chosen explanation. Unless you have taken full instructions on the explanation before the hearing and you are confident that the client will give that explanation, the result may simply be an increasingly confused, worried, and exhausted witness who cannot understand what you are getting at.

Benefits of re-examination

37.7 The prime aim of a good cross-examination is to force the witness to accept propositions or make admissions which assist the cross-examiner's case. The cross-examiner achieves this aim through leading questions which, one by one, compel the witness towards accepting the facts which the cross-examiner needs to build his argument. He avoids open questions which might allow the witness an opportunity to place her answers in a more favourable context.

37.8 If the HOPO has elicited a series of answers which are on their face damaging but you are aware that the witness has an explanation that she has not yet had the opportunity to give, re-examination provides that opportunity. If successful, it can be exceptionally effective.

37.9 Re-examination can also be highly effective in other circumstances. Your client will have had only a limited opportunity to expand on her witness statement in examination in chief. Cross-examination may have touched on much of the statement, but in a manner aimed at damaging your client's credibility rather than enabling her to put her case in the best light to the adjudicator.

37.10 If matters have been opened up in re-examination and there is further related evidence that your client can give, you are entitled to elicit it in re-examination. This is the last the adjudicator will hear from your client and leaving him with a good impression can sometimes alter the course of the case – as, of course, may leaving him with a bad impression.

37.11 What distinguishes a good re-examination from a bad (or disastrous) re-examination is the conduct of your pre-hearing conference – how thoroughly you explored the strengths and weaknesses of the case and the factual issues that cross-examination could throw up. You should be aware of what explanations your client can and cannot give, and what her capabilities are. More so even than examination in chief, you must be confident of the answer you will receive before you risk a question in re-examination.

37 Re-examination
Key points

■ The invitation to re-examine is not an order. Declining the invitation may highlight how little damage the HOPO's cross-examination has inflicted.

■ If your client has performed badly in cross-examination, beware of digging her deeper into a hole.

■ If she has provided new and potentially prejudicial information in cross-examination, re-examination is not the time to take instructions on it.

■ If done properly, re-examination can be exceptionally effective in both undermining the HOPO's cross-examination and enabling your client to put her case to the adjudicator.

■ What distinguishes a good re-examination from a bad re-examination is the thoroughness of your pre-hearing conference. It is especially important never to ask a question in re-examination unless you are confident of the answer you will receive.

38 Interventions from the adjudicator

38.1 In *Mohammadiani-Abolvardi*, the IAT stated that:

> *There is no doubt in our mind that it was for the Presenting Officer, and not for the Adjudicator, to make the Respondent's case.*

38.2 The *Surendran* guidelines governing the role of an adjudicator where the Home Office is unrepresented are quoted in full in chapter 40. The IAT stated in *Mohammadiani-Abolvardi* that 'the guidelines apply even more strongly' to an appeal where the Home Office is represented.

38.3 These guidelines emphasise that it is not the function of the adjudicator to 'expand upon' the Home Office refusal letter, 'nor is it his function to raise matters which are not raised in it, unless these are matters which are apparent to him from a reading of the papers', in which case the representative should be invited to address them in submissions or examination in chief. Neither is it his function to raise matters that the HOPO might have raised in cross-examination.

38.4 It is of equal importance that the adjudicator does not intervene inappropriately during your evidence in chief. The IAT noted in *Mohammadiani-Abolvardi* that:

> *The problem goes deeper than that, because there is no doubt that the Adjudicator was openly adopting a challenging attitude to the evidence long before the beginning of the cross-examination. There is a series of questions at the beginning of the examination-in-chief (by the time the Appellant had been asked 19 questions, 13 of them had been from the Adjudicator), including questions beginning 'Why', and 'I thought you said'. How the Appellant's counsel was expected to present his evidence in that atmosphere is far from clear.*

38.5 The correct approach was explained by the IAT in the same case as follows:

> *Where both parties are represented and evidence is taken, it is a sound rule for the Adjudicator to make no intervention at all until both parties*

have examined the witness. An interruption is justified only if there is some difficulty about taking the evidence, for example if the Adjudicator cannot hear what is said. In any event, an Adjudicator should never at that stage ask questions whose purpose is to develop a point. The Adjudicator can easily keep a note of any problems that arise in his or her mind. By the time the evidence has been given such problems may well have been resolved by the evidence being given and (if appropriate) challenged in an orderly way by the parties. If questions are to be asked by the Adjudicator, they should be at the end of the evidence, and should be followed by an opportunity offered to the Respondent and then the Appellant to ask any further questions arising out of the Adjudicator's questions. Only so can the parties be assured that the Adjudicator's impression of the evidence is fair, and not mistaken.

38.6   In **Oyono**, the IAT said that:

When evidence is being taken from a witness and where there is representation on both sides, an Adjudicator's role is of silent listening. It may very occasionally happen that an Adjudicator is so unclear as to what he has heard that he needs to ask for something to be repeated and, of course, there may occasionally be difficulties with interpreters causing the Adjudicator's general control over the proceedings to come into play. But it is for the parties to bring out evidence in the order they think appropriate and it is for the parties to put whatever contradictions in the evidence need to be put to the witness. When the evidence has been finished, in the sense that there has been examination-in-chief and cross-examination and re-examination, it may be that the Adjudicator wishes to put matters arising out of the evidence to the witness: but the time for that is after re-examination. If the Adjudicator does ask the witness any questions, he must then always give an opportunity to the parties to ask any further questions which arise from his. An Adjudicator who intervenes during the course of evidence is running the risk that he will be seen to be taking the side of one party or the other

38.7   The adjudicator should not be discouraged from raising his concerns at the hearing: on the contrary, fairness may well require this. But he should do so through the appellant's representative and should not himself embark on a series of questions resembling a cross-examination. In the past, adjudicators have been known to conduct a quasi cross-examination themselves even where the HOPO has declined to cross-examine the witness at all. It is particularly inappropriate of the adjudicator to make any intervention that suggests that he has already formed a view on credibility.

38.8   If you are concerned about the adjudicator's interventions, you should object politely. A failure to do so may prejudice a subsequent appeal.

38 Interventions from the adjudicator
Key points

- The *Surendran* guidelines (chapter 40) apply even more strongly where the Home Office is represented.

- It is for the HOPO not the adjudicator to put the Home Office's case.

- If the adjudicator has any concerns of his own, he should raise these with you but should not himself embark on 'cross-examination' of the witness.

- If the adjudicator does wish to put questions to the witness, he should do so at the end of the evidence and then give both representatives the opportunity to ask any further questions that arise from his own.

- If you do not raise your concerns about the adjudicator's interventions at the hearing, you may prejudice a subsequent appeal.

39 Closing submissions and post-hearing steps

39.1 If there is no oral evidence, you will be asked to make opening submissions, followed by the HOPO's submissions, followed by your reply. (Note that as appellant, you are entitled to the last word.)

39.2 If oral evidence was heard, the HOPO will normally be invited to make his submissions first, and will not reply to your submissions. The disadvantage of this procedure is that it helps the HOPO to avoid facing up to the attack on his case. He should have received your skeleton argument, but is unlikely to engage much with the arguments contained in it. (Some adjudicators have commented that a more sensible approach would be to start with your submissions: this would mean that the HOPO would see exactly how you put your case in the light of the oral evidence. It would also expose any failure to answer your case in his response.)

The HOPO's submissions

39.3 The HOPO will nearly always start by 'relying' on the refusal letter, even where much of it has been be overtaken by events. He will usually make submissions on the oral evidence. He will often ignore the country evidence apart from the Home Office's own Country Assessment.

39.4 His closing submissions ought not raise new issues of which notice could have been given in advance. While the HOPO should not raise new points at the hearing at all, it is especially inappropriate to do so in closing submissions after the evidence has been completed. The obvious exception is where they arise out of oral evidence. However, any challenge to the evidence should have been made in cross-examination.

39.5 Take a full note of the HOPO's submissions. The adjudicator may not record the submissions in his determination fully (or sometimes at all).

It may be important on appeal (whether by you or the Home Office) to be able to show what submissions were and were not advanced. If the Home Office appeals, it will be particularly useful if you can demonstrate that the points that the adjudicator is alleged to have failed to consider were actually not raised by the HOPO at the hearing.

39.6 It is only occasionally appropriate to interrupt the HOPO's submissions: essentially to avoid wasting time while the HOPO develops an argument to which there is a fundamental objection. The circumstances where it may be helpful to interrupt are if the HOPO:

- embarks on a submission based on a mistake which is apparent from the documents, for example the date of an interview or the date the appellant entered the country;
- misquotes either the interview notes or the evidence given at the hearing;
- misrepresents your case, for example by claiming that you advance an argument that you do not, or accept something that you do not;
- raises an entirely new issue, or makes a point which is inconsistent with a concession or agreement made earlier;
- disputes the credibility of a witness when he raised no challenge by cross-examination.

Your own submissions

39.7 It is usually best to prepare notes rather than a full speech. That way your delivery will be much more natural and you will be able to make eye contact with the adjudicator. More importantly, you will be better able to adapt your submissions to the issues that have arisen at the hearing if you are working from notes rather than a prepared speech.

39.8 Respond to each of the HOPO's arguments. It may help to note the HOPO's submissions down one page, and pointers to your counter arguments on the facing page. You will not usually be offered any time to consider his submissions before making your own.

39.9 You should have checked at the start of the hearing whether the adjudicator had read your skeleton and if not, you should have invited him to do so. To some extent, the nature of your submissions will depend upon the nature of your skeleton argument. If you have made detailed submissions in your skeleton on the country of origin evidence, and quoted the relevant passages, you will be able to move more quickly through these points in submissions.

39.10 Many adjudicators (particularly if they did not have long to consider your skeleton) prefer you to go through the skeleton in closing so that they have an opportunity to raise any point which occurs to them. Others will ask you not to repeat these points in closing.

39.11 An adjudicator should never refuse to listen to oral submissions unless they are plainly irrelevant. In particular, he should not limit oral submissions on the basis that you have submitted a skeleton argument. On the contrary, the IAT stated in *Klajic* that:

> *Practitioners should not rely on [skeleton arguments] as a substitute for dealing with any significant feature of their case in oral argument.*

39.12 The best structure for your submissions may change from case to case, so long as they have a structure. One example might be:

- summary of the appellant's evidence;
- any corroborating evidence;
- summary of factors establishing present risk;
- country and expert evidence;
- how the case engages the UK's obligations and other legal arguments;
- rebuttal of refusal letter and HOPO's oral submissions;
- any human rights issues not embraced by the above submissions (e.g. family life in the UK).

39.13 Some advocates prefer to start by responding point by point to the HOPO's oral submissions as these will be fresh in the adjudicator's mind. The additional advantage of this is that you can finish on a positive note stressing your own case. You must deal at some stage with each point in the HOPO's submissions, showing how they are either wrong or irrelevant.

39.14 Where the HOPO has relied upon the refusal letter without addressing the flaws identified in your skeleton, you should point that out. Highlight other points in the skeleton that the HOPO has been unable to answer in his submissions. Invite the adjudicator to draw an appropriate inference. Remind the adjudicator of evidence that the HOPO did not challenge. If the HOPO's submissions on credibility are unsustainable in light of his failure to challenge a corroborating witness, point this out; similarly where his submissions on risk are inconsistent with a witness' unchallenged evidence of continuing interest in the appellant. If the HOPO has questioned the credibility of a witness called to give evidence when he raised no challenge in cross-examination, you should object in the strongest terms (if you did not interrupt his submissions to do so).

39.15 You do not normally need to refer to basic authorities in closing submissions, any more than in your skeleton. However, you should ensure that your submissions on the facts reflect the basic caselaw (e.g. following *Karanakaran*, the adjudicator cannot reject the appellant's evidence unless he can exclude any real doubt that it is true).

39.16 Remember that adjudicators hear cases day after day, and see the same allegations put forward day after day by the Home Office, often without serious challenge. You need to engage the adjudicator's attention and explain forcefully why a case built on allegations without evidence (or even explanation) should be rejected by any court. Attack the Home Office presumptions about the reasonable refugee individually, discrediting where appropriate by demonstrating the 'Damned if you do, damned if you don't' philosophy which lies behind them. Point out the alternative standard allegation that the Home Office would have deployed had your client acted differently.

39.17 Make your submissions at a speed which allows the adjudicator to make a proper note. Issues may arise because the adjudicator does not accurately record your submissions in the determination. If you have not given him a chance to make a proper note, you have yourself to blame. If the adjudicator does not appear to have made a note of a submission which is central to your case, there is nothing wrong with asking the adjudicator politely whether he has a note or whether he would like you to pause while he notes the submission.

39.18 Always conclude by asking the adjudicator whether there is any matter of concern upon which you have not already addressed him.

Further submissions and evidence following the hearing

39.19 As an alternative to going part heard at the end of the court day, it may on occasion be suggested that submissions be completed in writing. This may also be proposed where an unforeseen issue has arisen upon which submissions and/or documentary evidence are required. (You can also suggest this course as an alternative to adjournment where a discrete piece of documentary evidence is not yet available – see para 8.42).

39.20 However, the Chief Adjudicator has warned that the IAA administrative systems have often failed to transfer further submissions or evidence to the adjudicator in time, and indicated that adjudicators should accept post-hearing submissions or documents only in exceptional circumstances (Adjudicator Guidance Note No 4). That note sets out the procedure to ensure that post-hearing material reaches the adjudicator, namely that there should be a formal written direction which should include a requirement that submissions are marked urgent and for prompt transfer to the named adjudicator.

After the hearing

39.21 Few people can take a note of what they say as they speak. But you will need to know what your submissions were if you are called upon – maybe months down the line – to draft grounds of appeal or respond to a Home Office appeal.

39.22 You need not note points contained in your skeleton. If you are dealing with arguments which you have prepared earlier, then you need only tick off each submission in your notes as you make it. Otherwise, unless you are accompanied by someone who has made a note of your submissions, you should make your own note after the hearing. It need not be verbatim. But the summary should enable you to identify whether the adjudicator has misunderstood or failed to address any of your submissions. It is, of course, crucial that you have a legible and comprehensible note of the evidence that was given at the hearing. You should also note any other point which may be important later (e.g. if an objection was over-ruled, or any indication by the adjudicator or the HOPO on which you relied).

39.23 Once the adjudicator has risen, ask your client and any other witnesses whether they have any comments about how the hearing went, and about the evidence they gave. It may transpire that there were misunderstanding or concerns about the interpreting which you had not picked up during the hearing. Ask about any evidence that appears to contradict the information the witness gave you in interview or conference. If it transpires that there was some very significant misunderstanding, it may be worth seeking to re-open the hearing rather than simply storing the information up for the IAT.

39.24 If important evidence comes to light, or if there is a substantial change of circumstances in the country of origin between the hearing and the promulgation of the determination, you should submit it. It will be open to an adjudicator to reopen proceedings if satisfied that it is in the interests of justice to do so (see e.g. *Keskin*). It is also safest to submit any important new caselaw which emerges between the hearing and the determination (*Pinter*).

39 Closing submissions and post-hearing steps
Key points

- Take a full note of the HOPO's submissions: it may be required for any appeal brought by you or the Home Office.

- Only interrupt the HOPO's submission if there is a fundamental objection to an argument that he is starting to develop.

- Neither you nor the adjudicator should treat the skeleton argument as a substitute for oral submissions.

- Ensure you respond to the refusal letter and to each of the HOPO's arguments. Emphasise submissions in your skeleton to which the HOPO was unable to respond.

- Point out if the HOPO's submissions are unsustainable in light of evidence that he did not challenge, especially from witnesses who gave oral evidence.

- Object strongly if the HOPO chooses not to challenge a witness in cross-examination but then attacks his credibility in closing submissions.

- The adjudicator may direct further submissions in writing but note the procedure for this established by the Chief Adjudicator.

- You must retain a note of your submissions as well as a full note of the oral evidence.

- After the hearing, ask your client and any other witness about any unexpected problems in their evidence.

- Significant new evidence or caselaw that emerges between the hearing and the determination should be submitted.

40 Hearings where the Home Office is unrepresented

40.1 The number of appeal hearings that the Home Office fails to attend has increased markedly in recent years. The IAT has repeatedly expressed concern about the practice. In *Surendran*, it set out guidelines for adjudicators where the Home Office was unrepresented. These were approved and annexed to the starred decision of *MNM*. They are as follows:

> 1 ... The Home Office... requests that the... adjudicator deals with the appeal on the basis of the contents of the letter of refusal and any other written submissions which the Home Office makes when indicating that it would not be represented.

> 2 [We do not] consider that the appeal should be allowed simpliciter. The function of the adjudicator is to review the reasons given by the Home Office for refusing asylum within the context of the evidence before him and the submissions made on behalf of the appellant, and then come to his own conclusion as to whether or not the appeal should be allowed or dismissed. In so doing he must, of course, observe the correct burden and standard of proof.

> 3 Where an adjudicator is aware that the Home Office is not to be represented, he should take particular care to read all the papers in the bundle before him prior to the hearing and, if necessary, in particular in those cases where he has only been informed on the morning of the hearing that the Home Office will not appear, he should consider the advisability of adjourning for the purposes of reading the papers and therefore putting the case further back in his list for the same day.

> 4 Where matters of credibility are raised in the letter of refusal, the Special Adjudicator should request the representative to address these matters, particularly in his examination of the appellant or, if the appellant is not giving evidence, in his submissions. Whether or not these matters are addressed by the representative, and whether or not the Special Adjudicator has himself expressed any particular concern,

he is entitled to form his own view as to credibility on the basis of the material before him.

5 *Where no matters of credibility are raised in the letter of refusal but, from a reading of the papers, the Special Adjudicator himself considers that there are matters of credibility arising therefrom, he should similarly point these particular matters out to the representative and ask that they be dealt with, either in examination of the appellant or in submissions.*

6 *It is our view that it is not the function of a Special Adjudicator to adopt an inquisitorial role in cases of this nature. The system pertaining at present is essentially an adversarial system and the Special Adjudicator is an impartial judge and assessor of the evidence before him. Where the Home Office does not appear the Home Office's argument and basis of refusal, as contained in the letter of refusal, is the Home Office's case purely and simply, subject to any other representations which the Home Office may make to the Special Adjudicator. It is not the function of the Special Adjudicator to expand upon that document, nor is it his function to raise matters which are not raised in it, unless these are matters which are apparent to him from a reading of the papers, in which case these matters should be drawn to the attention of the appellant's representative who should then be invited to make submissions or call evidence in relation thereto. We would add that this is not necessarily the same function which has to be performed by a Special Adjudicator where he has refused to adjourn a case in the absence of a representative for the appellant, and the appellant is virtually conducting his own appeal. In such event, it is the duty of the Special Adjudicator to give every assistance, which he can give, to the appellant.*

7 *Where, having received the evidence or submissions in relation to matters which he has drawn to the attention of the representatives, the Special Adjudicator considers clarification is necessary, then he should be at liberty to ask questions for the purposes of seeking clarification. We would emphasise that it is not his function to raise matters which a Presenting Officer might have raised in cross-examination had he been present.*

8 *There might well be matters which are not raised in the letter of refusal which the Special Adjudicator considers to be relevant and of importance. We have in mind, for example, the question of whether or not, in the event that the Special Adjudicator concludes that a Convention ground exists, internal flight is relevant, or perhaps, where, from the letter of refusal and the other documents in the file, it appears to the Special Adjudicator that the question of whether or not*

the appellant is entitled to Convention protection by reason of the existence of civil war (matters raised by the House of Lords in the case of **Adan**). Where these are matters which clearly the Special Adjudicator considers he may well wish to deal with in his determination, then he should raise these with the representative and invite submissions to be made in relation thereto.

9   There are documents which are now available on the Internet and which can be considered to be in the public domain, which may not be included in the bundle before the Special Adjudicator. We have in mind the US State Department Report, Amnesty Reports and Home Office Country Reports. If the Special Adjudicator considers that he might well wish to refer to these documents in his determination, then he should so indicate to the representative and invite submissions in relation thereto.

10 We do not consider that a Special Adjudicator should grant an adjournment except in the most exceptional circumstances and where, in the view of the Special Adjudicator, matters of concern in the evidence before him cannot be properly addressed by examination of the appellant by his representative or submissions made by that representative. If, during the course of a hearing, it becomes apparent to a Special Adjudicator that such circumstances have arisen, then he should adjourn the case part heard, require the Home Office to make available a Presenting Officer at the adjourned hearing, and prepare a record of proceedings of the case, which should be submitted to both parties up to the point of the adjournment, and such record to be submitted prior to the adjourned hearing.

40.2   If you are proceeding on the basis that credibility has not been put in issue by the Home Office in its refusal letter, say so to the adjudicator. If that is the case, and the adjudicator does not indicate that he is considering an adverse credibility finding, there will often be no need to call the appellant.

40.3   If credibility has been put in issue by the Home Office, it will usually be appropriate to call the appellant. Where the Home Office is represented, the majority of a witness' oral evidence is spent dealing with cross-examination. You may decide to ask more questions than usual in evidence in chief in order to give the appellant a reasonable opportunity to put her case to the adjudicator. You can often do this by inviting the appellant to comment on those allegations in the refusal letter to which she can respond in her own words, and to express her current fears.

40.4   However, if the Home Office's grounds for disputing credibility are weak and are fully addressed by your skeleton and/or the appellant's witness statement, you may simply ask the appellant to confirm her statement and then ask the adjudicator if there is any matter upon which he would like to hear oral evidence. This gives the adjudicator every opportunity to raise his concerns without risking stepping into the arena by conducting the examination himself.

40.5 In *Aksonov*, the IAT emphasised that an adjudicator should raise his concerns via the representative and invite him to deal with them in examination in chief or submissions. Only if the representative fails to deal with the points or if the answers are obscure should the adjudicator try to clarify matters through questioning the witness himself. He should never indulge in a lengthy cross-examination.

40.6 Where the adjudicator starts questioning the appellant in a manner resembling a HOPO's cross-examination, it will be appropriate to remind the Adjudicator that this is inconsistent with the *Surendran* guidelines (para 7).

40.7 While the adjudicator is entitled (and obliged) to raise adverse matters which are apparent from the papers, it is not his role to seek to elaborate upon or develop the Home Office's refusal letter. If his point seems closer to the latter than the former, you should again remind him that the *Surendran* guidelines confirm that the process is adversarial and the Home Office's case (unless it has submitted written representations) is the refusal letter 'purely and simply' (para 6).

40.8 If you are concerned that the adjudicator does not appear to be following the *Surendran* guidelines, it is important to raise your concerns politely at the hearing. You should make a full note during, or immediately after the hearing of any indications or interventions from the adjudicator and of your own submissions.

40 Hearings where the Home Office is unrepresented
Key points

- The *Surendran* guidelines govern the conduct of the hearing where the Home Office is unrepresented. These provide that:

  - [ ] The function of the adjudicator is to review the Home Office reasons for refusal in light of the evidence and to decide whether to allow or dismiss the appeal.
  - [ ] If a credibility challenge is raised in the refusal letter, the adjudicator should invite the appellant's representative to deal with it in examination in chief or submissions. The adjudicator is entitled to form his own view.
  - [ ] Where no credibility challenge is raised in the refusal letter but the adjudicator considers that credibility issues arise from the papers, he should point these out to the representative and invite him to deal with them in evidence or submissions.
  - [ ] The hearing is adversarial and the adjudicator should not adopt an inquisitorial role.
  - [ ] The refusal letter is the Home Office's case purely and simply. It is not the adjudicator's function to expand on the Home Office's case or to raise matters that it has not raised, unless these are apparent to him from the papers.
  - [ ] While he can ask questions for the purposes of clarification following examination in chief, it is not his function to raise matters that a HOPO might have raised in cross-examination.
  - [ ] If the adjudicator intends to refer to country reports, he should invite submissions on them.
  - [ ] He should not adjourn the hearing by reason of the Home Office's failure to attend other than in exceptional circumstances.

- You may wish to conduct a longer examination in chief, so as to give the appellant a reasonable opportunity to put her case to the adjudicator.

- If there is no credibility challenge in the refusal letter (and the adjudicator does not raise any concerns) you may choose not to call the appellant. Alternatively, you may call her simply to confirm her statement and ask the adjudicator if there are any matters on which he would like to hear evidence.

- If the adjudicator starts to 'cross-examine' your client, object. Ensure that you make a full note of indications and interventions from the adjudicator and of your own submissions.

41 Post-appeal directions and recommendations

41.1 An adjudicator may be asked to give either a direction or a recommendation following his determination of the appeal. But the similarity ends there. The 2002 Act empowers an adjudicator to issue a direction to 'give effect to his decision' where he has allowed the appeal. The direction is binding on the Home Office unless it successfully appeals against it.

41.2 A recommendation on the other hand is extra-statutory and can be made whether the adjudicator has allowed or dismissed the appeal. If he allows the appeal, he may 'recommend' a particular form and period of leave (sometimes in circumstances where he could actually have made a direction). If he dismisses the appeal, the adjudicator may recommend that leave be granted on other grounds. However, recommendations are not binding and Home Office policy is now to the effect that they will not be followed unless the Home Office agrees with them.

41.3 While the Home Office is not bound by a recommendation, it *will* normally be bound to accept the adjudicator's findings of fact as to the appellant's particular circumstances when it comes to consider any future application from the appellant. Obtaining findings of fact that can support such an application is often much more useful than obtaining a recommendation that the Home Office should grant the application.

Directions

41.4 Section 87 of the 2002 Act states:

> *Successful appeal: direction*
>
> *(1) If an adjudicator allows an appeal under section 82 or 83 he may give a direction for the purpose of giving effect to his decision.*

> *(2) A person responsible for making an immigration decision shall act in accordance with any relevant direction under subsection (1).*
>
> *(3) But a direction under this section shall not have effect while an appeal under section 101 or a further appeal –*
>
> > *(a) could be brought (ignoring any possibility of an appeal out of time with permission), or*
> >
> > *(b) has been brought and has not been finally determined.*
>
> *(4) A direction under subsection (1) shall be treated as part of the determination of the appeal for the purposes of section 101.*

41.5 The utility of seeking such a direction following firstly a successful asylum appeal, and secondly a successful human rights appeal (where the asylum appeal has been dismissed) is discussed below.

Successful asylum appeal

41.6 In **Merzouk**, the IAT declined to follow previous authorities to the effect that an adjudicator could direct the Home Office to backdate the grant of refugee status:

> *What directions, if any, could a Special Adjudicator give when allowing an appeal in an asylum case? The answer to that question is: such a direction as is necessary to give effect to his determination that the appellant's removal would be contrary to the United Kingdom's obligations under the Convention. Therefore, the Special Adjudicator could, if necessary, direct that the Secretary of State should grant the appellant leave to enter the United Kingdom under the 1971 Act, and/or direct the Secretary of State not to deport the appellant from the United Kingdom in contravention of the United Kingdom's obligations under the Convention - but that is the extent of his power in asylum cases.*

41.7 The Home Office is under a legal duty to give effect to the determination of an adjudicator regardless of whether it is accompanied by directions: it is not entitled to reconsider the matter afresh (**Boafo**). In **Saribal**, Moses J held that following a successful asylum appeal,

> *[t]he Secretary of State is not entitled to… refuse a claimant's right to indefinite leave to remain as a refugee unless he can set aside that determination by appropriate procedure founded on appropriate evidence.*

41.8 If the Home Office does not seek to appeal the determination, then the only basis upon which it can be set aside is if the Home Office uncovers 'fresh evidence of fraud which is relevant, credible and not previously available with due diligence' (**Saribal**).

41.9 There is therefore no need for a direction from the adjudicator in order to impose a duty on the Home Office to give effect to the determination by granting indefinite leave as a refugee.

41.10 In the past, there have been unreasonable delays on the part of the Home Office in processing the grant of leave to successful asylum appellants (see *Mersin*). You might therefore consider a direction that the Home Office act upon the determination within a specified period. But if the Home Office does not act expeditiously to implement the adjudicator's determination, it will in any event be open to you to bring judicial review proceedings against the Home Office.

Successful human rights appeal

41.11 The Home Office's policy on granting Humanitarian Protection following a successful article 3 claim is as follows:

> *Subject to certain exclusion grounds, Humanitarian Protection (HP) will be granted to anyone who is unable to demonstrate a claim for asylum but who would face a serious risk to life or person arising from:*
>
> *the death penalty,*
> *unlawful killing,*
> *torture, inhuman or degrading treatment or punishment.*
>
> *Serious Criminals, including war criminals; terrorists or others who raise a threat to national security and anyone who is considered to be of bad character, conduct or associations will be excluded from these provisions.*
>
> *Even if they can not be removed they will still be excluded from HP and given less favourable terms of stay.*
>
> *HP should be granted for up to 3 years, less in specific cases as directed. If at the end of 3 years, following an active review, it is decided that further protection is needed, a claimant will usually receive ILR. If protection is no longer needed and a person has no other basis of stay in the UK they will be expected to leave.*

41.12 There is also a subsidiary category of 'Discretionary Leave', the policy on which is as follows:

> *Discretionary Leave (DL) may be granted for a limited number of specific reasons. These people will either not be considered to be in need of international protection, or will have been excluded from such protection.*
>
> *DL may be granted to an applicant who:*
>
> - *has an Article 8 claim.*
> - *has an Article 3 claim only on medical grounds or severe humanitarian cases.*

- is an Unaccompanied Asylum Seeking Child (UASC) for whom adequate reception arrangements in their country are not available.
- would qualify for asylum or Humanitarian Protection but has been
excluded.
- is able to demonstrate particularly compelling reasons why removal
would not be appropriate.

An individual grant of DL should not be made for more than 3 years, or
less in specific cases as directed by the API's or separate notices which
may be issued from time to time. UASCs should normally be granted for
3 years or until their 18th birthday, whichever is earlier, although there
may be some exceptions. After the DL period has expired the claimants
situation will be reviewed with further leave granted if appropriate. A person on DL will normally become eligible to apply for ILR after 6 years.
However a person who has been excluded from asylum and/or HP but
granted DL will be excluded from ILR under the DL provisions. They will
only be able to apply for ILR under the long residence concessions and
even then they may be excluded. A person who no longer qualifies for
leave will be expected to depart from the UK.

41.13 There is a further residual category of 'Leave outside the Rules' (LOTR).
The Home Office states that:

LOTR should only be granted after the full consideration of whether
someone first qualifies under the provisions of the Immigration Rules,
and the new Humanitarian Protection and Discretionary Leave system.
There are a number of immigration policy concessions under which someone may apply for limited LOTR. There may also be other particular compelling circumstances where someone may request either limited or indefinite LOTR. (Home Office briefing to ILPA)

41.14 If the appeal has been allowed under article 3 on the basis of a real risk
of 'the death penalty, unlawful killing, or torture, inhuman or degrading treatment or punishment', the effect of this policy is that unless
one of the listed exceptions applies, the Home Office is obliged by law
to grant Humanitarian Protection to give effect to the adjudicator's
determination (by analogy with the position following a successful
asylum appeal). You may seek a direction to that effect, although as
with a successful asylum appeal, you can in any event seek judicial
review if the Home Office fails to grant Humanitarian Protection.

41.15 If any issue arises about whether your client falls within the listed
exceptions to the policy, then you may ask the adjudicator to determine any factual dispute. The Home Office will be bound by his findings of fact (**Danaie**, below). You may argue that the adjudicator is
obliged to make such findings in order to assess whether the decision
appealed against was in accordance with the law. If he finds that your

client does not fall within the exceptions to the policy, he may direct that Humanitarian Protection be granted.

41.16 The Discretionary Leave policy oddly states that a person may be granted such leave if he 'has an Article 3 claim only on medical grounds or [in] severe humanitarian cases'. However, if your article 3 claim was *allowed* by the adjudicator on medical/humanitarian grounds, you would necessarily have established a real risk of inhuman or degrading treatment which entitles you to Humanitarian Protection according to the terms of the policy. It is not easy to reconcile the two. You can argue that the fact that the lesser form of leave 'may' be granted to someone who has an 'article 3 claim' can only sensibly be understood as referring to a claim which has not been proven but is perceived to have sufficient merit to permit a favourable exercise of discretion.

41.17 There is certainly no sensible reason why someone who has *won* their appeal under article 3 on medical grounds should be given a lesser form of leave than someone who has succeeded on article 3 on any other ground. On the contrary, someone who has succeeded because of severe mental health risks (e.g. a significant risk of suicide) may be in *more* need of stability than other successful appellants. Given the equivocal wording of the Discretionary Leave policy, it may be useful to seek a direction that Humanitarian Protection be granted as the appellant has established a real risk of inhuman or degrading treatment.

41.18 In **Sharif**, the adjudicator had directed that the appellant be granted indefinite leave on the basis of his finding that 'the Appellant will be at risk indefinitely'. The IAT considered this finding of fact to be one to which no reasonable adjudicator could come. One can understand why.

41.19 However, the evidence may establish that the risk of suicide cannot be managed or treatment successfully administered while the appellant believes that she may in the future be expelled to her country of origin. In those circumstances, it may well be that a failure to grant indefinite leave would be inconsistent with the appellant's human rights. You could invite the adjudicator to issue such a direction not because of his assessment of what the factual position will be in the future but because to grant only limited leave would interfere with the claimant's human rights *now*. The direction will be based on a legal duty arising not from the Home Office's policy (as in the examples above), but directly from the requirement to respect the appellant's human rights.

41.20 In **Sharif**, the IAT considered that the only direction that the adjudicator could have issued was that the appellant should not be removed. However, the decision pre-dated the Humanitarian Protection policy and *Saribal* was not cited.

Appeals arising from directions

41.21 The effect of s.87(4) is to enable an appeal to be brought to the IAT against such a direction. On its face, it might be construed as only enabling an appeal to be brought against the *making* of a direction and not against a refusal to make a direction. However, there would be no apparent basis to differentiate in this way and it is unlikely that that was the intended effect.

Recommendations

41.22 Prior to the Human Rights Act, adjudicators regularly made a recommendation when dismissing an asylum appeal to the effect that the appellant should be permitted to remain on other grounds. The Home Office told Parliament in 1988 that recommendations by adjudicators were 'invariably' accepted by the Home Office unless they were perverse or otherwise unlawful, and representatives consequently put much effort into pursuing such recommendations.

41.23 Despite that indication, the Home Office in practice increasingly rejected such recommendations, and eventually altered its public policy to reflect that. The IDIs now state that:

> *The Secretary of State is not bound to accept a recommendation made when an appeal is dismissed or withdrawn. Such recommendations should be acted upon only where the determination and/or recommendation discloses clear exceptional compassionate circumstances which have not previously been considered and which would warrant the exercise of the Secretary of State's discretion outside the Immigration Rules.*

41.24 The APIs state that:

> *Recommendations must be considered (before we commence any enforcement action) by an experienced caseworker, usually within the [HOPO Unit]. The caseworker will assess whether they contain clear exceptional compassionate circumstances which have not previously been considered. Consideration should not be delayed pending the outcome of any application for leave to appeal to the Tribunal where an appeal has been dismissed by an adjudicator.*

41.25 An adjudicator's recommendation will therefore be *rejected* by the

Home Office even where the adjudicator has found that there are exceptional compassionate circumstances unless the Home Office has not already considered these circumstances *and* it agrees with the adjudicator that they justify permitting the appellant to stay. This policy severely limits the utility of seeking a recommendation.

41.26 In **Berisha,** the IAT held that:

> *[E]xtra-statutory recommendations are no longer an appropriate way of dealing with any serious difficulty in the way of returning someone to his country of origin. If that would result in a breach of human rights, then the appeal should be allowed; otherwise it should be dismissed. If there is still any room at all for extra-statutory recommendations, it can only be in the most exceptional cases, if they can be imagined, where fairness requires them without the appellant's human rights being engaged. They ought not to be seen as a sort of compromise solution, allowing the appeal to be dismissed without actually facing the consequences.*

41.27 In **Gokteke**, the IAT concluded that the adjudicator's decision to make a recommendation despite dismissing the human rights appeal raised concerns about whether he had properly considered the human rights issues when determining the appeal. It sought to discourage adjudicators from making extra-statutory recommendations.

41.28 In **Shillova,** however, while Silber J agreed that an adjudicator 'cannot make a recommendation when the reasons for it would at the same time justify allowing a human rights claim', he stated that:

> *I consider that there remain circumstances after the coming into force of the Human Rights Act in which it is possible and proper for a Special Adjudicator to make a recommendation where he is dismissing Human Rights Act and asylum claims.*

41.29 Your primary argument will normally be that the appeal should be allowed on human rights grounds rather than a recommendation made. If you can establish an interference with private or family life then removal is prohibited unless the Home Office can show that it meets a pressing social need. At least if the adjudicator is assessing proportionality for himself (see para 42.99), a recommendation to the Home Office that it permit your client to stay is arguably inconsistent with the pressing social need to remove her from the jurisdiction which is a prerequisite to dismissing the appeal on article 8 grounds.

41.30 If you consider that the Home Office's decision is unlawful on public law grounds (for example, because it is inconsistent with Home Office policy), then this can constitute a ground of appeal against the immigration decision (s.84(1)(e) of the 2002 Act) so that it is unnecessary to rely on a recommendation.

41.31 If you do decide to request a recommendation, point out the Home Office's policy on recommendations, and emphasise the factors which have not yet been considered by the Home Office upon which you want the adjudicator to base his recommendation. There is no appeal against a refusal to make a recommendation.

Findings of fact relevant to future applications

41.32 Far more useful than a recommendation is any relevant finding of fact by the adjudicator concerning the appellant's particular circumstances. Unlike a recommendation, the Home Office is bound to accept any such factual finding (at least where the adjudicator heard oral evidence) unless fresh evidence has come to light that undermines the finding (*Danaei*).

41.33 The Home Office will then have to consider any subsequent application on the basis of the findings of fact made by the adjudicator, even if he has previously disputed these facts. This may bring your client within a beneficial Home Office policy from which you otherwise would have been excluded. It may also provide the essential basis for any application outside the Immigration Rules on compassionate or humanitarian grounds.

41.34 Recent restrictive caselaw on the protection guaranteed by the ECHR and the Refugee Convention has also highlighted the scope that remains for discretionary humanitarian protection outwith the strict requirements of international law. In *Ullah*, the Court of Appeal held that a human rights appeal based solely on feared treatment in the country of origin could not succeed unless the article 3 threshold was met, but added that:

> *Where such treatment falls outside Art 3, there may be cases which justify the grant of exceptional leave on humanitarian grounds. The decision of the Secretary of State in such cases will be subject to the ordinary principles of judicial review but not to the constraints of the European Convention.*

41.35 Similarly, in *AE and FE*, the Court of Appeal restricted the factors relevant to assessing the reasonableness of an internal flight alternative, noting that:

> *The 'unduly harsh' test has... been extended in practice to have regard to facts which are not relevant to refugee status, but which are very relevant to whether exceptional leave to remain should be granted having regard to human rights or other humanitarian considerations.*

41.36 Such findings may also be relied upon if conditions subsequently change in the country of origin. For example, the adjudicator may have made a positive credibility finding but dismissed the appeal because there is insufficient evidence of present risk. If conditions subsequently deteriorate in the country of origin, the Home Office will normally have to consider any fresh application on the basis of the adjudicator's positive credibility finding as to past events.

41 Post-appeal directions and recommendations
Key points

- A direction can be given only where the adjudicator allows the appeal. It is binding on the Home Office. A recommendation can be given whether the adjudicator allows or dismisses the appeal but is not binding.

- Regardless of whether the adjudicator gives a direction, his decision to allow the asylum appeal confers on the appellant a right to indefinite leave as a refugee which the Home Office can defeat only if it uncovers fresh evidence of fraud.

- Judicial review proceedings can be brought if the Home Office does not process the grant of leave as a refugee within a reasonable period.

- Where the adjudicator allows a human rights appeal under article 3, the Home Office must grant Humanitarian Protection unless the appellant comes within exceptions to its policy including war criminals, terrorists, and people 'of bad character'. Findings of fact by the adjudicator relevant to whether the appellant falls within these exceptions will be binding on the Home Office. The adjudicator may be called upon to determine the issue in order to decide whether the immigration decision is in accordance with the law.

- If you can establish a real risk of inhuman or degrading treatment on medical grounds, you should be entitled to Humanitarian Protection and can seek a direction to this effect.

- Medical evidence may establish that a grant of limited rather than indefinite leave would be inconsistent with the appellant's human rights.

- The Home Office will not comply with extra-statutory recommendations unless it agrees with them.

- The adjudicator's reasons for making a recommendation may be inconsistent with his reasons for dismissing the human rights appeal.

- Unlike recommendations, the Home Office will normally be bound to accept findings of fact as to the appellant's particular circumstances.

- Such findings can be relied upon in making any further application pursuant to Home Office policies, or on compassionate or humanitarian grounds, or on the basis of a change of circumstances in the country of origin.

42 Assessing the adjudicator's determination

42.1 This chapter discusses some of the principal issues that you should be checking in assessing a determination dismissing the appeal. As with the rest of the book, it is not intended as a substitute for a sound and contemporary understanding of the law relating to asylum and human rights and to procedural fairness.

42.2 Drafting grounds of appeal to the IAT is dealt with in chapter 43. The assessment of the determination is obviously a prior exercise to formulating grounds of appeal, but less obviously, the latter does not simply flow from the former. You need to start by working out for yourself what (if anything) is wrong with the adjudicator's determination. You will then need to consider the most effective way of presenting it to the IAT.

Preparation

42.3 Start by checking the date on which the adjudicator prepared the determination. If it was prepared more than three months after the hearing, and the adjudicator has relied upon a total or partial adverse credibility finding, it will normally be unsafe (*Sambasivam*). Sometimes, the determination will state the date on which it was dictated or signed. If not, you can only go by the date on which it was promulgated.

42.4 If you presented (or attended) the adjudicator hearing, you ought to have good notes of evidence and submissions. If you did not attend the hearing, then it is *imperative* that you obtain both notes of the hearing (whether from the advocate or someone accompanying him) *and* the advocate's comments on the determination. There may be procedural challenges available to the conduct of the hearing that are not apparent from either the determination or the available notes. (See para 43.25 for procedure where objections are to be made about the conduct of the adjudicator hearing.) The advocate may also have points to contribute based on his pre- and post-hearing conferences.

42.5 Some flaws will be obvious from the face of the determination. But many others will not. You cannot assess the determination adequately without being fully familiar with the evidence, both oral and documentary. Make sure you have:

- all statements and interview notes;
- all country and expert evidence;
- any documentary evidence submitted by the Home Office;
- any skeleton arguments;
- a list of authorities submitted by both parties.

42.6 Again, this should be checked with the advocate where applicable. He may have submitted country reports or authorities of which his instructing solicitors are unaware (although this ought to be obvious from his notes of the hearing).

42.7 If you relied on expert evidence, ask your expert to comment on the treatment of his evidence (see below). Also invite any other comments on the determination. Even if they do not fall within the expert's area of expertise, they may provide valuable pointers for your grounds, or for further evidence worth pursuing.

42.8 Last *but not least*, ensure that the determination is translated to your client and her comments invited. It is far from unknown for the appellant to spot mistakes or misunderstandings which were missed by the lawyers (see e.g. *Haile*, para 42.23 as an example of the importance of this exercise).

Analysing the findings of fact

42.9 A common structure for an adjudicator's determination is:

- a summary of the evidence, both documentary and oral;
- the submissions of the parties;
- self-direction as to the relevant law (often pro forma);
- findings as to past events;
- conclusions on the risks flowing from expulsion.

42.10 Check that the evidence – both oral and documentary has been accurately summarised. The record of oral evidence should be checked against your own notes. Also check that any summary of the submissions made by the parties is accurate.

42.11 The next stage is to analyse what the adjudicator's factual findings actually were. These may not be as they appear at first glance. An adjudicator may make adverse comments on credibility – sometimes in damning terms – yet accept important parts of the appellant's evidence. Or he may make a positive credibility finding but downplay or ignore important parts of your client's history when recounting it. In **Demirkaya**, the IAT had made a positive credibility finding on an appellant who had been severely tortured in detention. However, in summarising his history, the IAT merely noted that the appellant had been arrested twice but released without charge, and then reached conclusions on risk on the basis of that summary. On appeal to the Court of Appeal (which was allowed), Stuart-Smith LJ described the IAT's summary as 'a masterpiece of understatement'.

42.12 You may find that the evidence that the adjudicator rejected was limited to, say, her past history, and did not include her ethnicity. He may have accepted that the appellant had the scars claimed, but not how they were inflicted. Or you may find that certain parts of the factual history were not actually rejected. (A determination will be flawed where the adjudicator purports to make a blanket adverse credibility finding when he has in fact accepted significant parts of the appellant's evidence.)

The correct approach to factual disputes

42.13 The correct approach to the resolution of factual disputes has now been authoritatively established by the Court of Appeal in **Karanakaran**. It held that the adjudicator should focus upon the ultimate question of whether there is a real risk of serious harm in the country of origin. In answering that question, the decison-maker

> must not exclude any matters from its consideration when it is assessing the future unless it feels that it can safely discard them because it has no real doubt that they did not in fact occur (or, indeed, that they are not occurring at present). Similarly, if an applicant contends that relevant matters did not happen, the decision-maker should not exclude the possibility that they did not happen (although believing that they probably did) unless it has no real doubt that they did in fact happen. (per Brooke LJ)

42.14 Most adjudicators include a pro forma self-direction to the effect that they have applied 'the lower standard of proof'. However, more important than the direction is whether the correct approach is applied in practice. In **Faustino**, the IAT stated that:

> We do not wish to leave this appeal without remarking about the frequency upon which adjudicators having correctly stated the criteria for the establishment of the facts appear to apply in practice much more stringent tests.

42.15 When analysing the adjudicator's findings of fact, bear in mind that he may not disregard any factual contention made by the appellant unless he can say beyond real doubt that it is untrue. Therefore, phrases such as 'it may be the case that...' indicate that he has not disregarded the evidence according to the *Karanakaran* standard and so must take it into account when he goes on to assess present risk. Similarly, a comment that 'I have doubts about the appellant's claims' does not amount to a rejection of these claims.

42.16 Having analysed the adjudicator's findings of fact in relation to the appellant's history and characteristics, you next have to consider whether the adjudicator was *justified* in rejecting any evidence about these matters. Also bear in mind the *Karanakaran* criteria when assessing the sustainability of the adjudicator's findings. If the adjudicator has clearly *disregarded* evidence of past events when he comes to assess present risk, that will be sustainable only if his reasoning justifies the dismissal of a real doubt that the appellant's contentions might be true.

Adverse findings as to characteristics and past events
Credibility findings: reasons

42.17 Both the High Court and the IAT have indicated that determinations which rest upon an adverse credibility finding must be the subject of careful scrutiny, and have warned of the dangers in making adverse credibility findings in cross-cultural situations and on evidence given through interpreters. In *Hussain* (1995), Turner J stated that:

> Credibility is not in itself a valid end to the function of an adjudicator. There is a risk... that over emphasis on the issue of credibility may distort the findings of an adjudicator.

42.18 In *Guine*, the IAT commended the above passage in *Hussain* to adjudicators and stated that:

> [A] decision which concentrates primarily on findings of credibility for its outcome is in general more likely to be found to be flawed...

42.19 In *Charuruka*, the Tribunal stated that:

> The Tribunal... simply comments that if an adjudicator is to express complete disbelief in the appellant's story it is for the adjudicator to state why this is so and not to rely on a general description of the evidence, particularly when it is certainly arguable that the description (e.g. vague and inconsistent) would not stand up to scrutiny.

42.20 Similarly, in **B (DR Congo)**, the IAT noted that:

> [The adjudicator] disputed or disbelieved the genuineness of the motiva-
> tion underlying the publication of the article. This he did because he
> thought that in his evidence before him the appellant 'was vague and
> hesitant'. The adjudicator has given no indication about the areas in
> which he found the appellant to be vague. Given that the appellant
> appeared before him, if he had thought that the appellant needed to give
> more detail than he had, he should have sought such details and if the
> appellant had not provided the detail then the adjudicator could properly
> have concluded that he had been evasive in his evidence. To describe a
> person's evidence as vague and use that as a ground for disbelief is, in our
> view, quite unsatisfactory unless of course the areas of lack of detail,
> which cause concern, are clearly spelt out. The adjudicator also disbe-
> lieved the appellant's evidence about how the article came to be pub-
> lished because he was 'hesitant'. Again such a description is far from sat-
> isfactory without more. One can be hesitant for perfectly bona fide
> reasons and one can be perceived to be hesitant for a number of bad rea-
> sons. As hesitancy is so closely linked to demeanour and judging
> demeanour across cultural divides is fraught with danger, the less it is
> used to disbelieve a person, the less likely is the chance of being criticised
> for unfair judgment.

Mistake as to the contents of the evidence

42.21 The adjudicator cannot make proper findings on the evidence before
him unless he has a proper understanding of what that evidence is. If
he makes a factual mistake about the contents of the evidence which is
before him, the determination will be flawed unless his reasoning can
be shown to be unaffected by the mistake.

42.22 Such mistakes as to the *contents* of the evidence are to be distinguished
from errors that you may assert in the adjudicator's conclusions as to
whether that evidence should be accepted or rejected. The latter may
be questions of evaluation upon which different views are possible.
But unless there is a dispute about what evidence was actually before
the adjudicator (e.g. if it is denied that a witness made a particular
statement in oral evidence), a misunderstanding as to the contents of
the evidence will usually be uncontroversial once identified.

42.23 The adjudicator may attribute a statement to the appellant that does
not appear in the evidence. He may assume that a statement refers to a
particular organisation when in context it is clearly referring to a different organisation. A good example of the importance of such mistakes is the case of **Haile**. The adjudicator had dismissed Haile's appeal,
Haile had been refused leave to appeal, and judicial review proceedings

in the Administrative Court had been unsuccessful. It emerged only on appeal to the Court of Appeal that the adjudicator had in the words of Simon Brown LJ 'misheard or misnoted and in the result misunderstood a significant piece of evidence which was before him', namely the identity of a particular political party named by the appellant in cross-examination. Simon Brown LJ concluded that:

> This was really a most regrettable mistake for the special adjudicator to have made. True, it produced only one of six reasons for disbelieving the appellant, but it must inevitably leave a sense of deep injustice in the appellant and it cannot confidently be said to have made no ultimate difference to the result. It is of course most unfortunate that this mistake was not uncovered until it was when and plainly it could and should have been.

42.24 This also illustrates the point that any such mistake will render the determination flawed unless the adjudicator's reasoning is such that it is *inevitable* that he would have reached the same result had he not made the mistake. Similarly, in *Fessahaye*, the IAT concluded that the adjudicator's reliance on an inconsistency was undermined by her failure to have regard to an interview transcript. Although she also rejected the account as inherently implausible, the IAT concluded that while it would have been slow to interfere with the finding of implausibility had it stood alone, 'it is at least possible that the adjudicator was influenced on it (consciously or not) by her views' on the claimed inconsistency.

42.25 There is a further category of error, often described as mistake of fact, where the adjudicator makes a factual finding which was reasonable on the evidence before him but which can be shown to be false by reference to evidence which was not before him. This is discussed at para 42.81 below.

Assessing credibility in the context of the country of origin

42.26 An adjudicator must assess the appellant's evidence of her past experiences in the context of the contemporaneous country conditions. He must not reach his credibility finding in isolation from his assessment of the country evidence. Refer to the authorities quoted at para 18.2 as to the importance of this requirement, and to para 42.51 below in relation to *how* the adjudicator should approach the country evidence.

Implausibility

42.27 The IAT has consistently warned against assessing evidence based on the assumptions of an examiner in the country of asylum (see e.g.

Kasolo (quoted at para 1.5), *Mendes*; *Sokoto*). That applies particularly to instances where an adjudicator rejects evidence simply because he believes that the appellant or other parties would have acted differently in the circumstances. For example, in *Toro*, the IAT lamented as 'dangerous' an adjudicator's speculation to the effect that an assassin would have chosen a different spot in which to strike (on the basis of which speculation, he had rejected the appellant's account).

42.28 There may be a number of concerns: firstly, that it is unsafe to reject an account on the basis of the adjudicator's assumptions as to how such people would act absent any evidential basis (or any basis whatever except the adjudicator's instincts as to how he would have acted in the same scenario). Secondly, the evidence may be consistent with country evidence that the adjudicator has failed to consider. Thirdly, even addressing the adjudicator's speculation on its own terms, his reasoning may indicate that he has misunderstood the position or failed to take account of an obvious explanation.

42.29 Always obtain your client's comments on such issues. Get your expert's comments as well if you have instructed one. If you had not anticipated the evidence being rejected as implausible, you may now wish to consider obtaining expert evidence on the point even if you had not previously instructed an expert.

Discrepancies

42.30 See chapters 1 and 12 for a general discussion as to how to counter alleged discrepancies. Consider firstly whether the discrepancy identified by the adjudicator is in truth a discrepancy or whether one or other of the appellant's statements may have been misunderstood, taken out of context, or is open to a different interpretation.

42.31 It may well be unjustified to identify a 'discrepancy' based purely on the fact that detail emerged progressively over time in the course of the proceedings. (see para 1.11 and cases such as *Kasolo* and *Salim*).

42.32 It may also be inappropriate to rely on a discrepancy on a peripheral issue in order to reject the centrepiece of the appellant's account (see e.g. *Chiver*). The discrepancy is only material if it is indicative that the appellant has fabricated her evidence. If it relates to a matter upon which there would have been no need nor reason to concoct evidence, it will often be unjustified to conclude that the discrepancy pointed to fabrication as opposed to confusion, mistake, or forgetfulness. It may assist to demonstrate that the discrepancy is on a par with others which are plainly innocent, such as dates of marriage or birth. If medical evidence has been submitted which addresses the appellant's ability to give consistent evidence, has it been given proper weight?

42.33 Is it unfair for an adjudicator to rely on an alleged discrepancy which was not raised at the hearing without inviting the appellant to address his concerns? The caselaw suggests that this will not always be unfair. If an appellant has made clearly inconsistent statements for which she has no good explanation, she may decide for tactical reasons that the best course is to concentrate on stronger elements of the case. On the other hand, it may be unfair to rely on a discrepancy without inviting the appellant's comments if it is reasonable to suppose that the appellant may not have appreciated that there is a perceived inconsistency and if the adjudicator cannot exclude that a satisfactory explanation will be available if he raises his concern (see also chapter 12).

Medical and country expert evidence

42.34 Check whether the adjudicator has given proper consideration to medical and country expert evidence that is relevant to credibility, and whether he has assessed credibility in the light of the expert evidence or as a separate exercise (see the discussion and authorities in chapter 26 as to medical evidence).

Specific documentary corroboration

42.35 Assess the adjudicator's approach by reference to the discussion and authorities in chapter 16. Consider in particular the following questions:

- Did the adjudicator consider the documentary evidence along with the other evidence in the round, or did he reach an adverse credibility finding as a prior exercise, and then infer from that finding that the documentary evidence must be unreliable?
- Did he give reasons why he found the evidence unreliable?
- Are his reasons sustainable?
- If he did not consider that the document was a forgery, but nevertheless found that it was unreliable, was there evidence to support a conclusion that the proper source would have published false information?

42.36 If you have not already obtained expert comment on the documents (which you normally should have done if you were not able to authenticate them through other means), you should seek it now if the documents have been rejected.

Subjective fear

42.37 Occasionally, an adjudicator will appear to accept the appellant's historical account, yet purport to dismiss the appeal on the strength of an adverse credibility finding in respect of the appellant's claimed fear. In *Gashi and Nikshiqi*, the IAT said it would be hard to contemplate a scenario where it would be justifiable to dismiss an appeal on a finding that there was no subjective fear when there was the required objective risk. There is even less justification for doing so in the context of a human rights appeal.

Witnesses of fact other than the appellant

42.38 Check firstly that the adjudicator has made findings of fact in relation to any evidence given by witnesses other than the appellant. The IAT has consistently held that a determination will be 'fatally flawed' where the adjudicator has failed to make a finding on a witness' evidence (see *Liang; Daramola; Zulqarnian*).

42.39 If the witness' evidence has not been challenged, the adjudicator ought not to reject it without giving notice that he is minded to do so. This will apply particularly where a witness is offered for cross-examination and the HOPO fails to challenge her evidence (see authorities quoted at para 36.4).

42.40 It may well also apply where a witness statement is filed, that statement is not challenged, and so the witness is not called to give oral evidence. In *Seri*, Smedley J stated that:

> It seems to me that if an adjudicator is intending to reject such evidence as the statement of this witness…, he should at least give the Applicant the opportunity to either make representations about it as to why he should not reject it or, provide an opportunity for the Applicant, if he wished, to call the witness to give live evidence…

> In my judgment, the Tribunal, when considering the Notice of Appeal and the obvious importance which the applicant attached to the evidence of [the witness], should have granted leave so that the evidence could be heard orally and evaluated and put in the scales with the remaining evidence. Not to provide that opportunity is, in my view, unreasonable.

Alternative/inconsistent findings

42.41 An adjudicator may make alternative findings (e.g. an adverse credibility finding on the one hand, and in the alternative, a finding that the appellant would be at no risk even were his factual evidence true). If he gives clear alternative bases for dismissing the appeal, it will usually be necessary to show that *both* are flawed in order to appeal the determination (although it is also possible that a flaw in respect of one part of his determination may raise such concerns about his grasp of the case or his general approach that the determination as a whole will be unsafe).

42.42 However, there may well be an issue over whether alternative findings were actually intended. If they are not clearly expressed as alternatives, then the adjudicator's consideration of one issue may suggest that he has accepted the preconditions for that issue arising. A good example is *Gnanam*. The appellant sought to challenge findings on internal flight, but the Home Office argued that any error in the assessment of internal flight was immaterial to the ultimate outcome because the IAT had held that 'the appellant is not a credible witness and... he has not established a well-founded fear of persecution for a Convention reason if returned to Sri Lanka.' Tuckey LJ concluded that.

> *the short answer to [the Home Office's point] is this: the Tribunal did consider the question of whether it would be reasonable or unduly harsh to expect the applicant to live in Colombo. They could only have done so on the basis that their findings that the appellant did not have a well-founded fear of persecution related only to Colombo and not to Sri Lanka as a whole.*

The adjudicator's assessment of country conditions and risk

42.43 The adjudicator needs to reach findings about country conditions for two reasons:

- to make a proper assessment of the evidence relating to the appellant's own circumstances and history (see above);
- to assess the consequences of expulsion in light of these findings.

42.44 You need to decide whether the adjudicator's assessment of the consequences of expulsion was justified on the appellant's individual facts as he found them to be. Do not fall into the trap of rushing to dispute adverse credibility, without considering what you can do with the findings that the adjudicator did make about the appellant's circumstances and history. Adjudicators themselves sometimes fall into the trap of regarding an adverse credibility finding as an end in itself (see para 42.17 above). It is not uncommon for them to make an adverse credibility finding in respect of some of the evidence and then fail to make any risk assessment on the basis of the remainder of the evidence, or else a sloppy assessment.

42.45 In considering the adjudicator's risk assessment on the basis of the findings as to history and characteristics that you have analysed, you need to check the following:

- Which of the appellant's submissions on risk depended upon facts that the adjudicator rejected?
- Has the adjudicator dealt adequately with the remaining arguments?
- Were his findings as to risk justified by the extraneous evidence (i.e. excluding the appellant's own testimony)

42.46 Recurring examples are where the adjudicator:

- *rejects the appellant's past history but not her claimed ethnicity/religion/sexual orientation*
  Was there evidence/submissions before the adjudicator that this alone would be sufficient to place her at risk?

- *rejects the appellant's account of ill-treatment, but not that she was detained*
  Was there evidence/submissions that a record of past detention would now place her at relevant risk, regardless of how she was treated during the detention?

- *rejects the appellant's claimed activities in her home country but not in the UK (perhaps because corroboration was available of the UK activities)*
  Was there evidence that she would be at risk because of her UK activities alone? (Remember that it is not determinative whether these activities were 'reasonable' or even whether they were carried out in bad faith – see **Danian**.)

42.47 How much the adjudicator has to do to justify an adverse conclusion will depend upon the cogency of the evidence and submissions which you put before him. This highlights how important it is, without detracting from your primary case, to ensure that any secondary arguments which may survive a complete or partial adverse credibility finding are properly set out.

42.48 If the adjudicator has relied upon internal relocation, check whether he has dealt with all relevant issues concerning viability and accessibility (see the discussion at para 1.71).

42.49 Consider whether the adjudicator has satisfactorily explained any change of circumstances on the basis of which he finds that a victim of past persecution is not now at real risk (**Demirkaya**, para 1.59). Note also that it is insufficient simply to show that there has been some improvement. In **Djebari**, Schiemann LJ emphasised that:

> [I]t is not helpful for the determination of the essential issues in the case to say that the risk of ill-treatment is less than it was a few years ago. The Tribunal will be concerned with whether the risk now is a real risk, not with whether that risk is less than it was a few years ago.

42.50 You should also check that the adjudicator has not overlooked aspects of the evidence as to past facts when determining future risk. It is not uncommon for the adjudicator to find that there is no real risk that the authorities retain an adverse interest in the appellant without having regard to evidence from the appellant or another factual witness to the effect that the authorities have been looking for the appellant since she fled her country.

Treatment of the country of origin material

42.51 You need to review the country evidence that was before the adjudicator to determine

- what evidence supported the appellant's contentions;
- what evidence contradicted the appellant's contentions.

42.52 The more you have spelt out, with clear references, why the background evidence points to one conclusion, the more difficult it will be for the adjudicator to identify a satisfactory basis for a different conclusion. If there was independent evidence to support the appellant's contention, and no independent evidence to support the contrary finding reached by the adjudicator, his conclusion will be flawed.

42.53 As discussed in chapter 17, the Home Office often submits no independent evidence but simply relies on its own statements and reports, whether described as country assessments, operational guidance, or bulletins. Often, these reports will claim to paraphrase independent evidence but the independent evidence will not be submitted. The adjudicator's determination ought to be unsafe if he relies upon claims from one of the parties as to the content of independent reports that are not put in evidence before him in preference to independent evidence from reputable sources which is submitted in evidence by the opposing party.

42.54 It follows from the approach required by **Karanakaran** (above) that an adjudicator should not disregard the appellant's claims unless he can say beyond real doubt that the evidence is untrue. Where the adjudicator is faced with contradictory reports from reputable sources, he may be unable to reject *either* beyond real doubt, and he will not therefore be entitled to disregard the appellant's evidence, simply because he prefers other evidence.

42.55 Do not overlook the possibility that the adjudicator's findings are inconsistent even with the Home Office's Country Assessment (particularly if the HOPO advanced submissions that were more extreme than his own evidence). The HOPO may argue that the appellant has not shown that the risks detailed in the Country Assessment will apply to her. In **Mohammed Adam**, the issue was whether the appellant, a draft evader, would be imprisoned for draft evasion and thereby placed at real risk of ill-treatment contrary to article 3. The appellant pointed to the Home Office Country Assessment which noted ill-treatment of the appellant's ethnic group, ill-treatment in prisons, and that the penalty for draft evasion was up to three years imprisonment. The IAT held that there was no evidence to show that the appellant would be subject to that penalty, stating that 'evidence that a particular form of punishment is prescribed by law should be accompanied by evidence to show that there is a real risk that such penalty would be imposed upon the particular appellant.' In the Court of Appeal, Schiemann LJ accepted that 'to place a burden on the appellant to show that there is a real risk that this penalty will be imposed on him is unfair'. He stated that:

> In the light of the Country Assessment it seems to me that the evidential burden passed to the Home Office. If it was going to be part of the Home Office case that there is no real risk that the penalties prescribed by law would be exacted then they should have produced the relevant evidence in advance so that the appellant might know what case he had to meet. The statement in... the (Country) Assessment that a deserter will usually be re-conscripted does not meet the point – particularly when the appellant is a member of a persecuted minority and might thus be expected to be a candidate for the unusual. To expect him to do more than point to the law is in my judgment unfair and unrealistic – c.f. **Modinos v Cyprus**.

42.56 Check also that the **Karanakaran** approach has not been turned on its head. It has been known for adjudicators to dismiss the appeal on the basis that 'I think there is a reasonable likelihood that she will be able to return to her village in safety.' The necessary implication of such a finding is that there is equally a reasonable likelihood that she will not.

IAT determinations relating to country conditions

42.57 Check that any relevant IAT determinations which were before the adjudicator were given 'careful consideration' in accordance with

Manzeke (see para 29.5). This may apply not only to findings about level of risk, but also to the plausibility of various common scenarios.

42.58 You may also be able to point to IAT determinations which post-date your own appeal hearing. In *Shyam Gurung*, the IAT had dismissed the claimant's appeal but another division of the IAT had issued a determination days later in which it reached factual findings about the country of origin which appeared to indicate that someone such as the claimant would be at risk. The Court of Appeal held that although the IAT's determination would otherwise have been unimpeachable, the inconsistent factual findings reached by another division of the IAT in a contemporaneous determination raised sufficient doubts to justify remitting the appeal to the IAT.

42.59 The citation of IAT authorities is discussed in chapter 29.

Treatment of expert evidence

42.60 A court is not obliged to accept expert evidence (which for current purposes includes publicly available country reports). But if it rejects expert evidence, it must give reasons for doing so, and these reasons must disclose an adequate evidential basis for so doing. It follows that the adjudicator will have erred if he failed to consider relevant expert evidence.

42.61 In *Cherbal*, the IAT described as a 'worrying and fundamental error' the rejection of an expert report on grounds of 'partiality', explaining that:

> The decision in *Slimani* provides no authority whatsoever for rejecting an expert's report simply on the basis of partiality without explaining why that label is to be attached to the particular expert. Further, it does not provide authority for simply rejecting one report as against another without any comparison of the two of the reports.
>
> In this case, the adjudicator indicated that he would accept the [Home Office Country Assessment] as Mr Joffe [the expert] had no specific evidence to the contrary without indicating whether the [Country Assessment] itself included specific evidence. The Tribunal in *Slimani* thought that in an appropriate case an expert's feelings should not be spared but that course could only properly be taken after indicating the evidence in relation to which the conclusion is reached, if the report is to be rejected because of inconsistency with another report which is to be accepted, the nature of the inconsistencies and the reason why one is preferred to another. Finally, just as the Tribunal did in *Slimani*, we would add that in consideration of reports in other decisions dealing with similar reports, it has to be borne in mind that the time factor will in many cases be different. The situation in the country concerned may well have changed for

> *the better or for the worse. Caution must be exercised therefore in reject-ing expert evidence in a particular case because somewhat similar evi-dence was not accepted in an earlier case.*

42.62 In **Kilic**, the adjudicator had stated that 'In coming to this decision, I have placed little weight on the expert evidence presented by the appellant. The reason for this is that I have found such expert evidence to be self-serving and as the experts in question were not called to give evidence (even if they have the credentials which qualify them in that role) they were acting more as advocates than expert witnesses – **Slimani**.' The IAT said that:

> *We agree with the grounds that the adjudicator was wrong to reject the expert evidence in these terms. It may be that experts who give oral evi-dence should carry more weight than those who give only written evi-dence. However, be it written, oral or both, their evidence is entitled to be treated with the respect due to persons who possess relevant expertise. Precisely why the adjudicator thought the evidence of the witnesses in question to be 'self-serving' is unclear. The epithet was quite misplaced. Even if she had cause to think them partisan, we cannot see that justified describing them as self-serving. As regards her description of them as advocates, she was entitled to rely on **Slimani** for the proposition that expert witnesses with strong views about a country (as were all four experts in this case) can act more as advocates rather than expert wit-nesses. However, as **Slimani** makes equally clear, an adjudicator must give reasons rather than mere epithets for accepting or rejecting an expert's view.*

42.63 It is also an error to reject an expert opinion simply as 'speculation' (**Karanakaran** and see generally the Court of Appeal judgments men-tioned in chapter 19 as to the importance of expert evidence).

42.64 The scope for the adjudicator to reject an expert report will depend upon the extent to which it is contradicted by other evidence of com-parable quality. It will also depend upon the extent to which the guid-ance in chapters 22–23 was followed.

Fairness

Conduct of the hearing

42.65 Was the hearing conducted fairly? Consider whether your examina-tion in chief and/or re-examination was unjustifiably limited (see chapters 35 and 37) and whether unfair cross-examination was permit-ted despite your objection (see chapter 36). The adjudicator's own questions and interventions must also be fair.

42.66 Assess the adjudicator's interventions according to the guidance in chapters 38 and 40. Sometimes, inappropriate interventions from the adjudicator will be apparent from his determination, e.g. 'I challenged the witness about...' But more usually, you will need to refer to notes of the hearing. It is obviously essential in order to assess these points that you have the advocate's notes of the hearing if you did not attend.

Relying upon evidence without inviting submissions on it

42.67 An adjudicator will often err if in dismissing the appeal, he relies upon a point that was not raised at the hearing. This will always be the case where he relies on material which was not in evidence before him, and upon which he did not invite the comments of the parties (see *Junaid*). It will often be the case where he relies upon an alleged implausibility which was not suggested at the hearing, and to a lesser extent where he relies upon an alleged discrepancy.

42.68 The risk of unfairness is particularly acute where the Home Office was unrepresented at the hearing and did not challenge the point in its refusal letter or written submissions. In *Junaid*, the IAT said that:

> There is no reason why an adjudicator, even in the absence of a Presenting Officer, should accept the account given if he or she takes the view that there are matters which are, on the face of them, difficult to accept. But if an adjudicator takes that view, it is essential that the appellant and his representative is put on notice that the adjudicator has those concerns. And so far as specific matters are concerned, the adjudicator must, if they are considered to be of importance, give the appellant an opportunity to deal with them.

> Not only did this adjudicator not inform the appellant and his representative that she was concerned about credibility, but she relied in deciding against him upon material which she looked at later and which she did not draw to the representative's attention. The result was that the appellant's representative had no opportunity to deal with those matters...

> We hope that we will never again see a determination such as this or an Adjudication where matters have not been referred to in the hearing upon which reliance is then placed [to] make adverse credibility findings.

42.69 In *Lopez-Zapata*, the IAT stated that:

> Any judicial officer is in these circumstances placed in a delicate position because he would act unfairly if he failed to raise an issue which appeared on the face of the evidence before him and which will require to be addressed. At the same time, we accept that in making those legitimate enquiries to clarify issues before him, he should be careful not to

overstep the mark so as to espouse or to appear to a neutral observer to espouse the cause of one party or the other.

42.70 Note that if the Home Office has conceded a point, it is not open to the adjudicator to reach a different finding, regardless of what notice he has given (**Carcabuk & Bla**).

Fairness: interim decisions

42.71 You cannot bring an appeal to the IAT against a procedural decision, e.g. the refusal of an adjournment or refusal to make a direction, or against a decision on a preliminary issue unless it results in the dismissal of your appeal. However, you can challenge such decisions as part of your appeal against the adjudicator's final determination if there is a realistic prospect that the result might have been different had the procedural decision been different.

42.72 If you were refused an adjournment by the adjudicator to enable you to submit evidence on a point on which he subsequently made an adverse finding, this may be challengeable. You will also want to appeal if the appellant was forced to proceed with the appeal when unfit to do so, or where the interpreting was inadequate (see chapter 34). The raising of new issues by the Home Office at the hearing on which you are not given the opportunity to take instructions or obtain evidence may also found an appeal, as could any refusal to issue directions against the Home Office which could have assisted you, or any direction preventing you relying on evidence or submissions.

42.73 You may also wish to challenge the grant of any application made by the Home Office. One example is where you oppose a Home Office adjournment application because a witness has attended to give evidence and will not be able to attend in the future. The prejudice in those circumstances may depend upon whether the witness' written statement is rejected. Unless it is possible to remedy the problem immediately through judicial review while the witness is still available, you can raise the issue, if necessary, when appealing the final determination.

Where the appellant was unrepresented or badly represented before the adjudicator

42.74 There is – unsurprisingly – not a great deal of caselaw on what fairness requires of an adjudicator (and the HOPO) when the appellant is unrepresented. The prospects of an unrepresented appellant lodging an application to the IAT (with appropriate grounds) are slim.

However, in the IAT's *Surendran* guidelines to adjudicators on how to conduct appeals where the Home Office is unrepresented, it held that the adjudicator's role would be different where it was the appellant as opposed to the Home Office that was unrepresented:

> *In such event, it is the duty of the Special adjudicator to give every assistance, which he can give, to the appellant.*

42.75 An adjudicator may therefore be entitled, and indeed obliged to take the initiative in identifying relevant evidence. Any such evidence must nevertheless be brought to the attention of both parties who must have the opportunity to comment, and a challenge may be founded on any reference in the determination to evidence that was not brought to the attention of the parties.

42.76 If the Home Office was represented, there will also be a particular duty of fairness on the HOPO to disclose weaknesses in his case. See para 9.29 as to the Home Office's duty not to mislead. The HOPO's duty to refer to adverse assessments of the Home Office's evidence in other cases, or evidence in the possession of the Home Office which contradicts its case (see *Ezzi*) will be especially important where the appellant is unrepresented.

42.77 If you are instructed by a client who was unrepresented before the adjudicator, you will have to try to establish to what extent the adjudicator complied with his duty to assist the appellant. The only way to do this is to take the fullest possible instructions from the appellant and then, if appropriate produce a witness statement.

42.78 Bad representation may well be worse than no representation at all because the duty upon the adjudicator to make allowances for bad representation is not as clear-cut and the bad representative may do actual damage which would not have occurred had the appellant been left to her own devices. However, the Court of Appeal has recognised that:

> *Of course, the appellate structure in asylum cases must be astute at every stage to detect, of its own motion if need be, any instance where the applicant may have been put at obvious risk of injustice in the presentation of his case through inadvertence or ignorance on the part of the applicant or his advisers.* (*Packeer*)

42.79 The IAT has taken the same view. In *Minta-Ampofo*, it emphasised that:

> *In our view, by placing the matter in the hands of solicitors, the Appellant had done what could justly be required of him. The Solicitor's failures must be regarded as not to be expected by him and hence beyond his control: he would not envisage a need to supervise his solicitors. In an asylum appeal, which has potentially very serious implications, we do not*

> *think it is appropriate to leave the Appellant to pursue any remedy against his representatives.*

42.80 In *Haile* (above), the Court of Appeal admitted fresh evidence even though it considered that the appellant's representatives ought to have appreciated the adjudicator's mistake and presented the further evidence before the IAT or at least the High Court on judicial review (from which the appeal had come). The Court of Appeal distinguished *Al-Mehdawi* (in which the House of Lords had held that the claimant must bear the consequences of his representative's mistake) on the ground that that case concerned an immigration rather than an asylum case. It held that it was not prevented from having regard to the wider interests of justice where evidence had not been put before the decision maker through the fault of the representative.

Relying on evidence which was not before the adjudicator

42.81 Even if the adjudicator's findings were justifiable on the evidence that was before him, there may be further evidence available which could show that his conclusions were mistaken. Such evidence falls into two categories:

- evidence establishing that his findings of fact were wrong when he made them;
- evidence that the position has changed since the adjudicator made his assessment.

42.82 If an adverse credibility finding rested in part upon a mistake of fact, it is unsafe and unlawful. (See chapter 43 as to the criteria for admitting such evidence in the IAT.) As is apparent from *Haile*, this will be so regardless of whether there are other reasons supporting the adverse credibility finding which are unaffected by the mistake unless it is inevitable that the adjudicator would have reached the same result had the fresh evidence been available.

42.83 If fresh evidence has become available since the hearing indicating that country conditions have changed for the worse, this is a matter which the IAT will be able to consider, and upon which it should grant leave unless, again, there is no realistic prospect that the changed circumstances could affect the result of the appeal.

Errors as to substantive law

42.84 Identifying substantive legal errors depends upon a proper knowledge of substantive asylum and human rights law. Areas where errors may occur in an asylum appeal include:

- identification of Convention reason;
- prosecution as persecution and article 1F;
- the assessment of sufficiency of protection;
- issues relating to internal protection.

42.85 Human rights law is newer and in a greater state of flux, and therefore more likely to give rise to error. The Court of Appeal ruled in **Ullah** that:

> Where the European Convention is invoked on the sole ground of the treatment to which an alien, refused the right to enter or remain, is likely to be subjected by the receiving State, and that treatment is not sufficiently severe to engage Art 3, the English court is not required to recognise that any other Article of the European Convention is, or may be, engaged.

42.86 An appeal is pending in the House of Lords (permission to appeal having been granted by the Court of Appeal).

42.87 Consider whether the adjudicator has properly appreciated the scope of article 3. In **Q**, the Court of Appeal accepted that the effects of destitution could engage article 3 (and see also **S, D & T**). The Court in **Q** quoted the European Court's guidance in **Pretty**:

> Where treatment humiliates or debases an individual showing lack of respect for, or diminishing, his or her human dignity or arouses feelings of fear, anguish or inferiority capable of breaking an individual's moral and physical resistance, it may be characterised as degrading and also fall within the prohibition of Article 3. The suffering which flows from naturally occurring illness, physical or mental, may be covered by Article 3, where it is, or risks being, exacerbated by treatment, whether flowing from conditions of detention, expulsion or other measures, for which the authorities can be held responsible.

42.88 In **Razgar**, the Court of Appeal held that a significantly increased risk of suicide following expulsion would give rise to an arguable appeal under article 3.

42.89 It should also be noted (as was emphasised by the IAT in **Bushati**) that the Court of Appeal's ruling in **Ullah** was limited to cases where human rights are invoked *solely* on the basis of feared treatment in the country of origin. The Court said that:

> There is a difference in principle between the situation where Art 8 rights are engaged in whole or in part because of the effect of removal in disrupting an individual's established enjoyment of those rights within this jurisdiction and the situation where Art 8 rights are alleged to be engaged

solely on the ground of the treatment that the individual is likely to be subjected to in the receiving state.

42.90 Check that the adjudicator has not applied an unduly restrictive interpretation of family life when deciding whether it is enjoyed in the UK. Family life can exist where there is 'the real existence in practice of close personal ties' (*K v UK*). In *Marckx*, the European Court stated that:

> *In the Court's opinion, 'family life', within the meaning of Article 8, includes at least the ties between near relatives, for instance those between grandparents and grandchildren, since such relatives may play a considerable part in family life. 'Respect' for a family life so understood implies an obligation for the State to act in a manner calculated to allow these ties to develop normally.*

42.91 Consider also whether the adjudicator has appreciated the scope of the relationships which may fall within private life. In *Nhundu*, the IAT stated that:

> *[The adjudicator] should have borne in mind that the Court views the private life concept as a broad one that includes not only the idea of an 'inner circle' in which individuals may live their personal lives as they choose without interference from the state; it also covers the right to develop one's own personality and to create and foster relationships with others: Niemietz v Germany. In the context of immigration and asylum cases, the Court has come to view the right to respect for private and family life as a composite right. This approach requires the decision-maker to avoid restricting himself to looking at the circumstances of 'family life' and to take into account also significant elements of the much wider sphere of 'private life' ... One consequence of this approach is that a person may be able to establish a protected right under Article 8 either by reference to significant elements of family life or significant elements of private life or a mixture of both.*

42.92 In *Razgar*, the Court of Appeal set out the following test by which to determine whether article 8 was engaged simply on the basis of the appellant's mental health:

> *We suggest that, in order to determine whether the article 8 claim is capable of being engaged in the light of the territoriality principle, the claim should be considered in the following way. First, the claimant's case in relation to his private life in the deporting state should be examined. In a case where the essence of the claim is that expulsion will interfere with his private life by harming his mental health, this will include a consideration of what he says about his mental health in the deporting country, the treatment he receives and any relevant support that he says that he enjoys there. Secondly, it will be necessary to look at what he says*

*is likely to happen to his mental health in the receiving country, what treatment he can expect to receive there, and what support he can expect to enjoy. The third step is to determine whether, on the claimant's case, serious harm to his mental health will be caused or materially contributed to by the difference between the treatment and support that he is enjoying in the deporting country and that which will be available to him in the receiving country. If so, then the territoriality principle is not infringed, and the claim is capable of being engaged. It seems to us that this approach is consistent with the fact that the ECtHR considered the merits of the article 8 claim in **Bensaid**. It is also consistent with what was said in paragraphs 46 and 64 of **Ullah**.*

42.93 Check, however, that the adjudicator has not focussed only on the implications of the appellant's mental health for her moral and physical integrity without also considering whether she enjoys private life in the wider sense explained by the IAT in **Nhundu** (above).

Article 8(2)

42.94 The IAT has suggested in the past that 'it will be virtually impossible for an applicant to establish that control of immigration will be disproportionate to any breach' (**Kacaj**). The Court of Appeal held in **Razgar** that 'We are in no doubt that in **Kacaj**, the IAT overstated the position.' The Court quoted extensively from the guidance given by the European Court in **Boultif** which is equally applicable to cases involving family life and those involving private life.

42.95 In **Boultif**, the European Court said that it was 'called upon to establish guiding principles in order to examine whether the measure was necessary in a democratic society'. The guidance included that:

In assessing the relevant criteria in such a case, the Court will consider the nature and seriousness of the offence committed by the applicant; the length of the applicant's stay in the country from which he is going to be expelled; the time elapsed since the offence was committed as well as the applicant's conduct in that period; the nationalities of the various persons concerned; the applicant's family situation, such as the length of the marriage; and other factors expressing the effectiveness of a couple's family life; whether the spouse knew about the offence at the time when he or she entered into a family relationship; and whether there are children in the marriage, and if so, their age. Not least, the Court will also consider the seriousness of the difficulties which the spouse is likely to encounter in the country of origin, though the mere fact that a person might face certain difficulties in accompanying her or his spouse cannot in itself exclude an expulsion.

42.96 It is instructive to note how the European Court applied its guidance to the individual case:

> The Court has considered, first, whether the applicant and his wife could live together in Algeria. The applicant's wife is a Swiss national. It is true that the applicant's wife can speak French and has had contacts by telephone with her mother-in-law in Algeria. However, the applicant's wife has never lived in Algeria, she has no other ties with that country, and indeed she does not speak Arabic. In these circumstances she cannot, in the Court's opinion, be expected to follow her husband, the applicant, to Algeria.

42.97 The adjudicator must therefore have regard to difficulties which will be experienced in the country of origin when conducting the art 8(2) balancing exercise even if they would not, taken in isolation, raise any human rights issue.

42.98 Consider also whether the adjudicator has had proper regard to the interests of others who would be affected by the proposed expulsion. In *AC*, Jack J held that an adjudicator must have regard to the impact of the appellant's expulsion on her family members when considering interference with family life in a human rights appeal:

> In my judgment, where in a deportation case an interference with family life is under consideration in the context of the deportee's right to freedom from interference with the exercise of family life under Article 8, it is right to consider and take into account the effect of the interference on all those sharing the family life in question, and not simply the effect upon the individual who is subject to possible deportation... It seems to me artificial and unsatisfactory that, where a right to family life is established as existing, the effect of the interference on only one individual should be taken into account. That must particularly be so where the effect of the decision to be made, if made one way, is likely to be to destroy the family life in question. The purpose of the Article is, in relation to family life, to conserve that life. As I have pointed out, the impact on one family member in turn impacts on another. So I consider that it is the effect of the proposed interference on the family life as a whole which should be taken into account.

> In the context of [a human rights appeal], however, it has particular advantages. It means that the impact of the decision on other family members can be taken account of under section 65. This may avoid the need for other proceedings in which the rights of those family members can be asserted. It also means that the adjudicator and the Appeal Tribunal carry out the same task in relation to the impact on family life as did the Secretary of State in making the decision appealed against.

Otherwise, to take the facts of this case as an example, the impact on [the appellant's child] would be relevant to the decision of the Secretary of State but irrelevant and to be removed from the balancing exercise on the appeal under section 65.

42.99   You should also examine whether the adjudicator has adopted the correct approach to the 'margin of discretion' when assessing proportionality. This may differ from case to case, as has now been clarified by the Court of Appeal in **Razgar**. The Court stated that where there was 'no issue of fact' or 'the adjudicator finds the facts to be essentially the same as those which formed the basis of the Secretary of State's decision', the adjudicator's approach will be the same as that of a judge on judicial review: i.e. deciding whether the Home Office's decision is within the range of reasonable responses open to him. Where, however, the facts are in dispute and the adjudicator finds the facts to be materially different from those asserted by the Home Office, the adjudicator should decide for himself whether the decision is proportionate by carrying out the requisite balancing exercise himself, although paying due deference to the Home Office's policies.

42.100   As indicated in chapter 1, the Home Office will often rely upon bald generalisations about the need to maintain immigration control without relating these to the facts of the case. Check that the adjudicator has not adopted the same approach. Check also that the adjudicator has assessed properly whether the mischief to which the Home Office's policy is directed is one that arises on the facts of the case.

42.101   In **Shala**, Schiemann LJ stated that:

I am of course conscious of the importance of having uniform policies consistently enforced and the difficulties in giving decision takers at a relatively lowly level a wide discretion. However, I would wish to emphasise the need for adjudicators to bear in mind the reasons for the policies which they are enforcing and not just the wording of the policies.

42.102   The case involved a Kosovan Albanian who arrived in the UK while Kosovo remained under Serb control (so that he was at the time entitled to refugee status) but whose asylum claim was not determined until after the NATO occupation (and so was rejected). The Home Office's submissions were directed to the fact that the separation of the family while the appellant sought entry clearance in Kosovo would be only temporary so 'did not require much by way of justification' and that it was 'important to go through the usual procedures'. Keene LJ noted that:

*The facts of this case bear a marked similarity with those of **Xhacka**, an IAT decision where the Tribunal was presided over by Collins J. There the* *appellant was also an ethnic Albanian from Kosovo whose claim for asylum was not dealt with for some two and a half years. During that time, he met and married a British woman, though the adjudicator found that that there were no insurmountable obstacles to the family living together in Kosovo. The IAT took the view that the claim under Article 8 should have been allowed, Collins J. saying at paragraph 3:*

'In the circumstances of this case, the fact is that the appellant did have a legitimate claim to enter, namely that he was at that time a refugee, and that coupled with the delay in dealing with his claim as an unaccompanied minor until the situation changed, is capable of amounting to exceptional circumstances and does in the circumstances of this case justify a decision that he is entitled to remain here because to remove him would be a breach of Article 8 of the European Convention on Human Rights.'

*That reference to 'a legitimate claim to enter' derives from a passage in **Mahmood**, where at para. 23, page 318, Laws LJ said this:*

*'Firm immigration control requires consistency of treatment between one aspiring immigrant and another. If the established rule is to the effect – as it is – that a person seeking rights of residence here on grounds of marriage (not being someone who already enjoys a leave, albeit limited, to remain in the UK) must obtain an entry clearance in his country of origin, then a waiver of that requirement in the case of someone who has found his way here without an entry clearance and then seeks to remain on marriage grounds, **having no other legitimate claim to enter**, would in the absence of exceptional circumstances to justify the waiver, disrupt and undermine firm immigration control because it would be manifestly unfair to other would-be entrants who are content to take their place in the entry clearance queue in their country of origin.' (Emphasis added)*

*The significance is that, both in **Xhacka** and in the present case, the appellant **did** have a legitimate claim to enter at the time when, on any reasonable basis, his claim should have been determined. Put another way, the fact that the delay by the Home Office has deprived him of that advantage should be seen as an exceptional circumstance which takes the appellant's case out of the normal run of cases where a person with no leave to enter seeks such leave on the basis of marriage: see **Mahmood**, para. 26.*

42.103 An example of a fact sensitive approach can be seen in the IAT's decision in **Harunaj**:

[W]e have to consider whether interference with the appellant's rights under Article 8(2) would be justifiable. Considerations of interest of

national security, prevention of disorder or crime, the protection of health or morals or the protection of freedom of others, is an essential element in weighing up on one side the rights of the appellant and on the other the Secretary of State's obligations to maintain a legitimate immigration policy in this country.

The adjudicator has not in our view carried out this balancing exercise. We do so and we come to the conclusion that it would be disproportionate in the circumstances of this appellant, bearing in mind that nothing in his background since coming to this country would lead to any concern for national security, the prevention of disorder or crime, or the protection of health or morals or the rights and freedoms of other citizens in this country. It would therefore be disproportionate for this appellant to be returned to Serbia. His appeal is accordingly allowed.

42 Assessing the adjudicator's determination
Key points

Preparation

■ Ensure you have notes of oral evidence and submissions and copies of all the documentation placed before the adjudicator by both parties.

■ Get the determination translated for your client and invite her comments.

■ Check the date: has there been more than three months delay between the hearing and the preparation of the determination?

Analysing the findings of fact

■ Has the adjudicator accurately summarised the evidence?

■ Analyse what factual findings the adjudicator has actually made (or not made) on the basis of *the whole of the determination*, not simply an adverse comment on credibility in the final paragraph.

■ Has the adjudicator correctly applied the *Karanakaran* approach to factual findings?

Adverse findings on characteristics and past events

■ Has the adjudicator made a mistake as to the content of the evidence before him (as opposed to whether that evidence should be accepted)?

■ Are his credibility findings properly reasoned?

■ Has he assessed credibility in the context of a proper assessment and understanding of the country evidence or has he engaged in speculation based on assumptions drawn from his own standpoint?

■ Are any discrepancies identified by the adjudicator real?

■ Does the discrepancy go to a central or peripheral issue?

■ Is the discrepancy more consistent with a fabricated than a truthful account?

■ Was it raised at the hearing?

■ Has the adjudicator taken proper account of any medical and other expert evidence relevant to credibility?

- Has he made findings on the evidence of factual witnesses other than the appellant?

- Has he rejected the evidence of a witness whose evidence was not challenged in cross-examination?

- Where he has rejected specific documentary corroboration, has he considered the evidence in the round or did he reach an adverse credibility finding as a prior and separate exercise?

- Did he give sustainable reasons for concluding that the document was unreliable?

- Did he deal with any expert evidence you had advanced to show the document was authentic?

- Has he given alternative bases for dismissing the appeal, or does his consideration of any further issue indicate his acceptance that it arises on the facts of the case?

Assessment of country conditions and risk

- On the basis of the appellant's individual facts as the adjudicator found them to be, does the country evidence show she is at risk?

- Have your submissions on the documentary evidence been adequately addressed?

- Has the adjudicator pointed to independent evidence which justifies his rejection of your case?

- Has he relied upon Home Office documents in preference to independent reports?

- Has he overlooked aspects of the Home Office evidence that support your case?

- Has he dismissed the appeal because there is no evidence confirming that a penalty prescribed by law will be imposed in practice, rather than recognising that the evidential burden lies with the Home Office to show that there is no real risk that such a penalty will be enforced?

- Has he given proper consideration to relevant IAT determinations which were before him?

- Has he given sufficient reasons, supported by evidence, to reject any expert country evidence upon which you relied?

■ Has he explained any change of circumstances justifying the conclusion that a victim of past persecution will not be at future risk?

■ Has he simply asserted an improvement in the situation or a lessening of the risk without focussing upon whether the remaining risk is a real one?

■ Has he taken account of any evidence from the appellant or other witnesses about continuing adverse interest in the appellant since she fled her country?

Fairness

■ Were any procedural decisions unfair? Could they have adversely affected the result?

■ Was the hearing conducted fairly, in terms of the leeway given to each advocate, and the nature of the adjudicator's interventions?

■ If the Home Office was unrepresented, did the adjudicator follow the *Surendran* guidelines or did he question the appellant in a manner resembling a cross-examination?

■ Did the adjudicator place adverse and unfair reliance upon a point which was not raised at the hearing?

■ If the appellant was unrepresented before the adjudicator, did he give her 'every assistance which he can give'? Did the HOPO act fairly by disclosing adverse points?

■ Can the appellant be shown to have been prejudiced by bad representation?

Relying on evidence which was not before the adjudicator

■ Is there further evidence which shows that the adjudicator reached incorrect findings on past facts?

■ Have there been relevant developments either in general country conditions or the appellant's own situation since the hearing?

Error in legal characterisation

■ Has the adjudicator correctly identified points of legal characterisation such as 'Convention reason', the distinction between prosecution and persecution, and the approach to non-state risks?

■ Has he appreciated the scope of article 3, including whether it will be engaged by the effects of destitution or a significantly increased risk of suicide?

- Has he correctly recognised the circumstances in which article 8 may be engaged in an expulsion case?

- Has he considered the full scope of family and private life? In a family life case, has he properly considered the impact of the appellant's expulsion upon a family member?

- If he reached findings of fact materially different from those of the Home Office, has he assessed proportionality for himself?

- Has he had regard to the reasons rather than simply the wording of any policies claimed by the Home Office to justify an interference pursuant to article 8(2)?

43 Grounds of appeal and evidence

43.1 The IAT deals with a high volume of applications for permission to appeal. The application will be considered by a legally qualified member of the IAT (r.18(1)), normally a Vice President. It can be assumed that he will be familiar with asylum and relevant human rights law, and with determining applications for permission. You can also assume that yours will be one of a large number of applications for permission on his desk, and that he will spend a limited amount of time on each one. The previous President of the IAT, Collins J, has stated that a single Chairman may be given 120 permission applications to determine in a single week (Middle Temple lecture, 7 April 2003). If one assumes a 35 hour working week, this leaves the Chairman with a startling average of little more than 15 minutes to consider and determine each permission application.

43.2 The test for granting permission to appeal is set out in r.18(4):

> *The Tribunal may grant permission to appeal only if it is satisfied that –*
>
> *(a) the appeal would have a real prospect of success; or*
> *(b) there is some other compelling reason why the appeal should be heard.*

43.3 Only in exceptional cases will permission be granted under limb (b). For the rest, you must show that the appeal has a real prospect of success. Success involves the IAT either allowing the appeal outright or remitting it. You need not decide at this stage which disposal to aim for. Your priority is simply to convince the IAT that you deserve a hearing. You should present your grounds of appeal in a manner which can persuade the IAT of this as quickly and clearly as possible.

43.4 If you are refused permission to appeal, the quality of your grounds will affect the prospects of success in an application for statutory review (chapter 45). The better the grounds, the more should be required from the IAT by way of reasoning if permission is refused. In *Lal*, Crane J stated that:

> *If the grounds are cogent, the use of formulaic reasons may point to a conclusion that the grounds did not receive sufficient consideration.*

43.5 Generalised assertions that the adjudicator has not followed the proper approach will not do. You must focus upon the reasons for which the adjudicator dismissed your appeal and demonstrate how his failure to follow the correct approach renders all or some of them unsafe. Similarly, it is not enough to assert that a particular finding is contrary to the evidence. You must justify this assertion by reference to the evidence.

43.6 It is often unnecessary to set out the facts of the case in detail. The extent to which you will do so depends upon the extent to which they are relevant to the grounds you are advancing. If the adjudicator has accepted (or not rejected) material facts, you may be arguing that he should have found that your client would be at risk on these facts. It will be particularly important to set out the material facts where that is not done adequately in the determination. Your client's credibility may be accepted, but the adjudicator's summary of her account may downplay her ill-treatment, activities, or the degree of adverse interest shown in her (see para 42.11). The grounds should then start with a proper summary of the relevant history.

43.7 Not every flaw in the adjudicator's determination will justify permission to appeal. You must both 'identify the alleged errors of law in the adjudicator's determination' *and* 'explain why such errors would have made a material difference to the outcome' (r.17(3)).

43.8 If the error could have made no difference to the result, the IAT will not grant permission. But remember that it is unnecessary to show that the determination *would* have been different, just that it *might* have been. In *Jude*, Schiemann LJ set out the correct test where an error has been shown in one aspect of a determination:

> *[M]y task, if I am to refuse relief to the Claimant in this case, is to be satisfied that had the IAT not made the clear error that it did, it would inevitably have reached the same conclusion. That is, of course, a very high hurdle for the defendant to leap over, and it has to be borne in mind that it arises in the context of an asylum case which demands that there be given the most anxious scrutiny to the claim.*

43.9 Similarly, in **Gashi (2002)**, Munby J stated that:

> *[T]he matter has got to go back to a different adjudicator for a fresh hearing unless [the Home Office] can demonstrate to me that no sensible adjudicator, properly directing himself or herself to all the relevant factors, could possibly arrive at any conclusion other than the conclusion at*

which in fact this Adjudicator arrived. In other words, in this particular context the test for resisting what would otherwise be the granting of a quashing order is the classic Wednesbury test.

Putting it slightly differently, [the Home Office] accepted that if [it] is to resist the remittance of this matter to the fresh adjudicator, the case would have to be one in which, had this Adjudicator in fact found for the claimant rather than, as he did, against him, the Secretary of State would have been able in this court to quash that decision on the ground of irrationality. That is, and appropriately, as it seems to me, a high test. It is a difficult hurdle to overcome in any context, and all the more so in the context of asylum, where this claimant is entitled in this court, as elsewhere, to the most anxious scrutiny of his claim.

43.10 You should refer to this high test if there is any possibility that the IAT might otherwise conclude that the error made no difference to the result.

43.11 Given the high volume of applications, the IAT appreciates clear, concise grounds. But it is not uncommon for the IAT, like other courts, to confound your expectations as to what are your best and worst points. An important additional danger in omitting potential grounds is that it renders it more difficult for any future representative to run the point on an application for statutory review. The Court of Appeal has held that the merits threshold is higher if the ground was not included in the application for permission (**Robinson**). You should therefore hesitate before omitting a ground of challenge entirely.

43.12 A compromise between the conflicting dangers of losing your best point in a sea of more difficult ones and omitting grounds which a court might consider to be arguable is to emphasise your best points at the start of the grounds and then set out the remaining grounds in shorter form towards the end.

43.13 Always quote any authorities which support your argument, whether higher court or IAT. If there is clear IAT authority supporting your submission, then that ought to prevent the IAT dismissing the point at the permission stage even if it disagrees with the point. The same should apply if there is conflicting IAT authority (unless one is starred) until the conflict is resolved by a higher court. If the IAT refuses permission on grounds which are supported by clear IAT or higher authority, you may well have good grounds for statutory review. If an IAT determination is unreported, you will have to comply with PD No 10 (see the discussion in chapter 29).

43.14 The IAT's jurisdiction is now restricted to appeals on points of law (s.101(1)). If you state that the decision was 'against the weight of the evidence', the response may be that this does not amount to a point of law. However, your grounds need not claim that a decision is perverse. What is required is that you point to the evidence that is inconsistent with the adjudicator's findings and explain why he had no sufficient basis to reject that evidence.

43.15 The requirements of anxious scrutiny and rigorous examination result in a considerably more intrusive review of whether factual findings are flawed. The more important the right at stake, the more is required from the decision maker by way of justification. In *Turgut*, the Court of Appeal held in a (pre-HRA) article 3 case that the decision maker's 'discretionary area of judgment... is a decidedly narrow one'. An asylum appeal may succeed on the law where 'the Tribunal's conclusions were not expressed with the requisite degree of clarity or did not deal adequately with the main submissions' (*Jain*) and where it is 'not sufficiently reasoned for it to be safe for this court to uphold it' (*Singh (2000)*). These tests were developed in the context of common law jurisprudence. The test for determining an error of law in an HRA case is certainly no lower and may well be higher. Note also that an adjudicator's determination will be unlawful where it is based on a mistake of fact (see *Haile*, para 42.23). Never lose sight of the need to focus the challenge on the reasons given by *this* adjudicator, and how the challenge renders *this* particular decision unsafe.

43.16 You will sometimes wonder upon receipt of the determination whether the adjudicator saw the same appeal you did. Remember that the IAT did not see it at all. Nor will it have time to read the evidence in any detail. It may well be necessary to set out evidence and submissions at some length if they were not properly set out in the determination, and if you rely upon the adjudicator's failure to appreciate them. But avoid the impression that you are simply copying and pasting your original submissions into the grounds of appeal. You must explain what you are doing and how it supports your challenge to the decision.

Some other compelling reason

43.17 A grant of permission to appeal because 'there is some other compelling reason why the appeal should be heard' (r.18(4)(b)) presupposes that your appeal has no real prospect of success on the merits. The compelling reason will normally be either to determine a point of general importance in the public interest, or to challenge findings by the adjudicator which may jeopardise some future proceedings by the appellant. An example of the former is *Noruwa*.

Evidence in support of an application for permission to appeal

43.18 Notwithstanding the limitation of the IAT's jurisdiction to one of law, s.102(2) of the 2002 Act states that:

> In reaching their decision on an appeal under section 101, the Tribunal may consider evidence about any matter which they think relevant to the adjudicator's decision, including evidence which concerns a matter arising after the adjudicator's decision.

43.19 There are, in any event, a number of authorities for the proposition that even the Court of Appeal should consider fresh evidence in an asylum/human rights case where it is in the interests of justice to do so. In *Haile*, the Court admitted fresh evidence to demonstrate a mistake by the adjudicator even though the mistake 'could and should' have been spotted earlier by the claimant's advisers and brought to the attention of the IAT or the Administrative Court. While the fresh evidence would have failed the *Ladd v Marshall* test (as it was previously available), the Court held that the test did not apply to public law cases, and it should instead be guided by 'the wider interests of justice'.

43.20 In *Tataw*, the IAT had rejected an application for permission to appeal out of time. On judicial review, the claimant asserted for the first time that the adjudicator's determination had been received late so that the application to the IAT had actually been made within the time limit. The Administrative Court held that it had no power to intervene as this information had not been before the IAT. On appeal to the Court of Appeal, the Home Office argued, and the Court of Appeal accepted that the decision of the IAT was unimpeachable on the material that had been before it. However, the Court held that it was unnecessary that there be any fault on the part of the IAT in order to identify a procedural error, and that the IAT's decision should be quashed in the interests of justice. It relied on the earlier case of *Rahmani* where an adjudicator heard an appeal in the appellant's absence as her representative had not contacted her. Quashing the decision in that case, Fox LJ held that:

> What happened here was that, without any fault by the adjudicator or the applicant, the adjudicative process failed and the applicant was wholly denied the oral hearing she had asked for and to which she was entitled.

43.21 In *A*, the Court admitted three expert reports and a further statement from the appellant which showed that the IAT had been wrong to conclude that there was an internal flight alternative. It allowed the appeal outright on the basis of the fresh evidence. Keene LJ said that:

> As a matter of principle it would be difficult to achieve [anxious] scrutiny whilst closing one's eyes to relevant evidence.

43.22 In **Khan**, the Court of Appeal admitted court documents from the country of origin as fresh evidence. In **Polat**, the Court admitted expert evidence analysing the factual guidance given by the IAT. It rejected the Home Office's submission that it was not entitled to have regard to fresh evidence, May LJ stating that:

> I have no doubt at all but that in an asylum case such as the present, which requires the court's most anxious scrutiny and where the appellant's basic human rights are central, the court should have regard to material of this kind.

43.23 These decisions demonstrate that where the consequences of an inaccurate result may be death or torture, the imperative is to get the decision right. They highlight the importance of submitting any relevant evidence which either establishes a procedural injustice or shows that the adjudicator's reasoning or conclusions are unsafe.

43.24 It is also worth repeating the advice given in para 8.71, namely that if you are refused an adjournment by an adjudicator in order to produce specific evidence, you must not abandon your efforts to produce it. Any challenge to the refusal to adjourn is likely to be met with suspicion if you do not present the evidence which you were refused an adjournment to submit, or at least detail your continuing efforts to obtain it. The benefits of submitting the evidence are illustrated by the Administrative Court's judgment in **Dirisu**.

43.25 If you are complaining about the conduct of the hearing, the facts on which you rely should be established by evidence. In **Aftab Ahmed**, the IAT stated that:

> Grounds of appeal do not prove themselves. Where criticisms are made about the conduct of an Adjudicator those matters must be established before the Tribunal. That can be done in a number of ways. A statement, or if need be an affidavit, can be produced from a representative or another person who attended the hearing who can state what happened so far as his or her recollection is concerned.
>
> If there are criticisms of an Adjudicator it may be that the Tribunal of its own motion will ask the Adjudicator for comments. Those comments will be put to the parties and will form part of the material which is considered by the Tribunal. But some material, other than the mere statement in the grounds, must be placed before the Tribunal.

43.26 Problems sometimes arise where you represented your client at the hearing and you are the only person who can confirm what happened at the hearing. This may be the case where the appellant does not speak English, you were the only lawyer present, and you did not have your own interpreter (which ought not to be the case – see chapter 34).

43.27 The ordinary rule is that an advocate should not continue to act in a case in which he is giving evidence, especially if that evidence may be subject to challenge. But given the present pressure of work in this field, it will often be difficult to find another lawyer able to draft grounds of appeal within the time limit. If it is not possible to pass the case to someone else to draft grounds, the best available course may be to include a witness statement confirming the grounds and to indicate in the application for permission that if your account of the hearing is disputed either by the Home Office or the adjudicator, you will cease to act as advocate so that you can appear, if necessary, as a witness. (Note also the guidance in *Goonawardena* that if the advocate before the adjudicator is not the drafter of the grounds of appeal, and these grounds include assertions as to what transpired at the hearing, he should at least be shown the grounds for approval either before they are lodged or as soon as practical thereafter.)

43.28 The previous 2000 Rules included a provision relieving the IAT of a duty to consider fresh evidence unless satisfied that there was a good reason for not adducing it before the adjudicator (r.18(11)). The provision was clearly inconsistent with *Haile* and has been omitted from the present Rules. (Note that PD No 4, para 2(ii), which explained how the IAT would apply the provision, is therefore out of date.)

43.29 Rule 21(2) requires an explanation of why fresh evidence was not submitted to the adjudicator, but it is addressed to evidence submitted following the grant of permission (r.21(3)). You should nevertheless provide an explanation of why the fresh evidence was not before the adjudicator unless it is obvious (e.g. because it deals with events during or post-dating the hearing, or it responds to a point taken in the adjudicator's determination). If the reason it was not before the adjudicator was a mistake on your, or your client's part, you should own up to this and refer to *Haile* and the wider interests of justice. In *Azkhosravi*, Keene LJ stated that:

> [T]he Tribunal is entitled to look with scepticism at new material which could have been adduced before the special adjudicator and it is entitled to an explanation as to why it was not put before him. But what it cannot, in my judgment, properly do is to focus entirely on that aspect and to pay no attention to the credibility of the fresh evidence or to the impact which, if it is credible, its receipt might have on the issues in the case.

The reason for that is that very important and apparently credible evidence might otherwise be excluded from consideration, evidence which indeed might in some cases produce a different result on the appeal, solely because of the lack of any proper explanation for its non-production at the original hearing. That could sometimes lead to injustice and this is why the balancing exercise is required.

43.30 You should be particularly careful to explain why evidence was not submitted before the adjudicator if adverse inferences may otherwise be drawn as to the credibility of the evidence. This will apply especially where you are seeking to rely upon a new witness statement from the appellant which the Home Office may challenge as a late embellishment. If the explanation for not having led evidence on the matter is that you did not foresee the point being taken against you or you overlooked the matter, it may be safest for you also to serve a witness statement to this effect.

43.31 If you cannot obtain the necessary evidence within the ordinary time limit for applying for permission to appeal, you will have to make a formal application to extend time for appealing under r.16(2) (para 44.12). Although the application may appear in the body of the grounds, you must state that you are making the application and identify the special circumstances justifying it. It is not sufficient simply to indicate when the further evidence will be available: *Sahin*. In that case, Henriques J held that:

[S]o soon as the claimant learned that the expert's report was not available within the time limit, he should have made formal application to the Tribunal to extend the time limit for making the application for leave to appeal.

43.32 You should nevertheless lodge such grounds and evidence as are available within the time limit in case your application to extend time is refused.

43 Grounds of appeal and evidence
Key points

■ The IAT may grant permission only if the appeal has a real prospect of success or if there is some other compelling reason why the appeal should be heard.

■ Generalised assertions that the adjudicator adopted the wrong approach or reached a conclusion that is contrary to the evidence will not do. Any challenge must be justified by specific reference to his reasoning and to the evidence.

■ It is unnecessary to show that the error *would* have led to a different result, but you should show that it is not inevitable that the error would have made no difference.

■ Highlight your best points but exercise caution before omitting a ground altogether.

■ Notwithstanding the limitation of the IAT's jurisdiction to one of law, it should admit fresh evidence if it is in the interests of justice to do so. That evidence may go to establish a procedural error or to demonstrate that the adjudicator's reasoning or conclusions are unsafe.

■ Where assertions are made about the conduct of the hearing, these must be established. If you presented the adjudicator hearing and nobody else can give evidence about what occurred, you should indicate that if your account of the hearing is disputed, you will cease to act as advocate so that you can appear as a witness.

■ Unless it is obvious, an explanation should be provided of why fresh evidence was not adduced before the adjudicator, especially if adverse inferences may otherwise be drawn as to credibility.

■ If material evidence cannot be obtained within the time limit then make an application to extend time. But lodge such grounds and evidence as are available in case that application is refused.

44 Lodging the permission application

Time limits

44.1 An appeal to the IAT may be brought only with permission (r.15(1)). The IAT will decide the permission application without a hearing (r.18(1)).

44.2 The time limit for seeking permission is 10 working days after service of the adjudicator's determination or five working days if the person is in detention (r.16(1)(a–b)).

44.3 The date of promulgation of the determination should appear on the notice to which it is attached and should also be stamped on the first page of the determination. Any earlier date entered by the adjudicator on which he signed the determination is irrelevant for the purposes of calculating the time limit. Similarly, if the adjudicator announces his decision at the end of the appeal, time will still run only from service of the written determination. However, if a written determination is handed down at a hearing, time will start to run immediately, and any subsequent service of the determination by post will not start the period running again.

44.4 Where the determination is sent by post, service is deemed to be effected on the second day after it was sent, unless the contrary is proved (r.54(5)(a)). The IAT will in practice accept any application for permission to appeal which is submitted within 12 working days of the date of promulgation of the adjudicator's determination (PD No 4, para 2(iv)).

44.5 At time of writing, applications for permission to appeal are served on the IAA's Leicester administrative office. There is a dedicated fax number for permission applications (0116 249 4214). Always check the notice attached to the front of the determination which will contain the present procedures for lodging the application.

44.6 Although there is nothing in the rules or practice directions concerning the time by which an application must be received, the IAT's practice is to accept faxed applications up to midnight on the last date for appealing (and there is no provision in the Procedure Rules indicating any earlier time). This practice was confirmed without objection by the RLC at a meeting with the IAT administration on 14 February 2002 (Symes & Jorro, chapter 14).

44.7   If the fax number is not working on the day time expires and it is not possible to speak to the IAA by telephone, the best course is to send it to another IAA fax with an explanation and then pursue the matter the next day. By r.54(1), a document is delivered to a person, including the IAA, when it is sent to a postal or email address, or fax number 'specified for that purpose'. One would not expect the IAA to rely on this rule to assert that an application is not served if it is directed to other than the preferred fax number. If it did, it is likely that a formal extension of time would be justified (see below). The IAT has suggested that a liberal approach has been taken to applications which are not significantly out of time (see para 44.14 below).

44.8   If you have lodged grounds by fax, the IAA has expressed a preference not to receive a further copy by post (Symes & Jorro, chapter 14). But ensure you retain the fax confirmation sheet and that your fax machine is set to the correct date and time.

Lodging the application late

44.9   If you lodge your application more than 12 working days after promulgation (assuming your client is not in detention), you should explain why it should not be rejected as out of time.

44.10 The 10 working day time limit in r.18(2) runs from actual service (or receipt) of the determination. But if it was received more than two working days after promulgation, the onus is on you to establish this. Practice Direction No 3 (as amended) provides that:

> (4) If any application is made after [12 working days have expired following the date of promulgation of the adjudicator's determination], it will be assumed that it is out of time unless the contrary is proved. Accordingly, there must accompany any such application all material relied on to seek to prove that the notice of the adjudicator's determination was not received within 2 days. An assertion that it was not so received is not by itself likely to persuade the Tribunal that the burden of proof is discharged.

> (5) It is not possible to give an exhaustive list of what material should be

served. *The applicant must be aware that he must prove that the application was made in time so must include everything (including statements of witnesses and documents) which he wishes the Tribunal to take into account. The Tribunal will not receive any further material.*

(6) Any application which contains no explanation will be summarily rejected.

44.11 If the determination arrives within 12 days of promulgation, it may be simpler (if practical) to submit the application within these 12 days, rather than going to the trouble of preparing the evidence necessary to establish late receipt. While you do not actually require an extension of time from the IAT if you lodge within 10 working days of actual receipt, you would normally apply in the alternative for an extension of time in case the IAT is not convinced by your evidence of late receipt.

44.12 Rule 16(2) states that time for applying for permission to appeal may be extended by the Tribunal:

if it is satisfied that by reason of special circumstances it would be unjust not to do so.

44.13 This is the same test as is applied by adjudicators when determining whether to extend time for lodging the notice of appeal. Error by a representative is capable of amounting to a special circumstance (para 4.24). In *Tofik*, the Court of Appeal held that there was a duty to give reasons for refusing to extend time under this provision.

44.14 The IAT indicated in *Kutchouk* that there was a practice amongst some of its members of considering any application for permission to appeal on the merits if it was submitted 'roughly in time'. However, at time of writing, the Court of Appeal has in the same case ordered the IAT to reconsider whether an extension of time can be deemed to have been granted in circumstances where no application to extend time was included with the notice of appeal. See para 43.31 for applying for an extension of time where evidence is not yet available.

The notice of appeal

44.15 Rule 17 states:

> *Form and contents of application notice*
>
> *(1) An application notice for permission to appeal must be in the appropriate prescribed form and must –*
>
>> *(a) state the appellant's name and address; and*
>> *(b) state whether the appellant has authorised a representative to act for him in the appeal and, if so, give the representative's name and address.*
>
> *(2) The application notice must state all the grounds of appeal and give reasons in support of those grounds.*
>
> *(3) The grounds of appeal must –*
>
>> *(a) identify the alleged errors of law in the adjudicator's determination; and*
>> *(b) explain why such errors made a material difference to the decision.*
>
> *(4) The application notice must be signed by the appellant or his representative, and dated.*
>
> *(5) If an application notice is signed by the appellant's representative, the representative must certify in the application notice that he has completed the application notice in accordance with the appellant's instructions.*
>
> *(6) There must be attached to the application notice a clear and complete copy of the adjudicator's determination together with a copy of any other material relied on.*

44.16 If a defect is subsequently discovered in the notice, refer to the Court of Appeal's judgment in *Jeyeanthan*. Judge LJ stated that:

> *[I]n the context of applications in asylum cases it would be wholly unrealistic not to recognise that errors, omissions and simple oversight by individuals, many without any proper grasp of English, or any understanding of the legal processes, are inevitable. To exclude them irrevocably from the appeal process, notwithstanding an application for leave brought in time, on the basis of incurable non-compliance with the mechanics of the appeal procedure, would be entirely inconsistent with a fair and just system for dealing with their cases.*

44.17 One respect in which non-compliance with the Rules has very serious consequences is a failure to include grounds of appeal with the notice of appeal. In the past, it was common practice to submit the notice with pro forma grounds and a note stating 'Further grounds to follow'. That is no longer permissible. Rule 17(2), quoted above, indicates that the application form should 'state all the grounds of appeal'. Rule 18(2) states that:

> *The Tribunal is not required to consider any grounds of appeal other than those included in the application.*

44.18 Practice Direction No. 4, para 2(ii) reflects this:

> *Applications must set out all the grounds relied on. Only those grounds will normally be considered by the Tribunal when deciding whether to grant leave to appeal. Further grounds will not be considered. Accordingly parties should not serve notices of appeal which indicate that grounds will follow but must decide before serving a notice what grounds they wish to rely on in any appeal.*

44.19 It is therefore extremely important that the application is not submitted until you are in a position to include all the grounds upon which you intend to rely. The practice of solicitors sending off the form and counsel sending the grounds on a later date (within the time limit) is no longer possible.

44 Lodging the permission application
Key points

- An application for permission must be made within 10 working days of service of the adjudicator's determination or five working days if your client is detained.

- The determination is deemed to be served on the second working day after posting unless you can establish by evidence that you received it later.

- The IAT may extend time for appealing if satisfied by 'special circumstances' that it would be unjust not to do so. Special circumstances may include a representative's error. The IAT must give reasons if it declines to extend time.

- You **must** serve all grounds of appeal along with the notice of appeal.

45 Statutory review

45.1 Statutory review is the sole means of challenging the IAT's decision on an application for permission to appeal. (The only exception, under transitional provisions, is where the *adjudicator's* determination was promulgated prior to 9 June 2003, in which case any challenge will be brought by judicial review – see Nationality, Immmigration and Asylum Act 2002 (Commencement No. 4) (Amendment) (No. 2) Order 2003.) Section 101 of the 2002 Act states that:

> *(2) A party to an application to the Tribunal for permission to appeal under subsection (1) may apply to the High Court or, in Scotland, to the Court of Session for a review of the Tribunal's decision on the ground that the Tribunal made an error of law.*
>
> *(3) Where an application is made under subsection (2) –*
>
> > *(a) it shall be determined by a single judge by reference only to written submissions,*
> > *(b) the judge may affirm or reverse the Tribunal's decision,*
> > *(c) the judge's decision shall be final.*

45.2 The rules governing an application for statutory review are set out in Section II of Part 54 of the CPR:

> *APPLICATION FOR REVIEW*
>
> *54.22 (1) An application under section 101(2) of the Act must be made to the Administrative Court.*
>
> *(2) The application must be made by filing an application notice.*
>
> *(3) The applicant must file with the application notice –*
>
> > *(a) the immigration or asylum decision to which the proceedings relate, and any document giving reasons for that decision;*
> > *(b) the grounds of appeal to the adjudicator;*
> > *(c) the adjudicator's determination;*
> > *(d) the grounds of appeal to the Tribunal together with any documents sent with them;*

(e) the Tribunal's determination on the application for permission to appeal; and

(f) any other documents material to the application which were before the adjudicator.

(4) The applicant must also file with the application notice written submissions setting out –

(a) the grounds upon which it is contended that the Tribunal made an error of law; and

(b) reasons in support of those grounds.

TIME LIMIT FOR APPLICATION

54.23 (1) The application notice must be filed not later than 14 days after the applicant is deemed to have received notice of the Tribunal's decision in accordance with rules made under section 106 of the Act.

(2) The court may extend the time limit in paragraph (1) in exceptional circumstances.

(3) An application to extend the time limit must be made in the application notice and supported by written evidence verified by a statement of truth.

SERVICE OF APPLICATION

54.24 (1) The applicant must serve on the Tribunal copies of the application notice and written submissions.

(2) Where an application is for review of a decision by the Tribunal to grant permission to appeal, the applicant must serve on the other party copies of –

(a) the application notice;

(b) the written submissions; and

(c) all the documents filed in support of the application, except for documents which come from or have already been served on that party.

(3) Where documents are required to be served under paragraphs (1) and (2), they must be served as soon as practicable after they are filed.

DETERMINING THE APPLICATION

54.25 (1) The application will be determined by a single judge without a hearing, and by reference only to the written submissions and the documents filed with them.

(2) If the applicant relies on evidence which was not submitted to the adjudicator or the Tribunal, the court will not consider that evidence

unless it is satisfied that there were good reasons why it was not submitted to the adjudicator or the Tribunal.

(3) The court may affirm or reverse the Tribunal's decision.

(4) Where the Tribunal refused permission to appeal, the court will reverse the Tribunal's decision only if it is satisfied that –

> *(a) the Tribunal may have made an error of law; and*
> *(b) either –*
>> *(i) the appeal would have a real prospect of success; or*
>> *(ii) there is some other compelling reason why the appeal should be heard.*

(5) Where the Tribunal granted permission to appeal, the court will reverse the Tribunal's decision only if it is satisfied that –

> *(a) the appeal would have no real prospect of success; and*
> *(b) there is no other compelling reason why the appeal should be heard.*

(6) If the court reverses the Tribunal's decision to refuse permission to appeal

> *(a) the court's order will constitute a grant of permission to appeal to the Tribunal; and*
> *(b) the court may limit the grant of permission to appeal to specific grounds.*

(7) The court's decision shall be final and there shall be no appeal from that decision or renewal of the application.

Where permission to appeal has been granted

45.3   The effect of s.101(2) is that *any* party to the permission application can seek statutory review. This means that you can challenge a decision by the IAT to limit the grant of permission to specific grounds (see para 46.13). Note, however, that the Court itself has a similar power to limit the grant of permission (r.54.25(6)(b) of the CPR).

45.4   Rule 54.25(5) of the CPR confirms that the *respondent* to the appeal before the IAT can seek statutory review of the decision to grant permission to appeal. See chapter 48 for the issues that arise when objecting to the grant of permission to appeal to the Home Office. These apply equally to formulating an application for statutory review.

45.5   The remainder of this chapter focusses on statutory review of a refusal to grant permission to appeal. The procedure, however, is the same when challenging a grant of permission.

Where permission to appeal has been refused

45.6 The 'application notice' on which the application for statutory review should be made is form PF 244 RCJ (Statutory Review). The form states that:

> *If you are seeking to file this application more than 14 days after the deemed date of receipt [of the IAT decision], you must apply for an extension of time. The Court will only extend time in exceptional circumstances. Your grounds for extension of time should be set out in Part B below.*

45.7 The deemed date of receipt is the second working day after posting *unless the contrary is proved* (r.54(5)). If you are filing the application within 14 days of *actual* receipt, you do not need an extension of time as long as you submit evidence that proves the date of receipt. However, it is safer to make an application to extend time in the alternative.

45.8 Part B of the form requires you to state:

> *Grounds upon which it is contended that the Tribunal made an error of law and reasons in support of them.*

> *(This Part should be used to set out grounds for extension of time in which to file the application.)*

45.9 You will normally attach a separate document containing the grounds upon which you seek statutory review.

45.10 The form states that:

> *It is the responsibility of the applicant to serve a copy of this notice on the Immigration Appeal Tribunal as soon as practicable after it has been filed in the Administrative Court.*

45.11 There is a two limb test under r.54.25(4) of the CPR for granting the application for statutory review. The first limb is whether the IAT 'may' have made an error of law. This is presumably intended to correspond with the previous threshold for granting permission to seek judicial review (i.e. an arguable error of law). The second limb mirrors the test that the IAT applies in determining an application for permission to appeal (i.e. real prospect of success or other compelling reason why the appeal should be heard).

45.12 Appeal now lies to the IAT only on a point of law. If the IAT identifies an arguable error of law in the adjudicator's determination, it should not refuse permission to appeal unless it is inevitable that the appeal would fail (see para 43.8).

45.13 One would expect the Court on statutory review to be even more cautious than the IAT about rejecting the application on the basis of the underlying merits of the appeal. In *Tataw*, the Court of Appeal emphasised that where it identified an error of law, it would only be in 'the most plain and obvious case' that it would refuse relief because the appeal had no merit. Brooke LJ noted that he did not have the expertise available to 'the expert appeal tribunal' to consider the merits of the appeal.

45.14 The requirement that the Court determine the application without a hearing means that everything may hinge on how you draft your grounds. Much of the discussion on drafting grounds of appeal to the IAT will also be relevant to the grounds for statutory review. The judge is likely to be less familiar with the IAT's caselaw – so you will have to take more care to set this out – but he will (hopefully) have more time to consider a statutory review application.

45.15 The formal focus at this stage is on the IAT's decision to refuse permission. Your grounds for statutory review may raise:

- arguable errors of law in the adjudicator's determination which ought to have triggered the grant of permission to appeal, *or*
- misdirections or other flaws disclosed by the reasons that the IAT gave for refusing permission, *or*
- both.

45.16 Check whether the IAT's reasons disclose errors: for example, they may demonstrate that it misunderstood the evidence or the adjudicator's determination. They may show that the wrong test was applied, e.g. by refusing permission because it was not satisfied that the error *would* (rather than *might*) have altered the result. As indicated at para 43.4, the standard of the grounds of appeal before the IAT may set the standard of reasoning required of the IAT.

45.17 The IAT has a duty to consider potential challenges that have not been raised in the grounds of appeal only if the point is obvious in the sense that it has a strong prospect of success if it is argued (*Robinson*). This is contrasted with the test of arguability which applies to a challenge that *did* appear in the grounds. (Note that r.17(2) does not limit the IAT's duty to consider obvious points for itself: *Naing*, declining to follow an earlier comment to the contrary.) If a challenge was omitted from the grounds of appeal, your grounds for statutory review will have to demonstrate that the *Robinson* test is met.

45.18 As with an application for statutory review, the IAT must decide whether to grant permission without a hearing (r. 18(1)). It ought not refuse permission to appeal on the strength of points which you might reasonably be able to address at a full hearing. This applies especially where the IAT relies on a point which did not form part of the adjudicator's reasoning. In **Shafiq**, the adjudicator had decided to proceed with the hearing in the absence of the appellant in the face of medical evidence stating that she was unfit to attend. In refusing permission to appeal, the IAT concluded that the adjudicator was entitled to proceed for the reasons that she gave. However, it also took a further point upon which the adjudicator had not relied:

> *The Tribunal further notes that the medical note produced as evidence of the Applicant's inability to attend is written with two different pens and apparently by two different hands.*

45.19 On judicial review, Kay J noted that the implication was that the medical evidence was bogus and concluded that:

> *If points of that kind are going to be taken, particularly at that late stage, the ordinary rules of fairness and natural justice require that there should at least be an opportunity for the Applicant to deal with any such matter.*

45.20 Kay J thought that the IAT would have been entitled to uphold the adjudicator's determination simply on the basis of her reasoning. But having taken a new point on the authenticity of the medical evidence in a manner that was unfair, the decision should be quashed unless it would not have been open to a reasonable member of the IAT to grant permission to appeal.

45.21 Where fresh evidence is submitted to the IAT in support of the application for permission to appeal, the IAT will normally err if it rejects that evidence as a matter of fact for the purposes of refusing permission. In **Kanthasamy**, Stanley Burnton J stated that:

> *It seems to me that a chairman on an appeal where fresh evidence is raised, where he decides to look at that evidence in the exercise of his discretion, generally is not deciding a primary question of fact at the leave to appeal stage. He is deciding whether the new matters put before him are such as to justify the matter going to the full tribunal. That is to say whether there is an arguable ground of appeal, bearing in mind that one of the matters now put forward was not before the adjudicator in the first place and therefore there may have to be either a primary finding of fact by the Immigration Appeal Tribunal, or a remission to the adjudicator, or some other adjudicator, to decide that question of fact... The chairman in this case did not put it in that way. He put it as a primary question. He said in the view of the tribunal it would not put her at risk on return as if*

he were dealing with the matter for the first time.

...

This was a primary finding of fact. It was a finding that there was no risk, which is not the same as saying there is no arguable risk. It seems to me that except in a very clear case, the chairman should, in a case such as this where the matter is being considered for the first time, either say in terms that the new facts put forward do not raise any arguable ground, or give permission to appeal.

45.22 There is no procedure equivalent to the Acknowledgement of Service in judicial review proceedings whereby the respondent may state his grounds for opposing an application for statutory review. At an Administrative Court Users Group meeting on 30 July 2003, mixed views were expressed from the judiciary as to whether, despite the lack of any provision in the CPR, there might be rare cases in which a judge would invite the Home Office's comments. If so, it follows that there may be rare cases in which a judge would seek further information from the applicant before disposing of the application.

45.23 The requirement to determine the application for statutory review without a hearing raises obvious concerns in the context of the gravity of the issues involved and the potential finality of the decision. Amongst other things, it prevents the applicant from addressing the judge's concerns and resolving any misunderstandings through oral argument. The Government responded to these objections by emphasising that any doubt would be resolved in favour of granting the application for statutory review so that the matter could be resolved by the IAT. Baroness Scotland QC (the Minister responsible at the Lord Chancellor's Department) offered the following justification:

I recognise that some may argue 'people only [presently] get permission [to judicially review the IAT's refusal of permission to appeal] once they have made oral argument to a judge [after permission was refused on the papers] and that is the very point of our concern'.

However, that tends to overlook the important point that the judge made the decision to refuse the written application within a system where there is the possibility of the application being renewed orally or adjourn for oral hearing. The decision is taken within the context that the applicant may have a 'second chance' before the judge.

Under statutory review, the context will be different. The judge will be making his decision within a system where there will be no possibility of an oral renewal or adjournment for oral hearing. If the judge decides to refuse the statutory review application, that will be the final decision. There will be nowhere else to take the challenge against the permission decision. Although, of course, any subsequent removal action against the failed asylum seeker could still be the subject of a new judicial review application. But, in respect of challenging the Tribunal permission decision, this is the end of the road.

I am sure the judges will be mindful of this, and as I said previously at Committee, it will weigh heavily indeed upon the judges who make that determination. If there is doubt or a matter needs to be considered, that is an arguable case. I would expect this would be the trigger for the judge to send the case back to the IAT where the matter can be resolved properly.
(letter to Lord Joffe, 29 October 2002)

Fresh evidence in statutory review

45.24 Rule 54.25(2) of the CPR states that the Court 'will not' consider fresh evidence on an application for statutory review unless there is a good reason why it was not submitted before the adjudicator or the IAT. This is repeated in the application notice. The provision reflects the old r.18(11) of the 2000 Rules which purported to relieve the IAT of any duty to consider fresh evidence absent a good reason why it was not adduced before the adjudicator. However, that provision was inconsistent with *Haile* and has been omitted from the present Rules (para 43.28). Taken literally, r.53.25(2) of the CPR is even stricter than the old r.18(11) of the 2000 Rules in that it mandates rather than permits the Court to disregard such evidence.

45.25 This raises manifest dangers given that this remedy is intended to be one of last resort. The restriction on considering fresh evidence does not appear in the 2002 Act (unlike the requirement to determine the application on the papers) and comes only from the CPR.

45.26 In a fundamental rights case where there is no good reason for not having adduced evidence earlier but the interests of justice nevertheless require that it be considered (as in *Haile*), you may argue that too strict an interpretation of r.54(25)(2) of the CPR would constitute an unlawful fetter on the Court's powers. However, this argument should only be required if it is impossible to interpret the provision consistently with the requirements of justice.

45.27 Where relevant and available evidence was not adduced before the adjudicator or the IAT, the reason will often be error by the representative rather than error by the appellant personally (as in *Haile*). The IAT has been prepared, when interpreting similar provisions of the procedure rules, to focus on the conduct and capabilities of the appellant rather that her representatives (see paras 4.24, 42.79, 46.69). You may therefore argue that injustice can be avoided in a *Haile* type situation by focussing on whether the applicant rather than her representative had a good reason for not having adduced the evidence: it will usually have been reasonable for her to rely on her representatives to conduct proceedings properly.

The decision

45.28 If the Court allows the application for statutory review, the Court's order will have the effect of granting permission to appeal to the IAT. There is no scope for the Court to remit the matter to the IAT for reconsideration of the permission application.

45.29 A decision *refusing* statutory review of a refusal of permission to appeal by the IAT will be served only on the Home Office. The Home Office is then responsible for serving it on your client. Rule 54.26(2–3) of the CPR states that:

> *(2) Where –*
>
> > *(a) the application relates, in whole or in part, to a claim for asylum;*
> > *(b) the Tribunal refused permission to appeal; and*
> > *(c) the court affirms the Tribunal's decision,*
> >
> > *the court will send a copy of its order to the Secretary of State, who must serve the order on the applicant.*
>
> *(3) Where the Secretary of State has served an order in accordance with paragraph (2), he must notify the court on what date and by what method the order was served.*

45.30 A similar procedure was introduced for refusals of permission to appeal by the IAT by the Immigration and Asylum Appeals (Procedure) (Amendment) Rules 2001. However, it has not been replicated in the current Rules. Under the old procedure, the Home Office served a very small proportion of such decisions personally rather than by post where it planned to detain the appellant immediately with a view to removing them. Presumably, the intention of r.54.26 of the CPR is to permit a similar practice.

45.31 You will have to warn your client of the risk that she may be detained if the Home Office serves the decision on her personally. Some indicator of the risk may be provided by any unusual delay in receiving the decision. Your client should be given advice about what to do if she is detained and provided with emergency contact numbers.

45.32 The Administrative Court Users Group was informed on 20 March 2003 by Maurice Kay J, the Lead Judge of the Administrative Court, that as statutory review of a refusal of permission to appeal would constitute a remedy of last resort, this may mean that decisions of the Court refusing the application would tend to be far longer than the decisions on written permission applications for judicial review.

45.33 One view of the effect of s.101 is that if a judge refuses statutory review, the only remedy left is an application to the European Court in Strasbourg. Given that a significant proportion of refusals of permission on the papers under the old judicial review procedure were subsequently overturned on renewal, this has the potential to create a sizable increase in business for the Strasbourg Court (at least if applicants could find competent representatives able to fund the initial application).

45.34 Baroness Scotland QC stated that any subsequent removal action by the Home Office against the claimant could still be the subject of a new judicial review application (above). If you receive a refusal of statutory review which you believe to be wrong (and especially if the application has been refused on the basis of a misunderstanding resulting from the absence of a hearing), you should seek specialist advice immediately.

45 Statutory review
Key points

- The only means of challenging the IAT's decision on an application for permission to appeal is by statutory review.

- The application must be made within 14 days of deemed receipt of the IAT's decision, failing which you will have to apply for an extension of time.

- The criteria for granting statutory review of a refusal of permission to appeal are that:

  ☐ the IAT 'may' have erred in law, *and*
  ☐ the appeal has a real prospect of success or there is some other compelling reason why the appeal should be heard.

- The requirement that the Court determine the application without a hearing means that everything may hinge on how you draft your grounds.

- The challenge may be directed to

  ☐ arguable errors of law in the adjudicator's determination which ought to have triggered the grant of permission to appeal, *and/or*
  ☐ misdirections or other flaws disclosed by the reasons that the IAT gave for refusing permission.

- Fairness requires that the IAT should not refuse permission to appeal on the basis of points which the appellant might have been able to address at a hearing, especially if they did not form part of the adjudicator's reasoning. Permission should not normally be refused on the basis of adverse findings of fact as to fresh evidence.

- Where the refusal of statutory review will bring a final end to the proceedings, the judge should resolve any doubt in favour of the applicant.

- Rule 54.25(2) of the CPR states that the Court 'will not' consider fresh evidence on an application for statutory review unless there is a good reason why it was not submitted. An overly literal or rigid interpretation of this provision may conflict with the interests of justice. The Court should be urged to focus on the conduct of the applicant personally rather than on her representatives.

- A decision refusing statutory review of a refusal of permission to appeal to the IAT will be served on the Home Office which is then responsible for serving it on your client: warn her of the risk that she may be detained when the decision is served and provide emergency numbers.

- If the decision appears to be wrong, you should seek specialist advice immediately.

- Statutory review can also be used to challenge a decision to grant permission limited to specific grounds and a decision to grant permission to appeal to the Home Office.

46 Preparing for the hearing

46.1   The first thing you have to decide is what you want (or what you would accept) out of the appeal. What you aim to achieve will influence how you prepare the appeal.

46.2   Section 102 of the 2002 Act provides that:

> *(1) On an appeal under section 101 the Immigration Appeal Tribunal may –*
>
>> *(a) affirm the adjudicator's decision;*
>> *(b) make any decision which the adjudicator could have made;*
>> *(c) remit the appeal to an adjudicator;*
>> *(d) affirm a direction given by the adjudicator under section 87;*
>> *(e) vary a direction given by the adjudicator under that section;*
>> *(f) give any direction which the adjudicator could have given under that section.*
>
> *...*
>
> *(4) In remitting an appeal to an adjudicator under subsection (1)(c) the Tribunal may, in particular-*
>
>> *(a) require the adjudicator to determine the appeal in accordance with directions of the Tribunal;*
>> *(b) require the adjudicator to take additional evidence with a view to the appeal being determined by the Tribunal.*

What to aim for

46.3   Consider at an early stage whether to invite the IAT to decide the appeal itself or just to remit it to the same or a different adjudicator. Plainly, the best result is for the IAT to allow your appeal outright, but that will often be unrealistic.

46.4   It will be most realistic where the adjudicator has made credibility findings in your favour. If so, your challenge will usually be that he applied the law wrongly or that his assessment of present risk is flawed. As long as further oral evidence is not required, the appeal should be capable of determination by the IAT on the basis of the documentary evidence and the adjudicator's findings on the oral evidence. Indeed, any suggestion of remittal for a fresh hearing should normally be strongly opposed if you won a positive credibility finding from the adjudicator. There should be no justification for making your client prove his credibility all over again simply because the adjudicator made errors in other aspects of his determination.

46.5 In other circumstances, remittal will be preferable to the IAT deciding the appeal itself. The most obvious example is where your client has been denied a hearing before the adjudicator, for example because the adjudicator unjustifiably determined the appeal without a hearing. You would not usually want the IAT to decide the appeal itself because your client would be unfairly deprived of a first instance hearing and the only possibility of appeal would be to the Court of Appeal.

46.6 If you are challenging an adverse credibility finding, you have to decide whether it is realistic to invite the IAT to reverse the credibility finding without hearing evidence. It might be realistic where the sole basis for the adverse credibility finding was alleged inconsistency between your client's account and the country evidence. If you can show that the adjudicator misunderstood the country evidence upon which he relied, and particularly if the Home Office can point to no other significant doubt as to credibility, you may argue that there is no need for oral evidence to be reheard.

46.7 You may argue in the alternative that the appeal should be allowed outright or, failing that, remitted. The IAT may be prepared to consider these alternatives at the outset of the hearing. But if deciding the appeal itself will involve consideration of substantial submissions and documentary evidence, it may indicate that while it is prepared to embark on the task, there is no guarantee that it will end in the appeal being allowed, in which case the alternative is more likely to be dismissal rather than remittal. You must be clear at the outset of the basis upon which the IAT is going to decide the appeal itself (e.g. that the appellant's account is accepted).

46.8 In other cases, it will not be realistic to substitute a positive credibility finding without hearing further oral evidence, for example where the adjudicator's adverse credibility finding is flawed because he adopted an unfair approach at the hearing, e.g. by rejecting concerns about the interpreter or questioning the appellant in a one-sided manner. Where oral evidence has to be reheard, remittal will normally be preferable so that the appellant is not denied a tier of appeal. In *Karunakaran (IAT)*, the IAT said that:

[I]t is not in general terms satisfactory that an appellate Tribunal should become the effective decision maker by reason of matters arising from the conduct of the appeal before the adjudicator which render it necessary that the appeal be completely reheard.

46.9 The IAT now tends to remit appeals wherever it would otherwise have to hear substantial factual evidence. (It is more ready to hear expert evidence.)

46.10 It will be unusual to seek remittal to the same adjudicator since the fact that he has already dismissed your appeal may make it difficult for him to approach a second hearing with an open mind. Circumstances where you might ask for remittal to the same adjudicator include where he has held that he is bound by IAT authority to dismiss your appeal, and where you rely upon fresh evidence but do not dispute the original findings. If it is not necessary to rehear the original oral evidence, remittal to the same adjudicator should preserve a positive credibility finding. But it might well be appropriate to ask the IAT to decide the appeal itself in those circumstances.

The grant of permission

46.11 Rule 18(7) provides that:

Where the Tribunal grants permission to appeal –

(a) its determination must indicate the grounds upon which permission to appeal is granted; and

(b) the appellate authority must serve on the respondent, together with the determination, a copy of the application notice and the documents which were attached to it.

46.12 Rule 18(6) states that 'The Tribunal's determination must include its reasons, which may be in summary form.' Decisions granting leave vary considerably in what they offer by way of reasons. Sometimes, they will simply state that 'the grounds merit further consideration'. Other decisions will identify which issues most concerned the IAT, and may offer what is in effect a reasoned preliminary view.

Limited permission

46.13 Rule 18(5) states that:

Where the Tribunal grants permission to appeal it may limit the permission to one or more of the grounds of appeal specified in the application.

46.14 If the IAT grants limited permission, consider firstly whether you remain satisfied that the remaining grounds are arguable and secondly, how important the remaining grounds are to the development of your appeal. If you conclude that the grounds on which permission was refused are both arguable and important, the choice of procedure by which to seek a reconsideration of your grounds is not straightforward.

46.15 By r.20(1), the IAT can grant an appellant permission to vary his grounds (see para 46.74 below) but r.20(2) states that:

> Where the Tribunal has refused permission to appeal on any ground, it must not grant permission to vary the grounds of appeal to include that ground unless it is satisfied that, because of special circumstances, it would be unjust not to allow the variation.

46.16 In *Gokteke*, permission to appeal had been granted on human rights grounds but refused on asylum grounds. No reason was given for the refusal of permission on the asylum grounds. The appellant gave notice that he would seek to renew his asylum grounds at the full hearing because he maintained that they were arguable. The IAT held that this did not constitute a reason for 'undermining' the refusal of permission, adding that:

> We would emphasise that we do not decide that it would, in this case or in any other, have been impossible to raise further grounds of appeal: but the present application, merely asserting the original purpose for submitting the original grounds, was not, in our view, one which in fairness to the Presenting Officer ought to have been allowed to be pursued. We emphasise that the basis of that conclusion is simply that the letter [from the appellant] which we had gives no reason at all for undermining the [refusal of permission]. If there had been a reason, we should perhaps have considered it.

46.17 It would appear therefore that the IAT does not accept that a submission that the grounds are arguable so that the Chairman was wrong to refuse permission can constitute a valid reason for renewing these grounds at the full hearing. The result might have been different if, for example, some procedural irregularity could be shown in the consideration of the permission application or if reasons had been given for refusing permission which disclosed some misunderstanding or misdirection. However, the latter is obviously unfeasible where no reasons have been given in respect of the grounds on which permission was refused (as was the case in *Gokteke*). You might argue that the failure to give reasons breaches r.18(6) and so amounts to 'special circumstances' justifying a reconsideration of these grounds at the full hearing.

46.18 At time of writing, permission has been granted in **Gokteke** to judicially review the IAT's refusal to entertain the application to renew the grounds on which permission was refused. Pending an authoritative ruling, you have something of a dilemma in deciding whether to apply to the IAT to vary your grounds or to seek statutory review of the decision to grant only limited permission (see chapter 45). If you do not apply for statutory review, the time limit will usually have expired by the time the IAT considers your variation application. The safest advice at present must be to seek statutory review. The procedure is not restricted to cases in which you were refused permission to appeal outright. However, you should explain in your grounds for statutory review why it is necessary to proceed in this way rather than using the variation procedure under r.20.

Starred appeals

46.19 If the IAT has decided to 'star' the appeal, you should receive notification of this with the grant of leave, together with the issues which the IAT wishes to use your appeal to resolve. The status of starred determinations is discussed in chapter 29. A starred determination is likely to have considerable implications for many other cases. ILPA and the RLG will welcome advance notice of a coming starred appeal, and other representatives should be happy to offer input in view of the potential ramifications.

46.20 The decision to star the appeal does not necessarily mean that the IAT will decide your individual appeal itself rather than remitting it. On at least one occasion, the IAT has also starred the appeal where it considers the individual case to be doomed to failure (**Noruwa**).

Remittal without a hearing

46.21 Rule 22 provides that:

> (1) The Tribunal may remit an appeal to an adjudicator for him to determine in accordance with any directions given by the Tribunal.

> (2) The power in paragraph (1) may be exercised by a legally qualified member of the Tribunal without a hearing.

46.22 Note that the provision does not expressly require the consent of either party in order to remit without a hearing. However, fairness ought to require at least the opportunity to make representations on the correct disposal and probably a hearing. There is of course no objection to the power being authorised if the parties consent.

46.23 That is reflected by the procedure by which the IAT has invited agreed remittals. The notice states that:

> *The Chairman is of the view that this is a case which is suitable for a remittal for a fresh hearing by another adjudicator. The Chairman would be grateful if you would consider this proposal, and, if you do not agree, inform the Tribunal of your objections within fourteen days of the date of this letter. If we do not hear from you within fourteen days, the Chairman will assume that you are in agreement, and a determination will be issued accordingly. If there is an objection to the Chairman's proposal, the matter will be listed.*
> (TRIB 12, v.2.09)

46.24 Your stance will be determined by the considerations set out above. The provisional view that the IAT has formed should be considered carefully. (The member who granted permission may not sit on the division that hears your appeal, but the tribunal may give weight to the view that he formed.) Remittal may be all you want. But if you take a firm view that the appeal should be allowed outright, do not be dissuaded from rejecting the summary remittal offered.

Seeking a pre-hearing review or disposal by consent

46.25 Even if the summary procedure is not suggested, the reasons for granting leave may point towards remittal. You can take the initiative in seeking to dispose of the appeal without a full hearing. The first step ought to be to ask the Home Office whether it will accept remittal. However, as with adjudicator appeals, you are unlikely to persuade anyone at the Home Office to give a sensible answer until the appeal is allocated to a HOPO shortly before the hearing. This problem may be best overcome by asking the IAT to list the matter for a mention accompanied by an explanation of the issues that you propose to use the mention hearing to clarify or resolve. The Home Office will then be obliged to adopt some position.

46.26 If no view is expressed by the IAT when granting leave, you will have no advance warning of how the IAT intends to conduct the hearing. This can be a serious problem. There are many cases where the appropriate disposal is not clear-cut. You may consider the appeal capable of being decided by the IAT, but you would not object to remittal – or vice versa. The tribunal members might enter the hearing room and indicate a preference for remittal which you accept. Or they might have determined that they will not only decide it themselves but conduct an exhaustive review of the law and country evidence. You ought to receive notice with the grant of leave if the appeal is formally starred, but there are many unstarred appeals where it gives wide-ranging legal and factual guidance.

46.27 If you do not have advance notice of its approach, you may be in genuine doubt about whether your hearing will last a couple of minutes or several hours, and correspondingly in doubt about the degree of preparation it is appropriate to undertake. This is not only frustrating. It is wasteful of public funds if extensive bundles and submissions are prepared in order to argue the merits of an appeal which ends up being remitted in a five minute hearing.

46.28 Again, you can try to resolve this by asking the IAT to list the hearing for a mention in order to determine how the hearing will be conducted. If the IAT favours remittal and the parties agree, the matter can be disposed of there and then. If not, you can ask for warning of any specific plans to use the appeal to examine any particular issue. This should avoid you being taken by surprise by a decision to treat the appeal as a test case on a recurring issue. (If you think it appropriate, you may actually propose that the IAT treats the matter as a test case.) As discussed above, it also has the important benefit that the Home Office can be compelled to take a view and let you know what it is. Since skeleton arguments are not required by the IAT's standard directions, you may otherwise have no indication of the respondent's position on your appeal until the start of the hearing.

46.29 HOPOs at IAT level are usually more willing and able to engage in sensible discussion about the issues and appropriate disposal of the appeal than are those who represent the Home Office at adjudicator level. You should always try to speak to the HOPO once he is briefed (usually a day or two before the hearing). It may be possible to reach an agreement even at this late stage, but it may then be more difficult to obtain the IAT's approval in time to avoid a hearing.

46.30 In *Senigeur*, the IAT indicated that where the parties were agreed in advance to seek remittal, that agreement 'should be submitted in advance in the form of a consent order'. If they did not obtain the IAT's consent in advance, 'they should not count on the outcome being in accordance with any agreement they may have reached' and 'they must not excuse themselves from attendance, without getting confirmation from a chairman that this is acceptable'.

'Keeping in touch'

46.31 Practice Direction No 4 is self-explanatory in this regard:

> *(7): Keeping in touch with the Tribunal*
>
> (i) *All parties to appeals and their representatives must provide an address for service and are reminded that unless they notify the Tribunal of any change of address documents sent to the address for service are deemed to have been properly served (r.47).*
>
> (ii) *Individual appellants or respondents must also keep in touch with their representatives. If they fail to do so and as a result do not receive any material documents, the Tribunal will not regard such non-receipt as a good excuse for any action or inaction.*
>
> (iii) *The Tribunal is obliged to proceed with a hearing in the absence of a party where no satisfactory explanation has been provided for the absence [now r.44(1)]. A failure to attend because documents have not been received although no change of address has been notified will not be regarded as a satisfactory explanation.*

46.32 Note also in this regard r.46(6-8) – para 4.28.

Notice of hearing and standard directions

46.33 Along with the grant of permission, you should receive a notice of hearing. The IAT, unlike adjudicators, regularly hears appeals by video link pursuant to r.38(5)(h). If you are not in London and a video link has not been directed, you may wish to apply for one. You will also receive the TRIB 14 forms which contain standard directions. Form TRIB 14b states:

> 1 *This form must be completed and returned within 14 days.*
>
> 2 *What is your TIME ESTIMATE for this appeal?*
>
> 3 *Are you seeking PERMISSION to CALL the CLAIMANT or any WITNESS(ES) to give oral evidence? If so give their names. If you are seeking permission to call any oral evidence, you MUST ENCLOSE FULL WITNESS STATEMENTS WITH THIS FORM, and explain why you think the Tribunal should hear oral evidence.*
>
> 4 *Would an interpreter be required for any of these witnesses if permission were granted? If so, state the language/dialect.*

What is your time estimate?

46.34 As indicated at para 46.27, you may be in genuine doubt whether the hearing will last minutes or hours. If an application to call oral evidence is outstanding, the difficulties in giving an accurate time estimate are exacerbated further.

46.35 The best advice is to give an estimate based on how you propose to conduct the hearing and to state that basis: for example, '30 minutes, based on our request for remittal for fresh hearing' or '3 hours, as we are inviting the IAT to determine the appeal itself and hear oral evidence'.

Are you seeking permission to call any witnesses?

46.36 This can also be a difficult decision (see below). If you are briefing an advocate for the hearing, you ought to obtain his input before answering it as it may be fundamental to how the appeal is run.

46.37 Practice Direction No 1 states that:

1   *It will be unusual for an appellant or respondent to be permitted to give evidence before the Tribunal.*

2   *Interpreters will not be provided in hearings before the Tribunal unless a witness who has been granted leave to give evidence requires his or her evidence to be given with the assistance of an interpreter. 'Witness' includes a party or any other person who is to give evidence.*

3   *A request to call evidence and for an interpreter must be made at the earliest possible opportunity (preferably in the application for leave to appeal) and in any event not later than 14 days before the hearing.*

4   *Reasons must always be given for the request which may need to be dealt with in a directions hearing. If no reasons are given, the request will be refused.*

46.38 While the Practice Direction countenances an application being made up to 14 days before the hearing, you should strive to comply with the direction in the TRIB 14 to make your application and provide witness statements within 14 days of receipt of the form.

46.39 If you fail to give your reasons for wishing to call oral evidence, you will almost certainly be refused permission to do so. The ability to consider fresh evidence in the interests of justice in an asylum/human rights appeal, even where the jurisdiction is restricted to points of law, is discussed at para 43.18.

46.40 The most obvious case in which you would wish to lead further evidence from the appellant is where she has learnt of material facts of which she was unaware when she gave evidence before the adjudicator. The relevant facts should be set out in the witness statement. You should not therefore actually need your client to give oral evidence in order to put the new facts in evidence. However, where credibility is in issue, then as with adjudicator hearings, you will normally want to offer her for cross-examination.

46.41 Another example is where you have complained that the adjudicator relied upon some matter without giving notice so that the appellant was denied the opportunity to deal with his concern during her evidence. You will often want to submit a supplementary witness statement offering the explanation and offer the witness for cross-examination.

46.42 You should state in your application to call oral evidence if permission is sought simply to make the witness available for cross-examination or questions from the tribunal. If the IAT then refuses the application, and the HOPO does not make representations in support of your application, it cannot be held against you when considering the credibility of the witness statement that the further evidence was not subject to cross-examination.

46.43 The IAT has in the past been prepared to hear oral evidence from an appellant who was found credible by the adjudicator in order to fill gaps in his evidence (e.g. *Yesil*). However, there is sometimes a risk in leading further evidence that the IAT will make an adverse credibility finding in respect of the further evidence which it may then use to cast doubt upon the adjudicator's positive credibility finding in respect of the rest of it. The HOPO may also attempt to cross-examine on matters which were accepted by the adjudicator (though you will argue that cross-examination should be restricted to the fresh evidence). Where you have a positive credibility finding from the adjudicator, you should therefore consider carefully whether the fresh evidence which the witness can give justifies any risk to the adjudicator's positive credibility finding.

46.44 Your primary argument may be that there is no need for the IAT to hear oral evidence in order to reverse the adjudicator's decision. The following are examples:

- You maintain that you can show by reference to extraneous evidence that each point taken by the adjudicator on credibility was bad.
- A dispute may have arisen about the extent to which credibility was

in issue at the hearing, whether evidence was challenged by the HOPO, or as to the adjudicator's recording of the evidence.

- The parties may disagree as to what credibility finding the adjudicator actually reached in his determination.

46.45 Yet another example is where the appellant did not give oral evidence before the adjudicator. The adjudicator's determination will be flawed if he regarded that fact alone as pointing towards an adverse credibility finding (para 30.12). But he may have taken other adverse points upon which he claimed he was entitled to rely in the absence of oral evidence.

46.46 While your primary argument in each of these cases may be that the appeal should be allowed outright with no need for further oral evidence, you may be worried that the IAT might disagree, and hold against you your failure to seek to call oral evidence to resolve the disputed points. The IAT will normally remit an appeal if substantial oral evidence would otherwise need to be heard, but you cannot guarantee in advance that it will take this course. Because the IAT does not book interpreters for hearings unless it has granted permission to call oral evidence, it will not normally be possible for oral evidence to be heard absent prior application.

46.47 If you think that the absence of an application to call oral evidence may be held against you, you should make it. But state in the application that your primary submission is that the appeal can be allowed without oral evidence, and that your application is designed to assist the IAT by giving it the option of hearing oral evidence should it consider that necessary, and should it not wish to remit the appeal. Regardless of the result of the application, you will have covered the appellant against any criticism that she did not offer further evidence.

46.48 Since the IAT does not routinely book interpreters for hearings, you need not usually worry that the IAT will reverse its decision at the hearing and ask to hear oral evidence for which your client is not prepared (unless, of course, she speaks good English).

46.49 Where an adjudicator has rejected expert evidence (whether medical or country), it is often valuable to submit a supplementary expert report to address the adjudicator's reasons. You may also wish to seek to call oral evidence from your expert. The same may apply where you are adducing expert evidence for the first time before the IAT.

46.50 See chapter 48 for circumstances in which you would apply to lead oral evidence as the respondent to a Home Office appeal.

Bundles of the evidence that was before the adjudicator

46.51 The standard directions currently being issued with the notice of hearing require that the parties:

> serve all other parties and in triplicate on the Tribunal a full, paginated bundle containing all the documents on which you ask the Tribunal to rely, even if you think they were available to the Adjudicator. The only documents that you do not need to send are the Home Office refusal letter or explanatory statement, the Adjudicator's determination, Notice of Appeal to the Tribunal, and the Tribunal's Grant of Permission.

46.52 You will often find that the Chairman has access to the full adjudicator file at the hearing, and sometimes he will be willing to look in it where it becomes necessary to consider a document that was not included in the parties' bundles. *But you must not rely on this.* It is important in order to safeguard your client that you include in the bundle everything which is relevant to the appeal.

46.53 Practice Direction No 1 states that 'only relevant pages of country reports need be served' (para 3). This can assist greatly in keeping down the size of the bundles. However, despite the express permission to use extracts, you should be careful that the choice of extract does not leave you open to accusations of misleading the IAT. In particular, if another part of the report qualifies the extract upon which you rely, you should not include one without the other.

46.54 If one of your grounds of appeal is that there was no evidence before the adjudicator which could support one of his findings, then deciding the contents of the bundle can be particularly problematic. Some courts have criticised representatives for not including everything which was before court below, regardless of whether they have any intention of referring to it specifically. The rationale for this criticism is as follows: if your case is that there was no evidence before an adjudicator to support a finding, you must present all the evidence which was before the adjudicator in order to establish that none of it is capable of supporting the conclusion. The opposing view is that the hearings are adversarial and if the Home Office claims that there was evidence to support the adjudicator's finding, it should submit that evidence in its own bundle. In the absence of judicial guidance, it is safer to include all the material in your own bundle.

46.55 If you decide to include all or much of the material which was before the adjudicator, and the adjudicator has referred extensively in his determination to the pagination of the bundles which were before him, it is helpful to everyone if you simply submit the bundles in the same form (i.e. with the same pagination) as was before the adjudicator.

46.56 Where you did not represent the client before the adjudicator, you may experience difficulty in extracting from the previous representatives copies of the evidence which was submitted by each party – or in getting a clear indication of which parts of the material with which you have been provided was actually submitted in evidence. The problem can be particularly acute if the appellant was represented by counsel and the solicitor is not entirely sure what counsel submitted.

46.57 If you are not confident that you have the correct material either from the previous solicitor or counsel, you can write to the Home Office asking for copies from its file and (if necessary) offering to pay photocopying costs. However, Home Office files are often equally fallible and the best option is to persuade the IAA to give you access to the material, again offering to pay photocopying costs. If the IAA refuses, then at least you cannot be blamed if you submit in good faith material which turns out not to have been before the adjudicator.

46.58 The present TRIB 14 does not state any time limit within which the bundle must be lodged. The previous version of the form required the appellant to serve a bundle not less than 14 days before the hearing and the respondent not less than seven days. The IAT has indicated orally to the author that it now expects each party to submit its bundle not less than 14 days before the hearing. Although there is presently nothing in writing to that effect, the TRIB 14 is apparently in the process of being amended to reflect this. Though the prospects of a HOPO looking at your bundle 14 days before the hearing are remote, it is nevertheless important to submit it within this time frame. Some divisions of the IAT used to apply the time limit strictly, although it is unclear whether they can continue to do so while no clear time limit is stated in the standard directions. You should check for yourself the present position in this respect.

Fresh documentary evidence

46.59 Rule 21(2–4) governs the submission of evidence which was not before the adjudicator:

> (2) If a party wishes to ask the Tribunal to consider evidence which was not submitted to the adjudicator, he must file with the appellate authority and serve on the other party written notice to that effect, which must –

> *(a) indicate the nature of the evidence; and*
>
> *(b) explain why it was not submitted to the adjudicator.*
>
> *(3) A notice under paragraph (2) must be filed and served as soon as practicable after the parties have been notified that permission to appeal has been granted.*
>
> *(4) If the Tribunal decides to admit additional evidence, it may give directions as to –*
>
> *(a) the manner in which; and*
> *(b) the time by which,*
>
> *the evidence is to be given or filed.*

46.60 Refer to the above discussion for submitting fresh evidence from witnesses. The most obvious circumstance in which you will have to submit further documentary evidence is to deal with developments in the country of origin. Another common scenario is where previous representatives handled the adjudicator appeal and submitted inadequate country evidence.

46.61 Fresh evidence may also be required to meet an unforeseen point taken by the adjudicator. The primary submission may be that he should not have taken the point at all, but the IAT may think that now you are aware of the point, you ought to respond. It can only add to your case if it can be shown that the point was anyway a bad one. Where, for example, the adjudicator has claimed that an aspect of the appellant's account was so implausible that it could not have happened, country or expert evidence can be submitted to refute this.

46.62 If you are complaining about the manner in which the hearing was conducted, you will have to submit evidence of how it was conducted unless this is apparent from the determination or record of proceedings. (You should normally have submitted such evidence with the application for permission to appeal.)

46.63 Remember that unlike material which was before the adjudicator, you *must* give written notice of an application to adduce the fresh evidence in accordance with r.21(2). With your notice, you should explain the relevance of the evidence and (unless it is obvious) why it was not submitted prior to the hearing.

Failure to comply with rules or directions on submission of evidence

46.64 The provision to the effect that late evidence should not be considered absent good reason (r.48(5)) is discussed at para 27.8.

46.65 The IAT can however be considerably stricter in dealing with late evidence than many adjudicators. PD No 4, para 6(ii) states that:

> *Any evidence (including witness statements) which is not submitted in accordance with the time limits set out in the TRIB 14 Directions will not be considered by the Tribunal unless the party seeking to make use of it establishes a good reason why he was in default. Parties must always disclose any such evidence to the Tribunal and any other party as soon as possible and must never wait until the hearing.*

46.66 As discussed above, the present TRIB 14 directions contain no express time limit for submission of evidence (other than witness statements where permission is sought to lead oral evidence). The IAT has generally taken a common sense view (at least in the absence of any objection from the opposing party) and accepted evidence as submitted in accordance with r.21 so long as it is submitted at least 14 days before the hearing (the time limit traditionally applied to submission of bundles). This avoids having to submit evidence piecemeal to the IAT. However, this has not been formally confirmed by the IAT, so the safer course must be to submit any fresh evidence as soon as you receive it and then submit it again in a paginated bundle 14 days before the hearing.

46.67 In *Macharia*, the Court of Appeal held that the IAT did not have power to grant an application to submit fresh evidence where written notice had not been provided. This applies regardless of whether the evidence is in the public domain. However late you submit the evidence, it must be accompanied by a written notice. If you are within 14 days of the hearing, you must submit the fresh evidence *immediately* with the written notice. Even if you get the evidence the day before the hearing, submit it with a written notice rather than bringing it to the hearing. If you wait until the hearing, the IAT will have no power to grant your application to submit the evidence – regardless of good reason – unless it adjourns in order to enable r.21(2) to be complied with.

46.68 If evidence is submitted late, you must also show that there is a good reason for admitting it. 'Good reason' may include lack of prejudice to the Home Office (and the IAT) or the importance of the evidence or a combination of the two. You will often argue absence of prejudice because the evidence would not have been considered by the

HOPO any earlier, however early you had submitted it. Call the HOPO Unit the day after you have served the bundles/evidence and enquire about the HOPO's views. If the HOPO says it will be some time before he looks at it or no HOPO has been allocated, you have precluded the HOPO from arguing at the hearing that he was prejudiced by late service (see also para 27.13). You should put forward any mitigating circumstances to the IAT in a covering letter with the evidence.

46.69 The IAT has indicated a willingness to make allowance for representatives' mistakes. In *Shanthakunavadivel*, the IAT said that:

> *The phrase 'as soon as practical...' is evidently elastic and might no doubt be interpreted to cover a situation where early notice is not given because a party, through no fault of his own, is not properly represented; it is also apt to cover the situation of documents which come into existence only shortly before a hearing.*

46.70 Of greatest weight should be the importance of the evidence. Point to Lord Woolf's guidance in *Macharia* to the effect that particularly where the evidence is being submitted on behalf of the asylum seeker rather than the Home Office, the IAT should take such procedural steps as are necessary to admit important evidence where justice required it (see also at para 8.40).

The Record of Proceedings

46.71 Rule 21(1) states that:

> *The Tribunal may consider as evidence any note or record made by the adjudicator of any hearing before him in connection with the appeal.*

46.72 The chairman who grants leave may direct that the record of proceedings is provided to the parties. If the chairman has not so directed, you should normally request it if it is potentially relevant, most usually because there is some issue about what occurred at the hearing before the adjudicator.

46.73 If you do not accept that the record of proceedings is accurate in some material respect, you will need to establish this. In *Goonawardena*, the IAT gave the following guidance:

> *In the Tribunal's view where any appeal to the Tribunal is brought on the basis of a challenge or amendment to the record of proceedings the following procedure should be adopted:*
>
> *(1) A typescript version of the proposed amendment should be drawn-up by the appellant or his or her advisers;*

(2) The proposed amendment should be supported by an original note taken at the proceedings, a minute on the file or an affidavit [presumably now a witness statement];

(3) Both the amendment and the supporting documentation should be served on all other parties to the appeal and submitted as a courtesy to the adjudicator through the usual channels, and;

(4) The respondent to the appeal should cause any amendment of his own to be drawn-up in typescript and supported in like fashion, served on the appellant and submitted as a courtesy to the adjudicator.

Obviously the fourth step in the proceedings would only be taken where the respondent neither agrees with the record of proceeding nor the proposed amendment by the other side. It is of course open to a respondent to indicate both to the other side and the Tribunal that the amendment is resisted and that the record of proceedings is accurate.

Variation of grounds

46.74 By r.20(1),

A party may vary his grounds only with the permission of the Tribunal.

46.75 See para 46.13 above for applying to vary grounds in order to renew grounds upon which you have been refused permission.

46.76 The procedure for applying to vary your grounds of appeal is set out in PD No 4, para 4:

(i) *An appellant who wishes to vary his grounds of appeal must make an application to the Tribunal to do so.*

(ii) *Such an application must be in writing, must set out the variation sought, must be made as soon as practicable after leave to appeal was granted and in any event not later than 21 days before the date fixed for the hearing of the appeal and must be served on any other party to the appeal.*

(iii) *Any party who wishes to object to such an application must do so in writing within 7 days of receipt of the application and must give reasons for such objection.*

(iv) *The Tribunal will decide on the material submitted without an oral hearing whether the application should be granted.*

(v) *If for good reason the application cannot be made in accordance with subpara (ii) above, the Tribunal at the hearing may*

> *decide to permit a variation but will not do so unless notice is given to the Tribunal and to any other party as soon as practicable.*

46.77 The intention of the Practice Direction appears to be to discourage parties arguing, without prior notice, points which they did not raise in their grounds of appeal. If you are using an advocate not previously involved in the case, this is yet another reason why it is important to brief him well in advance, and to ensure that the advocate reviews the grounds of appeal.

46.78 Not every new argument, of course, constitutes a new ground of appeal. You do not need to apply to vary simply to elaborate on a contention that is present in the grounds. One would hope that the procedure would be applied sufficiently flexibly to prevent injustice, particularly where asylum seekers are concerned.

46.79 If you wish to raise a new ground and have not complied with the Practice Direction, you will have to argue, as with late evidence, some combination of the importance and merits of the point, and absence of prejudice to the other side. You may wish to refer to the Court of Appeal's decision in *Haile* in support of the proposition that asylum seekers should not suffer the consequences of mistakes by their lawyers where this would be unjust to the asylum seeker. You may in the alternative be able to argue that the original grounds of appeal are sufficiently wide to embrace your new submission.

Skeleton arguments

46.80 Skeleton arguments for adjudicator hearings are addressed at chapter 28. Unlike adjudicator appeals, the standard directions from the IAT require skeleton arguments from neither appellant nor respondent.

46.81 There will often be less need for a skeleton argument before the IAT. Unlike adjudicator appeals (where the grounds of appeal are often pro forma), you will already have formulated your arguments in your grounds of appeal. These will have impressed the IAT sufficiently to grant you permission. In adjudicator appeals, the evidence may also have changed considerably since the grounds of appeal were drafted, whereas submission of fresh evidence following the grant of permission by the IAT will be less common.

46.82 The extent to which a skeleton argument is useful in the IAT will depend firstly upon the extent to which your arguments are covered in your grounds of appeal, and secondly upon what you want the IAT to do. If you are simply seeking remittal and your case is fully set out in the grounds of appeal, there may be little point in producing a skeleton.

46.83 On the other hand, if you are asking the IAT to determine the appeal itself, and particularly if you want it to consider a large amount of documentary evidence, the IAT will normally appreciate a skeleton. Even if you submitted very full grounds of appeal, the simple addition of page references for the appeal bundles will be a worthwhile effort. It may be useful to incorporate the skeleton that you produced before the adjudicator hearing. However, if you wish to use that skeleton to identify submissions which the adjudicator failed to address, avoid confusion by leaving it as a separate document, and refer back to it in your skeleton for the IAT. You should still provide the new page references for the IAT bundle if these are not the same as before the adjudicator.

46.84 If your case has developed since you were granted leave to appeal, a skeleton ought to be submitted. An obvious example is where you have been granted or are seeking permission to adduce fresh evidence. It may also be wise to deal with any points of concern raised in the grant of permission to appeal.

46.85 One way of discovering the Home Office's stance is to seek a direction from the IAT that the Home Office lodges a skeleton argument in response to your grounds of appeal and/or skeleton. The common objection from the Home Office to producing skeletons before adjudicators is that its position is sufficiently set out in the refusal letter (para 9.2). However, there is no alternative document available to detail its stance with respect to the IAT proceedings. If you do receive a skeleton argument from the Home Office, check whether the arguments ought to have been raised by way of respondent's notice (see para 48.22).

46.86 The Home Office very seldom lodges a respondent's notice – whether in good time or at all. But the HOPO often seeks to argue points at the hearing which ought to have been the subject of a respondent's notice (e.g. challenging a positive credibility finding). It is important to remind the IAT that such challenges should not be entertained.

Authorities

46.87 See chapter 29 for general guidance about citation of authorities, and in particular unreported determinations of the IAT. PD No 4 states:

viii Citation of authorities

(i) *Parties are reminded of their obligation to notify the Tribunal of any authorities they intend to cite and, in the case of decisions not reported in the Immigration Appeal Reports or the Immigration and Nationality Law Reports, to provide copies of the authority. Provision of copies is particularly necessary in the case of determinations of the Tribunal. The Tribunal will not accept citations of extracts from cases without being able to see the whole decision in order to appreciate the context.*

46.88 The Practice Direction does not specify any time limit by which authorities, *other than Strasbourg authorities*, are to be notified. However, if you are not intending to supply copies of authorities which are reported in the Imm ARs or INLRs, you should provide a list at least a day in advance. The norm is now to provide copies of all authorities relied upon, whether or not they are reported. It will usually be more convenient to the panel to have copies which they can highlight and take away with them.

46.89 The following provision of PD No 4 applies to Strasbourg authorities (decisions of the European Court of Human Rights and the now defunct European Commission on Human Rights):

(ii) *Where an authority referred to in s.2 of the Human Rights Act 1998 is to be cited at a hearing*

(a) *the authority to be cited shall be an authoritative and complete report;*
(b) *The Tribunal must be provided with a list of the authorities it is intended to cite and copies of the reports not less than 14 days before the hearing; and*
(c) *Copies of the complete original texts issued by the European Court or the Commission, either paper based or from the Court's judgment database ('HUDOC') which is available on the internet, may be used.'*

46.90 You are therefore required to provide copies – not simply a list – of Strasbourg authorities two weeks before the hearing. It is likely that some representatives will find themselves in breach of this requirement. It is unlikely that the IAT would exclude reliance upon a material Strasbourg authority simply because a copy was not submitted two weeks in advance.

46.91 Clearly, however, the aim should be to comply with the direction. The direction will certainly be of assistance in challenging the past practice of some HOPOs of asking the tribunal to 'take judicial notice' of a Strasbourg authority which they do not produce even at the hearing.

46.92 Common sense suggests that you are unlikely to be criticised for failing to produce multiple copies of leading authorities such as *Chahal* simply to illustrate the well established application of article 3 in an expulsion case. But you should copy even as well-known an authority as *Chahal* if you wish to cite it for any less obvious purpose. The determining factor should be whether there is any risk that the IAT (or the HOPO) might actually need to look at the authority during the hearing. Particularly since the Direction does not expressly allow for exceptions, it is preferable to err on the side of caution and provide copies if you are in any doubt. See also the IAT's guidance in *Dominguez* (para 28.18).

Adjournments

46.93 Practice Direction No 2 states that:

> *1 Applications for the adjournment of cases must be made not later than 48 hours before the date fixed for the hearing. Full reasons and any supporting material must be lodged with the application and copies served on the respondent. Such applications will normally be dealt with on the papers by a legally qualified chairman.*

> *2 Any application made later than 48 hours before the hearing date will normally be considered by the Tribunal at the hearing and will require the attendance, unless any notification to the contrary is given, of the party or the representative of the party seeking the adjournment. Such applications will only be granted if there are compelling reasons such as last minute illnesses.*

> *...*

> *4 Parties and representatives must never assume that an application, even if made more than 48 hours before the hearing, will be successful and must always check with the Tribunal the outcome of any application. The Tribunal will not hesitate to hear an appeal if a party or representative fails to attend notwithstanding that an application for an adjournment has been refused or when it has been lodged less than 48 hours before the hearing and no notification has been given that there is no need to attend.*

46.94 Refer to chapter 8 for general advice concerning adjournments. The test under r.40(2) is the same, as are the requirements in r.40(3) as to what an application must contain. The provisions on closure (r.13) apply only to adjudicators and not the IAT. See the discussion of *Macharia* (para 8.47, 46.67) as to the need to offer an adjournment if the IAT is minded to admit evidence from the opposing party of which written notice has not been provided.

46 Preparing for the hearing
Key points

■ Decide whether it is realistic to invite the IAT to allow the appeal outright or whether you should be aiming for a remittal. Consider any provisional view expressed by the Chairman in the grant of permission.

■ If you have been granted permission on limited grounds and you maintain that the grounds upon which you were refused permission are arguable and important, it is safer to seek statutory review than to rely upon an application to the IAT to vary your grounds.

■ If the IAT has decided to star your appeal, the determination may have considerable implications for other cases, and you are encouraged to inform ILPA and the RLG.

■ The IAT has power to remit an appeal without a hearing, but fairness should entitle you to an opportunity to make representations and the IAT has in the past dispensed with a hearing only where the parties consent.

■ Applying for a pre-hearing review may force the Home Office to disclose its stance on the appeal and avoid wasteful preparation.

■ Any agreement between the parties as to disposal must be approved by the IAT, failing which the parties must attend the hearing.

■ If your time estimate is dependent upon how the hearing is conducted (e.g. whether oral evidence is permitted) then state this in your reply.

■ Any further factual evidence from the appellant or another witness should be set out in a witness statement, but it will ordinarily be appropriate to apply for permission to call oral evidence so that the witness is available for cross-examination. Your application must state your reasons.

■ Although the present standard directions do not state a time limit by which you must file your bundle, you should comply with the traditional requirement that it be submitted not less than 14 days before the hearing.

■ Fresh evidence may be required in particular to deal with recent developments and to address unexpected points taken by the adjudicator. Written notice must be provided of any application to adduce fresh evidence.

- Ask for the record of proceedings before the adjudicator if this has not been directed by the Chairman when granting permission, and the record may need to be examined at the hearing.

- If you wish to raise a new ground of appeal (rather than elaborate upon existing grounds), written notice should be given not less than 21 days before the hearing.

- The utility of a skeleton argument depends upon the degree of detail in your grounds of appeal and whether you are inviting the IAT to determine the appeal itself rather than remit it. It may be particularly useful where there is a substantial amount of evidence to consider, where your case has developed since the grant of permission, or to address concerns raised in the grant of permission.

- PD No 4 requires copies of Strasbourg authorities to be submitted 14 days in advance.

- The test for granting an adjournment is the same as before an adjudicator but the provisions on statutory closure do not apply. Any application to adjourn should be made not less than 48 hours in advance.

47 The IAT hearing

47.1   This chapter deals with presenting the case as appellant. Refer to chapter 48 for advice on responding to a Home Office appeal.

47.2   The standard procedure is that the appellant makes submissions, followed by the respondent, followed by the appellant's reply. However, different divisions of the IAT vary in their approach to the hearing. The tribunal will often have discussed the case amongst themselves before entering the hearing room. The Chairman may even start by indicating the disposal that they provisionally favour (most commonly, in those circumstances, remittal to a different adjudicator for a fresh hearing) and enquire whether either party wishes to argue against that course. If nobody does, the hearing is over.

47.3   Once your submissions are underway, you will find that many divisions of the IAT are far more interventionist than adjudicators, interjecting repeatedly with comments and opposing arguments. Other divisions may hear your submissions in relative silence.

47.4   Do not be afraid of an interventionist tribunal. It is often far better to face a tribunal willing to reveal its hand and engage in argument, rather than one which hears you out while giving little indication of its views or concerns. You may feel you are being given little opportunity to develop a prepared submission in the face of these interventions. If you are concerned that you cannot fully address a point raised by the tribunal without developing other points first, you can explain the intended order of your submissions and ask if you can come back to the point later.

47.5   If you end up abandoning the order of your submissions in order to address the points being put to you from the tribunal, it is important that you review your notes before completing your submissions – if necessary, asking for a moment to do so – to ensure that every significant point has been covered.

47.6   Where you have submitted very full grounds or a detailed skeleton it may be difficult when preparing for the hearing to know what else to add in submissions. This is particularly so if the Home Office has not lodged a skeleton and you do not yet know what its case will be. It is of course possible simply to indicate that while you are happy to deal with any points on which the IAT would like elaboration, you otherwise have nothing to add to your grounds or skeleton.

47.7 Sometimes the IAT will pre-empt your submissions by asking if you are merely intending to rehearse points contained in your skeleton. This may be a good sign (indicating that they are already with you, subject to anything the HOPO may say) or a bad sign (that they think your appeal is so weak that they do not believe that oral submissions could improve it). Either way, if your written submissions are so detailed that you do not actually have anything significant to add, it may be best to stop and save further submissions for your reply to the HOPO. But bear in mind the guidance in *Klajic* (para 39.11) to the effect that a skeleton argument should not be seen as a substitute for developing significant features of the case in oral submissions.

47.8 If the IAT invites oral submissions without qualification, it is advisable to accept the invitation and develop your case fully. The IAT may not be completely familiar with your grounds or skeleton, and may prefer to go through the papers as you make your submissions, thereby allowing them the option of putting questions which occur to them. Or they may simply prefer to pose their questions at the appropriate point in your argument rather than confront you with them at the start. Your oral submissions also have an advantage over your grounds in that you make them in the knowledge of who is sitting on your tribunal and you may emphasise or de-emphasise points in light of the views that the members of your tribunal have expressed in previous cases. You may also have a clearer idea as to whether an outright win is a realistic goal or whether you should be concentrating your efforts on a remittal. Even if you decide that remittal is your best bet, it may do your chances no harm to emphasise that if it were not remitted, you would be presenting substantial arguments to the effect that the appeal could be allowed outright.

47.9 After your opening submissions, it is the HOPO's turn. As with the HOPO's closing submissions in an adjudicator appeal, you should object if improper arguments are advanced (see chapter 39).

47.10 The HOPO almost never produces a skeleton argument. A specific concern in the IAT is to ensure that the HOPO does not raise arguments in oral submissions which ought to have been made by way of a respondent's notice (e.g. an attack on a positive credibility finding). If he does, you should interrupt. It will normally be more convenient to everyone to make the objection immediately rather than allow him to develop a full argument before you complain that he was not entitled to embark on it. He may also make points which, while not such as would require a respondent's notice, are prejudicial when raised for the first time at the hearing without you having had the opportunity to consider further evidence or take instructions.

47.11 Submissions in reply are particularly important if you were unable to address the Home Office's case in opening (because you did not know what it was). If you had little to add in opening to your grounds, your reply may be your main speech. Deal with each of the HOPOs points, though avoid simply repeating the points made in opening. Note carefully any interventions by the IAT during the HOPO's submissions as they may indicate concerns which you can usefully address or add to.

47.12 As with adjudicator hearings, you must ensure an adequate note is taken of the HOPO's submissions as it may be important for any appeal to the Court of Appeal to demonstrate which points he did and did not take. Make a note of your own submissions after the hearing if you did not have anyone else to note them. Also note any material interventions from the tribunal, for example if they indicated that there was no need to address them on a particular point or that they had already reached a provisional view on an issue.

47.13 Though the majority of decisions are reserved, the IAT gives its decision at the hearing more frequently than do adjudicators. Chairmen vary as to whether they give an oral determination or reserve their reasons.

Oral evidence

47.14 Where you have been granted permission to call oral evidence, the way the hearing is conducted will vary according to the nature of the oral evidence. If (unusually these days) the IAT has agreed to hear full evidence from the appellant, the hearing will proceed in much the same way as an appeal before an adjudicator. If you are calling new witnesses – whether expert or factual – on a discrete issue, the IAT may prefer to hear opening submissions before taking the evidence at an appropriate point.

47 The IAT hearing
Key points

■ The IAT is often far more interventionist than adjudicators during submissions. This opportunity to address its concerns should be welcomed, but be careful not to omit significant aspects of your submissions due to taking points out of order.

■ Develop your arguments fully in oral submissions, regardless of the detail contained in your grounds or skeleton argument, unless the IAT indicates otherwise.

■ Object if the HOPO raises points in oral submissions which ought to have been the subject of a respondent's notice.

■ The HOPO almost never serves a skeleton argument and you will therefore have to make your opening submissions without knowing how the Home Office puts its case: your reply to the HOPO's submissions may therefore be particularly important.

48 Opposing Home Office appeals

48.1 Much of the discussion in chapter 46 on evidence, procedure, and adjournments will also be relevant if you are the respondent to an appeal by the Home Office. This chapter gives advice on specific issues that arise when the Home Office appeals.

48.2 The Home Office's APIs claim that 'we must accept adjudicators' decisions with good grace; we will only appeal where there are strong grounds for doing so'. Even by Home Office standards, the gap between policy and practice is striking. The Home Office has appealed increasingly large numbers of adjudicators' determinations in recent years. Its grounds for doing so are often problematic.

Home Office grounds of appeal

48.3 Grounds alleging that the adjudicator was 'perverse' or 'irrational' commonly amount to a reiteration of the factual arguments that the adjudicator had rejected. It is also far from uncommon for the Home Office to criticise an adjudicator for failing to address an argument which the HOPO had not even advanced at the hearing, e.g. an internal flight alternative. It may complain that the adjudicator failed to draw inferences from the country evidence that the HOPO had not invited him to draw, or that he should have had regard to IAT determinations that the HOPO did not rely on.

48.4 The grounds of appeal may be positively misleading by criticising the adjudicator for accepting a point which the HOPO had indicated at the hearing was not in dispute, or for adopting a procedural course to which the HOPO initially objected but after discussion accepted. The adjudicator may be criticised for accepting oral evidence which was not challenged by the HOPO in cross-examination.

48.5 This emphasises the importance of retaining copies of all the evidence submitted by both parties and a full note of the hearing in order to establish whether the point on which the Home Office is appealing was raised before the adjudicator in cross-examination and submissions. In *El Mustafa*, the IAT stated that:

> [T]he failure of a representative to cross-examine effectively and to make appropriate submissions before the adjudicator cannot impose on the adjudicator a duty to carry out a word by word analysis of the written and oral accounts of the asylum claim in search for potential discrepancies which may give rise to alternative interpretations.

48.6 How far the Home Office will go in criticising an adjudicator is illustrated by the case of *Mjekiqi* in which the Home Office complained that the adjudicator should have recognised an improvement in the country of origin as of the date of the hearing, albeit that no such improvement was reflected in the Home Office's own evidence. The IAT unsurprisingly concluded that:

> It is quite impractical for an Adjudicator to be criticised on the basis that he relied on the evidence put before him by the Secretary of State, rather than on some other evidence contradicting that evidence, on which the Secretary of State now says that the Adjudicator should have relied.

48.7 Under the IAT's previous jurisdiction to hear appeals on the facts as well as the law, the Home Office regularly argued that it was entitled to rely upon any improvement in country of origin conditions since the adjudicator hearing, even where it accepted that there had been nothing wrong with the approach or the decision of the adjudicator. In *Oleed*, Schiemann LJ rejected this approach:

> I accept that the Tribunal examines the situation in the country from which the refugee is fleeing as at the date of its determination. However, in the present case in my judgment there was nothing wrong with the Adjudicator's determination, there was no reason to appeal it and it would be wrong for the Home Secretary, on the back of the appeal which has been dismissed, to seek to re-examine the threat to the refugee with reference to a date later than the adjudicator's determination. To permit this would merely encourage appeals by a party who has no ground for appeal but hopes that the situation would change sufficiently to enable him to advance different arguments on different facts on appeal. Such procedures would not be in anyone's interest.

48.8 This decision was followed (with reluctance) by the IAT in *S (Sri Lanka)*. Given that the IAT's jurisdiction is now limited to one of law, you would in any event argue that it has no power to overturn an adjudicator's determination unless an error of law is identified.

48.9 Particularly incongruous with its claimed policy is the Home Office's increasing practice of not bothering even to attend before the adjudicator and then lodging grounds of appeal in which the real complaint is that the adjudicator did not do the Home Office's job for it. You will want to emphasise the IAT's disquiet about this practice. In *Beteringhe*, the IAT stated that it is

> *absolutely clear that it is not open to the Respondent to absent himself without explanation from a hearing before an Adjudicator and then challenge credibility findings by making submissions which ought to have been made by way of cross-examination at the hearing.*

48.10 In *Muwyinyi*, it said that:

> *[T]he respondent must appreciate that, if he has refused an application because he has not believed the applicant to be credible, he may be disabled from upholding that belief if he chooses not to test or seek to contradict the evidence given by the applicant to an adjudicator on appeal.*

48.11 In *Gjurgjei*, it said that:

> *We hope that our decision will make it perfectly clear to those responsible at the Home Office that they cannot simply leave it to adjudicators to make bricks without straw on their behalf. Any place where adjudicators sit will have been the subject of advance consultation with the Home Office, whose duty it is to find presenting officers, or else instruct counsel to appear there before them. (In these cases, there have been sittings at Cardiff for many years; and there is of course a large local Bar). Far too high a proportion of Home Office appeals result from cases where no presenting officer has appeared before the adjudicator. Adjudicators have a duty to deal with cases, if they possibly can, and they are entitled to help from both sides. If the Home Office are unable to provide it through some last-minute emergency, then no doubt any adjournment application will be dealt with on its merits. However, mere lack of resources (if that was the problem here) would neither seem to justify an adjournment; nor an appeal based on mistakes caused by failure to appear, unless (perhaps, because we are not deciding such a case) the correction is pointed out at the earliest possible stage. Every resources equation has an outcome side, as well as an input one; and the outcome must be a negative one in cases of this kind.*

48.12 In *Shafiei*, it said that:

> *We deprecate the practice which we have noticed of late where following non-appearance of a Presenting Officer before an Adjudicator who allows an appeal it is alleged that Surendran guidelines have not been followed… It would be grossly unfair to remit this appeal for a fresh hear-*

ing before an Adjudicator simply to allow the Secretary of State a second opportunity to field a representative.

48.13 In such cases, you may find that the refusal letter – which the *Surendran* guidelines state should be treated as the Home Office's case 'purely and simply' – actually contradicts the Home Office's grounds of appeal. For example, the refusal letter may claim that the authorities have a legitimate interest in your client whereas the grounds of appeal claim that the adjudicator erred in finding that the authorities had *any* interest in her. Few other litigants would dare to appeal a decision on the ground that it was 'irrational' for an adjudicator to agree with a factual proposition that had been a part of that litigant's case.

48.14 An adjudicator may be criticised for accepting the appellant's attack on the refusal letter without exploring the potential arguments that could have been deployed to defend it. This again is inconsistent with the *Surendran* guidelines which state that it is not the function of the adjudicator to expand on the refusal letter or take on the role of the HOPO. You may refer to authorities indicating that it is sufficient for an adjudicator to agree with the refusal letter where the appellant has not attended or presented any substantial case at the hearing (e.g. *Mavemba*).

48.15 If the Home Office makes inaccurate claims about what occurred at the hearing without producing evidence, reference may be made to the rule that grounds of appeal do not prove themselves: *Aftab Ahmed* (para 43.25).

Challenging Home Office grounds at the permission stage

48.16 It is in no-one's interest to prolong proceedings to a full hearing before the IAT on grounds which are unarguable. For your client, it prolongs the agony of uncertainty. The delay in resolving her status also means that she remains unable to work or study and unable to be reunited with any immediate family stranded abroad.

48.17 The IAT has bemoaned the consequences that flow from the 'wholly inappropriate' behaviour that it has encountered from the Home Office. In *Mefaja*, it noted that:

It means that cases which ought not to clutter the Tribunal and the Adjudicators do so. It means that time and money is wasted and it is particularly unfortunate in circumstances where there is enormous pressure

> *on the Appellate Authorities to deal with cases as speedily as possible. How the Home Office can expect the IAA to deal with its cases with appropriate speed when they do nothing to assist is beyond our comprehension.*

48.18 It can only assist the efficient operation of the appeals system as well as protecting the interests of your client if you point out the flaws in the Home Office grounds of appeal before permission is granted. The IAT stated in **Sivanesan** that while it has no power to set aside permission once it has been granted,

> *there appears to be nothing to prevent a potential respondent to an appeal to the Tribunal seeking to make representations prior to the grant of leave.*

48.19 The fact that the grant of permission can now be challenged by statutory review (para 45.4) highlights the sense in the IAT considering the respondent's objections *before* it grants permission. It is particularly important to do so if the Home Office has not disclosed that its grounds are inconsistent with the case it presented at the hearing: the IAT may otherwise fail to appreciate this.

48.20 Rule 15(5) states that:

> *As soon as practicable after an application notice for permission to appeal is filed, the appellate authority must notify the respondent that it has been filed.*

48.21 One practical obstacle is that the IAT presently complies only with the literal requirement of r.15(5). It will notify you that permission has been sought but will not include a copy of the Home Office's grounds of appeal. You need to act promptly to request a copy of the grounds from the IAT, and to lodge any representations before a decision has been reached on whether to grant permission. Tell the IAT that you are proposing to make representations and indicate when it can expect them.

Respondent's notice

48.22 If you are notified that the Home Office has been granted permission to appeal, you should give immediate consideration to whether to lodge a respondent's notice. Rule 19 provides that:

> *(1) A respondent who wishes to –*
>
> > *(a) apply for permission to appeal to the Tribunal against the adjudicator's determination; or*

(b) ask the Tribunal to uphold the adjudicator's determination for reasons different from or additional to those given by the adjudicator,

must file a respondent's notice with the appellate authority.

(2) A respondent's notice must be filed –

(a) within such period as the Tribunal may direct; or

(b) where the Tribunal makes no such direction, within 10 days,

after the respondent is served with notice that the appellant has been granted permission to appeal.

(3) A respondent's notice must be served on the appellant at the same time as it is filed.

48.23 If, say, the adjudicator allowed the appeal on human rights but not on asylum grounds, you may wish to reconsider whether to appeal the findings on asylum if the Home Office has been granted permission to appeal against the human rights findings. This will require a respondent's notice. Similarly, you may believe that a legal argument that the adjudicator rejected is in reality stronger than those on which he relied. Again, you should produce a respondent's notice.

48.24 On the other hand, it is not necessary to serve a respondent's notice simply in order to expand upon an argument that was accepted by the adjudicator. Whether the submission of fresh evidence should be accompanied by a respondent's notice may depend upon whether the evidence supports a point that the adjudicator decided in your favour, or whether you are seeking to reopen a point that he decided against you.

Preparation for the full appeal

48.25 As appellant, the Home Office ought to prepare a bundle of those documents upon which it relies. It regularly fails to do so. It is no part of your job to assist the Home Office to prepare its appeal. If the Home Office fails without good reason to provide the IAT with the material necessary to dispose of the appeal then the appropriate course is to invite the IAT to reject its contentions.

48.26 Nevertheless, there are circumstances in which you may wish to submit a bundle where the Home Office has submitted none. The IAT will have the Home Office's grounds and determination. If the Home Office submits that there was no evidence before the adjudicator which could justify his findings of fact, you may argue that the Home Office ought to include all the documentary evidence before the adjudicator in order to make out that ground of appeal. However, it may be safer to submit a bundle containing the evidence which you say is capable of supporting the adjudicator's finding.

48.27 If the Home Office disregards directions, you can ask for its appeal to be dismissed without consideration of the merits pursuant to r.45(2). Reference may be made to the comments of the IAT in *Tatar*:

> [W]hen we sat this morning we discovered that [the HOPO], who has the misfortune to appear on behalf of the Home Office, had not been provided with the file, was not even aware what the grounds of appeal were, and was not in a position to present the appeal at all. This is the more surprising since the grounds of appeal were lodged by the Treasury Solicitor. We suffer this sort of incompetence from the Home Office again and again. Files are not provided, documents are not available, they do not put in evidence that they ought to put in, they fail totally to produce any skeleton arguments, the list goes on and on and the Tribunal is simply getting fed up with it. We have issued directions, the Home Office disobey them in, I am bound to say, most cases. They do not seem capable of dealing with the appeals in the manner in which they ought to be dealt with...

> We have of course considered whether we ought to adjourn the matter, but this case has been listed now for some time. It has been hanging over Mr Tatar's head for nigh on two years now and he is entitled to have the matter brought to a conclusion. There is no basis upon which it would in our view be proper to grant an adjournment, particularly as we are encouraged not to grant adjournments unless satisfied that it is in the interests of justice so to do. The whole tenor of our rules is that we should get on with it; indeed we are told by the Secretary of State that we must do all we can to ensure that appeals are heard speedily. If the Home Office are incapable of producing material so as to enable those presenting cases on their behalf to do what they ought to do, then we are not going to be able to fulfil those requirements and we see no reason why we should accommodate the Home Office yet again.

> In all those circumstances, as we say, without being able to consider the merits of this appeal, we are bound to dismiss it.

Oral evidence

48.28 A similar dilemma may arise as respondent to that discussed at paras 46.36–46.49 when deciding whether to apply for permission to call oral evidence. Your primary submission will often be that the Home

Office's grounds of appeal do not justify the IAT's intervention in the first place. However, you may wish to reserve a secondary submission to the effect that any potential defect or omission can be dealt with by oral evidence at the hearing. Again, you should make clear why you are making the application, and that it supports a secondary rather than a primary submission.

Skeleton arguments

48.29 Even if you are not directed to do so, *it is important as respondent that you submit a skeleton in advance.* If you do not do so (and assuming you have not lodged submissions at the permission stage), the IAT will have no idea how you put your case until you reply to the HOPO's oral submissions. The IAT will often have discussed the case between themselves before the hearing starts, and may start the hearing by proposing a means of disposal to the parties (e.g. remittal). It can then be considerably more difficult to persuade the IAT from scratch that the provisional view they have reached is wrong.

48.30 When drafting the skeleton, remember that you are the respondent. You do not have to prove your case all over again (unless you accept that the adjudicator's determination is flawed). Keep your skeleton tight and focussed on the Home Office's grounds of appeal. It is the Home Office which has to establish that the adjudicator's decision is flawed. You simply have to knock down the arguments raised by the Home Office. The more your skeleton descends into argument about the merits of the case, the more you encourage the IAT to embark upon a fresh review of the merits, rather than focussing upon whether there is a sufficient basis to overturn the decision that you have already won.

48.31 While your argument will often be to the effect that the Home Office's grounds are so hopeless that they did not deserve permission, beware the possibility that you find the same Chairman who granted permission sitting on the tribunal which hears the full appeal. It is politic to concentrate your fire upon the Home Office for having advanced such grounds of appeal rather than the IAT for having granted permission.

48.32 If the adjudicator's determination was promulgated prior to 9 June 2003, the IAT will be able to exercise its historic jurisdiction to entertain an appeal on the facts (Nationality, Immigration and Asylum Act 2002 (Commencement No. 4) (Amendment) (No. 2) Order 2003). However, you can still refer to the high test established by the IAT for overturning an adjudicator's determination on the facts. In *Isik & Bingol*, it stated that:

> *An appeal to this tribunal is not a rehearing. We can reconsider matters of fact as well as points of law, but we approach our task in much the same way as does the Court of Appeal. We will not reconsider findings of fact made by adjudicators unless persuaded that they were clearly wrong. That means we must be persuaded that there was insufficient evidence to support a finding, that it was one which the adjudicator could not reasonably reach on the material before him or that his reasons did not support the findings made. The fact, if it be so, that we might not have made the same finding does not of itself entitle us to interfere; if there was sufficient material to entitle the adjudicator to make his finding, we will not overturn it.*

48.33 In **Sharif**, the IAT said that:

> *[T]his Tribunal will not interfere with findings of fact unless persuaded that they are findings which are based on no evidence or which are clearly and manifestly erroneous. Provided there is evidence which entitles an Adjudicator to reach a particular conclusion that is sufficient and in our judgment the conclusions which the Adjudicator has reached, albeit the reasons are in certain respects unsatisfactory, are conclusions to which he was entitled to come.*

Variation of grounds

48.34 The Practice Direction governing variation of grounds is set out at para 46.76. As respondent, you have seven days to object to any application by the Home Office to vary its grounds. You should use that opportunity, particularly if no good reason has been given why the grounds could not have been included in the application for permission, and especially if you consider that the proposed new grounds would not have merited permission.

48.35 Having said that, it is rare for the Home Office to comply with the Practice Direction. The more usual scenario is for the Home Office to attempt to raise new grounds at the hearing. The HOPO who presents the appeal is unlikely to be the person responsible for drafting the grounds of appeal. It is therefore particularly useful to speak to the HOPO prior to the hearing. If he indicates that he wishes to advance a new ground of appeal and has not complied with the Practice Direction, you will normally object.

Opposing interim applications by the Home Office

48.36 This section deals with responding to interim applications from the Home Office, and applies equally to responding to such applications when you are the appellant.

48.37 The most common interim application by the Home Office is to adduce fresh evidence. Unless it is obvious that the material became available only after the adjudicator determined the appeal, it will have to explain why it was not submitted to the adjudicator.

48.38 The HOPO may try to submit documentary evidence that was clearly available to the Home Office when the appeal was determined by the adjudicator. If there is no good explanation why it was not submitted to the adjudicator, you may object. The IAT's caselaw indicates that where evidence was in the possession of a party when the appeal was heard by the adjudicator, and the party chose not to submit that evidence, any attempt to rely upon it before the IAT will be viewed unsympathetically (e.g. *Murugiath*).

48.39 In the past, the Home Office has often argued that it can disregard the notice requirements in the Rules where the material is in the public domain. *Macharia* establishes that it may not (see para 46.67).

The hearing

48.40 The HOPO will normally make his opening submissions first. But if the IAT indicate a provisional view in favour of remittal at the outset, then you may have to dissuade them from that view before the hearing goes any further. If you won a positive credibility finding before the adjudicator and the only flaw relates to the adjudicator's conclusions on the country evidence or his assessment of risk, you will normally wish to oppose remittal. The IAT should be able to determine the appeal itself in those circumstances without hearing oral evidence and remittal (other than to the same adjudicator) puts your positive credibility finding at risk. If the challenge is simply to some ambiguity in the adjudicator's reasoning, you may wish to argue for remittal to the same adjudicator.

48.41 If the HOPO's submissions depart from his grounds of appeal, and there has been no successful application to vary the grounds, you should object (see above).

48.42 As with your skeleton argument, keep your reply focussed on whether the adjudicator was *entitled* to reach his decision, rather than rearguing the merits. If the tribunal is putting points on the merits, then while addressing them, you should also remind the tribunal that it is not a sufficient basis for intervention that it would have come to a different decision on the facts. If you accept that the adjudicator's determination is flawed, then you will, of course, have to present your case on the merits (or else concede a remittal).

48.43 The HOPO will have a right of reply to your submissions, but object if he raises any new point in his reply which does not arise from your own submissions.

48 Opposing Home Office appeals
Key points

■ Obtain and analyse the Home Office's grounds of appeal prior to the grant of permission.

■ Check whether its grounds of appeal are:

☐ rearguing the facts in the guise of a rationality challenge,

☐ relying on arguments, evidence, and caselaw which were not put before the adjudicator,

☐ criticising a finding by the adjudicator while failing to disclose that the Home Office did not dispute the point before the adjudicator,

☐ complaining that the adjudicator did not look for points adverse to the appellant when the Home Office did not attend the adjudicator hearing to oppose the appeal.

■ If there are flaws in the grounds of appeal, and especially where the grounds are inconsistent with the case put by the Home Office before the adjudicator, representations should be made opposing permission. If permission is granted, this may be challenged through statutory review.

■ Give immediate consideration following the grant of permission to whether a respondent's notice is appropriate.

■ The Home Office often fails to produce a bundle of those documents relevant to the presentation of its appeal. It is not your role to do the Home Office's job for it, but you should in those circumstances produce a bundle of documents to which you may need to refer.

■ If the Home Office disregards directions, it may be appropriate to invite the IAT to dismiss the appeal without consideration of the merits.

■ You may wish to protect your position by seeking permission to call oral evidence while maintaining (and emphasising) your primary submission that such evidence is unnecessary in order to dispose of the appeal.

■ A skeleton argument is particularly important when you are the respondent as the IAT may otherwise have no prior notice of your case. Focus on whether the Home Office has identified a flaw in the adjudicator's determination rather than rearguing the merits (unless you accept that the determination was flawed).

- Object if the Home Office seeks to raise new grounds without complying with the Practice Direction on variation of grounds, or if it seeks to adduce fresh evidence without complying with the notice requirements.

- If you won a positive credibility finding from the adjudicator, you will normally argue that the IAT should decide the appeal itself rather than remitting it for fresh hearing.

49 Appeal from the IAT

49.1   The route by which to challenge the IAT's determination will depend upon whether the IAT decided the appeal itself or remitted it.

49.2   Section 103 of the 2002 Act states:

Appeal from Tribunal

(1) Where the Immigration Appeal Tribunal determines an appeal under section 101 a party to the appeal may bring a further appeal on a point of law –

(a) where the original decision of the adjudicator was made in Scotland, to the Court of Session, or

(b) in any other case, to the Court of Appeal.

(2) An appeal under this section may be brought only with the permission of –

(a) the Tribunal, or

(b) if the Tribunal refuses permission, the court referred to in subsection (1)(a) or (b).

(3) The remittal of an appeal to an adjudicator under section 102(1)(c) is not a determination of the appeal for the purposes of subsection (1) above.

49.3   A further statutory appeal can therefore be brought only if the IAT decided the appeal itself. For challenging a remittal, see below.

49.4   Note also that it is the location of the adjudicator who determined the appeal at first instance – and not the location of the parties, representatives, IAT or anyone else – that determines to which court a further appeal is brought. If the adjudicator determined the appeal in Scotland, then the appeal *must* go to the Court of Session rather than the Court of Appeal: *Gardi (No 2)*. For the sake of brevity, this text refers to the Court of Appeal.

49.5 The application for permission to appeal must be made in the first instance to the IAT. It is governed by Part 4 of the Rules:

Scope of this Part

26 This Part applies to applications to the Tribunal for permission to appeal on a point of law to the Court of Appeal or the Court of Session from a determination of an appeal by the Tribunal.

Applying for permission to appeal

27 (1) Subject to paragraph (2), an application to the Tribunal under this Part must be made by filing with the appellate authority an application notice for permission to appeal.

(2) A person who is in detention under the Immigration Acts may apply for permission to appeal either –

(a) in accordance with paragraph (1); or

(b) by serving an application notice on the person having custody of him.

(3) Where an application notice is served in accordance with paragraph (2)(b), the person having custody of the applicant must endorse on the notice the date that it is served on him and forward it to the appellate authority.

(4) As soon as practicable after an application notice for permission to appeal is filed, the appellate authority must notify the other party to the appeal to the Tribunal that it has been filed.

Time limit for application

28 (1) An application notice under this Part must be filed in accordance with rule 27(1) or served in accordance with rule 27(2)(b) –

(a) if the applicant is in detention under the Immigration Acts when he is served with the Tribunal's determination, not later than 5 days after he is served with that determination; and

(b) in any other case, not later than 10 days after he is served with the Tribunal's determination.

(2) The Tribunal may not extend the time limits in paragraph (1).

Form and contents of application notice

29 (1) The application notice must –

(a) be in the appropriate prescribed form;

(b) state the grounds of appeal; and

(c) *be signed by the applicant or his representative, and dated.*

(2) *If the application notice is signed by the applicant's representative, the representative must certify in the application notice that hc has completed the application notice in accordance with the applicant's instructions.*

Determining the application

30 (1) *An application for permission to appeal must be determined by a legally qualified member of the Tribunal without a hearing.*

(2) *The Tribunal may –*

(a) *grant permission to appeal;*

(b) *refuse permission to appeal; or*

(c) *subject to paragraph (3), set aside the Tribunal's determination and direct that the appeal to the Tribunal be reheard.*

(3) *An order under paragraph (2)(c) –*

(a) *may only be made by the President or Deputy President of the Tribunal; and*

(b) *may not be made without first giving every party an opportunity to make written representations.*

(4) *The Tribunal's determination must include its reasons, which may be in summary form.*

49.6   The IAT may not extend the time limit for appealing (r.28(2)). The imperative is therefore to get an application lodged with the IAT within the time limit: *never* risk exceeding the time limit in order to perfect your grounds or seek further evidence. The ordinary position under the CPR is that permission to appeal can be sought directly from the Court of Appeal where no application was made to the lower court (CPR, r.52(2-3), White Book commentary, para 52.3.3). However, it may be argued that s.103(2)(b) precludes the Court of Appeal from granting permission to appeal from the IAT unless the IAT has itself refused permission on the merits (rather than on the basis that the application was out of time). If the Court of Appeal accepts that argument, the only means of challenging the IAT's determination of the appeal will be by judicial review. In *Amina Ahmed*, the Court of Appeal was prepared to entertain judicial review proceedings in respect of an adjudicator's determination where the time limit for seeking permission to appeal to the IAT (which could not at that time be extended) had been missed by one day as a result of solicitor's error.

49.7   The test for granting permission to appeal to the Court of Appeal is set out in r.52.3(6) of the Civil Procedure Rules. It is the same as the test for granting permission to appeal to the IAT (r.18(4)), i.e. either real prospect of success or other compelling reason.

49.8   Many of the points discussed in chapter 42 on analysing the adjudicator's determination will also be relevant to your consideration of the IAT's determination, especially if it considered the matter itself on the merits. If you were the appellant before the IAT, check that the IAT dealt with each of your grounds of appeal and that it did not adopt the adjudicator's reasoning without addressing your criticisms of it. If you were respondent before the IAT, consider whether the IAT has identified an error of law in the IAT's determination or whether it has interfered impermissibly on the basis of its own contrasting view of the facts. Note the quotations in *Oleed* as to concerns about the IAT appearing to interfere more readily with an adjudicator's findings on an appeal from the Home Office than from an asylum seeker.

49.9   Refer to the discussion at para 43.19 about relying on fresh evidence in an appeal on a point of law where it is in the interests of justice to do so. As with appeals from adjudicators' determinations, you should consider urgently whether there is any evidence available, including expert evidence, that may demonstrate that any conclusions reached by the IAT on the merits are wrong or unsafe.

49.10   It is unusual for the IAT to grant permission to appeal to the Court of Appeal. The application is often (though not always) considered by the Chairman of the division which heard the full appeal. Unsurprisingly, the Chairman will not commonly accept that he may have acted irrationally or unfairly.

49.11   The circumstances in which there is a significant prospect of the IAT granting permission to appeal against itself are where it accepts that the issue is one of high importance, where it wishes the Court of Appeal to consider a decision of the High Court which is binding on the IAT, where its determination may have been affected by subsequent caselaw from the higher courts, or (less often) where there are conflicting IAT determinations.

49.12   It is good practice to raise all grounds of appeal that you have identified (though not necessarily in the detail which will subsequently appear in your grounds and skeleton to the Court of Appeal). Unlike statutory review of the IAT's refusal of permission to appeal from an adjudicator (see para 45.17), the Court of Appeal will not usually apply a higher threshold when considering a renewed permission application simply because the grounds were not fully aired in the initial permission application to the IAT.

49.13 Rule 30(4) requires the IAT to state 'its reasons, which may be in summary form' for refusing permission to appeal. But corresponding to the above, you cannot bring a discrete challenge before the Court of Appeal based on a failure by the Chairman to fully address your grounds (see e.g. *Gashi (2001)*).

49.14 The limited circumstances in which the IAT is inclined to grant permission do not, however, mean that the application and the decision on the application are unimportant. The Court of Appeal will look at the IAT's reasons for refusing permission. It may well be helpful if the Court can see that the IAT had an opportunity to comment on your criticisms of its determination and what (if any) response it gave.

49.15 This will be particularly so if you rely on any matter relating to the conduct of the hearing before the IAT. If it is not apparent from the determination, you should ensure that your account is fully set out in your application for permission to the IAT. That way, the IAT has notice of the allegation you are making, and can state in its reasons for refusing permission to appeal if it considers that the factual basis of your complaint is incorrect.

49.16 Note also the guidance given by Sir Christopher Staughton in *Macharia* for dealing with potential disputes about what took place at the hearing. He said that:

> For the future, a party to an immigration appeal or his representative who feels that there has not been a fair hearing should record the circumstances in writing immediately and send a copy to the Home Office and the Tribunal. That would at least go some way to avoiding the problem that we face today.

49.17 The normal rule is that if you have a statutory appeal route available, then you should use it. But in *Macharia*, Sedley LJ indicated that judicial review was more appropriate where the challenge raised potentially contentious issues of fact as to what happened at the IAT hearing. He noted that the Court of Appeal 'manifestly' had jurisdiction to deal with the case. However, he gave the following guidance for future cases:

> The [Administrative Court] is the natural forum for questions of natural justice, arising from tribunal proceedings. Any allegation that there has been, for want of fair procedure, typically raises questions both of law and of fact, in other words, questions, not only of what the relevant rules were, but of what happened. The latter ordinarily requires evidence, but evidence is ordinarily given on affidavit. While this Court has power to admit fresh evidence, this is normally only in relation to the issues canvassed below.

The present case is not of this kind. It concerns not what was argued but what happened. The preferable course in such a case would have been and should be in future to put the applicant's account of events on affidavit in this case it would be [counsel for the appellant's affidavit] and another counsel would have to conduct the case. If leave is granted, both the Home Office and the Immigration Appeal Tribunal will be served with notice of motion, and each, if so advised, may put in its account of events, this may be important, where, as here, the conduct of the Tribunal itself is in question. If there is a conflict, the Court of Judicial Review has means of resolving it.

49.18 If your challenge raises both substantive and procedural issues, the appropriate avenue is likely to be appeal to the Court of Appeal. Even if your case falls within the type indicated by Sedley LJ as more suitable for judicial review, it would be advisable at least to apply to the IAT for permission to appeal to the Court of Appeal. This will minimise the scope for argument about alternative remedy and, as discussed above, will also provide an early opportunity to ensure that the IAT is on notice as to what you say took place at the hearing and has a formal opportunity to respond.

49.19 It should not be open to the IAT to seek to cure a defect in its determination of the substantive appeal through its reasons for refusing permission. In *He*, the IAT had stated in its reasons for refusing permission to appeal to the Court of Appeal that 'such problems as the appellant claimed to have experienced did not amount to persecution.' Schiemann LJ held that:

I do not regard it as permissible to treat that statement as independent evidence of what the Tribunal thought. The Tribunal's determination must contain its reasoning. The reply to an application for permission to appeal is not an appropriate place to supplement the reasoning as revealed in the determination. It should be remembered that... such an application is to be determined by a legally qualified member on his own, not even necessarily someone who took part in the hearing. The person taking the decision as to whether or not to give permission to appeal must, in a case like the present, limit himself to looking at the determination.

49.20 In *Krayem*, while the Court of Appeal left open whether there might be circumstances in which the IAT could supplement its reasoning when refusing permission to appeal, Richards J (with whom the other members of the Court agreed) held that:

It is true that the tribunal, if asked for leave to appeal, must give reasons for its decision on that request... But the reasons given [when refusing permission to appeal] are plainly intended to be directed to the question why an appeal is or is not appropriate, not to why the tribunal reached its substantive decision. Reasons relating to the grant or refusal of leave to appeal are not intended to supplement the reasons why the tribunal reached its substantive decision. Moreover I note that such reasons are to be given by the legally qualified member of the tribunal rather than by the lay membership of the tribunal... and that if the tribunal considers that there is a deficiency in its reasons it may, instead of granting leave to appeal, set aside its decision and direct that the matter be re-heard... All those matters tend towards the view that the correct place to look for the reasons for the substantive decision is in the substantive determination itself rather than in the decision as to the grant or refusal of leave to appeal.

The IAT's power to set aside its determination

49.21 By r.30(2)(c) and r.30(3), as an alternative to granting or refusing permission to appeal, the President or Deputy President may set aside the determination of the IAT and direct a rehearing. One assumes that this power will only be exercised where there is a clear error, no significant point of principle arises, and neither party objects. See **Bushati** for an example of the similar power under the 2000 Rules being exercised. It has also been used where there has been an unreasonable delay between the hearing and the promulgation of the IAT's determination.

49.22 If you think your application for permission to appeal would be suitable for disposal in this way, you should say so and give your reasons in your grounds of appeal. In **Polat**, the Court of Appeal considered that it would have been appropriate on the facts of that case for the IAT to exercise its power to set aside the determination in view of the fresh evidence that had been adduced with the application for permission.

49.23 If you succeeded before the IAT and the IAT proposes this means of disposal in response to a Home Office application for permission to appeal, be sure to respond within the time set by the IAT. You will normally object if you believe there is a realistic prospect of defending the IAT's determination in the Court of Appeal (unless, perhaps, it is proposed to remit the matter to the same division of the IAT). If the determination is set aside by the President or Deputy President in circumstances where you maintain that there was nothing wrong with it, judicial review will be the only remedy.

Challenging a remittal

49.24 As indicated above, a remittal cannot be appealed to the Court of Appeal. Any challenge must be by judicial review.

49.25 The most common circumstances in which you might wish to challenge a remittal for fresh hearing are where you were successful before the adjudicator and you submit that the Home Office's appeal was unfounded. Alternatively, you might argue that any flaw in the adjudicator's determination was capable of being rectified either by the IAT or by remittal to the same adjudicator thereby avoiding credibility being reopened.

49.26 Lodge the judicial review as soon as possible. A judicial review claim challenging remittal does not automatically stay proceedings before the IAA. If the remitted hearing before the adjudicator is listed before your judicial review application has been determined, you will have to apply for an adjournment. The IAA normally agrees to adjourn provided you supply an Administrative Court reference number. If it does not agree to adjourn, this would be one of the unusual circumstances in which you would be justified in seeking an injunction to prevent the hearing going ahead (see also para 8.56).

49 Opposing Home Office appeals
Key points

■ A further statutory appeal can be brought (with permission) only if the IAT decides the appeal itself rather than remitting it. If the *adjudicator* sat in Scotland, the appeal must go to the Court of Session.

■ The time limit for seeking permission to appeal from the IAT is 10 days (or five days if your client is detained). The IAT has no power to extent the time limit. If you are out of time, the only option is to make the permission application directly to the Court of Appeal.

■ If you were the appellant before the IAT, check that it has dealt with each of your grounds of appeal. If you were the respondent, consider whether the IAT has identified a genuine error of law in the adjudicator's determination.

■ It is good practice to raise all your grounds in the initial permission application to the IAT so that the Court of Appeal can see what response the IAT gave. It is especially important to do so if you make assertions about what took place at the hearing.

■ If your challenge relates solely to alleged unfairness at the hearing, the appropriate avenue may be judicial review rather than statutory appeal.

■ As an alternative to granting or refusing permission to appeal, the President or Deputy President may set aside the determination. If you are proposing this course, say so in your grounds and give reasons.

■ If you oppose this course, you are entitled to make representations. If these are rejected, judicial review is the only remedy.

■ Any challenge to a remittal must be by judicial review. You should act promptly as judicial review proceedings do not automatically stay proceedings in the IAA.

50 Remitted hearings

50.1 This chapter deals with specific issues that arise when presenting a new adjudicator hearing following the remittal of the appeal by the IAT. Remittal may be either to the same adjudicator who originally determined the appeal, or to a different adjudicator.

Same adjudicator

50.2 If the remittal has been directed to the same adjudicator, it will usually be to consider further evidence or to expand upon his reasoning. It will ordinarily be unreasonable (and pointless) to remit to the same adjudicator for him to consider the appeal afresh: he is unlikely to be able to approach the matter uninfluenced by his previous determination.

50.3 You may have invited remittal to the same adjudicator rather than a different adjudicator where he had already reached a positive credibility finding which had not been challenged before the IAT. Unless the IAT's directions envisaged further evidence from your client, you would not usually call her at the remitted hearing: to do so might provoke the HOPO to try to reopen credibility.

50.4 The adjudicator may originally have allowed your appeal on the strength of one aspect of your case and consequently declined to reach findings as to the remaining aspects. If the Home Office successfully appeals, then you become entitled to a determination of those remaining elements of your case that the adjudicator had left undecided: *McPherson*. You may argue that this is best achieved through remittal to the same adjudicator.

50.5 There ought to be clear directions from the IAT as to what the adjudicator is expected to add to his previous consideration of the appeal. But problems may arise where one or other party urges the adjudicator to consider developments outwith the scope of the directions given by the IAT when remitting the appeal. In *Sivaloganathan*, the matter was remitted to the same adjudicator to reconsider his decision solely in the light of fresh medical evidence. He expressed concern that the direction prevented him considering changes in country conditions since he initially determined the appeal. On the second appeal to the IAT from the adjudicator's redetermination of the matter, the IAT commented that :

> *While we can well understand the very laudable attempt by the Tribunal to prevent this appeal being heard all over again, with the greatest of respect we do think that as things turned out it was impossible to expect the adjudicator to perform the task hedged in as he was by the restrictive terms of the remission to him.*

50.6 You may argue in such circumstances that s.85(5) of the 2002 Act gives the adjudicator an overriding power to consider evidence about present country conditions relevant to the determination of the appeal.

50.7 In *Kazmi*, Lawrence Collins J considered whether an adjudicator on remittal could consider claims under articles of the ECHR other than the one which the IAT had directed him to consider. He noted that on ordinary legal principles, a tribunal to which a particular question is remitted should consider only that question. He nevertheless concluded that it was 'strongly arguable' that the adjudicator should consider a claim under another article of the ECHR if there were 'strong grounds' for the claim. He derived the qualification 'strong' from an analogy with *Robinson* and *Xhejo*. However these cases concerned the circumstances in which an adjudicator or the IAT were obliged to consider asylum and human rights points which had not been raised at all by the appellant. There is no obvious reason to apply the same high test where the appellant has raised the contention before the adjudicator.

Different adjudicator

50.8 Remittal to a different adjudicator will normally be for fresh hearing, and it is much less common for such a remittal to be accompanied by any further direction limiting the scope of the new adjudicator's enquiry. (If such a direction is issued, then the above discussion will apply.)

50.9 While unusual, the IAT may direct that the adjudicator adopt one or more of the first adjudicator's findings of fact where they have not been challenged before the IAT. In *Girmay*, the IAT disposed of a Home Office appeal by remitting the appeal for fresh hearing before a different adjudicator, but directed that the new adjudicator should adopt the first adjudicator's finding as to the appellant's age (which was disputed by the Home Office, but which had not formed part of its grounds of appeal to the IAT). You may wish to suggest this course in similar circumstances.

50.10 Even if the remittal is for fresh hearing with no further directions, the adjudicator will read the IAT's determination. You obviously need to consider it in detail too. (This may appear obvious, but it is overlooked with remarkable regularity: if you are briefed as the advocate at a remitted hearing in a case in which you were not previously involved, ensure that the solicitors have supplied you with the IAT's determination.)

50.11 If the IAT has commented adversely upon the previous adjudicator's reasons for dismissing the appeal, that is plainly something you will wish to emphasise (as effectively precluding the new adjudicator from relying on the same reasons). On the other hand, if the IAT indicated that while some of the reasons given by the previous adjudicator were flawed, it would have been open to him to rely on the remaining reasons, particular attention must be paid to how these aspects of the case are addressed.

50.12 Where the remittal is for fresh hearing, the adjudicator should not normally read the determination of the previous adjudicator, and certainly should not do so without the consent of the parties. In **Devaseelan**, the IAT stated that:

> It is well established that when an appeal is remitted for rehearing an Adjudicator should have no regard to any previous determination, and should not even look at it except with the consent of all parties.

50.13 In **Gashi (2001, IAT)**, the IAT said that:

> For guidance…, we state the following as a set of principles to be followed:
>
> (1) As a general rule it is best practice for an adjudicator hearing an appeal de novo not to read the Determination of a previous adjudicator unless expressly invited to do so, so as to avoid any misunderstanding of what has influenced him. There is no prohibition, however, on reading the Determination.
>
> (2) If the adjudicator considers it appropriate to read the Determination, he should not do so until he has told the parties of his intention, and invited their comments.
>
> (3) There will be instances where parties invite him to read the Determination because, for example, the findings of fact have been accepted, and the re-hearing is to consider the conclusions to be

*drawn from those findings. This invitation should be recorded in his
Determination.*

*(4) The previous record of proceedings, and not the earlier Determination,
can if necessary provide confirmation of what evidence was given at a
previous hearing.*

*(5) If an Appellant does not attend the de novo hearing, an adjudicator
may rely on the evidence given at the previous hearing when forming
his independent view of the case, but without reference to an earlier
Determination.*

*(6) Parties seeking to challenge a Determination on the basis that an
adjudicator has read a previous Determination should only do so
where there are clear grounds for challenge, other than the mere fact
of reading the Determination. Reading a previous Determination of
itself is not a proper ground of appeal.*

50.14 It follows that the adjudicator should normally be aware of the previous adjudicator's reasons only to the extent to which they are set out
in the IAT's determination. However, you should still have regard to
the first adjudicator's reasons when preparing for the hearing: the
HOPO will have the previous determination and may have read it for
guidance as to what weaknesses he can now exploit.

50.15 It is open to the HOPO to raise what your client said at the first adjudicator hearing as an inconsistent statement. Given that consideration
of the previous determination is normally precluded, the HOPO will
have to do this by obtaining the record of proceedings.

50.16 Where the first adjudicator had made a positive credibility finding
which was not criticised by the IAT, you may wish to consider whether
you need to call your client rather than relying upon the original credibility finding.

50.17 In **Mario**, the original adjudicator had made a positive credibility finding and allowed the appeal. The Home Office appealed and the IAT
remitted the appeal for fresh hearing. The appellant was not called
before the second adjudicator, yet the second adjudicator reached an
adverse credibility finding based on the evidence that the appellant
had given before the first adjudicator. On the second appeal to the IAT,
the IAT pointed out that the failure of an appellant to give oral evidence did not preclude an adverse credibility finding. However, it
accepted the submission that faced with two credibility findings, one
on the basis of oral evidence and one without that benefit, the IAT
should prefer the credibility finding of the original adjudicator who
heard the evidence, even though it was formally hearing an appeal
from the second adjudicator.

50.18 If you decide not to call oral evidence and instead refer the adjudicator to the positive credibility finding made by the first adjudicator, you will obviously invite him to read the previous determination. You may argue that it is both unfair and inefficient for the appellant to have to prove his credibility twice if there was nothing wrong with the first finding. However caution should be exercised where, despite the positive credibility finding of the first adjudicator, substantial grounds for doubting credibility are apparent from the papers.

50 Remitted adjudicator hearings
Key points

- Remittal may be either to the same adjudicator who originally determined the appeal, or to a different adjudicator.

- Remittal to the same adjudicator will usually be for the purpose of considering further evidence or expanding upon his reasoning. It has the advantage of preserving a positive credibility finding.

- The IAI can direct the adjudicator as to the scope of his consideration on remittal. But there may be circumstances in which the adjudicator would be justified in embarking on a wider consideration of evidence and/or submissions.

- Where remittal is to a different adjudicator, he will have read the IAT determination, but should not normally read the original adjudicator's determination unless invited to do so by the parties.

- At the remitted hearing, the HOPO may raise statements made in oral evidence before the first adjudicator, but he will have to rely on the first adjudicator's record of proceedings to establish these.

- If the first adjudicator reached a positive credibility finding and the appeal has been remitted to a different adjudicator, it may be appropriate not to call oral evidence and instead to rely on the original credibility finding.

51 Second appeals

51.1 The term 'second appeal' is used where a previous appeal by the same appellant has already been dismissed. Circumstances which might call for a second appeal include where the first appeal was limited to a particular issue (e.g. asylum but not human rights) or where there have been developments in the country of origin or other relevant evidence is now available that was not before the first adjudicator.

51.2 Access to a second appeal will depend in part upon the provisions under which the first appeal was dismissed. This chapter discusses firstly the provisions governing access to a second appeal (which may also prevent an appeal where your client had a previous right of appeal that she did not exercise), before going on to discuss the conduct of a second appeal.

'Pardeepan appeals'

51.3 The IAT held in *Pardeepan* that an adjudicator could not consider human rights issues in an appeal against a decision that pre-dated 2 October 2000. In so holding, the IAT relied on specific assurances which it requested and received from the Home Office to the effect that no appellant caught by its ruling would be removed without being able to bring a separate human rights appeal. The Home Office briefly reneged from its assurance during 2001, but backed down in the face of judicial review proceedings and concerns from the IAT (expressed both to the Home Office and to ILPA).

51.4 If your client is covered by the *Pardeepan* assurance, the Home Office should be prepared to 'generate' a human rights appeal (i.e. issue a new immigration decision), regardless of whether it considers that the appeal raises any new issue or has any prospect of success. If the asylum appeal was finally determined prior to 2 October 2000, the Home Office will not co-operate voluntarily in 'generating' a human rights appeal unless it accepts that the human rights claim meets criteria analogous to a fresh claim for asylum.

Certification under s.96

51.5 Section 96 of the 2002 Act is intended to enable the Home Office to prevent appeals being brought or continued where the appellant has previously been subject to one stop procedures under either the 2002 Act or the 1999 Act (the latter included by para 4 of sch 6 to the 2002 Act). Unlike its predecessor, s.73 of the 1999 Act, a certificate may be issued even if no previous appeal has actually been brought (provided that there would have been an opportunity to appeal at some stage).

51.6 Section 96(1) states that:

(1) An appeal under section 82(1) against an immigration decision ('the new decision') in respect of a person may not be brought or continued if the Secretary of State or an immigration officer certifies –

(a) that the person was notified of a right to appeal under that section against another immigration decision (whether or not an appeal was brought and whether or not any appeal brought has been determined)

(b) that in the opinion of the Secretary of State or the immigration officer the new decision responds to a claim or application which the person made in order to delay his removal from the United Kingdom or the removal of a member of his family, and

(c) that in the opinion of the Secretary of State or the immigration officer the person had no other legitimate purpose for making the claim or application.

51.7 Many have struggled to understand numerous provisions in the wealth of immigration and asylum legislation promoted by the Home Office over the last decade. It is nevertheless some testament to the drafting of section 96(1) that the Home Office's own APIs describe the criteria for certification as 'convoluted'. The interpretation that it offers of the terms for certification are 'essentially' that:

- *the person against whom the decision has been made was notified of a right of appeal against another immigration decision (whether or not the right of appeal was exercised); and*

- *the new application was made to delay the removal from the United Kingdom of the applicant or a family member; and*

- *there was no other legitimate purpose for making the application.*

51.8 It adds that:

> *This is saying that, following on from a right of appeal which gave the opportunity to raise the matter earlier, the application was made in the hope that removal would be delayed without any reasonable belief that it could succeed.*

51.9 Unsurprisingly, the Court has been particularly puzzled by the phrase 'no other legitimate purpose for making the claim'. Five different judges have expressed doubts about how to interpret the identical phrase in s.73 of the 1999 Act, leading to four different formulations. In **Ngamguem**, Ouseley J held that:

> *In order for there to be a legitimate purpose there has to be some new material of substance placed before the Secretary of State which goes beyond what has been presented to the Special Adjudicator.*

51.10 In **Vemenac**, Burton J decided that:

> *what (the phrase) means is that the Secretary of State must be shown reasonably to have been satisfied that in his opinion the appellant had no legitimate purpose because the case put forward was so hopeless that it was not properly arguable.*

51.11 He invited Parliament to clarify the meaning of the phrase, but that invitation was not taken up in the 2002 Act. Davis J in **Soylemez** applied Burton J's formulation while expressing doubts. In **Balamurali**, however, Mitting J declined to follow the analysis of either Burton J or Ouseley J, concluding that:

> *'Legitimate purpose' seems to me to focus on the purpose for which the claimant makes his claim, not on its soundness nor on the prior availability or lack of availability of material relied on for the first time in his new appeal. Other phrases could easily have suggested either proposition.*

51.12 Mitting J 'struggled to discern what the draughtsman might have had in mind' before concluding that 'the only acceptable construction of that phrase' was that 'the words were there to accommodate situations not foreseen by the draughtsman as a long-stop against potential injustice'. However, he emphasised that the Home Office had a discretion whether or not to certify if the statutory criteria are made out, and that the exercise of that discretion

> *is governed by administrative law principles. It is not possible in this judgment for me to attempt to identify all factors which the Secretary of State should or may take into account… The list that follows is, therefore, both incomplete and tentative. But it seems to me that the Secretary*

of State must take into account two factors: first, the scheme of this part of the Act, which is intended to produce finality resulting from a single appeal; and secondly, by virtue of section 6 of the Human Rights Act 1988, the human rights of the claimant. Factors which it will commonly be appropriate to take into account are likely to be the strength or weakness of any new claim and the reasons why such a claim was not advanced in the original appeal.

51.13 In **Duka**, Collins J noted the conflicting decisions and indicated that he disagreed with Burton J. His formulation was as follows:

The starting point is for the Secretary of State properly to take the view that one of the purposes was to delay. Of course, in one sense every claim made has a purpose of delaying removal, but the word 'delay' is important because the distinction is drawn between delaying removal and preventing removal. As I read it, what Parliament has in mind was that in the knowledge of the inevitable result, namely that removal would take place because there was no good claim to remain, the process amounts to a delaying tactic. When Parliament uses the expression 'the appellant had no other legitimate purpose', it means no more than it says: namely, that there is no good reason, no legitimate reason, for pursuing the claim, and that is because it is a bad claim, and if the Secretary of State's view that it is a bad claim and thus there is no legitimate reason for pursuing it is correct, then he is entitled to certify.

51.14 Mitting J gave permission to appeal in **Balamurali** on the 'other compelling reason' basis because of 'the need for an authoritative ruling' on the interpretation of the phrase. The Court of Appeal has not considered the matter at time of writing.

51.15 What each of the judgments has in common is that the Home Office must have regard at some point to the merits of the appeal. It follows therefore that while necessary, it is not sufficient for the Home Office to demonstrate that the new claim could reasonably have been raised in previous proceedings.

51.16 The difficulties in interpretation do not end with s.96(1) because the Home Office can also issue a certificate under s.96(2). This states that:

An appeal under section 82(1) against an immigration decision in respect of a person may not be brought or continued if the Secretary of State or an immigration officer certifies that the immigration decision relates to an application or claim which relies on a ground which the person –

(a) raised on an appeal under that section against another immigration decision,

(b) should have included in a statement which he was required to make

> *under section 120 in relation to another immigration decision or application, or*
>
> *(c) would have been permitted or required to raise on an appeal against another immigration decision in respect of which he chose not to exercise a right of appeal.*

51.17 The Home Office this time restricts itself to noting that the criteria are 'a little involved'; the APIs suggest that a certificate can be issued under s.96(2) if the claim:

- *was raised on an earlier appeal; or*
- *should have been included in a statement that was required under section 120 (i.e. a statement of additional grounds in response to a one stop warning); or*
- *could have been raised at an earlier appeal, had an appeal been lodged.*

51.18 The criteria for certification under s.96(2) largely overlap with the criteria for certification under s.96(1). The Home Office offers no explanation either in the Explanatory Notes to the Act or the APIs for the dual provisions. Nor is there any explanation for the absence from s.96(2) of the criterion that there be 'no other legitimate purpose for making the claim or application'. Resolving this puzzle is not helped by the fact that the Home Office has issued certificates under *both* provisions in the same case.

51.19 It cannot be right that by certifying only under s.96(2), the Home Office can shut its eyes to the merits of the appeal that it is seeking to oust. The issue of a certificate is discretionary under s.96(2) as under s.96(1). The merits must be relevant to the discretion whether or not to certify which, as Mitting J pointed out (above), will be governed by administrative law principles.

51.20 The Home Office's IDIs (which have not been updated to refer to s.96 rather than its narrower predecessor, s.73 of the 1999 Act) state that:

> *We will need to consider the case with great care before issuing such a certificate. The consequences for the appellant could be extremely serious.*

51.21 The Home Office is correct about the consequences, which renders all the more unfortunate the fact that the provisions are so impenetrable.

51.22 There is yet another power to issue a certificate in order to limit the grounds that the adjudicator can consider in an appeal which has not been precluded entirely by a certificate under s.96(1–2). Section 96(3) states that:

> *A person may not rely on any ground in an appeal under section 82(1) if the Secretary of State or an immigration officer certifies that the ground*

was considered in another appeal under that section brought by that person.

51.23 On its face, this would appear to suggest that one of the parties to the appeal can direct the adjudicator, even during the course of the hearing, as to what issues he may and may not consider.

51.24 Note that the Home Office can issue a certificate pursuant to s.96(1–3) even if the claimant has been outside the UK since his previous right of appeal (s.96(5)), including where she was expelled to her country of origin following a previous appeal. The Home Office has in one case utilised this provision to seek to preclude any new appeal where the claimant relied upon treatment in his country of origin following which those authorities expelled him back to the UK.

Challenging a s.96 certificate

51.25 Apart from establishing the prospects of success in the appeal that the Home Office is trying to prevent, you will also have to explain why your client did not take previous opportunities to raise the issue. This may be because the purpose of a one stop notice was not properly explained to her, or because she was badly represented.

51.26 In **Cakabay**, Peter Gibson LJ noted that:

> *it is trite law that tribunals and courts with limited jurisdiction do have collateral jurisdiction to determine whether in any particular case they have jurisdiction to deal with applications before them.*

51.27 Plainly, if a certificate is issued in response to a notice of appeal, then an adjudicator must reach some decision as to whether there remains a live appeal before him. The Home Office would be unlikely to dispute this. However, it is likely to contend that the adjudicator's power is limited to examining the certificate to check that it complies with the statutory wording (regardless of how little relation these words may bear to the reality of the case).

51.28 There might be scope to argue that the adjudicator is obliged, in order to determine whether he retains jurisdiction, at least to consider whether the certificate is lawful. However, the point was not taken in any of the judgments discussed above (it being assumed that judicial review was the only remedy). The additional danger in pursuing this course before the adjudicator is that the Home Office may seek to remove your client before an adjudicator has had a chance to rule on the issue (if it does not accept that the adjudicator has jurisdiction to rule on the lawfulness of the certificate). Given the often inadequate notice of removal, the safer course will be to lodge judicial review proceedings.

51.29 That danger does not apply where the certificate is issued under s.96(3) since the appeal will in any event be proceeding on the uncertified grounds. Apart from the affront to judicial independence which s.96(3) presents, it is plainly absurd on public policy grounds for the adjudicator to be considering some of the issues in the case while other issues are tested in concurrent proceedings in the Administrative Court challenging the certificate. Both the adjudicator and the courts may therefore be readier to contemplate a wider jurisdiction on the part of the adjudicator to consider whether a certificate under s.96(3) has been correctly issued.

Conduct of a second appeal

51.30 In the starred determination of **Devaseelan**, the IAT gave guidance to adjudicators on the correct approach to a second appeal. Adjudicators presently treat this guidance as their starting point so it is set out at length below:

> *d. Our guidelines on procedure in second appeals*

> 37. *The first Adjudicator's determination stands (unchallenged, or not successfully challenged) as an assessment of the claim the Appellant was then making, at the time of that determination. It is not binding on the second Adjudicator; but, on the other hand, the second Adjudicator is not hearing an appeal against it. As an assessment of the matters that were before the first Adjudicator it should simply be regarded as unquestioned. It may be built upon, and, as a result, the outcome of the hearing before the second Adjudicator may be quite different from what might have been expected from a reading of the first determination only. But it is not the second Adjudicator's role to consider arguments intended to undermine the first Adjudicator's determination.*

> 38. *The second Adjudicator must, however be careful to recognise that the issue before him is not the issue that was before the first Adjudicator. In particular, time has passed; and the situation at the time of the second Adjudicator's determination may be shown to be different from that which obtained previously. Appellants may want to ask the second Adjudicator to consider arguments on issues that were not, or could not be, raised before the first Adjudicator; or evidence that was not, or could not have been, presented to the first Adjudicator.*

> 39. *In our view the second Adjudicator should treat such matters in the following way.*

(1) The first Adjudicator's determination should always be the start-ing-point. It is the authoritative assessment of the Appellant's sta-tus at the time it was made. In principle issues such as whether the Appellant was properly represented, or whether he gave evi-dence, are irrelevant to this.

(2) Facts happening since the first Adjudicator's determination can always be taken into account by the second Adjudicator. If those facts lead the second Adjudicator to the conclusion that, at the date of his determination and on the material before him, the appellant makes his case, so be it. The previous decision, on the material before the first Adjudicator and at that date, is not inconsistent.

(3) Facts happening before the first Adjudicator's determination but having no relevance to the issues before him can always be taken into account by the second Adjudicator. The first Adjudicator will not have been concerned with such facts, and his determination is not an assessment of them.

40. *We now pass to matters that could have been before the first Adjudicator but were not.*

(4) Facts personal to the Appellant that were not brought to the atten-tion of the first Adjudicator, although they were relevant to the issues before him, should be treated by the second Adjudicator with the greatest circumspection. An Appellant who seeks, in a later appeal, to add to the available facts in an effort to obtain a more favourable outcome is properly regarded with suspicion from the point of view of credibility. (Although considerations of credi-bility will not be relevant in cases where the existence of the addi-tional fact is beyond dispute.) It must also be borne in mind that the first Adjudicator's determination was made at a time closer to the events alleged and in terms of both fact-finding and general credibility assessment would tend to have the advantage. For this reason, the adduction of such facts should not usually lead to any reconsideration of the conclusions reached by the first Adjudicator.

(5) Evidence of other facts, for example country evidence, may not suffer from the same concerns as to credibility, but should be treated with caution. The reason is different from that in (4). Evidence dating from before the determination of the first Adjudicator might well have been relevant if it had been tendered to him: but it was not, and he made his determination without it. The situation in the Appellant's own country at the time of that determination is very unlikely to be relevant in deciding whether

the Appellant's removal at the time of the second Adjudicator's determination would breach his human rights. Those representing the Appellant would be better advised to assemble up-to-date evidence than to rely on material that is (ex hypothesi) now rather dated.

41. The final major category of case is where the Appellant claims that his removal would breach Article 3 for the same reason that he claimed to be a refugee.

(6) If before the second Adjudicator the Appellant relies on facts that are not materially different from those put to the first Adjudicator, and proposes to support the claim by what is in essence the same evidence as that available to the Appellant at that time, the second Adjudicator should regard the issues as settled by the first Adjudicator's determination and make his findings in line with that determination rather than allowing the matter to be re-litigated. We draw attention to the phrase 'the same evidence as that available to the Appellant' at the time of the first determination. We have chosen this phrase not only in order to accommodate guidelines (4) and (5) above, but also because, in respect of evidence that was available to the Appellant, he must be taken to have made his choices about how it should be presented. An Appellant cannot be expected to present evidence of which he has no knowledge: but if (for example) he chooses not to give oral evidence in his first appeal, that does not mean that the issues or the available evidence in the second appeal are rendered any different by his proposal to give oral evidence (of the same facts) on this occasion.

42. We offer two further comments, which are not less important than what precedes them.

(7) The force of the reasoning underlying guidelines (4) and (6) is greatly reduced if there is some very good reason why the Appellant's failure to adduce relevant evidence before the first Adjudicator should not be, as it were, held against him. We think such reasons will be rare. There is an increasing tendency to suggest that unfavourable decisions by Adjudicators are brought about by error or incompetence on the part of representatives. New representatives blame old representatives; sometimes representatives blame themselves for prolonging the litigation by their inadequacy (without, of course, offering the public any compensation for the wrong from which they have profited by fees). Immigration practitioners come within the supervision of the Immigration Services Commissioner under part V of the 1999 Act. He has

*power to register, investigate and cancel the registration of any
practitioner, and solicitors and counsel are, in addition, subject to
their own professional bodies. An Adjudicator should be very slow
to conclude that an appeal before another Adjudicator has been
materially affected by a representative's error or incompetence;
and such a finding should always be reported (through arrangements made by the Chief Adjudicator) to the Immigration Services
Commissioner.*

*Having said that, we do accept that there will be occasional cases
where the circumstances of the first appeal were such that it would
be right for the second Adjudicator to look at the matter as if the
first determination had never been made. (We think it unlikely
that the second Adjudicator would, in such a case, be able to build
very meaningfully on the first Adjudicator's determination; but we
emphasise that, even in such a case, the first determination
stands as the determination of the first appeal.)*

*(8) We do not suggest that, in the foregoing, we have covered every
possibility. By covering the major categories into which second
appeals fall, we intend to indicate the principles for dealing with
such appeals. It will be for the second Adjudicator to decide which
of them is or are appropriate in any given case.*

51.31 Prior to the IAT's decision in **Devaseelan**, adjudicators regularly
accepted that they had a statutory duty to reach their own conclusions
on an appeal rather than simply adopting the findings of fact of
another adjudicator who heard a different appeal against a different
decision. However, the guidance in **Devaseelan** has not been challenged in the Court of Appeal.

51.32 The guidance renders second appeals more difficult where the issues
overlap with those that were considered in a previous unsuccessful
appeal. Your primary task may be to put as much distance as possible
between your new appeal and the adverse findings in the old one. The
first step should always be to obtain your client's detailed comments
on the first determination. It may reveal misunderstandings on the
part of the original adjudicator. Where the previous adjudicator made
an adverse credibility finding, investigate whether there is any evidence which can be obtained to corroborate any part of the rejected
account. If one of the facts found by the adjudicator can be shown to
be inaccurate, his credibility finding will normally be unsafe.

51.33 If there is relevant evidence relating to past history which was not put
before the adjudicator, it is essential to explain the reasons carefully. If
it is attributable to fault by a previous representative, you ought to

consider whether it is appropriate to notify the OISC and/or the previous representative's professional body (see also para 13.19).

51.34 If you are alleging that the factual findings reached by the previous adjudicator are unsustainable, you are likely to be asked whether they were the subject of appeal or judicial review. It may be that the factual findings were not challenged because it was concluded that the legal test applicable to the original appeal could not be met even were those facts overturned. For example, findings of fact as to risk may not have been challenged in an asylum appeal because a view was taken that a Convention reason could not be established. In those circumstances, it would be unreasonable to rely upon the failure to challenge the original factual findings as evidence of waiver of some kind.

51.35 If there was no good reason why the factual findings in the previous appeal were not challenged, you will be back in the representative's fault scenario discussed above. If the adjudicator accepts that the representative was at fault in not challenging the previous findings, then he ought to consider whether these findings were flawed. In practice, the two questions may be different sides of the same coin.

51.36 Note that while the IAT appeared to be sceptical of representatives identifying mistakes in the conduct of the previous appeal where none had been made, it did not suggest that where a mistake had been made, the appellant should suffer the consequences of his representative's mistake. Any such proposition would be contrary to *Haile* and the IAT's consistent caselaw.

51.37 A second adjudicator will, in certain circumstances, be entitled to disagree with the inferences drawn by the first adjudicator as to risk. Such an approach is appropriate where there are serious concerns about the inferences that the adjudicator drew from these primary facts in order to reach his conclusion on 'the question of safety upon return'. This was established by the IAT in the case of *Gill*, in which it rejected the Home Office's challenge to the effect that the second adjudicator's approach had been inconsistent with *Devaseelan*. The IAT held that:

> *Although [the Home Office] is technically correct in stating that the Adjudicator in the second case has reversed the findings of the Adjudicator in the first case on precisely the same facts, it is certainly arguable that the Adjudicator's findings in the first case with regard to the question of safety upon return, are insufficiently clear and warrant the re-examination of the question of safety upon return by the second Adjudicator considering the human rights claim…*
>
> *In some circumstances we think it was open for the second Adjudicator to consider in somewhat greater detail the question of the safety of return*

but within the context of the first Adjudicator's findings that return would not be a breach of this country's Refugee Convention obligations. We think that it was proper for the second Adjudicator to consider the question of adequacy of protection within the Horvath guidelines in view of the rather sweeping findings of the first Adjudicator.

51.38 Expert analysis of the first adjudicator's findings may well be useful.

51 Second appeals
Key points

■ If an asylum appeal against a decision pre-dating 2 October 2000 was dismissed after that date, the claimant is entitled to a separate human rights appeal.

■ If the claimant has already been subject to the one stop procedure under the 1999 Act or 2002 Act, the Home Office may be able to issue a certificate under s.96 of the 2002 Act preventing any appeal being brought or continued. The wording of these provisions is convoluted and subject to conflicting decisions of the Administrative Court.

■ The Home Office can also issue a certificate preventing the adjudicator considering particular issues in the appeal where it claims that these were considered in a previous appeal.

■ A certificate under s.96 can be challenged by judicial review, although there may be scope to argue that an adjudicator has jurisdiction to consider the lawfulness of a certificate.

■ The IAT has given guidance on the role of an adjudicator hearing a second appeal.

■ He should have regard to relevant facts that post-date the first adjudicator's determination and to facts that pre-dated the first adjudicator's determination but were irrelevant to the issues in the first appeal.

■ Evidence from the appellant that could have been presented to the first adjudicator but was not may be treated with suspicion (in the absence of corroboration).

■ The adjudicator should consider whether there is a good reason for not having adduced evidence before the first adjudicator. If the reason is error by the representative, the adjudicator should report that error.

■ Where the appellant relies on the same facts on the same evidence to prove the same issues, the second adjudicator should normally regard the issues as settled by the first adjudicator.

■ Always get your client's comments on the first determination. Look for corroboration of facts that the adjudicator rejected. Expert analysis may be useful.

- You will need to provide an explanation if any errors in the previous determination were not appealed and for why available evidence was not adduced before the first adjudicator.

- It will be open to an adjudicator to reach different findings as to safety upon return upon the same facts and evidence where he concludes that the first adjudicator's findings are insufficiently clear and warrant re-examination.

52 Upgrade appeals

52.1 This chapter deals with bringing an asylum appeal where your client has been refused asylum but granted leave on other grounds (most commonly Humanitarian Protection, Discretionary Leave, or the old 'exceptional leave'). These appeals are commonly known as 'upgrade appeals'. They are governed by s.83 of the 2002 Act which provides that:

> *(1) This section applies where a person has made an asylum claim and –*
>
> > *(a) his claim has been rejected by the Secretary of State, but*
> > *(b) he has been granted leave to enter or remain in the United Kingdom for a period exceeding one year (or for periods exceeding one year in aggregate).*
>
> *(2) The person may appeal to an adjudicator against the rejection of his asylum claim.*

52.2 In **Saad**, the Court of Appeal pointed to the extensive rights to which refugees are entitled under the Refugee Convention and emphasised that to deny a refugee these rights would violate the UK's international obligations. The Court specifically emphasised that to grant a refugee some lesser form of leave would place the UK in breach of the Convention.

52.3 The Court of Appeal left open the issue of whether entitlement to refugee status could ever be determined by the courts, but it noted the practical disadvantages of challenging a refusal of asylum through judicial review proceedings which were not designed to test evidence. It held that the appeals provisions then in force must be construed so far as possible on the basis that the UK intended to comply with its international obligations. This involved interpreting the provisions so as to permit an *effective* appeal against the refusal of refugee status for those granted leave on other grounds.

52.4 Section 83(1)(b) of the 2002 Act denies this effective right of appeal to anyone granted leave on other grounds for a year or less. Unlike the provisions considered in *Saad*, it is impossible to interpret s.83 as permitting an effective asylum appeal to such persons.

52.5   It is perplexing that despite having the benefit of the guidance in *Saad*, the Home Office nevertheless promoted legislation through the 2002 Act which has the effect of rendering judicial review the only means of testing the refusal of refugee status for a significant category of claimants. Challenging the refusal of asylum by judicial review is outside the scope of this text. But the discussion below about ascertaining the basis upon which leave was granted on other grounds will also be relevant to a judicial review claim.

52.6   If the Home Office grants leave on other grounds while you have a pending asylum appeal under s.82, that appeal shall be treated as abandoned (s.104(4) of the 2002 Act). The same applies to appeals (other than upgrade appeals) under the 1999 Act (s.58(9)). You cannot avoid deemed abandonment by varying your notice of appeal so as to continue the appeal under s.83 (*Kanyenkiko*).

52.7   You can, of course, immediately lodge a new asylum appeal under s.83 if your asylum appeal under s.82 (or a provision of the 1999 Act) is treated as abandoned in this way. However, there is no conceivable public policy reason for imposing this delay and multiplicity of proceedings. Where the Home Office grants leave shortly before the hearing of the appeal, there might be scope – if everyone involved were to adopt the constructive approach illustrated by *Saad* – to issue a new notice of appeal under s.83 and retain the hearing as listed.

52.8   Note also that the HOPO cannot trigger the deemed abandonment provision simply by announcing at the hearing (or beforehand) that the Home Office will be granting leave on other grounds. Considering the equivalent provision under the 1999 Act, the IAT stated in *Diriye* that:

> *Section 58(9) is, in some senses, of penal effect. Although the context of the abandonment imposed by that section is that the Appellant has been granted leave, the effect is that his present endeavours in pursuing his appeal are wasted. He must... begin again. It follows that an Adjudicator should not apply the provisions of s.58(9) unless confident that the conditions of that sub-section have occurred. The condition is 'If the Appellant is granted leave to enter or remain in the United Kingdom'. A promise is not a grant...*

> *What then should an Adjudicator do if, during the course of a hearing, a Presenting Officer indicates that he or she proposes to grant leave? First,... the proposal to grant leave does not ipso facto cause the appeal to be abandoned. In many cases, it will be appropriate for the*

Adjudicator to adjourn the hearing in order for the grant to be made and to cause it to be brought back for mention in an appropriate period of time. We are told... that the Appellant is sometimes invited to withdraw his appeal. That, it appears to us, is not appropriate. The grant of leave will cause his appeal to be abandoned and no other action is required by the Appellant.

... Until leave is granted, the Appellant is at liberty to pursue his appeal. An Appellant who... has been given an indication that... he will have a limited grant [of leave] may nevertheless, until that grant is made, choose to pursue his appeal. He may be confident that he can, quite apart from the grant, persuade the Adjudicator that he is a refugee. Under those circumstances, it appears to us that if the grant has not yet been made, an Adjudicator should be very cautious before granting the adjournment and effectively prohibiting him from pursuing the appeal which he has begun and which has not yet been statutorily concluded by abandonment.

52.9   If the HOPO announces that leave is to be granted on other grounds and applies for an adjournment to allow the Home Office to formalise it, you will normally voice strong opposition if your client wishes to pursue her asylum appeal. The Home Office would have to satisfy the adjudicator under r.40(2) that the appeal could not be justly determined without an adjournment. It is difficult to envisage how the fact that it has promised to grant leave could possibly enable the Home Office to meet this test: on the contrary, an adjournment would mean that the appeal could not be determined on the merits at all.

Conducting an upgrade appeal

52.10 Under r.7(3), the time limit for bringing an appeal under s.83 is the same as applies to an appeal under s.82 (para 4.12). But if leave is granted at some point after asylum has been refused, time runs not from the date of the decision against which you are appealing (which under s.83 is the refusal of asylum) but from the date on which the appellant is served with notice of the decision to grant leave on other grounds.

52.11 Your client may leave the UK while her upgrade appeal under s.83 is pending without that appeal being treated as abandoned. (Section 104 applies only to appeals under s.82.) But note that the position is different in respect of upgrade appeals under s.69(3) of the 1999 Act: these *will* be treated as abandoned if she leaves the UK (s.58(8)).

52.12 The issue in an upgrade appeal is the same as in any other asylum appeal: whether, as of the date of the hearing, expulsion would violate the Refugee Convention (**Saad**).

52.13 The basis upon which the Home Office has concluded that the claimant qualifies for leave on other grounds yet is not a refugee may be obscure. Often there will be no apparent justification for the grant of leave other than the facts upon which she has sought refugee status.

52.14 It is perhaps not unrelated to this point that the HOPO often refuses to disclose voluntarily the basis upon which leave was granted. Some elucidation can now be obtained from the form of leave that the Home Office has granted. For example, if it grants Humanitarian Protection, that indicates its acceptance that your client will be at real risk of treatment contrary to article 3 (see the policy at para 41.11). The position will be less clear if your client was granted the old form of 'exceptional leave' prior to 1st April 2003. You may have to seek a direction in order to clarify its reasons.

52.15 The efficacy of directing the Home Office to disclose the basis upon which it granted leave is illustrated by the case of *Hassan*. The IAT was told that the Home Office was granting six months exceptional leave to Libyan asylum seekers. This resulted from advice from the Foreign Office to the effect that:

> Any Libyans returning to that country after an absence of six months or more are subject to an interrogation by the Libyan security authorities. Failed asylum seekers are routinely imprisoned by administrative (as opposed to judicial) order for 'having shown disloyalty to the state'.

52.16 The Home Office had therefore concluded that:

> We do not believe that we can at present safely enforce removals of failed asylum seekers to Libya. Any representation made under Article 3 of the Human Rights Act against the removal to Libya of a refused asylum applicant, and based on information currently available in the public domain is likely to succeed...

52.17 The appellant argued that the information presented by the Home Office demonstrated that it ought to have granted asylum rather than exceptional leave. The IAT agreed:

> If returned to Libya, there is clearly a real risk that the appellant will suffer imprisonment and so persecution because he has 'shown disloyalty to the State' by absenting himself. The persecution will be for a Convention reason, namely imputed political opinion. Thus the [Home Office] Bulletin itself establishes that the appellant is a refugee...

52.18 Where family reunion is dependent upon the outcome of the upgrade appeal, you will often wish to press the IAA for a prompt listing. Note however that the family can make a direct application for entry clearance relying upon article 8, followed by a human rights appeal if that is refused. There may well be a strong case where Humanitarian Protection has been granted to the UK sponsor, notwithstanding the Home Office's restrictive policy on family reunion. There is no need to await the result of the upgrade appeal.

52.19 Conversely, if you require an adjournment to permit further preparation of the upgrade appeal, adjudicators will normally be more ready to grant it. That is because the public policy arguments in favour of speedy determination of asylum claims do not apply where the appellant already has leave on other grounds.

52.20 It is arguable that article 6 should apply to upgrade appeals because unlike ordinary immigration appeals, upgrade appeals are not concerned with disputes over whether someone should be expelled but simply with the rights that the appellant enjoys within the UK. However, the same procedural safeguards can be derived from the common law duty of fairness (*MNM*).

52 Upgrade appeals
Key points

- The UK will violate its international obligations under the Refugee Convention if it grants a lesser form of leave to someone who is entitled to refugee status.

- Someone granted leave for a year or less will have no appeal against the refusal of asylum and must challenge the decision by judicial review.

- An appeal (other than an upgrade appeal) will be deemed abandoned if the Home Office grants leave. You may not vary your grounds to continue the appeal under s.83.

- A promise to grant leave is not the same as the grant of leave. You should have good grounds for opposing any adjournment sought by the Home Office to enable it to grant leave and so prevent the appeal being determined on the merits.

- An upgrade appeal under s.83 is against the refusal of asylum, but the time limit for appealing will run from the grant of leave on other grounds if that post-dates the refusal of asylum.

- The basis upon which the Home Office has granted leave on other grounds may in reality demonstrate entitlement to refugee status.

53 Fast track appeals

53.1 Fast track appeals are governed by the Immigration and Asylum Appeals (Fast Track Procedure) Rules 2003. In this chapter only, references to rules are to the Fast Track Rules unless otherwise stated. The standard procedure rules are referred to as the 'Principal Rules'.

53.2 The Fast Track Rules apply extraordinarily tight time limits throughout the appeal process. They do not deal with the treatment of the initial application to the Home Office. But Home Office practice in cases which it hopes will be subjected to the Fast Track Rules is to detain the claimant on arrival, conduct the asylum interview on the day after arrival, and decide the claim on the day after that. The result is that the only opportunity for the claimant to be interviewed by her representative prior to the Home Office decision is either on the same day she arrives (often following a traumatic journey) or on the same day as her asylum interview. This raises grave concerns relating to fairness.

53.3 ILPA's position is that it 'opposes wholly and in principle the new fast track procedure' (response to consultation on PD CA2 of 2003). Commenting on the pilot introduced in 2002, it stated that:

> *ILPA's position, following intensive consultation with our members, is that it is not reasonably possible for a solicitor's firm operating under a General Civil Contract with the LSC to prepare and present (or instruct counsel to properly present) appeals according to best practice within the expedited timetable you propose. The fact that a client has been detained since arrival and that advice at initial stage was limited by... draconian time limits... only exacerbates the obstacles in this respect.*

> *ILPA has had a great deal of feedback on the proposals. That is the universal response of our members who include the most experienced representatives in the field, and in particular members who act as reviewers in quality standard assessments by the LSC, assessors for the Law Society Immigration Panel, and examiners for the Bar Council Immigration Accreditation Board.*

> *Our members, including those appointed as assessors by the LSC, Law Society, and Bar Council, have told us that proper representation in this timescale is not reasonably possible.*

53.4 Home Office policy is that only 'straightforward claims' are appropriate for the fast track procedure (press statement, 18 March 2003). It will withdraw the claim from the fast track if the Medical Foundation accepts a referral. The Medical Foundation will deal with requests relating to fast track cases as a priority. However, given that the Home Office's own procedure permits only one clear day between arrival and decision, this may well be impractical. The Home Office has indicated to NGOs, including the RLC, that it will consider representations at any stage to the effect that a case should be removed from the fast track procedure. A need to obtain supporting evidence may well indicate that the appeal is not 'straightforward' and thus unsuited to the fast track procedure. In *ZL*, the Court of Appeal noted in the context of the week long decision making process under the Oakington procedure that where medical evidence was required to support a claim – and in analogous cases – the Court would expect it to be recognised that a fast track procedure was inappropriate (para 3.13). Depending on the circumstances of the case, you may wish to judicially review an unreasonable refusal to remove a claim from the fast track prior to the Home Office's decision on the claim.

Bail

53.5 An adjudicator appeal will be subject to Part 2 of the Fast Track Rules by r.4 if:

(a) *the appellant was in detention under the Immigration Acts at a place specified in the Schedule to these Rules when notice of that immigration decision was served on him; and*

(b) *the appellant has continuously been in detention under the Immigration Acts at a place or places specified in the Schedule since that notice was served on him.*

53.6 It will be seen that an appellant can be subjected to the fast track procedure only if she was detained when the decision was served by the Home Office *and* has been detained continuously since. While Home Office policy envisages that claimants may be detained pending the initial decision simply to facilitate the determination of their claim under a fast track procedure, *further* detention pending appeal must be justified according to the ordinary detention criteria (as reflected by the Home Office's press statement of 18 March 2003).

53.7 Once an appeal has been lodged, there is a 'presumption' in favour of liberty that can be displaced only by 'strong grounds for believing' that the appellant will abscond . If detention is inconsistent with published Home Office policy in this regard, it will be unlawful. An adjudicator will act unlawfully if he refuses bail to an appellant who is unlawfully detained (see generally chapter 55).

53.8 It is therefore imperative that a bail application is lodged immediately following the Home Office's decision. In practice, there may not be time to have a bail application listed before the substantive hearing is listed under the fast track. In that case, it will be listed on the same day as the appeal. It is understood that some adjudicators have declined to entertain a bail application until after the substantive appeal has already been heard under the fast track procedure. It is difficult to see how an adjudicator could lawfully take this course. Whether it is lawful to subject an appeal to the fast track procedure must depend upon whether the appellant is lawfully detained. Clearly, this question must be addressed *before* the appeal is heard in the fast track.

53.9 The Home Office has on occasion argued that the detention is justified *because* the appeal is being heard in the fast track procedure, as a result of which it claims that the appellant is likely to abscond if released. That argument is obviously flawed: the appellant can only be subjected to the fast track procedure in the first place if the Home Office can justify her detention according to the ordinary criterion of 'strong grounds for believing' that she will otherwise abscond. You should argue that to reverse the correct test in this way is itself evidence of an unlawful approach on the part of the Home Office. For the consequences of the appellant ceasing to fall within the scope of the Fast Track Rules, see para 53.23 below.

Procedure before the adjudicator

53.10 The time limit for lodging notice of appeal is two days (r.6(1)). Upon receipt of the notice of appeal (whether or not served within the time limit), the Home Office has two days in which to lodge the appeal papers with the IAA and serve them on the appellant (r.6(3)).

53.11 The IAA must then fix a hearing date not later than two days after it receives the appeal papers 'or as soon as practical thereafter if the appellate authority is unable to arrange a hearing within that time' (r.7). In practice, the IAA is presently listing hearings within the two days.

53.12 The notice of hearing must be served on each party and representative 'not later than noon on the day before the hearing' (r.7(3)). However, the IAA need not serve the notice on the representative unless he has provided a fax number for this purpose (r.21).

53.13 Rule 6(2) states that:

> *An adjudicator may not extend the time limit in paragraph (1) unless he is satisfied that, because of circumstances outside the control of the appellant or his representative, it was not practicable for notice of appeal to be given within that time limit.*

53.14 This test differs critically from that which applies to appeals under the Principal Rules (i.e. whether, by reason of 'special circumstances', it would be unjust not to extend time). 'Special circumstances' may include an error on the part of the representative for which the appellant is not responsible (para 4.24). That is consistent with the approach of the Court of Appeal in having regard to the wider interests of justice where an appellant has been prejudiced by a representative's error (para 43.19). Were the provision to be interpreted as precluding the adjudicator from having regard to the interests of justice in determining whether to extend time, there would be scope to argue that it was unlawful. The adjudicator should, however, strive to construe the provision consistently with human rights and with the standards of fairness required by the common law by, for example, holding that an inadvertent error by the representative was one that was beyond his control.

53.15 Documentation can be lodged at the hearing of a fast track appeal unless it is practical to lodge it beforehand. Practice Direction CA2 of 2003 states that:

> *The Standard Directions provided for in Practice Direction CA8 of 2001 dated 27th July 2001 will not apply in relation to cases under the Fast Track Procedure Rules 2003. Standard Directions in Fast Track cases will be:*

> > *Documents, including witness statements, country reports, skeleton arguments and any chronology to be relied on at the hearing must be filed in a paginated bundle at the hearing or where practicable twelve hours before. Copies of all such documents are to be provided to every other party to the appeal. Copies of documents in a language other than English must be accompanied by a full certified translation.*

> > *Witness statements are to stand as evidence in chief at the hearing.*

53.16 The commentary to the Practice Direction states that:

> *If documents are to be relied on they must be filed and served 12 hours*

> *before or at the hearing. Without them they cannot be relied on. To that extent their production is mandatory. Best practice requires that there should be a witness statement ready for the hearing. Both sides will need to have available background information for the adjudicator if that is to be relied on in support of the case.*

53.17 Under the fast track procedure, the same Home Office official may conduct the asylum interview, write the refusal letter, and conduct the appeal hearing. This has advantages in that you will be able to query the basis for allegations in the refusal letter directly with its author. However, if a dispute of fact arises as to what was said at the interview, the HOPO will not be able both to continue to conduct the appeal and to give evidence as to what took place at the interview (para 36.36, 43.27). If he wishes to give evidence to dispute the appellant's account of the interview, he will have to apply for an adjournment or cease to act as representative.

53.18 The test for adjournment is set out in r.8(2):

> *An adjudicator may only adjourn the hearing of an appeal where –*
>
> *(a) it is necessary to do so because there is insufficient time to hear the appeal;*
>
> *(b) a party has not been served with notice of the hearing in accordance with these Rules;*
>
> *(c) the adjudicator is satisfied by evidence filed or given by or on behalf of a party that –*
>
> > *(i) the appeal cannot be justly determined on the date on which it is listed for hearing; and*
> >
> > *(ii) there is an identifiable future date, not more than 10 days after the date on which the appeal is listed for hearing, by which the appeal can be justly determined; or*
>
> *(d) the adjudicator makes an order under rule 23.*

53.19 The basic test ('whether the appeal can be justly determined without an adjournment') is the same as applies under the Principal Rules. However, an adjudicator may not adjourn a fast track appeal for more than 10 days unless he removes it from the fast track (see para 53.21 below).

53.20 The fact that the hearing will be listed little more than a week after the appellant's arrival (and she will have been in detention throughout) renders it more likely that an adjournment will be required in order to permit a fair opportunity to present your case. The common objection to an adjournment under the ordinary procedure – namely that there has already been sufficient time to obtain expert evidence, documentary corroboration etc. – is far less likely to apply to fast track appeals. The Court of Appeal concluded in **ZL** that a week would ordinarily provide a fair opportunity to present an initial claim to the Home Office in the Oakington procedure. But it emphasised that it reached that conclusion in the context that the claimant need establish no more than an arguable case within that period (para 3.12).

53.21 Apart from challenging your client's continued detention, the only means of getting out of the fast track is to seek an order under r.23. This states that:

> *(1) Where Part 2 or 3 of these Rules applies to a pending appeal, an adjudicator or the Tribunal may order that that Part shall cease to apply to the appeal –*
>
> *(a) if all the parties consent;*
>
> *(b) in exceptional circumstances, if the adjudicator or the Tribunal is satisfied by evidence filed or given by or on behalf of a party that the appeal cannot otherwise be justly determined; or*
>
> *(c) if –*
>
> > *(i) the respondent has failed to comply with a provision of these Rules, or the Principal Rules as applied by these Rules, or a direction of the appellate authority; and*
> >
> > *(ii) the adjudicator or the Tribunal is satisfied that the appellant would be prejudiced by that failure if the appeal were determined in accordance with these Rules.*
>
> *(2) An adjudicator or the Tribunal may, when making an order under paragraph (1) –*
>
> *(a) adjourn any hearing of the appeal; and*
>
> *(b) give directions relating to the further conduct of the appeal.*
>
> *(3) Where an adjudicator adjourns a hearing in accordance with paragraph (2), rule 13 of the Principal Rules (closure date) shall apply.*

53.22 Rule 23(1)(b) will apply where the appeal cannot justly be determined within 10 days of the date fixed for hearing (this being the maximum period for which an adjudicator can adjourn a hearing).

53.23 The effect of removal from the fast track is addressed by r.24:

> *(1) This rule applies where any of Parts 2 to 4 of these Rules ceases to apply to a pending appeal or application because –*
>
> *(a) the conditions in rule 4, 9 or 15 cease to apply; or*

(b) an adjudicator or the Tribunal makes an order under rule 23.

(2) Subject to paragraph (3), the Principal Rules shall apply to the appeal or application from the date on which that Part of these Rules ceases to apply.

(3) Where –

(a) a time period for something to be done has started to run under a provision of these Rules; and

(b) that provision ceases to apply,

if the Principal Rules contain a time limit for the same thing to be done, the time period in the Principal Rules shall apply, and shall be treated as running from the date on which the time period under these Rules started to run.

53.24 It follows therefore that if your client is granted bail or an order is made under r.23, the Fast Track Rules, including any fast track time limit then running, will cease to apply, and be replaced by the equivalent procedure under the Principal Rules.

53.25 The IAA must serve the adjudicator's written determination on the parties not later than one day after the hearing (r.8(3)).

Procedure before the IAT

53.26 Rule 9 states that Part 3 of the Fast Track Rules (governing appeals to the IAT) applies:

to an appeal (including an application for permission to appeal) to the Tribunal where –

(a) the appeal is against the determination of an adjudicator upon an appeal to which Part 2 of these Rules applied; and

(b) the party appealing against an immigration decision has, since being served with notice of that immigration decision, continuously been in detention under the Immigration Acts at a place or places specified in the Schedule to these Rules.

53.27 It does not follow that an appeal to the IAT will be governed by the Fast Track Rules simply because they applied to the adjudicator appeal. They will apply only if the appellant has remained continuously in detention. It is therefore valuable to proceed with a bail application even after the adjudicator has heard the appeal.

53.28 The Fast Track Rules provide that an application for permission to appeal must be lodged within two days of service of the adjudicator's determination (r.11(1)). The IAT can extend time 'if it is satisfied that, by reason of special circumstances, it would be unjust not to do so' (r.11(4)). Unlike adjudicator appeals, the test for extending time is therefore the same as applies under the Principal Rules.

53.29 Rule 11(2) states that the appellant must -

> (a) *state in his application notice whether he seeks an oral hearing of the appeal if permission to appeal is granted, giving reasons if he does so; and*

> (b) *file with the application notice (whether or not he seeks an oral hearing) –*

>> (i) *any written submissions upon which he wishes to rely if the Tribunal grants permission to appeal and decides to determine the appeal without a hearing; and*

>> (ii) *any notice under rule 21(2) of the Principal Rules asking the Tribunal to consider additional evidence.*

53.30 The IAT will serve these papers on the respondent. The respondent then has a day to indicate whether he seeks an oral hearing if permission is granted (giving reasons if he does so) and to file any written submissions upon which he would rely if the appeal is determined without a hearing; any respondent's notice; and any application to adduce fresh evidence (r.12).

53.31 Rule 14 provides that if the IAT grants permission to appeal, it must decide (having regard to any written representations) whether to determine the appeal on the papers or to fix a hearing (r.14(2)). If it determines the appeal on the papers, it should do so at the same time as it grants permission or as soon as practicable thereafter (r.14(3)). If it fixes a hearing, the hearing date should be not later than two days after permission was granted (or as soon as practical thereafter), and notice of hearing must be served not later than noon on the day before the hearing (r.14(4)). The test for adjournment before the IAT (r.14(5)) is the same as applies before an adjudicator (r.8(2)).

53.32 The standard procedure before any appeal tribunal (including the IAT) involves a right of reply for the appellant to the respondent's submissions. However, there is no provision for you to reply to the respondent's submissions where the appeal is determined without a hearing. This will in itself be a good reason to fix the appeal for hearing unless no issue is raised by the respondent's submissions. It will, in any event, be appropriate to seek a hearing in all but the simplest of cases. The opportunity to address the IAT's concerns in oral argument is often invaluable. The submission of any fresh evidence will be a further reason for fixing a hearing.

53.33 If permission to appeal is refused, you may seek statutory review (see chapter 45). You will have the ordinary 14 days in which to lodge the application, whether or not your client remains in detention. You should always maintain your efforts to obtain any relevant evidence. If it becomes available while you are preparing your application for statutory review, you may submit it in support of that application.

53.34 Part 4 of the Fast Track Rules (governing applications for permission to appeal to the Court of Appeal) again applies only if your client has remained in detention continuously since she was served with the immigration decision (r.15). The time limit for seeking permission to appeal is two days (r.17(1)) and the IAT may not extend time (r.17(2)). The IAT must serve its decision on the permission application not later than one day after it was lodged (r.18).

53.35 If permission is refused, you may renew the permission application to the Court of Appeal. The time limit for doing so is 14 days (CPR, r.54.4(2)). The appeal will remain pending until the time limit expires (s.104(2) of the 2002 Act) so that your client cannot be removed within that period. As with statutory review, if relevant evidence becomes available during this period, it may be considered by the Court of Appeal if it is in the interests of justice to do so.

53 Fast track appeals
Key points

- Representations may be made to the Home Office at any stage to the effect that the claim is not (or is no longer) 'straightforward' and is thus unsuitable for the fast track procedure.

- An appellant can be subjected to the Fast Track Rules only if she was detained when the decision was served by the Home Office AND has been detained continuously since.

- Once the Home Office has made a decision on the claim, any further detention pending appeal must be justified according to the ordinary detention criteria. The fast track procedure is the result of the appellant being detained, not a justification for her detention.

- It is imperative that a bail application is lodged immediately following the Home Office's decision. A successful bail application will result in the appeal being removed from the fast track procedure.

- The time limit for lodging a fast track appeal is two days. The test for extending time for appealing is stricter than under the Principal Rules. A too rigid application of the test may be unlawful.

- Documentation may be lodged at the hearing unless it is practical to lodge it earlier.

- The test for adjournment is the same as under the Principal Rules but an adjudicator cannot adjourn an appeal for more than 10 days unless he removes it from the fast track.

- An appeal may be removed from the fast track if:
  - ☐ all parties consent, or
  - ☐ 'in exceptional circumstances', if the appeal cannot be justly determined within the fast track,
  - ☐ or if the respondent has failed to comply with a provision of the Rules or with directions and the appellant would be prejudiced by the appeal continuing in the fast track.

- Proceedings in the IAT will continue under the Fast Track Rules only if the appellant has remained continuously in detention.

- The time limit for seeking permission to appeal is two days. The test for extending time is the same as under the Principal Rules.

- There is no automatic right to a hearing if the IAT grants permission. You must provide reasons in support of a request for a hearing, together with any written submissions on which you will rely if the appeal is determined on the papers. The respondent may also make written submissions but there is no right of reply to the respondent's submissions if the IAT determines the appeal on the papers.

- The time limit for applying to the IAT for permission to appeal to the Court of Appeal is two days.

- The standard 14 day time limit applies both to applications for statutory review and to applications to the Court of Appeal for permission to appeal.

54 Representing children

54.1 A child of any age may make an asylum or human rights claim. UNHCR states that:

> *The problem of 'proof' is great in every refugee status determination. It is compounded in the case of children. For this reason, the decision on a child's refugee status calls for a liberal application of the principle of the benefit of the doubt. This means that should there be some hesitation regarding the credibility of the child's story, the burden is not on the child to provide proof but the child should be given the benefit of the doubt.*
> (Refugee Children, Guidelines for Protection and Care)

54.2 The UNHCR Handbook repeats that determination of claims by children requires liberal application of the benefit of the doubt (para 219).

54.3 The UN Convention on the Rights of a Child defines 'child' as any person under the age of 18, and the Immigration Rules provide accordingly that:

> *[A] child means a person who is under 18 years of age or who, in the absence of documentary evidence establishing age, appears to be under that age.* (para 349, HC 395)

Disputes over age

54.4 The Home Office regularly disputes that someone is a child. Establishing this is important on a number of grounds: special procedures apply to the determination of children's asylum claims (below); it is Home Office policy not to detain unaccompanied children (para 55.14); children cannot be denied support on the same basis as adults; the Home Office will grant an unaccompanied child at least Discretionary Leave if she is refused asylum (unless adequate reception arrangements are available in her own country). If the Home Office does not concede that your client is a child prior to the appeal hearing, it will therefore be valuable to obtain a finding of fact to this effect even if the adjudicator dismisses the appeal on asylum and human rights grounds. The Home Office will be bound by the adjudicator's finding of fact that the appellant is a child (para 41.32) and, if she is also unaccompanied, will ordinarily be bound to grant her Discretionary Leave in accordance with its policy (see para 54.31).

54.5 If you presented your client's initial application to the Home Office then you should already have addressed any failure by the Home Office to recognise your client as a child. UNHCR states that:

> When the exact age is uncertain, the child should be given the benefit of the doubt. (Refugee Children)

54.6 In *B (2003)*, Stanley Burnton J quoted the Home Office policy as follows:

> If the applicant claims to be a minor but his/her appearance **strongly** *suggests that s/he is over 18 the applicant will be treated as an adult until such time as credible documentary or medical evidence is produced which demonstrates that s/he is the age claimed. In borderline cases the Immigration Service will continue to give the applicant the benefit of the doubt and to deal with the applicant as a minor. In accordance with existing policy they will continue to inform the Refugee Council's Panel of Advisors of anyone who has claimed to be a minor, even when the age is disputed and the decision has been taken to treat the applicant as an adult.* (emphasis as in original)

54.7 The judge considered draft local authority guidance on age assessment which he said made 'sensible suggestions'. He noted that:

> the form comments that 'A medical opinion and view on age will always be helpful', a statement with which it is difficult to quarrel. Side notes make helpful but common sense suggestions, such as 'Life experience and trauma may impact on the ageing process.'

54.8 You should normally seek an expert medical opinion where age is disputed, while being aware of the limitations of such medical evidence. Stanley Burnton J quoted from the *Guidelines for Paediatricians* published by the Royal College of Paediatrics and Child Health:

> In practice, age determination is extremely difficult to do with certainty, and no single approach to this can be relied on. Moreover, for young people aged 15–18, it is even less possible to be certain about age. There may also be difficulties in determining whether a young person who might be as old as 23 could, in fact, be under the age of 18. Age determination is an inexact science and the margin of error can sometimes be a much as 5 years either side. Overall, it is not possible to actually predict the age of an individual from any anthropometric measure, and this

should not be attempted. Any assessments that are made should also take into account relevant factors from the child's medical, family and social history.

54.9 The medical report will therefore offer an age *range* into which your client falls rather than an exact age. This may be sufficient for your purposes given the Home Office's acceptance that the benefit of the doubt should be accorded in borderline cases.

54.10 Medical evidence may be particularly useful where the Home Office is disputing your client's age on the basis of travel or other identity documents which indicate that she is an adult. If the date of birth shown on such a document is outside the range identified by the medical evidence, this will corroborate your client's claim that the stated date of birth is false and should render further reliance on the document by the Home Office unsustainable.

54.11 Stanley Burnton J noted that:

> *Given the impossibility of any decision maker being able to make an objectively verifiable determination of the age of an applicant who may be in the age range of, say, 16 to 20, it is necessary to take a history from him or her with a view to determining whether it is true. A history that is accepted as true and is consistent with an age below 18 will enable the decision maker in such a case to decide that the applicant is a child. Conversely, however, an untrue history, while relevant, is not necessarily indicative of a lie as to the age of the applicant. Lies may be told for reasons unconnected with the applicant's case as to his age, for example to avoid his return to his country of origin. Furthermore, physical appearance and behaviour cannot be isolated from the question of the veracity of the applicant: appearance, behaviour and the credibility of his account are all matters that reflect on each other.*

54.12 He gave the following guidance:

> *[E]xcept in clear cases, the decision maker cannot determine age solely on the basis of the appearance of the applicant. In general, the decision maker must seek to elicit the general background of the applicant, including his family circumstances and history, his educational background, and his activities during the previous few years. Ethnic and cultural information may also be important. If there is reason to doubt the applicant's statement as to his age, the decision maker will have to make an assessment of his credibility, and he will have to ask questions designed to test his credibility.*

54.13 You should therefore take a detailed statement covering these issues where the medical evidence is not clear-cut.

Ethics

54.14 Membership of the Children's Panel of the Law Society requires the following personal undertaking:

> *I undertake that, when representing a party in proceedings covered by the Children Act 1989:*
>
> 1 *Subject to paragraph 2, I will not normally delegate the preparation, supervision, conduct or presentation of the case, but will deal with it personally.*
>
> 2 *In each case I will consider whether it is in the best interests of my client to instruct another advocate in relation to the presentation or preparation of the case.*
>
> 3 *If it is in the best interests of my client, or necessary, to instruct another advocate, I will consider and advise my client or the Children's Guardian (if applicable) who should be instructed in the best interest of my client.*
>
> 4 *I agree that, save in exceptional circumstances, any advocate that is instructed will either be:*
>
> > a) *another Children Panel member (approved as a Children Representative if my client is the child); or*
> > b) *a member of the Bar on my Practice's approved Counsel list.*
>
> 5 *I will obtain an undertaking from that advocate to:*
>
> > a) *attend and conduct the matter personally unless an unavoidable professional engagement arises;*
> > b) *take all reasonable steps to ensure that so far as reasonably practicable a conflicting professional engagement does not arise.*

54.15 The same standards should wherever possible be applied to the representation of children in asylum and human rights appeals. It is not acceptable for a child to be switched between representatives without good reason. You should ensure that your client is accompanied to any hearing or interview by someone she knows and trusts. It is not acceptable to send a clerk who does not know your client or her case. You must ensure that any advocate has a full conference well before the date of the hearing.

54.16 Ideally, you should have a working knowledge of family and child care law and practice. (See *Putting Children First* by Coker, Finch, & Stanley (LAG, 2002) for a guide aimed at immigration practitioners.) You must, as a minimum, ensure that specialist advice is obtained. Membership of the Law Society's Children's Panel also requires a basic knowledge of child development.

54.17 It is your responsibility to ensure that both the Home Office and the courts recognise their duties to your client as a child. But while recognising that your client is a child, it is equally important to recognise that the child is your client. She is as entitled as an adult client to independent representation, to realistic advice to enable her to make informed choices, and to have her instructions respected and effected to the fullest extent to which you are able. It is because a child is entitled to the same standard of representation that you must adapt to her age, mental development, and experience so as to provide it.

Taking instructions

54.18 UNHCR advise that a child should be assessed by

> an expert with sufficient knowledge of the psychological, emotional, and physical development and behaviour of children... When possible, such an expert should have the same cultural background and mother tongue as the child. (Refugee Children)

54.19 If this has not already been done, then you should consider obtaining such an assessment. Apart from its potential evidential value in your client's appeal, it will assist you in determining how you can best take your client's instructions. Whatever the expert's conclusions, however, it cannot absolve you of your ultimate duty to assess your client's ability to give instructions, and to follow them so far as that assessment allows.

54.20 You should also assess the degree of support available to your client from responsible adults, and check that the Refugee Council's Panel of Advisors has been notified. If the age or development of your client does not allow you to take detailed direct instructions, you will have to make an assessment of the extent to which you can accept instructions from any adult on your client's behalf.

54.21 Detailed research on country of origin conditions should be conducted prior to taking instructions. Children will be less likely than adults to be able to make an accurate assessment of those aspects of their experiences which will require explanation to someone unfamiliar with their country. Some children will have only the vaguest idea of why they have been sent to the United Kingdom. Paragraph 351 of the Immigration Rules states that:

> A person of any age may qualify for refugee status under the Convention... However, account should be taken of the applicant's maturity and

in assessing the claim of a child more weight should be given to objective indications of risk than to the child's state of mind and understanding of his situation. An asylum application made on behalf of a child should not be refused solely because the child is too young to understand his situation or to have formed a well-founded fear of persecution. Close attention should be given to the welfare of the child at all times.

54.22 Consider what practical steps you can take to make it easier for your client to give instructions. Your client may prefer to meet you at a venue other than your office. She may prefer to be accompanied at meetings by someone whom she trusts. But she may equally want to consult her representative privately and you must ensure that such opportunities are made readily and tactfully available.

54.23 The way in which you take instructions will depend on the maturity and experience of your client. Children will manifest fear in different ways. Children even more than adult asylum seekers are likely to express themselves best if given freedom to do so in their own way in their own time, rather than in response to structured interview questions. You can also refer to UNHCR's *Guidelines for Interviewing Unaccompanied Refugee Children and Adolescents and Preparing Social Histories.*

One stop procedure

54.24 The one stop procedure applies to children of any age and poses a particular risk to them. They may be served with a one stop notice when an adult relative makes an asylum claim and/or has that claim refused. There is no provision to ensure that children obtain independent advice. There is equally no safeguard to exclude penalties being applied for failure to comply with a one stop notice. The penalty could be a certificate under s.96 preventing any subsequent appeal being pursued by the child (para 51.5). One would hope that the Home Office would not seek to impose such a penalty on the basis that a child had not responded to a one stop notice but experience suggests otherwise.

54.25 If you are representing an adult with dependent child relatives, it is essential to be clear about who is your client. You should always warn your adult client about the potential consequences of the one stop procedure for her children. If you are instructed by her children, you must give them full advice including (unless they are very young) the opportunity to give instructions in the absence of other relatives. The importance of being clear about whether or not the child is your client cannot be over-stated. If the child is represented, that fact could be used by the Home Office to justify its implementation of future penalties against the child for failure to comply. Incomplete or half-hearted advice to the child may be worse than no advice at all.

Home Office policies

54.26 The Home Office operates a number of policies in respect of children. The most significant is the seven year rule which provides that a family will not normally be removed from the UK where one of its members is a child who has resided in the UK for at least seven years. The policy was explained to Parliament as follows:

> *For a number of years, it has been the practice of the Immigration and Nationality Directorate not to pursue enforcement action against people who have children under 18 living with them who have spent 10 years or more in this country, save in very exceptional circumstances. We have concluded that 10 years is too long a period. Children who have been in this country for several years will be reasonably settled here and may, therefore, find it difficult to adjust to life abroad. In future, the enforced removal or deportation will not normally be appropriate where there are minor dependent children in the family who have been living in the United Kingdom continuously for 7 or more years. In most cases, the ties established by children over this period will outweigh other considera- tions and it is right and fair that the family should be allowed to stay here. However, each case will continue to be considered on its individual merits. (Hansard, 24 February 1999, HC Col 310)*

54.27 Note that you should not agree to adjourn an appeal for consideration under this policy if the child is approaching her 18th birthday: the Home Office may argue that the policy ceases to apply on her 18th birthday regardless of the fact that she had spent more than seven years in the UK before reaching 18.

54.28 Such polices are relevant on two bases. Firstly, where the decision against which you are appealing is inconsistent with a Home Office policy, it may be unlawful on public law grounds. This is a matter which the adjudicator will be obliged to consider if you have raised it as a ground of appeal. It is also a requirement of article 8(2) that the decision be lawful in domestic law terms as well as proportionate.

54.29 Secondly, if the Home Office operates a policy which permits children to remain in the UK in similar circumstances to those of your client, it should be far more difficult for it to establish that the removal of your client is necessary in order to maintain an effective immigration control.

54.30 If a child has been in the UK for close to seven years and there are additional factors supporting your argument that expulsion would constitute a disproportionate interference with her private life, it will still be useful to refer to the seven year policy. It demonstrates the Home Office's acceptance that seven years residence alone will render removal inappropriate, and inferentially that there is no 'pressing social need' for the removal of families with children who qualify. A slightly lesser period of residence with additional factors should lead to the same conclusion.

54.31 Home Office Ministers have consistently accepted that children cannot be expelled unless it is established that adequate reception and care arrangements are in place. Home Office policy is presently to grant unaccompanied child asylum seekers who are not refugees or entitled to article 3 protection 'Discretionary Leave' for three years or until their 18th birthday, whichever is earlier. (While Discretionary Leave can be refused if adequate reception arrangements are in place in the country of origin, that will seldom be the case. In practice, the Home Office generally grants Discretionary Leave as matter of course rather than attempting to investigate possible reception arrangements.) Indefinite Leave will only be granted after six years of Discretionary Leave. However, if you can establish that she will be at real risk of inhuman or degrading treatment in her country of origin, she should be entitled to Humanitarian Protection. She may then qualify for Indefinite Leave after three years rather than six (see para 41.11).

54.32 If a child is severely traumatised or suffers other serious mental health problems, medical evidence may indicate that she needs to feel secure about her future in order to rebuild her life and respond to treatment. There may then be scope to argue that a grant of Discretionary Leave rather than Indefinite Leave would be inconsistent with her human rights (see also para 41.19).

Conducting the appeal

54.33 The effect of the policy of granting Discretionary Leave to unaccompanied children means that most asylum appeals on behalf of such children will be upgrade appeals (see chapter 52). Just as a child's manifestation of subjective fear may be dissimilar to that of an adult, different criteria will often apply to the objective element. For example, the conscription of children into military service is very likely to constitute persecution in circumstances where it would not amount to persecution in respect of an adult. Similarly, the threshold for article 3 ill-treat-

ment is likely to be lower. You should have regard to the rights protected by the UN Convention on the Rights of the Child.

54.34 Paragraph 352 of the Immigration Rules provides that:

> *An accompanied or unaccompanied child who has claimed asylum in his*
> *own right may be interviewed about the substance of his claim or to*
> *determine his age and identity. When an interview is necessary it should*
> *be conducted in the presence of a parent, guardian, representative or*
> *another adult who for the time being takes responsibility for the child and*
> *is not an Immigration Officer, an officer of the Secretary of State or a*
> *police officer. The interviewer should have particular regard to the possi-*
> *bility that a child will feel inhibited or alarmed. The child should be*
> *allowed to express himself in his own way and at his own speed. If he*
> *appears tired or distressed, the interview should be stopped.*

54.35 In **Omotayo**, the IAT held that while it would not remit an appeal simply because the adjudicator had overlooked a 'technical breach', the
determination would be flawed if the adjudicator placed adverse
reliance on an interview conducted in breach of this rule (i.e. without
a responsible adult being present). It stated that:

> *The plain fact of the matter is that this appellant should have been inter-*
> *viewed in accordance with... procedures on unaccompanied minors but*
> *was not. At her interview there was no-one representing her.*
> *Subsequently, however, the respondent sought to rely on what she had*
> *said in this interview in refusing her asylum appeal. At the hearing of her*
> *appeal the respondent proceeded in a similar vein. The Special*
> *Adjudicator, whilst making full allowance for the appellant's age and*
> *also demonstrating that he quite well understood why she would not*
> *have volunteered when interviewed that she had been raped, proceeded*
> *nevertheless to count against her that he would have expected her to have*
> *said a number of other things at that interview.*

> *The Tribunal cannot reiterate too strongly the need for those interviewing*
> *children to adhere strictly to the words and spirit of paragraph 352 of HC*
> *395... In the case of persons who have been wrongly denied the benefit*
> *of the special procedure for unaccompanied minors, the Tribunal consid-*
> *ers it vital that the evaluation of their claim does not place reliance on*
> *what is said at an initial interview conducted without a representative of*
> *any kind being present...*

> *The Tribunal recognises that the Special Adjudicator was not helped in*
> *this case by the fact that neither the respondent nor the appellant's repre-*
> *sentative seems to have identified to the Special Adjudicator the failings*
> *in the way in which this appellant was examined upon arrival. In cases*
> *involving unaccompanied minors the duty to ensure full adherence with*

procedural safeguards rests upon all of the parties involved in the refugee-determination process – the interviewing officers, the representatives as well as the Special Adjudicator.

54.36 If the Home Office refusal letter has placed adverse reliance on an interview conducted in breach of the Immigration Rules, you should challenge this in your grounds of appeal, lodge a complaint, and ask the Home Office to withdraw the offending paragraphs. You should then pursue the matter prior to or at the start of the hearing.

54.37 It may be unnecessary and inappropriate to tender a child for cross-examination, and preferable instead to deal by way of a written statement with any matters arising out of the refusal letter upon which your client can usefully comment. The statement should be taken through means and in an environment which are best suited to your client. You may wish to indicate to the Home Office that your client, because of her age, will not be giving oral evidence, and invite the Home Office to put in writing any questions which it wishes to address to her. You can then discuss these with your client and, if they are appropriate questions for your client to answer, answer them in the statement. You should also consider whether there are adult relatives or other witnesses who can explain the dangers your client faces. However, as with adult clients, if your client, despite your advice, wishes to give evidence and is competent to make the decision, then you must respect the decision.

54.38 It will often be unfair to question a child in the same manner as an adult. If you are minded to call her, consider requesting at the outset that she should be given the opportunity to express herself in her own way at her own pace, and that she should not be criticised if her evidence goes beyond the confines of the question to which she is responding. If the adjudicator indicates that this is not acceptable, then you and your client may wish to reconsider whether she should give evidence. If the appeal is dismissed in such circumstances, you may wish to raise the issue on appeal.

54.39 During any cross-examination, you must be particularly alert to object to inappropriate questioning. The same issues may arise as with adult asylum seekers (discussed in chapter 36). However, a style of questioning that might be acceptable to an adult might well be inappropriately aggressive to a child. There may also be an increased danger of the HOPO straying into irrelevancy. For example, if your client is at risk because of the political activities of her parents, the HOPO may launch into questions about their politics even where your client has never claimed any knowledge of these.

54.40 Much work has been done by the family courts to make the court room as unintimidating as possible for children involved in litigation. The IAA does not make special arrangements for child appellants as a matter of course. But if you request them, either at the first hearing or in writing, arrangements can be made such as holding the hearing in a smaller room, seating the adjudicator at the same level as the parties, and giving evidence by video link (see the IAA Gender Guidelines, para 5.6). You may request such steps whether or not the child intends to give oral evidence. See also chapter 32 as to exclusion of the public and anonymity.

54 Representing children
Key points

- Establishing that your client is a child is important because:

  - ☐ special procedures apply to the determination of children's asylum claims,
  - ☐ it is Home Office policy not to detain unaccompanied children,
  - ☐ children cannot be denied support on the same basis as adults,
  - ☐ the Home Office will grant an unaccompanied child at least Discretionary Leave if she is refused asylum (unless adequate reception arrangements are in place in her home country).

- Expert medical evidence should be sought where age is in dispute. It cannot identify a precise age, but Home Office policy is to accord the benefit of the doubt in borderline cases. It may establish that a date of birth contained in a document relied upon by the Home Office is false.

- Where medical evidence is insufficient to establish that your client is a child, a detailed statement should be taken dealing with family background and history, education, and activities during the previous few years.

- It is not acceptable for a child to be switched between representatives at a firm without good reason. You should obtain an undertaking from any advocate that he will conduct the matter personally and do everything possible to avoid conflicting professional engagements.

- You should have a working knowledge of family and child care law or else ensure that specialist advice is obtained.

- A child is as entitled as an adult to independent representation, to realistic advice, and to have her instructions respected and effected to the fullest extent possible. You need to assess your client's ability to give instructions and the extent to which it is appropriate to accept instructions from any adult on your client's behalf.

- Conduct detailed country of origin research before interviewing a child. Conduct the interview in surroundings in which your client is comfortable. She should be permitted to provide information in her own way in her own time, rather than simply in response to a structured interview.

■ You should warn any adult client of the risks posed by the one stop procedure for her children. You must be clear whether the children are also your clients. If so, you must advise them fully about the one stop procedure and take separate instructions from them.

■ Home Office policy is that a family will not normally be removed if it includes a child who has lived in the UK for at least seven years.

■ Unaccompanied children who are refused asylum will initially be granted Discretionary Leave for three years or until their 18th birthday (whichever is earlier). Those who establish a real risk of inhuman or degrading treatment should be entitled to Humanitarian Protection. There may be cases in which only a grant of indefinite leave would be consistent with the child's human rights.

■ The Immigration Rules provide that a child should not be interviewed by the Home Office without a responsible adult being present. An adjudicator will err if he places adverse reliance on an interview conducted in breach of the Immigration Rules.

■ It may well be inappropriate to tender a child for cross-examination. The Home Office can be invited to put any questions in writing in advance.

■ If you are minded to call your client, you should ask that allowance be made for her age when she gives evidence. Cross-examination that would be acceptable in respect of an adult may be inappropriate for a child.

■ The IAA can be asked to make practical arrangements including rearranging the hearing room and hearing evidence by video link.

55 Bail

55.1   This chapter deals with applying for bail for a detained appellant. Guidance on challenging detention prior to the Home Office's decision on the asylum/human rights claim, and more detailed guidance on applying for bail generally, can be found in the *Best Practice Guide to Challenging Immigration Detention* (to be published by ILPA, BID and the Law Society in late 2003).

55.2   Any appellant may apply for bail to an adjudicator (and subsequently to the IAT). It is a fundamental aspect of best practice in conducting an appeal that every effort is made to obtain your client's release. Not only is unjustified detention a violation of your client's human rights. It may also greatly complicate the preparation of the substantive appeal. If your client is in detention when served with the notice of refusal and remains in detention thereafter, she will be subject to the fast track procedure (chapter 53). This may severely prejudice the conduct of her appeal. In those cases, it is obviously imperative that a prompt bail application is made in order to facilitate the proper preparation of the appeal.

Criteria for detention

55.3   Once the Home Office has refused the asylum/human rights claim, Home Office policy permits detention either where removal is imminent or where there are strong grounds for believing that the person will abscond. In *Amirthanathan*, the Home Office accepted that once an appeal is lodged, the appellant cannot be detained on the basis of 'imminent removal'. (The judge held that the same would apply where the Home Office had been notified of an intention to appeal.)

55.4   Someone with a pending asylum/human rights appeal can therefore only be detained if there are strong grounds to believe that she would otherwise abscond. In *Brzezinski*, Kay J noted that it was the Home Office's policy to detain appellants only as a 'last resort' and held that 'any reasonable person' would conclude that such detention should be necessary only 'in a small minority of cases'. He held that:

> *One weighs all the various factors. One only restricts a person's liberty if it is essential to do so and one judges that by having regard to all the factors that are properly to be considered in the particular case.*

55.5 That passage from Kay J's judgment is quoted at the start of the IAA's *Bail: Guidance Notes for Adjudicators* (3rd Edition, May 2003). The Home Office's policy on detention, as set out in its Operation Enforcement Manual (OEM), is appended to the IAA Guidance. You should be familiar with both documents when making a bail application.

55.6 The Home Office accepted in **Amirthanathan** that detention would be unlawful where it was inconsistent with Home Office policy. The judge quoted extracts from the OEM, including the following:

- *There is a presumption in favour of temporary admission or temporary release.*
- *There must be strong grounds for believing that a person will not comply with conditions of temporary admission or temporary release for detention to be justified.*
- *All reasonable alternatives to detention must be considered before detention is authorised.*
- *Once detention has been authorised, it must be kept under close review to ensure that it continues to be justified.*

55.7 UNHCR's Guidelines on the Detention of Asylum Seekers (also appended to the IAA Guidance) are similarly to the effect that detention should be resorted to 'exceptionally'.

55.8 The IAA Guidance notes that 'There is a common law presumption in favour of bail...' (See also **B (1997, CA)** in which the Court of Appeal considered that the application both of Home Office policy and of 'normal bail criteria' prompted the conclusion that the appellant should be granted bail.)

55.9 The IAA Guidance notes that:

> *The burden of proving that the presumption in favour of liberty does not apply lies on the Secretary of State. As detention is an infringement of the applicant's human right to liberty, you [i.e. the adjudicator] have to be satisfied to a high standard that any infringement of that right is essential.*

55.10 It refers adjudicators to the test set out in the Home Office's policy (i.e 'strong grounds for believing' that the person will abscond) and states that the standard of proof that the Home Office must meet is 'higher than the balance of probabilities but less that the criminal standard of proof'.

55.11 The IAA Guidance also quoted the comments of Dyson LJ in the case of *I* to the effect that 'the relevance of absconding, if proved, should not be overstated', and lists other relevant factors identified by Dyson LJ including the length of the period of detention; the effect of detention on the detainee and her family; and the danger that, if released, she will commit criminal offences.

55.12 In **Amirthanathan**, it was noted that liberty was one of the 'bedrock principles' of the ECHR and that detention of asylum seekers must meet the test of 'proportionality'. The judge quoted the Home Office's acceptance that:

> In all cases detention must be used sparingly, and for the shortest period necessary.

55.13 It is a precondition to the lawfulness of detention that there would be a realistic prospect of removing the person but for her pending appeal (*I*).

'Persons unsuitable for detention'

55.14 The Home Office's OEM (para 38.7.3) states that:

> Unaccompanied minors must only ever be detained in the most exceptional circumstances and then **only overnight**, with appropriate care, whilst alternative arrangements for their safety are made. In circumstances where responsible family or friends in the community cannot care for children they should be placed in the care of the local authority. The same applies to all persons under the age of 18... (emphasis as in original)

55.15 The only exception relates to the detention of children as part of an 'entire family'. However, a family can be detained only where the normal detention criteria are satisfied. It will often be particularly unlikely that a family will abscond where, for example, the children are settled at school. Sometimes, the Home Office will just detain one of the parents raising additional issues under article 8.

55.16 The only circumstances in which you should have to challenge the detention of an unaccompanied child is where the Home Office is claiming that she is an adult. See para 54.4 for resolving age disputes.

55.17 There are other categories that the Home Office accepts are 'unsuitable for detention' (even where they would otherwise meet the detention criteria). The OEM (para 38.8) states that the following will be detained 'in only very exceptional circumstances':

- *the elderly, especially where supervision is required;*
- *pregnant women, unless there is the clear prospect of early removal and medical advice suggests no question of confinement prior to this;*
- *people with serious disabilities;*
- *those suffering from serious medical conditions or the mentally ill;*
- *those where there is independent evidence that they have been tortured;*

55.18 Expert evidence may well be necessary to establish the nature and degree of your client's ill-health. If your client has been tortured, she will *only* fall within the categories deemed unsuitable for detention if you obtain independent evidence. Most commonly, this will be a medical report. However, it could also be a statement from an independent witness who could corroborate her account of torture. Given the purpose of the enquiry, there should be no rationale for the Home Office applying any narrow, legalistic definition of torture.

Reasons for detention

55.19 Article 5(2) of the ECHR provides that:

> *Everyone who is arrested shall be informed promptly, in a language which he understands, of the reasons for his arrest and of any charge against him.*

55.20 That is reflected by assurances given by the Home Office to Parliament. It has undertaken to provide written reasons for detention when a person is detained and at regular intervals thereafter. The rationale for that undertaking was explained to Parliament as follows:

> *[W]ithout exception… the giving of written reasons is extremely important [because] if you have to give written reasons it improves the decision-making process, whether or not those reasons are to be published or scrutinised in a judicial process. But it is extremely important that those written reasons should be provided to any detained person so that he or she will know and have at least a degree of moral consolation that their detention is not an unthinking exercise of administrative power… I do not believe that it can be overstressed.* (Home Office Minister of State, 29 April 1998 , Col 357)

55.21 Rule 9(1) of the Detention Centre Rules 2001 confirms this duty:

> *Every detained person will be provided, by the Secretary of State, with written reasons for his detention at the time of his initial detention, and thereafter monthly.*

55.22 Immediately your client is detained or you receive instructions from a detained appellant, you should write to the Home Office requesting your client's release and requiring that it discloses all reasons relied upon for detaining your client.

55.23 It is essential to find out the reasons as early as possible. Without them, you cannot properly prepare your bail application. Rule 33(2) requires the Home Office to provide written reasons in response to an application for bail, but only the afternoon before the hearing (below). By that time, there may be insufficient opportunity to obtain the evidence you need to dispute them.

55.24 The Home Office's OEM states that:

> It should be noted that the reasons for detention given could be subject to judicial review. It is therefore important to ensure that they are always **justified and correctly stated**… It is important that the detainee understands the contents of the [reasons for detention]. If he does not understand English, officers should ensure that the form's contents are interpreted. Failure to do so could lead to successful challenge under the Human Rights Act (Article 5(2) of the ECHR refers). (emphasis as in original)

55.25 Notwithstanding the above, immigration officers have been known to refuse to provide written reasons to representatives and, on occasion, to refuse even to *read* the reasons over the telephone. Assuming he will at least read the reasons, get the immigration officer to stop while you write them down verbatim, and then read them back to him. Confirm these reasons in writing to the Home Office, and that they represent *all* the reasons for detention that you have been given. Problems have arisen where an immigration officer has refused to give written reasons and subsequently disputes in court that the oral reasons recorded by the solicitor are accurate. Also ask the Home Office for an explanation of the refusal to provide written reasons for detention.

55.26 The Home Office (or a Chief Immigration Officer) has power to grant bail on the basis of sureties. However, the sums that it requires from sureties tend to be exorbitant. There is no need to seek bail from the Home Office before making a bail application to an adjudicator.

55.27 You should also make written representations in response to any reasons for detention you have been given. It may not directly result in the Home Office releasing your client. But if you have fully addressed the Home Office's reasons for detention in correspondence, and the Home Office's reasons for opposing your bail application do not take account of your representations, that can only strengthen your case before the adjudicator.

Assessing the Home Office's reasons for detention

55.28 Once (or if) you get the Home Office's reasons, you must assess whether they indeed constitute 'strong grounds for believing' that your client will abscond. Some reasons with which you may be faced are discussed below.

- *'She did not claim asylum on arrival and/or entered the country clandestinely.'*
  A very large proportion of asylum seekers do not claim asylum at a port. Having successfully entered the country without claiming asylum, the fact that she then presents herself voluntarily to the Home Office can only tell in her favour. Refer to the discussion of the timing of the asylum claim at para 1 49.

- *'The majority of asylum seekers of her nationality have been refused.'*
  The High Court in **Brzezinski** found, not surprisingly, that to base risk of absconding simply on nationality was unacceptable.

- *'She has no ties with the United Kingdom.'*
  Most asylum seekers will have no ties with the United Kingdom. Indeed, such ties are often used by the Home Office to suggest an ulterior motive for the asylum claim.

- *'She possessed/presented false documents and is unable to prove her identity.'*
  Travelling to the UK on false documents is hardly inconsistent with the behaviour of a genuine refugee. In **Adimi**, Simon Brown LJ said that:

  > *Although under the Convention subscribing States must give sanctuary to any refugee who seeks asylum (subject only to removal to a safe third country), they are by no means bound to facilitate his arrival. Rather they strive increasingly to prevent it. The combined effect of visa requirements and carrier's liability has made it well nigh impossible for refugees to travel to countries of refuge without false documents.*

  Indeed, if an asylum seeker does possess travel documents properly issued in her own name, it is often alleged by the Home Office that this indicates that she has no genuine fear of the authorities in her home country.

- *'She has been convicted of a criminal offence in the United Kingdom while on Temporary Admission.'*
  This has in the past been advanced as a ground for detention even where the court imposed a non-custodial sentence (and where it is not asserted that there is a likelihood that the person will commit a

further offence). It was held in *Brzezinski* that a conviction for a minor offence of dishonesty could not justify a belief that an asylum seeker will abscond, and while not irrelevant to an assessment of her trustworthiness, could only be a minor consideration. If the court which tried the matter felt that imprisonment was appropriate then it would have imposed a custodial sentence (and could, if necessary, recommend deportation). Such reasons may be accompanied by assertions that 'She has abused her Temporary Admission'. If the court has not imposed a custodial sentence, it is not for immigration officers to impose some additional punishment.

The Home Office has on occasion sought to justify immigration detention because the person has been charged with a criminal offence, even where she has been released on police bail. If she was considered likely to commit a further offence, she could have been denied police bail. Immigration officers should not second guess or circumvent the criminal process.

• *'She has breached the terms of Temporary Admission.'*
This is less straightforward, but it by no means follows that any such breach should lead to detention. It may simply be that the asylum seeker has inadvertently failed to attend the Home Office on the correct date, but remains living at the address approved by the Home Office.

Asylum seekers are often part of extended families living at different addresses, and may periodically stay with these relatives. Problems can arise when asylum seekers are stopped by police and questioned, usually without proper interpreters, and give a relative's address rather than their own address. If this happens to your client, you should put the facts to the Home Office immediately, explaining why your client gave that address, pointing out the lack of a proper interpreter, and confirming that she continues to live at the approved address.

CLR for bail applications

55.29 The standard tests for granting CLR apply (see chapter 56). ILPA has expressed concern that some representatives are justifying a failure to apply for bail for detained clients on the basis of an incorrect application of the merits test. CLR should only be refused for a bail application if the merits of the application are poor (given that the fundamental right to liberty will always be engaged).

55.30 The onus is on the Home Office to justify detention. The prospects will be poor only if it has established strong grounds for believing that your client will abscond. If you have asked the Home Office to provide reasons for detention and it has refused to do so, that in itself is unlawful and a basis for seeking bail.

55.31 It is *never* acceptable to conclude that a bail application has insufficient prospects of success simply because sureties are not available (see below).

55.32 If you do refuse CLR funding on the basis that the merits are poor, your client is entitled to the same right of review of your decision as would apply if you refused CLR for the substantive appeal (para 56.18).

Applying for bail

55.33 Rule 32 deals with lodging a bail application:

> *(1) An application to be released on bail must be made by filing with the appellate authority an application notice in the appropriate prescribed form.*
>
> *(2) The application notice must contain the following details –*
>
> *(a) the applicant's –*
>
> > *(i) full name;*
> > *(ii) date of birth; and*
> > *(iii) date of arrival in the United Kingdom;*
>
> *(b) the address of the place where the applicant is detained;*
>
> *(c) whether an appeal by the applicant to an adjudicator or the Tribunal is pending;*
>
> *(d) the address where the applicant will reside if his application for bail is granted, or, if he is unable to give such an address, the reason why an address is not given;*
>
> *(e) the amount of the recognizance in which he will agree to be bound;*
>
> *(f) the full names, addresses, occupations and dates of birth of any persons who have agreed to act as sureties for the applicant if bail is granted, and the amounts of the recognizances in which they will agree to be bound;*
>
> *(g) the grounds on which the application is made and, where a previous application has been refused, full details of any change in circumstances which has occurred since the refusal; and*

> (h) *whether and in what respect an interpreter will be required at the hearing.*
>
> (3) *The application must be signed by the applicant or his representative or, in the case of an applicant who is a child or is for any other reason incapable of acting, by a person acting on his behalf.*

55.34 The indication in r.32(2)(d) that the appellant can provide either the address at which he would reside if bail were granted or 'if he is unable to give such an address, the reason why an address is not given' allows for bail to be granted where the appellant is to be accommodated by NASS under the asylum support regime at an address which has not yet been identified. The IAA Guidance states that:

> *Where an applicant is relying upon accommodation to be allocated by NASS, it will be necessary for written evidence from NASS to be produced at the hearing of the bail application confirming that NASS has accepted that the applicant is eligible for its support and that it will be allocating accommodation. NASS is aware of this requirement. If bail is granted, the condition of residence should read:*
>
> > *To reside at such accommodation as is directed by NASS in accordance with the terms and conditions of support given, and to notify the IAA, the Chief Adjudicator, and the Secretary of State for the Home Department of the address of such accommodation within 24 hours of being provided with it.*
>
> *This wording has been approved by NASS. Policy Bulletin 64 will also indicate that when allocating accommodation, caseworkers should have regard 'to the location of the person or organisation acting as surety'.*

55.35 The new version of Policy Bulletin 64 is, at time of writing, yet to be published. Check for information either on the Home Office website, or the excellent *www.asylumsupport.info.*

55.36 See para 55.77 for making a bail application where your client has already been refused bail. If making the first bail application, r.32(2)(g) requires you to state 'the grounds upon which the application is made'. As discussed above, the Rules make provision for the Home Office to give written reasons only after the bail application is lodged. If it has already disclosed its reasons, you should deal with these briefly in your application. If it has not disclosed reasons, you need state only that 'The Home Office has not established strong grounds for believing that the appellant will not comply with conditions of temporary admission/release.'

55.37 Note that an interpreter will not be booked automatically unless you request one. You should do so if either the appellant or any surety will require one.

55.38 The appellant will normally have no significant capital of her own. Rule 32(2)(e) can be satisfied by entering a nominal sum. The IAA Guidance indicates that:

> You should always enquire of the applicant or the representative if there are any assets. If the applicant has no assets, as is usually the case, the recognizance can be a nominal sum of £10.

Sureties

55.39 Contrary to what has sometimes been supposed, it is no precondition of a bail application that sureties are available. The detention of an appellant will only be consistent with Home Office policy where the 'presumption' in favour of liberty has been displaced by 'strong grounds for believing' that the appellant will abscond. If detention is inconsistent with Home Office policy, it will be unlawful (as the Home Office accepts). The adjudicator will himself act unlawfully if he refuses to grant bail to an appellant who is unlawfully detained.

55.40 In *Brzezinski* (and quoted in the IAA Guidance), Kay J stated that 'Clearly it would be wrong to require sureties, if there were no need for sureties'. The purpose of a surety is that it may enable 'a person who might not otherwise be granted his liberty [to] be granted it.' It will be an error of law for an adjudicator to refuse bail because of absence of sureties when the appellant should not be detained in the first place.

55.41 Sureties should be required only where there are strong grounds for believing that the appellant will abscond and where the provision of sureties can reduce the likelihood of absconding to an extent that will enable the adjudicator to grant bail. There will, of course, be cases where the evidence of the appellant's propensity to abscond is so strong that bail must be refused despite the availability of sureties.

55.42 The IAA Guidance includes a 'Surety Check-list' for adjudicators that states that:

> When you find that bail can be granted subject to suitable conditions, the question to ask yourself is whether or not there are such conditions that can be imposed without the need for sureties. If there is no need for sureties, there is no need to hear evidence from [any that have been offered].

Assessing suitability

55.43 You will have to determine whether any available surety is suitable. An unsuitable surety can be worse than no surety at all. The HOPO will seek to turn the bail hearing into a trial of your surety so as to distract attention from the fundamental question of whether he has shown good grounds for detention in the first place.

55.44 Any surety should preferably be a British citizen or have leave to enter/ remain. But for obvious reasons, it will often be the case that the only people in this country who know your client well enough to stand surety are also asylum seekers. If you offer another asylum seeker as a surety, or someone whose leave may not last the duration of the bail, you will have to make representations as to why they will nevertheless make suitable sureties. The Home Office accepted in *Brzezinski* that asylum seekers should not be rejected as sureties simply by reason of their immigration status and that the question should be decided according to the individual circumstances of the case. This should be pointed out if either the HOPO or the adjudicator assert that no asylum seeker can be a satisfactory surety.

55.45 You should also emphasise that the purpose of requiring a surety is to give that person a stake in ensuring that the detainee complies with conditions and that the amount of the surety can only sensibly be considered in relation to the surety's means. The IAA Guidance notes that:

> *What is a nominal sum to one person may be a substantial sum to another.*

55.46 You should take instructions on the surety's occupation (if any), home (even if it is not proposed that your client will live with him), and family ties. Obviously, the more stable his background, the better. If he has been a successful surety before, then that should be mentioned.

55.47 The surety must be able to provide evidence that he has sufficient funds to meet his obligations as a surety should the appellant abscond, and there should not be any apparent risk that he will lose those funds during the duration of the bail. An adjudicator should not require that the funds offered by the surety are immediately available, and equity in a property can therefore be acceptable (*Shamamba*). The adjudicator's 'Surety Check-list' states that:

> *If you are considering taking into account the value of the equity in a home, only do so if the money can easily be obtained, e.g. by way of an affordable re-mortgage or further charge.*

55.48 You should check any bank statement or savings book, preferably before the day of the hearing. If the surety offers a sum of £2000, and provides a bank statement which shows a balance of £2000, but that £1900 of it was deposited the day before the hearing, the HOPO will claim this to be evidence that the money has been given to the surety by someone else for the purposes of the bail hearing. Take instructions. Your surety may prefer to keep money in cash. He may have deposited his cash savings into a bank account to provide convenient evidence of his ability to meet the surety. Or he may have consolidated funds from different accounts for the purposes of the bail hearing. He may have sold something.

55.49   If the savings are from his salary, then be sure that you are clear as to how it has been feasible to save that amount from his salary, and how this is reflected in the bank statements provided. A surety should not be rejected simply because he has borrowed the money to stand surety (although he may well be asked about the terms of the loan). As stated above, the point is simply to demonstrate the stake the surety has in ensuring your client complies with bail, and the question is therefore to what extent the potential surety is responsible for funds offered, not how he came by them.

55.50   Establish why the person is prepared to stand surety. It is preferable if he knows your client personally and can vouch for her character. The adjudicator's 'surety check-list' suggests that the following may be relevant in assessing 'relationship with the applicant':

- *Is the surety a blood relative or related by marriage, or not related at all?*
- *How long has the surety known the applicant?*
- *How much contact has there been between the surety and the applicant in the United Kingdom?*
- *Will the applicant feel a sense of moral obligation towards the surety?*
- *Will the applicant live with the surety, and what arrangements have been made?*

55.51   Given the likely scarcity of possible sureties, a person who knows your client's family rather your client personally will often be acceptable. The surety should be prepared to maintain contact with your client on bail, and be confident of his ability to exert influence over her.

55.52   The IAA guidance recognises that a suitable surety in the traditional sense may well be unavailable to an asylum seeker:

> *It should be borne in mind that asylum seekers rarely have friends or relatives in the United Kingdom who can act as sureties. They may have no alternative but to rely on assistance from voluntary organisations to support their applications.*

55.53   The Churches Commission for Racial Justice has established the Bail Circle which maintains a register of people in the community (many from churches) prepared to act as sureties in bail applications. The IAA

Guidance notes that 'sometimes officers or senior figures from charities, churches and other organisations are offered as sureties'. It suggests that if an organisation is taking the applicant 'under its wing', it may be appropriate to impose conditions other than sureties.

55.54 Potential sureties should attend the bail hearing unless this is impossible. The IAA Guidance states that if the adjudicator concludes that sureties are required, then only in exceptional circumstances should he grant bail on the strength of a surety who has not attended the hearing.

55.55 The IAA's 'Notice to applicants, their representatives, and sureties' (appendix 4 to the IAA Guidance) states that:

> Representatives are reminded that it is their responsibility to ensure that the proposed sureties bring with them to the hearing suitable evidence to prove their identity, income and assets. In particular they are requested, where possible and relevant, to produce the following documents:
>
> a) passport or other means of establishing identity;
>
> b) if right to reside in the United Kingdom is limited, evidence of when that right expires;
>
> c) recent wage slips or, if self-employed, a copy of their latest set of accounts as submitted to the Inland Revenue or a letter from their accountants certifying their personal taxable income;
>
> d) Bank statements, and building society passbooks, preferably covering the last three months, with evidence of current balances;
>
> e) rent books or mortgage statements, together with other documentation showing the address of the surety, e.g. current driving licence or NHS Medical Card;
>
> f) any documentary evidence showing the value of any property or other assets belonging to the surety.

55.56 However, the failure to produce such documentation will not necessarily lead to the surety being rejected. The adjudicator's 'Surety Checklist' states that:

> You should seek some documentary evidence to support the oral evidence of the surety relating to his financial circumstances. The absence of such documentary evidence is not fatal, but may affect the weight you attach to such oral evidence.

The bail hearing

55.57 Rule 33(1) states that:

> Where an application for bail is filed, the appellate authority must -
>
> (a) as soon as reasonably practicable, serve a copy of the application on the Secretary of State; and
>
> (b) fix a hearing.

55.58 Article 5(4) requires that a detainee has access to a court which can determine 'speedily' the lawfulness of her detention and, if unlawful, order her release. Practice Direction CA6 of 2001 provides that:

> Bail applications are to be listed for hearing within three working days of receipt by the appellate authority of the notice of application.

55.59 The IAA Guidance states that:

> It should be the rule rather than the exception that the applicant attends the hearing. This will be necessary, in particular, if there is a dispute over the facts as set out in the bail summary. You may also wish to satisfy yourself that the applicant understands and is likely to comply with any conditions that may be imposed. Further, the applicant has a right to attend the hearing of his application, be legally represented, and have an interpreter provided if necessary.

Home Office's bail summary

55.60 Rule 33(2) states that:

> (2) If the Secretary of State wishes to contest the application, he must file with the appellate authority and serve on the applicant a written statement of his reasons for doing so –
>
> (a) not later than 2.00 p.m. the day before the hearing; or
>
> (b) if he was served with notice of the hearing less than 24 hours before that time, as soon as reasonably practicable.

55.61 The Home Office will usually comply by serving a document headed 'Bail Summary' containing its reasons for opposing bail. You may well need to take further instructions from your client upon receipt of the bail summary. This may have to be done by telephone if it is not possible to arrange a legal visit.

55.62 The IAA Guidelines state that:

> If [the Home Office] fails to file a bail summary within the required time,

or if there is no bail summary, how should [the adjudicator] proceed? If no bail summary is available, then you should proceed without it. This implies that bail would have to be granted. If it is provided late, then you can consider it. However, if the allegations contained in it are disputed, its late submission and the lack of time given to the applicant to prepare his response to it must affect the evidential weight you can attach to it and any evidence submitted in its support.

Conduct of the hearing

55.63 If, at the outset of the hearing, the adjudicator notes that the bail application has not been made on the prescribed form, the IAA Guidance indicates that he should provide a copy of the correct form for completion. The Guidance advises adjudicators to proceed to hear the bail application if any failure to comply with the Rules is minor and does not prejudice the Home Office. It suggests that where new details of sureties are provided which the HOPO wishes to check, the matter may be put to the back of the list to enable him to do so.

55.64 The HOPO will be asked whether he has anything to add to the bail summary. Usually, he does not. You will normally object if he seeks to raise fresh reasons which were not included in a bail summary served only the afternoon before. The IAA Guidance states that:

If you consider the bail summary to be inadequate, you should inform the Presenting Officer at the beginning of the hearing. If the Presenting Officer asks for time to make further enquiries, you may consider it appropriate to grant a short adjournment to enable him to make a telephone call to obtain additional information from the entry port.

55.65 The HOPO will usually attend without the Home Office file, and often without any evidence to support the Bail Summary. The onus is on the Home Office to establish that the appellant must be detained, not on the appellant to establish that she should be released. This fundamental point should be at the forefront of your case at the bail hearing. You should also remind the adjudicator of the IAA Guidance to the effect that:

If allegations in the bail summary are contested in evidence then the Secretary of State should adduce evidence, including any documents relevant to the decision to detain, to support his allegations.

55.66 If the HOPO cannot point to evidence to establish any allegation made by the Home Office which the appellant disputes, there will be no evidential basis upon which the adjudicator can accept that allegation.

55.67 If the Home Office has produced grounds and evidence capable of supporting detention, you will need to set out the positive factors in favour of release, such as family in the United Kingdom, settled accommodation, and ill-health. Remember that the overriding question is whether your client is likely to go to ground if granted bail. If this is impractical, for example because your client does not speak English or is elderly, then this should be pointed out.

55.68 You may lead oral evidence from the appellant in order to answer the Home Office's case or to establish positive factors to set against the Home Office's grounds for detention. You should object if the HOPO puts allegations in cross-examination for which he has produced no evidence. You may also present evidence showing that your client falls within a category that the Home Office accepts is unsuitable for detention, most usually independent evidence of torture.

55.69 The adjudicator will often wish to hear from any sureties that have been offered. Your examination in chief should deal with the surety's suitability. Depending upon how well your surety knows the client, you may also ask the surety for an assessment of your client's character, and what makes the surety confident that she will not abscond.

55.70 The HOPO will then have an opportunity to cross-examine your sureties. Any cross-examination will generally be designed to persuade the adjudicator of one or more of the following: that the surety does not know your client or does not know her very well; that the surety's immigration status in this country is uncertain; that the proof of funds which the surety has provided is suspect; that it is likely that the funds have been provided to the surety by someone else for the purposes of this application; that the surety is of bad character. Just as during cross-examination in substantive asylum appeals, you should object if you think any question asked by the HOPO is unfair or misleading, or if the HOPO's tone is hectoring, or he is interrupting the witness before he has finished his answers; you should also object if the HOPO starts asking questions which are irrelevant to the issue of whether the witness is an acceptable surety.

55.71 Adjudicators normally expect to impose conditions as to residence and reporting when they grant bail and you should be prepared to assist with these.

Refusal of bail

55.72 In *B (1997, CA)*, the Court of Appeal held (in granting bail to an asylum appellant) that:

> *When a judge makes an order curtailing the liberty of a subject it is essential that, for the benefit of the person concerned as well as of this court, he gives his reasons even if only in a few sentences.*

55.73 Rule 33 states that:

> *(3) The appellate authority must serve written notice of the adjudicator or the Tribunal's decision on –*
>
> *(a) the parties; and*
> *(b) the person having custody of the applicant.*
> *...*
> *(5) Where bail is refused, the notice must include reasons for the refusal.*

55.74 The 'reasons for the refusal' required by r.33(5) will be written by the adjudicator on the notice and given to you before you leave the hearing centre. The notice is appended to the IAA Guidance. It provides a blank page for the adjudicator to state his reasons why 'I am satisfied that there are substantial grounds for believing that if granted bail the applicant will abscond...'

55.75 Despite the requirement to provide reasons in writing, adjudicators sometimes give additional reasons orally that do not find their way into the notice. You must take a full and contemporaneous note of any oral reasons given by the adjudicator.

55.76 Your options following refusal of bail are to either make a fresh bail application or to bring judicial review proceedings. You have no right of appeal to the IAT against the adjudicator's refusal to grant bail.

Fresh bail application

55.77 Rule 32(2)(g) states that where a previous bail application has been refused, the application form should provide 'full details of any change in circumstances which has occurred since the refusal'. The Administrative Court has emphasised that any change of circumstances, which may include new evidence in support of the asylum/human rights appeal, should trigger 'careful reappraisal' of whether detention remains justified (*B (1997, AC)*; *Mohamed*). The IAA Guidance states that:

> *If a bail application is refused, an applicant has a right to make a fresh application on the same grounds and any further grounds that may have arisen. Renewed bail applications should not be a review of previous decisions. Adjudicators must have regard to the reasons for the decision given by previous adjudicators and should generally expect to see fresh additional reasons and/or some change in circumstances...*

> *The lapse of time between bail applications may well itself be a relevant factor. It is suggested that provided a fresh bail application is made at least 28 days after the refusal of the previous application and you find that the lapse of time is relevant to the particular case then you should be prepared to consider the arguments that were presented on the previous application as well as any fresh arguments.*

55.78 Adjudicators, given that they exercise an independent statutory discretion, are entitled to reach different decisions on the same circumstances, and would unlawfully fetter their discretion if they regarded themselves as bound by decisions of previous adjudicators to refuse your client bail. This ought to apply to a bail application made within 28 days of a previous refusal even in the absence of any fresh evidence or change of circumstances (other than lapse of time in detention). However, the more appropriate course, where you consider that a refusal to grant bail is unlawful, will be to seek judicial review.

Judicial review

55.79 The Court of Appeal held in **Cawley** that the same priority will be given to a judicial review of detention as is applied to habeas corpus (which takes precedence over any other court business). This is adhered to in practice, and High Court judges have on occasion expressed surprise at the failure of the IAA to hear bail applications on non-working days.

55.80 You may challenge both the adjudicator's refusal to grant bail and the Home Office's continuing detention of your client. Unlike criminal courts, an adjudicator may only grant bail, not remand in custody. It remains the Home Office's detention, and the Home Office retains a duty, recognised by its policy, to keep detention under review and release as soon as possible, regardless of whether the adjudicator has refused to exercise his independent statutory power to grant bail. (See e.g. **B (1997, AC)** in which the Home Office was found to have acted unlawfully in failing to release the claimant on the same date that he was refused bail by an adjudicator. It was ordered to pay damages in respect of its unlawful detention of the claimant from that date, despite a further bail application being refused by an adjudicator in the meantime.)

55 Bail
Key points

- There is a presumption in favour of liberty. It is for the Home Office to rebut it. An appellant may only be detained if there are strong grounds for believing that she will abscond if released.

- Detention will be unlawful if it is inconsistent with Home Office policy. An adjudicator will act unlawfully if he refuses bail to someone who is unlawfully detained.

- Unaccompanied children may only be detained overnight whilst alternative arrangements are made for their care.

- Other categories deemed unsuitable for detention include those with serious medical conditions or the mentally ill, and those who can produce independent evidence of torture.

- A detainee is entitled to written reasons for detention from the Home Office. Ask the Home Office to disclose its reasons, record them, and make any representations in response.

- CLR should be refused for a bail application only if the prospects of success are poor. CLR should never be refused simply because no sureties are available.

- Where your client cannot offer an address but is entitled to asylum support, bail can be granted to an address to be arranged by NASS.

- Sureties should be required only where there would otherwise be strong grounds to believe that the appellant would abscond.

- Assess the suitability of any surety: an unsuitable surety may be worse than no surety.

- The Home Office must serve written reasons for opposing bail (the 'bail summary') by 2pm on the day before the bail hearing. If no bail summary is served, bail should be granted.

- The onus is on the Home Office to justify continued detention, not on the appellant to establish that she should be released. The Home Office must adduce evidence at the hearing to support its allegations if they are contested.

- An adjudicator must give written reasons for refusing bail.

■ A fresh application for bail can be made following a refusal of bail, and will be the appropriate course if there has been a change of circumstances (including lapse of time) or fresh evidence is available.

■ If the refusal of bail is unlawful, it can be challenged by judicial review, as can the Home Office's continued detention of the appellant.

56 Public funding and costs

56.1   Your client is entitled to legal representation for her appeal funded through Controlled Legal Representation provided that she meets the means test, and her appeal meets the 'sufficient benefit' and merits tests.

56.2   Most asylum and human rights appellants qualify under the means test (particularly given the increasingly draconian restrictions on them working). It is normally straightforward to apply the relevant criteria.

56.3   The sufficient benefit test should also be straightforward in most asylum/human rights appeals. The criterion is expressed as follows in the GCC:

> *Do the likely benefits to be gained from the proceedings justify the likely costs, such that a reasonable privately paying client would be prepared to take proceedings having regard to the prospects of success and all the other circumstances?*

> *If the answer to this question is no, then you should not grant Controlled Legal Representation unless the case has a significant wider public interest. In practice most immigration cases will satisfy this question, although it could, for example, justify a refusal in relation to a limited application to remain in the country.*

Virtually all asylum and human rights cases should satisfy this test.

The merits test

56.4   The merits test is less straightforward and more closely linked to the preparation of the appeal. Section 5 of the GCC specification sets out the following criteria:

> *Question 1: What are the prospects of the appeal being successful?*

> *These must be estimated in one of the following three categories:*

(a) *Moderate or better – prospects are clearly over 50%. If so, Controlled Legal Representation may be provided (assuming that all the other criteria are satisfied).*

(b) *Unclear – where it is not possible to predict the chances of success because further investigation is needed, or Borderline where those chances appear to be 50:50.*

> *In those circumstances, you should refuse Controlled Legal Representation unless any of the following three factors apply:*

> i)   *the case is of overwhelming importance to the client, that is, it concerns the life, liberty or physical safety of the client or his or her family, or the roof over their heads. This will often be true of asylum cases; or*
> ii) *the case raises significant issues of human rights; or*
> iii) *the case has a significant wider public interest, that is, the proceedings have the potential to produce real benefits for members of the public other than the client and their family, other than any benefits which normally flow from proceedings of the type in question.*

> *Where these factors apply, you will usually grant Controlled Legal Representation provided all other criteria are satisfied. To clarify if the case falls within (c) below then CLR should be refused or withdrawn even if (i) to (iii) above apply.*

(c) *Poor – prospects are clearly below 50%. Controlled Legal Representation must be refused where the appropriate advice to the client would be that in the circumstances of the case their appeal is more likely to fail than to succeed.*

5   *Examples of where the prospects of success will be poor are where:*

(a) *In light of all the evidence the reasons for applying to remain in the United Kingdom are, in the case of an asylum application outside the criteria laid down in the 1951 Convention relating to the Status of Refugees or in the case of a human rights application, outside the criteria in the ECHR.*

(b) *In a second or subsequent asylum or human rights application, where the same facts have already been determined before an Adjudicator on a previous application and dismissed and there has been no relevant change of circumstance.*

(c) *The client's circumstances and/or the circumstances within her/his country of origin have changed since the initial application was made such that any claim on the basis of asylum or human rights would be likely to fail.*

> (d) *The client's credibility is significantly in doubt and the client is unable to provide a satisfactory explanation for any discrepancies or provide relevant corroborative evidence of his/her statement.*
>
> (e) *Where in light of recent case law based on similar facts the appeal would be likely to fail.*
>
> (f) *Where the client has unreasonably failed to provide the necessary information such as to enable the supplier to properly prepare the case despite the reasonable efforts of the supplier to obtain that information.*

> 6 *A successful outcome for the purpose of estimating success will not except as set out below, include a situation where the appeal may result in a recommendation by the Adjudicator. The exception will be where you estimate that there is a good or borderline chance (as defined above) that the determination and/or recommendation of the Adjudicator will disclose clear exceptional compassionate circumstances which have not previously been considered and which will lead to the exercise of the Secretary of State's discretion outside the immigration rules.*

56.5 An asylum or human rights appeal will ordinarily be of overwhelming interest to the client and/or raise significant human rights issues. So to authorise CLR, the prospects of success should *either* be 50% or above, *or* not possible to predict or borderline.

56.6 Clearly, the prospects of success will be easier to predict where credibility is not in issue, and not possible to predict in many cases where credibility *is* in issue. The following process is suggested:

- On the basis of your client's account, is there a realistic case that expulsion will violate the UK's obligations? If not, CLR should be refused.
- If so, are there any arguments in the Home Office refusal letter upon which it is likely to be successful in defeating the appeal regardless of credibility? If so, CLR should be refused.
- If not, and credibility has not been put in issue in the refusal letter, you should grant CLR.
- If not, and credibility is in issue, is your client's account inconsistent with available country information to an extent that renders it incapable of belief? If so, refuse CLR.
- If not, are there other credibility points in the Home Office's refusal letter which are central to the case and which cannot be answered? If so, refuse CLR.
- If not, grant CLR.

56.7 If the points made in the refusal letter are weak, you will probably conclude that the chances of success are at least 50%. If the points made in the refusal letter are arguable but not conclusive, then the prospects of success are likely to depend upon two variables, neither of which can be safely predicted in advance.

56.8 The first is the performance of your client on the day (assuming you call her). Clients who perform badly in conference may perform well in oral evidence – and vice versa. The second is the identity of the adjudicator who is allocated to hear the appeal. In the real world, and given the variety of approaches taken by adjudicators, this may have an even greater impact upon the result.

56.9 The issue you must address is the prospect of the *appeal* being success-ful, not merely the prospect of it being successful at first instance before the adjudicator. Therefore, higher authority that renders the immediate prospects of success poor (or even non-existent) does not necessarily represent a bar to granting CLR.

56.10 If the adverse authority is recent, you should first check whether it is under appeal. If public funding has been granted to pursue that appeal, that should be sufficient evidence of the prospects of success to justify the grant of CLR. If it is not being appealed, you will have to consider the prospects of challenging it once you reach a court with the power to reverse (or reinterpret) the decision. Obviously, that will be more likely if the adverse authority is from the IAT or Administrative Court rather than the Court of Appeal or above.

56.11 You cannot leap-frog the adjudicator stage, even if you accept that he will be bound to dismiss your appeal on the present state of the author-ities. But you will have to consider whether attendance at the adjudica-tor hearing is justifiable on CLR in those circumstances. One option is to explain, either in writing or at the first hearing, why you consider that the adjudicator is bound to dismiss the appeal, and invite him to dismiss it summarily in order to clear the way to a further appeal.

56.12 There will however be many cases in which there is a danger of the adjudicator reaching adverse factual findings which could prejudice your case on a subsequent appeal from his determination. In those cir-cumstances, you will usually be justified in attending the hearing.

56.13 The GCC gives the following additional guidance on the application of the merits test to an application for permission to appeal to the IAT:

> An application for leave to appeal to the Tribunal should not be auto-matic. An Adjudicator has already considered both issues of fact and law. CLR should only be granted where the prospects of success are good or borderline as defined above. When considering the prospects of success

you should look at the prospects of the appeal succeeding before the Tribunal and not simply the prospects of getting leave. Where the issue is of a technical nature you should carefully consider whether the outcome is one which will ultimately benefit the client and not merely prolong his/her stay in the country in a case which on the facts is likely to fail.

You should not proceed to grant CLR at the leave stage on the grounds that the prospects of success are unclear. A supplier should be aware of all relevant issues by this stage. Exceptionally the prospects of success may be unclear where further investigation is needed, for example, where fresh evidence has come to light since the Adjudicator hearing that would be admissible before the Tribunal. In such cases CLR may be granted to enable further investigation to be carried out. However once this investigation is concluded then the merits test should be reconsidered and the prospects should no longer be said to be unclear.

56.14 The IAT will refuse permission to appeal even where an error is identified in the adjudicator's determination if the appeal as a whole is unmeritorious. There should therefore be few cases in which you conclude that permission to appeal will be granted but there are insufficient prospects of the appeal succeeding in order to grant CLR.

56.15 See the discussion in chapter 43 concerning the circumstances in which fresh evidence may be relevant to the prospects of success before the IAT.

Reviewing and refusing CLR

56.16 There is a continuing duty to keep the merits of the appeal under review for the purposes of CLR. The GCC states that:

> 7 *The criteria for CLR should be applied as soon as practicable after the right to appeal has arisen and before the appeal is filed provided sufficient information is available to undertake the merits test at that stage and it is practicable to sign the form within the time limits for appeal. An example of where it may not be practicable would be where a client is in detention and the supplier is unable to secure an appointment with the client before the time limit to appeal has expired. Where CLR is granted in connection with an appeal before an Adjudicator and the prospects of success are unclear as further investigation is required, then the merits test should be reapplied as soon as the information necessary to properly determine the prospects of success are available to the supplier. If after further investigation the prospects of success are poor then CLR should be withdrawn.*

8   *The criteria should continue to be reviewed where practicable in advance of the hearing. If therefore after you have decided to grant Controlled Legal Representation in any particular case circumstances change or new information arises such that the merits test is no longer satisfied, you should cease to provide Controlled Legal Representation save to the extent of any professional duty owed (including in particular to inform your client, the Home Office and the appellate authority of your ceasing to act). Likewise, you may grant Controlled Legal Representation to a client to whom you have previously refused it where further information arises or circumstances change such that the criteria are now satisfied.*

56.17   Adverse developments rendering the prospects of ultimate success poor may include higher adverse authority being confirmed on appeal and an improvement in the country of origin. You may equally grant CLR despite it previously having been refused if legal or evidential developments have increased the prospects of success.

56.18   If you decide not to grant CLR or you withdraw it, you **must** give your client proper notice of the review procedures (regardless of whether you go on to represent her on any other basis). The GCC states that:

Right of Review

Where you refuse an application for Controlled Legal Representation or having granted the application, subsequently withdraw Controlled Legal Representation you should inform the client of their right to seek a review of your decision by the Regional Director and the Funding Review Body, and if so requested by the client, provide them with the review notification form. A record of this advice must be kept on the file.

1   *Clients will have the right to seek a review by the Regional Director and Funding Review Body of your decision not to provide or continue Controlled Legal Representation. The appeal notification must be in the form specified by us from time to time and should be submitted to the Regional Office within 14 days of your decision.*

2   *The review notification form will include a section which you must complete, recording your reasons for the refusal. The review will be determined in accordance with the procedures set out in the Funding Code*

56.19   If you refuse CLR, you may not continue to prepare the appeal under Legal Help. The GCC provides that:

If the criteria for Controlled Legal Representation are not satisfied then suppliers should not continue to provide Legal Help to the client in connection with that appeal except to inform the client of their situation and advise on rights of appeal... Carrying on the case under Legal Help defeats the purpose of the merits test. If an application for review is filed at the Regional Office against the decision to refuse CLR then only limited Legal Help may be provided in order to undertake urgent work pending a decision on the review. Legal Help may also continue to be available to enable you to make representations on the client's behalf which are not in connection with the appeal.

Bail

56.20 The same criteria and procedures (including the right of review if CLR is refused) apply to funding a bail application through CLR. The GCC confirms that CLR may be used to fund a bail application (provided the relevant tests are met) even where you are not providing representation at an appeal under CLR. See para 55.29 for comments on the application of the CLR criteria to a bail application.

Enhanced Rate CLR

56.21 The GCC provides for CLR to be paid at higher rates where the case involves an 'exceptionally complex or novel point of law' or 'a matter of Significant Wider Public Interest'. It states:

> **Enhanced Payment rates for Controlled Legal Representation**
>
> *You may apply to us for prior authority to exceed the rates for payment for Controlled Legal Representation set by paragraph 7(b)(i) of Annex A to the Contract Schedule in any case which:*
>
> *(a) raises an exceptionally complex or novel point of law, or*
>
> *(b) raises a matter of Significant Wider Public Interest (as defined in the Funding Code).*
>
> *We may at our discretion grant such prior authority in any case where we consider the above criteria to be satisfied. The prior authority will specify the enhanced rate payable and will not apply to any work carried out before the date of grant.*
>
> 1 *... The prior authority should be sought by letter from the appropriate Regional Office. The authority will not be retrospective; any work carried out before the grant of authority must be remunerated at the Schedule rates for Controlled Legal Representation.*
>
> 2 *The purpose of the rule is to allow a higher rate of pay to be agreed in what amounts to 'test cases'.*

56.22 The two criteria for enhanced CLR are in the alternative. As to the first, the GCC states that:

> 3   *For criterion (a) the point of law raised must be 'exceptionally novel or complex' when compared to the points raised in other immigration or asylum cases. The case must not only raise the point of law – but there must be merit in pursuing it in line with the merits test... Note that the criterion does not cover cases where the facts (but not the law) are exceptionally novel or complex.*

56.23 While factual issues will not qualify under the first criterion, they may qualify under the second, 'Significant Wider Public Interest'. The GCC states:

> 4   *'Wider Public Interest' is defined in paragraph 2.4 of the Funding Code as 'the potential of proceedings to produce real benefits for individuals other than the client (other than benefits to the public at large which normally flow from proceedings of the type in question).' The wider public interest must be significant and further guidance on this issue is contained in paragraphs 5.2 and 5.3 of the Funding Code Guidance...*

> 5   *Cases designated as 'starred' appeals before the Immigration Appeal Tribunal will normally come within the criteria, but there will be other cases where they are relevant.*

56.24 The Funding Code Guidance indicates that ''wider public interest' refers to the potential of the proceedings to produce real benefits for individuals other than the client' and that it will be unusual for there to be a 'significant wider public interest' if less than 100 people would benefit, although this will vary according to the importance of the benefit. Clearly, the stakes – and so the potential benefits – in asylum and human rights litigation will be substantial, so one will expect the threshold for the number of people to be affected to be at the lowest end of the scale. The Guidance recognises that the potential beneficiaries may be difficult to identify and that an estimate may have to be made. A legal precedent in particular may have a continuing beneficial effect for years to come. That continuing benefit is relevant in justifying 'significant wider public interest' for so long as it may last.

56.25 As to the actual enhanced rates, the GCC states that:

> 6   *The rates agreed for the work will be specified in the authority. They will not in any event exceed the CLS rates payable for other complex work – such as High Court litigation.*

What CLR will cover

56.26 CLR will cover any work reasonably undertaken in order to progress the case. If the work would be authorised by a reasonable private paying client in the same circumstances, this indicates that it is reasonable. Given the overwhelming importance of most human rights and asylum appeals to the client, work is likely to be reasonable wherever it progresses the case positively.

56.27 The GCC states that:

> Determining reasonableness will involve, in general terms, taking into account all the relevant circumstances of the case including the nature, importance, complexity or difficulty of the work and the time involved; and allowing a reasonable amount of time in respect of all Controlled Work actually and reasonably done...

56.28 There are no set rules as to how long it takes to perform any particular task. Figures given by the LSC are guideline figures for a notional average case, but few cases will in reality be average. The only work upon a case that cannot be covered, even in circumstances where a private client would authorise it, is attendance by a solicitor at a hearing which counsel is conducting.

56.29 CLR *does* cover attendance of an interpreter along with the advocate at a hearing. This will normally be *essential* (see chapter 34).

56.30 CLR ought to cover any interim application which progresses the case, including attendance at a first hearing, unless the matter can be satisfactorily dealt with on the papers.

Certificates of no merit

56.31 Rule 24 deals with the IAT's power to issue 'certificates of no merit':

> (1) If, when it determines an appeal or an application for permission to appeal under this Part, the Tribunal considers that –
>
> (a) the appeal or application to the Tribunal is vexatious or unreasonable; or
>
> (b) where the appellant was the party who appealed to an adjudicator, that appeal was vexatious or unreasonable,
>
> it must issue a certificate to that effect (a 'certificate of no merit').
>
> (2) Where the Tribunal issues a certificate of no merit, the appellate authority must –

(a) *serve a copy of the certificate on –*

  (i) *every party; and*

  (ii) *any legal representative acting for the party against whom the certificate is issued; and*

(b) *serve on the body specified in paragraph (3) a copy of –*

  (i) *the certificate; and*

  (ii) *the determination of the Tribunal upon the appeal or application for permission to appeal.*

(3) *The body referred to in paragraph (2)(b) is –*

(a) *the Legal Services Commission, if the certificate relates to an appeal or application which was determined in England and Wales;*

(b) *the Scottish Legal Aid Board, if the certificate relates to an appeal or application which was determined in Scotland; and*

(c) *the Legal Aid Committee of the Law Society of Northern Ireland, if the certificate relates to an appeal or application which was determined in Northern Ireland.*

56.32 Section 101(3)(d) of the 2002 Act gives a similar power to the Administrative Court on statutory review:

[I]f, in an application to the High Court, the judge thinks the application had no merit he shall issue a certificate under this paragraph (which shall be dealt with in accordance with Civil Procedure Rules).

56.33 Rule 54.26(4) of the CPR states that:

(4) If the court issues a certificate under section 101(3)(d) of the Act, it will send a copy of the certificate together with the order to –

(a) *the persons to whom it sends the order under paragraphs (1) and (2); and*

(b) *if the applicant is in receipt of public funding, the Legal Services Commission.*

56.34 The GCC gives the following guidance on how the LSC will treat these certificates:

If such a certificate is issued in relation to work you have carried out under this Contract you must send a copy of the certificate to us (whether or not you intend to make any claim under the Contract for work you have carried out in the case). You must ensure that any such certificate is made available on any assessment of costs for such work, whether the assessment is carried out by the court or by us.

1   *Certificates issued under this Rule are issued under the above statutory provisions where an adjudicator, tribunal or court considers that the particular application before it has no merit. The fact that the certificate has been issued does not mean that you will necessarily not be paid for work done under the case. However the certificate will be taken into account on assessment of costs in determining what sum if any is reasonable to pay. In general however it will not be reasonable to pay solicitor or counsel fees for work carried out in such a case after it should have been clear to the legal representatives concerned that the case had no merit. We may be prepared in an appropriate case, to treat the issues of solicitors' or counsels' costs separately according to who was responsible for the case proceeding despite its lack of merit.*

2   *If significant numbers of certificates are issued under this Rule in respect of your contract work we may take that as evidence that such work is not being carried out with reasonable skill and care, such that there may have been a breach of other obligations in the Contract...*

56.35 The certificate itself does not affect the outcome of the case or the course of proceedings before the IAT or the Administrative Court. There is no procedure for making representations to either tribunal against the issue of a certificate. This, together with the fact that a certificate may be issued following a paper application for permission or statutory review rather than following a hearing, creates an obvious risk that the certificate could be based on a misunderstanding or error.

56.36 The procedure rules and the CPR simply provide that the certificate should be sent to the LSC. There is no provision as to what steps the LSC should take upon receipt. However, it is clear from the GCC that the LSC intends such certificates to have potentially serious consequences for public funding. If it is going to place adverse reliance on a certificate, it ought to entertain (and you ought to make) any representations to the effect that the certificate was issued in error.

Costs of a statutory review application

56.37 There is no provision for an adjudicator or the IAT to award a party their costs of the appeal. But r.54.27 of the CPR provides that the Administrative Court may reserve the costs of a statutory review application to be determined by the IAT. Rule 25 states that:

(1) This rule applies where –

(a) a party has applied to the High Court or the Court of Session under section 101(2) of the 2002 Act for a review of a decision of the Tribunal; and

(b) the High Court or the Court of Session has reserved the costs (or, in Scotland, expenses) of that application to the Tribunal.

(2) The Tribunal has discretion whether to order one party to pay the costs or expenses of that application to another.

(3) If the Tribunal orders one party to pay costs of an application to the High Court to another, it must refer the case to a costs judge to assess the amount of costs to be paid.

(4) If the Tribunal orders one party to pay expenses of an application to the Court of Session to another, it must refer the case to an Auditor of the Court of Session for the taxation of those expenses.

(5) In paragraph (3), 'costs judge' means a taxing master of the Supreme Court of England and Wales.

56.38 You have a duty to the LSC to make any appropriate application for costs against the Home Office. You should make such an application if you succeed in your appeal before the IAT following a successful application for statutory review. Where there is provision for a court to award costs, the ordinary expectation is that the loser will be directed to pay the winner's costs. That is not dependent upon the losing party being blameworthy, so it ought to be no answer for the Home Office to say that it was not responsible for the IAT's decision on the permission application that precipitated the application for statutory review.

56 Public funding and costs
Key points

- You may grant CLR subject to satisfying the means test, 'sufficient benefit' test, and merits test.

- Virtually all asylum and human rights appeals will satisfy the 'sufficient benefit' test.

- The merits test will be satisfied where the prospects of success are moderate or better.

- If the merits are unclear or borderline, you should grant CLR if the case is of overwhelming importance to the client and/or involves significant human rights issues and/or has a significant wider public interest. An asylum/human rights appeal will normally satisfy at least the first two criteria.

- CLR should be refused only if the prospects of success are poor.

- The question relates to the prospects of the *appeal* being successful, not merely the prospects of initial success before the adjudicator.

- An application for permission to appeal to the IAT should be funded by CLR only if the prospects of success are moderate or better. CLR may, however, be used to fund investigation of fresh evidence where the prospects are unclear.

- There is a continuing duty to keep the merits of the appeal under review. Legal and/or evidential developments may result in CLR being granted (where it has previously been refused) or withdrawn.

- If you refuse or withdraw CLR, you must give your client proper notice of the review procedure. You cannot continue to prepare the appeal under Legal Help in these circumstances.

- The same criteria and procedures apply to granting or refusing CLR for a bail application. It is not a precondition to the grant of CLR for a bail application that representation for an appeal is being funded by CLR.

- CLR may be granted at enhanced rates if the appeal involves exceptionally complex or novel points of law or a matter of significant wider public interest.

- CLR will cover any work reasonably done to progress the case (except for the attendance of a solicitor at an appeal which is being conducted by counsel).

■ The IAT or the Administrative Court may issue a 'certificate of no merit'. There is no provision to make representations to either tribunal against such a certificate. The certificate may have serious consequences for public funding. The LSC ought to consider (and you ought to make) any representations to the effect that the certificate was issued in error.

■ There is no provision for an adjudicator or the IAT to award a party her costs of the appeal. But the Administrative Court may reserve the costs of the statutory review application to be determined by the IAT. You should apply for these costs against the Home Office where you succeed before the IAT.

Index

Notes

Notes

Notes

Notes

Notes

Notes

Notes

Notes

Notes